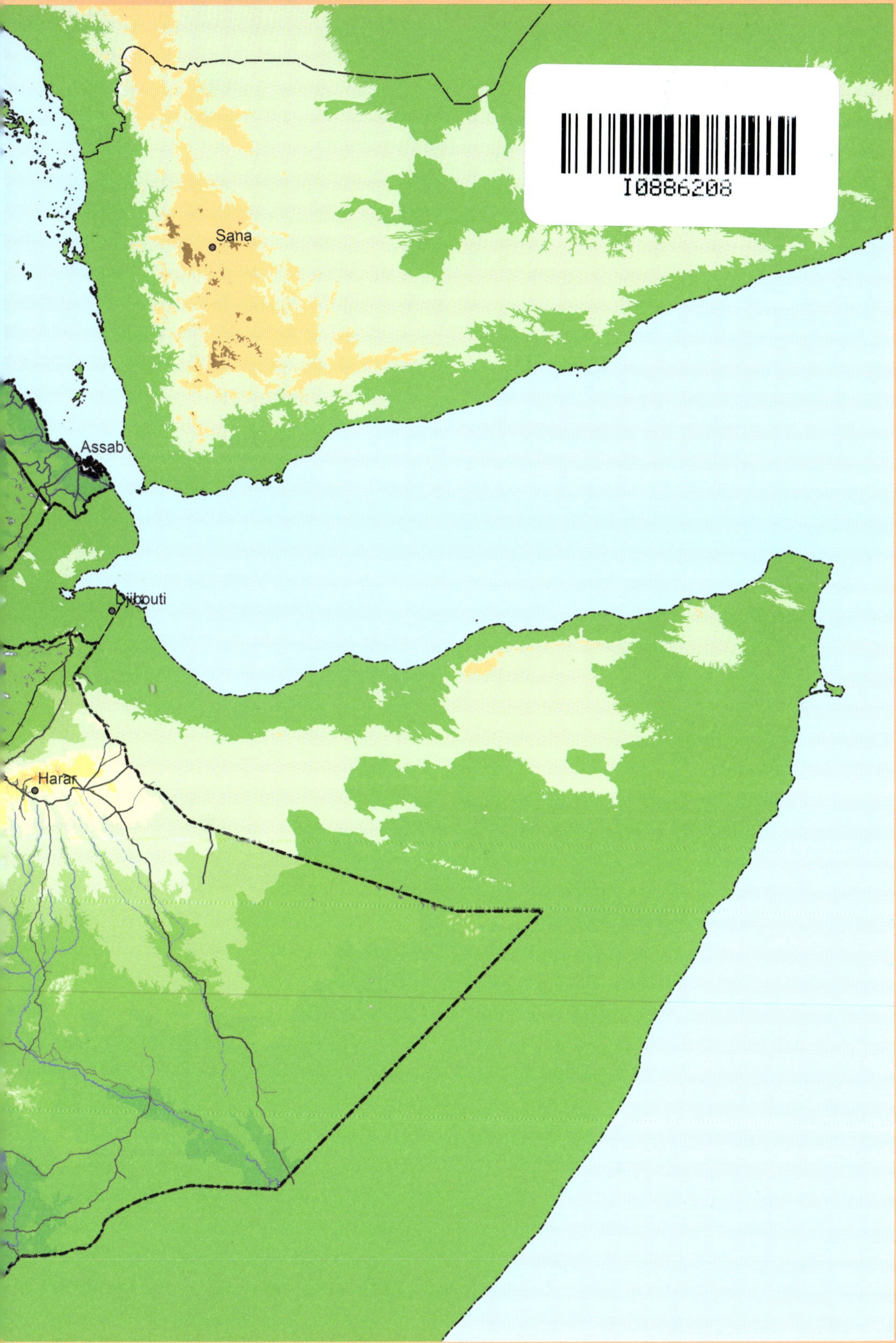

I0886208

ETHIOPIA

ETHIOPIA

History, Culture and Challenges

edited by

Siegbert Uhlig, David Appleyard,
Alessandro Bausi, Wolfgang Hahn,
and Steven Kaplan

LIT

Michigan State University Press

Published with the support of the German-Ethiopian Foundation.

Cover image: Beta Medhana Alam on Sunday morning, © Serge Dewel-Mouton
Back cover: Market day, southern Ethiopia, © Martina Drewes
OMaps:
Physical map of Northeast Africa, © Hiob Ludolf Centre for Ethiopian Studies, Hamburg
Political map of Northeast Africa, © Luisa Sernicola

∞ The paper used in this publication meets the minimum requirements of ANSI/NISO Z39.48-1992 (R 1997) (Permanence of Paper).

First published in Europe by LIT Verlag
(World Rights except North America)
Fresnostr. 2 D-48159 Münster
Tel. +49 (0) 2 51-62 03 20 Fax +49 (0) 2 51-23 19 72
e-Mail: lit@lit-verlag.de – http://www.lit-verlag.de

First published in North America by
Michigan State University Press
(North American Rights only)
1405 S. Harrison Rd., Ste. 25
East Lansing, MI 48823-5245 USA
e-Mail: msupress@msu.org – www.msupress.msu.org

Bibliographic information published by the Deutsche Nationalbibliothek
The Deutsche Nationalbibliothek lists this publication in the Deutsche Nationalbibliografie; detailed bibliographic data are available in the Internet at http://dnb.d-nb.de.
ISBN 978-3-643-90892-6 (LIT Verlag)
ISBN 978-1-61186-275-1 (Michigan State University Press)

A catalogue record for this book is available from the Library of Congress
A catalogue record for this book is available from the British Library

In Germany: LIT Verlag Fresnostr. 2, D-48159 Münster
Tel. +49 (0) 2 51-620 32 22, Fax +49 (0) 2 51-922 60 99, e-mail: vertrieb@lit-verlag.de
In North America: Michigan State University Press, 1405 S. Harrison Rd., Ste. 25
East Lansing, MI 48823-5245 USA
Tel (517) 355-9543, Fax (517) 432-2611; (800) 678-2120
secure fax for orders only (517) 432-7484
email: msupress@msu.org www.msupress.msu.org
In Austria: Medienlogistik Pichler-ÖBZ, e-mail: mlo@medien-logistik.at
In the UK: Global Book Marketing, e-mail: mo@centralbooks.com
e-books are available at www.litwebshop.de

To the ignorant man, a small garden seems like a forest.
If you want to know how business is going in the market, you have to go there.
(Ethiopian proverbs)

Preface

The idea for this small general-readership compendium arose even before the appearance of the *Encyclopaedia Aethiopica*, when representatives of the cultural, business, and political sectors, especially students and supporters of charitable organizations but also travel organizers, expressed the feeling that the time was ripe for a clear and comprehensible introduction to the past and present of northeastern Africa and above all of Ethiopia, a book that would be more than just a travel guide.

You hold in your hands the result. More than 85 scholars from over 15 countries have presented here brief but reliable sketches giving information on the region and its most important peoples, their languages, history, and religions, and the challenges now facing it. All chapters were introduced by some introductory words written by the editorial team and Jon Abbink (chapter III). The authors are cognizant that this small book can only provide an overview, in which it would be impossible to treat all themes of importance. They have undertaken to stimulate readers to ask questions and to explore further.

For those who wish to learn more, brief references to further literature can be found at the end of every article. Readers would likewise do well to consult the five volumes of the *Encyclopaedia Aethiopica*, which are abbreviated herein as '*EAE* I–V':

EAE I *Encyclopaedia Aethiopica*, Volume I: *A–C*, Wiesbaden: Harrassowitz Verlag 2003

EAE II *Encyclopaedia Aethiopica*, Volume II: *D–Ha*, Wiesbaden: Harrassowitz Verlag 2005

EAE III *Encyclopaedia Aethiopica*, Volume III: *He–N*, Wiesbaden: Harrassowitz Verlag 2007

EAE IV *Encyclopaedia Aethiopica*, Volume IV: *O–X*, Wiesbaden: Harrassowitz Verlag 2010

EAE V *Encyclopaedia Aethiopica*, Volume V: *Y–Z, Addenda, Index*, Wiesbaden: Harrassowitz Verlag 2014. I–IV ed. by Siegbert Uhlig (IV in cooperation with Alessandro Bausi), V ed. by Alessandro Bausi in cooperation with Siegbert Uhlig.

The *Encyclopaedia Aethiopica* (*EAE*), which brings together the research of 600 experts on the Horn of Africa, was published at one of the few university centres of research on Ethiopian Studies, the Hiob Ludolf Centre at the University of Hamburg.

Northeastern Africa, including Ethiopia, is in a radical state of flux. In the past the region has made negative headlines, with catastrophic famine, political upheavals and social fermentation, with dictators, waves of refugees, state collapse and corruption. The region is surely anything but politically homogeneous – Somalia, for example, cannot be compared with Ethiopia or Eritrea. But there are many geopolitical and cultural-historical commonalities that unite the countries of northeastern Africa. Here Ethiopia can be considered the political and economic nexus, and indeed it, too, stands at the centre of our book. Now and then we bring the neighbouring countries into the picture. With all the unsolved problems, however, it is easy to lose sight of the extraordinary cultural richness that northeastern Africa encompasses.

Fascination with the land and people of northeastern Africa goes back to antiquity. This small introductory compendium also seeks to arouse the curiosity of its readers, whether students, prospective tourists in search of interesting people, landscapes, and unique sites, or businessmen seeking new markets to invest in, but above all anyone who is willing to confront Africa with all of its paradoxes and paradises.

The challenges facing the region are truly immense. The rich diversity of the Ethiopian peoples also involves manifold forms of social development: on the one hand archaic rituals and gerontocracy, on the other hand the fundamentally democratic forms of decision-making found among many extended clans and ethnic groups; on the one hand well-functioning women's associations, on the other hand groups of women who are denied any participation in society.

There are huge social challenges: the juxtaposition of traditional and modern legal systems; both fundamental progress and continuing inadequacies in medical care; successful anti-poverty programmes alongside the insuperable threat of famine; a well-nigh unstoppable, decades-long stream of emigration; efforts to raise the gross national product and to improve the infrastructure. We will address many of these themes, approaching them frankly and openly, and at the same time advertising the goal of further development of the region, which can only be achieved through top-level education.

Whatever profits are realized from this book will go in full towards the creation of an endowed professorship for contemporary issues in northeastern Africa, conceived with the goal of furthering progress in this part of Africa. Many prominent personalities share this goal with us and are enthusiastically committed to it: for example, the former Federal President of Germany, Horst Köhler, who has said, 'I am pleased at the initiative of the DeutschÄthiopischeStiftung and the University of Hamburg to establish an endowed professorship. Africa is changing much more quickly ... We need therefore to create places where it will be closely observed and our perception sharpened. A professorship in contemporary issues of the Horn of Africa offers this chance. I wish the Foundation many sponsors'. Information about this junior professorship, its goals, and funding possibilities can be found at *www.daes.info*.

The nature and scope of the book unfortunately preclude scientific discussion, and so the opinions of scholars may differ on some points. We make use of a simplified transcription system for names and concepts: instead of Ḫaylä Śəllase (I) we write Hayla Sellase and instead of Zär'a Ya'qob we write Zara Yaeqob. Readers seeking more precise information are referred to the glossary of selected terms. A small index will provide further assistance; here there will also be found a list of abbreviations of the principal organizations. A number of maps, some of which have already appeared in the five-volume *Encyclopaedia Aethiopica*, give additional information. Almost all of the photographs were provided free of charge, and our sincere thanks go to the donors. We got material from Matthias Ansel, Horst Böge, Serge Dewel-Mouton, Martina Drewes, Philipp Hedemann, Wilfried Hofmann, Clemens Schlüter, Christian Sefrin, Wolbert Smidt, Stefan Warwas and some other contributors, also from institutions like 'Ethiopia Travel' and 'Depositphotos'. We are very grateful for their support, also to Luisa Sernicola and Matthias Schulz who prepared the maps for the book, previously published in *EAE* V.

We thank Maija Priess for her extensive support in many fields. We would also like to thank Douglas Johnson, Hilke Meyer-Bahlburg and Silke Sophie Ebert for their reading of the completed manuscript.

Some of the articles were written in French, others in German; Bernard Liger, Orin Gensler, and David Appleyard kindly undertook the translations into English. Andreu Martínez was responsible for developing and maintaining the database, which was of fundamental importance due to the large number of authors. Thomas Rave handled the layout and prepared the camera-ready copy for the printer. Finally we thank LIT Verlag and Michigan State University Press for their collaboration.

The authors have striven for conciseness, and not infrequently issues are simply summarized which in a scientific exposition would require many pages. This is brevity, but not at the expense of clarity. Nonetheless there are some articles in our book where the content cannot be expressed in simple language. Many keywords and topics are treated several times and in different contexts. This is intended so as to be able to document the many substantive aspects. The placing of several articles in specific chapters may seem arbitrary, as perhaps in the chapters on material and spiritual culture, society and religion. This could have been done differently, even though there are reasons for the chosen context. Similar is the mention of Ethiopia in article titles; usually only reading reveals whether the content refers exclusively to Ethiopia. In this way, the editors have had to make compromises. We intend to publish the German version of this small compendium.

A number of supporters of the endowed professorship have contributed significantly to the financing of this popular introduction. We would like to thank the executive board of the DeutschÄthiopischeStiftung (DÄS) and above all Karl-Dieter Broks (Hamburg) and Honorary Consul Thomas Gerkmann (Bremen) for their generous support. They and other friends of Ethiopia have made this book project possible, realised in cooperation with the Hiob Ludolf Centre for Ethiopian Studies and the German-Ethiopian Foundation.

Ya-Adwa del torennat (Adwa Victory Day) = 23 Yakkatit 2009 (Ethiopian calendar) = 2 March 2017 (European calendar)

The editors

German-Ethiopian Foundation

Research. Educate. Preservate.

Table of contents

I Ethiopia and the Horn of Africa

Culture contact between Europe and northeastern Africa

In search of paradise – or the fascination of a meeting of two worlds. Europe and northeastern Africa – what do we know of one another? What draws us to this part of the world, pregnant with legends, the cradle of mankind? A land like Ethiopia with dozens of peoples – what holds them together? And what connects us with them?

We cannot learn this from a distance. We have to meet the land and its people, look into the big eyes of the children, and drink coffee seated in a circle with the women; we have to sit under a tree with the wise men and await a furrow-faced elder's pronouncement after a long parley; we must think about the 'wax and gold poetry' – to us a closed book – about the proverbs; we must walk through the teeming jam-packed city of Addis Ababa, wait at the taxi stand and watch the wildly gesticulating boys shouting their hearts out; we have to see the traffic policeman come down from his box to kiss the grille of the church; we must stand hesitantly at the street-crossing confronted by the crowds of curly-haired schoolchildren who twice a day pour out of school and bring traffic to a halt – the pulsating, laughing future of Africa.

What secret is it that draws us here and will not let go its hold on us once we have begun to try to understand it? This magical, almost magnetic force which for centuries has drawn us to this land and its people – behind it lies a long history. And this we want to retell here.

The Byzantine Empire already had close contacts with the Ethiopian rulers of Aksum. But even before this some basic facts were known, thanks to such figures as the anonymous author of the 'Periplus of the Erythrean Sea', who navigated the Ethiopian coast in the first century BCE. In the 6th century, Cosmas Indicopleustes ('he who sailed to the Indies') wrote his richly detailed 'Topographia Christiana', which reproduced the text of two Ethiopian stone inscriptions.

Even in Antiquity there were decisive encounters between the Arab-influenced African culture of the Mediterranean and its Christian counterpart. Although we cannot fully distinguish truth from legend, it is clear that in the first half of the 4th century Christianity was brought to Ethiopia through the agency of Greek traders; the Aksumite ruler Ezana, as we learn from monumental inscriptions, converted to Christianity and made it the religion of his kingdom.

In the following centuries reports reached Europe of fantastic wealth and of a Christian kingdom at the ends of the 'civilized' world that was threatened by its Muslim neighbours. The reports drew upon fabulous tales of late Antiquity – for example, from the 12th century on, the story of the priest-king 'Prester John' and the peaceful land which he ruled. Only in the 15th and 16th centuries did the growing body of factual information lead to a fundamental change in Europe's picture of Africa. Letters between Ethiopian emperors and European rulers or the Pope helped to put knowledge on a more precise footing. Travellers to the Holy Land told of meetings with Ethiopian monks. The first Ethiopians to come to Europe contributed further information. Europeans themselves, initially the Portuguese, began to explore Ethiopia and to compose eyewitness accounts of the land and its people.

Older written sources. The curiosity of the European bourgeoisie, hungry for knowledge, bore fruit in the age of seafarers and explorers in reliable accounts about hitherto unexplored parts of the world. As early as the 13th century, travellers like Marco Polo began to exploit the then-available information in their writings, though without ever having set foot themselves in the country. One of the first works devoted to Ethiopia is the travel journal of the Portuguese Francisco Alvares, 'The Prester John of the Indies. A True Narration about the Lands of the Prester John', printed in 1540.

In the same year of 1540 there also appeared a short book by Damião de Góis on the beliefs and customs of the Ethiopians. This work is based on a document by the Ethiopian cleric Sagga Za-ab and on interviews with the envoy of the Ethiopian emperor, whom Damião had met in 1533. Educated readers eagerly snapped up this little book and made it a bestseller, which was reprinted again and again and whose Latin version was translated into the main European languages. Leading intellectuals such as Erasmus, Luther, Melanchthon, Thomas More, and Johannes Magnus discussed this work and Damião who brought it to light. The book is a compendium of Ethiopian culture, focusing on themes dealing chiefly with religious practices such as festivals, circumcision and baptism, monks and priests, dietary prescriptions, and the Sabbath. Ethiopian history and government are also dealt with.

Several other reports are also worthy of mention in this context, e.g. the account, which appeared 1565, of Christovão da Gama's military campaign of 1541 against Ahmad Grany.

About a century after Damião de Góis, a meeting of far-reaching import took place between an educated Ethiopian and a German diplomat and scholar. In 1649, while in Rome on a political mission, Hiob Ludolf made the acquaintance of the monk Gorgoryos (Gregory), who had fled Ethiopia for religious reasons and was living in a monastery in the Vatican. Ludolf quickly learned Old Ethiopic (Ge'ez) and Amharic and held intensive discussions with the Ethiopian. He invited him to Germany, where in 1652, drawing upon the existing literature, he worked with him as informant under the patronage of his German reigning prince. The Ethiopian monk's responses were written down and later appeared in the brief work 'Theologia Aethiopica'.

In the following decades, employing the scientific methods of his time, Ludolf continued to publish groundbreaking works dealing with Ethiopian languages, literature, geography, history, and culture. These served to stimulate further the ever-growing interest in the fascination of Ethiopia (see also the article 'Travel and exploration in Ethiopia and the Horn of Africa').

Excerpts from the literature. After Ludolf the stream of works on Ethiopia swelled to a flood. Here we can only give a few examples, chosen essentially at random, of English-speaking authors from various periods.

In the mid-18th century Samuel Johnson, the renowned man of letters, scholar, lexicographer, and much-cited author, wrote a didactic novel which has become known under the short title 'Rasselas'.

Samuel Johnson, 'The History of Rasselas, Prince of Abissinia' (originally titled: 'The Prince of Abissinia. A Tale'), London 1759 (quoted from the 1889 London edition).

[13] 'Here the sons and daughters of Abyssinia lived only to know the soft vicissitudes of pleasure and repose, attended by all that were skilful to delight, and gratified with whatever the senses can enjoy. They wandered in gardens of fragrance, and slept in the fortresses of security. Every art was practised to make them pleased with their own condition. The sages who instructed them told them of nothing but the misery of public life, and described all beyond the mountains as regions of calamity, where discord was always racing, and where man preyed upon man. To heighten their opinion of their own felicity, they were daily entertained with songs, the subject of which was the Happy Valley'.

After a fruitful voyage of research and discovery that lasted several years, James Bruce published a five-volume account of his journey with a wealth of observations on what he had learned about the land and people of Ethiopia.

James Bruce of Kinnaird, 'Travels to Discover the source of the Nile, in the Years 1768, 1769, 1770, 1771, 1772, and 1773', Edinburgh 1790.

[Volume III, 264] 'The crown [of the king] is made in the shape of a priest's mitre, or head-piece; it is a kind of helmet, covering the king's fore-head, cheeks, and neck. It is lined with blue taffety; the outside is half gold and half silver, of the most beautiful filigrane work … [265] The king goes to church regularly, his guards taking possession of every avenue and door through which he is to pass, and nobody is allowed to enter with him, because he is then on foot, excepting two officers of his bed-chamber, who support him. He kisses the threshold and side-polls of the church-door … [282] The king of Abyssinia never is seen to walk, nor to set his foot upon the ground, out of his palace; and when he would dismount from the horse or mule on which he rides, he has a servant with a stool, who places it properly for him for that purpose. He rides into the antichamber to the foot of his throne, or to the stool placed in the alcove of his tent'.

Nathaniel Pierce, a British adventurer, lived for some 15 years in northern Ethiopia, served at the court in Tegray, and during his stay wrote a two-volume account of his experiences.

[Nathaniel Pearce,] 'The Life and Adventures of Nathaniel Pearce, written by himself, during a Residence in Abyssinia, from the Year 1810–1819', London 1831.

[Volume I, 317] 'The [Marriage] festival then begins, and the raw meat is handed about, while it still reeks and shivers under the large two edged knife, with which every man is furnished. The girl, whom, perhaps, the husband has never seen in his life, is seated on a couch, surrounded by her female servants and her *arkeys* [body of troops], who hold their clothes before her, to conceal her from his sight. Before the festival arrives at its height, and when the parties are beginning to be intoxi[318] cated, the husband again jumps up, boasting as before, while his *arkeys* fly to the girl, take hold of her, drag her away, as if by force, and put her upon a mule, one of the *arkeys* jumping up behind her. The husband and his followers then mount their horses, and ride off together'.

The British traveller Mansfield Parkyns spent three years in Ethiopia and described his stay in a two-volume work which he published twice, in 1853 and 1868.

[Mansfield Parkyns,] 'Life in Abyssinia … Three Year's Residence and Travels in that Country. By Mansfield Parkyns', London 1868.

[Volume II, 9] 'Before sleeping, the men take off their belts and trousers without disarranging their cloth, which is of itself sufficient to keep them perfectly covered; and the women likewise divest themselves of their shirts. A bachelor rolls himself up in his cloth – head, feet, face, and all completely covered up… [10] Married couples sleep in the same manner; that is, quite naked, but rolled up close together in a sort of hydropathic dry pack, or double mummy fashion'.

Evelyn Waugh was a successful upper-class writer who, as an avowed admirer of colonialism and Mussolini's politics, can be classed as a radical conservative. In his sometimes cynical travelogue of Africa and especially Ethiopia, he narrated his impressions at the beginning of Emperor Hayla Sellase's reign.

Evelyn Waugh, 'Remote People. A Report from Ethiopia and British Africa 1930–1931'.

[23] 'Addis Ababa is a new town; so new, indeed, that not a single piece of it appears to be really finished. Menilek the Great chose the site forty years ago and named it, when it was still a hillside encampment, 'The New Flower' … [26] At every corner were half-finished buildings; some had been [27] already abandoned; on others, gangs of ragged Guraghi were at work … The usual way for an Abyssinian gentleman to travel is straight down the middle of the road on mule-back with ten or twenty armed retainers trotting all round him; [28] there are continual conflicts between the town police and the followers of the country gentleman, from which the police often come out the worse'.

Dr Marion Stone, the fictional hero of Abraham Verghese's novel 'Cutting for Stone', enjoyed a carefree childhood in Addis Ababa during the reign of Hayla Sellase. This autobiographical, sometimes melancholy novel by the Indian-American physician Verghese had a long run on the bestseller list.

Abraham Verghese, 'Cutting for Stone', New York 2009.

[82] 'Even now Hema [Dr Hemlatha] felt a bit like a David Livingstone or an Evelyn Waugh exploring this ancient civilization, this stronghold of Christianity which, until Mussolini's invasion in '35, was the only African nation never to be colonized. Waugh, in his dispatches to the London 'Times' and in his book, referred to His Majesty Hayla Sellase the First as 'Highly Salacious', seeing cowardice in the

The volcano Erta Ale, © Christian Sefrin

Emperor's leaving the country in the face of Mussolini's advance. Hema's reading of Waugh was that he could not accept that the bloodlines of Emperor Hayla Sellase, extending back as they did to the Queen of Sheba and King Solomon, made the Windsors or the Romanows look like carpetbaggers. She didn't think much of Waugh or his book'.

We are trying to know better this unfamiliar world whose uniqueness so captivates us, this culture with its fascinating secrets. And so we walk on past the regiment of shoeshine boys hanging around the hotel entrance with plastic bowls of some unidentifiable substance; we go to see the new dam, with its promise of economic miracles for Ethiopia; we turn to look at a woman pulling a plough through the red earth, or walking barefoot by the roadside carrying a 100-pound bundle of firewood to the city; we participate in the happy pandemonium of Christian and Muslim pilgrimages; we observe a sluggish crocodile in the river; and we enjoy the chilly mornings with the smell of wood smoke floating up from the courtyards, and the bewitching aroma of the flowers and the calls of birds which are so exotic to our ears.

Literature: RED., DONALD CRUMMEY, 'Ethiopia', *EAE* II, 393–397; SIEGBERT UHLIG, 'Ethiopian Studies', *EAE* II, 433–438; RICHARD PANKHURST, WENDY LAURA BELCHER, 'Ethiopia in English-language literature', *EAE* V, 401–405.

Siegbert Uhlig, Hiob Ludolf Centre for Ethiopian Studies, Hamburg

The mystery of Ethiopia

In 1943 a long debate was brewing among British officials in Ethiopia. It concerned the future of that country, and inevitably also her history. On the one hand there were the British army officers who had liberated Ethiopia from the Fascist occupation, which had lasted from 1936 to 1941. Most of them had served in British colonies throughout the empire, in Asia and Africa. Ethiopia, they argued, was something strange, abnormal. True, she had existed independently from time immemorial, but it was high time to restore common-sense; namely, to divide the country and put it under 'a proper' British government. Facing these officers were British Foreign Office officials, who were advising Emperor Hayla Sellase. They stood for fulfilling the British 1941 declaration that Ethiopian sovereignty should be fully restored. The real driving force behind the latter was Colonel R.E. Cheesman, who had stayed in the country long enough to know her better than the army officers. On 17 June 1943 he reported to London, and in a few lines perhaps outlined the best introduction to our volume:

'During the reign of [Emperor] Menilek II [1889–1913] and since then, the foreign policies of England, France, and Italy in regard to Ethiopia have been based on the assumption that she must break up, yet she did nothing of the sort. She survived the reign of *Lej* Iyasu [1913–1916], Zawditu, [1916–1930] and Hayla Sellase, and showed a united, if ineffectual front to the Italians in 1935–1936. Yet the theory of disintegration persisted… It is not surprising that the military view could not realize that a national unity existed in Ethiopia, and that a government that was not visible and was so different from their own, could possibly last more than a few months'. Cheesman himself had no doubt that Ethiopian statehood would prevail. He analyzed what he called 'the crazy structure of the Ethiopian empire' as held together by a 'mysterious magnetism, which is incomprehensible to one who has no more than a superficial knowledge of Ethiopia'.

The riddle of history. Indeed, what kept Ethiopia going, and on her own feet, for more than two thousand years? What was the 'magnetism' which kept her so long as a free, independent, 'mysterious' African empire? For many outsiders Ethiopia remained a strange enigma, an intriguing curiosity, even a deviation from the logical course of history. It was to some extent due to this line of thinking that, much to the discredit of the entire world, Ethiopia had been sacrificed to Mussolini in 1935, even though it was a member of the League of Nations.

There is, no doubt, a lot curious about Ethiopia, the legendary, biblical 'land of Kush'. How was it born some two millennia ago as a defined, real political entity to survive until today? How did a royal dynasty emerge in the ancient city of Aksum to lead the country for nearly a thousand years, until declining around the 9th century? How did local African culture combine with Oriental Christianity, joining the cross and the crown in the year 333, and in a way, which lasted until 1974? How were Hebraic, Old Testament dimensions added, already in ancient Ethiopia, to this kind of political Christianity, linking it to an Ethiopian-Israelite self-awareness? How did Ethiopia's unique version of Christianity keep to its own path at the same time connected to the greater Christian world by being a branch of the Church of Egypt from its very beginning until 1959? What enabled the continuity of Ethiopia after the decline of the Aksumite dynasty, and what brought about a full-fledged medieval renaissance, especially under the Solomonic dynasty (1270–1529)? How did the Solomonic emperors manage to revive and expand the kingdom, rebuild and renew a variety of political, military, cultural and other institutions, which have continued to this day? What was the 'magnetism' which held the country together during centuries of political decline, during days in which, according to the rich Ethiopian biblical-oriented literature, 'there was no king in Israel, everyone did what was right in his own eyes'? How did the inheritance of that long history help Ethiopia recover on the threshold of the modern era, first by the tragic Emperor Tewodros II (1855–1868), then by Emperor Yohannes IV (1868–1889), and by those already mentioned, from Menilek II to Hayla Sellase I (1930–1974)?

Veterans celebrating Adwa 'Victory Day', © Dereje Belachew

Breakup and unity. To be sure, the 'theory of disintegration' persisted all along. For many, Ethiopia has remained until today a mystery to be explained. In 1974 she began to experience a military revolution which turned into a communist-oriented regime under Colonel Mengistu Haile Mariam. The country was exposed to internal wars and external pressures which seemed to tear her apart. Eritrea, which had been an Italian colony from 1890–1941, then under a British administration before being returned to Ethiopia (a federal arrangement in 1951, full annexation in 1962), was again lost to Ethiopia. Upon the fall of Mengistu Haile Mariam in 1991 Eritrea became practically independent and was declared officially a state on its own in 1993. Yet, the rest of Ethiopia survived the years of fratricidal wars and also the country's redefinition as of 1991.

The current leadership of Ethiopia departed from the centralizing ethos of the imperial days and of the later Marxist regime. It rather proposed to rebuild the country on its human diversity, and declared Ethiopia (practically from 1991, officially as of 1995) a federation. Today's Ethiopia consists of nine 'states' demarcated along ethnic lines. This new structure seems to have put the 'theory of disintegration' to its ultimate test. According to the new 1995 Constitution every 'state' has the right to secede, following a legally defined procedure. Many observers, as in old days, thought that this daring experiment would lead finally to the dismemberment of old Ethiopia. Yet, as these lines are being written, some two and a half decades later, none of the nine 'states' has sought separation. The federal structure did redefine Ethiopia, but she is surely still there. So what about the 'theory of disintegration'?

We want at this point to push the question even further. The rulers of the country, even at their prime, were never able to build a strong and regular standing army, nor a powerful state machinery really capable of imposing centralisation around the periphery of the state. Ethiopia was and still is a vast territory, mountainous, full of deep gorges, always difficult to cross. Nothing in her geography facilitated communication or helped political unity. Nor did Ethiopia develop an economy dependent on a central administration. While, for example, the Nile in Egypt (and later, the cultivation of cotton) was the hub of such a central system, the Blue Nile in Ethiopia forms a deep canyon that divides people. Amharic never developed as a single pan-Ethiopian language at the expense of dozens of other languages, and this has enhanced local and sometimes centrifugal identities. At the end of the 19th century Ethiopia conquered and annexed the south, doubling its territory and its ethnic diversity. Yet, Ethiopia did not lose her integrity, but rather was strengthened.

Moreover, 'mysterious' Ethiopia did not only survive, but faced two of the most powerful forces in history. These challenged her existence, and yet she defeated them. First was imperial Islam. Islam, as a formidable religious and political power emerged in the 7th century in Arabia, on the opposite shore of the Red Sea. It soon expanded in all directions to become one of the greatest empires in human history. Yet, Ethiopia survived on its very doorstep. When Islam presented its harmonious combination of state and religion, the Ethiopians had long had their own, and they did not accept political Islam as an alternative to their identity. They did accept Muslims as communities and individuals, and today's Ethiopia is the home of many Muslims and Christians: Ethiopian Orthodox 43.5%, Muslim 33.9%, Protestant 18.5%, traditional 2.7%, Catholic 0.7%, other 0.6% (2007 est.), but they would not allow Islam to dominate their state politically. Whenever an Islamic army challenged Ethiopia, it was defeated. With the exception of one important 16th-century case – the conquest by Ahmad ibn Ibrahim 'Grany', 1529–1543, practically all military encounters with armed Muslims, from all directions, ended with Ethiopian victories. Still Christian-Muslim relations within Ethiopia remained relatively tolerable, and for many Muslims, following a famous message of Prophet Muhammad, the country is even a model of intra-religious co-existence.

Secondly, early modern, as well as modern Europe has also challenged Ethiopia and her systems. First, missionaries arrived from various European countries aiming to teach the Ethiopians their versions of Christianity. The missionaries were mostly received well, but not always, and contributed to Ethiopia in many ways, but they hardly changed the hegemony of Ethiopian Christianity and the Church. Then, during the last quarter of the 19th century, during the age of 'the Scramble for Africa', whilst European powers occupied practically the whole of the continent, they did not conquer Ethiopia. The British and the French had their good reasons to think it was too costly, the Italians, who thought otherwise, paid dearly. Though they did manage to get control over Eritrea in 1890 by employing their modern army, and as much due to internal Ethiopian rivalries, they were soundly defeated by the Ethiopians when an head-on collision finally happened. On March 1, 1896, at Adwa, a well-organized, pan-Ethiopian army of nearly a quarter of a million fighters, the majority with modern arms, practically annihilated the imperial Italian army. The fact that 40 years later Mussolini enjoyed some revenge did not change the historical significance of Adwa: Ethiopia did not come under the yoke of European imperialism. She rather entered the 20th century as an independent African empire, and in time would also be a founder member of the UN. Thus with the exception of 13 years in the 16th century (the Ahmad Grany Islamic conquest), and five years in the 20th (1936–1941 under the Fascists), Ethiopia continued to enjoy independence. She has done so from nearly the dawn of history until this very day.

The victories of Ethiopia arguably added another dimension to the question of this 'mysterious magnetism'. They ensured the country's independence, but came at a heavy price. When other African or Asian societies, which succumbed to European domination, had to undergo changes, Ethiopia remained on its old traditional track. For the generations inspired by the legacy of Adwa, the West was not a source of fear, nor a source of imitation. The old conservative elite of Ethiopia had little motivation to adopt innovations and borrow new models from Europe. Consequently Ethiopia underwent only slight political, social and economic modernisation prior to the 1974 revolution. When Hayla Sellase was deposed, many aspects of Ethiopia's life were still reminiscent of biblical days. Ethiopia remained full of medieval charm and magic, but also poverty and misery. The image of walking skeletons, the victims of hunger and thirst, seemed to strengthen the idea that the country was going to die with them. Colonel Mengistu's period, though introducing the terminology of revolutionary change, helped little. Plunging the country into endless internal wars, it even worsened the situation.

Yet, as we go deeper into the 21st century Ethiopia continues to disprove the old 'theory of disintegration'. She even seems to be changing more quickly now. Though major problems are still all too evident, few would define today's Ethiopia as 'a failing state', like some other neighbouring countries. In any case, this book offers no analysis of contemporary affairs, and surely no predictions. We do not even claim to have full answers to all questions related to the unique, wonderful and intriguing story of Ethiopia's two millennia. We shall also leave the question of 'the mysterious magnetism' open to answers by anyone interested. What we do offer is a treasure of information and insights about a country which has survived from ancient times, and is still the focus of much curiosity.

Literature: HAGGAI ERLICH, *Ethiopia and the Challenge of Independence,* Boulder 1986; PAUL B. HENZE, *Layers of Time: A History of Ethiopia*, New York 2000; SVEN RUBENSON, *The Survival of Ethiopian Independence*, London 1976.

Haggai Erlich, Tel Aviv

'The most populated mountain' — an introduction

'The most populated mountain in the world' [*la montagne la plus peuplée du monde*], Jean Gallais (1989)

At the beginning of the 20th century the French geographer Fernard Maurette invented the term '(Oriental) Horn of Africa' to refer to the peninsula separating the Gulf of Aden from the Indian Ocean. The term generally describes the area covering Ethiopia, Eritrea, Djibouti, Somalia and Somaliland. In this introduction the 'Horn of Africa' only refers to the countries of the peninsula.

States	2015 population	2050 population	Surface area in km^2
Djibouti	900,000	1,200,000	23,000
Eritrea	5,200,000	10,000,000	118,000
Ethiopia	98,100,000	165,000,000	1,104,000
Somalia	11,100,000	27,000,000	638,000
Somaliland	*3,500,000*	–	*137,000*
Total	115,300,000	203,200,000	1,883,000

Table 1: Population in the Horn of Africa (*Population & Sociétés*, no. 525)

The highlands of Ethiopia and Eritrea are home to the second densest concentration of population in sub-Saharan Africa after Nigeria. This is because they offer natural conditions favourable to human settlement: cool and humid plateaus and their fertile soil provide a healthy environment free from malaria and trypanosomiasis which can affect cattle as well as humans. During the Neolithic, sedentary populations developed plough-based cereal farming systems in the north and arboriculture systems based on the 'false banana' (*ensat*) further south. In the peripheral lowlands nomadic cattle herders circulated in the search for water between piedmont oases and seasonal pastures.

Until the 1960s population numbers were kept constant by recurrent food shortages caused by an irregular rainfall worsened by political unrest. But the current demographic revolution has radically changed the economic and political context in the Horn. The 1970 census counted 25 million inhabitants in Ethiopia and Eritrea and by 1984 a new census counted 42 million. Despite the thousands of victims of the dramatic 1973–1974 and 1984–1985 famines surprisingly demographic expansion did not slow down. In 1994 there were 57 million people in Ethiopia alone (without Eritrea) and in 2007 the figure reached 75 million, tripling in almost 40 years. Given the fact that the population is very young (under-15s form 34% of the population in Djibouti, 43% and 41% in Eritrea and in Ethiopia, respectively and

47% in Somalia) and with the decreasing pattern of infant and adult mortality experts expect the population will have almost doubled by 2050! But the demographic pressure is higher than it seems because 80% of Ethiopian-Eritreans live in regions above 1,800m and only occupy a third of the country. On the plateaus the average density is above 200 inhabitants/km^2 and in Ethiopia the size of farms has decreased from 1.4ha in 1988 to 0.8ha in 2006. Despite the population increase, however, and according to the Food and Agriculture Organization (FAO) data the proportion of Ethiopians dependent on food aid remains stable ranging from 7% in good years to 11% in more difficult times. Eritrea does not release any figures on the food situation in the country using the state of emergency as an excuse. In Somalia the civil war has been the cause of a number of local food shortages. A severe food crisis is still threatening the Horn of Africa given the added factors of a more erratic rainfall and the growing tendency to cultivate dryer and steeper land. The food crises of the last third of the 20th century have shaken the different governments who were accused of keeping silent on their catastrophic consequences and of failing to help the victims. The 1973–1974 famine hastened the fall of Hayla Sellase and radicalized Siyaad Barre's dictatorship. In 1984–1985 Mengistu, who used to say that collectivization would protect Ethiopia from famines, requested international aid when it was too late and forced the peasant communities to resettle and in many cases to join the villagization programme. He lost his legitimacy and fell under the coalition of the Eritrean and Tigrean fronts. Twenty years before Hayla Sellase was confronted with Eritrean separatism in the Organization of African Unity (OAU) and with Somali irredentism in Ogaden. In 1974 the mutinies which were to lead to the Ethiopian revolution occurred in the Asmara and Metsewa garrisons in the north and under the pressure of the Western Somalia Liberation Front in the south.

The period after Hayla Sellase. The fall of the *negus* encouraged regional separatist claims among the peoples who had been conquered by Menilek (Oromo, Afar, Somali) but also among Amhara and Tegreans. The 1975 Agrarian Reform widened the split between the south which supported it and the north which bitterly opposed it. The leaders of the neighbouring countries tried to exploit the shaky territorial stability of Ethiopia. Sudan supported the Eritrean People's Liberation Front (EPLF) and the Tigray People's Liberation Front (TPLF) whereas Hayla Sellase and Mengistu in Ethiopia sheltered the rebels of South Sudan. Siyaad supported the Western Somali Liberation Front and he tried to rally the Bale Oromo who had risen against the *negus* between 1963 and 1967. But in 1977–1978 the Somali army who had come in support of the rebels in Ogaden was defeated on the highlands of Harar and Bale. From 1988 onwards Siyaad had to fight the Somali National Movement in the north of Somalia. In 1991 he had to flee from Mogadishu and Somaliland seceded from Somalia even though its population was entirely Somali.

After Mengistu's fall many observers expected 'the break-up of Ethiopia' even though the United States had imposed Isayas Afewerki, the EPLF leader, in Eritrea and Mallas Zenawi, the TPLF leader, in Addis Ababa. In 1991 the UN, the OAU and the Arab League immediately recognized the independence of Eritrea long before the 1993 referendum. However these organizations denied such a recognition to Somaliland which has engaged in a nation building process with the efforts of its own people and of the diaspora. It still remains a 'phantom state' whereas South Sudan acquired international recognition in 2011. Up to now the former Italian Somalia is still administered by a provisional government and despite repeated foreign interventions it keeps breaking up into semi-autonomous regions where warlords and *Al-Shabaab* political movement are in constant warfare. Surprisingly Somalia, seen by Western eyes as the only homogeneous State in sub-Saharan Africa, has been unable to reach stability. Conversely the 1995 Ethiopian federal Constitution guarantees substantial autonomy to every 'people, nation and nationality' which includes the right to secede. It was expected that the various Ethiopian nationalities would follow the steps of Eritrea and secede in the broader context of the break-up of the Soviet Union (USSR). Isayas thought the struggle for independence had obliterated the religious and linguistic differences between the citizens of a unitary state. After seven years of close military and economic alliance Ethiopia and Eritrea engaged in a relentless and uncompromising conflict from 1998 to 2000. The result was Ethiopia's becoming a land-locked country, though it gained undisputed borders while Eritrea lost Ethiopian trade in transit and found itself in an isolated position. In Ethiopia the difficulties strengthened the control over state-regions by the federal government which imposed a national plan against poverty and since 2010 has conducted a strict enforcement of the new Growth and Transformation Plan (GTP).

Under the leadership of Mallas, the late Prime Minister, and of the coalition in power (Ethiopian People's Revolutionary Democratic Front), Ethiopia has turned towards foreign direct investment (FDI) whilst Eritrea, still under a state of emergency since 1991, retreats into a sort of splendid isolation. The Eritrean diaspora is constantly increasing due to significant emigration and the government is using considerable pressure to force émigrés to pay the 'patriotic' tax. The Ethiopian government has a totally different approach and resorts to loans from international institutions, foreign states and private organizations to finance an ambitious building programme of urban housing, roads, railways, telecom networks, schools and universities. In Addis Ababa and in the regional capitals there is a speculative property boom on land made vacant by the expulsion of poor residents with precarious tenancies in return for modest compensation. The city centres now boast high-rise buildings, office blocks and condominiums for the 'middle' class whereas the outskirts are dotted with less elaborate housing estates for rural migrants and resettled city residents. These urban renovations face strong opposition and were the cause of the massive vote against the government in 2005 in the capital. For a long time, urban residents formed only 15% of the total population but the recent acceleration of the rural out-migration is pushing thousands of young qualified and mostly landless people every year towards the towns and in particular to Addis Ababa which has seen its population rise from 800,000 to 4 million in 40 years. In the last ten years the capital has been for young migrants a mere stop-over on their way to the Middle East, the Arabian Gulf, Europe or America.

Recent developments. On the basis of the measure of frustration among the younger generation, of persisting food shortages and a continuing high population increase which brought about the result of the 2005 elections, Mallas hurriedly launched the GTP which makes a clear choice in favour of a high speed industrialization policy. This relies on three pillars: an improved transport system, big industrial farms and the construction of huge dams. These enormous plants are supposed to provide enough energy to make Ethiopia self-sufficient while at the same time attracting a substantial amount of foreign currency in return for the sale of electricity to the neighbouring countries. Since the closure of the aging 'Chemin de fer djibouto-éthiopien', the Djibouti-Addis

Ababa highway, which concentrates almost 90% of Ethiopia's foreign trade, has been saturated with an endless succession of heavy goods vehicles. In 2013 the government started the construction of a 4,500km electrified standard gauge railway network. The contract was awarded to a consortium of Chinese, Turkish and Indian companies. At first it will follow the route of the previous Addis Ababa-Djibouti railway. At a later stage the network is to link the highlands of the north to Tadjoura. 2015 saw the opening of two tram lines in the capital, built and equipped by Chinese firms. Already in 2009, the Ministry of Agriculture had announced that 3 million hectares were available for investors. This 'vacant' or 'underused' land – i.e. one seventh of the total cultivated land – is located in the sparsely populated lowlands in the west. In return for a small rent investors will have a 20 or 30-year lease (or more) to develop mechanized agriculture for export (cotton, rice and palm oil) on plots of thousands of hectares. Besides Ethiopian investors, foreign agro-industrial groups (from Saudi Arabia, India, Korea and China) have been awarded tens of thousands of hectares. They enjoy tax relief for their expatriate staff, for the repatriation of profits and capital and the imports of machinery and inputs. Protests broke out among the indigenous populations who were deprived of the land of their ancestors in the Beni Shangul, 'South', Oromiyaa and Gambela *kellel*: over 40% of the surface area of the latter region was leased out (2012). Due to insufficient short-term results the Indian group 'Karaturi' has given up while 'Saudi-Star' (Ethiopia-Saudi Arabia) is thriving and the French firm 'Castel' is planting a new vineyard.

A comparison between the demographic, economic and military weight of Ethiopia in the Horn and the peripheral countries leads to the conclusion that Ethiopia has reaffirmed its status as a regional power. However the political bases of the industrial development initiated by Mallas after the 2005 riots remain uncertain even though his death in 2012 did not affect the coalition that has been in power since 1991. Despite the pervasive resentment caused by the land grab, by the increasing control by the government over all sectors of society and the economy and by disillusioned qualified young people forced to emigrate to the Gulf, the international image of Ethiopia has changed: the country is seen as a stable and reliable emerging state for investors and a land of culture and heritage.

Literature: GÉRARD PRUNIER, ÉLOI FICQUET (eds.), *Understanding contemporary Ethiopia. Monarchy, Revolution and the Legacy of Meles Zenawi,* London 2015; JEAN-BAPTISTE JEANGÈNE VILMER, FRANCK GOUÉRY, *Érythrée. Un naufrage totalitaire,* Paris 2015; ALAIN GASCON, *Sur les hautes terres comme au ciel. Identités et territoires*, Paris 2006.

Alain Gascon, Paris

II Land and environment

Introduction

The East African Rift Valley runs diagonally across the Horn of Africa from the Gulf of Aden and the so-called Afar Triangle and crosses into Kenya in the area of Lake Turkana. This huge feature, which is part of the 6,000 km long Great Rift Valley, has determined the geomorphology of much of the region. On the one hand, in Ethiopia mountains rise to around 4,500 m, whilst on the other hand the lowest point in Africa can be found at Lake Asal in Djibouti at 155 m below sea level. The Rift Valley is rimmed by active and dormant volcanoes, whilst the Ethiopian highlands are scored by deep river valleys and gorges and the land is dotted with distinctive steep-sided plateaus.

This highly varied geomorphology gives rise to a wide array of climatic zones, ranging from the African Alpine Zone above 3,300 m with an average temperature of only 10°C to hot lowlands just above or even below sea level where temperatures may range from 25°C to as much as 48°C in the Danakil depression, amongst the hottest places on earth. The highlands catch the rain-laden monsoons coming from the Indian Ocean providing a mix of rainy and dry seasons in the year with rainfall ranging from 750 mm to 1,000 mm per annum in the central highlands. Elsewhere, especially towards the east, in the Somali and Afar regions, desert or semi-desert conditions prevail.

This huge variety of environments has at one and the same time produced a challenge to human livelihood in some areas, whilst also providing a rich and fertile context for agriculture in others. By no means is the sometimes popular image of Ethiopia as a land of drought and famine a true one, though millennia of agriculture has led to the loss of forests and soil erosion in several regions. In much of the region, however, agriculture remains the rule. Fields tend to be small and are worked with ox ploughs, and small flocks and herds graze the land. In the drier regions nomadic pastoralism prevails. Ethiopia is an ancient centre of plant domestication and two species, *tef*, a kind of millet, and *ensat* ('false banana') are ancient cultivars peculiar to the region. The wide range of environments also allows the cultivation of a host of other food crops, from wheat, barley and oilseeds to semi-tropical plants such as sugar cane, bananas and other fruits. Domestic animals include cattle, sheep, goats, horses, donkeys and, in the warmer regions, camels. Amongst wild fauna nowadays there are few large animals, though in the past elephants, rhinoceros and hippopotamus existed; however, a few lions are still to be found. The commonest wild animals today are various species of antelope and caprids, baboons and monkeys.

Geology and geomorphology

The Horn of Africa is a vast mountainous peninsula of 1,883,000 km^2 coinciding with a series of horsts (raised blocks between two faults) that appeared on the intersection of the east-west graben (tectonic ditch) of the Gulf of Aden and the North-South Rift of East Africa. The Great Rift is more than 6,000km long, 40–60km wide and has a depth ranging from a few hundred to more than 1,300m. It extends from the Middle East in the north to Mozambique in the south. In the north of Eritrea a system of faults diverges from the Red Sea rift in a southerly direction to follow the edge of the horsts of the Ethiopian-Eritrean plateaus. The Red Sea rift extends as far as the straits of Bab al-Mandab where it hits the southern edge of the Arabian Plate on the Gulf of Aden and the Gulf of Tadjourah. The Gulf of Aden rift extends into the Indian Ocean and is limited to the south by an east-west mountainous escarpment from Soqotra Island through Cape Gardafui to the mountains of Somaliland and Harar. Created by the separation of the Nubian Plate to the west and the Somali Plate to the east, the Afar Triangle lies between the Red Sea, bordered by a mountain range sometimes called 'the Danakil Alps', the escarpment of the Tegray and Amhara horsts and the Ahmar Mountains. South of Addis Ababa these two branches of the Rift unite to form one big graben which fractures the southern highlands of Ethiopia. It extends beyond the Ethiopian-Kenyan border and its bottom is dotted with a number of lakes, from Lake Zway in the north to Lake Turkana in the south.

A peninsula created by volcanoes. The Rift was formed during the Cenozoic era causing the eruption of vast lava fields that constitute the substratum of the Ethiopian highlands and the mountainous spines of Bale and Harar. As the plates were moving apart, the Rift deepened and filled with volcanic flows and debris torn off by erosion from the horsts nearby. In the graben these sediments settled to form a thousand metre-thick layer at the bottom which is covered by lakes containing water rich in minerals. However the lava flows did not affect Tegray and Eritrea where Mesozoic sedimentary strata can be seen on the surface. To the southwest, beyond the plateau escarpment begin the sedimentary formations of the Sudanese depression. To the east (Somaliland, Puntland and Somalia) the Mesozoic marine transgressions have brought thick sedimentary layers (limestone and sandstone). After the volcanic eruptions during the formation of the Rift in the Cenozoic era the highlands started to move upwards, the grabens widened and these movements have continued to this day. The Afar Triangle was submerged by the sea but the recent formation of a coastal mountain range has protected it from further marine transgression. Later, new volcanoes appeared in the Afar Triangle on the edge of the Rift and sometimes in the highlands and these are still active. The succession of more humid and cooler palaeoclimates left traces of glacial erosion on summits above 4,000m and residual glaciers above 5,000m. Rainy and warmer periods aggravated fluvial erosion that accelerated the digging of deep canyons and the accumulation of alluvial cones on the piedmonts. In the Holocene age the development of cattle breeding and plough-based cereal culture had a deep impact on vegetation; perhaps human populations accelerated the negative effects of erosion when they cleared the 'primitive' forests that probably covered the highlands. Although an unstable tectonic zone, the Horn of Africa in recent times suffered only a couple of earthquakes (Dase in 1953 and Eritrea in 2011), which caused some damage but far less than droughts and floods. Experts reckon Ethiopia has important geothermal potential because of its numerous thermal springs.

The geomorphology follows a regional pattern in accordance with the substratum and climatic erosion processes. In the sedimentary, volcanic and granitic strata differential erosion has carved out impressive tablelands (called *amba*). In Tegray and Eritrea lofty *amba* made of Antalo limestone and Addigrat sandstone, occasionally form a rocky chaos towering above the softer Mesozoic layers. Further north the Paleozoic and Precambrian granitic basement constitutes the substratum of the Eritrean mountains. South of the Takkaze river the highlands coincide with the thick lava flow which was emitted in the Miocene age and was deeply transformed by soil formation. These basalts extend on the western side of the Afar Triangle and the rift as far south as Lake Chamo and on the eastern side from Harar to Bale. These plateaus (between 2,000 m and 3,000 m) are deeply carved and fragmented by the Takkaze, Abbay, Didessa and Gibe canyons interrupted by spectacular waterfalls (Tis Esat, Sor). They are dominated by enormous Miocene volcanic cones, now eroded, which rank among the highest peaks in Ethiopia (e.g. Ras Dashan 4,620m, Abuna Yosef 4,284 m, Choqqe 4,154 m, Amba Farit 4,247 m, Kaka 4,190 m, Tulluu Dimtu 4,377 m). To the north and south of the Lake Tana depression (1,850 m) the plateaus are fragmented by faults which steer the course of the Gudar and Abbay rivers and are dominated by recent volcanoes (Dandi, Wanchi, Jibat).

Dallol, Danakil depression, © Philipp Hedemann

The Horn of Africa Rift. South of Nazret the Rift was filled during the Quaternary era by lacustrine sedimentation and was compartmentalized by fault escarpments, craters and lava flows. It diverges to the west with a succession of faults forming steps with the Zeqwala (2,989 m) and Yarar volcanoes and the Dabra Zayt crater lakes on each side with, at the end, the Wachacha (3,385 m) cone, the Mannagasha dome and the Entoto (3,198 m) escarpment overlooking Addis Ababa. On the bottom lie lakes without outlets (Zway, Abiyataa, Langano, Shalaa, Awasa, Abbayya, Chamo, Chaw Baher) as far as the Ethiopian-Kenyan border which runs north of Lake Turkana (375 m). The Afar Triangle was connected to the Red Sea but this connection disappeared in the Quaternary era and was split by intense faulting. The region has been subjected to recent volcanic activity and has been filled with thick lacustrine and fluvial sedimentation where fossils such as 'Lucy's' skeleton are particularly well preserved thanks to the hot and arid climate. The centre of the Afar Triangle where the Fantale (2,007 m) has resumed its activity is crossed by the middle and lower Awash terminating during the summer high waters in an interior delta that includes Lakes Gamari, Adobed and Abhe (260 m) on the border with Djibouti. In the northern tip of the Triangle between the edge of the Tegray plateau and the Red Sea coastal range, in Eritrea, lies the Afar/Danakil depression which reaches a depth of -120 m in the Dallol area and includes a volcano (-48 m) surrounded by salt and sulphur lakes and geysers. In the south a lava lake in the Erta Ale crater (613 m) has been boiling since 1967. These depressions are separated by small mountain ranges following a NNW-SSE direction and extend into the Republic of Djibouti with Lake Assal at an altitude of -155 m. Above the lake, the Ardoukoba volcano erupted in 1978 and completed its formation within a few months at the contact point of the NS rift and of the extension of the Gulf of Aden faulted rift forming the Gulf of Tadjourah. This gulf lies between the lava horsts of the Mabla Mountains to the North and the Ali-Sabieh lava plateaus to the South.

On the southern side of the Harar and Bale volcanic plateaus the Cenozoic sedimentary layers appear on the surface west of the town of Harar. These folded and faulted layers constitute the mountainous spine on the edge of the Somali Plate. This range extends into Somaliland as far as Cape Guardafui. The sandstone has produced chaotic formations (Harar-Jijjiga) and the limestone has generated karst plateaus where the Wayb river disappears into the Soof Omar caves. The Cenozoic layers follow a regular incline towards the Indian Ocean and the water system is centred around the Wabi Shabelle, the Jubba and their tributaries. The summer high waters originating in Bale and Harar flood the lower valleys in their arid environment. In the Benaadir region near Mogadishu/Xamar the Wabi Shabelle hits the sand bar, redirects its course in a southerly direction and runs parallel to the coast for 400 km. It diverges into numerous meandering branches and eventually meets the Jubba before crossing the dunes in Kismaayo. The flat Indian Ocean coastline bordered by a succession of swamps is very different from the straight rocky coast of Puntland, Somaliland, Djibouti and Eritrea. There, steep mountainous escarpments overlook an arid and torrid coastal plain which is particularly inhospitable.

Literature: ALAIN GASCON, AMINA SAÏD CHIRÉ (eds.), *Atlas de Djibouti*, Paris 2007; ETHIOPIAN MAPPING AUTHORITY, *National Atlas of Ethiopia*, Addis Ababa 1988.

Alain Gascon, Paris

Climate

The Horn of Africa is a vast peninsula which juts out between the Indian Ocean and the Gulf of Aden. It is situated south of the Tropic of Cancer and extends over 2,100km in latitude from 18°N (Ras Kassar, Eritrea) to 1°40'S (Kaambooni, Somalia). It covers a distance of over 2,200km in longitude from 31°E (the Baro Salient, Ethiopia) to 51°15'E (Cape Guardafui, Somalia/Puntland). The highlands rise in the centre to altitudes ranging from 1,800m to 3,000m with enormous volcanic formations towering above them and reaching altitudes of over 4,000m.

The Indian Ocean monsoon. The hot and humid air from the Indian Ocean brought by the summer monsoon winds hits the Ethiopian-Eritrean barrier and releases its moisture over the Somali peninsula. In winter the trade winds blow hot and dry air from the Arabian Peninsula. At the end of winter and in spring humid winds from the north follow the Red Sea, reach the eastern edge of the northern plateaus and spread over the southern highlands. The frequency and volume of rainfall increase with altitude and depend on latitude. The volume of rain generated by the low pressures of the Inter-Tropical Convergence Zone is greater as the regions come closer to the equator. Near the tropic the dry season is longer in relation with the Sahara high pressures: as the air descends, it becomes dryer. There, regional variations in the frequency and intensity of the rainfall caused by the mountains occur in connection with the exposure to humid winds. The Rift Valley enjoys a climatic shelter and has lower rainfall than the neighbouring areas. On the leeward slopes, sheltered from the dominant humid winds, the air has lost its moisture over higher ground and gets warmer and dryer as it descends. Rainfall maps have shown the absence of symmetry in the continental and regional distribution of precipitation. Although on the same latitude as Gabon and its rain forest, the region of Kismaayo is a surprising 'Sahel on the Equator' with an open forest of thorn trees related to a mean annual rainfall under 400 mm concentrated within a period of three months. Although isolated from the Indian Ocean by the Ethiopian mountains the equatorial South Sudan depression receives 800 mm–1 m of rain every summer.

In sum, if we consider the Horn of Africa as a whole the rainfall pattern does not coincide with altitude. But on a regional scale temperature patterns seem to match more closely the altitude contours. In tropical latitudes temperatures fall with altitude (approx. -5° C per 1,000 m) but contrary to regions in 'temperate' latitudes the difference between the length of night and day does not exceed 30 minutes. Moreover the sun is always close to its zenith and consequently the angle formed by its beams and the ground surface is always close to 90° C. Solar radiation depends on rainfall distribution during the course of the year. In the rainy season the clouds form a screen restricting solar and ground radiation and consequently the temperature differences within a single day tend to decrease. On the peaks, geologists have identified traces of glacial erosion dating back to cooler and sometimes more humid episodes in the Holocene age. In the 19th century some travellers reported snowfall in the Semen Mountains but climatologists reckon they were more likely to have encountered hail showers.

Three altitudinal zones. The fact that Amharic terminology for different altitudinal zones has been adopted by the academic world reflects the fact that observations were carried out in the peripheral regions of the northern and central highlands. The plateaus (above 2,400 m) belong to the *daga* zone where average annual temperatures range from 10° C to 15° C with frequent frost in December and January above 3,000 m and every night above 4,000 m. Permanent human settlement is rarely found above 3,300 m (Bale, Wallo, Wanchi) since it depends on the highest limit of cereal cultivation (here barley) and cattle breeding. Some experts propose a further altitudinal zone, *werch* ('frost'), to include the volcanic summits but they have been unable to reach an agreement. The piedmonts and the valleys on the high plateaus belong to the *qwalla* zone generally situated under 1,600–1,800 m and receive less than 600 mm mean annual rainfall within a period of three months. On average, temperatures vary between 18° C and 25° C. These regions are spared frost but are also prone to malaria and sleeping sickness along the perennial rivers and during the rainy season. They do not have much in common with the hot and arid lowlands (called *baraha,* meaning 'desert') in the Afar Triangle and the Red Sea coastal plains with temperatures above 30° C in Metsewa, Djibouti and Boosaaso. Climatologists cannot decide whether to add *baraha* to the three 'recognized' zones. Be-

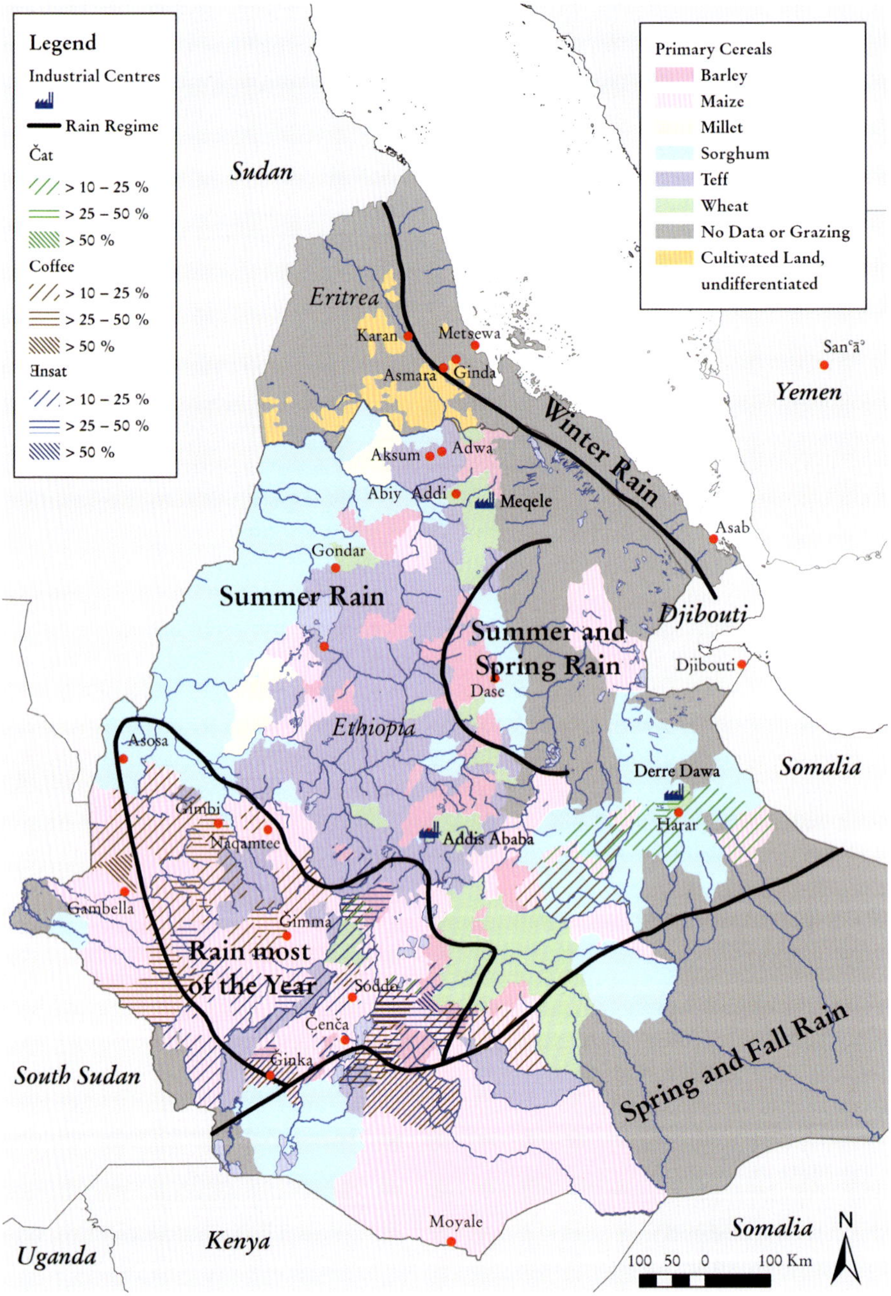

Map 2: Climate and agriculture, © Hiob Ludolf Centre for Ethiopian Studies, Hamburg

tween the *qwalla* and *daga* zones there is an intermediate level called *wayna daga* ('vine' *daga*). It draws its name from the vines grown in some monasteries for the celebration of the Eucharist and from the place-name '*Wayna daga*', a district north of Lake Tana. In this zone the average annual temperatures range from 18°C to 20°C with possible frost for a few days in winter. The risk of malaria and sleeping sickness is low even in the summer rains. Annual precipitations are under 600mm in the north (Eritrea, Tegray,

Wallo) but increase to 1m in the centre and to 1.4m south of the capital. To the southwest observations show a regular increase in the volume and duration of rainfall, which tend to obliterate the distinctions between *qwalla* and *wayna daga*.

We might ask whether these 'recognized' three tiers apply in southwestern Ethiopia and probably in Harar, too. There, the intermediate zone is very small and sometimes disappears, leaving only two levels: an upper level where it is impossible to grow coffee and a lower one well adapted to its culture. We must also bear in mind that in the Horn, until at best 50 years ago, regular climatic data were unavailable. Fortunately, more recently, new progress in air traffic control and an increasing number of meteorological observation satellites have enabled us to broaden our knowledge.

Analysts now have mathematical models at their disposal to forecast the weather, which made it possible to predict the severe rainfall deficit of 1984–1985. We also need rely on a denser grid of weather stations and on a better knowledge of the vernacular terms in all the languages of Ethiopia.

The main climatic regions. Since we lack precise regional and local climatic maps, we can only produce a general description of the main climatic regions of the Horn. Besides altitude, one of the most relevant criteria for a regional description is without doubt the duration and the distribution of rainfall throughout the rainy season, essential for precipitations to be efficient. This is because very heavy rains are needed to recharge aquifers adequately when the ground surface is prone to intense drying out during dry periods, which cause a halt to the growing season. The regions where the heavy rains (*Keramt*) come in one continuous period (July–September) extend on the western plateaus from the Ethiopian-Eritrean border to the north of Addis Ababa, then further south including the Rift and the Bale Mountains. It also extends in a kind of west-east appendix along the mountainous backbone of Arsi and Harar. The rainfall map shows areas to the east with two spring and summer rainfall peaks: on the southern and western edges of the Afar Triangle and along the mountains of Somaliland the total annual rainfall reaches 800–900mm but drops to under 600mm in the centre of the triangle and is down to 400mm, concentrated over a three-month period, on the Red Sea coast of Eritrea, in the Ogaden and in the Hawd. West of the rift the wettest 'pole' of the country, south of Lake Tana, receives over 1,600mm and the south of Wallaga (Jimma-Kafa) over 2,000mm. North of Gondar over 2,000mm fall over the Semen Mountains, while the plateaus of Tegray, Eastern-Wallo and Eritrea lie on either side of the 600mm precipitation line below which cereal crops are uncertain. In contrast, the escarpment of the Eritrean highlands overlooking the Red Sea has a short winter rainy period generated by local depressions. In Somalia the amount of rain drops even further and is fragmented into four periods. The main dry season from November to March is followed by the main rainy season from March to June, which may be interrupted by a short dry season in July-August before the rains reappear in the short rainy season in September-October. The 400mm line only concerns the area situated between the Wabi Shaballe and Jubba rivers where dry farming is possible though unreliable. Along the Indian Ocean coast aridity is reinforced by the cold Somalia current reducing evaporation and home to abundant plankton which guarantees fishing resources (see also 'Ecological zones' in article 'Ecology and environment').

The climatic irregularities. It is estimated that in Ethiopia the inter-annual coefficient of rainfall variability is 14% in the west and 65% in the east. We speak of an 'Arid crescent' which includes the regions with irregular and barely sufficient rainfall. Its centre corresponds to the eastern lowlands, its southern tip veering westwards towards the Kenyan border, while the northern end (north of Dase) includes the Ethiopian-Eritrean plateaus as far as the Sudanese frontier. It was there that the population was victim to the last two subsistence crises of 1973–1974 and 1984–1985. Recent improvements in water management and local irrigation have developed dry season cultivation and limited the effects of rainfall irregularities. The extension of the road network made food distribution possible in the most affected areas such as Tegray and Walaytta during the 2008 food crisis.

Some of the media went so far as to blame the Mengistu regime for deliberately organizing the food shortage and for using the climatic irregularities as a pretext to keep the farmers under control. However climatologists had shown that the 1973–1974 and 1984–1985 famines were caused by a succession of years with insufficient rainfall.

The 1984–1985 deficits showed 30% of the average rainfall on windward slopes and 50% on leeward sides. The erratic pattern of rainfall as the cause of recurrent food shortages is well established in the Horn, as testified over the centuries by royal chronicles. Thanks to their Nile meter, the ancient Egyptians had discovered that about every ten years a 'good Nile' cycle was followed by a 'bad' one – the seven handsome and fat cows and the seven ugly and thin cows of the Old Testament account. We know that 86% of the Nile waters come from the Ethiopian highlands. The reversal of the 1940–1970 favourable rain configuration in the Sahel, which affected Ethiopia and Somalia in 1973–1974, has confirmed the relevance of the 30-year rainfall cycle theory. Historians have pointed to centennial variations with exceptional droughts or floods after many 'good' or 'bad' years. For the time being, because of insufficient precise data, it is impossible to predict how the climatic system of the Horn will evolve in the more general context of global warming. It is even more difficult to risk local and regional predictions. Global warming will not necessarily entail higher temperatures if rainfall increases as is suggested in a number of scenarios.

Literature: Central Statistical Agency, International Food Policy Research Institute, *Atlas of the Ethiopian Rural Economy*, Washington, Addis Ababa 2006; Jean Gallais, *Une géographie politique de l'Éthiopie. Le poids de l'État,* Paris 1989.

Alain Gascon, Paris, Jon Abbink, Leiden

Ecology and environment

Ecology means the interaction of organisms with each other, their environment, as well as the outcome of this interaction. So, examining the interaction between physical conditions and land-use patterns and cultural practices in different regions of Ethiopia we may speak of 'agro-ecological zones'.

Ecological zones. The variety of ecological zones in Ethiopia is a particular result of its topography, from lowlands lying below sea level to mountains of more than 4,500m. There are six agro-ecological zones in Ethiopia, which are rooted in the local languages and are also used by the rural population at least in relative terms. Here average altitudes given across the highlands: *baraha* (below 500 m), *qwalla* (500–1,500 m), *wayna daga* (1,500–2,300 m), *daga* (2,300–3,200 m), *werch* (3,200–3,700 m), high *werch* (more than 3,700 m). Depending on the mean annual rainfall and evaporation some of these zones can be subdivided into different sub-zones (dry, moist and wet).

From *baraha* to high *werch,* soils change sequentially through yellow and sandy to red, then brown and black. According to climate, the natural vegetation varies, again sequentially, from Acacia to members of the Cordia and Ficus families and bamboo through juniper, African redwood (*hagenia*), podocarp conifers to heathers and hypericums, and lastly mountain grassland.

Altitudinal belts	Major crops	Altitudinal boundaries
I Werch:	No cultivation	
		A: Upper limit of barley and (rarely) potato cultivation (due to temperature)
II High daga:	Barley (potato)	
		B: Upper limit of wheat/pulses (due to temperature)
III Daga:	Wheat, barley, pulses	
		C: Upper limit of maize/tef (due to temperature)
IV Wayna daga:	Tef, maize, wheat, pulses	
		D: Approximate lower limit of maize/tef (due to rainfall)
V Qwalla:	Sorghum, tef (rarely)	
		E: Approximate lower limit of sorghum (due to rainfall)
VI Baraha:	No rainfed cultivation	

(Amharic denotations and dominant crops are listed by belt)

Table 2: Key to altitudinal belts and rainfed crops, © Hans Hurni

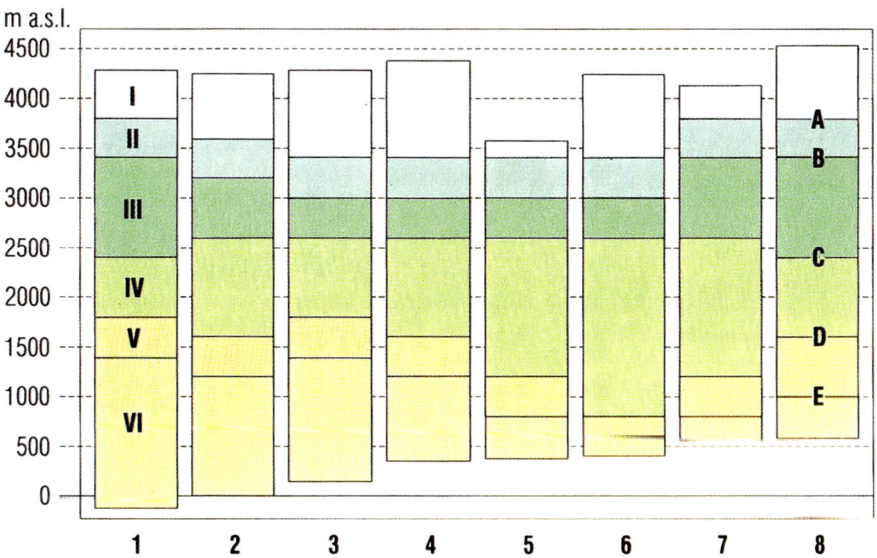

Source: Field survey, H. Hurni, GDE

Agro-climatic regions: 1 = Northeast, 2 = East, 3 = East/Southeast, 4 = South, 5 = Southwest, 6 = West, 7 = Northwest, 8 = North

Table 3: Altitudinal agro-ecological belts in each agro-climatic region, © Hans Hurni

From the lowest to the highest zones mean temperatures differ considerably, and in the Semen Mountains even snow is possible. Rainfall is relatively high in the middle and upper zones because of topographical effects. In general the annual rainfall is higher in southern than in northern Ethiopia. The variation of temperatures throughout the year increases from south to north along with rainfall variability. So the risk of drought is higher in the northern than in the southern highlands, but is generally high in the semi-arid and arid lowlands (*baraha* and *qwalla*). Besides the desert and semi-desert climates, there is also quite a substantial difference in length between dry and rainy seasons, varying regionally from about four to eight months a year.

Land-use can be divided into two main types: agriculture based on the ox-plough, and cattle breeding, as part of a nomadic or semi-nomadic system, sometimes combined with some basic agriculture. In general land-use is linked heavily to factors of the physical environment such as water supply, temperatures and soils, but there are also various modifications of this because of ethnic, cultural or politico-economical particularities. Agriculture is dominant between around 1,000m to 3,500m. The most productive zones are *wayna daga* and the lower parts of the *daga* with two or even three harvests a year. Irrigation in general is not very common. Irrigated land can be found in areas with low annual rainfall and/or high evaporation, especially along rivers like the Awash and in valleys, as well as in areas with market-oriented production.

The most important crops are cotton, fruits, sugarcane, sorghum, *tef*, maize, *ensat*, coffee, various vegetables, barley, wheat and pulses. Outside agricultural areas, where it is an integrating part of the system, cattle breeding is concentrated in the low productive parts of the lowlands and the highlands. In the highlands smaller livestock, especially sheep, are dominant.

Environmental challenges. The great famines of the 1970s and 1980s resulted in increased interest in the environmental processes of the Horn of Africa. Environmental degradation is seen as one of the most acute problems in Ethiopia and the surrounding countries, because of its effects on agriculture, which is crucial for the nutrition and economy of the region as a whole.

Domestication of important agricultural crops, such as *tef* and finger millet, is believed to have begun about 7,000 years ago. The Aksumite culture was a primary centre for the diffusion of several cereals, pulses and oil-seed crops. The development of the ox-plough (500–1,000 BCE) was an important step in environmental history. Open space for ploughing and for crops and pasture was needed, which is one reason why long-term change of the vegetation structure is severe. There is evidence that the Aksumite civilization declined because of soil erosion and the associated decline in agricultural productivity.

Today biodiversity is under pressure in many places, because of deforestation as indigenous trees and crops are replaced by other, imported species and the extension of land-use into formerly sparingly cultivated or uncultivated areas arising from population growth. Wood is a basic and widely used resource of an agricultural society with almost no fossil fuel reserves. The analysis of travel reports proves that the wide destruction of forests and woodlands in central and northern Ethiopia and Eritrea started decades, in some places even centuries before 1900. In the eastern highlands large-scale deforestation began with the expansion under Menilek II from the end of the 19th century. For the western and southern regions various studies show overall deforestation since the 1950s. Because of the shortage of wood in central and northern Ethiopia, eucalyptus trees were introduced in the 1890s to help solve in particular the energy problem in many areas, but the tree's high need for water has provoked soil erosion.

The major causes of deforestation and the degradation of forest resources are the clearing of forests and woodlands for cultivating crops and the felling of trees and shrubs for fuel, charcoal, construction material, and so on. The causes of deforestation are, however, closely linked with the vicious cycle of mutually reinforcing factors, poverty, population growth, poor economic growth and the state of the environment. In 1994 it was estimated that high forests covered less than 2.7% of the country. Deforestation of natural woodland still continues, although thanks to the planting of eucalyptus, cypress and

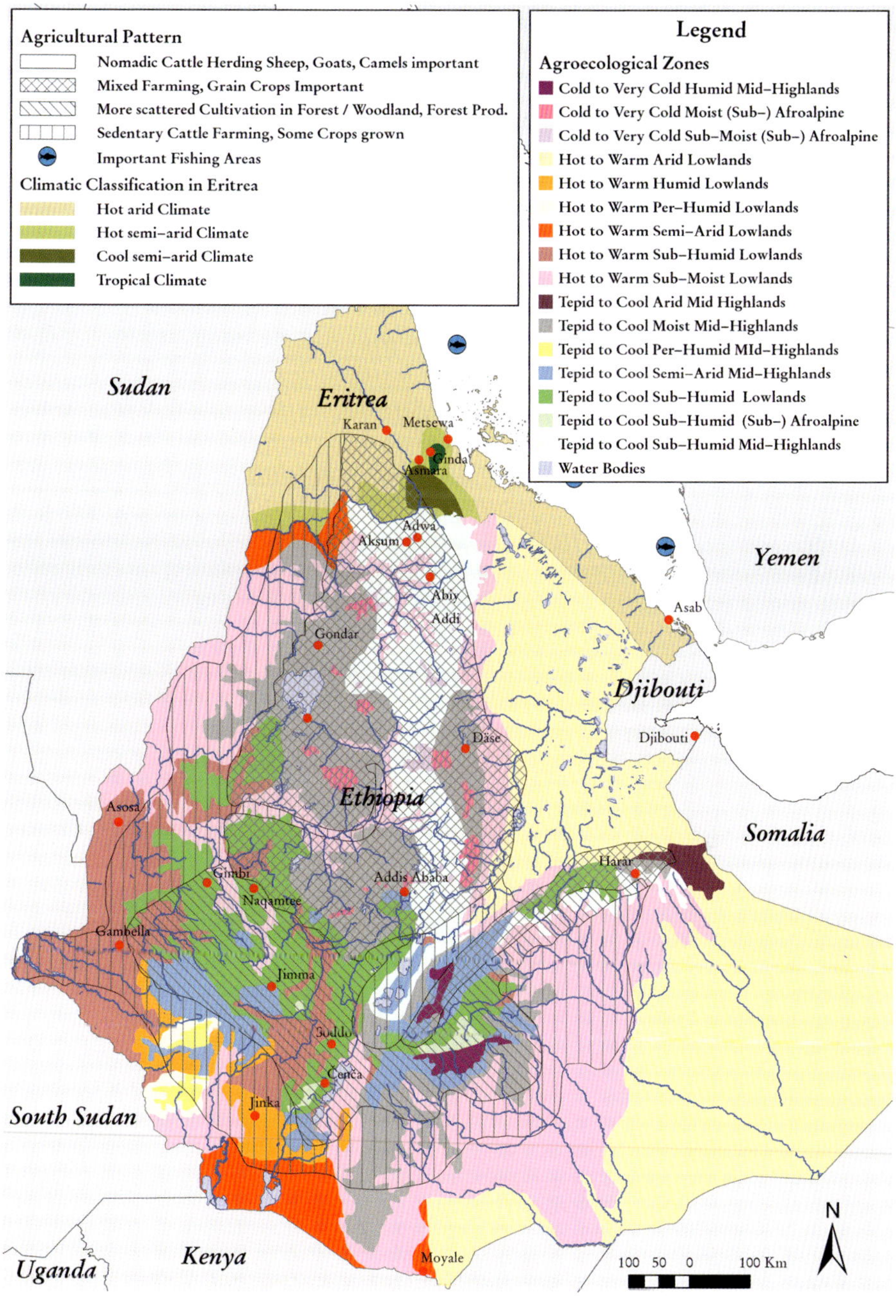

Map 3: Ecology and agro-ecological zones, © Hiob Ludolf Centre for Ethiopian Studies, Hamburg

pine the total forest cover has been increasing for some years, at least in some areas. The introduction of exotic species may cause several unforeseen risks, when an introduced species becomes a competitive weed thereby reducing crop yield and replacing local flora, causing an adverse effect on the environment, and introducing susceptibility to disease.

The degradation of soils is clearly linked to rainfall patterns, topography and vegetation cover or land use, respectively. Soil erosion is a very old phenomenon: the fertility of the Nile in Egypt since ancient times is mainly due to soil loss in Ethiopia. A severe problem for the farmers is that in several places soil depth will reach a critical level for agriculture in the next few decades, if this process cannot be slowed down or stopped through conservation measures. Land degradation involves both soil erosion and loss of soil fertility. While the soils in the highlands have a high inherent fertility, the continuous removal of nutrients without replacement as well as the steep and dissected terrain with extensive areas of slopes, coupled with the high intensity of rainfall have led to accelerated soil erosion. Due to the scarcity of wood for fuel, animal dung and crop residues are used as fuel instead of being used as fertilizers, which further increases fertility loss.

The availability and quality of water in general, its patterns of flow and the seasonal variation of rainfall all play an integral part in the system of environmental processes. Degradation of water resources involves both silting and the deposition of sediment, which leads to changes in the physical, chemical and biological conditions of resources. Deforestation, poor agricultural practices and soil erosion increase surface runoff and reduce the amount of rainfall infiltrating the soil and eventually percolating into groundwater aquifers. About 74% of the annual runoff of more than 110 billion cubic metres goes into the rivers that flow into Sudan, Egypt, Somalia and Kenya. Lower levels of infiltration and water storage in soils also affect the availability of water for human use. This, in turn, leads to higher peak flows in streams and rivers causing greater flood damage. Where soils are better at retaining moisture, spring and river flows are extended and evened out. This is important for irrigation development. Soil erosion also leads to the reduced life of storage dams due to silting, and may change the conditions for transport and hydropower production.

The carrying capacity of the rangelands, 42% of the country's total area (above 1,700m; average annual rainfall above 600mm) is severely limited by the inadequate watering facilities and by a consequent inefficient utilization of vegetation. The cutting of fodder instead of letting the animals range freely could be an improvement in order to reduce overgrazing and increase productivity.

Due to the expansion in irrigated crop cultivation in some of the traditional pastoral areas, partly by 'land grabbing', some grazing lands have been lost. Huge grazing areas have been reduced for parks (19,767km^2), wildlife reserves (28,100km^2) and sanctuaries (9,536km^2). This situation has led to conflicts between pastoralists and animosity towards government organizations and export-oriented agro-enterprises. Pastoralists have been forced to live in and utilize marginal areas for livestock production and have, therefore, become more vulnerable to drought. The continuing succession of droughts has affected livestock populations as well as the ability of highland farmers to produce crops. It has also led to catastrophic livestock losses as well as deterioration in rangelands.

Especially since the 1990s pollution has become a severe problem in rapidly modernizing regions and economic sectors. Air pollution is caused mainly by the addition of poisonous gases and particulate matter. In most cases these are the products of the combustion of fossil fuels. In particular, inhabitants of towns and areas around industry are affected, as well as several crops. For example, in 2011 more than 50% of the cars in Addis Ababa were more than 20 years old, and so not up to modern emission standards. Together with increasing industry, transport and domestic use of fuel in the last two decades, these factors have led to rising cases of acute respiratory infection. During recent years fresh water streams in Ethiopia have turned into open sewers due to the addition of domestic sewage, agricultural waste and industrial effluents resulting in death or impairment of the lives of both man and animals. Rubbish disposal is an unsolved problem in many towns. Pollution of soils results from the use of excessive fertilizers, pesticides and herbicides which adversely affect the physical, chemical and biological properties of the soil, which in turn affects plant growth.

Literature: DEMEL TEKETAY, ALFONS RITLER, 'Environment', *EAE* II, 323–327; ALFONS RITLER, 'Ecological Zones', *EAE* II, 213–215; HANS HURNI, *Agroecological Belts of Ethiopia. Explanatory Notes on 3 Maps at a Scale of 1:1,000,000*, Berne 1998; SOIL CONSERVATION RESEARCH PROGRAMME ETHIOPIA, *Research Report 43*, Addis Ababa, Berne 1998.

Alfons Ritler, Centre for Development and Environment, University of Berne

Ethiopian biomes

Biomes are natural formations of plants and animals; they are defined by structure of the natural vegetation and the species composition of the wild plants and animals that occur there. Altitude, climate and other environmental conditions vary significantly from biome to biome. Ethiopia has a high number of biomes due to variation in altitude, from the Dallol Depression, *c.*130 m b.s.l., to the peak of Ras Dashan, *c.*4,600 m a.s.l., and to different rainfall patterns on the eastern and western side of the highlands. Ethiopian farmers have traditionally recognized agricultural zones, which approximate widely defined biomes: *qwalla*, *wayna daga*, *daga* and *werch*. Newer studies of Ethiopian vegetation have defined the following biomes: (1) Desert and semi-desert scrubland – occurring in the dry parts of Afar and the Ogaden. (2) *Acacia-Commiphora* woodland and bushland – covering most of the south-eastern lowlands, parts of Afar and the Rift Valley. (3) Wooded grassland of the western Gambela region – tall grasslands south of the Baro River, inundated during the rainy season. (4) *Combretum-Terminalia* woodland – occurring on the entire western slopes of the highlands up to *c.*1,500 m. (5) Dry evergreen Afromontane forest and grassland complex – the natural biome of the central, northern and eastern highlands up to *c.*3,500 m, with an upper zone dominated by *Hagenia-* and *Hypericum-*trees. (6) Moist evergreen Afromontane forest – occurring from *c.*1,500 m and upwards in south-western Ethiopia, west of the Gibe/Omo and south of the Abbay rivers. (7) Transitional rain forest – found in the highest rainfall areas of south-western Ethiopia up to *c.*1,500 m). (8) Ericaceous belt – a belt on most of the high mountain massifs above the Afromontane forests from *c.*3,500 to 4,000 m. (9) Afroalpine belt – above the Ericaceous belt from *c.*4,000 m. A number of biomes are associated with rivers or lakes: (10) Riverine vegetation – along rivers, except where they pass very dry habitats. (11) Freshwater lakes, marshes and swamps. (12) Salt lakes, salt wetlands and salt pans – mainly in Afar, for example Dallol Depression, and in the Ogaden.

Literature: IB FRIIS, SEBSEBE DEMISSEW, PAULO VAN BREUGEL, 'Atlas of the Potential Vegetation of Ethiopia', *Biologiske Skrifter, Biological Series of the Royal Danish Academy of Sciences and Letters*, 58 (2010), 1–307.

Ib Friis, Natural History Museum of Denmark, Copenhagen

Wild flora

Ethiopia has a rich flora of wild plant species compared with many other African countries. In tropical Africa, Cameroon and Gabon have the highest richness

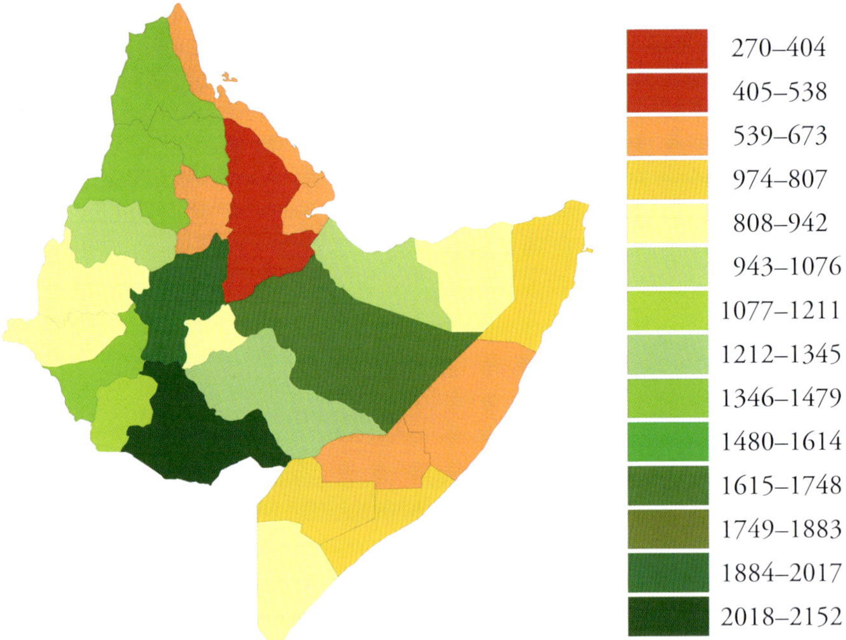

Table 4: Richness of plant species; the colours indicate the number of all wild plant species per region, © Ib Friis

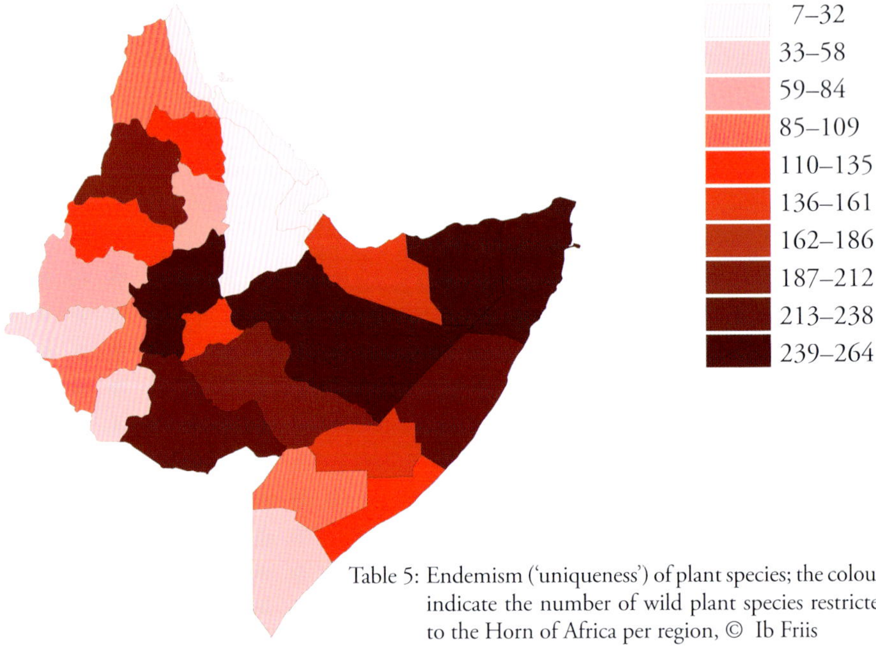

Table 5: Endemism ('uniqueness') of plant species; the colours indicate the number of wild plant species restricted to the Horn of Africa per region, © Ib Friis

(4,000–5,000 species/10,000 km^2). The average richness in Ethiopia is 1,500–2,000 species/10,000 km^2.

This contrasts with a markedly lower richness in countries at the same latitude west of Ethiopia: 500–1,000 species/10,000 km^2 in the Sudanian savannah zone, a broad belt of savannah that runs east and west across the African continent, from the Atlantic Ocean to the Ethiopian highlands. The richness in the semi-arid Sahel zone between the Sudanian zone and the Sahara Desert is 200–500 species/10,000km^2; this zone continues to the Red Sea and crosses the northern Eritrean lowlands.

The higher richness of plant species in Ethiopia and Eritrea than in the Sudan and the Sahel is due to a more varied climate, topography and geology than in the countries west of Ethiopia, where mountains and montane climate are absent.

Acanthus sennii (acanthus family), only found in the Ethiopian highlands. © Ib Friis

Composition of the flora. The wild flora of the Horn of Africa is here taken to include all species of plants not cultivated by man: local, indigenous species or species which have arrived by natural dispersal, formerly cultivated and naturalized species and weeds. In this sense the wild flora includes more than 6,500 species, amongst which are five species of gymnosperms (including conifers and the ephedra [shrubby horsetail] family) and around 200 species of ferns and fern-allies. The wild flora of the Horn of Africa is complex also at higher levels than the level of species, consisting of around 230 families, of which there are three families of gymnosperms and 36 families of ferns and fern allies. Several large plant families are economically important: grasses (around 700 species), legumes (around 550 species) and the sunflower family (around 500 species). Other plant families with over a hundred species are: the acanthus family, spurges, sedges, milkweeds, orchids, labiates, the mallow family, bindweeds, figworts and the coffee family. The grasses and legumes are ecologically important in woodlands and wooded grasslands, while the conifer0s podocarpus and juniper are important in the dry forests in northern and central Ethiopia, and members of the family Sapotaceae, the olive family, the rose family and the coffee family are important in the moist southern and southwestern forests. In the dry shrubland of south-eastern Ethiopia and Somalia the frankincense or myrrh family is important and represented with many species of myrrh and frankincense. The latter is also common in the northern part of the western lowlands.

Grasses	Poaceae	Olive family	Oleaceae
Legumes	Fabaceae-Papilionoideae	Rose family	Rosaceae
Acanthus family	Acanthaceae	Myrrh family	Burseraceae
Spurges	Euphorbiaceae	Myrrh	Commiphora
Sedges	Cyperaceae	Frankincense	Boswellia
Milkweeds	Ascepiadaceae	Rose	Rosa
Orchids	Orchidaceae	Saxifrage	Saxifraga
Labiates	Lamiaceae	Cyclamen	Cyclamen
Mallow family	Malvaceae	Orpine family	Crassulaceae
Bindweeds	Convolvulaceae	Lady's Mantle	Alchemilla
Figworts	Scrophulariaceae	Clover	Trifolium
Coffee family	Rubiaceae	Giant Thistle	Echinops, Cirsium
Podocarpus	Podocarpus falcatus	Giant Lobelia	Lobelia rhyncopetalum, Lobelia achrochilus
Podocarpus	Podocarpus falcatus		
Juniper	Juniperus procera	Arabica coffee	Coffea arabica

Table 6: Wild plants in the Horn of Africa, © Ib Fries

Distribution of the flora. In Ethiopia and Eritrea the species richness is unevenly distributed: the highest richness (3,000–4,000 species/10,000 km^2) is found in the former Sidamo region, which has around 2,000 species, while the former Shawa and Hararge regions have around 1,500 species each (all biome 2 and 5). The Eritrean coastal zone, with just over 500 species, has a richness of only about 1,000/10,000 km^2. The variation in species richness in the wild flora correlates with variation in altitude, rainfall and geology. The medium altitudes of the Ethiopian highlands, between approximately 1,500 m and 3,000 m a.s.l., have the highest species richness, while this drops significantly towards the highest peaks of the Ethiopian mountains. The lowest richness is found in the lowland deserts of the Afar region, with a species richness of only around 400 species/10,000 km^2, in the semi-deserts along the Red Sea coast and in a number of dry areas along the Ethiopian border with Somalia and Kenya (all biome 1). Higher species richness is found in the fire-prone woodlands near the border with Sudan (biome 3 and 4), where the richness drops along a gradient from Gambela towards north-western Ethiopia and western Eritrea. The mosaic of moist lowland forests and moist woodlands in southwestern Ethiopia (biome 7) has species richness comparable to that of similar areas further to the west in Africa.

Connections to floras in other parts of the world; floristic uniqueness of the Horn of Africa. A number of widespread European and Asian plant genera have their natural southern limit in Ethiopia or northern Somalia; well-known examples are rose, saxifrage and cyclamen. However, the greatest similarity between the flora of the highlands of Ethiopia and Eritrea is with the highlands of East Africa, whilst a small number of genera or species, especially at higher altitudes, are not found wild anywhere else, e.g. the genus *Hypagophytum* (orpine family), which is only found in the Semen and the mountains of Tegray. The wild flora of Ethiopia and Eritrea is therefore mainly transitional, with some elements shared with Europe and temperate Asia, while others are shared with tropical Africa and the East African mountains. However, the percentage of species of wild plants not found anywhere else but in the

Horn of Africa is rather high compared with other countries; only the tropical African countries Angola and the Democratic Republic of Congo have higher percentages, while Madagascar and extratropical South Africa have significantly higher percentages. These endemic species occur mostly in south-eastern Ethiopia and Somalia, while others occur in the Ethiopian highlands, e.g. many species in the genera Lady's Mantle, clover, giant thistle and the Ethiopian giant lobelia. These highland endemics are usually widespread in areas of suitable altitude. Relatively few endemic species occur in the moist forests of southwestern Ethiopia, though these areas are supposed to be the natural home of Arabica coffee, which probably does not occur in the wild anywhere else. The flora of Somalia has the highest degree of endemics, over 25% unique plant species, and the proportion of endemic species increases towards the tip of the Horn of Africa, but the total flora of Somalia contains only around 3,200 species. 17% of the species in Ethiopia and Eritrea are endemic or have a limited extension into Somalia. The endemic species in the lowlands are normally rather restricted in distribution. Narrowly distributed endemic species are most frequent in the Ogaden and in the lowlands of the old Sidamo and Bale regions.

The rich flora of wild plants in the Horn of Africa were already valuable natural resources in the Pre-Aksumite and Aksumite periods and have sustained the high diversity of agricultural practices among many ethnic groups in later periods. Ethiopia is considered one of the important centres for domestication of plants.

Literature: Ib Friis, Mats Thulin, Henning Emil Adsersen, Anne-Marie Christiansen Bürger, 'Patterns of plant diversity and endemism in the Horn of Africa', *Biologiske Skrifter, Biological Series of the Royal Danish Academy of Sciences and Letters,* 55 (2005), 289–314; Jens Mutke, Wilhelm Barthlott, 'Patterns of vascular plant diversity at continental to global scales', *Biologiske Skrifter, Biological Series of the Royal Danish Academy of Sciences and Letters,* 55 (2005), 521–553.

Ib Friis, Natural History Museum of Denmark, Copenhagen

Cultivated flora

Overview of plant diversity. The flora of Ethiopia and Eritrea is rich and contains diverse types of cultivated plants, making it one of the six plant-wealthy countries of Africa. The region exhibits abundant and unique overall biodiversity, and is a place of early plant cultivation, domestication and introduction, which stands out especially for its genetic richness and the uniqueness of its cultivated flora. The region's location at the gateway to Asia and Europe, situated in the tropical upland of the Horn of Africa, is believed to have facilitated the exchange of crops and genetic material over an extended period. The indigenous crops of the region were subsequently joined by those received from Asia, South and Central America, Europe and the rest of Africa. The area is home to over 6,000 species and/or varieties of higher plants of which about 841 are listed as 'useful' plants and close to 170 are cultivated. Many crops are drawn from wild species or from external sources through long processes of experimentation, innovation, domestication and introduction. Prolonged manipulation of crops has produced a collection of ancient cultigens referred to as farmers' varieties or 'landrace' varieties of the crops cultivated on a regular basis as staple foods; others are cultivated in a rather intermittent manner and still others less frequently by a few cultures.

Exploration, origin and genetic resources. Early descriptions of the cultivated plants of the region are by and large hidden in explorers' accounts, personal diaries, and the writings of historians, cultural and human anthropologists and biologists. These accounts show that Ethiopian farmers were experts in raising and utilizing the plants that they so painstakingly cultivated. The accounts of the traveller James Bruce included drawings of some crops, such as *ensat* ('false banana'), safflower, and *anchoote* (a vine producing an edible tuberous root). Explorers and scholars of Ethiopia in the late 1800s and early 1900s included many crops in their botanical accounts.

In the late 1920s the Russian Nikolai Vavilov made extensive collections of plant genetic material. This and later studies on the origins of Ethiopian crops and the description of agricultural systems included more complete records of cultivated plants.

Ethiopia soon became a centre of global attention as an important source of crops and plant genetic material such as genes resistant to barley yellow dwarf virus and coffee berry disease, as well as types of barley and sorghum rich in protein and lysine, an essential amino acid. Such genes have had profound impacts on the development of modern agricultural technologies. Some crops that are believed to have been introduced into Ethiopia early on have diversified, making the region an important secondary gene accumulation centre.

Typical farm homestead with *ensat* and other crops around the house, © Manfred Metz

Ethiopia is a historic centre of crop plant origin and diversity. An interesting example is the discovery of coffee, which is believed to have happened when a herdsman observed the unusual behaviour of one of his goats that had nibbled a coffee bush. He took some coffee berries home, and subsequently from Ethiopia coffee was taken first to Yemen, then to Europe and beyond. Other Ethiopian domesticates, such as *tef*, *ensat*, and sorghum, are believed to have emerged when humans inhabiting the grasslands were forced to move to the highlands due to an extended dry period around 13,000 years ago. The region has rich diversity in four of the world's most widely grown food crops (wheat, barley, sorghum and peas), three industrial crops (linseed, castor oil and cotton), one cash crop (coffee) and in other crops of more national and local importance. Ethiopia is recognized as a primary gene centre for *nug* (Niger seed), *tef* and Ethiopian mustard, as well as for subspecies and local varieties. Alongside indigenous crops, cassava, tannia and some fruit trees (avocado, apple, plum, casimir) were introduced in the last 100 years, and some others in later years.

Crop cultivation, exchange and conservation. Widely cultivated plants include cereals (*tef*, sorghum, barley, wheat, maize, finger and pearl millet); roots and tubers (*anchoote*, *ensat*, yam, taro, tannia, Irish, sweet and Oromo or Walaytta potatoes); stimulants (coffee, *chat*, *gesho*); pulses (beans such as faba, haricot and lima, field peas, cowpeas, lentils, chickpeas, groundnuts); fruits (banana, orange, lime, mango, papaya, grape, custard apple, peach, tree tomato, avocado, casimir), oilseeds (*nug*, sesame, linseed, rapeseed, safflower, sunflower); vegetables (peppers, shallot, onion, garlic, tomato, cabbage, carrot, beetroot, pumpkin); aromatics (myrtle, basil, artemisia, lemon grass); sugarcane, bottle gourd and many others. Not only is there a high number of species of cultivated plants but also diversity of horticultural complexes. The frequently cultivated cereals form the backbone of the region's agriculture and food economy. Conventional cultivated plants, cultivated trees (including the eucalyptus introduced from Australia) and shrubs as well as ornamental plants and hedge species make the cultivated flora truly sizeable. Some of the crops are staples, others are for industrial or commercial use and still others have minor roles. Variety in crop categories is a characteristic feature of the farming system as it is of dietary habits. Oils and spices are always important no matter what the staple food since they improve taste, texture and appearance. Some species are both cultivated and grow naturally while others are harvested from forests or occur as naturalized escapes, making Ethiopia a place where a full spectrum of cultivated flora can be seen.

Descriptions of the region's plant diversity have probably been responsible for the transfer of species to other countries through both official and unofficial channels. In this way, Ethiopia has contributed greatly to the world pool of cultivated plants and their genetic resources. An important gift from Ethiopia to the rest of the world is Arabica coffee, which soon became a significant international commercial crop. Other notable contributions include disease resistant varieties of barley and wheat as well as high-protein and high-lysine varieties of cereals (e.g. barley, sorghum); still other gifts include *tef*, *ensat*, *anchoote*, Oromo or Walaytta potato, *nug* and African finger millet. Crops introduced from outside the region that now appear entirely naturalized include chillies, maize, garlic, onions and Irish and sweet potatoes all of which are integral to local cuisine. While the rich and unique genetic resource of the region's cultivated plants is greatly valued, the biodiversity base is facing a serious threat mainly from the erosion of crop genetic resources and the on-going drive for growth and agricultural transformation. The impending consequences in today's world of climate change and the push for growth and transformation are posing challenges that need to be addressed. The way forward is a combination of *ex situ* and *in situ* conservation since the cultivated plants of the region are important national assets as much as they are global resources to be preserved for posterity.

Literature: Jack Rodney Harlan, 'Ethiopia: a Center of Diversity', *Economic Botany* 23 (1969), 309–314; A. Poncet, Inga Hedberg, M. Melander, Eva Persson, 'Useful plants in the flora of Ethiopia and Eritrea area according to volumes 1–7', Inga Hedberg, Ib Friis, Eva Persson (eds.), *Flora of Ethiopia and Eritrea*, VIII, 39–95, Addis Ababa University, Uppsala University 2009.

Zemede Asfaw, Addis Ababa University

Fauna

Ethiopia is a country characterized by a variable climate highly modified by topography and has many biomes (see Ethiopian biomes). These diversied biomes support a varied fauna.

However, the large population of the country with over 100 million inhabitants, has an impact on the distribution of the fauna through habitat destruction. Moreover, high population growth has forced people to cultivate more and more land. The natural vegetation on most of the highlands (see biome 5) was earlier closed-canopy forest in moister areas, and grassland, bushland, and thicket in drier areas. However, these hillsides have good fertile soil and are now heavily populated by farming communities. Therefore most of biomes 5 and 6 have been converted to agriculture with a few areas of natural vegetation remaining.

The invertebrate fauna is not completely documented and needs immediate attention, but the vertebrate fauna is mostly well known, though the number of species is constantly increasing as more roads are opened up facilitating the exploration of new areas. The same time, new applications of modern techniques of taxonomy are available. So far, the record shows 200 species of fish, containing about 40 endemic fish species. Lake Tana alone harbours 27 native species of which 22 are endemic. From the few localities that have been explored, there are 63 amphibian species known of which 26 are endemic. There are over 100 species of reptiles recorded, at least 16 being endemic.

Birds. The number of bird species within Ethiopia is 872 of which 26 are endemic.

Mammals. Over 320 Mammal species have been recorded with over 50 endemic species known solely in Ethiopia. Over the last 20 years, loss of habitat and poaching have reduced the population of several species of wild animals in Ethiopia, but the decline is most marked in larger mammals like the African elephant (*Loxodonta africana*). Ethiopia has lost nearly 90% of its elephant populations since the 1980s and now hardly 1,000 are left. Ethiopian lion (*Panthera leo roosevelti*), compared to other African lions, has darker mane and smaller body.

Among the endemic mammals are the endangered Walia Ibex (*Capra walie*) restricted to the Semen Mountains and the Mountain Nyala (*Tragelaphus buxtoni*), in the Ethiopian highlands east of the Rift Valley, found in biome 8, but more common at slightly lower elevations. The Menelik's Bushbuck (*Tragelaphus scriptus meneliki*) lives in high-altitude forests over a larger area, but is endangered as well. The Ethiopian Wolf (*Canis simensis*) with the largest population in the Bale Mountains is the most researched of all the endangered mammals in Ethiopia and yet critically endangered.

The Gelada or Bleeding-heart Monkey (*Theropithecus gelada*) is concentrated in the Ethiopian highland, with the largest population in the Semen Mountains. More widespread are the Mantled Guereza or Abyssinian Black-and-white Colobus (*Colobus guereza*) and the Hamadryas Baboon (*Papio hamadryas*), native to the Horn of Africa. The Olive Baboon (*Papio anubis*) inhabits savannahs, steppes, and forests. The Big-headed Mole-rat (*Tachyoryctes macrocephalus*) is endemic on the Sanetti Plateau in the Bale Mountains (biome 9). Furthermore, there are endemic species of small mammals such as the Shrew (*Crocidura harenna*) and the Narrow-footed Woodland Mouse (*Grammomys minnae*).

Despite having the largest livestock resource base in Africa the meat and live animals export business is much lower than Somalia's or Sudan's. Pastoralism is a way of life and livelihood system for more than 10 million pastoralists in Ethiopia. Pastoral livestock is also increasingly sought for breeding purposes. Government and donor-funded development programmes and commercial farmers are buying large numbers of heifers from pastoral marketing cooperatives.

Considering all of these trends, it can be safely assumed that 40-50% of the cattle and goats supplied to domestic markets originate from the pastoral system, while the proportion of sheep is lower. Pastoral camels from the eastern part of the country are also increasingly sought in domestic markets in mid- and highland areas, as farmers see their value as a drought-tolerant pack animal.

Gelada baboon, Semen Mountains, © Philipp Hedemann

Camels. In spite of the importance of the camel, it remains a gloomy fact that this valuable animal has been and is still neglected by planners and scholars, and the camel herders are marginalized in their own society. Because of the seasonal migrations, crossing of national boundaries and reluctance of herders to give exact herd sizes, it is difficult to estimate the camel population. The importance of the dromedary arises primarily, however, from its provision of milk, blood, and meat within a subsistence economy and its use as a beast of burden. Besides its economic importance, the camel has social and cultural importance to the pastoral herders of the region. Camels are prized according to their role in the traditional social relations for payment of bride wealth and compensation of injured parties in tribal feuds. Camels can also be seen as a sort of banking system or security against drought, diseases and other natural calamities that affect smaller stock more severely. Camels can go without water for 19–30 days; salt is given to camels every 6–8 months. Camel herders clearly understand that the camel is their basic means of survival. Because of the semi-arid and arid conditions and the seasonal concentration of water and grazing, nomadic camel pastoralism characterizes the livestock husbandry patterns of most of the region; and it represents a highly rational adaptation of human life to this environment. It constitutes the only efficient way of exploiting many areas where cultivation and small stock raising are impossible.

Equines. Equines including donkeys, mules and horses are important animals in Ethiopian agriculture and in the national economy. Ethiopia has one of the highest donkey populations in the world (about four million). The small-scale farmers of the highlands have the largest share with two to three animals per family and with female donkeys being most common (70%). In the country as a whole, donkeys provide pack services, carrying commodities weighing 60–100kg and covering distances of 15–20km up to five hours. In the northern areas their contribution in terms of firewood trade to the family income is decisive. Constraints to improved donkey use are discussed, including health problems, nutrition and policy issues. Besides, Ethiopia has 65% of all African mules and almost half of horses. The mule has more stamina than a horse, can carry heavier burdens while eating less, and is surer of foot in the mountain passes.

Cattle. In some areas of Ethiopia access to oxen is considered to be a more important production resource than land. The reasons for oxen's strong position there are related to the predominance of cereal cultivation, dry climate and heavy soils. In parts of Ethiopia there are more oxen than cows. Households with a pair of oxen are in general the rich households and those without oxen have to pay up to 50% of the harvest to have their land ploughed.

The majority of milking cows belong to the indigenous eight cattle breeds of the Zebu types. However, their potential for milk production is low with the average age at first calving being 53 months. But also a very small number of crossbred animals are milked to provide the family with fresh milk, butter and cheese. Surpluses are sold, usually by women, who use the regular cash income to buy household necessities or to save for festival occasions. Both the pastoralist and smallholder farmers produce 98% of the country's milk.

Ethiopian sheep can be categorized into four groups based on their ecological distribution, tail types and fibre type. There is high morphological and ecological diversity among the major sheep groups as well as among the sheep types. There is also a strong relationship between sheep types, ethnic groups and production systems. At the national level, sheep and goats account for about 90% of live animals/meat and 92% of skin and hide export trade value. For some farmers, goats and sheep are like their saving accounts and their insurance policies; whenever they need immediate cash, they sell a few goats or sheep to cover their costs.

Backyard poultry is the predominant system in Ethiopia and represents nearly 98% of the poultry population. Farmers directly sell their chickens to consumers or to small retail traders who take them to large urban markets. Governmental rural improvement programmes use poultry as intervention component to target women. The consumption of poultry products is more common in urban than in rural areas, and especially high during holidays. Chickens have special values in welcome feasts for visitors, a source of food for women post-birth, payment to villagers for local health services, gifts to newly married couples, and they strengthen social networks between women.

Beekeeping. Beekeeping in Ethiopia is an ancient tradition which stretches back into its early history. It is an important activity for many rural people and is carried out in forests, home gardens and houses in all parts of the country. Honey and beeswax play a big role in the cultural and religious life of the Ethiopian people. The collection and selling of honey and other bee products, is a major economic activity. Ethiopia with over 10 million honeybee colonies has the highest honeybee population in Africa. It is one of the leading producers of honey and beeswax in Africa and in the world. The country is endowed with a botanically diversified honey source of 800 bee plants.

Literature: FISSEHA GEBREAB, 'Animals', *EAE* I, 268–273; AFEWORK BEKELE, DEREK WILLIAM YALDEN, *The Mammals of Ethiopia and Eritrea,* Addis Ababa 2013.

Afework Bekele, Addis Ababa, Maija Priess, Universität Hamburg

Agriculture

Agriculture is the mainstay of the Ethiopian economy. It provides income and employment for about 80% of the population, accounts for almost half of the gross domestic product (GDP) of the country and generates more than 80% of the export earnings. About 15% of the total surface of the country is used for cultivation, mainly for seasonal crops, about 1.5% for perennial crops, and almost 50% for pasture.

Due to a great variety of climatic and agro-ecological conditions (as expressed by the 12 biomes), Ethiopian agriculture is highly diversified. Crop cultivation, mainly by smallholder farmers, is concentrated in the densely populated central highlands which constitute 40% of the land area and accommodate some 80% of the population. The majority of the population in the highlands depends on mixed farming on small plots of land. Livelihoods in the less populated lowland areas are mainly dependent on pastoralism and agro-pastoralism (Somali, Afar, parts of Oromia Regional States) or shifting cultivation (Benishangul-Gumuz, Gambella and parts of Southern Nations, Nationalities, and People's Regional States).

Major crops grown are cereals, pulses, oil-seeds and coffee. Although large parts of Ethiopia have fertile land and generally adequate rainfall, agricultural production is constrained by poor technology, land fragmentation, overutilization, soil erosion and recurrent droughts, leading to low productivity and repeated shortfalls. Only about 1% of the cropping area is irrigated.

There are two distinct cropping seasons, the main (*Mahar* or *Keramt*) season during the summer rains, when about 95% of the crops are produced, and the small (*balg*) season during the short spring rain period.

Food crops, cash crops and livestock. Grains are the most important field crops, occupying about 86% of the cropping areas. Principal grains are *tef* (an indigenous

Landscape in Agame, Tegray, © Wolbert G.C. Smidt

cereal used for making *enjara*, the local pancake-like bread), wheat and barley grown in cooler climates (of biome 5) and maize, sorghum and millet grown at lower altitudes and warmer climates. *Tef*, wheat and maize are the main staples for the majority of Ethiopians. Cereals are largely grown as non-market crops to serve the subsistence needs of farmers' households.

Yields per hectare are lowest for *tef* (about 1 ton per hectare on average) and highest for maize (around 2tons per hectare on average). While cereal production at the national level almost stagnated at 5–7 million tons during the 1970s to 1990s, after the fall of the *Darg* regime promotion of agriculture and liberalization of the grain markets brought about a substantial increase in production of more than 3 % annually during the 1990s, which further accelerated with growth rates of above 7 % after 2000. Since 2000, annual cereal production has averaged more than 10 million tons. With improved seed varieties, fertilizers and proper cultivation practices there is still a high potential for further substantial increases in yields and production.

Pulses (chickpeas, lentils, haricot beans) and oil-seeds come second and third after cereals in crop production. They are grown at all altitudes from sea level up to about 3,000 m (biome 5), but are particularly prevalent in the northern and central highlands. Apart from serving primarily subsistence needs, pulses and oil-seeds used to be important cash crops in the past. Among the oil-seeds, sesame has gained importance as a high-value cash crop in recent years.

Ensat ('false banana') is an important food crop in Ethiopia's southern and south-western highlands. Since the *ensat* plant can withstand short drought periods and *ensat* flour can be stored for many years, it is also a suitable food security crop.

Coffee is indigenous to Ethiopia and the most important cash crop (see 'Coffee'), generating income for more than 300,000 farmers' families and about two thirds of the export earnings of the country. Other cash crops of some significance are *chat*, a mild stimulant, cotton, citrus, other fruits and sugarcane. In recent years, flowers have also become an increasingly important cash crop and export item.

Livestock production is an important area, contributing about one third to agricultural GDP. Hides and skins are the second largest export earner after coffee. Ethiopia is said to have the largest livestock population in all of Africa, comprising some 30 million cattle, 42 million sheep and goats, 7 million equines, 1 million camels, 50 million poultry and 5 million bee colonies (2012/2013). Livestock serves several purposes, such as provision of draught animals, food, cash, savings, transportation, manure, fuel as well as social protection and prestige.

Ethiopia has great potential for increased livestock production, both for the local market and for export. However, expansion is constrained by inadequate animal feed, diseases, and lack of veterinary and support services.

Main features: traditional smallholder mixed farming. Agricultural production in Ethiopia is organized into four types of farm: smallholder peasant farms, group/cooperative farms, state farms and private commercial farms. Although group/cooperative and state farms enjoyed particular promotion under the former *Darg* regime, they remained relatively unimportant and contributed less than 5% to overall agricultural production. However, state farms and private commercial farms account for a higher share of industrial crops like cotton, sugarcane as well as vegetable, fruit, coffee, tea and sesame production.

Smallholder peasant farms have remained the predominant farm type in Ethiopia. They are characterized by subsistence orientation, mixed crop-livestock farming, rain-fed agriculture, low inputs, traditional technologies and low productivity. Peasant farms occupy about 95% of the cultivated land and produce 96% of national agricultural output. Average farm size is less than two hectares and 50% of the holdings are below one hectare, often split up into several tiny plots. Peasant farmers are mainly subsistence oriented, with only small amounts of cash income derived from occasional sale of crops or livestock. Farming practices have remained very traditional, with ox-ploughing for cereal cultivation in large part and hand tools for other crops. Population pressure and lack of alternative income earning possibilities have forced many farmers to cultivate steep slopes and marginal land, causing soil erosion, water run-off and land degradation.

In contrast to such general and unfavourable features of peasant farming, which are typical for large parts of the northern and central highlands, some ethnic groups in the southern highlands (Burji, Konso-Gidole, Dullay) have developed an intensive and sustainable farming system, with terracing as a marked feature. The terraces, usually built with stones, allow the cultivation of slopes, prevent soil erosion and increase the water retaining capacity of the soil. Complemented by water-retention and irrigation facilities, by the use of animal dung and human faeces as manure, and by adapted systems of crop rotation and mixed cropping, the soil fertility is maintained and the terraces can be cultivated throughout the year. In spite of such striking advantages, this more intensive and sustainable farming system has not spread to other areas of the Ethiopian highlands, where soil erosion and water scarcity are constraining agriculture.

Major challenges: low productivity, exposure to drought and sustainable land use. The Ethiopian government has acknowledged agriculture as the main source of economic growth for the country (Growth and Transformation Plan), and has launched various initiatives to further boost agricultural production, including:

- Land registration, to provide land tenure security to farmers which is expected to encourage them to invest in the land and apply sustainable land use practices;
- Promotion of integrated watershed management;
- Expansion of small, medium and large scale irrigation (e.g. the construction of the 'Grand Ethiopian Renaissance Dam' is expected to allow development of 500,000 hectares of irrigated land);
- Facilitating the commercialization of agriculture, through promoting high value crops, intensifying production in high-potential areas and developing agricultural marketing infrastructure;
- Promotion of large-scale private commercial agriculture in (so far) only extensively used or underused lowland areas.

Some of these initiatives have been widely appreciated as necessary, useful and successful, such as land registration, watershed management and small-scale irrigation, while others, particularly the promotion of large-scale irrigation and large-scale commercial agriculture, have still to prove themselves and have raised major concerns as to their actual and potential harmful environmental and social impacts.

Population depending on agriculture	80 %
Contribution of agriculture	
to GDP	50 %
to exports	50 %
Share of total land surface:	
used for cultivation:	*c.* 15 %,
irrigated:	*c.* 1 %
under perennial crops:	*c.* 1.5 %
used for livestock:	*c.* 50 %
Typical features of Ethiopian agriculture	95% smallholder peasant farms, mixed crop-livestock farming, rain-fed agriculture, low inputs, traditional technologies, low productivity, low yields
Major crops	Cereals (maize, *tef*, wheat, sorghum, millet), pulses, oilseeds, coffee
Livestock	Largest livestock population in Africa; ca. 54 million cattle, 30 million sheep and goats

Table 7: Ethiopian agriculture – facts and figures, © Manfred Metz

Literature: MANFRED METZ, 'Agriculture', *EAE* I, 2003, 148–153; ALEMAYEHU SEYOUM TAFFESSE, PAUL DOROSH, SINAFIKEH ASRAT, *Crop Production in Ethiopia: Regional Patterns and Trends, International Food Policy Research Institute, Ethiopian Development Research Institute, Ethiopia Strategy Support Program II, Working Paper No. 0016,* Addis Ababa (March) 2011.

Manfred Metz, Berlin

III Peoples

Introduction

Ethiopia (including Eritrea before 1991) has a fascinating diversity of peoples and cultures. This makes both for cultural 'richness' and for problems.

The long history of Ethiopia, with its political origins in the old Aksumite empire (until the 9th century CE), is strongly marked by this diversity, which was not influenced by Western colonial rule. The Ethiopian state and regional-political structures have their socio-cultural roots in the traditions of these many peoples and ethnic groups, who emerged, developed, moved, split off or migrated as a result of different adaptations to the physical and geographical environments. The people of today's Ethiopia are still tied to these historical and cultural traditions, which are dynamic, partly 'reinvented', and often maintained with pride.

The country's population of 100 million (the most recent figure of December 2016, from UN estimation) includes about 75 ethnic groups and peoples, depending on the definitions used. On these separate ethnic groups (see below), no statistical breakdown is available beyond the last (2007) census. But a safe estimate is that all groups have increased with at least 10%, giving the average annual population growth of 2,6%. Next to ethnicity, religion is important, adding important dimensions to the picture of diversity, conflict, and cultural exchange that one sees today. Remarkable in the history of Ethiopia is the relative harmony with which these communities and peoples of different faiths have co-existed and interacted, despite the fact that religious identity seems to be a growing 'fault line' in today's Ethiopia.

Peoples and languages. In the historical sources it is often difficult to distinguish between names of peoples, regions and languages, as they often became coterminous, as in the case of Tegrennya. But language and ethnic boundaries are not always identical. A language tends to expand and be adopted beyond a specific ethno-linguistic group, leading to a blurring of boundaries, so it is difficult to assert full overlap between the two identities. Additionally there are always mixed populations or some that fall outside any classification, e.g. urban populations, who already in the past have often lived for several generations in the towns, intermarried with others, mixed socio-cultural traditions, and come to speak the locally dominant language, such as Amharic or the Oromo language Oromiffa in Ethiopia or Tegrennya in Eritrea. If asked, however, many people will often identify themselves under a variety of ethnic labels. So while the first guide to, or criterion by which to distinguish, ethnic groups/peoples is perhaps language, this is only a starting point, complicated by multiple interactions. Ethnic groups and languages in Ethiopia have been well researched over the past decades, with work ranging from scientific to policy studies to popular books. This diversity and the cultural richness also led to growing 'ethnic tourism' in Ethiopia, for example in the southwest.

In Ethiopia and Eritrea two of the four large language groups of Africa are represented: Nilo-Saharan and Afroasiatic (or Afro-Asiatic). Within Afroasiatic, three large units are found: Semitic (represented by Ethiopian-Semitic and Arabic), Cushitic, and Omotic. Nilo-Saharan languages are the smallest group, spoken predominantly in the western areas of Ethiopia and Eritrea. For further discussion see the section on languages.

The Nilo-Saharan group, estimated to total about 1.3 million, comprises some 20 peoples, among whom are the Nara and Kunama in southwest Eritrea, and the Berta, Gumuz, Nuer, Anywa, Me'en, Mursi and others in Ethiopia. They vary in number from more than 200,000 (Berta) to only about 300 (Kwama), and they are mostly agro-pastoralists and small-scale cultivators, with a few hunter-gatherer minorities. Many also engage in cross-border trade with Sudan. They show the entire range of 'religious variety', from Muslim to Christian (Orthodox or Evangelical) to traditional or tribal religion. These peoples, living historically on the margins of the Ethiopian state, were never well-connected to the centres of political power.

Within the Afroasiatic language family, there are three major groups, of which Omotic is only found in southern Ethiopia. The Omotic-speaking peoples comprise about 32 named groups, although again dialectical differences are contested and may increase the number. Numerically (and based on the last national census of 2007), the most important ones are the Walaytta (1.75 million), the Kafa (or Kaficho, around 1.1 million), and the Gamo (1.4 million). Among these groups, mixed agriculture is the dominant activity, and the livelihood of many peoples is centred around the cultivation of *ensat* ('false banana').

The two other groups, with the largest populations, are the 'Semitic speakers' and the 'Cushiticspeakers'. The Ethiopian-Semitic-speaking groups comprise the Amhara (19.8million in 2007), the Tegrennya-speakers (around 4.5million), the Tegre (in Eritrea 1.2million with various subgroups), the 'Gurage' groups (again with several sub-divisions, some1.8million), and the Silt'e (about 1million), who were until 2003 identified as part of the Gurage. All these groups live in and around the Ethiopian central highlands.

Among Cushitic-speakers we find the largest ethnic group/people in Ethiopia, the Oromo, with perhaps 25.4million (in 2007, incl. many subgroups), and also the Somali (4.5million in Ethiopia), Sidaama (about 1.9million), Afar (1.2million), and Hadiyya (1.2 million), not taking into account the past decade of 2,6% annual population growth.

There are also minority (caste) groups, such as the Wata, Fuga, Manja or Band, Shabo and Sabuye. It is often difficult to say whether they are part of their 'host societies' or different groups. Many still suffer discrimination and exclusion.

Language communities, especially the large ones, may also include people from different ethnic origins who have adopted the regionally dominant language as their first language. Next to this language divergence, the peoples of Ethiopia have different origin trajectories and socio-cultural profiles, with characteristic indigenous political structures, ritual and religious ideas, kinship systems, or art/material culture traditions. These have been described in a wealth of anthropological literature. While such variety cannot be denied and has produced the cultural complexity of today, the peoples cannot be neatly placed in categories of 'essential' difference, because interaction and exchange have been frequent, and peoples' identifications can shift or be used opportunistically. In the 20th century a stronger Ethiopian national state arose and led to political centralisation, military and educational modernisation, and to a new framework of state laws (since the 1950s), which challenged the customary law traditions of ethnic groups.

Ethnicity in modern times. Due to economic and political inequalities in the imperial state and the 'modernisation process', ethno-linguistic and ethno-regional identities were 'reproduced' in regional disparities, hierarchies of power, lack of access to central resources, and also cultural prestige ranking. These processes contributed to the durability of ethnicity.

During the *Darg* period (1974–1991), 'ethnicity' was de-emphasized, in line with Marxist-Socialist policy. But rebel movements based on ethno-regional identities emerged in many parts of Ethiopia to combat the government and the perceived lack of equality or respect for ethno-cultural rights. The metaphorical 'family identity' suggested by the appeal to ethnicity often had more resonance among people than any other identity.

In post-1991 ethno-federal Ethiopia, the political regime was guided largely by conceptions of ethno-linguistic identity. The ruling Tigray People's Liberation Front (TPLF), the core of the post-1991 government, had its roots in an ethno-regional resistance movement against the central government. Under the TPLF-EPRDF regime, since 1991 ethnic identities and languages have been given explicit recognition, and 'nationalities' became units for decentralisation, district borders, educational reform and local autonomy. Ethnicity has become a vehicle of identity politics and serious disputes. The political use of ethnicity tended to overshadow *cultural* ethnicity. Not unsurprisingly, the realities of ethnic and linguistic diversity in Ethiopia do not quite correspond to their 'official' delineation in state laws and documents. A new map of the 'ethno-linguistic regions' of Ethiopia in 1992 showed 63 units. The Ethiopian Constitution of 1995 declared Ethiopia to be a federation of Nations, Nationalities and Peoples, and in various policy documents the numbers 70 or 72 were mentioned. Again, in the last population census of 2007, 86 groups were enumerated. So the (self-)classification is shifting. Since 2005, ethnic diversity is officially celebrated in the country in an annual state-sponsored 'Nations, Nationalities and People's Day'.

In the present era of globalization, many Ethiopian ethnic groups also have 'migrant communities' abroad, often with their own specific websites. Their elites are engaged in the discursive (re)shaping of their historical ethnic identities. This often leads to (over)emphasizing ethnic boundaries and identities, although these may not always bear close resemblance to the facts on the ground in the home country.

Literature: ELOI FICQUET, DEREJE FEYISSA, 'Ethiopians in the twenty-first century: the structure and transformation of the population', in GERARD PRUNIER, ELOI FICQUET (eds.), *Understanding Contemporary Ethiopia: Monarchy, Revolution and the Legacy of Meles Zenawi,* London 2015; PAULOS MILKIAS, *Ethiopia,* Santa Barbara 2011; SOLOMON ADDIS GETAHUN, WUDU TAFETE KASSU, *Culture and Customs of Ethiopia,* Greenwood 2014.

Jon Abbink, Leiden

Languages

The region of Ethiopia and the wider Horn of Africa has one of the largest and more diverse arrays of languages in the continent. Ethiopia itself has between 70 and 90 spoken languages, whilst Eritrea has nine, and the greatest diversity is found in the west and southwest of Ethiopia. It is difficult to be precise about the exact number of languages in Ethiopia for a number of reasons. Firstly, linguists as well as the speakers of language varieties do not agree about what is a language with a number of dialects, or a group of closely related languages. A case in point is Oromo, which is regarded in some accounts not as a single language but as a group of related spoken dialects, some of which are not readily mutually intelligible. This is not unusual in the case of unwritten languages, and even when one variety or dialect is selected as the base for the form of a language, an array of spoken dialects may be and often is retained. Secondly, as linguists make better descriptions, 'new' languages may be identified where before they proposed only dialect variation.

So, for instance, the variety of Tegre spoken on the Dahlak islands is often regarded as a separate language, Dahalik, now that it has been better described.

Lastly, in the less accessible parts of the country, especially in the west and southwest, 'new' languages are even today occasionally still being discovered. It is equally difficult to be precise about the number of speakers of some languages. This, too, can be for various reasons. So, many people in Ethiopia may speak more than one language, often two but commonly three or more, for use in different contexts. One language may be used at home, another in dealing with officialdom, and yet another in interaction with neighbouring villagers or at the market. This kind of situation is especially common in the countryside. Still, even in big cities like Addis Ababa, you may hear people using a range of languages. Linguists often talk of a person's 'mother-tongue', which is ideally the language learned by a child at home, but even here there are instances where more than one language is used in the home. Two languages that are widely used in the region as a *lingua franca* (as a language of wider currency) are Oromo and Amharic, which considerably increases the number of speakers in some censuses. Yet again, the statistics can be complicated by a mismatch between ethnicity, between which ethnic group an individual identifies him or herself with and the first language that he or she speaks. So, the number of speakers of all varieties of Oromo is stated in the 2007 census as almost 25 million, whilst the number of people who identified themselves as ethnically Oromo is as much as 26.5 million. On the other hand, in the same census, over 21.5 million individuals indicated that they spoke Amharic, though the people claiming membership of the Amhara ethnic group numbered a little over 19.8 million. These census figures are almost certainly now outdated.

The languages. Almost all of the languages of Ethiopia, Eritrea, Djibouti and Somalia belong to one of four major language families. There is a handful of very small languages, spoken in the southwest of Ethiopia, the affiliation of which is disputed, and a variety of Bantu is spoken in the far south of Somalia. Of the language families represented in the region, two are found only in the Horn of Africa: Omotic in Ethiopia, and Cushitic in all four countries of the Horn together with pockets in Sudan, Kenya and Tanzania. Another group, Ethiopian-Semitic (or Ethiosemitic), spoken in Ethiopia and Eritrea, forms a branch of the wider Semitic family, which is represented across North Africa and the Middle East. The largest member of this family is, of course, Arabic in all its varieties and one form of Arabic is spoken as a mother tongue in Eritrea, where it was introduced from the Arabian peninsula in the mid-19th century. Together, Omotic, Cushitic and Semitic are generally considered as members of a much wider superfamily called Afroasiatic (or 'Afro-Asiatic'). The

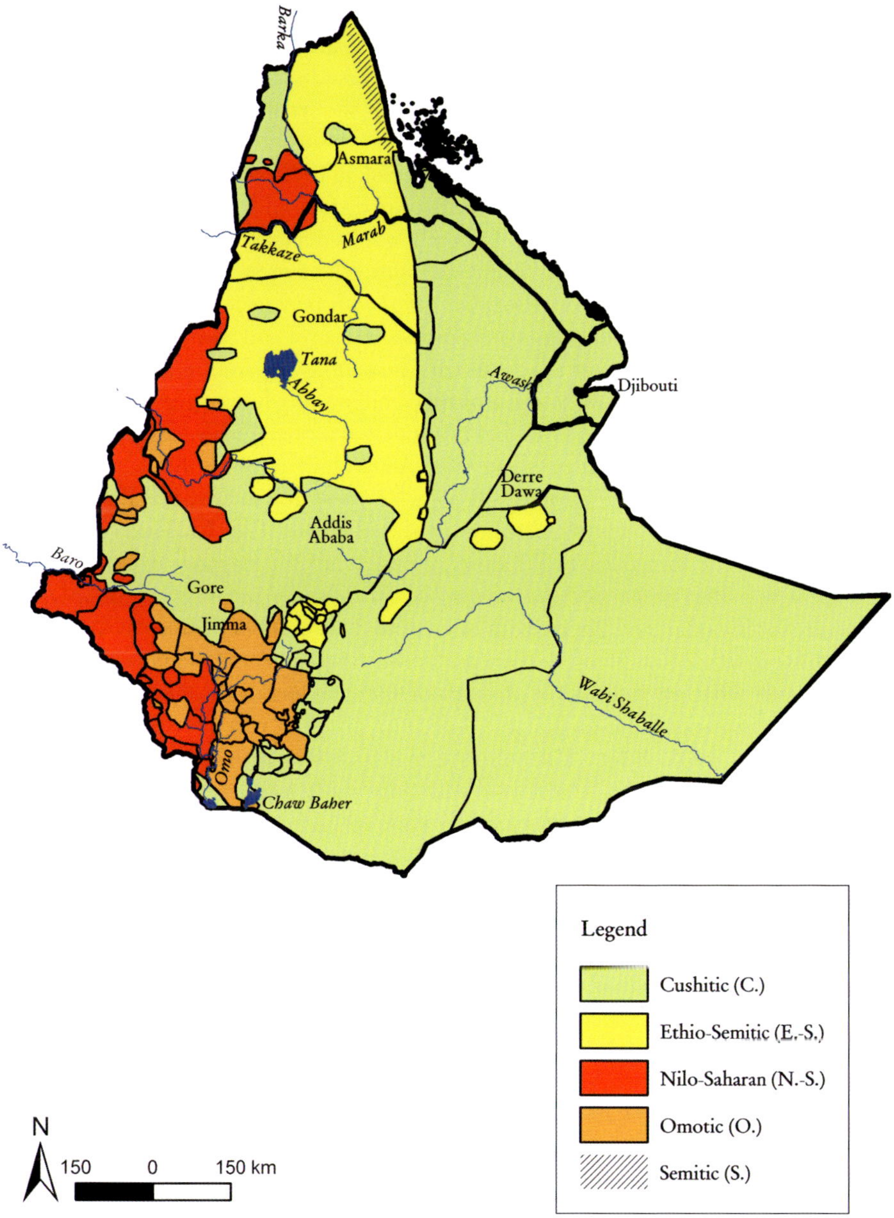

Map 4: Languages of Ethiopia and Eritrea, © Hiob Ludolf Centre for Ethiopian Studies, Hamburg

fourth major family of languages represented in the region is Nilo-Saharan with a number of relatively small languages found chiefly along the western frontiers of Eritrea and Ethiopia. Most Nilo-Saharan languages are spoken further west, across Sudan, South Sudan and Chad, and as far west as Mali.

There are around 30 Omotic languages, divided into between two and three major subgroups, all spoken in Ethiopia. Most of the Omotic languages have relatively small numbers of speakers, ranging from a few thousands to tens of thousands. Three languages, Kafa, Gofa and Kullo (or Dawro), have several hundred thousand, but only

Walaytta and Gamo have more than a million. The question of what is a language and what is a dialect arises in this last instance, as Gamo, Gofa and Kullo/Dawro are sometimes grouped together as varieties of what could otherwise be considered as a single language. The differing ethnic awareness of the speakers, however, contradicts this clumping together.

There are also around 30 Cushitic languages spoken in all four countries of the Horn excluding those in Kenya and Tanzania. Linguists divide the family into around six or seven branches or sub-branches. Again, there is a considerable range in the numbers of speakers, from a few thousand to several millions. The largest Cushitic languages are Oromo (self-name *Oromiffaa* or *Afaan Oromoo*), with perhaps over 30 million speakers in Ethiopia alone, not counting communities in Kenya and Somalia, but including all varieties. The second largest is Somali (*Af Soomaali*), with around 16 or 17 million speakers, again counting all varieties, around 6 million of whom are in Ethiopia, with the rest in Somalia, Djibouti, Kenya and the Somali diaspora. Other large Cushitic languages with more than a million speakers are Afar (*Qafar af*), in Ethiopia, Eritrea and Djibouti; Afar together with Oromo and Somali belongs to the Lowland East Cushitic branch. Sidaama and Hadiyya, members of the Highland East Cushitic branch, are both spoken in the Rift Valley of Ethiopia. Another Cushitic language with over a million speakers is Beja (self-name *Bidhaawyeet* or *Tu-Bdhaawi*), most of whose speakers, however, live in Sudan and Egypt, with only around 160,000 in Eritrea.

Turning to Ethiopian-Semitic, there are between twelve and 20 languages depending again on what are considered dialects or independent languages. This particularly applies to the smaller languages sometimes grouped together under the name 'Gurage' (e.g. Chaha, Selte, Walane), a term which in fact has more geographical than scientific reality. The largest and culturally most important members of this family are Amharic (*Amarennya*), probably with around 26 million speakers including those who use it as a language of wider communication across much of Ethiopia, and Tegrennya with a little under 7 million speakers in Ethiopia and Eritrea together. Aside from Tegre in Eritrea, all the other Ethiopian-Semitic languages have less than a million speakers, typically several tens of thousands at most or just a few thousand at least. A special case is that of Ge'ez (also called Ethiopic or Classical Ethiopic), which is no longer a spoken language in the true sense, but has great importance as the language of the literature and traditional culture of the Ethiopian Orthodox Church, fulfilling the role that Latin played until recently in the Roman Catholic Church.

Lastly, the Nilo-Saharan languages of the region number less than 20 and none has more than around 200,000 speakers, most being much smaller. The largest languages are Berta, Kunama and Nara in Eritrea, and Gumuz, Me'en and Nuer in Ethiopia.

Typology and nature of the languages. At the same time that the majority of the languages of the region are quite distinct, many show certain patterns and structural features in common. This may be partly because most, i.e. those belonging to the Cushitic, Omotic and Semitic families, are ultimately related, albeit distantly, being members of the Afroasiatic superfamily. The similarities are also doubtless due to the fact that these languages have been spoken side by side for millennia and have inevitably influenced one another. Cushitic and Omotic are assumed to be indigenous to the Horn, and Semitic languages were introduced sometime during the 1st millennium BCE. We can see this influence at work when we compare Ge'ez, dating roughly to the first half of the 1st millennium CE, with the modern Ethiopian-Semitic languages.

Ge'ez has structurally much more in common with non-Ethiopian-Semitic languages like Arabic, for instance.

Amongst the features that typify many languages of the region are: the presence of 'glottalized' consonants contrasting with plain ones – a glottalized *k* being represented in this book by *q*: Walaytta *qamma* 'night' but *kamma* 'cover!'); complex verb systems which express in one word what most European languages express in several (so, Tegrennya *aywasaduwwon* 'they did not take it'); order of words different from European languages, especially with the verb at the end (so, Oromo *intalli mana keessaa hojii qabdi* 'the girl has work at home', lit. 'girl house inside work she-has'). These are just three of the most obvious examples and many more have been identified.

As a result, the region has been called a 'language area', that is to say a geographical region in which the languages spoken share a number of features which, taken together, distinguish them from any other geographically defined group of languages in the world. However, no one language shows all the features in the longer lists, and indeed the usefulness of the idea of 'language area' is sometimes disputed.

Literacy and language policy. The history of writing and literacy in Ethiopia goes back over two millennia to the time of the most ancient Ge'ez inscriptions. Little is known, however, of how widespread literacy was in the proper sense of the word. Even with the introduction of Christianity and the beginning of the long process of translating the Bible and other Christian literature into Ge'ez, then the spoken language of Aksum, knowledge of reading and writing was probably fairly restricted. Ge'ez remained virtually the sole language of literacy in the Christian kingdom long after it had ceased to be spoken, though there are isolated survivals of written Amharic from the 14th century, increasingly so during and after the 18th century. Amharic was the spoken language of the court and the ruling élite from the late 13th century; it was even called 'the language of the king'. This situation continued into modern times as the language increasingly attained high prestige and 'amharicization' became a necessity for social and political advancement. During the Italian occupation of 1936–1941 the idea of a national language for Ethiopia and Eritrea was rejected and teaching in schools could be in any of the main local languages, including Arabic in Muslim areas. Before this, only missionary schools had used local languages. However, following the Liberation the Imperial government introduced policies requiring the use of Amharic, and the 1955 Constitution stated that Amharic was the official language of the Ethiopian Empire. All official documents were published in Amharic and in English as the official language of international communication. Other languages, such as Oromo, Afar, Arabic, Somali, Tegre and Tegrennya were still used sporadically in radio broadcasting. Amharic was the language of instruction in schools up to the sixth grade, after which English took over.

After the 1974 revolution this strict Amharic-only policy was relaxed. In theory different nationalities were allowed to choose whether to use their own languages in local matters and in education. In practice, however, only a few languages were in a position of development in terms of standardization and literacy to adopt such roles. The government therefore promoted a programme of developing alphabets for hitherto unwritten languages. Of the modern languages only Amharic and Tegrennya had a tradition of being written, along with Oromo which had had some support from the missions. The then government decided in favour of using the Ethiopian script (*fidal*) for writing other languages, seeing it as a sign of national unity. The Ethiopian script, however, is not suitable for all languages of the area and sometimes clumsy adaptations had to be made. Around the same time the government undertook an energetic literacy campaign and delegated responsibility for the study and standardization of languages to the Ethiopian Language Academy. Nonetheless, the government of the People's Democratic Republic of Ethiopia still retained Amharic as 'the working language of the State'.

The Language Academy also undertook an extensive programme of terminological development for Amharic to bring it up to the standard of a modern means of communication. The vocabulary and richness of the language expanded exponentially in directions that it had not seen before.

Following the change of government in 1991, the Federal Democratic Republic of Ethiopia declared in 1994 for the equal rights of all languages. As part of this literacy movement, many languages advanced as they dropped the use of the Ethiopian script and shifted to adaptations of the Roman alphabet. Opposition to the use of *fidal* had been strong in some quarters, and most notably Oromo had for some time been written in the Roman alphabet (called *qubee*) in expatriate communities. This was now adopted in Ethiopia itself and Oromo is now written in the Roman alphabet.

Elsewhere, since independence in 1991, Eritrea has been developing literacy in its nine indigenous languages, though de facto official status applies just to Tegrennya, Arabic and English (as the international language). The *fidal* is used for writing only Tegrennya and Tegre, whilst for the others Roman alphabets have been developed, except of course for Arabic. Djibouti retains Arabic and French as its official languages, though Somali and Afar are the most widely spoken languages. Somalia has Somali and Arabic as its official languages, and a Roman alphabet was developed for writing Standard Somali in 1972.

Literature: JON ABBINK, 'Languages and peoples in Ethiopia and Eritrea', *EAE* V, 381–388; DAVID APPLEYARD, MARTIN ORWIN, 'The Horn of Africa', in ANDREW SIMPSON (ed.), *Language and National Identity in Africa*, Oxford 2007, 267–290; MARVIN LIONEL BENDER et al. (eds.), *Language in Ethiopia*, Oxford 1976.

David Appleyard, SOAS, London

Tegray

Tegrennya-speakers are an important ethnic and regional group in Ethiopia and Eritrea, unified principally by their language, Tegrennya, a major Ethiopian-Semitic language. They are often called Tegray in Ethiopia (in Amharic *Tegre*, in English also Tegrayans, which is the term used in this article when referring to Ethiopian Tegrennya-speakers). Tegray is only one of the names they use for themselves (also in the form *Tegraway* and in the plural *Tagaru*). Many people, especially in rural areas, prefer to use the name of their particular subgroup, often derived from the traditional name of their region (e.g. *Walqayte*). They mostly live both in the Ethiopian region called Tegray and in central Eritrea, where they are often called *Tegrennya*, the same as the commonest name of the language. The only self-designation recognized by almost all urban and rural Tegrennya-speakers is *Habasha*, which term is also used in the form *(H)Abasha* by the Amhara to refer to themselves or, more recently, to Ethiopians in general. The potential confusion of names is exacerbated by the existence of the Tegre, speakers of the related Tegre language, who live in Eritrea and who also occasionally call themselves Tegray. Tegrennya-speakers number around 6.5 million, around 4.5 million of whom live in Ethiopia with the rest in Eritrea, where they form between 40% and 50% of the population.

History. An ethnic designation, clearly linked to the name 'Tegray', occurs first in the 10th century in the form *Tigretai*, though it is more likely that the term refers to the ancestors of the Tegre living on the Red Sea coast in the area of the ancient port of Adulis. The Tegray region has been densely populated since ancient times with a diverse mix of populations, both Semitic and Cushitic-speaking. Inscriptions from Aksumite times and before, as well as the diversity of place names suggest that the area has always been marked by migrations and the interaction of various ethnic groups. For example, oral traditions record that the Tegrennya-speakers of Hamasen and Akkala Guzay in Eritrea migrated from the Tegray region in the 13th century.

One of the last such important migrations took place in the 19th century, when Emperor Yohannes IV placed Tegrayan lords as governors of the Marab Mellash, i.e. mainly in the Eritrean highlands, and many Tegray from Tamben settled in the Asmara area, becoming a significant minority there.

The Tegray region formed the core of the Aksumite kingdom and in many senses the Tegray are the inheritors and, in part, the descendants of the population of Aksumite times. Indeed, the spiritual core of the region was and is the town of Aksum itself, and some names of Tegrennya-speaking groups and settlements have persisted from Aksumite and Post-Aksumite times until the present. Over the ensuing centuries, after the centre of power in Ethiopia shifted further south under the Amhara, a 'Tegrayan dynasty' in the proper sense never came into existence, the competing rulers of individual provinces being too strong. At times, however, local provincial rulers managed to establish their rule over most provinces of the Tegray region. Occasionally, these northern provinces were temporarily united under one or two rulers, for instance, since at least the 14th century under the *tegre makwannen* ('Lord of Tegray') in the Hawzen or Adwa area and, further north, under the *baher nagash* ('Ruler of the sea[coast]'), who controlled the trade routes to the Red Sea. Rarely were all territories of Tegrennya-speakers unified in the hands of one individual, perhaps most notably, in the 19th century, under the future Emperor Yohannes IV who later reigned over the whole of Ethiopia (1872–1889). The inherited tendency of separation continued in a new form when Eritrea was founded in 1890 as an Italian colony, with Hamasen as its political centre, now separated from Ethiopia. Yohannes's descendants held parts of the Tegray region as a fief under Amhara rule forming the first 'Tegrayan' dynasty.

Different branches of this family held important positions as governors or sub-governors and repeatedly attempted to defend local autonomous structures in different ways until the 1970s, sometimes in confrontation with the central government, sometimes partially collaborating.
However, in a brief attempt to exploit discontent with Amhara rule for his own interests, Hayla Sellase Gugsa from that dynasty, sided with the Italians in the war of 1935–1936. This proved to be a miscalculation when the Tegray region, instead of becoming an autonomous princedom, was absorbed into Eritrea under the Italians.

In many respects the Tegrayans have in the past viewed their relationship with the wider Ethiopian nation in the light of their legitimacy as the heirs of Aksum controlling the sacred site of Aksum.

In modern times, measures of centralisation, aggressive marginalization, economic decline and political suppression at the hands of the Ethiopian state led to the creation of local armed resistance movements in the 1970s, especially the Tigray People's Liberation Front, which from 1989 onwards fully controlled the Tegray region. With the separation of Eritrea from Ethiopia in 1991, Tegrennya-speakers were again split between Eritrea and the Tegray region of Ethiopia. Subsequently, during the Eritrean–Ethiopian war of 1998–2000, they suffered greatly.

Society. Most Tegrennya-speakers are traditional agriculturalists, practising plough agriculture and cultivating *tef*, sorghum, millet, wheat, maize, etc., and keeping cattle, sheep and goats, and in many areas bees. Their society is marked by a strong ideal of community and, especially in rural areas, by egalitarian principles. Some groups have a strong sense of local identity and have traditionally had their own semi-autonomous organizations dominated by assemblies of elders or leading families and, in the past, local feudal dynasties. Tegrennya-speakers have been described as 'individualistic' because of elements of competition, rivalry and local conflicts in their society. This reflects more a marked tendency to defend one's own community and local rights against perceived interference from powerful individuals or the state.

Landscape in Tegray, © Wolbert G.C. Smidt

Tegrennya-speaking communities are characterised by numerous social institutions of a marked networking nature, where relations are based on mutual rights and bonds. Economic and other support is mediated by these institutions, which continue to function fully especially in rural areas. For instance, the institution of 'brotherhood' or *hawennat* comprises all descendants in the male line from an ancestor at least seven generations in the past. All members of this extended family are linked by mutual obligations. Villages are in addition usually perceived as genealogical communities, consisting of several lineages. Village assemblies, called *bayto,* decide on local political matters, nowadays in accord with principles of the modern state both in Ethiopia and in Eritrea. Another important association in major rural parts of the Tegray region is the *sewa sanbat* ('Sunday chalice'), in some areas named after saints, and of which there may be several in each village. Every man is a member of such an association which meets on Sunday and where economic and other problems are addressed, based on the principles of consensus and mutual aid. Also important as a cultural and social institution are assemblies of elders (*shemagelle*), who pass on an often-detailed oral history of their groups and oral registers of land tenure and rights and genealogies. Land rights were traditionally inherited not just by families, but also by entire village communities, with differences from region to region. The Tegrennya customary laws are a remarkable heritage. In Eritrea several groups have elaborated these as written law codes, which are still valid locally though subsidiary to state laws. In the Tegray region, customary law is still partially practised, especially in marriage and inheritance practice, as well as occasionally in penal cases. Customary law is also an important factor in conflict resolution.

Despite a general impression of homogeneity, Tegrennya-speakers are composed of numerous subgroups with their own socio-cultural traditions. Among these are the Agama of eastern Tegray, the autonomous Tsanadagla and Maratta of Akkala Guzay in Eritrea, the Hamasenay, agriculturalists in Hamasen and cattle herders in Humara, the egalitarian Wajjarat of south-eastern Tegray, and so on. There are many others, sometimes numbering only a few members and scattered across several districts. Usually they define themselves through common descent, but in some cases also as a political confederacy uniting several groups.

Assimilation processes have led to the inclusion of other ethnic groups; for example, Agaw settlers in Saraye became Tegrennya-speakers several centuries ago, and some Bilin villages near Karan in Eritrea also now belong to the Tegrennya-speaking population.

Religion. The great majority are Orthodox Christians, though there are minorities of Muslims and, since the 19th century Protestants and Catholics, principally in Eritrea. The daily life of Tegrennya-speakers is greatly influenced by religion. For example, fasting periods are strictly observed, especially in the Tegray region of Ethiopia; at the same time, traditional local beliefs, particularly in spirits, are widespread. Muslim Tegray are both merchants and peasants with traditional land rights, and form a special subgroup within Tegrennya speaking society. Some of them, especially in Eritrea, call themselves Jabarti. In the past, many Muslim Tegrennya-speakers also acted as servants for wealthy farmers and nobles, many settling near important trade routes and in towns. They follow Sunni Islam which shows diverse influences from the Sudan, Egypt, Yemen and Saudi Arabia, whilst Eritrea and the Tegray region are the home of the oldest Muslim populations in the Horn of Africa supposedly dating back to the earliest times of the religion.

Over the centuries, small groups of Tegrennya-speakers have migrated southwards across Ethiopia. In the 19th century, Tegray were employed as riflemen in the Oromo kingdoms and Muslim Tegray traders settled in the Gibe states. As a result ethnic terms related to 'Tegray' appear across Ethiopia in different ethnic contexts today. Some clan names such as Tigeroo, Tigre or Tigrii amongst Naggaadee (i.e. *naggade* 'merchant') groups within the Oromo bear witness to this, as do the Nagado Tigroch family amongst the noble clans of the Kafa in southwestern Ethiopia, and even today there is a clan bearing the name Tegera amongst the Walaytta. There are numerous other groups who claim origins from Tegray immigrants, notably amongst some Gurage lineages.

Literature: WILLIAM A. SHACK, *The Central Ethiopians: Amhara, Tigriña and Related Peoples,* London 1974; Wolbert Smidt, 'Təgrəñña-speakers', *EAE* IV, 908–911; WOLBERT SMIDT, 'Təgray', *EAE* II, 888–895.

David Appleyard, SOAS, London, Wolbert G.C. Smidt, Mekelle University

Amhara

The native speakers of the Amharic language (*Amarennya*) constitute the Amhara ethnic group in Ethiopia. Amharic is an Ethiopian-Semitic language, which is first recorded in the 14th century. The Amhara came to prominence with the change of dynasty under Yekunno Amlak (r. 1270–1285) and their language became the spoken language of the court and government thereafter. Today Amharic is widely spoken across the country, outside the Amhara region, especially in urban centres.

They are the second largest group in the country (nearly 30%), and they make up the predominant part (more than 90%) of the population of the Amhara National Regional State. This is a region with strong sub-regional identities, and many of its inhabitants still refer to themselves by the name deriving from their sub-region (e.g. *Gojjame, Gondare, Manze*). Many Amhara also live in other regions of Ethiopia, and especially in towns and administrative centres, as a result of the central role the Amhara have held for centuries in state administration and governance.

Daily life and the land. Most Amhara live in an extraordinarily beautiful landscape. The Amhara region consists of wide plateaus in the highlands, intersected by deep river gorges, wide valleys with pastures and farmland, and steep slopes covered in bush or forest. The climate varies, depending on altitude and season, and most farmland depends on rain, at the right time and in reasonable measure. In the highlands, the nights are cool, while in the dry season, the days can be rather warm, and really hot in the lowlands. Much of the countryside is occupied by farms whose houses are scattered across the landscape, on the land they farm. Churches are a common sight in Amhara communities, usually found on a high point in the landscape, surrounded by old trees. The few highways that exist cater for motorized transport, but many Amhara live far from roads. Everywhere, webs of footpaths criss-cross the landscape, connecting homesteads with each other and with the open places where peasants gather to buy and sell agricultural produce from each other at the local weekly markets, and where itinerant traders, who travel from market to market, offer items for sale, or buy products from the peasants in larger quantities. Small towns have grown up around these markets, both along the highways and in places inaccessible to trucks and cars. In such places there is a hint of urban life, in particular on market days, when small kiosks, cafés and restaurants offer coffee, food, and the popular home-brewed beer and liquor.

The beauty of the landscape contrasts with the hardship of peasant life. At daybreak, before 6am, women get up to start their daily chores. In the countryside, the nearby fields are commonly used to relieve oneself, and after a quick wash, a simple meal may be prepared. Sometimes live coals have to be collected from a neighbour, carried in a piece of broken pot, to kindle the fire, and soon the morning air is seasoned with the crisp smell of the smoke emanating from the numerous household fires round about.

The division of labour varies according to gender and age. Men do the heavy agricultural work, such as ploughing, and women are responsible for cooking, cleaning, childcare, water fetching, and a multitude of other daily chores around the house. Children are gradually introduced to the working life of adults, first by helping with looking after small animals and chasing away birds and vermin from the fields. As they grow up, they follow the gender-oriented pattern of work, where girls gradually take on more womanly responsibilities and boys follow their fathers and older brothers in the work of farmers. Old women can assist the younger with cooking, and old men make themselves useful by looking after grazing animals around the house.

The ideal peasant household is self-sufficient in labour and food, with a surplus that can be sold at the market to cover the costs of the replacement of plough oxen, a milking cow, market goods (clothes, utensils, sugar, salt and coffee), and the annual taxes of the state. The basis of the ideal household unit is the union of a husband and a wife, and their children. As a production unit, it is at its peak when the children have reached an age when they can participate fully in the daily work, and their parents still have their full working capacity. Such households are typically relatively well off, with plough oxen, one or two milking cows, and some sheep and goats and perhaps a donkey or two. Land is the limiting factor, and households with full working capacity will typically sharecrop the land of households with less capacity, in particular widowed or divorced women with no capable male in the household.

Amhara elders in Bahrey Gemb, near Gondar, © Wolbert G.C. Smidt

The family (*betasab* = 'people of the house') is closely associated with the land. Boys and girls have equal rights to inheritance, including of land. Ideally, when a young boy matures and becomes ready for marriage, he should get a share of his family's land to plough by himself, and by saving from the produce he gets from the land, become economically independent and able to marry. Similarly, girls should get a share of the family's land at marriage, to add to that of her husband. Land shortage has made this practice less common, and youngsters who take up a living as farmers depend on other means of getting access to land, such as renting land from widows, old people, or others who cannot work the land themselves. Through such arrangements women can form households without men. For men it is more problematic to live alone, without a woman in the house to care for cooking, cleaning, and other household chores. While ploughing is almost exclusively men's work, most men are helpless at housework. The women's role in farming is mainly weeding, and, to a lesser extent, harvesting.

The Amhara region has suffered a number of famines, and periodic food shortage has been common in many areas. The staple food is *enjara*, a sour, flat, soft bread made of cereal flour, of which *tef* (an indigenous grass-like cereal with tiny grains) is the most prestigious. *Tef* is very labour-intensive and climatically sensitive, and is a valued cash crop. The daily *enjara* is often made of sorghum, barley, or wheat (barley is the only grain grown at the highest altitudes). Meat is a luxury that most peasants cannot afford other than on festive occasions. Commonly, the *enjara* is eaten with a stew made of pulses, onion, garlic, and red pepper, sometimes supplemented with vegetables.

Traditionally in Amhara society, boys should marry when they are 18 or 19 years old, and girls at 14 or 15. In some regions there were practices, now forbidden, of very early marriages, in particular for girls, and parents would arrange marriage ceremonies for girls as young as six to eight years. In such instances, the girl would move to the home of her young husband (who would be a little older and sexually mature), but continue to live under the protection of her parents-in-law, until she was considered mature and ready for marital life. Marriage is an economic union more than a relation between lovers. The first marriage of two young people is arranged in agreement with their respective families, primarily the fathers. The first marriage is fragile and easily breaks down. Many older Amhara women tell how they do not even remember the name of their first husband, running back home after a few days. It is the first marriage that has most ceremony and festivity and which involves a wedding party (*sarg*) and ceremonial visits by the bride's family to the groom's homestead, and later the other way round. The couple ideally receives a share of their families' land at marriage, as well as household utensils and animals. The costs involved are high. One way to circumvent the costly gifts and ceremonies is to abduct a girl. Traditionally, this was a forceful way to get a wife, but today it can be a means for young people both to avoid the authority of their parents and to save expenses. With increased attention to education and prospects of a life different from that of their parents, many youngsters, including girls, now oppose the tradition of arranged marriages and take up independent lives in small towns, trying to get as much education as possible.

Daily life and the Church. The local community is organized around a church with its particular *tabot* (an altar tablet representing the Ark of the Covenant), consecrated to one of the saints of the Ethiopian Tawahedo Orthodox Church. Every saint has his monthly (minor) and annual (major) day of celebration. On such days heavy work, in particular ploughing, is forbidden, and the annual celebration is a day of communal festivity, often with competitive games and mock combats between neighbouring groups, and always, if affordable, plenty of meat and drink (the most popular drink is *talla,* a beer with low alcoholic content brewed by women in most households).

The church is an important institution in the lives of most Amhara. Its complex ritual calendar regulates their daily lives. In addition to the monthly saint's days of the *tabot*, there are a number of major religious holidays. The most important are Easter (*Fasika*), the Feast of the Cross (*Masqal*), and Epiphany (*Temqat*), among which Easter is the most prominent. Christian Amhara observe a fast (*tsom*) every Wednesday and Friday during most of the year, when they abstain from eating any animal products, and the most virtuous eat only one meal in the afternoon. They also observe *Lent* with about 55 days of fasting leading up to Easter. Then the fast is broken after a nightlong liturgy with a lavish feast on Easter Sunday.

The importance of the church becomes particularly evident at times of life crises, in particular death. The rituals for the deceased start with the burial in the church graveyard, which is followed by requiem masses and social gatherings at prescribed intervals during the first year after death (the 40th day the most important), and then annually. The funerary rites involve high, and often unexpected, expenditure for the bereaved family, and because of this, the burial association (*edder* or *qere*) is a very important social institution. The burial association is an organized group of members who pay regular contributions into the fund and who are obliged to participate in, and assist at funerals of relatives of the co-members of the association.

Social organization. Neighbours are linked to each other by a great variety of symbolic and practical bonds. There are religious fraternal associations (*mahbar*) devoted to a particular saint and small-scale savings clubs (*equb*), all with some formal structure and membership and regularity over time. Neighbourhoods may also be gathered around a protective, communal spirit (*adbar*), often represented by a tree of particular size and age, to which regular offerings are made to ensure the peace and tranquillity of the community. Neighbours also help each other practically in more or less formalized ways. For example, labour-intensive agricultural tasks can be done by semi-formal reciprocal work parties (*dabo*), and neighbours with one ox each combine their oxen to make the necessary pair to pull the plough, and take turns in using the pair to plough their fields.

In general, the peasant Amhara community is characterized by a high degree of cooperation, but also interdependency, and this can to some extent conflict with Amhara self-esteem and pride. As a result, suspicion and envy can emerge in the community, and sometimes result in open, violent conflict and in fear of attack by magic. Along with the devotion to the church, many rural Amhara also believe in a multitude of spirits, supernatural forces, and magical powers of spells, magic or healing scrolls, herbal concoctions, sooth-saying, and curses. Many people seek advice from specialists in spiritual matters, such as spirit mediums, astrologists, exorcists, herbalists, healers and other knowledgeable people. The men of the church, and in particular the 'scribes' (*dabtara*), are also believed to command mystical powers of a potentially harmful nature. A destructive force, the evil eye (*ayna tela* or *buda*), is associated with envy and selfishness, and is potentially inherent in any person. Traditional handicraft specialists, primarily blacksmiths and potters, are believed to be especially disposed to carry the evil forces of *buda*, and often live in their own villages, separated from the rest of the community.

The Amhara of today are a very varied group, and many have lived in urban centres for several generations. The Amhara have played a central role in the long history of Ethiopia, and the culture and customs of the group include and combine elements from the 'great traditions' of Ethiopia, including the church and the state, as well as smaller, vernacular ones from the various sub-regions from where they originate. In Ethiopia, as elsewhere, ethnicity is not only a matter of identity but also of politics, and the concept of 'Amhara' has become a basis for political mobilization at national and federal state levels.

In present-day Ethiopia people are experiencing a tremendous process of change towards increased urbanization, a market-oriented and monetized economy, new forms of communication through the spread of mobile phones and internet access, and a general attention to rights to education, health and welfare. People who consider themselves as Amhara, just like any other Ethiopian, participate in this great transformation from a myriad of different positions, from the poor peasant farmer in the northern highlands to the wealthy merchant in Addis Ababa. Each of them may identify himself differently, some in a politicized manner, others in terms of their relation to the land and kinship group to which they belong, but the reference point for Amhara culture and custom remains the traditional life of the farming households in the northern highlands, to which many urbanized Amhara regularly return for memorial services for long deceased relatives, and for major church holidays.

Literature: DONALD N. LEVINE, 'Amhara', *EAE* I, 230–232; SIMON D. MESSING. *The Highland Plateau Amhara of Ethiopia*, New Haven 1985; WILLIAM A. SHACK, *The Central Ethiopians Amhara, Tigriña and Related Peoples*, London 1974.

Harald Aspen, NTNU, Norwegian University of Science and Technology, Trondheim

Beta Esrael

The Beta Esrael or Falasha are a group who resided in northern and northwest Ethiopia for hundreds of years. They lived in more than 500 villages scattered throughout the Gondar area. Smaller groups resided in Tegray, Lasta, and Qwara. Since 1977 the vast majority of the Beta Esrael have emigrated from Ethiopia to Israel.

Religious practice. At the heart of Beta Esrael identity in Ethiopia was a system of religious beliefs and practices which combined Hebraic-biblical, Christian and pan-Ethiopian elements. They expressed particular devotion to the *Orit* (Torah/Old Testament). From the 15th to the 20th century their supreme religious leaders were monks, who in the 20th century were replaced by 'priests'. They presided over the liturgy in the prayer house, officiated at sacrifices and served as spiritual advisors.

Their annual cycle consisted of festivals and fasts observed according to a lunar calendar. Some of their most important holidays such as the New Year, the Day of Atonement and Passover were celebrated at the same time as and shared religious associations with biblical festivals observed by Jews elsewhere in the world. The Beta Esrael observed the Sabbath with particular strictness as a day of rest. Unlike most other Jews they were not familiar with the Talmud or later rabbinic writings. Nor did they observe Chanukah, celebrate a Bar Mitzvah or wear phylacteries or prayer shawls.

Prior to the 20th century the Beta Esrael religious system reflected their unique identity in the context of Christian Ethiopian society. Over the course of time, their contacts with outside Jews produced a system much closer to that of 'normative Judaism'. Holidays were modified or added to stress those elements found elsewhere in the Jewish world. Distinctive customs such as monthly observances, sacrifices, monasticism and certain purity laws declined or were eliminated. Hebrew came to be used alongside Ge'ez and Torah scrolls were held alongside Orit manuscripts.

In Ethiopia, the Beta Esrael lived both in their own villages and in mixed villages alongside other ethnic groups. They usually resided near rivers and streams, which were necessary not only for their daily needs, but also for purposes of ritual purification. Their women separated themselves and lived in special huts during menstruation and after giving birth. The Beta Esrael also observed strict social segregation, which required them to purify themselves following contact with outsiders.

In many ways, the lives of the Beta Esrael resembled that of their Christian neighbours. Their dress, physical appearance, and languages (Amharic and Tegrennya) closely resembled those of their neighbours. There were, however, also aspects, which distinguished the Beta Esrael and served to mark the border between them and their neighbours. They consumed the same foods and beverages as other Ethiopians, although unlike the Christians the Beta Esrael refused to eat raw meat. Like their Muslim and Christian neighbours, the Beta Esrael did not eat pork or food, especially meat, prepared by outsiders.

History. Traditions attribute the presence of a recognizable Jewish group in Ethiopia to migrations of Israelites in the time of King Solomon (10th century BCE), or the dispersion of the ten Lost Tribes, particularly the Tribe of Dan (*c.* 722 BCE). However, since the mid-1970s, a new scholarly consensus has emerged which, although conceding the existence of early Jewish influences on Ethiopian culture, views the Beta Esrael as an Ethiopian ethnic group and dates their earliest appearance in Ethiopia to the 14th century.

Whatever the origins of the Beta Esrael, there is little evidence for their presence in Ethiopia prior to the 14th century. There are a number of references to Jews in the Red Sea area in the works of travellers (none of whom actually visited Ethiopia) or accounts of legendary figures such as Prester John or the warrior Jewish Queen Esata (or Gwedit, Gudit, wrongly 'Judith').

The first reliable reference to the people later known as the Falasha appears to be in the chronicle of the wars of Emperor Amda Tseyon I (r. 1314–1344). According to this source the emperor sent troops against people 'like Jews'. Indeed, this period appears to mark the beginning of 300 years of intermittent conflict between the Beta Esrael and the Christian rulers of Ethiopia.

During 15th and 16th centuries the Beta Esrael emerged as a distinctive ethnic group by acquiring new skills and developing new institutions. As they gradually lost the right to own land, they began to supplement their income as blacksmiths, weavers, and carpenters, and in the case of women, as potters. Both blacksmithing and potting were despised professions, which led to the Beta Esrael being viewed with suspicion and fear by their neighbours.

Although the 16th-century Muslim conquest of Ethiopia was initially welcomed by the Beta Esrael, they later suffered considerably at the hands of the conquerors. One reflection of their ill fortunes throughout the 15th and 16th centuries is the frequent mention by Hebrew authors of Ethiopian Jews sold into slavery and redeemed by Jews in Egypt.

By the early 17th century, following their conquest by the Emperor Susenyos (r. 1607–1632), the Beta Esrael no longer had a military or political autonomy. However, they were able to exploit their distinctive religious, economic and social patterns to ensure their survival as a people. Indeed, they appear to have been employed intensively as craftsmen in the construction of the imperial capital of Gondar.

Modern times. For the Beta Esrael the encounter with the modern Western world began in the mid-19th century with the arrival of Protestant missionaries under the auspices of the London Society for Promoting Christianity amongst the Jews. In response to this missionary 'threat' several well-known Jewish figures called for assistance for the Beta Esrael.

In 1867 the orientalist Joseph Halévy travelled to Ethiopia to investigate their situation. Despite his unequivocal recommendation on their behalf, no action was taken for 40 years when his student Jacques (Ya'acov) Faitlovitch arrived in Ethiopia.

Faitlovitch more than any other person was responsible for their entry into the consciousness of Jews elsewhere in the world. He sent a small number of students abroad and attempted to reform their religious practice. Although his activities were suspended during the Italian invasion of Ethiopia, he returned after the restoration of the Emperor Hayla Sellase. No attempt was made to bring the Beta Esrael en masse to Israel in the period from 1948 to 1977, when only a handful were brought. In 1973 diplomatic relations between Ethiopia and Israel were suspended.

Beginning in 1977, small numbers of Beta Esrael were brought to Israel after they had succeeded in fleeing Ethiopia for the Sudan, Kenya or Djibouti. In 1984–1985 thousands of Beta Esrael were airlifted to Israel from the Sudan in what became known as 'Operation Moses'. After the restoration of diplomatic relations between Ethiopia and Israel in 1989 a legal system of immigration was put in place. In May 1991 as the Marxist government fell, over 14,000 Beta Esrael were airlifted to Israel in less than two days. Although widely estimated to have numbered around 30,000 people, since 1977 over 80,000 members of the community and their relatives have migrated to Israel. When children born in Israel are included in the figure, the population of the group today is about 130,000.

While no organized Beta Esrael community exists in Ethiopia today, hundreds and even thousands of people continue to claim the right to emigrate to Israel as relatives of those already in the country.

Literature: Steven Kaplan, *The Beta Israel (Falasha) in Ethiopia*, New York 1992; Kay Kaufman Shelemay, *Music, Ritual and Falasha History*, East Lansing 1989; Hagar Salamon, *The Hyena People, Ethiopian Jews in Christian Ethiopia,* Berkley–Los Angeles 1999.

Steven Kaplan, The Hebrew University of Jerusalem

Oromo

The Oromo (obsolete name 'Galla') are the largest Cushitic-speaking people of the Horn of Africa, living primarily in Ethiopia, northern Kenya and parts of Somalia. In Ethiopia, they are the single largest ethnic group, constituting between 33% and 40% of the population, and currently inhabiting nearly all areas of the country. According to one of the Oromo myths of origin, the name 'Oromo' derives from Horo, the paradigmatic man and first ancestor of the Oromo. His descendants came to refer to themselves as *ilmaan Oromoo* ('sons of Oromo'). Oromo tradition suggests that this has been the Oromo self-name since they began to develop a separate identity sometime in the early centuries of the 2nd millennium CE.

Origins. Scholars agree that the Oromo descended from some of the earliest inhabitants of the Horn of Africa. Linguistic and archaeological evidence suggests that the period between 3500 and 1000 BCE witnessed a continuous movement of Cushitic peoples within northeastern Africa, particularly in the Ethiopian highlands. Perhaps beginning in the early 1st millennium BCE, two distinct Cushitic-speaking peoples, the Konso-Oromo and the Omo-Tana, moved to occupy the southern edges of the Ethiopian highlands along the Rift Valley floor. Over the second half of the millennium, the ancestors of the Oromo gradually split from the Konso-Oromo family and emerged as a separate linguistic group. Around the turn of the 1st millennium CE, this proto-Oromo group moved southwards, crossed the Rift Valley and occupied the wide plains between the Wabi-Shaballe and Ganaalee Dorya rivers. In time, they extended their grazing pastures to the Dawa river, and perhaps to the Lake Turkana region. Until recently, many specialists identified a specific area named *Walaabu* in this latter region as the cradle of the Oromo from where they migrated to the rest of what is today's Ethiopia. This interpretation arises from misunderstanding the Oromo creation myth that 'creation came out of *Walaabu*'. The creation story holds that *walaabu* is the primordial water from which the creator fashioned all creation, including humans.

Many mistake the Oromo myth of origin for actual history and erroneously suggest that the Oromo left Walaabuu and appeared for the first time in the Ethiopian highlands in the 16th century. In fact, by this time the Oromo had emerged as a community of speakers of a distinct language, followers of an indigenous Oromo religion, and practitioners of a distinct form of livelihood governed by a unique social organization called the *gadaa* system.

Language. The Oromo speak *Afaan Oromoo* or *Oromiffaa*, a Cushitic language of the Afroasiatic family closely related to the Konso, Somali and Afar languages. Currently, it is considered the second largest African language in terms of number of speakers. Not only the single common mother tongue of the Oromo nation, which comprises at least four mutually intelligible dialect groups, *Afaan Oromoo* also serves as a *lingua franca* in the southern part of Ethiopia, among members of various ethnic groups. The Oromo language remained an unwritten language until the mid-19th century when some Europeans began studying it from Oromo living in Europe and produced the first written works on the language using the Latin alphabet. Early Oromo written literature comprised Christian scriptures as well as non-religious publications including dictionaries, grammars, collections of short stories, proverbs, poems, school books and so on. The missionary writers, some of whom were trained linguists, used the Latin alphabet arguing that this was better suited to writing *Afaan Oromoo* than the Ge'ez script. In 1871, the Gospel of Luke was printed using the Ge'ez script, marking a turning point in Oromo literary history. The switch was made primarily to please King Menilek of Shawa who had permitted the establishment of a German Oromo mission in his kingdom, but also because the few literate Oromo in Shawa also used this script. The use of the Latin alphabet, though deemed phonetically more suited for writing *Afaan Oromoo,* remained prohibited in Ethiopia for more than a century.

Religion. Before they came into contact with Christianity and Islam, the Oromo adhered to a distinctly monotheistic indigenous Oromo belief system. As early as the 17th century, European travellers described the Oromo as people who were neither Muslim nor Christian who worshipped no idols. Indeed, the Oromo were worshippers of *Waaqa*, a supreme spirit-being who they believed created the universe and guided humans along the path of justice, truth and harmonious social order. The Oromo indigenous religion contained fundamental truths about the divine and a view of the created universe but without established creeds, canonized revelations or an ordained priesthood.

The belief system maintained a conception of a cosmos divided into the physical world and an invisible realm inhabited by deities, spirits and ancestors. Revelations, the main avenue of communication between the physical and spiritual realms, were continuous and updated the belief system. In fact, the Oromo believe that *Waaqa* appears to all persons regularly in nature and is manifested in dreams, visions and augury. *Waaqa* is said to communicate with humans mainly through *ayyaana,* spirit-forces manifested in the physical world in a multiplicity of ways. While *ayyaana* are apparently of the same nature as *Waaqa*, they are viewed as independent divinities that serve as the creator's link to creation. A more personal and direct relationship with *Waaqa* is maintained through the *qaalluu,* a religious and ritual expert known to have a special insight to *Waaqa* through the power of *ayyaana*, which possess him at regular intervals.

In the last two centuries, a large number of Oromo have converted to Christianity and Islam through both peaceful means and forced conversion. In the 19th century, Oromo in the northern part of Ethiopia were forcibly converted from Islam by Emperor Yohannes IV (r. 1872–1889) and many in the central parts were forced to accept Orthodox Christianity by Emperor Menilek II (r. 1889–1913). Those who lived in the east, north, and the central and southwestern part of Ethiopia converted to Islam through trade and proselytization, or as a protest against forcible conversion to Orthodox Christianity. In the 20th century, the majority of Oromo in the western region embraced the Protestant faith through evangelization by indigenous and European missionaries. Accordingly, nearly half of Oromo in Ethiopia are Muslims, a third Orthodox Christians, and about a fifth Protestants. A little over 3% are followers of the Oromo indigenous religion now known as *waaqeffanna*. Adherence to traditional practices and rituals is still common among many Oromo regardless of religious affiliation.

Transfer of power at the *chaffee* ('assembly') of the Tuulama-Oromo 2013, © Ezekiel Gebissa

Social organization. Studies show that the Oromo *gadaa* system took shape sometime in the 11th or 12th century and developed to maturity on the plains of southern and south-eastern Ethiopia as a result of five centuries of legislative transformation. By the 16th century, this complex system was fully operational among the pastoralist Oromo in the extensive region between the Wabi Shabelle valley and Lake Turkana. Under the *gadaa* system, Oromo society is organized into ten classes based on the social age of fathers and sons that succeed each other every eight years in assuming economic, military, political and ritual responsibilities. Formal transfer of power was held in front of a national assembly where laws were established for the following eight years. As a social organization, the *gadaa* system guided the lives of individuals and served as a mechanism of socialization, education, religious expression, maintenance of peace, judicial administration and social cohesion.

The *gadaa* system was supported by a complementary and equally complex religious organization headed by the *qaalluu*, the ritual leader whose residence served as a focal point of the Oromo indigenous religion. The *gadaa-qaalluu* system functioned essentially as the organic constitution of the Oromo nation through which the society administered itself, defended its territory, and organized its economy.

As the Oromo moved to different parts of the Horn of Africa, the *gadaa* system was replicated at the clan level. In time, major *gadaa* centres were established across the Oromo regions. In these places, *gadaa* remained the common foundation of the Oromo nation and a distinctive social system that held it together as a unified society. Representatives took an annual pilgrimage to the grand *qaalluu*, Abba Mudaa, to pay homage and affirm the unity of the Oromo.

History. Today, the Oromo live over a vast area stretching from the Sudanese border to the Hararge highlands near Somaliland, and from the Eritrean border to inside Kenya. This distribution of the Oromo is the result of the last four centuries of population movements and settlement patterns. In the early 16th century, Oromo society was organized into two groups or 'moieties' called Boorana and Barentuu who lived to the west and east of the Rift Valley, respectively. These groups were governed by the *gadaa* system with pastoralism as their primary mode of production. Earlier in the century, these two groups left the plains and moved to other areas in large numbers: the Barentuu migrated in an eastern and north-eastern direction, eventually settling in today's Arsi, Bale, Harar, Gojjam and Wallo regions. The Boorana migrated in northwest, west and south-western directions towards the regions of Shawa, Wallaga, Illubabor, Gojjam, and Gondar. In the Ethiopian highlands, the pastoralist migrants joined Oromo who had settled there at different times prior to the 16th century practicing sedentary agriculture. As a result, the Oromo today are the largest and most widely spread ethnic group in Ethiopia.

Beginning in the early 17th century, those Oromo who had settled in the region north of the Abbay river gradually became integrated into the Christian kingdom. Many joined the political establishment as employees of Ethiopian emperors, serving in high-level positions. Emperor Susenyos was an important emperor of the early 17th century who grew up among the Oromo, spoke their language and employed Oromo military tactics both in his rise to power and in defending his empire. In time, many of these Oromo, in particular those who lived in Gojjam and Gondar, embraced Christianity and assimilated to highland Ethiopian culture. Eventually, they lost their language and culture becoming virtually indistinguishable from the highland peoples.

The Oromo who settled south of the Abbay river saw their history unfold in a different direction. They settled and cultivated lands that were richly endowed with natural resources and agricultural produce. The region was connected to the world economy through long-distance trade routes. Within a few decades of their settlement, their primary mode of production became mixed agriculture. As demand for the region's products rose, the value of land increased, leading to the emergence of Oromo landowning and merchant classes. In the process, *gadaa* officials used their positions to acquire more authority and private wealth. Gradually they converted their elective offices into permanent institutions resembling monarchies. By the middle of the 19th century, five Oromo states (e.g. Limmu-Ennarya and Jimma) had emerged in the Gibe River region, and two more in Wallaga.

In the southern and south-eastern part of the country, especially in Bale, Arsi, and Boorana, the Oromo practiced a pastoralist livelihood. Further east, those who had settled in the immediate periphery of the city of Harar practiced agriculture as their main occupation, primarily as the result of an agricultural commodity exchange relationship with Harari city dwellers. The Oromo who lived further away from Harar remained pastoralist and governed themselves by their own *gadaa* system until the late 19th century. Among the pastoral Boorana in the southernmost part of Ethiopia, the *gadaa* system has remained the dominant sociopolitical organization until the present.

In the last third of the 19th century, King Menilek of Shawa, armed with modern European firearms, conquered and annexed the Oromo kingdoms and most of the territories of the pastoralists. Shawan forces removed the indigenous rulers of the Oromo kingdoms, occupied their lands and placed them under the administration of the conquering generals. The retinue of these generals moved in as soldier-settlers known as *naftannya*. In the newly conquered regions, these governors and the soldier-settlers were allotted land and local farmers as labourers called *gabbar* in lieu of salaries. Thus, in the conquered areas, there developed a lord-serf relationship known as the *naftannya-gabbar* system. The kingdoms that submitted peacefully were made tributaries and their rulers were left in place in return for recognition of the Shawan king as suzerain.

This post-conquest political arrangement remained in place for the next few decades. Once Hayla Sellase (r. 1930–1974) ascended the throne, he embarked on a policy of centralisation. Even the semi-independent status that Emperor Menilek II (r. 1889–1913) had granted to the former kingdoms and states was gradually undermined and eventually abolished. Under Hayla Sellase, Oromo elites were assimilated and co-opted while farmers became landless and pastoralists were evicted to make room for mechanized farming.

The discontent emanating from political marginalization, economic exploitation, and cultural alienation of the Oromo engendered revolts throughout the period of Hayla Sellase's rule. The dissatisfaction initially manifested in the Rayyaa-Aseebuu revolt in 1928–1929 culminated in the Bale uprising of 1964–1970 and the establishment of the Macha-Tuulama Self-help Association in 1963, both of whose declared aim was a struggle for economic justice, political equality and civil rights. The Macha-Tuulama Association was quickly disbanded, but the ideas of self-reliance, ethnic identity, and citizens' rights for the Oromo people within the empire essentially launched Oromo cultural and political nationalism. The demands and activities of the movement in part paved the way for the popular 1974 Ethiopian Revolution, which dealt a mortal blow to the imperial regime's economic base through the nationalization of land. The nationalist Oromo Liberation Front was part of the 1991 rebellion, which overthrew the *Darg* military dictatorship and obliterated the superstructure of domination.

The fall of the military regime marked the apogee of the Oromo political struggle against political, economic and cultural injustice. Today the territory inhabited by Oromo has been named 'Oromia' and exists as a federal entity with demarcated boundaries and institutions of governance recognized by the Ethiopian government. Aside from some specialized use of Arabic script (*ajami*) by Muslim Oromo, the *qubee* script which utilizes a Latin alphabet is today the principal means of writing

Afaan Oromoo, which is the medium of administration, instruction, and commerce in Oromia. The Oromo people have embraced their heritage as a nation and individual Oromo express pride in their identity within the Ethiopian polity.

Literature: Tsega Etefa, *Integration and Peace in East Africa: A History of the Oromo Nation*, New York 2012; Ezekiel Gebissa, 'Oromo History', *EAE* IV, 61–64; Mohammed Hassen, *The Oromo of Ethiopia: A History 1570–1860*, Cambridge 1990; Ezekiel Gebissa, *The Oromo and the Christian Empire of Ethiopia 1300–1700*, Woodbridge, Suffolk 2015; Asmarom Legesse, *Oromo Democracy: An Indigenous African Political System*, Lawrenceville 2006.

Ezekiel Gebissa, Kettering University

Some peoples of northwest Ethiopia

Along the north-western border with Sudan extends the regional state of Beni Shangul-Gumuz of the Federal Democratic Republic of Ethiopia. Together with the Southern Nations, Nationalities and Peoples Region and Gambella it is one of the constitutionally recognized multi-national states of Ethiopia. In 1991 the region was amalgamated from the two former administrative regions Beni (formerly known as Bela) Shangul, or the Asosa *awrajja*, later forming parts of Wallaga, as well as the former Matakkal district. Beni Shangul-Gumuz today comprises three zones (districts) and one special *warada* (sub-district). These are Matakkal, Kamashi, Asosa and the Mao-Komo special *warada*. The constitutionally recognized population comprises Gumuz, Berta, Shinasha, Mao and Komo. Additionally many Oromo and Amhara live in the region. Beni Shangul-Gumuz is an area of extraordinary cultural and demographic diversity. Its history is framed by inter-ethnic encounter, migration and trade. The inter-ethnic histories have led to a unique mix of cultural and religious contacts and relations.

Berta. The Berta are speakers of a Nilo-Saharan language, whose own language shows marked influence from Sudanes Arabic. The Berta originated from the multi-ethnic Funj sultanate (1504–1821). They migrated into the Ethiopian highlands approximately during the late 17th century. According to their oral traditions there they first encountered the Gwama (see below under Mao) around the River Tumat, whom they pushed further south. Their country of origin lies between Fazughli and Roseires in present-day Sudan. Sudanese Arab traders followed the Berta, which led to the spread of Islam in the region. The influx of these traders, who knew the Berta as *jebellawin* ('mountaineers'), led to mixed marriages from which emerged a feudal ruling class that came to be known as the *watawit*. When the Ethiopian Empire expanded and incorporated the shaykhdoms of Bela Shangul in 1898, *Shaykh* Khojali al-Hasan became the most influential regional ruler. Khojali was a vassal of Addis Ababa until the 1930s and managed to maintain a semi-autonomous rule over Beni Shangul.

As the second biggest group in Beni Shangul, the Berta today occupy many political posts in the capital Asosa. The rural population depends on subsistence agriculture based mainly on sorghum and maize. The Berta own goats and sheep but few cattle. The donkey is a major means of transportation in the region and a symbol of Berta identity. For many families gold panning, which is mainly a task of the women, is still an important means of additional income.The traditional music of the Berta is very famous. Well known are the wind instrument ensembles playing the *wasa* (calabash trumpet) or the *zumbara* (bamboo flute). Christianity generally plays a subordinate role in the region but the Berta are mostly Muslims.

Gumuz. North of the Berta, in the area of Matakkal as well as in the Dabus valley, live the Gumuz. Like the Berta, the Gumuz are also speakers of a Nilo-Saharan language. For centuries the Gumuz suffered from predatory raids from the Ethiopian highlands and the kings of Gondar. The Gumuz, being the closest to Gondar of the borderland groups, already suffered from the raids of King Sartsa Dengel (r. 1550–1597). The use of the name *shanqella* derives from this period. It was first used for the Gumuz and later became a collective name for the whole 'black' population of the western lowlands of Ethiopia. The term has a racist connotation and is forbidden today.

Like the Berta the Gumuz of Gubba also formed an aristocratic class with historical links to the Funj sultanate. The last leader of Gubba, *Shaykh* Hamdan, also known as *Dajjazmach* Banja, was, like Khojali, a vassal of the central government in Addis Ababa. His palace was used as a fort during the Italian occupation and was later bombed by British air raids during the War of Liberation (1941).

Contrary to the other Nilo-Saharan groups of the region, the Gumuz have, to a certain degree, retained the tradition of sister exchange marriage. According to this tradition the groom has to give his sister or cousin to the family of the bride in exchange. The exchange substitutes for bride wealth. With the penetration of Christianity and government policies the Gumuz have increasingly given up this tradition. Contrary to the Berta, many Gumuz still follow traditional religions. Islam is most prominent among the Gumuz of Gubba.

Mao and Komo. Several groups in western Ethiopia are subsumed under the term Mao. The term was probably introduced to the region by the Oromo and Busase of Anfillo who migrated into the area in the course of the 18th century. Still today, the Mao live as a minority in Anfillo *warada*. Further to the north, on the border with Oromia as well as inside Oromia live other Mao groups. These are the Bambasi Mao, the Hozo and Sezo. Like

Komo men during a ballgame, Pokung, Gambella, © Alexander Meckelburg

the Anfillo Mao, these groups speak Omotic languages. Also partially identified as Mao are the Gwama (incorrectly also called Kwama). The Gwama of highland Wallaga are referred to as Mao, while in the lowlands of Beni Shangul they are identified as Gwama.

The Gwama of Oromia refer to themselves as *sith chwala* ('black men' in Gwama). *Twaa gwama*, the Gwama language, like *taa komo*, the Komo language, is also a Nilo-Saharan language. Both are spoken in the Sudan and there are some speakers of both languages further south in Ethiopia in the Gambella Regional State.

The political history of the Mao and Komo was strongly influenced by the expansion of the Berta from the north and the Oromo from the south. In the area of Gidamii, the Komo were displaced from their ancestral homeland around Mount Gewa (today called Gemi in Oromiffa) and assimilated by the expanding Leeqaa Oromo. Especially in the region around Begii the regional power struggle of the Oromo and Berta was apparent. Around Begii ran the border between the country of Khojali and the Oromo leader Jote Tullu. At times, Begii, also the seat of Khojali, belonged to the area of Beni Shangul/Asosa *awrajja* until the end of the *Darg* era. After the civil war and the fall of the *Darg* in 1991, the Oromo claimed Begii *warada* and in the course of a referendum it was incorporated into the newly established federal state of Oromia. Hence large parts of the Mao/*sith chwala* came under Oromo administration. The administrative centre of the Mao and Komo is today the neighbouring town of Tongo, the central town of the Mao-Komo *special warada*.

Literature: ALFREDO GONZÁLEZ-RUIBAL, *An Archaeology of Resistance: Materiality and Time in an African Borderland*, Lanham 2014.

Alexander Meckelburg, Hiob Ludolf Centre, Hamburg

Gurage and Selte

Introduction. The Gurage and Selte belong to the most important ethnic and linguistic groups of modern Ethiopia. This is based not only on a population of almost 3 million, but also on their sizeable presence in Addis Ababa as well as in many smaller central and southern Ethiopian towns. In Walqitte and Werabe, the administrative centres of Gurage and Selte respectively, newly created universities are in the process of being established. In the capital they are the third largest population group after the Amhara and the Tegrennya-speakers. Their home region is amongst the most densely populated regions of the whole of Ethiopia. It lies south of the Awash and Wabi rivers in today's administrative zones of Gurage and Selte, in the northernmost part of the Southern Region of Ethiopia. The region includes various ecological and climatic zones between around 1,700m and somewhat above 3,000m.

The term 'Gurage' conceals a fascinating complexity. It does not describe a single group with a unified language, culture, religion and economy sharing a territory and a common history. Rather, it covers, depending on varying definitions, at least 14 territorial groups that each speak different but closely related Ethiopian-Semitic languages. Western Gurage languages are spoken by the Chaha, Endagan, Enor/Ennamor, Enar, Ezha, Geto, Dobbi/Gogot, Gumar, Masqan, Muher and Kestane/Soddo. The Selte, Walane and Zay speak Eastern Gurage languages. Whilst 'Gurage' is applicable as a linguistic term for all these groups, it cannot be assigned to the whole ethno-political unit of the Gurage in terms of their own sense of belonging. This also is true in the case of the Selte, who from at least the late 1990s have firmly rejected being assigned to the Gurage. At the same time there are groups who in fact do not speak a Gurage language but who nevertheless belong to the present Gurage administrative zone and count politically as Gurage, as for instance the Cushitic-speaking Qabeena and Libido. All of the groups listed here have each created their own local histories and various cultural particularities because each of them was an independent political unit until the conquest of the Gurage region by the Ethiopian Empire in the second half of the 19th century.

Economy. When Addis Ababa became the new capital at the end of the 19th century, the Gurage were playing an important role as carriers and building workers. Moreover, Muslim Gurage and Selte especially also worked for foreign trading companies. Since the Italian occupation and more so in the 1950s-1970s, they successfully established their own businesses, which they have steadily expanded since then notably as small enterprises in the towns of central and southern Ethiopia. Consequently their names are today considered in Ethiopia almost as synonyms for business acumen. With the improvement of infrastructure the Gurage and Selte are today increasingly developing entrepreneurial activities in their home regions, as well. However, the vast majority of the rural population operates a largely traditional peasant mixed economy with horticulture, agriculture and animal husbandry. A central role is played by the cultivation of *ensat*, which is harvested after about eight years. Most of this exacting work is considered the job of the women, while the men are chiefly responsible for the cattle and cereal farming. The large underground tuber of the *ensat* serves as a source of starch. This starch can only be used for food preparation after an elaborate traditional fermentation process. Of the variety of tasty dishes based on *ensat* only '*ensat* bread' (*qocho*) is found in other parts of Ethiopia. Producers use every part of the *ensat* plant. For example, the large leaves are suitable as packaging material, and from the pseudostem fibres are obtained for making ropes.

Gurage women at an *ensat* pit, © Dirk Bustorf

Alongside farmers, traditional society included blacksmiths, tanners, potters and woodworkers, who in spite of excellent craftsmanship and specific ritual roles in the past occupied a low social rank. Originally they were denied land ownership. Their situation has now somewhat improved.

Religion. Religious boundaries run right across the boundaries of territorial groups. The Selte, Walane, Qabeena and Libido are almost entirely Muslim. Whilst the older generation has grown up in a mystical folk Islam, younger Muslims often adapt to a modern Islamic education and a puristic or scriptualist interpretation. The vast majority of the Kestane, Muher, Enar and Endagan belong to the Ethiopian Orthodox Church. Although Christianity had probably already arrived in the area in the 14th century, it then became largely forgotten and took root again only after the Ethiopian conquest in the 19th century. The other groups are very mixed in respect of religion. In central Gurage there are some Catholics. Various Protestant churches have proselytized with some success only in recent decades. Alongside the Abrahamic religions there exist today local remnants of the old socio-religious systems of the Gurage. They are, however, today under strong pressure from other religions and the authorities, who want to categorize them as 'backward' and 'pagan' or reduce them to folklorism. Their central practices and ideas revolve mainly around the three mighty guardian spirits of the Gurage as well as the spirits of individual clans.

Early history. The earliest mention of the names Gurage and Selte is found in the chronicle of Emperor Amda Tseyon I (r. 1314–1344). He led a series of campaigns into the south. His chronicle mentions that he installed governors in several places in Gurageland. Some oral traditions mention one of the emperor's commanders as *azmach* Sebhat. He allegedly came from the line of the biblical King Solomon and became the ancestor of many western Gurage clans. In order to secure the southern borders of the Christian kingdom, under his leadership military colonies from what is now Eritrea were settled in northern Gurageland. According to tradition they are considered to be the ancestors of the Gurage. From their colonies Ethiopian Orthodox Christianity is also said to have first spread into the region. However, by the 18th century it had become almost forgotten.

The Muslim Gurage and Selte tell a different migration myth. According to this it was Muslim scholars of Arab descent and the troops of Ahmad Ibrahim al-Ghazi of Adal (Ahmad Grany) who, coming from east of the Rift Valley, settled in the region after the end of the war against the Christian kingdom in the 16th century. The origin of some of these ancestors, such as Hajji Aliyye of Selte and *Shaykh* Nasrallah, is traditionally traced directly to the family of the Prophet Muhammad. In addition to the Christian and Islamic traditions there are also a number of other origin legends. One of these speaks of a further immigration from the north in the time of Emperor Zara Yaeqob (r. 1434–1468), and traditions of individual clans mention historical roots in southern Ethiopia as well as amongst the Oromo. Concerning such legends one can only speculate about the early origins of the Gurage. In any case, their origins are ethnically and culturally very heterogeneous. More detailed written sources are extant only from the time of Emperor Susenyos (r. 1604–1632), who undertook campaigns in the region.

Modern history. In the 19th century, amongst the fragmented and regularly warring groups, progressively larger political formations developed out of a very loose system of alliances and non-aggression pacts. These were far removed from centralized structures. They had, however, institutionalized common councils that were conducted nominally by the high priest of a powerful Gurage guardian spirit. They were able to achieve peaceful markets and a shared customary law (*seera*), which is partially valid up to the present. They also organized joint military operations. First, amongst the western Gurage the *Ammest Bet Gurage* ('Five Houses of Gurage') were formed, which were later widened to the *Sabat Bet Gurage* ('Seven Houses of Gurage'). The *Sabat Bet Gurage* are today often understood as the 'Gurage proper'. Amongst the Selte the Gogot confederation was founded which is not to be confused with the ethnic subgroup of the Dobbi.

A further phenomenon of the 19th century was a wave of islamization in the region, which was directly and indirectly inspired by anti-colonialism and religious awakening in the Islamic world. Under their leader Hasan Enjaamo the Qabeena established a sultanate, which many Muslims joined. For a brief while they succeeded in subduing large parts of Gurageland and for a short time repelling conquest by

Emperor Menilek II. After the defeat of Hasan Enjaamo in 1889 Menilek was again able to take by force the region that had already once submitted to him in 1888. Kestane-Gurage had for the first time already in 1876 joined the Ethiopian empire.

Under Ethiopian rule the regions of Gurage and Selte were integrated into the province of Shawa. A feudal system was established to exploit their productivity, which was supported by local leaders and northern Ethiopian troops and led to several rebellions until its abolition after the revolution of 1974. The poverty of the rural population caused by this system contributed significantly to the migration of many Gurage and Selte to the city. Migration continues today because the area of arable land per family is mostly too small to be distributed to the next generation through inheritance. Nowadays many families can survive only with the support of their urban members. Most families have in this way become so-called translocal groups, i.e. it is part of their survival strategy that they are economically active and organize their lives in multiple places at the same time – in the city and in the countryside.

Literature: DIRK BUSTORF. *Lebendige Überlieferung. Geschichte und Erinnerung der muslimischen Silt'e Äthiopiens. With an English Summary*, Wiesbaden 2009; GABREYESUS HAILE MARIAM, *The Guragué and their Culture*, New York, Los Angeles 1991; WILLIAM A. SHACK, *The Gurage. A People of the Ensete Culture*, London–New York–Nairobi 1966.

Dirk Bustorf, Hamburg

Hadiyya

Hadiyya was the name of a political entity which belonged to the Muslim federation of Adal and comprised a large territory in southeastern Ethiopia between the 13th and 16th centuries. It was inhabited by heterogeneous ethnic groups speaking different Cushitic and Semitic languages, but sharing a number of common cultural features, such as a strong Islamic impact and an agro-pastoralist economy. The groups which are presently to be labelled Hadiyya proper are part of the Highland East Cushitic group and thus linguistically related to the Qabeena, Allaaba, Kambaata, Timbaaro, Sidaama, Gideo and Burji. They occupy a territory between the sixth and the eighth parallels reaching from the upper Omo river to the plains west of Lake Zway. Most of this area was allocated the administrative status of the Hadiyya Zone within the Southern Nations, Nationalities and Peoples' Region in the 1990s.

History. In the 14th century parts of the Adal federation including Hadiyya were subjected to the sovereignty of the Christian Ethiopian Empire which secured its rule by settling military colonists. The Ethiopian royal chronicles, for example from the early 14th to 17th centuries, record various struggles of the Hadiyya to obtain their independence as well as describing diplomatic relations. Oral traditions have preserved numerous details about a civil war among the Hadiyya, in which the leader Booyyaamo, called Bamo in the chronicle of Emperor Zara Yaeqob, supported the emperor against a rebellion of his tribesmen. This has recently become a hotly debated issue among the present-day Hadiyya, and the claim of Booyyaamo's descendants to hold a notable position in Hadiyya society is being increasingly challenged. It is considered a source of honour by the majority of the Hadiyya, however, that Emperor Zara Yaeqob married a Hadiyya princess who, under her Christian name Eleni, played an important role in Ethiopian history until her death in 1522. During the Adalite 'holy war' of 1527–1568, led by Ahmad ibn Ibrahim (Ahmad Grany) and Nur ibn Mujahid against the Christian empire, a large part of the Hadiyya migrated from the western area of the Harar plateau and present-day eastern Arsiland to the region of the Rift Valley as far as Gurageland, Kambaata and Walaytta. From the second part of the 16th century onwards the Hadiyya east of the Rift Valley were largely conquered and assimilated by the Oromo who were expanding from their original home in the south.

In the second half of the 20th century, a numerically important part of the Oromo subgroups of the Arsi and the Ittuu could still be recognized as having descended from the original Hadiyya population of those areas, and about two thirds of the Arsi clans were in fact classified as having originated from the former Hadiyya.

In the regions west of the Rift Valley a number of ethnic groups claim descent from the ancient Hadiyya, such as the Qabeena, the Selte, Welbarag, and other peoples formerly called East Gurage, as well as the modern Hadiyya proper, the Allaaba and factions of the Sidaama such as the Qeweena. Since the late 20th century, the name has increasingly been restricted to the Hadiyya proper, who have adopted it as the name of their administrative zone. The ensuing remarks on history and ethnography from the 19th century onwards will focus on this area and its inhabitants. The Hadiyya comprise the major subgroups of the Agara, Leemo, Sooro, Shaashoogo and Baadawwaachcho and amount to a total population of around 1.5 million. The common ethnic consciousness that these subgroups share has developed in the course of historical events and experiences since the 19th century. The Hadiyya have often been on hostile terms with the neighbouring Kambaata, but they have at the same time frequently intermarried and maintained an intensive network of cultural and economic relations with them.

Hadiyya men dancing at a funeral, © Ulrich Braukämper

Between the 1870s and the 1890s the Hadiyya were subjugated by the Ethiopian empire and allocated to a province called Kambaata. Like all the inhabitants of the conquered lands of the south, they were degraded to the status of serfs, who had to provide the military colonists, who were mostly of Amhara origin, with taxes and other services. Because of this oppressive situation the Hadiyya did not develop much in the way of loyalty towards the Ethiopian state and openly revolted during the civil war of 1916–1917 and the period of the Italian occupation.

Until the restoration of Hayla Sellase the majority of the Hadiyya adhered to a folk religion called *Fandaanano* and characterized by elements taken from their Muslim past. After the emperor had issued a decree in 1944 demanding 'pagan' citizens adopt one of the world religions as a symbol of modernisation, the Hadiyya gradually converted to Islam, Orthodox Christianity or to one of the Mission Churches. Protestant and Catholic missionaries had first appeared in central-southern Ethiopia in the late 1920s and were particularly successful among the Hadiyya, Kambaata and Walaytta. At the beginning of the 21st century *Fandaanano* finally vanished as a functioning socio-religious system. Its high priests were deprived of their previous position and status as mediums.

Society. The sociopolitical organization of the Hadiyya has always been characterized by egalitarian patterns. Unlike their Kambaata and Walaytta neighbours they had neither kings nor the age-grade system of the Oromo. Men could achieve prominent status by warlike deeds, wealth or by skill in councils, eloquence and wisdom. Numerous categories of honorary titles existed, but were generally not inherited. Men who killed dangerous animals or human enemies were rewarded with special insignia and spectacular funeral ceremonies. So-called feasts of merit, performed when a man amassed a hundred head of cattle, have also now become extremely rare. Alongside the common people there were and still are groups of 'outcast' craftsmen, who marry within their group and observe a particular division of labour. The women of one of these, the *fuga'a,* produce pottery and the men are tanners and woodworkers. Another group specializes in leather working and yet another in blacksmithing. Slavery, which existed until the Italian occupation, never reached an extent comparable with neighbouring kingdoms.

Today the Hadiyya are a typical example of the peoples of the *ensat* ('false banana') culture alongside the Gurage, Selte, Kambaata, and others, who practice an intensive type of cultivation particularly of the *ensat*, and are known for an extraordinary population density exceeding 500 people per square kilometre in some areas. People live in scattered groups of houses surrounded by gardens and plantations that constantly have to be manured. *Ensat* and cereals such as barley and wheat are mainly grown above 2,000m, whereas in lower areas maize and millet prevail. Up to the second part of the 19th century, however, the Hadiyya mainly practised a mixed economy based on livestock and an extensive cultivation of barley as the most appreciated crop. They then adopted the cultivation of *ensat* from their Gurage and Kambaata neighbours and thus benefitted from the high productivity of this plant, which has so far saved them from serious food shortages. After the Ethiopian conquest the plough was introduced as an important agricultural innovation, but traditional tools, the digging-stick and the hoe, have retained a basic importance. Livestock are also highly esteemed, but ownership has been considerably reduced because of the dramatically increasing lack of pastureland.

Because of overpopulation and ecological challenges the Hadiyya, like the Gurage, have a notable tradition as entrepreneurs and migrants to urban centres and factories outside their home country.

Literature: Ulrich Braukämper, 'Hadiyya History', *EAE* II, 963–965; Ulrich Braukämper, *Fandaanano: The Traditional Socio-Religious System of the Hadiyya in Southern Ethiopia,* Wiesbaden 2014.

Ulrich Braukämper, Göttingen

Sidaama

Sidaama (previously also known as Sidamo) is the self-name of an ethnic group who live in southern Ethiopia. Their language is known as *Sidaamu afoo* ('tongue of Sidaama') and belongs to the Cushitic language family. The Sidaama inhabit the highlands on the edge of the Ethiopian Rift Valley, between the town of Hawaasa (Awasa) to the north and Dilla to the south. The neighbours of the Sidaama are Oromo-speaking Gujji and Arsi, and the Walaytta who speak an Omotic language. The Sidaama zone is located in the Southern Nations, Nationalities and Peoples' Region and comprises 19 districts. According to the 2007 national census of Ethiopia, the number of Sidaama mother-tongue speakers is 2,925,171. The Sidaama territory is dominated by a plateau that is interrupted by small valleys and rivers. The area has three ecological zones: lowland, midland, and highland. The vegetation is lush enough to support cattle grazing, *ensat* ('false banana') e.g. and other crop cultivation. The year is roughly divided into the dry season (November-March) and a rainy period (April–October).

A Sidaama elder in front of his *ensat* garden, © Anbessa Teferra

Origins. Some Sidaama elders claim that the Sidaama came from overseas, settled in various places in Ethiopia and then moved south to settle in Bale. Other oral sources oppose this view and posit that the Sidaama came from the south. They claim that the original home of the Sidaama was the River Dawa area. Their two main ethnic components were the Maldiya and the Bushshe. Both were pastoralists, though the Bushshe may have been familiar with horticulture. The Sidaama word *bushsha* ('soil') may attest to this fact. The land, however, was already occupied by a people called Hoofa and the Sidaama became their subjects. As demands for tribute from the Hoofa increased, the Bushshe joined forces with the Maldiya and succeeded in defeating the Hoofa who later on were assimilated to the Sidaama. Decades later conflict arose between the Bushshe and Maldiya. However, eventually peace was restored thanks to marriage exchange, a common language and culture, bonds that still hold the people together.

Economy. In the highlands most Sidaama are subsistence farmers while in the lowlands they also practice pastoralism. The number of pastoralists, however, is decreasing rapidly because of overpopulation and the associated lack of open grazing lands. Overpopulation is also causing farming to be less productive because of decreasing plot sizes. The Sidaama mainly cultivate *ensat*. Of its products, *waasa* (fermented *ensat* pulp) in particular is the main staple food which is supplemented by dairy products, vegetables, and occasionally meat. In addition to *ensat*, maize, barley, sorghum, sugar cane, pulses, etc., are grown. The Sidaama live in small hamlets in which the *ensat* gardens surround the thatched houses. Coffee has been the main cash crop since the 1950s. Today, the Sidaama region is one of the major coffee-producing areas and provides up to 40% of the washed coffee on the Ethiopian market. Sidaama coffee, being organic, is one of the premium coffee brands in the world. The other important cash crop is *chat*.

There are also artisans such as tanners, potters, blacksmiths, and weavers. Traditionally, these professions have been despised and intermarriage between the ordinary Sidaama and the first three artisan groups was prohibited. A portion of the educated population is engaged in government jobs while others are involved in trade.

Social and political organization. The Sidaama are divided into a number of clans. The Maldiya are the largest group comprising nine sub-clans, while the *Bushshe* consist of five sub-clans. The family forms the lowest nucleus of social organization. Since the Sidaama have a patriarchal system, the husband is the one who administers the family, which he supports by farming and cattle rearing. The wife is responsible for all household chores including bringing up children. A group of families form the village and the village collective forms the neighbourhood, which cooperates in various tasks such as house building, farming, pond maintenance, etc. The council of elders administers the neighbourhood. They handle local affairs and resolve various conflicts. The Sidaama did not have one elected leader. Instead, a 'traditional chief', called *moote*, administered each clan. The traditional Sidaama system is patrilineal with males inheriting property. The sociopolitical structure was based on a system of generation grades called *luwa*, which has five sets, alternates every eight years, and includes only males.

Religion and rituals. Sidaama traditional religion is based on honouring *magano* ('God') and belief in the spirits of powerful clan founders and deceased elders. One of the main ways of respecting God is by adhering to *halaale* ('truth') which emphasizes kindness, honesty and respect for elders. Ancestors, in particular a deceased father, act as mediators between God and the family. In order to elicit the assistance of ancestors or pay respect to them, a ritual of feeding the spirit is performed. It involves pouring honey and milk or pouring the blood of a slaughtered bull on the ancestor's tomb. The rich system of Sidaama tradition and customary practices is gradually changing due to various forces. For instance, during the *Darg* regime traditional songs were discouraged. In addition, Evangelical churches that have rapidly expanded since 1991, as well as creeping globalization, are responsible for the decline of traditional customs. Traditional leather dresses, ornaments, pouring honey and milk on an ancestral tomb, openly weeping in funeral ceremonies, etc., are becoming a rarity.

Tourist Attractions. The Sidaama zone is endowed with various sites which are a good source of tourist attractions. These include *Wando Gannat* hot water spring and forests, Hawaasa fish market, and *Gidabo* hot water spring. In Aragash Lodge (near Yergalam), besides the natural habitat, one can also observe food preparation of the staple known as *waasa* and also a coffee ceremony. There are also the waterfalls of *Logita* and *Bonora*. The colourful Sidaama New Year festival of *Fichchee-Cambalaalla* attracts tourists and was inscribed in 2015 by UNESCO on the Representative List of the Intangible Cultural Heritage of Humanity.

Literature: JOHN HAMER, ANBESSA TEFERRA, 'Sidaama Ethnography', *EAE* IV, 655–658; ARNE TOLO, *Sidama and Ethiopian: the Emergence of the Mekane Yesus Church in Sidama*, Uppsala 1998.

Anbessa Teferra, Tel-Aviv

Somali

The Somali form one of the largest ethnic groups of the Horn of Africa, including eastern Ethiopia. The total Somali population worldwide is difficult to estimate, because Somali have a long history of migration and, more recently, flight, within the region and globally. As a consequence, Somali are found across eastern and southern Africa, but also in the Arabian Peninsula, Europe, North America, South Asia and Australia. The last official census inside the Somali Republic was conducted in 1985 and 1986, but its results were not published.

Today the population inside Somalia is estimated at around 10 million; a further four to five million reside in Ethiopia (mainly in Region 5), another 2.5 million live in Kenya (mainly in the northeast, but also in Nairobi, Nakuru and Mombasa) and around half a million live in Djibouti. Additionally, around one million are refugees in Ethiopia, Kenya and Yemen. Approximately another million Somali reside around the globe as diaspora communities. Against this backdrop, Somali have aptly been called a 'globalized nation'. Many Somali hold passports from several states and speak, besides Af-Soomaali (an Eastern Cushitic language) and Arabic, which is learned in Koranic school, numerous other languages.

Origins. Some origin myths link Somali to pious travellers or *shaykh*s coming from the Hadhramaut in the 14th and 15th centuries who settled in the north of the Somali peninsula. These are credited with spreading a Sufi-version of Sunni Islam among many Somali and are recognized as the founding fathers of large descent groups such as Isaaq, Dir and Darood. Linguistic research suggests that the ancestors of the Somali moved into the northern Horn of Africa from around Lake Turkana in today's northwestern Kenya. The name 'Somali' was first mentioned in a written source in the 14th century CE, in the Ethiopian *Kebra nagast* praising the victory of King Yeshaq over Islamic forces in the Horn.

Throughout the centuries Somali mixed with the Oromo, who also came from around Lake Turkana and invaded northeastern Africa in the 16th century. Moreover, since ancient times Arabian and Asian, and later European refugees, missionaries, merchants and adventurers landed on the Somali shores along the Gulf of Aden and the Indian Ocean and established trading posts, mosques and fortresses. They gradually became integrated into the local population, particularly along the Benaadir coast of today's southern Somalia. Finally, before the advent of Somaloid nomads from Lake Turkana, some of the southern parts of the Horn were most probably already inhabited by Bantu-speaking agriculturalists.

They as well as other indigenous groups inhabiting the northern Horn were absorbed by the newcomers. In the 19th century, Arab slave traders introduced more Bantu-speakers from eastern Africa into southern Somalia, where they were used as plantation workers. From a historical perspective, therefore, the Somali inhabiting the Horn of Africa today are a complex mixture of various groups. However, ethnic and cultural mixing was more intense in the south and along the coast than in the north and the hinterlands.

At present, in the late 20th and early 21st centuries, Somali adhere to a strong ethnic ideology of 'Somaliness' which serves to distinguish them from other 'African' people as much as from 'Arabs' and others. Key features of 'Somaliness' are adhering to Sunni Islam, speaking Somali, and reckoning descent in the father's line, establishing belonging to clan-families like Dir, Darood, Isaaq, Hawiye or Rahanweyn, which are subdivided into numerous clans, sub-clans, lineages and smaller groupings. While historical research has shown that patrilineal descent is frequently fictitious and genealogies are flexibly constructed and individuals and groups can be incorporated or excluded, the ideology of descent remains strong among many Somali. This, at least until the mid-20th century, automatically confned descendants of former slaves (in Somali *Jareer*) and 'mixed' groups (such as Madhibaan, Reer Xamar or, until recently, Rahanweyn) to inferior status and 'impure' Somaliness. Over the past decades, the social hierarchies in Somali society have been broken up to some degree; still, intermarriage between minority and majority groups and political participation of minority groups is restricted.. Also, specialist religious groups, such as Asharaf and Shekhal are, on the one hand, praised as direct descendants of the family of the Prophet Muhammad; but on the other hand, they are treated as dependants by economically and politically influential patrons from the majority groups.

Animal husbandry constitutes the backbone of many Somali family economies throughout the Horn and the camel has become an emblem of Somali identity. Export of Somali-owned livestock from eastern Ethiopia via the port of Berbera in Somaliland (north-western Somalia) to the Arabian Peninsula is an important source of income. Besides, in some areas of eastern Ethiopia and southern Somalia rainfed farming and irrigated plantations provide a source of income.

Somali market in Djibouti, © Wolbert G.C. Smidt

History. From the 19th century onward, Somali were divided between Ottoman-Egyptian, Ethiopian, French, Italian and British colonial powers. These powers encountered a society which was predominantly pastoral-nomadic (in the north) and agro-pastoralist (in the south). There had been powerful Islamic sultanates in the past (from the 12th to 18th centuries), in which Somali clans played a major political role and which were located along caravan routes between the interior and the coast. One of these was the sultanate of Adal with its capital Harar (in eastern Ethiopia). In 1527 Ahmad ibn Ibrahim al-Ghazi (called Ahmad Grany in Amharic or Axmed Gurey in Somali) seized power in Adal. He recruited many Afar and Somali fighters and led a *jihad* against the Christian Ethiopian kingdom. For more than a decade, his troops controlled vast territories and waged havoc in the Ethiopian highlands. However, Muslim power crumbled immediately after Axmed Gurey's death in battle in 1543. Over the following two centuries, the Somali sultanates gradually disappeared.

In the second half of the 19th century Somali came under numerous traditional authorities commanding, often only nominally, influence over their respective descent groups. But there was no overarching ruler. Only in religious settlements, which had been founded by Sufi 'brotherhoods' or 'orders' (Arabic *tariqa*, pl. *turuq*), had some stable hierarchical organization developed. The activities of the *shaykh*s and their followers in these settlements were focussed mostly on religious learning, teaching and agriculture. The general lack of cohesion among Somali facilitated external interferences and partition.

With the opening of the Suez Canal in 1869 the Somali coast marked the route of European ships to and from India and other parts of Asia. Italy acquired the port of Assab in modern Eritrea in 1869. At the same time, the Khedive Ismail of Egypt brought the Afar and Somali coast up to Cape Guardafui (Ras Asey) under his nominal control, including the important ports of Zayla and Berbera as well as Harar in the interior, which by then was famous as a centre of Islamic learning. However, when the Mahdi revolt broke out in Sudan in 1884, Egyptian troops retreated from the Somali Peninsula. This left the field open for the European powers and Ethiopia. Menilek II (r. 1889–1913) extended his rule into its eastern periphery from the 1880s onward. Imperial troops conquered Harar in 1887 and afterwards proceeded to the eastern lowlands. In this way Ethiopia underlined its claims to territory in the Horn. Through investment in its army and the import of large quantities of firearms, which facilitated the victory over the Italians at Adwa in 1896, Ethiopia had become a power on a par with the European colonizers. In 1897, the Anglo-Ethiopian treaty ceded one-third of the British-controlled areas in the north to Ethiopia, in return for Menilek's neutrality in Britain's competition with France over strategic positions in the Horn, along with some economic concessions. This area became known as Ogaden, Hawd and Reserved Areas, and covers the area of today's Region 5, between Jijjiga in the northwest and the Gumburu Hills in the southeast.

In regular raids Menilek's soldiers extracted 'taxes' through confiscating harvests and herds. The Europeans granted Somali very little protection against the Ethiopians. But some Somali groups also cooperated with the Ethiopians against fellow Somali. Colonial partition and oppression set the stage for *daraawiishta* ('the Dervishes'), a religiously and politically inspired anti-colonial resistance movement founded by the Somali *shaykh*, warrior and poet Mohamed Abdille Hasan (Maxamed Cabdille Xasan). Originally from the Ogaden region, he mobilized many Somali throughout the northern (and partly southern) Somali peninsula to fight Ethiopian, but also British and Italian colonizers and their Somali allies. Between 1899 and 1920 insurgency and counter-insurgency laid havoc to many areas, particularly in British Somaliland. The Dervishes were eventually defeated by massive British military operations. Later, Maxamed Cabdille Xasan, who had died whilst a refugee in Iimey, deep in today's Region 5 of Ethiopia, became a national hero in Somalia. Somali nationalism aimed at integrating all Somali in the Horn into one state, who after independence were divided between northern Kenya, eastern Ethiopia, Djibouti and the Somali Republic. This provoked repeated armed clashes and war between Somalia and its neighbours, particularly Ethiopia, with whom Somalia engaged in a conventional and very costly war in 1977–1978. This ended in Somali defeat after the Soviet Union had sided with Ethiopia. In the wake of this event, hundreds of thousands of Somali fled from Ethiopia into Somalia, fearing reprisals by the government in Addis Ababa.

Recent events. The Somali region inside Ethiopia, which is dominated by members of the Ogadeen clan (part of the Darood clan-family), has been characterized by protracted insecurity, economic marginalization and armed conflict. (See also chapter IX the article 'Ethiopia and its neighbouring states', here 'Somalia'.) State-sponsored violence and violence by various guerrilla groups has shaped the lives and experiences of Somali in Ethiopia for at least six decades since the 1950s. The most important Somali resistance movement in eastern Ethiopia is the Ogaden National Liberation Front (ONLF) which was founded in 1984. It fought the forces of the *Darg* regime until 1991. With the coming to power of the Ethiopian Peoples' Revolutionary Democratic Front, anti-regime activities were temporarily halted by the integration of ethnic-based guerrilla groups into the federal political framework. Soon, however, tensions between the government in Addis Ababa and the ONLF re-emerged and fighting started again. Also the collapse of the Somali state had negative consequences for Somali in Ethiopia. Among other forces, Al-Ittihad Al-Islamiya (AIAI), a Somali Islamist group, engaged in the Somali civil war. It had the proclaimed aim not only to take over Somalia but also to free Somali in 'Western Somalia' (eastern Ethiopia). In the 1990s, AIAI operated inside Ethiopia and conducted several attacks in Addis Ababa. Its stronghold in Luuq (southwestern Somalia) was bombed by the Ethiopian air force in 1996.

The Union of Islamic Courts (UIC) including *Al-Shabaab* ('The Youth') came to power in southern Somalia in 2006. It was in many regards a successor of AIAI. Some of its members combined an Islamist and a Somali nationalist agenda. Around 15,000 Ethiopian forces intervened in southern Somalia in late 2006, defeated the UIC and occupied Mogadishu, in cooperation with the Somali president Cabdullaahi Yuusuf. In January 2009, after two years of massive violence and human rights violations on all sides, the Ethiopian army officially withdrew from Somalia, only to re-intervene in October 2011. Since then, thousands of Ethiopian troops have been on the ground in southern Somalia, fighting *Al-Shabaab*.

In April 2007, the ONLF attacked the Abole oil field in Dhagaxbuur. Around 70 Ethiopian soldiers and oil workers, as well as nine Chinese employees of Sinopec Limited, a Chinese oil and gas company, were killed in the attack. The incident triggered a counter-insurgency campaign by Ethiopia's National Defence Forces (ENDF) to isolate the ONLF from local communities. In 2009, a special police force called the Liyu Police was founded, to assist the ENDF in its operations in the Somali Region. The Liyu Police consists mainly of ethnic Somali.

The years after the Abole oil field attack were marked by massive human rights violations. In 2012, Somali and non-Somali actors in Kenya with contacts to the Ethiopian government and the ONLF initiated peace talks between the two enemies. They were, as of early 2016, not yet concluded. Simultaneously, the Ethiopian government increased its investments in the Somali Region. A new university was established in Jijjiga, the capital of the Somali Region, already in 2005 and opened its doors for students two years later. Infrastructure projects including roads were built and added to the improvement of the regional economy. Nevertheless, Somali in Ethiopia remain a group that is frequently viewed with suspicion (as 'guerrillas' or 'terrorists') by other Ethiopians, particularly representatives of the state.

Literature: TOBIAS HAGMANN, *Talking Peace in the Ogaden. The search for an end to conflict in the Somali Regional State in Ethiopia,* Nairobi 2014 (*http://www.riftvalley.net/publication/talking-peace-ogaden#.VUZCJFP7tlc*); MOHAMED HAJI MUKHTAR, *Historical Dictionary of Somalia* (*New Edition*) Oxford 2003.

Markus Höhne, Universität Leipzig

Walaytta

The Walaytta (Wolaitta) people number about 1.75million and live in a region of the same name in south-central Ethiopia. They speak a language of the Omotic family. When the Ethiopian imperial state militarily expanded at the end of the 19th century, one of the regions it conquered (in1894) was Walaytta. It was then a prosperous kingdom. The people had little linguistic or cultural similarity to the Amhara-Tegray populations of the Ethiopian highlands, although there had been influence of royal traditions and religions since the 14th century. But the Walaytta kings always resisted too close a link with the Ethiopian empire, because they wanted to remain independent politically and economically.

The current Walaytta area is around 4,500 km². It has 1.75 million inhabitants and is densely populated. The capital, Soddo, has about 135,000 inhabitants. The scarcity of agrarian land and resources has led to significant emigration of young people to other places to find work and to focus on education, to 'escape' from their overcrowded land and the lack of employment.

In the past decade, the zone's economy has seen some investment, new infrastructure and the opening of a university in the capital in 2007. But it is still relatively poor and marked by agrarian stagnation. High population pressure tends to inhibit growth.

History. Walaytta had an interesting history as a kingdom. It is for many people still a nostalgic reference point of past glory. There were two dynasties in the historical Walaytta: the first one the Walaytta-Malla dynasty, that emerged in the 13th century, from the Walaytta-Malla clan, which still exists. The Tegre dynasty ruled after *c.*1710 until 1894. Under the Walaytta-Malla dynasty the state itself emerged. It was formed by gradual conquest and expansion to the north and east. The kingship later developed into a 'divine' form.

The most famous Walaytta king is reputedly Motolome, who reached fame through featuring in the medieval Christian religious text *Gadla Takla Haymanot* (although here reference is likely to a king of the same name in another area). At the time of this first dynasty, it is likely that the Walaytta followed a traditional local religion, despite the legend of Motolome's Christian conversion.

Orthodox Christianity was present well before the conquest of Walaytta by the Ethiopian Emperor Menilek's forces in 1894, and probably was brought by the ancestors of the second dynasty in Walaytta, the Tegre, who ruled from the early 1700s. Its founders were allegedly immigrants from the north, namely Tegray. As Christians from the north in possession of a literate-religious tradition they may have gained respect.

Under the Tegre kings, the state expanded significantly. The most notable expansion occurred under the conqueror King Sanna (r.1762–1790), who fought neighbouring peoples and incorporated areas beyond Damota (a mountainous area) into his realm. He was the most important conqueror king of the Walaytta and decisively shaped the Walaytta state. His son Ogato continued the expansion further northeast. The Tegre kings also elaborated the court system, with four advisors below the king, a head of defence, and a council of twelve councillors, who had a great say in confirming the successor king and were involved in general policy matters. Remarkable is the absence of any written legacy of the kingdom, despite the alleged North Ethiopian origins of the new elite.

The 19th century was the highpoint for Walaytta, especially under Kings Amado and Gobe. The last king was Tona (r. 1889–1894). King Tona refused to acknowledge Emperor Menilek's sovereignty and a war ensued in 1894, demolishing the Walaytta state structure and bringing steep economic decline and an identity crisis to the society.

In imperial times, up to 1974, the area was called 'Wolamo', an administrative unit in the Sidamo Province. It was a subsistence-oriented, underdeveloped agricultural area, with significant social inequality and little industry except for traditional crafts, and small markets. In the 1980s and 1990s the Walaytta area was part of the North Omo region and no longer a separate unit.

A Walaytta family in front of a typical house, © Jon Abbink

Society and economy. Walaytta society is traditionally composed of more than 100 patrilineal clans, with diverse origins. High-ranking clans are those of the former royals and nobles, followed by those of the free farmers known as *goka*, and the craftsmen and also former slaves at the lower end of the social ladder.

Walaytta oral tradition contains rich historical and family narratives. There is an indigenous genre of 'epic songs', called *gereesa*, in which the narratives are recited. These traditions are declining but still find resonance among the youth. However, young people have lost the art of reciting and are more preoccupied with modern educational achievement, economic survival, and religious modernisation. The Walaytta are known for their characteristic songs and dances, performed at weddings, religious gatherings and other ceremonial events. These are also regularly performed by national dance and theatre companies in Ethiopia and also featured on Ethiopian TV.

The Walaytta economy is still predominantly mixed agrarian and subsistence-oriented. *Ensat* is an important crop. Farmers sell ginger, wood, coffee and butter in the markets, which are also sold outside the region. The urban economy is slowly growing, with some investment in services, small-scale production facilities and food-processing, and education.

The main religions are Orthodox Christianity (25%), Pentecostal-Evangelical faiths (around 63%), Catholicism (5%), and Islam (around 5%) in the towns.

Since November 2000 the Walaytta region has been given separate administrative zone status in the Southern Region of Ethiopia after a wave of violent protests in

Soddo. The current (since 2012) Ethiopian Prime Minister Hailemariam Desalegn is from Walaytta (Boloso-Sore area).

Walaytta is struggling with environmental pressure and economic development. Land scarcity and high population growth are serious and have not abated. There are few alternatives yet to agriculture and small-scale trade, although an industrial zone was set up in Soddo. Agriculture has shown some growth in the past few years due to government stimulus. Walaytta is always vulnerable to weather changes, and in most years food aid is needed for thousands of people. Next to seasonal labour migration, there is growing permanent emigration to richer towns in the south and to Addis Ababa. The overall socio-economic picture of Walaytta is therefore still precarious.

Literature: JON ABBINK, 'Wolaitta livelihoods (Ethiopia): agricultural 'involution', identity, and prospects of growth', *Afriche e Orienti*, special issue, 13/4 (2011), 86–104; DATA DEA BARATA, 'Governance, language, politics and education in Southern Ethiopia: the tribulations of inventing WoGaGoDa', in PAULOS MILKIAS, MESSAY KEBEDE (eds.), *Education, Politics and Social Change in Ethiopia*, 117–128, Los Angeles 2010; DESSALEGN RAHMATO, *Development Interventions in Wollaita, 1960s–2000s: A Critical Review*, Addis Ababa 2007.

Jon Abbink, Leiden

Mursi (Mun)

The Mursi are an agro-pastoral people of southwestern Ethiopia with a population of 6,916 according to official figures. The name they use for themselves is 'Mun' (sg 'Muni') or 'Taama' (in ritual/historical contexts) and they speak 'Mun', a Surmic, Nilo-Saharan language that is closely related to but also distinct from that of the Suri to the west and northwest. Indeed, language, as well as clan relations and customs intertwine Mursi and Suri people and their histories. For example, the Mursi, like the Suri, are known for their extraordinary pottery and wooden lip plates, worn by adolescent girls and married women, and for the stick dueling competitions of boys and men. The Mursi herd mainly cattle but also goats and sheep. They cultivate sorghum and maize, beans and squash, and collect over 40 varieties of edible leaves.

Location. The Mursi live in an area of roughly 2,000 km^2 along and between the Omo and Mago Rivers in the Sala-Mago District of Southern Nations, Nationalities and Peoples' Region. It includes landscapes ranging from riverine forests and bushland thicket to open savanna grasslands. The main highland area, which runs from the southwest to the northeast reaches a height of about 1,666 m (known in Mursi as Dara Mountain). The Mursi live in a remote area that has become increasingly accessible in recent years. There are two national parks (Mago and Omo National Park), one sport hunting camp, and the Tama Wildlife Reserve in the area.

History. According to their own oral history, the Mursi originated from the South and began migrating north around the mid-19th century, crossing the Omo river from the west to the east at a place called Dorl. Despite a good deal of intermingling with their neighbours, especially, the Suri, Kwegu and Bodi, over the last half a century, the Mursi and Bodi have oscillated between friendly accommodation and outright warfare. Their changing relations have had much to do with struggles over land and water resources. The Mursi are believed to have acquired land throughout their long association and close proximity to the Bodi to the north and, more recently, the Ari to the east. In the 1980s a number of Mursi from the Mara area established themselves in the Mago Valley. Moving to the Mago Valley meant incorporation into capitalist forms of production and commerce. Mursi began to sell their cattle in the Ari highland markets, which provided a potential economic base for Mursi facing drought. Mursi still have little, if any, education and economic opportunities, despite tourism and agro-development in their area, and continue to be enjoined from participating in politics.

Ethnography. Anthropologist David Turton was the first to explore the social and political foundations of the Mursi. They have a sociopolitical system in which kin, clans and local groups are the most salient modes of organization. As Turton discovered, clans are dispersed amongst a number of local groups, called *buranyoga,* which can only be represented on a map by marking off discrete lengths of the Omo according to the flood cultivation sites used by their members. Throughout their history, the Mursi have practised an age-grade system that is still followed today. Mursi society is patriarchal in nature, with elder men (*bara*) deciding most major matters for each age group. Mursi boys are raised to defend and protect the interests of the community and to achieve the status of married adult men (*rora*), who are especially respected for their wise ways and capacities as peace-keepers. Mursi girls are raised to become strong girls (*bansanaa*), and, upon marriage, take on the age-grade status of their husbands. Anthropologists have explored many aspects of Mursi ethnography, such as the role of women, domestic relations, dress, rhetoric and culture change, the impact of tourism, praise songs and ritual, healing and healers, body painting, and so on.

Culture of the people. A body of oral customary law covers many aspects of Mursi behaviour and ritual life. Payment in cattle will settle most conflicts, just as healers or local priests can cure most afflictions or problems within the community. The central human figure in the Mursi religious system is the inherited position of the *komoru* or priest, whose roles include divination and prophecy, ensuring rainfall for cultivation, protecting livestock from disease, and people during times of war. The Mursi are

An unwed Mursi girl prepares for a bracelet competition, © Shauna LaTosky

monotheists who believe in a higher force called Tumwi. Some Mursi have also adopted Christianity but the majority remain loyal to their own brand of monotheism.

Bridewealth exchange is ubiquitous among the Mursi, involving the exchange of livestock. A herd of 38 cattle is required in order to marry and be deemed a respectable member of society. The measure of a person's wealth is in terms of cattle and children. To die a bachelor (*zigai*) is taboo among the Mursi. Girls and boys come together during harvest dances and stick dueling competitions (called *donga*). Girls also compete after men's stick dueling competitions in bracelet (*ula*) contests, also referred to as *donga a dholuiny* ('girl's *donga*). Men do not typically marry when they are young but instead they grow their herds in order to accumulate enough cattle to pay for a bride.

The Mursi's entire way of life depends not only on their cattle, but also on the cultivation of sorghum and maize. All subsistence needs are met by their crops and cattle bi-products. They drink the milk and, on occasion, drink the blood of their cattle, and eat sorghum or maize porridge, together with edible leaves called *kinnoi*. Bulls and oxen are slaughtered for meat on special occasions, for ceremonies, or if a person is ill. Mursi ingenuity and wisdom is expressed through their long and enduring relationship to the land as cultivators and cattle herders and through intergenerational legacies of stewardship, involving the protection of wildlife, livestock, grasslands, and sacred groves called *badhinya*. The Mursi, like their neighbours, would not have survived in this environment had it not been for their supreme resilience, adaptability and opportunistic responses to changing social and environmental conditions. The move to the Mago in 1979/1980 is the most obvious example of this in their recent history.

Plantations and resettlement. The Lower Omo is due to become the largest irrigation complex in Ethiopia. Since 2011, the state-run Ethiopian Sugar Corporation has set up the Omo-Kuraz Sugar Development Project, and resettlement sites are being built in order to transform the lives of the Mursi and their neighbours by turning them into settled cultivators with irrigated plots, but with few or no cattle. These plans are being carried out in the interests of national development and in the firm belief that it will also benefit the local population. Past experiences show that ambitious and well-meaning projects like this have often had tragic consequences for those they were intended to benefit, mainly because the planners failed to involve local people in project planning and thereby to respect local knowledge.

Literature: Shauna LaTosky, *Predicaments of Mursi (Mun) Women in Ethiopia's Changing World*, Köln 2013; David Turton, 'The Meaning of Place in a World of Movement: Lessons from Long-term Field Research in Southern Ethiopia', *Journal of Refugee Studies*, 18/3 (2005), 258–280.

Shauna LaTosky, Max-Planck-Institut für ethnologische Forschung, Halle/Saale

Hamar (Amar, Hamer)

Location. The ancient stronghold of the Hamar is a rugged mountain range that rises steeply from the low-lying Woyto Valley (400–600m) up to about 2,000m, from where it slopes gradually westward to the plains of the Lower Omo. From the direction of Jinka, the Hamar Range seems low and unimpressive, but if viewed from Lokitang or Illeret, the Hamar mountains tower high over the whole region between Lake Turkana and Chaw Baher. The highest peaks are Assile in the south and Baala in the north, both about 2,000 m. From this secure position the Hamar could watch whatever might come from the west. In early times, the traditional border to the west was the Kaeske, a dry riverbed flooded in the rainy season with the waters draining from the mountains and eventually emptying into the Omo Valley. Ever since the Ethiopian conquest at the end of the 19th century, however, the Hamar have gradually extended their territory westward and southward, coming into close contact with the Boorana, Dhaasanac, Nyangatom, and Kara (Karo).

History. The Hamar speak a group of dialects belonging to the Southern or Aroid branch of the Omotic family. They originated as an amalgamation of culturally different groups. According to Hamar tradition, their first ancestor came from Ari and was followed by others from Maale, Samay, Konso, and elsewhere. This formative period may well go back to the 17th or 18th century and lasted until the end of the 19th century when the first big game hunters and European explorers arrived, after whom Menilek II's armies entered the area. As a result of their eventual conquest the Hamar lost some of their traditional institutions, and whilst in exile, adopted some customs of their hosts, but they never lost their identity.

Economy. As long as anyone can remember the Hamar have practised a mixed subsistence economy based on slash and burn agriculture, augmented by raiding. From high up in their mountains they would spot the game or herds of the Boorana, Samay, or Arbore below in the valley, and would sweep down on them. In addition the Hamar raise cattle, sheep, donkeys and goats. These last are in fact the backbone of their economy. There may be years when the sorghum fails to ripen, but it is never so dry that the goats could not survive and carry the Hamar through the most difficult months of the year. Goats can also be traded for grain or taken to one of the two markets in Hamar, where they may be bartered for other commodities or converted into money.

Territorial organization. Of greatest importance is the *dele* or homestead consisting of a cattle kraal, a goat enclosure, one or more houses, and an open, cleanly swept place where relatives, friends and also strangers will at first be invited to rest before cowhides are spread out in front or inside the *dele* to receive the guests. Depending on how many generations or siblings inhabit the *dele,* the cattle kraal will have one or more gateways while the goat enclosure has only one. Both gateways are of utmost importance for all major rituals of the Hamar. Ideally, a homestead lies on an elevation that allows a good view of the surrounding terrain and one to observe the weather. Several homesteads together form a neighbourhood. Neighbours are called *zarsi*, alluding to a grass of the same name, which spreads on the ground and over time creates a network of connected roots. The next largest spatial unit is the *tsinti*, of which there used to be about a dozen, radiating out from sacred gateways through which all the inhabitants of a *tsinti* would pass once a year, if they had lived righteously. But according to Hamar tradition hardly anyone would ever dare to pass. Finally, all of Hamar territory is divided into the lands of the two ritual leaders who are responsible for peace and health in the country. Nowadays these traditional territorial divisions are supplemented with modern administrative categories, the same as all over Ethiopia. Together with the fast expanding roads and towns, these will eventually supersede the traditional forms of territorial organization.

Kinship organization. Unlike cattle or camels, goats allow a fast accumulation of herds and thus foster forms of kinship that need neither deep genealogies nor large corporate groups. Although the Hamar have clans, nine in one moiety (*Binnas*) and 16 in the other (*Galabu*), these are dispersed all over the country and have no economic or political function. Rather they provide a framework for marriage and the many rituals

Hamar wedding ceremony, © Matthias Ansel

associated with founding a family. Membership of a clan is inherited from the father, and although a member of one moiety generally marries a member of the other, the picture is complicated in that there is one clan, which belongs to both moieties and in that some *Galabu* clans may marry other *Galabu* clans. While the moieties with their reservoir of clans provide the over-all orientation for marriage choices, the actual marriages are conducted between specific families or 'houses' and lineages. As is to be expected, marriages involve the transfer of livestock and other goods like grain, honey, rifles etc., which may be extended over many years, even generations.

Political organization: the role of the spokesmen. The peoples of southern Ethiopia are rightly famous for their egalitarian and democratic politics, which contrast sharply with the hierarchical and authoritarian societies of the north. In Hamar only selected men are allowed to speak at public meetings. They are called *ayo*, which means 'those who get things done'. An *ayo* is selected by men of senior age-groups when there is need for a new spokesman. The privilege is provisional and lasts only as long as his leadership is good and fruitful. At public meetings the men sit in order of seniority, and the principle of seniority applies also to speaking. Old and experienced speakers usually begin with a noisy and stylized expression of anger, reprimanding the younger men. After finishing with his rhetorical anger, the speaker comes to the particular matter of the day, typically placing the current issue in a historical context. After the first speaker follows a second, a third and so on depending on how important the issue is and how many spokesmen are present. No speaker is listened to in complete silence, but when a meeting concerns matters of war and peace the men will begin to chant their war songs indicating their willingness to fight and their rejection of any prudence that might be interpreted as fearfulness.

Religion and the philosophy of *barjo*. In addition to the notion of spirits of the dead and associated sacrifices and divination, the Hamar aim to create good fortune or well-being (*barjo*), underlying almost all of what we might call Hamar 'religion'. The philosophy of *barjo* and its associated blessings are in accord with the Hamar egalitarian political system. According to the Hamar, creation goes on continuously and human beings have an active part to play in it. Every living being needs *barjo* to exist and achieve its natural state of well-being. Even such phenomena as clouds, rain, the stars, etc., need to have their *barjo* to appear in a regular and ordered way. People can actively engage in producing and augmenting the *barjo* of people, animals, plants, the soil, the seasons, etc., by calling forth *barjo*. Both men and women have *barjo*, but only the elders call forth *barjo* in an emphatic and stylized way with songs. Women call *barjo* in a quiet and unobtrusive way, for example, by sweeping the entrance to their goat enclosure and by putting on a belt decorated with cowry shells. Also, blessing may be done collectively as when neighbours or lineages celebrate and elevate an initiate by making him leap on to and run over a row of cattle. This event confirms and augments the *barjo* of the youth, turns him into a fully fledged man who may marry, and makes sure that his wife will bear him many children. Sometimes this is referred to as 'bull jumping' but bulls are not even allowed to be present! Only female cows, a calf and two oxen may take part in the event.

Literature: IVO STRECKER, *Ethnographic Chiasmus. Essays on Culture, Conflict and Rhetoric. The Hamar of Southern Ethiopia*, V, Wien, Berlin, Michigan 2010; IVO STRECKER, *Berimba's Resistance. The Life and Times of a Great Hamar Spokesman. As told by his son Aike Berinas. The Hamar of Southern Ethiopia*, IV, Berlin et al. 2013.

Ivo Strecker, Mainz and Arba Mench

Afar

The Afar (written Qafár in the official spelling) are a largely pastoral society of the arid lowlands of the Horn of Africa. Linguistically they belong to the eastern branch of the Cushitic language family. Nowadays, a large majority of about 70% of the Afar live in Ethiopia (*c.* 1.3 million). They are also established in the eastern lowlands of Eritrea (*c.* 0.3 million) and in the north and west of Djibouti (*c.* 0.3 million, representing one third of this country's population). Administratively, they form the Afar National Regional State in Ethiopia, with the capital city Samara, and in Eritrea they inhabit the Southern Red Sea Zone. In Tegrennya they are called Dankal (after the former Dankali kingdom of the coast), in Amharic Adal (and Udali in Somali, after the former Adal state). Europeans often refer to them as Danakil (derived from the Arabic). The newly constructed capital Samara houses a new university, and administrates a developing industry, comprising especially potash concessions, as well as huge agricultural projects based along the nearby Awash.

The territory. The territory of the Afar forms a wide triangle, comprising essentially barren and empty lowlands, mainly inhabited on the fringes. The first side of this triangle is formed by the coastline of the Red Sea, from the Bori peninsula in Eritrea, southeast of Metsewa, to the bottom of the Gulf of Tadjoura at the Bab al-Mandab in Djibouti. The second side is limited by the foothills of the escarpment of the Ethiopian highlands. At a relatively cooler altitude, these slopes offer more abundant pasture for transhumant seasonal migrations. Clashes often occur between pastoralists and mountain dwellers when one party raids the herds of the others as a response to the expansion of cultivated areas over seasonal grazing areas. Peaceful forms of exchange are nevertheless frequent through a series of markets established in intermediary zones and connected by trade routes. The camel caravan trade used to be the link between the mountains and the sea. For ages the Afar have specialized in the extraction and trading of salt, which was of vital importance to the highlanders. Afar camel herders have suffered competition from modern transport (the Ethiopian–Djiboutian railway, then roads) but their handling activity has been partially compensated by the traffic of smuggled goods. The third side of Afar country is formed by a large strip of land on the eastern banks of the Awash River including its terminal interior delta ending in a series of lakes, located on the present boundary between Ethiopia and Djibouti. The Awash and its non-permanent tributaries provide pastures and waterholes for cattle and camel herds in the dry season along the ways used during the transhumant migrations to higher altitude areas. The vital relation of Afar pastoralists to their environment, based on the availability of water resources, has been seriously disrupted by the clearing of extensive lands for irrigation all over the Awash basin with the multiple consequences of hindering access to river banks, reducing water flow, and contaminating water with pesticides and fertilizers. Since the 1970s the vicinity of the Awash has been a contested border zone with the Isa Somali who have settled in several spots across the riverine area.

Socio-political structure. The social organization of the Afar is a combination of two dimensions, genealogical and territorial. On the one hand they belong to a great number of patrilineal clans (*kedo*) intertwined through links of kinship and pacts of alliance. Clans and sub-clans bear the memory of a complex history of conflicts, natural disasters, population movements, integration of migrant minorities and incorporation of holy lineages of men of religion. On the other hand, the regulation of land rights, water use and trade are the prerogative of authorities in charge of large territorial units (*bado*) usually referred to as sultanates. In the 17th century, after the collapse of the Walashma dynasty which had ruled the multi-ethnic Islamic kingdom of Adal since the 13th century, the fertile lands of the terminal delta of the Awash River were reclaimed by migrant populations from the highlands (Haralla, Dobaa) who were integrated into Afar ethnicity. This process led to the formation of the sultanate of Awsa. Through its wealth derived from agricultural resources and its strategic position, this sultanate extended its influence over all southern Afar lands. To this day it has remained the largest and most powerful Afar polity. The current *amoyta* ('king') is Hanfadhe Alimirah, recognized by the state as a traditional ruler of the Afar, with his seat at Aysaiita nearby Samara. Besides the central position occupied by Awsa, the coastal area was divided between the sultanates of Baylul (north-east, in today's Eritrea), Rahayta (central, today partitioned between Eritrea and Djibouti) and Tadjoura (or Tagori, south-west, in Djibouti), all of which continue to exist today as traditional polities. The northern inland Afar territories were ruled by the sultanates of Bidhu and Teru; the sultanate of Gobaad covered the

Afar elders on the beach of Tadjoura, playing *gebeta*, © Wolbert G.C. Smidt

south-west territories. The ruler of Awsa established a friendly trade relationship with the Shawan kings, who profited from the secure connection to the Red Sea trade through Awsa territory. In 1875 Awsa defended its independence against an Egyptian expeditionary force coming from Tadjoura, and in 1883/1888 they signed international treaties of friendship with Italy. Awsa accepted a vassal relationship with Ethiopia only around 1896 after wars with the Shawan kingdom. However, they safeguarded their autonomy in a manner similar to the Oromo Jimmaa kingdom, and only fully submitted in 1944. From 1916–1921 the Awsa rulers hosted the deposed ruler of Ethiopia, *Lej* Iyasu.

In addition to clan and territorial divisions the majority of Afar groups are divided into two rival political coalitions, the Reds (*Asayammara*) and the Whites (*Adoyammara*). This dual structure resulted from conflicts for control of grazing lands along the Awash valley in the 18th century. Each of the above mentioned polities is headed by one of the two parties, and no party can pretend to have exclusivity over land resources and has the obligation to accommodate the opposite. Over time, intermarriage and admixture between the two moieties have made this distinction very vague in some areas.

Religion. In religion, the Afar are almost exclusively Muslim. Islam was spread along the coastal areas probably as early as the ninth century through clerics of Arabian origin. Their descendants and spiritual heirs formed holy lineages established in the permanent settlements of the political centres, from where they disseminated the tenets of Islam among the nomads who kept most of their traditional beliefs and ritual practices. Since the mythical founding figures of Islam among the Afar, like *Shaykh* Ibrahim Warufi, proselytization was performed by learned *shaykh*s who were credited with magical powers and whose shrines (on the summits of volcanoes) are considered as shields protecting the territory. The Qadiri Sufi movement played a significant role in fostering the incorporation of the Afar into the regional networks of Islam. In the 19th century, *Shaykh* Kabir Hamza Mahmud al-Awsiyi composed a number of mystical poems and treatises in Arabic and in the Afar language. The coexistence between formal obedience to Islamic faith and law and customary traditions has been an issue of contention between the compliant Hanafi law school, widely represented in Awsa, and the more reformist positions of the Shafii, dominant in northern parts.

Heritage sites and tourism. The Afar Triangle is the location of the most ancient paleoanthropological sites, where *Australopithecus* skeletons, such as 'Lucy', have been found. Tourists visit the Afar Depression, one of the hottest deserts of the world, its colourful sulphur springs at Dallol, with the lowest point at ca. 146 m below sea level, and areas of traditional salt extraction at the salt lakes north of Berahle. There is a range of volcanoes parallel to the coastline, one of which, Nabro, erupted in 2011. Erta Ale is one of the few active volcanoes in the world with an open lava lake. Security is tight, every trip is guarded by both locally stationed soldiers and professional guides, usually starting from Meqele in Tegray.

Literature: Didier Morin, 'Afar', *EAE* I, 2003, 115f.; Aramis Houmed Soule, *Deux vies dans l'histoire de la Corne de l'Afrique. Mahamad Hanfare (1861–1902) et Ali Mirah Hanfare (1944–) sultans afars*, Addis Ababa 2005; Didier Morin, *Dictionnaire historique afar (1288–1982)*, Paris 2003; Getachew Kassa, *Among the Pastoral Afar in Ethiopia*, Utrecht 2001.

Éloi Ficquet, École des hautes études en sciences sociales, Paris, Wolbert G.C. Smidt, Mekelle University

Peoples of southwest Ethiopia: Nuer and Anywaa

Nuer

Basic facts. The Nuer are agro-pastoralist cattle herders and cultivators, predominantly growing maize and a small range of vegetables along the river banks and in the upland savannah. Agricultural products constitute around 60% and dairy products 40% of their staple diet. During the dry season they settle in large groups in dry-season cattle camps along the Baro and Gilo rivers and their tributaries, while during the rainy season they move into the uplands into settlements of nuclear families. Fishing forms an important part of their subsistence economy, whereas hunting, formerly an important part of their economy, has now ceased due to the destruction of most of the wildlife in recent regional conflicts.

The overwhelming majority of the Nuer live in South Sudan, and by calculating from the 1956 census may have reached 1.8 million today. In the Ethiopian census of 2008, their number in the Gambela region of Ethiopia is given at 112,606.

The main Nuer tribes in Ethiopia are the eastern Jikanny, particularly the Gajaak, followed by the Gagjiok sections Kuek and Lang as well as Gaagwang. Neighbouring the Nuer to the west are the Dinka and to the east the Anywaa. To the south, they adjoin the Murle and to the north the two small ethnic groups of the Mabaan and the Komo.

Effects of Globalization: Colonialism, missionaries, war and outmigration. The Nuer started to expand from the area north of the Bahr al-Ghazal river, before the Turco–Egyptian invasion of South Sudan, towards Ethiopia at the end of the 19th century. With the signing of the boundary agreement in 1902 between colonial Sudan and imperial Ethiopia, some sections of the Eastern Jikanny officially became part of Ethiopia. Since the *Darg* era, the Nuer have been subsequently further integrated into the Ethiopian state system. Education became an issue for larger sections of the society in the 1980s when the refugee camps which were opened in the area offered access to schools. With the establishment of the Gambella regional state in the 1990s the first generation of educated Nuer have been further incorporated into the Ethiopian state as administrators.

The Nuer are known for their segmentary lineage system which consists of lineages that nest into larger tribes and through different mechanisms create a relatively balanced political system. The globalizing forces of colonialism, missionary activities and the civil war in Sudan and South Sudan have dramatically changed the Nuer political and cultural system. During the *Darg* they suffered under the presence of the government supported Sudan People's Liberation Army (SPLA) in Itang. In particular, the Ethiopian Gajaak Nuer experienced large population movements with marauding soldiers in their areas and a war launched against them by the SPLA (1985–1988). With a deterioration of their traditional ethics aimed at restraining fighting, the effects of war caused an escalation of violence in the Ethiopian Nuer areas, so that many of them fled into Ethiopian refugee camps. Here they gained access to education and converted to Christianity as a coping strategy against war and violence. In 2001 they established their own synod of the Ethiopian Evangelical Church Mekane Yesus. How-

When prayers fail: A Christian seeking advice at a Nuer prophet, Jikow, Gambella, © Christiane Falge

ever, Christianity has not completely replaced other religious movements and the place of Nuer prophets has not been erased.

After the fall of the *Darg* in 1991 the fragmented Nuer entered into intertribal warfare with their neighbours the Anywaa and the Murle. In 1992 many refugees returned to their home areas while thousands of Nuer were resettled to Western countries. From the US they started forming transnational lineage networks connecting churches and political groups with those in the homeland. The resultant flow of remittances, ideas and people enabled the globalization of the Nuer in Gambella. Currently they keep switching between their areas and Ethiopian refugee camps. In the context of renewed fighting after the Southern Sudan Peace Agreement in 2015 and the South Sudanese food crisis in 2017, Ethiopia is again home to more than 300,000 Southern Sudanese refugees, many of them Nuer.

Literature: EDWARD EVANS-PRITCHARD, *The Nuer*, Oxford 1940; CHRISTIANE FALGE, *The Global Nuer: Transnational Life-Worlds, Religious Movements and War*, Köln 2015.

Christiane Falge, Hochschule für Gesundheit, Bochum

Anywaa

The Anywaa (Anuak) are an indigenous people living in the lowlands of today's Gambella Peoples' Region. Historically and linguistically they are closely related to other Luo speaking peoples in South Sudan and East Africa, such as the Shilluk, Acholi and Luo of Kenya. According to the 2007 Ethiopian census, they number about 65,000. A further 100,000 live on the other side of South Sudanese border, in Pochalla and Akobo Counties of Jonglei State. The main geographical features of Anywaa country are the rivers, which rise on the western fringe of the Ethiopian highlands and all of which are tributaries of the Sobat river which flows into the White Nile. Traditionally most of their villages are located along the river banks. The Anywaa are sedentary agriculturalists, cultivating sorghum, maize and other crops, as well as engaging in fishing, hunting and collecting edible wild plants. Only a few cattle, goats and sheep are kept. They used to have two social strata, aristocrats and commoners, and of the former there were two types, namely nobles and village headmen. This system of political authority together with the marriage payment of special beads were banned by the socialist regime of Ethiopia. The socialist era also saw the advent of tens of thousands settlers from the highlands, a number of development programmes including a state farm and an irrigation project, and a huge influx of Sudanese refugees. A group of Anywaa dissidents who were against the socialist regime organized a liberation movement, the Gambella People's Liberation Movement (GPLM), and fought the regime. When the Ethiopian People's Revolutionary Democratic Front took over power, the GPLM was permitted to head the semi-autonomous region of Gambella. However, an uneasy relationship between the federal government and the Anywaa continued, often resulting in violent clashes. Tensions exist not only with the federal government but also with the ever-increasing numbers of highlanders and Nuer. The fact that in terms of population they have become a minority, at little more than 20% of the population in the region which they consider 'their home', is a major source of their grievance.

Literature: DEREJE FEYISSA, *Playing Different Games: The Paradox of Anywaa and Nuer Identification Strategies in the Gambella Region, Ethiopia*, New York, Oxford 2011.

Eisei Kurimoto, Osaka University

IV History

Introduction

Only in very few regions of Africa does historical knowledge reach back further than in the north-eastern parts of the continent. The idea that this region is the 'cradle of mankind' is supported by skeletal remains of hominids dating back millions of years. The construction of settlements dates to the first pre-Christian and the first Christian millennia. Various remains attest to a culture distinguished by written language (and eventually literature), hegemonic statehood, urban architecture, an expansive imperialism and a political-economic centre with trade-routes extending to the Mediterranean, into the interior of Africa and to the shores of India. With some interruptions, the rulers of this region were open to communication with Europe and Asia. The Nile and the Red Sea were both conduits for the transmission of information and the exchange of merchandise including animal products, precious metals and slaves.

The highly developed culture of writing, manifest since the 1st millennium BCE in inscriptions, is unique in sub-Saharan Africa. Thus the culture of Ethiopia and Eritrea was documented and widely preserved.

The dominant ideology from the 13th to the second half of the 20th centuries was the ruling classes claim to legitimacy based on the biblical ancestry BCE of their dynasty. They traced themselves to the legendary royal couple of King Solomon and Queen of Sheba (allegedly 10th century). This dynasty created a centre of might and culture in the Lake Tana region and, towards the end of the 19th century, further into the South, at the Entoto hill. The emperors of this dynasty were disempowered by rivalling provincial princes during a period of profound weakness in the later part of the 18th century, but after the middle of the 19th century imperial rule revived its power by modernising. The regenerated 'house of Solomon' opened the region to the world, led Ethiopia into the modern age and into the international community of nations until a violent revolution put an abrupt end to the dominance of the emperor. After a prolific advance in its early stage the revolution deprived itself of all moral justification by brutally climbing to power and causing a social and economic decline; thus the red regime vanished after a protracted civil war.

Palaeontology and prehistory

Island Africa. Along with deep space and the deep sea, the deep past of our planet is one of the most dizzying frontiers for human exploration. The rocks of Ethiopia offer a wonderful and unique opportunity to explore the tiny fragment of the deep past that comprises the evolution of humankind. Not that the ancient remains of human ancestors are found only in Ethiopia, but so far it is in this country that scientists have unveiled the most complete and richest human fossil record.

Fragments of Ethiopia's deep past can be glimpsed many millions of years before human ancestors started walking on two legs. In the Blue Nile River Gorge, fossils older than 140 MA (mega-annum = 1 million years) provide evidence of Jurassic fauna including giant carnivorous dinosaurs. Fifty million years later, on the central Ethiopian plateau, delicate remains of insects and plants were trapped in amber and have survived until today.

At this time, Africa and the Arabian Peninsula were separating from the other southern continents, and initiated a solitary journey toward the North. Long after dinosaurs vanished from Earth (65 Ma), the Ethiopian site of Chilga (27 Ma, near Lake Tana) preserves fossil plants and mammals that attest to this long isolation. They notably tell us about extinct relatives of elephants and hyraxes, then known nowhere else in the world, living in luxurious vegetation developing under a hot and rainy climate.

After Island Africa collided with Eurasia, new migrants populated the continent and most notably the Great Rift Valley. The Rift resulted from a major geological uplift (started by 30 Ma) that created the Ethiopian highlands. The combination of the gradual creation of a fault with volcanic activities in the Rift worked as a giant trap fossilizing organisms that lived and died in eastern Africa. From the Red Sea to Lake Malawi, this valley recorded the main phases of biological evolution that occurred in the region. Of this record, the Ethiopian segment is the most impressive for the last eight million years.

The earliest significant remains trapped in the Ethiopian Rift are found at Chorora (*c.* 8 Ma), near the southern edge of the Afar Triangle. Found with early hippos and three-toed horse relatives, *Chororapithecus* was a large ape identified from a handful of teeth. These teeth indicate that *Chororapithecus* was most probably a precursor of gorillas: they document an evolution that took place before the human lineage and the chimpanzee lineage split apart.

Early hominids. For the human lineage, the earliest known Ethiopian species are *Ardipithecus kadabba* at almost 6 Ma, and *Ardipithecus ramidus* at 4.4 Ma, both found in the Middle Awash Valley (Afar). *Ardipithecus kadabba* is known from a few remains, was most probably walking on two legs, and had somewhat smaller canines than those of chimpanzees. *Ardipithecus ramidus* is notably documented by the oldest skeleton of a human ancestor, nicknamed 'Ardi'. This is a wonderful discovery, because human ancestor remains are so rare: out of 1,000 fossil bones discovered in eastern Africa, less than ten belonged to human ancestors and are mostly isolated teeth. So 'Ardi', even incomplete, provides us with a wealth of information. From the moderate size of her canines compared with other specimens of *Ardipithecus ramidus*, we know that 'Ardi' was a female.

The crushed cranium indicates that her brain capacity was similar to that of chimpanzees. We know from her hip bones that she walked frequently on two legs (bipedalism), but also retained an ability to climb trees. In accordance with this ability, her big toe was opposable to the other toes, as in chimpanzees and gorillas. By contrast, her hands and wrists were more like those of humans, and she was not knuckle-walking as chimpanzees do. Alongside with *Ardipithecus*, many other animal remains have been discovered, suggesting that these 'ground apes' ('Ardi' = 'ground' in the Afar language) were living in habitats with abundant trees, differing from the modern landscapes of eastern African plains dominated by grasslands.

The following human ancestors from Ethiopia belong to genus *Australopithecus*, characterized as *Ardipithecus* by a moderate brain size, but with enhanced bipedal walk abilities. *Australopithecus afarensis* is a particularly well-documented species dated between 3.7 Ma and 2.9 Ma. The internationally renowned 'Lucy' – or *Denqenash* in Amharic – belongs to *Australopithecus afarensis* and was found in 1974 at Hadar, north of the Middle Awash. At the time, this partial skeleton was one of the oldest known human fossils. Today, although we know that Lucy was only midway in our evolutionary journey, she remains a major reference to which any new discoveries are compared. *Australopithecus afarensis* is also known through many other specimens from various Afar sites, including the partial skeleton of a baby nicknamed Selam, found at Dikika. Together, they depict an opportunistic species dwelling a diversity of habitats.

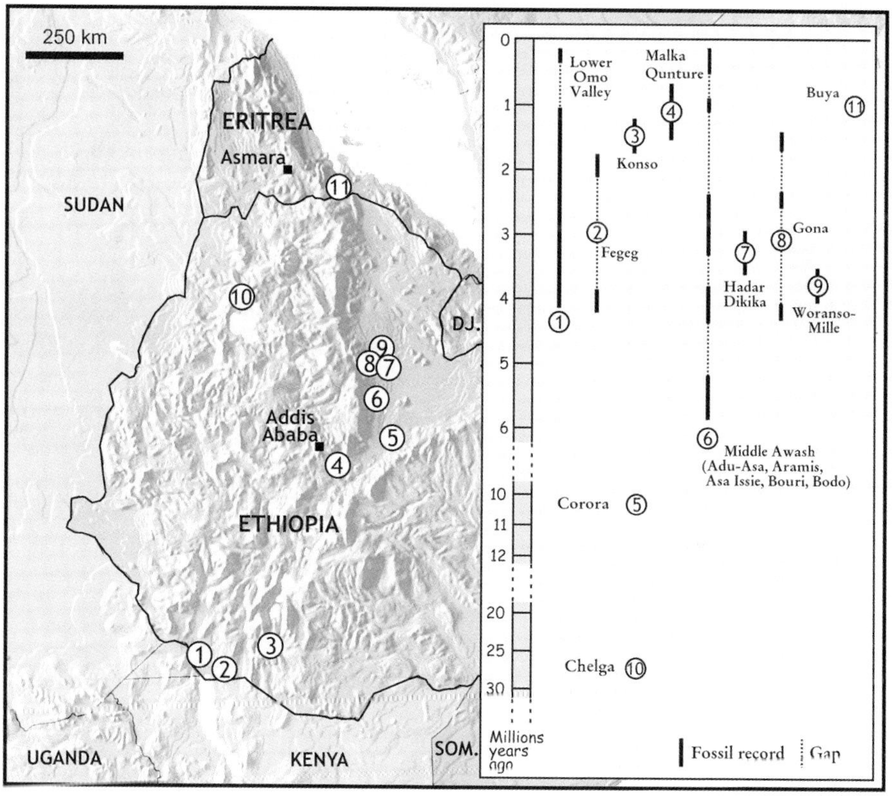

Table 8: Space and time distribution of the main Ethiopian and Eritrean palaeontological sites, © Jean-Renaud Boisserie

Becoming humans. From 3 Ma onward, fossil humans are found not only in the Afar, but also in the southern part of the Ethiopian Rift. Shungura, in the Lower Omo Valley, provides an outstanding fossil record from 3 Ma to 1 Ma. This remarkable record of human evolution and of environmental changes is almost continuous and particularly well dated. It is a source of information on this time period without parallel elsewhere in the world. It notably records the evolution of robust human relatives (including *Paranthropus aethiopicus* and *Paranthropus boisei*) that developed particularly large crushing teeth and went extinct from about 1.3 Ma. Some of the earliest known representatives of the genus *Homo* (the genus that includes our species, Homo sapiens) were also found at Shungura. The detailed geological setting of this site allows correlating these human ancestors, as well as other animals, and their morphological changes to the increasing aridity and cooling that marked the evolution of Earth since 2.8 Ma.

From roughly the same time period, the earliest known evidence of material cultures in Ethiopia are relatively crude tools made in basalt or in quartz, from Gona and Hadar in the Afar (2.6 Ma and 2.3 Ma, respectively), and from Shungura (2.3 Ma). It is not clear which species of human ancestor first started to make tools, but at 2.5 Ma in the Middle Awash, the remains of *Australopithecus garhi* were found in close relation with bones bearing cut marks made with stone tools.

New techniques of stone knapping emerged by 1.8 Ma and were recorded for the first time in Konso (southern Ethiopia). They were notably characterized by the production of hand axes. They are contemporaneous to the evolution of *Homo erectus*, recorded at Konso by 1.4 Ma, as well as in the Middle Awash and at Buia in Eritrea at 1 Ma. This larger-brained, tall human ancestor is the first one that has expanded to Eurasia, and is also the precursor to later human species.

Among these, the earliest known representatives of Homo sapiens, our species, have been recorded from 200,000 to 160,000 years ago in Ethiopia, in the Lower Omo Valley and at Herto in the Middle Awash. At the latter site, three crania of anatomically modern humans (two adults and a child) display marks suggesting that these individuals, known as *Homo sapiens idaltu*, were subjected to deliberate mortuary practices, predating the earliest known graves by 60,000 years.

From *Ardipithecus kadabba* to *Homo sapiens idaltu*, Ethiopia has therefore hosted most of the main phases of human morphological and cultural evolution, and has offered critical insights on our African roots. Many more discoveries will come to complete them, notably from the fossil sites of the Awash Valley in Afar and of the Lower Omo Valley, recognized as a UNESCO World Heritage site.

Literature: JEAN-RENAUD BOISSERIE, 'Palaeontology', *EAE* IV, 104–107; JEAN-RENAUD BOISSERIE, 'Ardipithecus ramidus and the Birth of Humanity', *Annales d'Éthiopie*, 25 (2010), 270–281.

Jean-Renaud Boisserie, Centre National de la Recherche Scientifique, Addis Ababa and Poitiers

Pre-Aksumite culture

Definition. 'Pre-Aksumite culture' is the conventional term used to indicate the archaeological evidence ascribed to a polity, perhaps at a state scale of complexity, with indisputable South Arabian features, which emerged in the mid-1st millennium BCE in Tegray and central Eritrea. Main sites are Yaha, Hawelti, Malazo, Kidana Mehrat, Seglamen in central Tegray, Mazbar and Maqaber Gaewa (Wuqro) in Eastern Tegray, and Matara, Addi Grameten and Kaskase in central Eritrea. Archaeological and epigraphic evidence suggest that at the very beginning the core of the polity was located in the region of Yaha and Aksum, where the earliest royal inscriptions were discovered. Pre-Aksumite culture is tentatively dated to *c.* 800/700–400 BCE on the basis of a few radiometric dates from Kidana Mehrat (Aksum). Settlements included large villages, hamlets, and ceremonial centres. A major ceremonial centre with a monumental temple and possibly a palace was located at Yaha.

The subsistence economy relied on cultivation of hulled barley, emmer (hulled wheat), linseed, pea, and perhaps oat, *tef*, noog, and lentils. Domestic cattle and a relatively small number of sheep/goats were the dominant component of livestock. A figurine of two yoked oxen from Hawelti, near Aksum, demonstrates the use of a plough. Main crafts were metalworking and stone carving for statues and votive altars, which were made for royal/elite use. Monumental inscriptions point to the existence of literate specialists working for the kings, as well.

Epigraphic evidence. Royal inscriptions in South Arabian script and Sabaean language record the name of the polity (*Dʿmt*) and several chiefs with the generic title *mlk* (king) and the Sabaean title *mkrb* (*mukarrib*), perhaps corresponding to paramount king. Queens are also recorded and most likely had a relevant dynastic role. Some inscribed votive altars from the Aksum-Yaha region record individuals from Saba (Yemen). They possibly formed a small minority in the society, and may have been regarded as part of the elite.

South Arabian and indigenous deities are recorded in the Pre-Aksumite inscriptions. In particular, stone, bronze and clay figures of bulls, maybe representing the Sabaean god Almaqah, sphinxes in an Egyptian/Meroitic style, and sitting ladies suggest that the bull, lion and possibly a female deity had a central role in the cult. The temples were a focal feature of the society.

Archaeological evidence. Administrative devices included zoomorphic, oval, rectangular, and circular bronze seals, and rectangular, ellipsoid and lozenge clay seals. The occurrence of seals in many Pre-Aksumite sites suggests a widespread administration. Zoomorphic bronze seals, sometimes with personal names, were only found in elite tombs at Yaha.

The remains of monumental temples are the most impressive features of the Pre-Aksumite culture. They include the so-called 'Great Temple' and the 'Grat Baal Gebri Palace' at Yaha, two quadrangular shrines with a projecting entry at Hawelti, and two small rectangular temples within an enclosure Malazo and Maqaber Gaewa, respectively. Two clay models of huts from Hawelti suggest that rural people lived in conical and rectangular huts, at least in the region of Aksum. The temples at Yaha exhibit some typical South Arabian features, such as the podium, square pillars with rectangular bases, pecked stone slabs, and architectural decorations.

Elite shaft-tombs were recorded at Yaha and Matara. They consisted of quadrangular or roughly circular shafts, over 2 m deep, with one or more burial chambers at the base. Small pit-graves, sometime associated with a stela, have been also recorded at Seglamen in central Tegray and may represent a different tradition in burial customs.

Art. Four statues from Hawelti, Maqaber Gaewa and Addi Galamo (Meqele), respectively, and a so-called throne from Hawelti are the main evidence of a sophisticated art. The statues represent sitting women with long robes. The 'throne', carved in one stone block, consisted of a quadrangular seat with bull's legs and a baldachin decorated with a male and perhaps a female standing figures carved on both sides and an ibex frieze along the edge. A few stone sphinxes, representing a lying lion with a male human head, from Addi Grameten, Feqya, and Dibdib (Eritrea) and some clay fragments of a similar sphinx from Hawelti (Tegray) are further evidence of figurative art in this period. These artefacts point to syncretistic art, which was exposed to different Achemenian, Greek and Meroitic, as well as South Arabian influences.

Small stone votive altars have been found at Yaha, Malazo, Feqya, Matara and Addi Grameten, and include cylindrical altars with a conic foot, cubic altars with a trapezoidal foot, simple offering slabs on a stepped trapezoidal base, offering tables with a rectangular basin and a spout in the shape of a lion head. At Feqya, in particular, an altar with a rectangular basin and two projecting sphinxes was recorded. The cylindrical and cubic altars are South Arabian in style, and some specimens could be

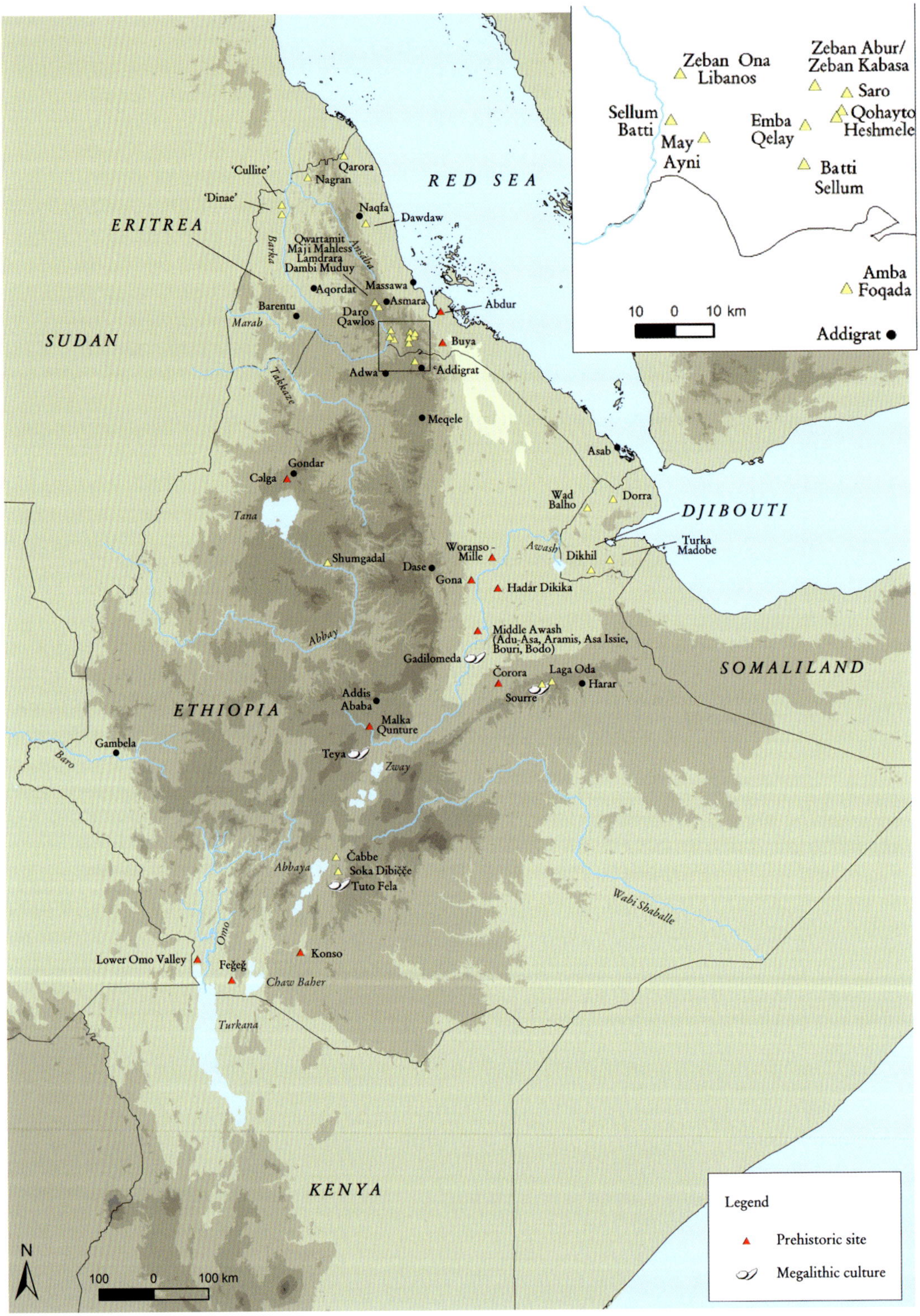

Map 5: Pre-Aksumite culture, © Hiob Ludolf Centre for Ethiopian Studies, Hamburg

imported from Yemen. The offering tables with a lion head spout can be compared to Egyptian and Meroitic prototypes, but they have been also found at Marib (Yemen). The altars with a simple offering slab may be compared to Meroitic specimens.

External contacts. Contacts with the Nubian kingdom of Kush are supported by a few Nubian objects from Yaha, Matara and Hawelti. They include an alabaster vessel similar to Nubian specimens of the 8th–7th centuries BCE from Yaha; two amulets from Hawelti, similar to specimens of the 6th–5th and 2nd centuries BCE from Meroe; some beakers from Yaha and Hawelti comparable to bronze, silver and clay beakers of the 7th and late 5th–mid-3rd centuries BCE from Meroe; and a carnelian amulet of Meroitic type from Matara.

Development of the polity. The ceramics from the lower strata at Matara and Yaha suggest that in the early 1st millennium BCE the Pre-Aksumite cultural area was initially divided into two regions with distinct traditions in pottery style, corresponding to central Tegray and eastern Tegray/central Eritrea, respectively. Both regions were probably included in a network of contacts with Yemen, as South Arabian vessels were collected at Yaha and Matara. Potsherds like the early Pre-Aksumite ones from the Yaha-Aksum region were also found in sites at Shurab el Gash, near Kassala, suggesting contacts between the highlands and the lowlands in the early 1st millennium BCE.

The same ceramics occur in the strata of all sites dating to the mid-1st millennium BCE suggesting that the highlands from central Eritrea to central Tegray were incorporated into one cultural area. The occurrence of temples, sophisticated art, elaborate craft of stone-carving (altars and offering tables), and bronze seals, together with the use of writing and a clearly-cut site hierarchy point to the consolidation of the state at this time. An impressive temple and an elite cemetery with very rich tombs were located at Yaha.

In the mid- to late 1st millennium BCE the Pre-Aksumite polity apparently collapsed in central Tegray, as the settlements decreased in size and monumental buildings were abandoned.

Yaha was no longer a major ceremonial centre, and the landscape was characterized by small rural settlements. Small shrines were located at Hawelti and Malazo, to the west of Aksum, but they most likely served rural people. The evidence of fire destruction of two monumental buildings at Yaha might point to warfare as a cause of the end of the Pre-Aksumite polity in Tegray. However, the continuity in occupation of Matara may suggest that an urban society survived in central Eritrea.

Origins. The origins of the Pre-Aksumite polity are still debated. Epigraphic and monumental evidence point to an indisputable South Arabian influence suggesting the hypothesis of a migration and/or colonization from Yemen in the early 1st millennium BCE as the main factor of state formation on the highlands. Actually, rock-inscriptions in Qohayto (Akkala Guzay, Eritrea) document the presence of single individuals (or very small groups) from Arabia on the highlands at this time. A few Pre-Aksumite inscriptions from the region of Aksum also record some Sabaean individuals in the mid-1st millennium BCE. These individuals surely contributed to introduce South Arabian cultural elements into Eritrea and Tegray, but their role in the formation of the Pre-Aksumite polity is unknown. The Sabaean title '*mukarrib*' (*mkrb*) may suggest that the Pre-Aksumite polity was organized on the Sabaean model, but the possible role of the queens may reflect a local tradition rather than a South Arabian one and suggest that the *D'mt* polity arose from an indigenous complex society.

The archaeological evidence, on the contrary, points to a distinction between the elite who used South Arabian (mainly Sabaean) symbols of power (monumental architecture, inscriptions and art) and ordinary people maintaining their local traditions, as most of the ceramics are local and suggest an indigenous origin of the population.

The present evidence, thus, suggests that the Pre-Aksumite culture emerged from the convergence of two main proto-historical local traditions in one culture: a western (Tegrayan) tradition and an eastern (mainly Eritrean) tradition. The South Arabian influence was a superficial – though impressive – component affecting only the upper strata of the population.

The same evidence suggests that an early state initially arose in the Yaha-Aksum region, as a consequence of contacts between the local population and the South Arabs, and later incorporated the eastern region. In the 4th century the Pre-Aksumite polity apparently collapsed in the western region, maybe because of conflicts, and a new polity emerged at Aksum.

Literature: FRANCIS ANFRAY, *Les anciens éthiopiens*, Paris 1990; ETIENNE BERNARD, ABRAHAM JOHANNES DREWES, ROGER SCHNEIDER, *Recuil des Inscriptions de l'Ethiopie des Périodes Pré-Axoumite et Axoumite*, Paris 1991; RODOLFO FATTOVICH, 'The northern Horn of Africa in the first millennium BCE: local traditions and external connections', *Rassegna di Studi Etiopici*, n.s. 4 (2012), 1–60.

Rodolfo Fattovich, Associazione Internazionale di Studi sul Mediterraneano e l'Oriente, Roma

Aksumite culture

Definition. 'Aksumite culture' is the conventional term to indicate the archaeological remains of the so-called Kingdom of Aksum, after the name of the capital city at Aksum in central Tegray (northern Ethiopia), which dominated the highlands in present Tegray and Eritrea from the late 1st millennium BCE to the late 1st millennium CE. Archaeological sites ascribable to this culture have been recorded over most of Tegray and Eritrea, suggesting that the territory of the kingdom occupied the whole highlands from the Red Sea coast and the edge of the Rift Valley to the Rore (northern Eritrea), Takkaze River (western Tegray) and Amba Alaji (southern Tegray). The Aksumite settlements included towns, villages, and isolated hamlets. Monasteries and churches became a relevant component of the Aksumite landscape after the introduction of Christianity in the 4th century CE. Urbanism was at its peak in the mid-1st millennium CE when the kingdom reached its maxim expansion. Beside Aksum, large settlements have been recorded at May Adrasha, Henzat, Hagaro Deragwe, Gulo Makeda in Tegray, and at Matara, Tokonda, Dara, Qohayto, Arattu and Adulis in Eritrea.

Archaeological evidence. The most distinctive aspects of the Aksumite culture are the residential and cult buildings, funerary monuments, and thrones. The residential architecture included large royal and/or elite compounds, urban houses, and rural houses. The elite compounds consisted of a central building separated with courtyards from an enclosure of rooms to form a discrete residential unit. They were built on a stepped podium (i.e. a constructed platform usually about 3.5m high) with an indented plan and could have two or more stories. Urban houses have been found at Kidana Mehrat (Aksum) and Matara. They included both upper and lower status houses forming quarters of close-packed buildings. Upper status houses were similar in plan to the central building of the elite compounds. Lower status houses were small arrangements of rooms separated by narrow lanes. Rural huts had a rectangular or quadrangular plan probably covered with a flat roof, and sometimes incorporated a small circular silo or cistern. In Christian time cult buildings included churches with

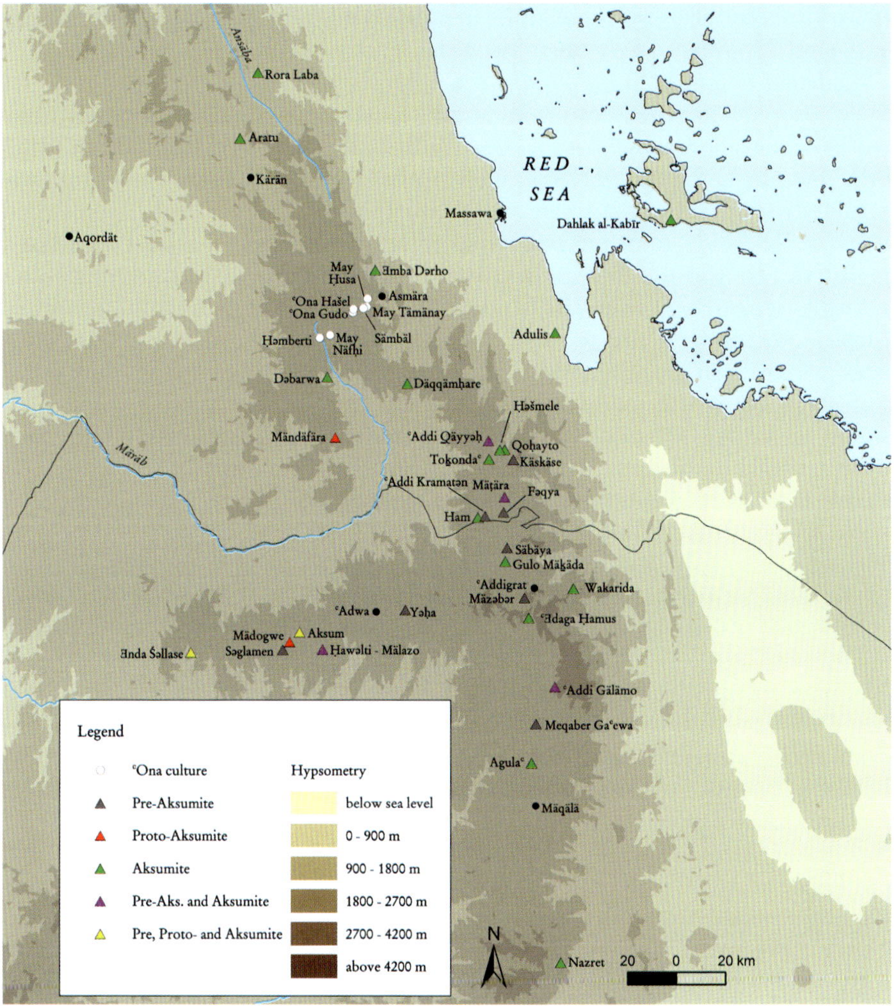

Map 6: Aksumite culture, © Hiob Ludolf Centre for Ethiopian Studies, Hamburg

a rectangular antechamber, a hall with three to five aisles, and a rounded or square apse with two lateral rooms, as well as most likely an upper gallery. They have been recorded at Aksum, Matara and Adulis. Cruciform churches have been recorded at Aksum and Tokonda. The churches were built on an indented podium and could be surrounded with an enclosure of rooms in conformity with the elite residential buildings. The funerary superstructures consisted of man-made stone platforms associated with stelae and tombs. The stone platforms, always associated with stelae, were erected as a superstructure to protect the elite tombs and as a place for the votive offerings to the deceased, as we can infer from the pottery basins which were often placed on the top of the platforms. The stelae varied from simple unshaped monoliths to dressed, symmetrical and sculptured stones, ranging in height from about 2–3 m to over 30 m. The tombs included pit graves, shaft tombs, staircase tombs, and hypogeal constructed tombs. To date, the oldest stelae, dating to late 1st millennium BCE, have been recorded on the top of Beta Giyorgis hill, to the northwest of Aksum. The thrones consisted of a stone base, two stone slabs at the side, and a stone slab at the back. The lateral slabs were sometimes inscribed, and the back one could be ornated at the top. Most likely, these monuments date back to the 3rd–5th centuries CE.

Different traditions in the style of the ceramics suggest that, up to the early 1st millennium CE, there were two cultural sub-regions corresponding to central Tegray and eastern Tegray/central Eritrea, respectively. In the mid-1st millennium CE (4th–6th centuries CE) the same material culture spread over the whole Aksumite area, suggesting that both sub-regions were incorporated into one cultural area. The recorded evidence also points to two distinct types of 'urban' landscape in central Tegray and in eastern Tegray/central Eritrea. In central Tegray the ancient landscape was characterized by a clearly-cut hierarchy in size of the settlements, ranging from the city of Aksum, over 100 ha in size, to small compounds less than 1 ha in area, and included large and small villages, elite residences, residential compounds, farming hamlets and workshops. Large settlements, ranging from 7 ha to over 11 ha in area, were located mainly at the base or sometimes on the top of the hills. Isolated elite palaces were often scattered in the open plain. Villages, hamlets and compounds were located on the top or along the slopes of the hills. Field terraces, wells, dams, paths, quarries and landmarks were other relevant components of the landscape.

The landscape in eastern Tegray and central Eritrea was characterized by scattered, affluent and/or elite residential buildings and churches, as we can infer from the archaeological areas at Gulo Makeda in Tegray, and Dara, Qohayto and Tokonda in Eritrea. Two towns with packed buildings were located at Matara (ca 20 ha in area) in central Eritrea and Adulis (ca 21 ha in area) on the Red Sea coast.

Aksumite ceramics included beakers, cups, open or closed bowls, plates, dishes and jars. Distinctive vessels in central Tegray were jars with a spheroid body and cylindrical neck, decorated vertical deep grooves, while cylindrical cups with one or two horizontal grooves along the rim were typical of eastern Tegray/central Eritrea. Lithics tools included knapped flakes, bladelets and scrapers. Administrative devices included clay or stone stamp seals, and pottery tokens. Coins were introduced in the late 3rd century CE and were used until the mid-7th century BCE. Imported artefacts, mainly glass vessels and beads, from Aksum point to contacts with Egypt, Gaul, India and Nubia in the early to mid-1st millennium BC, Syria, and Egypt in the mid-1st millennium CE, and Byzantine Egypt and Sassanian Persia in the late 1st millennium CE.

The absolute chronology of Aksumite culture is uncertain. Excavations on the top of Beta Giyorgis hill (Aksum) suggested a sequence of five phases of urban development of the capital city: a) Proto-Aksumite phase: 360 BCE (?)–120/40 BCE; b) Early Aksumite phase: 120/40 BCE–130/190 CE; c) Classic Aksumite phase: 130/190–360/400 CE; d) Middle Aksumite phase, 360/400 CE–550/610 CE; e) Late Aksumite phase, 550/610–800/850 CE.

The systematic survey of the territory of the capital city at Aksum suggests that the urban development of Aksum was characterized by: 1) A progressive increase in the size of Aksum from Proto-Aksumite to Early Aksumite time, when the town occupied an area of approximately 80 ha to 100 ha, and the settlement progressively shifted to the foothill of Beta Giyorgis and expanded from north (Beta Giyorgis and May Malahso) to south and west (Addi Keletta). At this time, an elite palace and cemetery still occurred at Beta Giyorgis, but elite palaces were also built at Addi Keletta and elite tombs were located along the May Hejja. 2) A larger expansion in Classic Aksumite to Middle Aksumite time, when the urban settlement occupied an area of about 180 ha; in particular, impressive elite palaces were built at Addi Keletta at this time, and hewn stelae up to 33 m in height were erected close to monumental tombs in the royal cemetery along the May Hejja in Classic Aksumite time. 3) A sharp decrease in the size of the town in Late Aksumite time, when the settlement occupied an area of approximately 60 ha. The only elite palace of this phase so far recorded was located at Dungur, to the west of Aksum. 4) A further reduction in the size of the town in Post-Aksumite time, when the settlement occupied an area of about 40ha and was located around the church of Maryam Tseyon.

Development of the polity. The analysis of the Aksumite material culture suggests that beginning in the 4th century CE, a new polity emerged at Aksum in central Tegray. The earliest archaeological evidence of this polity has been recorded on Beta Giyorgis hill to the northwest of Aksum, and has been ascribed to the Proto-Aksumite phase of the urban development of the ancient capital city. The origins of this polity are uncertain. The use of funerary stelae together with votive offerings in the elite cemeteries points to the cult of the elite ancestors as the focal ideological feature of the institutional authority in the local society, and might suggest some kind of cultural continuity with the traditions associated with the leadership dating to the 3rd–2nd millennia BCE in the Eritrean-Sudanese lowlands. The funerary evidence from Beta Giyorgis also points to some similarities in symbolic behaviour of Proto-Aksumite elite to that of the Napatan and Meroitic one.

Stelae field, Aksum, © Serge Dewel-Mouton

The continuity in ceramics and funerary stelae between the Proto-Aksumite and Early Aksumite phases at Aksum demonstrates that the kingdom of Aksum descended from the Proto-Aksumite polity. The erection of carved stelae up to 9-10m high on massive platforms associated with offering basins suggests that funerary cult was a very important component of the elite and royal ideology in Early Aksumite time. A distinctive model of Aksumite kingship emerged in Classic Aksumite time, when the throne surely was a relevant symbol of royal power, and was replicated in funerary and triumphal contexts. Spearheads, arrowheads and a fragment of archer's loose from royal funerary contexts of late Classic to Middle Aksumite time at Aksum are very similar in style to Nubian (Meroitic and post-Meroitic) specimens and may reflect a similar military symbolism in the ideology of kingship in both regions. The occurrence of a royal cemetery with elaborately hewn stelae and basins carved on the stone slabs supporting them at Aksum indicates that in the mid-1st millennium CE the funerary cult was still a very important component of the ideology of the kings and the elite. The carving of the more elaborated stelae in the shape of a palace suggests that the palace was an important symbol of the king and the elite in the late 3rd–early 4th centuries CE.

The disappearance of the funerary stelae in Middle Aksumite time points to an abandonment of funerary cult and a radical change in the royal and elite ideology. The construction of tomb superstructures representing a building may suggest that the palace still was regarded as a symbol of royal and elite power. In Middle Aksumite time the cross appeared as a royal symbol on the coins supporting a change in the ideology and the adoption of a Christian model of kingship. The archaeological record from Beta Giyorgis suggests that the period of transition to Christianity lasted at least 150 years, from the mid-4th to the early 6th centuries, as can be inferred from the progressive increasing use of the cross as a decoration of the ceramics. In the 5th century, the cross appears on the coins, used as a propaganda medium by the kings, but not on the pottery, suggesting that in the beginning Christianity was imposed by the king, but not yet completely accepted by the population. In the 6th century, on the contrary, the cross was the dominant decorative motive on the domestic ceramics, suggesting an extensive Christianization of the people.

Finally, the representation of the king with crowns very similar to those of the contemporary Byzantine emperors on coins dating to the 6th–7th centuries, and the construction of a church over royal or elite hypogeal tombs in the style of the *martyria* may indicate that the Aksumite kings and elite adopted some elements of Byzantine royal symbolism in Late Aksumite time. The throne still was a symbol of the royal ideology, as kings sitting on the throne appear on coins dating to Late Aksumite times.

The archaeological evidence of the decline of the Aksumite polity is still very scant. Aksum decreased sharply in area between the 6th/7th and 8th/9th centuries. Matara was apparently abandoned not later than the 8th century CE. Adulis in 6th/7th centuries was just a small village with a church and round huts, and was abandoned in the 8th century. No town probably existed on the highlands in Tegray and Eritrea in Post-Aksumite time, as the few sites of this period are mainly scattered small villages. The occurrence of many masonry and rock-hewn churches possibly dating to 11th–12th centuries, mainly in eastern Tegray, might suggest that this was an important region at this time.

Literature: FRANCIS ANFRAY, *Les anciens éthiopiens*, Paris 1990; RODOLFO FATTOVICH, *Kings and Farmers. The Urban Development of Aksum, Ethiopia: ca. 500 BC–AD 1500*, Boston 2008; DAVID W. PHILLIPSON, *Foundation of an African Civilisation. Aksum and the Northern Horn 1000 BC–AD 1300*, Woodbridge, Suffolk 2012.

Rodolfo Fattovich, Associazione Internazionale di Studi sul Mediterraneano e l'Oriente, Roma

History of Aksum

Importance of Aksum. The kingdom of Aksum was so named after its capital city of Aksum, located at the centre of the northern Ethiopian highland of Tegray, not far from the Ethiopian-Eritrean border. Already in antiquity it lay at the crossroads of trade and communication from the shores of the Red Sea with the ancient port of Adulis to the inland African territories extending to the lowlands far to the north and west of the northern highlands. The kingdom of Aksum is so important in Ethiopian history, that it is used as a benchmark for general periodization.

Archaeologists and historians distinguish between a) a Pre-Aksumite period (7th/8th centuries BCE to the 1st century CE), with the 7th to 4th centuries BCE characterized by a South Arabian phase attested by the presence of *c.* 200 Sabaean inscriptions, and b) a Proto-Aksumite phase from the 4th century BCE to the 1st/2nd centuries CE defined only by archaeological evidence; c) an Aksumite period (1st to 7th centuries CE); and a d) Post-Aksumite period (8th to 11th centuries CE), that precedes the e) Zagwe period (12th to 13th centuries CE).

Although earlier settlements from the 1st millennium BCE are attested by extremely abundant archaeological evidence in the whole of the Aksum area and especially on the hills nearby, the kingdom of Aksum as a political entity of its own is commonly believed to have emerged in the mid-1st century CE at the latest, when the name of Aksum is mentioned for the first time in the 'Periplus of the Erythrean Sea' (50/60 CE), a sort of trading guide for Roman merchants sailing down the Red Sea from the Mediterranean to the Indian Ocean.

'An African civilization of Late Antiquity', as it has been called by Stuart C. Munro-Hay, the kingdom of Aksum survived with the definite profile of a prominent political entity and at times of an important regional power, until at least the first half of the 7th century. Subsequently Aksum rapidly declined due to the prevailing influence of Islam on the trade routes it once controlled.

Among the major achievements that characterize the history of Aksum, one may count: (1) the emergence of a hegemonic kingdom, that gradually extended its direct or indirect influence far beyond the metropolitan boundaries, to the southern regions of Semen, to Meroe (in the 3rd century CE) and to South Arabia (in the 3rd century and from the end of the 5th to the 6th century continuously for some decades): this royal heritage has endured in Ethiopian memory as an ideal element and has played a major role in shaping the identity of subsequent Christian Ethiopian kingdoms; (2) the use of a language of its own, namely the Semitic Ge'ez (or classical Ethiopic), which remained the literary language in use until the 19th century and is still found today in church liturgy and taught as part of the traditional religious Christian education; (3) the Christianization of the country commencing in the first half of the 4th century and the lasting impact of Christian monophysite faith and institutions, including monasticism, primarily through the institutional dependence of the Aksumite Church on the bishopric and then Patriarchate of Alexandria of Egypt; (4) a literature, with its genres, including especially the translation of the Bible and other Christian religious writings, which shaped a large part of the subsequent literary production.

Sources for the history of Aksum. In contrast to the Pre-Aksumite period, that is characterized by a paucity of written evidence (only short South Arabian inscriptions) and by the absolute prevalence of archaeological sources, it is starting from the Aksumite period that – in addition to the vast and impressive archaeological remains that include the famous obelisks of Aksum and several monumental complexes – we also have a wide range of local and foreign written sources, including inscriptions in Ge'ez (both in Ge'ez and Sabaean script), and Greek issued by kings of Aksum and literary works of patristic authors on Aksumite events. For some events – particularly King Kaleb's expedition to South Arabia in 525 CE – a rich written documentation spanning several languages (Greek, Syriac, Arabic, and again Sabaean and Ge'ez inscriptions) of the Christian Orient exists. Moreover, starting from the late 3rd century CE onwards, an almost complete numismatic series of coins in gold, silver and copper was minted. The legends on the coins, in Greek and Ge'ez, attest to kings of Aksum until the first decades of the 7th century CE.

They also attest to, as do the inscriptions of King Ezana, the crucial passage from paganism to Christianity at the middle of the 4th century CE. A remarkable, recent discovery is the dating (confirmed by radio-carbon analysis) to the period of the kingdom of Aksum (*c.* 5th to 6th centuries) of two of the three codices of the 'Four Gospels' from Abba Garima, near Adwa, in northern Tegray. These would definitely be the most ancient Ge'ez manuscripts discovered to date and are among the most ancient illustrated Christian manuscripts in the world. Besides ancient written, archaeological, and numismatic evidence, another source for Aksumite history are the local traditions, both oral and in written form as historical, literary, and hagiographic narratives. These include half- or pseudo-historical documents, like kings lists, traditions of ancient foundations etc. the reliability of which is as a rule extremely doubtful.

A famous example is that of the legendary brother kings Abreha and Atsbeha, who are credited with the introduction of Christianity. The relevant event is calqued on the life of Ezana, who actually reigned with his brother, while the names recall Ella Atsbeha (one of the names of King Kaleb) and that the ruler in South Arabia, Abreha (see also the article 'History and faith of the Ethiopian Orthodox Tawahedo Church').

Underground tomb, Stelae field, Aksum, © Serge Dewel-Mouton

A chronology. A rough chronology of the Aksumite period can be sketched as follows:

From the 1st century CE (in the Early Aksumite archaeological period, *c.*50–150 CE) the 'Periplus of the Erythrean Sea' attests to the names of three cities, Aksum (*Aksomites*), Adulis (*Adouli*), and Qohayto (*Koloe*) connected by shared trade interests. It also mentions a King Zoskales in relationship either with Aksum or with a separate coastal kingdom and provides evidence for the extent of Hellenistic culture in the area.

In the 2nd/3rd (Classic Aksumite archaeological period, *c.* 150–400 CE) a king Sembrouthes is attested to by a Greek inscription (written in the 25th year of his reign). He may be the same king attested to in an acephalous inscription known as

'Monument of Adulis' (*Monumentum Adulitanum*, second part), written in the 27th year of the reign of an unnamed king. In this inscription the king describes his victories in inland, to the North and then to the South, and beyond the Red Sea. In the same century (*c.* 200–275 CE) the domination of Aksum over part of South Arabia is attested to by Sabaean inscriptions.

These mention Kings 'DBH (king of Aksumites), BYGT (son of the king), GRMT (son of the king of the Aksumites), DTWNS and ZQRNS (two kings of Abyssinia). Around the 3rd century CE the earliest inscription in Ge'ez on a metallic object (probably a sceptre) attests to GDR(T) (probably the same as the GDRT in South Arabian inscriptions), king (*ngsy*) of Aksum, and other inscriptions that are the earliest known evidence of the Ge'ez language.

In the last decade of the same century the earliest Aksumite coins were issued by King Endybis, who is the first of a series of kings for whom we have only the name, followed by Afilas and WZB. In the 3rd century the power of Aksum grows to the extent that it is named as one of the four most powerful kingdoms in the world in the 'Kephalaia', a Manichaean text.

During the 4th century, Ella Amida, father of Ezana and possibly of Ousanas (I), is attested to by inscriptions. It is probably at this time that Aksum conquered Meroe. In the first half of the 4th century (*c.* 330–340s) the Christian Frumentius of Tyre (or *Abba* Salama, as he is known in the Ethiopian tradition) is in Aksum and served as a secretary and archivist of King Ezana. The latter (*c.* 330–370) is attested to by coins and, together with his brothers S'ZN and HDF, by several inscriptions, both pagan (we know of the names of the divinities, which are peculiar in the Semitic pantheon) and Christian. He converted to the Christian faith through the initiative of the aforementioned Frumentius. It might also be at this time that the church (later known as cathedral) of Aksum (*Gabaza Aksum*) was founded and the translation from Greek into Ge'ez of the Bible was first undertaken.

Sometime after 346 CE, Frumentius was appointed bishop by Athanasius in Alexandria. Before and after this appointment the embassies of Theophilus the Indian, first to Himyar in South Arabia and then also to Aksum may have taken place.

Some years later, Athanasius of Alexandria mentions in his 'Second Apology to Emperor Constantius' (*c.* 357) Aizanas and Sazanas as rulers of Aksum. At the same time a Roman law directed to people of Aksum and Himyar forbade travellers to remain in Alexandria longer than one year. While Christianity was taking ground in Aksum, *c.* 380 on the opposite shore of the Red Sea another monotheism was adopted and a complete conversion to Judaism took place in the 6th century.

During the 5th century (Middle Aksumite archaeological period, *c.* 400–550 CE), the narrative of the Christianization of the kingdom Aksum by Frumentius is already inserted by the Church historian Rufinus of Aquileia (*c.* 402–403 CE) into his 'Ecclesiastical history'. Several kings of Aksum are attested exclusively by coins (Ouazebas, Eon, MHDYS, Ebana, Nezana, Nezool, Ousas, Ousanas, Ella Amida (II)) up to Tazena, Kaleb's father, who is also attested by an inscription.

In the same century (*c.* 420), a Moses, bishop of Adulis, is mentioned by Palladius ('On the Peoples of India and the Brahmans'). The ecumenical councils of Ephesus (431) and Chalcedon (451, rejected by the Alexandrian monophysite Church) probably provoked the redaction of the '*Qerellos*' patristic collection, that is one of the most important patristic writings from the Aksumite period. The canon-law collection known as the 'Aksumite collection' (*Sinodos*), probably also belongs to this period. Finally the monk Thomas of St Euthymius was appointed bishop of Abyssinia, *c.* 478–486.

The end of the 5th and the first decades of the 6th centuries were dominated by the religious events occasioned by the 'Edict of Union' (*Henotikon*, 482) and by the figure of King Kaleb (after 500–*c.*540 CE). The edict issued by Emperor Zeno (r. 474–475, 476––491) might have been the cause behind monks and priests from the Byzantine area coming to Aksum in a movement that is sometimes called the 'second Christianization' of Ethiopia.

This is connected to the foundation of churches and monasteries attributed to the 'Nine Saints', a tradition that actually took shape no earlier than almost ten centuries after the events themselves. (Despite local traditions to the contrary, the same is true for accounts related to St Libanos/Mata and St Yared). This is also the possible date of production of the oldest surviving Ge'ez manuscripts, namely two copies of the 'Gospels' from Abba Garima.

King Kaleb along with Ezana is the best documented Aksumite king, attested to by Ge'ez inscriptions, coins and abundant literary sources which focus on the expeditions he led against the Jewish king of South Arabia, Y(W)SF 'S'R YTH'R/Dhu-Nuwas, who had persecuted Christians, including Aksumites, in South Arabia.

The first expedition, which took place before 518, was led by HYN, probably a general of Kaleb, already during the period of Bishop Euprepius of Aksum (*c.*514–530). A second expedition was led after harsher persecutions of Christians took place *c.*522–523, that heavily involved the oasis of Najran and resulted in a massacre of several thousands of Christians, as documented in Sabaean inscriptions. The preparation for one Aksumite expedition was also reported (*c.*520) by Cosmas Indicopleustes at Adulis, which occasioned the copying of the 'Monument of Adulis' later inserted into Cosmas' 'Christian Topography'. Kaleb's decisive military expedition, supported by a Byzantine fleet, took place *c.*525/530, in the same years or little earlier than two Byzantine embassies led respectively by Julian (*c.*525/531) and Nonnosus (*c.*531/542) reached Aksum.

After the complete victory of the Aksumites and defeat and death of the Jewish king, eventually (*c.*530/535), South Arabia was ruled by a certain SMYF' 'SW', appointed by Aksum, but a few years later Abreha (*c.*535–*c.*565) took over the control of South Arabia and was able to rule there for decades, although probably paying a tribute to Aksum, until his rule (after the so-called 'year of the elephant' in the Islamic tradition, *c.*565) was in turn overthrown by the Sasanids (*c.*570/575).

In the course of the 6th century (Late Aksumite archaeological period, *c.*550–700), after Kaleb (who already bore a Jewish name), other kings are attested by coins, often with names that recall the Jewish heritage: Esrael, sometimes identified with the legendary Gabra Masqal, a son of Kaleb; W'ZB, a son of Kaleb, attested by an inscription, and also tentatively identified with Gabra Masqal; Gersem, Ioel, Hetaza (father of Ella Tsaham?), attested by coins. It is around this period (*c.*570/580), that Aksum is reported to have been exposed to the influence and preaching of the dissident followers of Julian of Halicarnassus.

Between the 6th and the 7th centuries, the decline of Aksum is apparent from the quality of its coins. Its last kings of the 7th century were – according to one of the hypothetical reconstructions – Ella Gabaz (II) and Armah. Ella Tsaham is attested by literary sources and is probably to be identified with *Najashi* al-Atsham b. Abjar (to be probably emended into al-Atsham b. al-Hataz) who offered shelter and protection to the first Muslims migrated to Aksum (*c.*615/616), during the so-called first *hijra*.

There is still no totally convincing hypothesis to explain the end or the decline at least of the kingdom of Aksum. It appears that the Islamic expansion played the major role, since Muslims took early control of the trade routes along the Red Sea: already in 702 CE even the Dahlak islands were occupied by Muslims and to 864 CE dates the earliest dated Islamic inscription from the same archipelago. At the same time, internal migrations (like the 8th-century migrations of the so-called Rom/Balaw to the Eritrean and northern Ethiopian highlands from the north) substantially changed the ethnic composition of the northern highlands.

Various sources from the following centuries report of destructions in Aksum and there was a general decay of the material culture (Post-Aksumite archaeological period, *c.* 750–1000). The late and very uncertain epigraphic records (so-called inscriptions of *hatsani* Daneel) are also eloquent evidence of this. For many centuries, Aksum was reduced to a small village and ceased to be the capital of the Christian kingdom.

Literature: STUART C. MUNRO-HAY, *Aksum: An African Civilisation of Late Antiquity*, Edinburgh 1991; DAVID PHILLIPSON, *Foundations of an African Civilisation. Aksum & the northern Horn 1000 BC–AD 1300*, Woodbridge, Suffolk 2012; PAOLO MARRASSINI (ed.), *Storia e leggenda dell'Etiopia tardoantica. Le iscrizioni reali aksumite*, Brescia 2014.

Alessandro Bausi, Universität Hamburg

Aksum, town and monuments

The ancient city of Aksum, located in north-central Tegray on Ethiopia's northern highland plateau, was a major political, economic, and religious centre during the first seven centuries CE. The city's position in a fertile agrarian landscape along an ancient trade route linking the northern highlands with the southern Red Sea and larger Indian Ocean World, the Great Rift Valley of eastern Africa, and the Nile Basin were central to its development as the capital of the Aksumite kingdom. With Aksum as its capital, the polity would eventually extend its reach from northern Eritrea to the margins of central Ethiopia and from the southern Arabian Peninsula to the Sudanese Nile borderlands. Aksum, a robust urban centre, was essential to the kingdom's involvement in the ancient geopolitics of Northeastern Africa, Eastern Mediterranean, and Southwestern Asia between the 3rd and 7th centuries CE. The ancient city is referenced in several Aksumite inscriptions and by external sources including texts from the Arabian Peninsula, diplomatic correspondence of the Byzantine Empire, and written accounts from the wider Mediterranean and Red Sea worlds, such as Pliny's 'Natural History', Claudius Ptolemy's 'Geography', the anonymous 'Periplus of the Erythrean Sea', and in the 'Christian Topography' of Cosmas Indicopleustes. Following the end of the Aksumite kingdom, Aksum experienced a long process of depopulation. While it retained a prominent place in the collective memories of many peoples in the Horn of Africa and continued to serve as a sacred centre for Orthodox Christians, the collapse of the Aksumite kingdom marked the end of Aksum as a paramount settlement and political centre until recent times. Today the city is experiencing sustained growth as a regional hub of economic development, something that has impacted the preservation and conservation of its historical and archaeological heritage.

Early settlement. The origins of ancient urban development at Aksum date back nearly three thousand years to the 1st millennium BCE when archaeological evidence for substantial village settlements appears in the Aksum area at the ancient settlement areas of Kidana Mehrat and Ona Nagast. At Kidana Mehrat, located in a wide valley just east of Beta Giyorgis hill in the northern periphery of Aksum, people occupied a stone-built village complex of angular rooms, produced pottery, used stone and copper alloy tools, cultivated wheat and barley, and kept domesticated cattle, goat, and sheep. Nearby at Ona Nagast on the top of Beta Giyorgis hill arose an ancient settlement with many households and a monumental elite building or 'palace' containing semi-subterranean rooms, stepped walls, carefully laid floors, and a podium. Adjacent to this settlement stands a cemetery at Ona Enda Abboy Zagwe containing pit graves, rock-cut tombs, and stelae several meters in height. Both Kidana Mehrat and Ona Nagast were vital precursors to the rise and early development of Aksum.

Stelae and tombs. By the early 1st century, the core of Aksum was concentrated in the valley between Beta Giyorgis hill and May Qoho hill. Here burials, platforms, and monolithic stone stelae mark the beginning of Aksum's initial development as the centre of a growing state polity. By the late 3rd century, the landscape between Beta Giyorgis and May Qoho would see the construction of a massive terrace feature, known today as the Stelae park and subterranean tombs marked by monumental monolithic stelae, including several over twenty meters in length and carved from single blocks of locally quarried granite-like nepheline syenite rock. More than one hundred standing and fallen stelae are found at the Stelae park and hundreds more are located in several areas at Aksum, including those along the west side of the May Hejja stream, in the May Aqno and May Cheqqa areas, and in the Gudit Stelae Field, an ancient cemetery on the south-western edge of Aksum containing about 600 stelae.

The most monumental stelae located in the Stelae park were likely the grave markers of royal tombs dating to the 3rd and early 4th centuries CE. Six of these are carved as representations of multi-storied buildings with low-relief depictions of window-frames and apertures, horizontal wooden beams, false doors, and inlayed metal plaques (now gone) set at the apex of each stela. Two of the standing stelae (referred to as Stela 2 and Stela 3) weigh 160/170 tons each and both measure about 24 m in total length. The largest stela at Aksum, Stela 1, weighing as much as 520 tons and measuring 33 m in length, is so massive that it is the largest single block of carved stone ever created by ancient people anywhere in the world. This enormous stela likely fell and broke into several pieces during the attempt to erect it in the fourth century.

Also in the Stelae park terrace area there are several monumental funerary complexes, most prominent of which are those named the Mausoleum, Nafas Mawcha, the Tomb of the Brick Arches, and the Tomb of the False door. The Mausoleum comprises a large subterranean tomb complex located adjacent and partially under the giant fallen Stela 1. The central features of the Mausoleum include a corridor running east-west measuring almost 17 m in length and about 2 m in width, with five rectangular chambers of about 3m in length on the north side of the corridor and five chambers on the south side arranged symmetrically. Located near the Mausoleum is Nafas Mawcha, a subterranean tomb building consisting of a massive capstone weighing about 360 tons and measuring 17 m by 6 m in dimension, set over a rectangular subterranean chamber 14.5 m wide on its north-south axis and 22.5 m long on its east-west axis, and surrounded on three sides by a passage. Excavations at Nafas Mawcha have produced, among other things, ceramic jars shaped as human heads, a gilded bronze square pendant featuring a rose-shaped design made of blue, green, and white glass, a clay model of an Aksumite house, and bronze decorative items. The high status grave goods and size and configuration of the tomb suggest that the tomb may have served as the final resting place of an Aksumite king or royal relative.

On the eastern side of the Stelae park lies the Tomb of the Brick Arches. This tomb complex is entered through a passageway roofed horizontally with rough stone lintels and containing a flight of eighteen stone steps. At the bottom of the steps is a horseshoe-shaped brick arch, followed by four rock-cut burial chambers, and two other clay brick arches. Archaeological excavations in the Tomb of the Brick Arches have revealed a number of high status artefacts, including a finely executed bird-shaped ceramic vessel, a metallic plate with a human face effigy, metallic plaques containing ornate polychrome geometrical designs, ivory panels for a chair or throne, red glass goblets, and more than four hundred pieces of elephant ivory.

On the opposite side of the Stelae park from the Tomb of the Brick Arches is the Tomb of the False door, a subterranean funerary complex named by archaeologists for its false door carved in rock over the access stairway. This complex possesses an open paved courtyard with stone blocks fixed by metal clamps, a 12 m square subterranean structure constructed of coursed masonry, and a burial chamber with a stone sarcophagus located at the base of a flight of stone stairs that had been robbed by tomb raiders in ancient times.

Beyond the Stelae park, other important Aksumite funerary areas are the Gudit Stelae Field, where non-elite tombs are located; the rock hewn 'Tomb of Bazen' on the southern slope of May Qoho hill; the 'Tomb of Menilek' northwest of Dungur on the south-western periphery of the city; shaft-tombs on the western side of the Abba Liqanos plateau; and the multi-chambered dressed granite block tombs of 'Kaleb' and 'Gabra Masqal' at the site of Enda Kaleb 2 km north of Aksum.

The latter may date to the 6th century CE and contain superstructures that take the form of twin churches set over each tomb and connected by a colonnaded courtyard and a broad flight of stone stairs. The northern tomb, traditionally attributed to the 6th century Aksumite King Kaleb, consists of a stepped adit (entrance), a central longitudinal chamber and three rooms. The southern tomb, attributed to Kaleb's son Gabra Masqal, also has a stepped adit, a central longitudinal chamber and five rooms, in one of which three sarcophagi are preserved.

Urban centre and royal capital. By the 3rd century Aksum's ancient urban configuration was characterized by a variety of loosely clustered buildings and monuments suggestive of a community comprising a range of socioeconomic statuses and specialized

Aksum in 1906, with a view of the Stelae field, Deutsche Aksum-Expedition 1906, © Messbildarchiv, Brandenburgisches Landesamt für Denkmalpflege, Wünstorf

in urban features. The ancient city of Aksum was linked to regions to its north through the May Gwodae and May Atela River corridors. The May Abak River Valley connected Aksum with the east and south and was the location of a large satellite village at Hamad Gabaz on the eastern periphery of the city. And the May Negus River linked Aksum with areas south and west, including ancient Aksumite communities at Seglamen, Medogue, May Abeqat, and with the Enda Sellase area and the great Takkaze River beyond. Two of the most intriguing qualities of ancient Aksum are the lack of a defensive wall surrounding the urban centre, or other fortifications, and the paucity of large-scale irrigation features, suggesting that the city did not suffer military incursions and relied upon seasonal rainfall and water conservation methods, utilizing small reservoirs and cisterns for localized water management and sustainable food production over the long term. A surviving example of Aksumite water management may be observed in the May Shum reservoir located north of the Stelae park area that still serves as a community cistern today. It is estimated that during the first 4 centuries CE, the city's core area covered 80ha to 100ha. By the 6th century, the urban core of Aksum was about 180ha in extent with additional related satellite settlements and rural hinterland communities extending at least 10km in radius and linked by a network of paved and unpaved roads. At its height, at least 50,000 people would have inhabited the ancient city's centre, with thousands more living in the urban periphery and immediate hinterland. The boundaries of the ancient city seem to have been marked by monumental stone throne bases and royal inscriptions. Throne bases are also found stretching from the city's Maryam Tseyon (Mary of Zion) cathedral to the Stelae park area and are distinguished by dressed slabs of stone measuring 2–3m square with a smaller seat block and slots for monolithic pillars at each corner that likely supported a canopy. While these thrones may have been used by Aksumite nobility, they may also have served as repositories of statues and as commemorations of royal achievements. Found at various locations at Aksum, royal inscriptions engraved on long stone slabs record the exploits of various Aksumite kings. These are written in the Ethiopic language of Ge'ez and sometimes in expressions that include Epigraphic South Arabian script and Greek, providing detail of royal titles, decrees, religious references, and accounts of military campaigns against foreign enemies. Such inscriptions seem intended for public viewing and at least two multiple-script examples attributed to the 4th-century King Ezana may have been free-standing monuments marking the northern and south-eastern entrances to the city.

Large Aksumite buildings were often set on a high stepped foundation or plinth, capped with slabs of slate and possessing recessed walls. Some buildings had two and three stories and occasionally contained basement storage areas. Elite structures, sometimes referred to as pavilions, were multi-story structures of a square plan with recessed walls and massive corner projections or towers with dressed cornerstones and an entrance accessed by broad steps set in an open courtyard and surrounded by a range of subsidiary square and rectangular shaped rooms. Famous examples of such pavilion complexes at Aksum include the sites of Taaka Maryam, Enda Semon, and Enda Mikael in the western section of Aksum, and Dungur to the south of Beta Giyorgis hill. Domestic buildings of lower-status Aksumite neighbourhoods were rectilinear in plan, built of undressed mud-mortared fieldstone walls, rubble filled cores, and connected by narrow alleys. Open-air activity areas were interspersed throughout the city, where pottery and stone tool production was carried out. Other specialist craft production included woodwork, the production of ivory figurines, cylindrical boxes, and intricate plaques, glass production, and a diverse range of metalwork in iron, copper alloy, silver, and gold.

Particularly important metalwork activity was the minting of coinage, as the Aksumite kingdom issued its own gold, silver, and copper coins from the second half of the 3rd century to the middle of the 7th century. Inscriptions on Aksumite coins in Greek and Ge'ez script record the names of about 20 kings of Aksum and examples of Aksumite coins have been found at archaeological sites as far away as southern Arabia and India.

During the 4th century Aksum became the centre of a Christian Aksumite state and was followed by a long process of church and monastery building throughout much of the Aksumite realm. At Aksum a church was built prior to the 6th century where the famous Maryam Tseyon cathedral now stands (identified in Ethiopian Orthodox traditions as the resting place of the Ark of the Covenant). This early church was likely basilican in form, with two aisles on either side of the central nave, and standing on a podium 3.4m in height and 66m by 41m wide, reached by a broad flight of steps. Other ancient churches at Aksum include the remains of twin basilican churches built over the tombs attributed to Kings Kaleb and Gabra Masqal; two church structures on Giyorgis hill; a 7th century church named Arbaetu Ensesa in the south-eastern section of Aksum's urban core that possessed three aisles, a sanctuary, a semicircular apse, and subsidiary rooms including a treasury; and Abba Pantalewon, a church and monastic site perched on a forty meter high rock pinnacle on the south-eastern slope of May Qoho hill where a sanctuary likely was constructed early in the Christian period over a previously existing pre-Christian temple dedicated to Mahrem, the ancient god of war.

Decline. The long decline of Aksum as an urban centre and imperial capital began as early as the mid-6th century when the ancient economy and population of the city and surrounding areas shrunk dramatically. Factors involved in this decline seem to have included changes in trade and political power in the southern Red Sea region and northern Horn of Africa linked with the Persian conquest of Himyar in South Arabia, the growing Arab control of Red Sea trade, challenges from other African polities, and environmental degradation impacting the carrying capacity of the landscape surrounding the city. By the 9th century the city of Aksum was no longer a royal capital and by the close of the 1st millennium, much of the remaining population lived in the western section focused around the Maryam Tseyon cathedral. Between the 10th and 15th centuries the central settlement of Aksum was scarcely more than 40 ha in size, and while it has never lost its prominence as a premier ecclesiastical site, and has served variously as a key regional market town, administrative centre, and tourist destination over the last five hundred years, it has not been until the past decade that Aksum has begun to regain its prominence as an integral urban centre in Ethiopia (see also the article 'Aksumite culture').

Literature: KATHRYN A. BARD, RODOLFO FATTOVICH, ANDREA MANZO, CINZIA PERLINGIERI, 'The chronology of Aksum (Tigrai, Ethiopia): a view from Bieta Giyorgis', *Azania: Archaeological Research in Africa* 49 (2014), 285–316; STUART MUNRO-HAY, 'Aksum: History of the Town and Empire' *EAE* I, 173–179; DAVID W. PHILLIPSON, *Foundations of an African Civilisation: Aksum & The Northern Horn 1000 BC–AD 1300*, Woodbridge, Suffolk 2012.

Matthew C. Curtis, University of California, Los Angeles

The Zagwe

After the rapid decline of Aksum in the 7th century, there is a scarcity of local sources that make it difficult to reconstruct subsequent events. What we know is mainly based on the reports of Arabic geographers and Church historians, but has little support from reliable local sources. Among the few events of which we are informed, there is the foundation of the monastery of Dabra Egziabeher on Lake Hayq (*c.* 869/871 CE), the mention of Kubar as the capital of Abyssinia (post 872 CE), and the report of a queen ruling Ethiopia (*c.* 930–980), who is credited with killing a king (*hatsani*) of Aksum (*c.* 970–980). This final event is also confirmed by a letter (post 969–ante 978) from the king of Ethiopia to King George of Nubia, detailing the devastation of the kingdom. But we also know of further important population movements, with a first Agaw migration from Lasta, resulting in the origin of the Bilin ethnic group in present day Eritrea (*c.* 9th/10th century).

Origin. The Zagwe period takes its name from a royal dynasty of king-saints, probably belonging to the Agaw linguistic group (Zagwe probably means 'of the Agaw'). They originated in Bugna, a district of Lasta, in Wallo (*c.* 200 km south of Aksum) at the northernmost limit of the present Amhara region. Their earlier capital Adafa was sited here, before a new capital was founded as the present Lalibala. The Zagwe ruled a major part of Christian Ethiopia from Lasta province including much of today's Eritrea to the north, with a special focus on Shimazana with the historical monastery of Dabra Libanos of Ham, to Wallaga and Bagemder to the west, but not including Shawa and territories to the south of it. According to the Ethiopian tradition, the Zagwe period lasted for more than 300 years, from the 10th to the 13th century. However, most historians believe that the dynasty reigned from the 12th (*c.* 1140 CE) to the 13th century (*c.* 1268/1270 CE), when they were overthrown by the Solomonic dynasty when King Yekunno Amlak, killed the last Zagwe king Yetbarak. Unlike at least some of the kings of Aksum, the Zagwe were virtually unknown to the coeval Mediterranean powers, but enjoyed regular relationships with Egypt and Jerusalem, as appears from documents and art motifs in the famous rock-hewn and grotto churches attributed to them.

Apart from documents attributed to King Lalibala (*c.* 1185–1225) and his successor Naakkweto Laab (d. *c.* 1250), and the date of the Zagwe's overthrow (*c.* 1268/1270 CE), there are few other certain elements. The later Ethiopian tradition considers the Zagwe 'usurpers' from the point of view of dynastic legitimacy, since they were not Israelites (so also in the *Kebra nagast*), and places them immediately after the destruction of Aksum (*c.* 9th/10th century). On the other hand, they are considered king-saints. In keeping with this, most of the Zagwe kings (all apart from Marari and Tataweddem) have been portrayed hagiographically with several texts devoted to Kings Yemrehanna Krestos, Harbay, Lalibala, Naakkweto Laab, and Queen Masqal Kebra, composed in the 15th century at the earliest. This was probably in connection with the accomplishment of the monumental complex of rock-hewn churches at the city of Lalibala, that followed the gradual normalization of their status as king-saints, which made them acceptable also to the newly established Solomonic dynasty.

The Zagwe hagiographies testify to a concept of kingship that appears to be oriented towards peace and prosperity (for example, 'rainmaking'), which is very different from both the Aksumite and the Solomonic ones. On the contrary, the intense activity of patronage and church foundation they are credited with, is no special feature of their own. From other sources like the historian Abu Salih (Abu l-Karim) it appears that the Zagwe boasted of an Israelite descent, but from the family of Moses and Aaron. The same author also attests to the tradition that the Zagwe possessed the Ark of the Covenant and that their kings were priests.

Zagwe kings. The number and names of the Zagwe kings cannot be asserted with certainty, since in the traditional king lists their number varies from five to sixteen

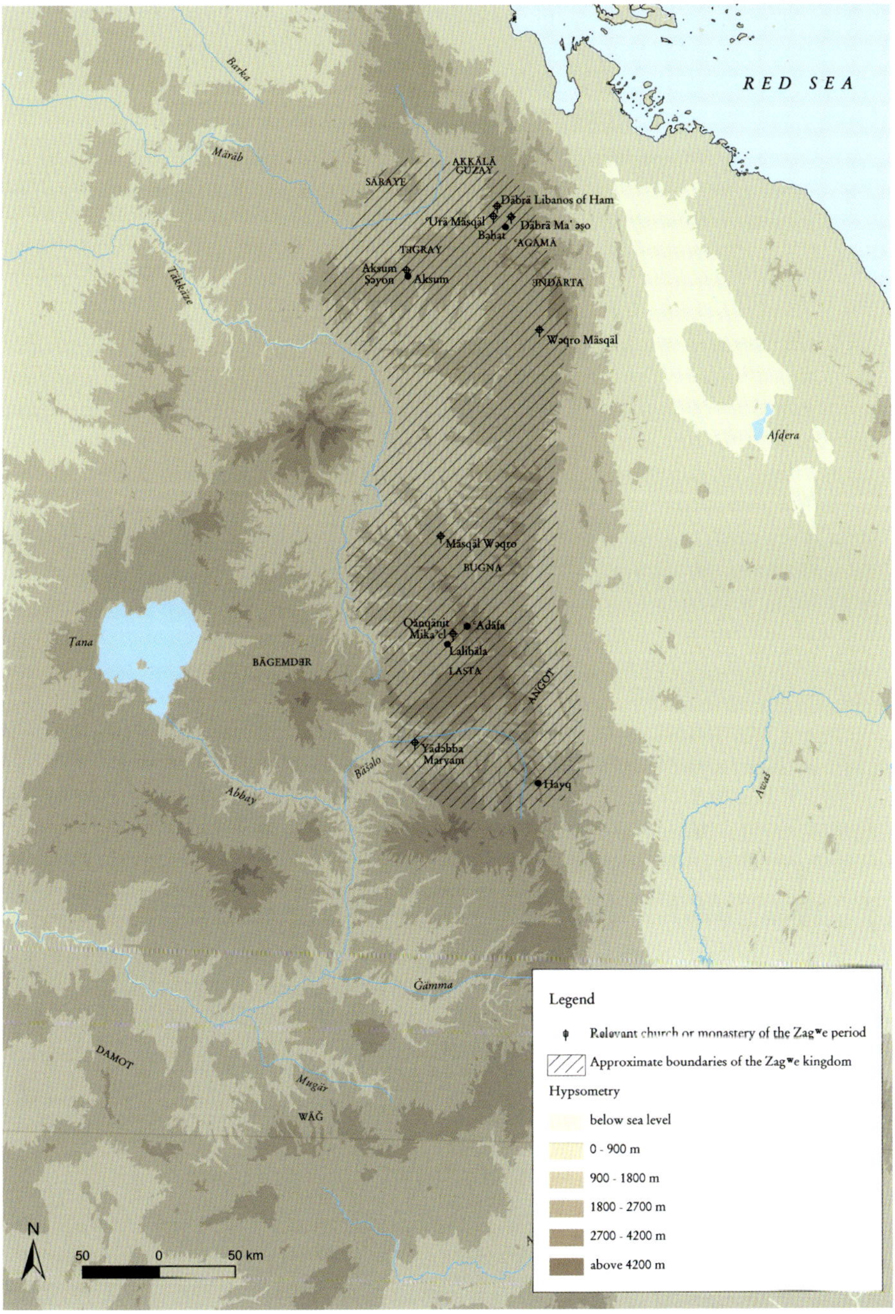

Map 7: The Zagwe period, © Hiob Ludolf Centre for Ethiopian Studies, Hamburg

and different dates are attributed to the dynasty. These uncertainties will probably be cleared up when a systematic archaeological excavation of Lalibala is undertaken. Moreover, the Zagwe seem to have followed the Agaw laws of inheritance, that implied a certain degree of matrilineality, with power passing to brothers and then to nephews of the king, and consequent terminological uncertainty.

For example, a list with eleven kings includes Takla Haymanot, Tataweddem/Tatadem, Germa Seyyum, Jan Seyyum, Yemrehanna Krestos, Qeddus Harbay, Lalibala, Naakkweto Laab, Yetbarak, Mayrari, and Harbay. In addition, the circumstances under which power passed to the Zagwe are totally unclear.

A later Ethiopian tradition has it that Mara (Takla Haymanot), a general of Delnaod (the last Aksumite ruler), married the latter's daughter and then rebelled against his father-in-law, killed him in battle and established a new dynasty. According to this tradition, the descendants of Delnaod of the Solomonic line, remained hidden for centuries, preparing the restoration of their line. (Other traditions still credit a woman, Terda Gabaz, the spouse of Degna Jan or Hezba Nany, the last Aksumite king, with being instrumental in the transfer of power to the Zagwe dynasty.)

The founder and first king of the dynasty was probably Marara (Takla Haymanot), followed by Tantaweddem (with the throne name of Solomon). The latter's fine inscribed metal processional cross is preserved in the church of Ura Masqal in northern Tegray, very close to Dabra Libanos of Ham and the present Eritrean border. This as well as other very informative documentary texts issued by Zagwe kings are probably the earliest authentic feudal deeds transmitted to us. Although some survive only in copies, they attest to the existence of a sophisticated administration which demonstrates substantial continuity with the protocols known from Aksumite inscriptions. Yemrehanna Krestos (whose hagiography particularly stresses the aspect of the 'priest-king' and who was also supposed to be the model for the Ethiopian location of 'Prester John'), preceded Harbay and the latter's brother Lalibala, both sons of Jan Seyyum. The last Zagwe king, Yetbarak, known as 'the hidden one', was killed by Yekunno Amlak (the founder or restorer of the so-called Solomonic dynasty) in Gayent, in the church of St Qirqos (Quiricus, the saint patron of his dynasty), where he had taken shelter.

The tentatively established genealogy can be given as follows: Marari (1) by whom Masoba Warq bore Tantaweddem (2) Gerwa Seyyum, and Jan Seyyum; Gerwa Seyyum was the father of Yemrehannä Krestos (3); the latter had in turn two sons, Harbay (4) and Lalibala (5), who were the fathers, respectively, of Naakkweto Laab (6) and Yetbarak (7).

Various evidence hints at pro-Zagwe resistance movements opposed to dynastic change. Whereas a decisive role in the overthrow of the Zagwe is traditionally assigned either to St Iyyasus Moa or, according to a later tradition, to St Takla Haymanot. Even later traditions from the 17th century connect the establishment of the new dynasty with the reward of 'one third of the kingdom' to the monastic 'house of Takla Haymanot'. Unable to unify the kingdom and patrons of the arts, the descendants of the Zagwe were locally recognized as 'kings' and enjoyed some autonomy as prefects of the Wag (*wag-shum*) still in the 17th and 18th centuries.

(1) Marari
(2) Tantaweddem
(3) Yemrehanna Krestos
(4) Harbay
(5) Lalibala
(6) Naakkweto Laab
(7) Yetbarak

Tentative genealogy of the Zagwe kings

Literature: Marie-Laure Derat, 'The Zāgʷē dynasty (11th–13th centuries) and King Yemreḥanna Krestos', *Annales d'Éthiopie*, 25 (2010), 157–196; Gianfranco Fiaccadori, 'Zagʷe', *EAE* V, 107–

114; PAOLO MARRASSINI, 'Un caso africano: la dinastia Zague in Etiopia', in SERGIO BERTELLI, PIETRO CLEMENTE (eds.), *Tracce dei vinti*, Firenze 1994, 200–229.

Alessandro Bausi, Universität Hamburg

Solomonic dynasty

Sheba's descendants. The term Solomonic dynasty has been coined by modern historians as a designation for the Ethiopian Christian dynasty which came to power in the late 13th century. The rulers of Ethiopia from that period until the overthrow of Hayla Sellase in 1974 were traditionally believed to be descendants of Solomon, King of Israel, and Makeda, the Queen of Sheba, who is claimed to have come from the ancient Ethiopian kingdom of Aksum. Menilek I, the legendary son of Solomon and Makeda is believed to have been the first of a line of Ethiopian rulers who continued in power until the second half of 20th century.

The classic formulation of the claim of Solomonic descent is found in the *Kebra nagast* ('The Glory of Kings') which is generally believed to date more or less in its present form to the 14th century. However, it is important to note that elements of this foundation legend may predate this version of the story. Certainly, the claim that the Ethiopian monarchs of ancient Israelite descent and possess the Ark of the Covenant both predate the 14th century.

According to the *Kebra nagast*, the Queen of Sheba travelled from Aksum to visit King Solomon in Jerusalem. During her stay, Solomon not only dazzled her with his wisdom, but also tricked her by a clever ruse into having sexual relations with him. The Queen conceived a son, whom she bore upon her return to Aksum. When he reached maturity, this son, Menilek, journeyed to Jerusalem to meet his father. At the completion of Menilek's visit, Solomon commanded that the first-born sons of the priests and elders of Israel accompany him to Aksum. Before setting out, however, Menilek and his companions led by the son of the High Priest, stole the Ark of the Covenant from the temple. Thus, the glory of Zion passed from Jerusalem and the Children of Israel to the New Zion, Aksum, and the new Israel, the Ethiopian people.

According to the *Kebra nagast*, members of the Solomonic dynasty ruled Ethiopia from the time of Menilek I. Other sources relate how they were overthrown by the 'Jewish' Queen Gudit (Judith). Ethiopia was then ruled by kings of the Zagwe dynasty, who were considered as non-Israelite 'usurpers'. They were overthrown around 1270 by Yekunno Amlak. Later Ethiopian royal historiography, which depended on the rulers of the Solomonic dynasty depicts Yekunno Amlak as a descendant of the last Aksumite ruler. Thus his rise to power came to be portrayed as the 'restoration' of the Solomonic dynasty. The claim was voiced repeatedly over the centuries in many royal chronicles. Several of the outstanding rulers of this period had names with strong biblical Israelite connotation including Amda Tseyon I ('pillar of Zion', 1314–1344) and Zara Yaeqob ('seed of Jacob', 1434–1468). There is, however, no credible evidence that any Aksumite ruler ever claimed Solomonic descent or that there was in fact a continuous bloodline from the kings of Akum to Yekunno Amlak and his descendants. Moreover, the reign of Solomon is generally dated to the 10th century BCE, centuries before the emergence of Aksumite civilization.

Solomonic hegemony. It is important to note that the idea of Solomonic descent was part of a wider network of associations in Ethiopian politics and church-state relations. Members of the Solomonic dynasty were keepers and defenders of the true faith and vital patrons of the church. A legitimate ruler had to be, not only a member of the dynasty, but also a Christian. These include special rituals of enthronement and symbols of authority. The lion, and more specifically the (conquering) Lion of Judah, was used as a symbol of the Ethiopian monarchy at least from the middle of the 16th century. Over the course of centuries it was elaborated and in a royal seal from the mid-18th century a crowned Lion appears with a large cross and a motto which identifies the emperor as a 'descendant of Solomon, son of David'. The central feature in the Coat of Arms of Emperor Menilek II is a Solomonic throne, on which is inscribed the motto 'Star of the House of David'.

An important testimony to the tenacity of the belief in the Solomonic dynasty is the fact that even in the 'Era of the princes', when the legitimate rulers were little more than puppets of the ruling nobles, they were not replaced by non-Solomonic emperors. Thus the ideal of rule by a member of the Solomonic dynasty was retained even if effective power of such ruler was virtually non-existent.

Succession did not necessarily pass from father to son, but could also include brothers, nephews, and in rare cases daughters. Of course this means that there were large numbers of claimants and succession struggles were common. From the 14th century until the 16th the problem of rival claimants was resolved by confining potential heirs to a 'royal prison'. Over time as the number of descendants grew, however, divisions arose between Shawan and Gondarine branches of the dynasty.

Similarly, several non-royal groups also developed traditions which associate themselves with the Solomonic traditions. Among the Beta Esrael (Falasha) there is a claim that some of the Israelites who accompanied Menilek I to Ethiopia, refused to travel on the Sabbath, separating themselves from the main party and thus becoming the ancestors of the Falasha. Some traditions report that the Zagwe were descendants of King Solomon and a slave/servant woman.

Although the overthrow of Hayla Sellase in 1974 put an end to effective rule of Ethiopia by a representative of the Solomonic dynasty, there are political groups, particularly in the diaspora, which still view his descendants the legitimate rulers of Ethiopia and advocate the 'restoration' of a Solomonic ruler as either a constitutional monarch or mere figurehead.

Literature: Ernest Alfred Wallis Budge, *The Queen of Sheba and her only Son Menyelek*, London 1922, 1932, 2001; Gerard Colin, '*La Gloire des rois* (*Kebra Nagast*)'. *Epopée nationale de L'Ethiopie*, Genève 2002; Sven Rubenson, 'The Lion of the Tribe of Judah: Christian Symbol and/or Imperial Title', *Journal of Ethiopian Studies* 3/2 (1965), 75–85.

Steven Kaplan, The Hebrew University of Jerusalem

Kingdom and city of Gondar

Azazo as a precursor of Gondar. While by no means the first permanent settlement of the Solomonic monarchy, Gondar was the first that claimed a continued presence of Solomonic rulers for generations. Its origins must be sought in Azazo, about 13 km to the south of Gondar. It was there that in 1621 Emperor Susenyos (r. 1607–1632), the father of Gondar's founder, Fasiladas, established a royal settlement. Reportedly, he chose the site, a strategic hill situated at the crossroads of important trade routes to Sudan, Gojjam and Tegray, with the help of one of his most trusted advisors, Spanish Father Pedro Páez, who since 1603 had been at the head of a small but influential Jesuit mission. The new settlement was christened as Gannata Iyasus ('Paradise of Jesus') and it was conceived of as a complex combining different purposes: defensive, recreational, residential and religious. Its chief architectural elements were a palace-garden, which was built with the help of Indian masons and engineers and was shaped on the model of Indian Mughal royal architecture, and a fortified church complex. Fasiladas came of age within this setting and, once the Jesuits had been banned from the country, he used Gannata Iyasus for some time as one of his royal residences, together with those in Libo (Danqaz) and Gondar.

Foundation and early developments. According to the historical record, King Fasiladas (r. 1632–1667) first settled in Gondar during the fourth year of his reign, that is in 1636 or 1637. By about 1641 he seems to have made Gondar his primary residence (madina in the royal 'short' chronicle), yet without fully abandoning the tradition of roving capitals. It can be assumed that by the middle of the decade Gondar was slowly taking the shape of a permanent settlement with an urban-like structure. In the mid-1640s, once he had managed to bring some 'rebel provinces' under effective control, amass considerable material wealth through periodic raids and initiate an activist foreign policy (thanks to diplomatic missions to Yemen, Ottoman Turkey, Mughal India and Dutch East India), Fasiladas sought to recreate in Gondar the architectural spaces he was so familiar with from his teenage days in Gannata Iyasus and Danqaz.

By about 1647, when the envoy of the Zaydi Yemen Hasan bin Ahmad al-Haymi offered the first attested description, the *Fasil gemb*, the most famous construction of the city, had been completed or was on the eve of completion.

The envoy described it as 'the castle of the king ... a high building and a lofty structure, among the most wonderful of splendid constructions and the most beautiful of glorious marvels, built of stone and lime. There is no other like that in that city, nay in the land of al-Habasha – it is a most perfect sight and has a most beautiful form'. The envoy further added that the castle was built by an Indian and, although it was 'outside of the city' it was surrounded by numerous buildings made of mud.

From the historical record, we can assume that from its foundation Gondar included a multi-ethnic and multi-confessional population. At its core were Christian Amhara, who may have occupied the highest state offices as well as their traditionally influential roles within the Church. A second important group were Muslims, who, as Hasan bin Ahmad reported, lived in 'special, enclosed quarters'. They must have belonged to different ethnic groups, such as Amhara, Sudanese, Arabs, Yemenis and Turks. They played a pivotal role in economic affairs (financing and trade) as well as in diplomacy. The royal court probably included a considerable number of its interpreters and advisors from within these groups. The Kemant and Beta Esrael (Falasha), probably speaking Agaw dialects and professing their own distinct religions, were involved since the foundation of the city as craftsmen and masons. Finally, a small Ethiopian-Portuguese militia, who had emerged during the rule of Galawdewos (r. 1541–1559), served as the ruler's private guard at the court.

While Gondar was growing as a city, the Gondarine state seems to have solidified its presence in the territory. Thus, at least a number of provinces, including Dambeya, Bagemder, Gojjam, Agaw Meder, Damot, Takusa and perhaps even Tegray would have been tightly integrated by way of a network of imperial roads (for this purpose several bridges of stone and mortar were built), royal churches (such as Azazo Takla Haymanot, Daga Estifanos, Qoma Fasiladas, Dabra Berhan Sellase, Egziabeher Ab,

Dafacha Kidana Mehrat, Aksum Tseyon, Martula Maryam) and provincial fortresses (Aringo, Yebaba, Abba Gish Fasil, Gemb Giyorgis, Gomar, Wahni Amba and perhaps also Guzara).

Fasiladas' castle from south, Gondar, © Serge Dewel-Mouton

Further transformations. Fasiladas's successors, in particular Yohannes I (r. 1667–1682) and Iyasu I (r. 1682–1706), and later Dawit III (r. 1716–1721) and Bakaffa (r. 1721–1730), for all the crises endured during their reigns, seem to have continued the policies of their predecessor. Thus, under Yohannes I the religious segregation policy at the capital was emphasized. The Christians claimed for themselves the higher areas of the main hill of Gondar, those around the royal palaces, while the Muslims and Falasha occupied the areas to the south of the city and on the banks of the Kaha river. The Muslim quarter was henceforth known as Eslam Bet (later also as Addis Alam), while the Beta Esrael resided in two areas, the Kayla Meda and Falasha Bet. The 'Turks' settled in the area known as Turkoch, where Baata Church today stands. Moreover, Orthodox religious leaders also had their quarters: the *echage* (the head of Dabra Libanos's monastic community) and his entourage occupied the *echage bet*, an area immediately opposite the royal castles to the northwest. The *abun*, the Coptic metropolitan, resided in the so-called *abuna bet*, where today Gabreel monastery stands. For their part, the Ethiopian-Portuguese and remnants of Catholic converts were forced to leave the kingdom.

During the reigns of Fasiladas's successors new sumptuous buildings were added to those erected by the city's founder. Yohannes built a palace of the chancellery and an elegant library while Iyasu erected a castle with an impressive barrel vault. Bakaffa, for his part, built an original, U-shaped, pavilion. The new buildings followed the Indian-inspired architectural tradition started by Susenyos and Fasiladas, but each showed variations and introduced new features, probably borrowing from such neighbouring areas as Yemen and Egypt. New churches were also built, such as Tsadda Egziabeher

Ab (Yohannes I), Dabra Berhan Sellase (Iyasu I), Hamara Noh (Tewoflos), Ledata (Yostos), Atatame Qeddus Mikael (Dawit and Bakaffa) and Dafacha Kidana Mehrat (Bakaffa).

By the turn of the 18th century, Gondar must have acquired a sizeable population and become the true political, cultural and economic centre of a large area. The city's area of influence might have stretched as far as to the Sudanese lowlands and the Red Sea. The city thus served as a market where the products of several regions were exchanged and brokered; from the crops of the fertile agricultural areas of Gojjam, Damot, Agaw Meder and Dambeya to the local cattle, from civet, to coffee, hides and slaves. Its churches also claimed a major role as centres of religious learning, where religious poetry (*qene*), liturgical chants and rituals such as *zema* and *aqqwaqwam* could be acquired as well as theology and exegesis (*andemta*).

Among the important civil officials ruling in the city were the *naggadras* and the *kantiba*. The former was the head of the merchants, collecting customs, supervising caravans and adjudicating civil matters. The *kantiba*, for his part, acted as a sort of mayor, dispensing justice and maintaining public order.

Mentewwab and the Qwaran period. In the central decades of 18th century, under the aegis of Queen Mentewwab (regnal name Berhan Mogasa), the Qwaran party, originally from the western province of Qwara near the Sudan, became an influential force within the city and the kingdom. In the 1720s Mentewwab married King Bakaffa and bore him a son, the future Iyasu III. Thereafter her relatives, including her brother Walda Leul, would be positioned in key roles of the kingdom while Mentewwab ruled as a regent. The official rulers, Iyasu II and Iyoas were never allowed to hold any effective power.

Yet, Queen Mentewwab also became a patroness of the arts in her own right, thus bringing Gondarine art and architecture to new heights. Under her auspices the castles of Iyasu II and her own castle were built at the royal compound in Gondar. But she is mostly remembered for the abbey and royal complex of Qwesqwam she ordered to build in the outskirts of Gondar; the complex included the church of Dabra Tsahay (= 'mount of the sun', an homage itself to her home region of Qwara, which in Qwarenna literally means 'sun') and a refined palace. In the Tana area she also funded the church of Narga Sellase, which, like Dabra Tsahay, contains an important collection of Gondarine-style paintings. It was from this period that we have one of the longest descriptions of the city, authored by the Scottish traveller James Bruce. According to his writings, towards 1770 Gondar was a city of 'about ten thousand families in times of peace; the houses are chiefly of clay, the roofs thatched in the form of cones'.

The *Fasil gemb* was said to be in ruins, but a succession of kings had built apartments 'by the side of it of clay only, in the manner and fashion of their own country; for the palace itself was built by masons from India, in the time of Facilidas'. The palace and all its contiguous buildings were 'surrounded by a substantial stone wall thirty feet high, with battlements upon the outer wall, and a parapet roof between the outer and inner'. To the south, on the other side of the Qaha River 'is a large town of Mahometans of about a thousand houses. These are all active and laborious people; great part of them are employed in taking care of the king's and nobility's baggage and field-equipage, both when they take the field and when they return from it'.

From decay to recovery in the 20th century. The regency of Mentewwab lasted until May 1769, when Mikael Sehul of Tegray murdered Iyoas and installed his own candidate on the throne. This is considered the official beginning of the so-called

Zamana masafent (= 'The Era of the princes'), when the Gondarine rulers were overshadowed by regional lords. The city remained the ceremonial, commercial and religious centre of the kingdom, but the kings were reduced to figureheads without the means to maintain their courts. The first of local lords was *Ras* Ali Gwangul, who governed from Dabra Tabor from the second decade of the 19th century.

By the early 1830s, Gondar's royal compound was reported to be in ruins; the reigning monarch holding court in quite modest quarters beside the once large castle. The city had shrunk to about 1,000 houses with perhaps 6,500 inhabitants. After the mid-1850s, no further emperors reigned in Gondar. King Tewodros II refused to live there and in 1864 and 1866 he famously sacked and plundered the city (in 2010, however, a statue was erected in his memory in Piasa, at the entrance of the city). In 1888 and 1889, the Sudanese Dervishes burned what was left of the city. By the early 20th century, the population had dwindled to perhaps one thousand or fewer people.

Gondar only began to recover with the Italian occupation. The city was taken in 1936 and it thereafter became the capital of the Amhara Province ('governatorato dell'Amhara'). A new city was built around the old one, with new commercial and government buildings, roads and public areas. At the same time, a tight segregation of the two populations – Italian and indigenous – was established. Additionally, a programme of restoration and management of Gondar's architectonic heritage was implemented for the first time.

After the defeat of the Italian forces in November 1941, Gondar became the capital of the Province of Bagemder and Semen. The imperial government took over the Italian government buildings and established a municipal administration under a *kantiba* and a council with both Christian and Muslim members. Muslims and, increasingly, Christians engaged in commerce and trade and the city's markets continued to flourish. Primary schools and a new secondary school were opened and in 1953 a public health college was established on the grounds of the former Italian Consulate. Foreign tourists began to visit the city's monuments, which in 1969 were undergoing major restorations with the help of UNESCO.

Today, thanks in part to investments by diaspora Ethiopians and to Ethiopia's economic boom the city is experiencing an important urban sprawl along the 10km stretch of road connecting Gondar to Azazo. In 2004 the health college was upgraded to a university and three campuses were established in the outskirts of the city, in the Maraki-Samunar Bar area. The city has maintained its role as the main gateway for the trade with Sudan and oversees the production of important cash crops, like sesame. Gondar has also become an important tourist destination, although without yet developing its potential to its maximum. As of 2012, its population peaked at about 300,000, far larger than that of the official capital of the Amhara regional state, Baher Dar.

Literature: GHIORGHIS MELLESSA, 'Gondar Yesterday and Today', *Ethiopia Observer*, 12/3, (1969), 164–176; RICHARD PANKHURST, 'Notes for the History of Gondar', *Ethiopia Observer*, 12/3 (1969), 177–227.

Andreu Martínez d'Alòs-Moner, University of Gondar

The Era of the princes

The period of the Ethiopian history known as *Zamana masafent* ('The Era of the princes') lasted from the mid-18th century to the mid-19th century. This period is characterized by the weakening of the coordinating (rather than central) power established in Gondar since the 17th century. The monarchy was not abolished, but the aged and powerless representatives of the royal Solomonic dynasty were placed under the tutelage of regional lords, and reduced to symbolical functions, hence designated as 'puppet kings' in general historical discourse.

This periodization refers to the biblical 'Book of Judges', translated in Ge'ez by the term of *masfen*, pl. *masafent* ('ruler, governor') that corresponds more closely to the Hebrew *shofet*, pl. *shoftim* ('ruler, military leader'), than the Greek version of *krites*, pl. *kritai* ('judge'). The construction of parallels with biblical history is a common feature in Ethiopian historiography. This depiction of the whole period as depraved and disordered was probably conceived in the late 19th century, when the broader narrative of national unification and restoration of imperial grandeur became part of the official propaganda under Menilek II. The latter, in the chronicle of his reign, is compared to King David, while his predecessor Tewodros II is described as Saul, thus referring to the 'Books of Samuel' (that follow 'Judges'). The Book of 'Joshua' (that precedes 'Judges') is associated with the figure of King Iyasu I, who represented the pinnacle of the Gondarine kingdom. If the latent eschatology behind the concept of *Zamana masafent* belongs obviously to the Ethiopian mindset, its appearance in Ethiopian historical literature and the way it was adopted into the historical studies of foreign scholars is an issue that has not been sufficiently analyzed to date.

A weakened monarchy. Conventionally, the beginning of the 'Era of the princes' is set in 1769, the year of the assassination of King of Kings Iyoas and the seizure of power by *Ras* Mikael Sehul of Tegray. These events dealt a final blow to the already weakened authority of the royal dynasty. They were followed by fierce competition between regional rulers to keep the remains of the kingdom under their control. These clashes of cultural identities and political legitimacies were exacerbated by religious struggles between Christian theological factions that reflected regional divisions. The territory of Gojjam was the core of the *qebat* (Unctionist) theological movement that was attractive to assimilated Agaw and Oromo populations. The partisans of an irredentist and conservative vision of the realm that should belong only to ethnic Abyssinians (Tegray and Amhara), supported the *Tawahedo* (Unitarian) dogma.

After the regicide of Iyoas, the years between 1769 and 1802 were a period of tremendous instability. The lords from different regions fought against each other for control of Gondar and used this temporary position of supreme governorship to distribute official positions and land grants to their kin and clients. In 33 years, nine Solomonic scions were made kings. Among them, Takla Giyorgis I was enthroned and deposed six times. He failed in his repeated attempts at restoring a dynastic authority hence his ironical labelling as *fatsame mangest* ('the accomplisher/concluder of the kingdom').

The rise of Muslim Oromo converts. This troubled context was propitious to the emergence of a dynasty of Muslim Oromo origin, the Warra Shekoch ('the house of the *shaykhs*'), who came from the territory of Yajju, to the north-east of Wallo. They assimilated the faith and the habits of the Christian kingdom after having concluded an alliance-through-marriage with the ruling family of Lasta. This mixed lineage reached the highest political functions in 1784 when Ali Gwangul was made *Ras* by King Takla Giyorgis. *Ras* Ali governed for only four years, but his position was passed on to his brothers and their descendants despite strong internal feuding between them.

From 1802 to 1825, the situation was more stable under *Ras* Gugsa's rule. He consolidated and extended the authority of his kin and allies. A new capital city was

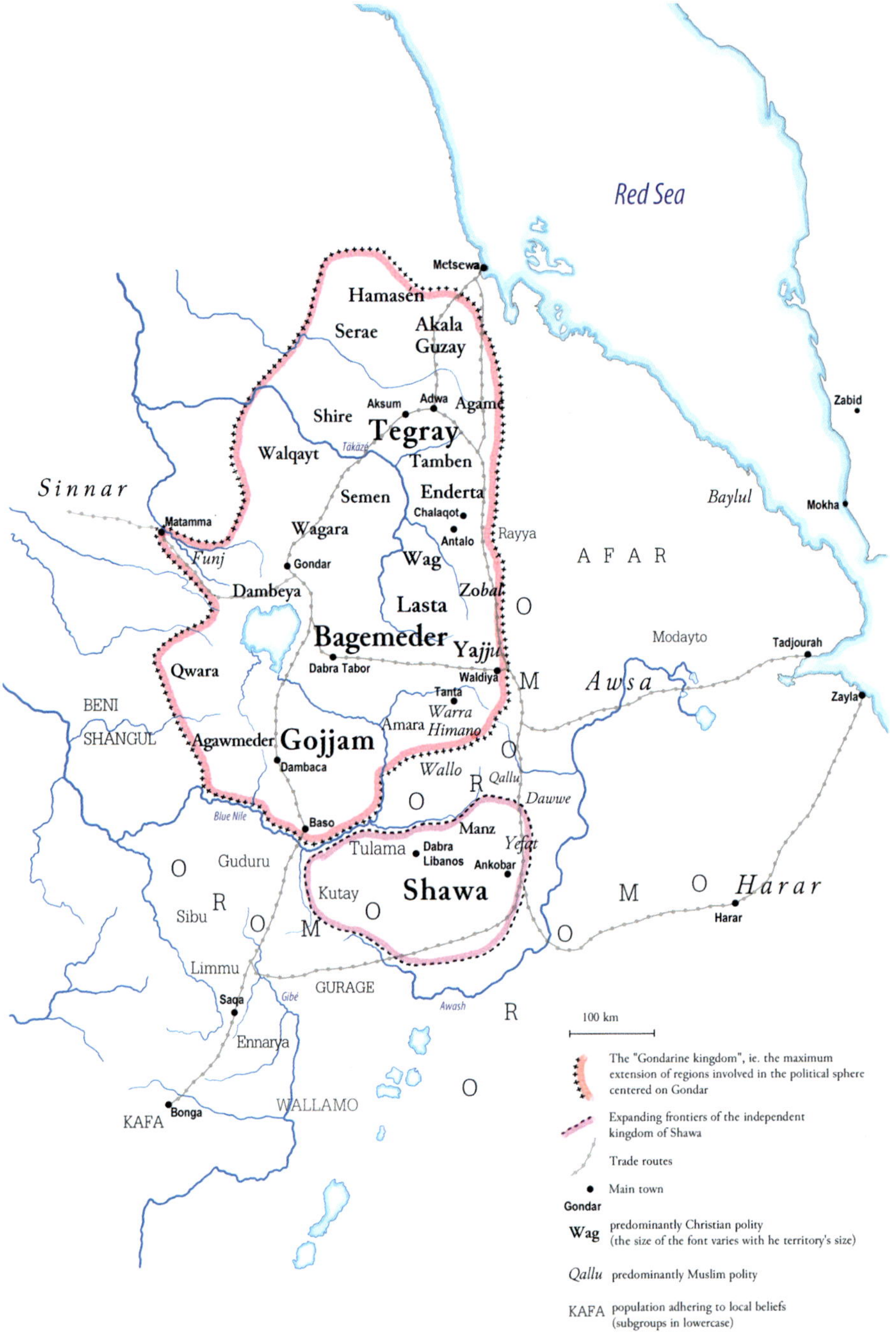

Map 8: Christian powers in central Ethiopia and their neighbours during the *Zamana masafent* ('Era of the princes', 1769–1855), © Éloi Ficquet

founded in Dabra Tabor, which occupied a more central position than Gondar. Some significant reforms were attempted, particularly regarding land tenure. Even if it was not fully implemented, this reform indicates that meaningful political issues such as the redistribution of resources were at stake behind the scene of regional conflicts. Meanwhile, Gondar castles were deteriorating and the city saw its population and activities decline, but it was not totally abandoned. It remained the seat of state and church administration organized around symbolic figures of national importance. Though deprived of executive power, the king (*atse*) was still essential to the ritual validation of acts. The presence of the Egyptian Metropolitan Archbishop (*abun*) was jeopardized by the theological disputes and by tensions with Egypt. His seat was vacant for many years, but lords were vying for his return as he could be instrumental in their strategy to impose themselves as supreme leaders.

Regional competitions. The long-standing supremacy of Yajju and Wallo ruling families disturbed the other lords. The ascension of outsiders and recent converts to the top of the political ladder was seen as a desecration of the ancestral legacy of the Christian kingdom of Ethiopia and as a threat to the country's independence. The most determined challengers of the Yajju lords of Dabra Tabor were the successive leaders of Tegray (namely Walda Sellase, Sabagadis, and Webe). Their ambition to regain control of the kingdom was served by their geographical situation commanding the trade routes to the Red Sea through which they could collect taxes and divert most of the supply in firearms to their own armies. They were weakened, however, by the same internal struggles as in the other regions. Meanwhile, the kingdom of Shawa kept its distance to the political developments of the *Zamana masafent* by not paying any kind of tribute nor consideration to the masters of Gondar and by developing its own commercial network connected to the sea through the eastern port of Zayla.

International context. If the period was dominated by unremitting internal competitions, it also witnessed increasing pressure from international actors. The Ottoman viceroy of Egypt, Muhammad Ali, claimed to take over the historically established, albeit remote, Turkish dominion over the whole African coast of the Red Sea. In the 1820s, the Turco-Egyptian troops invaded the territories of Sennar and Kordofan in the north-eastern areas of the present day Sudan. This led to skirmishes on the Ethiopian western borderlands. There was also a revival movement of Islamic Sufi mystical orders which made headway into Oromo-speaking areas (Wallo) through the proselytization activities of learned *shaykhs* who were credited with magical powers. Furthermore, the presence of Europeans gradually increased. In 1770, James Bruce made his way to 'rediscover' the source of the Blue Nile (pretending the Jesuit Páez did not). He witnessed the wars that led to the collapse of the kingdom. From the 1810s (with the sojourns of the British subjects Salt and Pearce) a growing number of scholars, missionaries, diplomats and adventurers travelled and stayed in different regions of Ethiopia. From these they reported the details of local politics, as understood from the point of view of the entourages of influential oligarchs under whose protection they were sheltered. There were some unsuccessful attempts at establishing diplomatic relations.

Messianic expectations. In the popular opinion of Christian Ethiopians of the time, the permanent state of political crisis and the feeling that the whole world was changing was expressed in religious terms by the expectation of a messianic king, named Tewodros, in remembrance of the 15th century king who disappeared in the 9th month of his reign in a war against the Islamic state of Adal. It was believed that he would 'come back' and restore peace through the reunification of the Christian territories

Solomonic kings of kings (*atse*)	Dominant lords/king makers
Yohannes II (r. May to Sep. 1769)	*Ras* Mikael Sehul of Tegray (*fl.* 1769–1771)
Takla Haymanot I (1st r. Oct. 1769–Sep. 1770)	
Susenyos II (r. Sep. to Dec. 1770)	Coalition led by *dajach* Wand Bawasan of Lasta, *dajach* Goshu of Gojjam and *dajach* Fasil of Damot
Takla Haymanot II (2nd r. 1770–1777)	*Ras* Mikael Sehul until 05/1771 (battle of Sarbakusa). Then shifting alliances and power struggle led by the 3 afore-mentioned lords.
Salomon I (r. 1777–1779)	*Ras* Haylu Yosedeq of Gojjam (*fl.* 1777–1784)
Takla Giyorgis I (1st r. 1779–1784)	
Iyasu III (r. 1784–1788)	*Ras* Ali of Yajju (*fl.* 1784–1788)
Takla Giyorgis I (2nd r. Apr. 1788–Jan. 1789)	
Hezqeyas (r. 1789–1794)	*Ras* Aligaz of Yajju (*fl.* 1788-1791)
Takla Giyorgis I (3rd r. Jan. 1794–Apr. 1795)	*Ras* Asrat and *Ras* Walda Gabreel, both of Lasta
Baeda Maryam II (r. Apr. 1795–Jun. 1796)	
Salomon II (r. Jun. 1796–Aug. 1797)	*Ras* Mared of Gojjam
Yonas (r. Aug. 1797–Feb. 1798)	*Ras* Asrat of Lasta vs *Ras* Walda Sellase of Tegray
Takla Giyorgis I (4th r. Feb. 1798 to Jul. 1799)	
Demetros (Jul. to Oct. 1799)	
Takla Giyorgis I (5th r. Oct 1799–May 1800)	
Demetros (May 1800 to Jul. 1801)	*Ras* Gugsa Marsa of Yajju (*fl.* 1801–1825)
Egwale Tseyon (1801–1818)	
Iyoas II (r. 1818–1821)	
Gigar I (r. 1821–1831)	
	Ras Yemam Gugsa (*fl.* 1825–1828)
	Ras Mareye Gugsa (*fl.* 1828–1831)
Iyasu IV (Feb to Sep. 1831)	*Ras* Dori Gugsa (*fl.* 02–05 / 1831)
Sahla Dengel (r. 1832–40; 1842–43; 1846–50; 1852–55) Yohannes III (r. 1840–42; 1843–46; 1850–52) The two nominal kings reigned concurrently and alternately during the 1840s and 50s	*Ras* Ali Alula (*fl.*1831–1853) and his mother: *Etege* Manan of Warra Himano.

Table 9: Ruling figures of the *Zamana masafent* ('The Era of the princes', 1769–1855)

into one kingdom. This providential role was eventually taken by a petty lord from the western frontier district of Qwara, *Dajjazmach* Kassa Haylu, who quickly came to prominence as a military leader through his exceptional fighting spirit. The Warra Shekoch ruling family tried to win his loyalty by marrying him to the daughter of *Ras* Ali II. The latter had been governing since 1830 under the authority of his mother Manan who acted as a regent queen, being the wife of *Atse* Yohannes III, one of the last holders of the non-executive position of 'king of kings'. Kassa's stubbornness and ambition were stronger than political machinations and he turned against all the *masafent*. The last supporters of *Ras* Ali were defeated in 1853. Then it was the turn of the powerful *Ras* Webe of Tegray, who was defeated in 1855. Kassa immediately took the advantage of this victory to have himself anointed and crowned as 'king of kings' under the name of Tewodros II. This event marked the formal end of the Gondarine Solomonic dynasty. After having broken with the balance of powers that had characterized the *Zamana masafent*, the new 'self-made king' laid down the principles of a new political order in which reforms and modernisation could be achieved only through the restoration of a strong royal authority.

Literature: MORDECHAI ABIR, *The Era of the Princes. The Challenge of Islam and the Re-unification of the Christian Empire, 1769–1855*, London 1968; DONALD CRUMMEY, 'Society and Ethnicity in the Politics of Christian Ethiopia during the *Zamana Masafent*', *The International Journal of African Historical Studies*, 8/2 (1975), 266–278; SOPHIA DEGE, 'Zämänä Mäsafənt', *EAE* V, 122–129; SHIFERAW BEKELE, 'Reflections on the Power Elite of the Wärä Seh Mäsfenate (1786–1853)', *Annales d'Éthiopie*, 15 (1990), 157–176.

Éloi Ficquet, École des hautes études en sciences sociales, Paris

The Ethiopian empire under Tewodros II and Yohannes IV

After experiencing a long period of disintegration and instability, Ethiopia had three outstanding political leaders in the second half of the 19th century who revived and maintained the power of the monarchy, unified its principalities, expanded its territorial size, defended its sovereignty against foreign invaders, and introduced western innovations, to mention only a few of their achievements. They were Tewodros II, Yohannes IV, and Menilek II, and all three were born within the chaotic period known as the *Zamana masafent* ('The Era of the princes'; see also the previous article).

Emperor Tewodros II

The initiator of Ethiopia's unity and modernisation was Emperor Tewodros II (1855–1868) who was physically energetic, quite intelligent according to the national and foreign sources of his time, well informed about national and international politics, and morally beyond reproach at least in the early years of his reign. He was born in Gondar or Qwara around 1820 and his name was Kassa Haylu. Hardly anything is known about his father, apart from the fact that he was a nobleman of Qwara in north-western Ethiopia. His mother Attetagab, who lived mostly in Gondar, brought him up and enrolled him at an early age in the church school of Takla Haymanot at Chenkar between Gondar and Lake Tana.

In the late 1820s, the monastery was attacked by soldiers returning from a campaign and several of the pupils were killed or wounded. Kassa escaped and joined a group of people heading for Qwara. His half brother, who governed the region, took care of him and continued his education in the monastery of Mahbara Sellase. How long he pursued church education is not known, but his later discussion with the clerics as well as others showed that he was versed in religious, legal and historical traditions of the country. He was equally well trained in military matters such as horse riding, operation of weapons and tactics of war. He probably perfected his military skills by participating in the intermittent campaigns against the encroaching Turkish and Egyptian contingents from the Sudan on which Qwara bordered.

Around 1840 he moved to Gojjam and entered the service of *Dajach* Gosshu for some time. He left with a few comrades for Tchilga where he became a rebel against

Throne of Emperor Yohannes IV in the royal palace in Meqele, carved by Naretti, Mekelle Museum, © Wolbert G.C. Smidt

the ruling notables of Gojjam and Bagemder. Here began his popularity as he attacked the rich and distributed his gains among the poor peasants. The number of his soldiers steadily increased. As the area under his control grew Empress Manan and her son, *Ras* Ali, the most powerful political leaders over what was left of the empire, sought reconciliation with him through mediators. Kassa accepted the proposal that he would marry a granddaughter of the empress and become governor of Qwara. The marriage was consummated, but the province was denied, allegedly because he was not of sufficiently high rank. Again he rebelled and in the years 1845–1855, he was victorious in several battles against *Dajach* Gosshu, *Etege* Manan, *Ras* Ali and *Dajach* Webe of Semen. Following the defeat of the last of these, in Semen he crowned himself Emperor Tewodros II at Darasge in February 1855.

At this time, he declared the precepts of his imperial policy: peasants and traders were encouraged to pursue their occupations; landowners should retain their properties; robbers, thieves and rebels would suffer severe punishments if they continued their practice; victims could appeal to him personally; emasculation of captives was forbidden; and the practice of holding responsible the relations of a murderer was abolished. In the Orthodox Faith only the doctrine of the *abun* was to be followed. As far as marriage was concerned, a man should have only one wife.

But he did not have the time to supervise and administer all the precepts he imagined and wished for his society. The unification of Ethiopia was far from being complete at the time of his coronation and he had yet to subdue Wallo and Shawa, not to mention the south. Even Tegray, which was governed by Webe, did not come automatically under his control. A nephew of the captured governor ruled it for the next five years. Nevertheless, Tewodros was far from being tired or discouraged. After the rainy season of 1855 he marched to Wallo and captured Maqdala which he made his store of government treasure and a prison for suspects and rebels. He also entered Shawa without encountering much resistance, as *Ras* Hayla Malakot fell ill and died before the emperor reached Ankobar. He appointed governors for both regions, took young prince Menilek with him and marched through Gojjam to Bagemder.

But he did not remain there. He had to march to the various regions to quell rebellions led by the notables (including many of his own appointees). Character-changing events coincided with these rebellions. In 1860 his most faithful wife, who accompanied him even in the crucial times of his campaigns, died of illness. The Catholic and Protestant missionaries, whom he had tolerated as long as they did not involve themselves in his politics, were found to be exchanging letters with the rebels or openly criticizing him in their books. Besides, his letters addressed to some of the European powers remained unanswered. In response he arrested all the Europeans in the country, including the British consul, and confined them to Mount Maqdala. The British government reacted by sending a huge expeditionary force to Maqdala to release the prisoners. Tewodros saw that most of his officers and soldiers had deserted him and chose to commit suicide rather than surrender to foreigners. Thus ended his life, but his initiative for the reform and unity of his country remained alive in the minds of writers and politicians of Ethiopia.

Emperor Yohannes IV

Yohannes' major policy was the revival of Ethiopia's unity and security. In this sense he was the real successor of Tewodros II, although viewed chronologically it was his brother-in-law, Takla Giyorgis II who acceded to the throne before him. He thus spent the greater part of his reign (1872–1889) trying militarily and politically to unify and pacify the state and to defend its independence against foreign threats.

Yohannes was born at May Beha (Tamben) *c.* 1831 and died in Matamma in March 1889. His original name was Kahsay, though he was better known by the Amharic version Kassa. His father was *Shum Tamben* Mirtcha Walda Kidan and his mother Sellas, a daughter of *Shum Agame* Waldu. Little is known about his early life and education. He began his political career as a rebel against the governors of Tegray whom he subsequently killed or took captive during the last years of Tewodros II. By 1867 the whole of Tegray was under his control.

When the British army marched to Maqdala through Tegray he concluded an agreement with them to the effect they would not occupy his country and he would allow his subjects to supply the expedition with provisions against payment. On their way back to the coast, the British supplied him with cannons, rifles and ammunition which raised his prestige and power.

He refused to submit himself to Takla Giyorgis or to send him the metropolitan he had brought from Egypt. When Takla Giyorgis marched against him in 1871, Kassa defeated and took him captive. Six months later, he crowned himself in Aksum 'Yohannes IV, King of Zion, King of Kings of Ethiopia'. The greater part of Ethiopia was not yet under his rule and, hence, after quelling a rebellion in Rayya Azabo, he marched to Bagemder, Gojjam and Wallo, all of which surrendered without serious resistance. But before he reached Shawa, he had to turn northward, as Egyptian forces assisted by European and American officers were marching from three directions toward the highlands. Yohannes utterly defeated them at Gundat and Gurae in 1875–1876, and gained from them a considerable amount of weapons and ammunition. In 1877–1878 he marched to Shawa and received the submission of *Negus* Menilek who agreed to regularly deliver annual tribute.

In the first five years of his reign, he thus succeeded in achieving the unity of the predominantly Christian provinces. He crowned Menilek of Shawa and Takla Haymanot of Gojjam regional kings and encouraged them to expand the empire to the south, east and west; he toured the other regions and appointed governors, usually from the local nobility, regardless of their former attitudes toward him, as long as they submitted and expressed to him their unflinching loyalty.

His next aim was to achieve the religious unity of the country. In this he succeeded only in the Orthodox Christian part of the society. He inherited an empire with three religious questions which had to be resolved: the internal dissensions within the Ethiopian Church, the threat of Islam to the state and Christianity, and foreign missionary activities. He regarded all three as menaces to the unity and stability of the state. By 1878, he was ready to tackle the problems by summoning a council at Boru Meda.

> Most of the high dignitaries and notables of Ethiopia were present at the council. The leading theologians of the three major disputing groups of the Orthodox Church attended the Council and tried to defend their respective doctrines. A letter from the patriarch of Alexandria was read at the end of the disputation which endorsed the imperial tenet. All those who did not adhere to the doctrine of Alexandria had to go into exile.

The policy transcended Yohannes' reign, though there were indications that the suppressed theologies had by no means been totally eliminated. Immediately following the Council of Boru Meda, Yohannes appointed a couple of church scholars to conduct the Christianization of Muslim Wallo. In the same year, a coercive decree was issued obliging Muslims to convert to Christianity. The consequences were ruinous:

Library of Yohannes I seen from the palace of Iyasu I, Meqele © Wolbert G.C. Smidt

many Muslims emigrated to the Sudan; foreign trade, which was predominantly in the hands of Muslims, sharply declined; and several dignitaries of the empire were unwilling to enforce the decree. The measure also attracted criticism from foreign powers, a circumstance which turned out to be detrimental to his foreign policy. Two years later, the project was abandoned and Yohannes began to deny in his correspondence that an application of force had ever taken place.

Another stumbling block to his foreign policy was his experience with foreign missionaries. Both Protestant and Catholic missions had been established in the distant north long before Yohannes IV was crowned. There is no indication that he resented their presence as long as they were not involved in politics.

Some of the French Catholic missionaries in Akkala Guzay could not, however, remain neutral. They exacted a particular annual tribute which was traditionally due to the *liqa kahnat* of the Orthodox Church. When Takla Giyorgis was defeated, a letter of the missionaries was found among his papers which encouraged him to oppose Yohannes. Hence, Yohannes expelled them from his dominion.

Another concern of Yohannes was the retrieval of lost territories, the delimitation of the boundaries of his empire, and the defence of the sovereignty of the state against the threat and interferences of foreign powers. He visualized his country as an island of Christianity in the sea of Islam. With this in mind, he made friendly overtures to several European powers soliciting their peaceful involvement in settling his dispute with Egypt through negotiation. The reaction of the foreign powers was, however, rather apathetic, as they had more interest in Muslim Egypt than in Christian Ethiopia.

On behalf of Egypt, Great Britain negotiated an agreement known as the Treaty of Adwa or the Admiral Hewett Treaty of 1884 in which Yohannes was promised the right to import weapons through the port of Metsewa and to take over some territories which were under Egyptian control provided that he granted safe conduct to the Egyptian garrisons threatened by the Mahdists of the Sudan. Yohannes fulfilled his obligation, but Great Britain conceded Italy's occupation of Metsewa, a non-signatory of the treaty. Still worse, Great Britain proposed that Yohannes cede certain coastal territories and apologize for the death of Italian soldiers at Dogali. Yohannes saw no reason why he should apologize for fighting the invaders of his country. In March 1889 Yohannes encountered the Mahdists at Matamma and was fatally wounded in the heat of the battle. The Mahdists cut off his head and brandished it in Khartoum. This event more than any of his achievements associates him with martyrs in Ethiopian literature.

Literature: SVEN RUBENSON, *King of Kings Tewodros of Ethiopia*, Addis Ababa–Nairobi 1966; ZEWDE GEBRE-SELLASSIE, *Yohannes IV of Ethiopia: a Political Biography*, Oxford 1975; RICHARD A. CAULK, *'Between the Jaws of Hyenas': A Diplomatic History of Ethiopia, 1876–1896*, Wiesbaden 2002.

Bairu Tafla, Universität Hamburg

Emperor Menilek II

Origins. Emperor Menilek II (1844–1913) was effectively the founder of the modern Ethiopian state. He was the grandson of Sahla Sellase, king of Shawa, southernmost of the major provinces of highland Ethiopia, and son of Sahla Sellase's successor Hayla Malakot (r. 1847–1855). The name Menilek referred to the legendary son of King Solomon and the Queen of Sheba, and prophesied for him a distinguished imperial future. At the age of eleven, he was taken into captivity by the new emperor Tewodros II, and raised at Tewodros' court. In 1865, as the emperor's power waned, Menilek escaped and was received with joy in Shawa as its rightful king. Self-proclaimed king of Shawa, Menilek showed signs of imperial ambitions, but after Tewodros' death in 1868 he lacked the military strength to challenge the ruler of Tegray, who became emperor Yohannes IV. When Yohannes advanced on Shawa, Menilek was obliged to submit to him in March 1878. During the period between 1866 and 1889, when Menilek was in effect the quasi-independent ruler of Shawa he laid the foundations of his subsequent rule as emperor. These were based on three elements. First, he established independent connections with Europe, through which to gain modern technology (especially weapons), expertise, and diplomatic support; second, he conquered neighbouring peoples to the southeast, south and southwest, in order to pre-empt European colonialism and exploit the considerable wealth that these regions offered; and third, he maintained his autonomy from the historic centres of national power to the north, until he was in a position to challenge them.

Emperor Menilek II, Ilg-Collection, Mekelle Museum, © Wolbert G.C. Smidt

Securing Ethiopian independence. Following Yohannes' death fighting the Mahdists at Matamma in March 1889, Menilek immediately declared himself emperor, and received the allegiance of the principal regional lords. Although his domestic standing was assured his international position was extremely precarious. On 2 May 1889, he signed a treaty with the Italians at Wechale, the Italian text of which deceitfully established an Italian protectorate over Ethiopia. The Amharic text made no such commitment, placing Menilek on a collision course with Italy. In the resulting contest for support, Menilek operated with great skill, securing arms and diplomatic support especially from France, Russia and Turkey, and the allegiance of a virtually united Ethiopia. As a result, he was able to put into the field a well-equipped army probably of over 100,000 men, with which he gained a crushing victory over the Italians at Adwa on 1 March 1896.

In the aftermath of victory, Menilek secured full European recognition of Ethiopia as a sovereign independent state – the only African state in the entire continent to achieve this vital status. He nonetheless accepted the Italian colony of Eritrea within its existing frontiers, rather than seeking to establish Ethiopian rule down to the Red Sea coast. This decision, later much criticised, is best explained by the exhaustion of the Ethiopian army after Adwa, and the fear of arousing European hostility if he attacked an existing colony. However, the expansion of Ethiopian territory to the south, east and west continued, establishing the country within the bounds that it retained a century later.

Building a modern state. Menilek then turned his attention to the establishment of a modern Ethiopian state. He had a very enquiring mind, and took an interest in external innovations of all kinds, using European advisers of whom the most important was a Swiss, Alfred Ilg. One critical development was the construction of a railway line from the French colony at Djibouti to the newly established city Addis Ababa, which gave Ethiopia access to the sea independent of Italy, which controlled the historic gateway to the highlands through Metsewa, and remained the principal threat to Ethiopia's independence. Addis Ababa formed a permanent capital, close to the centre of the empire, displacing the system under which the administration had moved with the ruler. Rulers of newly incorporated provinces, even in Muslim areas such as Jimma, were permitted to remain in office if they acknowledged Menilek's supremacy, but were ruthlessly suppressed if they resisted. At the same time, a ruling class of Christian highlanders, including retired soldiers known as *naftannya*, took over much of the conquered territory, establishing a highly exploitative system of quasi-colonial rule that created serious long-term problems for the maintenance of the Ethiopian state. While it was possible for individuals from the conquered peoples to reach the highest positions under the emperor, including the Oromo Minister of War *Fitawrari* Habta Giyorgis and the Gurage *Dajjazmach* Balcha, governor of Sidamo, these were assimilated in religious and cultural terms to the Amhara and Orthodox Christian core. Menilek's daughter Shawaraga was married to the Muslim Oromo ruler of Wallo, Mohammed Ali, who was however obliged to convert to Christianity and assume the name of Mikael; their son Iyasu briefly ruled as Menilek's successor.

Menilek likewise recognized the need to train a new class of administrators, and established Ethiopia's first European-style school, which was named after him, for the purpose. Other indicators of modernity included a postal system, which issued its first postage stamps in 1894, the start of a road network, several services, and the installation of telephones and telegraphs which, however unreliable, greatly improved communications both within the country and with the outside world. The principal foreign powers established permanent diplomatic missions in Addis Ababa, on large properties granted to them by the emperor. Government ministries were formally set up in 1907, though these functioned essentially as adjuncts to a highly personalised administrative system conducted through the palace. The ancient office of *tsahafe teezaz* ('writer of orders'), who was in effect the emperor's secretary, was for example formalised as the Minister of the Pen. More significant was the centralisation of the taxation system, under which provincial governors were under far greater pressure than before to send their revenues to the central government.

Decline and achievement. A tall, thickset man, much darker in complexion than most highland Ethiopians, Menilek cared little for the trappings of imperial rule, and in later life generally wore a simple cloak with a bandanna round his head, sometimes surmounted by a broad-brimmed hat. His long and tragic decline dated from mid-1906, when he sustained a mild apoplectic attack. Further strokes followed in May 1908 and in early 1909. A massive stroke in October 1909 brought him close to death, and although he was successful in achieving the transfer of imperial authority to his grandson *Lej* Iyasu, he was in no condition to exercise effective power until his eventual death in December 1913. He must rank among the greatest of not only Ethiopian but also of African leaders. Alone among his continental contemporaries, he possessed the vision, the political skills and the state capacity needed to protect his country and people against advancing colonialism, and in the process to carve out for his own state a massively increased territory and place in world affairs. That this proved to be deeply flawed may equally be laid at his door, though he did no more than other empire-builders of his era. In the longer run, land alienation in the south, and the discriminatory social relations that inevitably went with it, were to prove the greatest weakness of the state that he had founded, while his recognition of the Italian colony of Eritrea was likewise fraught with lasting consequences. He is remembered among Ethiopians both positively, as a great individual ruler and the founder of modern Ethiopia, and negatively for the legacies of economic exploitation and ethnic and religious inequality that followed from what was, effectively, a structure of internal empire-building.

Literature: HAROLD G. MARCUS, *The Life and Times of Menilek II: Ethiopia 1844–1913*, Oxford 1975; BAHRU ZEWDE, *A History of Modern Ethiopia 1855–1974*, London 1991; PAUL HENZE, *Layers of Time: A History of Ethiopia*, London 2000.

Christopher Clapham, Centre of African Studies, Cambridge University

Emperor Hayla Sellase and his era

On 2 November 1930 the eyes of the world were turned toward Addis Ababa: on this day *Ras* Tafari Makwannen, the regent, was crowned as Emperor Hayla Sellase I of Ethiopia – *negusa nagast*, King of Kings, Victorious Lion of Judah. Envoys from all over the world came to take part in the coronation festivities. The British royal family sent a delegation, as did Japan, Italy, the Netherlands, and Sweden. Proudly Hayla Sellase listed them in his memoirs. France, the US and Weimar Germany all sent high-ranking representatives. The word was out: in Ethiopia a veritable 'happening' was in the offing, and the international press gave it headline treatment. Ethiopia, for centuries well-nigh forgotten on the international political scene, was now front-page news.

Hayla Sellase's coronation ceremony drew upon a tradition and history reaching back more than 3,000 years, to the time of the biblical kings David and Solomon. According to the tradition, the founder of the Ethiopian imperial dynasty was Menilek I, the son of King Solomon and the Queen of Sheba. Hayla Sellase counted himself as the 225th successor of Menilek I on the Ethiopian throne in the Solomonic line. With his anointing – the heart of the coronation ceremony – Tafari Makwannen became the divinely chosen *negusa nagast*, the emperor of Ethiopia.

At that time no one could have dreamed that four and a half decades later, with the revolution of 1974, the death knell would sound for this millennia-long tradition. The events of 1974, which have gone down in the annals of Ethiopia as the 'creeping revolution', marked the end not only for Hayla Sellase but also for an empire which had endured, according to the tradition, for countless generations.

Hayla Sellase, who put his mark on the country like no other ruler before him, remains now, over 40 years later, a disputed figure – for some a ruthless dictator, for others (notably the Rastafarians) a saint. But it must not be forgotten that Tafari Makwannen was a child of the end of the 19th century, subject to all the influences at work in the Africa of that time. He was born in the city of Harar in eastern Ethiopia on 23 July 1892. It was by no means obvious or foreordained that this child would one day be emperor. It was a combination of fate and the unexpected turnings of history that ultimately brought him to the throne.

Tafari Makwannen's way to the throne. Tafari's father, *Ras* Makwannen, was a cousin of Emperor Menilek II and governor of the province of Harar since the end of the 1880s. Harar had become part of the Ethiopian empire only a short time before, and *Ras* Makwannen ruled it with prudence and – for an Ethiopian ruler of those times – an astonishing freedom and openness. He had gained nationwide fame on 2 March 1896 at the battle of Adwa. There the united Ethiopian troops under the command of *Ras* Makwannen dealt the attacking Italian military units a crushing defeat, thereby saving Ethiopia from the fate of becoming an Italian colony. This was one reason why, in 1898, Emperor Menilek formally named his cousin *Ras* Makwannen to be his successor. But Makwannen died unexpectedly of an illness in 1906.

Hayla Sellase with a palm frond on the Saturday before Palm Sunday, © Georg Gerster

Tafari Makwannen, now 13 years old, was left an orphan. His mother had died in childbirth when he was two years old. Emperor Menilek II took the orphaned boy under his wing and brought him to live at the royal court in Addis Ababa. Here he learned not only courtly etiquette, but also the intrigues of courtly society. By European standards the young Tafari Makwannen's education was fairly rudimentary. During his childhood years in Harar it consisted of traditional Ethiopian schooling and private instruction from French monks and Catholic priests. Yet here, in the open atmosphere of his father's house, he received a basic education which included not only the French language but also European thinking and the worldview of a practicing Christian. In everything that he learned later he was self-taught.

At the court in Addis Ababa, the young Tafari grew up together with his cousin *Lej* Iyasu, Menilek's grandson, whom the emperor had named as his successor soon before his death. That this was not in fact the way things turned out was due to a variety of factors. *Lej* Iyasu had the reputation of a dissolute playboy, and he hardly missed an opportunity to outwit the parvenu Ethiopian dignitaries. Also suspect in the eyes of the court and the church were his tolerant dealings with Islam, the religion of almost half the population of Ethiopia – an attitude in which he was undoubtedly ahead of his time. Most of all, however, he backed the wrong horse in foreign policy. Iyasu considered the colonial powers Britain and France as his adversaries, and prior to the First World War he sought alliances with Germany and the Ottoman Empire. This decision was soon to lead to his political undoing.

Thus it was that in 1916, at the age of 24, Tafari Makwannen assumed the regency over Ethiopia. The princes and powerbrokers of the land saw in him someone who could be bent to do their bidding. But they underestimated the strength of the young regent's will. *Ras* Tafari seized his opportunity, and was firmly determined to take up the legacy of his great role model Menilek II, who had reunited Ethiopia and steadfastly defended it against the European imperial powers. First as Prince Regent (for Menilek's daughter Zawditu), then from 1930 as Emperor Hayla Sellase, he opened up his land to the world despite the persistent resistance of the Ethiopian ruling elite, and led his country out of the Middle Ages into the modern world.

System of governing, domestic policy and initiated reforms. No one will deny Hayla Sellase's good intentions in seeking to serve his country, nor the historic successes that he achieved. In 1931, one year after his coronation he bestowed the first constitution on his country which transformed Ethiopia into a constitutional monarchy, however not limiting his power. The approaches to parliamentarism in the western sense were slim, e.g. that in spite of instituted elections political parties were not allowed. There was no separation of powers as all three were trusted to the emperor. This constitution was revised in 1955 at the occasion of Hayla Sellase's 25th anniversary of reign, with a transition from the traditional Ethiopian to Western law including some additions regarding human rights.

Cautious steps towards modernisation and reforms got stuck, like the decree on the abolition of serfdom (which had been a condition for being admitted to the League of Nations in 1923) because the big landlords did not comply with it. More successful was the building of roads, schools and hospitals albeit this was restricted to the capital Addis Ababa. Ethiopian students were sent abroad by the emperor at the expense of the state. According to his autobiography 32 proposed reforms had been implemented until 1935 so that Ethiopia was moving from Middle Ages to the 20th century.

Hayla Sellase tried to withstand the Italian Fascism and saved the unity and independence of his multi-ethnic state but his escape to Europe in 1936 was disapproved by many of his compatriots. He also violated international accords by incorporating Eritrea into Ethiopia.

Foreign affairs, travels and the Organisation of African Unity. Contrary to his domestic endeavours which were largely inefficient the emperor was brilliant at foreign policy. As soon as 1923 he induced the League of Nations to admit Ethiopia as a member state. He made a lasting contribution to the founding of the Organization of African Unity (OAU/AU), and played a fundamental part in the decolonising of Africa, urging it to solve her problems by herself. The leaders of African states were invited by the emperor to assemble in Addis Ababa's Africa Hall for a first Pan-African conference in 1963. With political discretion and diplomatic skill the emperor was able to bring the rival groups together under an African roof, thus taking the initiative leading to the foundation of the OAU. After achieving an agreement on The Charter of the OAU

Hayla Sellase was chosen its first president and called 'father of African unity'. Two years later Addis Ababa was appointed to be the permanent seat of the OAU.

Several important tours witness the emperor's intention to play a significant role in world politics. Already in his time as prince regent he visited Europe (Rome, Paris, London) in 1924. A six-month mission to the USA, Canada, Mexico and western Europe was undertaken in 1954. His official visit in Bonn was the first to be made by a foreign head of state in the German Federal Republic. Under Hayla Sellase Ethiopia joined the alliance of non-aligned states and in this connection he sought relations with the Eastern bloc and betook himself to the Soviet Union and China.

Coup d'état of 1960, crises and the famine of 1973. Over a long time Hayla Sellase remained an uncontested ruler. By and by cracks arose and the loyalty of his entourage began to crumble when he was no longer esteemed for what he had done but critized for what he had omitted to do.

During his tour to Brazil in 1960 officers of the Imperial Body Guard staged a coup against the emperor installing the Crown Prince as the new head of state. They seized the palace and took hostages who were detained and then killed; in the streets the regular troops fought against the insurgents. It became apparent that the putschists did not have the support of the people and the army as a whole behaved allegiant to the emperor. On his return to Addis Ababa he was cheered by the inhabitants. The crown prince who showed regret was pardoned but the leaders of the revolt were hanged in public. The whole affair lasted four days and claimed about 2,000 lives.

Another sign of discontent became obvious amongst the Ethiopian students who had been sent to study in Europe and the USA during the 1950s and 1960s. From 1965 onwards they took to the streets and demonstrated, together with teachers and bank employees. They compared the Western countries with the economic and political backwardness of their native country. In the early 1970s Ethiopia slipped into a dangerous crisis caused by manifold factors. The main reason was certainly a disastrous drought of several years and therefore dramatic crop shortfalls due to the climatic change. The feudal structures which still existed in the countryside (where the peasants suffered from the duties they had to pay to the landlords) added to the catastrophe. What was more, this situation was concealed from the world public; relief agencies were seldom or not at all admitted access to the ailing people. This, together with the helplessness and the inaction of the government led to mass demonstrations and waves of strikes. In autumn of 1973 there flashed around the world pictures of children starving in the Ethiopian provinces Wallo and Tegray where hundreds of thousands died and this was a highly visible beacon lighting the way to the emperor's downfall. Although various attempts were made to appease the demands of the Ethiopian students and the Ethiopian military, all the efforts to reform the country had come too late. On the morning of the 12th September 1974 a small group of *Darg* officers in combat fatigues entered the Jubilee Palace and summoned the emperor to his library. With his head held high he listened to the proclamation that one of the officers read out declaring that hitherto he was deposed from the throne. After his imprisonment firstly in the headquarters of the Army 4th Division and then in a small apartment within the walls of the Menilek Palace, the military junta declared on the 28th August 1975 that Hayla Sellase had passed away in the preceding night after failing to recover from a prostate operation.

Summing up. Hayla Sellase had set out to modernise Ethiopia following along western lines. But he proved unable to cope with the challenges of the second half of the 20th century. In the words of Ethiopian historian Bahru Zewde, 'Hayla-Selasse's greatest crime was that he ruled for far too long – and was not aware of it'. When in hindsight history passes its verdict on Hayla Sellase's 60-year reign as a regent and emperor, when his strengths and weaknesses are set in the balance, then his services to Ethiopia will perhaps outweigh the major mistakes which he undoubtedly made. Of him, too, it can be said, the greatness of a ruler can only be appreciated in light of the regimes and rulers who come after him. Or, to put it in the words of an Ethiopian proverb 'the truth and the morning come to shine inchmeal'.

Literature: Asfa Wossen Asserate, *Der letzte Kaiser von Afrika*, Berlin 2014; John H. Spencer, *Ethiopia at Bay: A Personal Account of the Haile Selassie Years,* Los Angeles 2006; Bahru Zewde, 'Hayla-Sellase. From Progressive to Reactionary', *Northeast African Studies* 2/2 (1995), 99–114.

Asfa-Wossen Asserate, Frankfurt am Main

Ethiopia after the fall of the emperor

From 1974 to 1987, state power in Ethiopia was exercised by the 'Provisional Military Administrative Council', the *Darg* (Amharic 'committee'). The radical military officers who toppled Emperor Hayla Sellase in September 1974 in the wake of nationwide protests took upon themselves the power-political role of guarantor of far-reaching and forward-looking reforms. Unlike more traditional military regimes, which typically limit themselves to replacing one small ruling élite with another, the *Darg* aimed at comprehensive, revolutionary social and political change. Within a few months the nationalist leftist junta had set in motion laws aimed at radical reforms. The 'shamefully underdeveloped' Ethiopian empire was to be developed, reformed, and modernized.

Military rule and ideological power struggle. The putschists who violently ended the 60-year reign of Hayla Sellase on 12 September 1974 started out as an anonymous opposition group of some 120 military officers. In February 1974, radical non-commissioned officers had begun to coordinate activities among the various fighting forces, and all army units received radio instructions to send three deputies to a 'coordination committee of the military, the police, and the territorial army'. The committee, later calling itself the 'Provisional Military Government', met for the first time on 28 June 1974. Young, low-ranking officers dominated; the highest-ranking person present was a major. The organizationally inexperienced committee was politically extremely heterogeneous, with little in common beyond a desire to overthrow the emperor. The political and ideological discussions that took place within the committee were of considerable importance. Plans to set up a 22-man military junta were rejected, as was a proposal to invest state power in an elected civilian government. In the words of an imperial ex-minister, '… some are half-baked radicals and Maoists … Some of the majors are very reactionary. The only thing the whole committee has in common is a general feeling of dissatisfaction. The armed forces have no crystallized opinions and no ideas'.

In mid-September 1975 the Provisional Military Government named General Aman Andom, a native of Eritrea, as its speaker. The general, who was not himself a member of the *Darg*, was trying to achieve a peaceful settlement of the Eritrean conflict. Two months later he was dismissed from his office and shot to death in his home when he offered resistance. With him died two *Darg* members and 57 senior representatives of the former regime, whose death sentences he had refused to sign. Aman Andom's successor was Brigadier General Tafari Banti from the central province of Shawa, a former Ethiopian military attaché in the USA, who had the reputation of a hardliner on the Eritrean question; as his deputies, Colonel Mengistu Haile Mariam and Major Atnafu Abbate were named. Two days after Tafari Banti took office, a 5,000-man contingent of the former imperial bodyguard was transferred to the Eritrean capital of Asmara.

Specific Ethiopian socialism. In December 1975 the military government, which upon seizing power had immediately declared all opposition illegal, published a declaration of basic principles which, despite all its vagueness, set a course for the future. In this ten-point programme the *Darg* expounded its revolutionary slogan 'Ityopya teqdam' ('Ethiopia first') and laid out the concept of a 'specifically Ethiopian socialism'.

Ethiopia must remain a united country, and there shall be no discrimination on the basis of ethnic origin, religion, language, or culture.

Ethiopia advocates economic, cultural, and social cooperation with Kenya, Somalia, and the Sudan.

1. The guiding principle of the Ethiopian revolution, 'Ityopya teqdam', is founded upon a specifically Ethiopian socialism.
2. Every region and every village shall develop its own resources and be self-sufficient.
3. A major political party is to be founded on a nationalist and socialist basis, inspired by the revolutionary philosophy of 'Ityopya teqdam'.
4. The economy shall be taken over *in toto* by the state. All wealth and property in Ethiopia belongs by right to the Ethiopian people. However, a number of economic sectors shall remain in private hands, insofar as they are considered useful for the public good.
5. The right to own land shall uniformly be restricted to those who till the land.
6. Industry shall be taken over by the state. However, a number of private enterprises that are useful for the public good shall remain in private hands until such time as the state deems their nationalization advisable.
7. The family, the basis of Ethiopian society, shall be protected from all harmful and unclean foreign influences.
8. Ethiopian foreign policy shall in essence be continued as it is now. However, the new regime shall make every effort to strengthen good relations with all its neighbours.

(Africa Committee, Materials, 1977, 14)

As a result of the uncompensated nationalization of agricultural land, the landed aristocracy was deprived of the economic basis of its political power. Banks, insurance companies, and large industries were nationalized, and the expropriation of second homes and apartment buildings led to a drop in rents and put a curb on property speculation. Moreover, all across the country the people were organized into assemblies of peasants and urban neighbourhoods (*qabale*). Together with other mass organizations such as youth and women's associations, these provided the institutional framework of a political system which in 1984 was augmented by a Marxist-Leninist workers' party.

It soon became clear, however, that the internal political power groupings in the conflict involved a central contradiction. On the one hand, it was in the power-political interests of the *Darg* to disempower the feudal aristocracy through social revolutionary intervention in the structure of property and ownership. On the other hand, in its striving for popular legitimation, the military government acted with intransigence and open violence against the very classes and social strata who stood to profit from its policy of redistribution, so long as their political demands involved any potential weakening of central authoritarian forms of government. The ruthless suppression of all opposition, the de facto ban on strikes, the authoritarian control of mass organizations, the refusal to grant democratic rights, and the government's intransigence on the question of nationalities – all this made it quite clear that the *Darg* was concerned above all to dictatorially secure its central state authority and to extend its bureaucratic control. In the face of demands for democratization and regional self-government, the military regime reacted with intimidation, mass arrests, and torture. During the 'Red terror' of 1977–1978 several thousand dissidents, mostly young people, lost their lives.

In early February 1977 Tafari Banti was killed in a shoot-out in the royal palace. Several days before, the general, whose position seemed assured as a result of the latest redistribution of governmental powers, had alluded in a public address to the possibility of a political accommodation with the oppositional Ethiopian People's Revolutionary Party (EPRP), who for their part had begun in September 1976 to murder adherents of the government. In November 1977 Atnafu Abbate was executed. At a meeting of the military government he had accused the regime of suppressing all opposition, had called into question the country's ties to the Soviet Union in the domains of foreign policy and security, and had expressed his support for a 'mixed economy'.

In retrospect, three phases of 'post-revolutionary developments' can be distinguished:

- In 1974, the year of the revolution, internal political groupings were determined by the power-political opposition between the feudal aristocracy and the spontaneous mass movement of the people, supported by factions of the military.
- Between 1975 and 1977 conflicts broke out between the civilian and the military sectors. The fundamental disagreements among the main political players (military, trade unions, intelligentsia) over the appropriate institutional forms for social conflict resolution led to civil war-like clashes, which the *Darg*, with its monopoly on state-controlled violence, resolved successfully in its own favour.
- After the crushing of all opposition (1977–1978), the military rulers set out to ideologically and institutionally secure the power they had won through violence, within the framework of an authoritarian programme of forced modernisation.

In hindsight, the decade and a half of Ethiopian military rule confirms the thesis that a predominantly military regime can only be successful in the initial phases of its rule, the stage when major decisions must be confronted. The *Darg* was unable to translate the impulses for reform into lasting economic and political gains. In September 1987 the 'Provisional Military Government' dissolved itself and handed over state power to a 'civilian regime' – still controlled by the military. Mengistu Haile Mariam, who had taken over the chairmanship of the *Darg* in 1977, continued as head of state and leader of the party.

Literature: AFRICA COMMITTEE, *Materials,* Berlin 1977; STEFAN BRÜNE, Äthiopien – *Unterentwicklung und radikale Militärherrschaft*, Hamburg 1986; CHRISTOPHER CLAPHAM, *Transformation and Continuity in Revolutionary Ethiopia*, Cambridge 1988; PLINY THE MIDDLE AGED (pseud.), 'The PMAC – Origins and Structure', *Ethiopianist Notes*, 2/3 (1978–1979),1–18 and *Northeast African Studies*, 1 (1979), 1–20.

Stefan Brüne, Hamburg

Selected chronology of Ethiopian history

8th–5th century BCE	Pre-Aksumite period, South Arabian civilization in Ethiopia
1st century CE	Rise of Aksum as a city state
3rd century	Aksum becomes a regional power, interventions in South Arabia
4th century–mid-7th century	Aksumite empire
mid-4th century	King Ezana adopts Christianity
c. 525	Expedition of King Kaleb in Yemen
late 6th century	Aksum's decline begins
640s	Aksum cut off from its Roman connections
mid-10th century	Aksum destroyed by a Queen Gudit (wrongly identified with a Jewish 'Judith')
1137?–1270	Zagwe dynasty in Lasta, rock churches in Lalibala
1270	Emperor Yekunno Amlak founds the Solomonic dynasty
1314–1344	Emperor Amda Tseyon I's consolidation and expansion
1434–1468	Emperor Zara Yaeqob, the apex of medieval Ethiopian kingship
1508–1526	Negotiations for an alliance between Ethiopia and Portugal
1527–1543	*Jihad* of Ahmad Grany
1541	Portuguese forces arrive in support of Emperor Galawdewos
1540s	Migration of Somali into Ethiopia begins
1557	Metsewa occupied by the Ottoman Turks
1622	Emperor Susenyos converted to Catholicism
1626	Enforced union of Catholic and Ethiopian Churches
1636	Gondar becomes the imperial capital
1769–1855	'Era of the princes' with puppet emperors
1855	Kassa Haylu crowned as Emperor Tewodros II
1868	British expedition against Tewodros II, suicide of the emperor
1871/1872	Kahsay Mecha becomes emperor as Yohannes IV
1882	Metsewa occupied by Italy (1890 'Colonia Eritrea')
1888	Djibouti founded by the French
1889	Death of Yohannes IV, fighting the Mahdists
	Emperor Menilek II builds a new Ethiopian empire expanding into the south
1896	Ethiopia victorious at the battle of Adwa
1913	Death of Menilek II, succeeded by his grandson Iyasu V
1916	Iyasu V deposed
1917	Menilek's daughter Zawditu enthroned with *Ras* Tafari Makwannen as regent
1923	Ethiopia accepted as a member to the League of Nations
1928	Coronation of *Ras* Tafari Makwannen as *negus*
1930	Coronation of *Ras* Tafari Makwannen as Emperor Hayla Sellase I
1935/1936	Ethiopia conquered by fascist Italy
1936	Flight of Hayla Sellase
1936–1941	Africa Orientale Italiana
1941	Defeat of the Italian forces by British troops and return of Hayla Sellase
1952	Affiliation of Eritrea as an autonomous region
1960	Somalia independent
1960	Failed military coup against Hayla Sellase
1962	Annexation of Eritrea, beginning of the insurrection
1974	Military coup, deposition of Hayla Sellase (1930–1975)
1975	Socialist *junta* (*Darg*) established
1977/1978	Ogaden war between Ethiopa and Somalia
1987	Constitution of the 'People's Democratic Republic of Ethiopia'
1991	Overthrow of the Mengistu regime
1993	Eritrean Independence
1995	Federal Constitution of Ethiopia

V Material culture

Introduction

Despite the importance of certain cultural, religious and historical bonds between the peoples of northeastern Africa, it has never been a homogenous region with almost one hundred ethnic groups, three monotheistic religions and a long history of conflicts. Accordingly, the material cultures of the region are diverse and varied.

The factors which have shaped material culture include ecological conditions (forests, waters, savannahs), modes of production, climatic zones or altitudes, as well as the impact of religion and other external influences. Affiliation to one of the three large Afroasiatic linguistic communities dissecting the territory also determine cultural expressions.

This diversity has affected, for example, the construction of houses and places of worship, the production of textiles, the manufacture of tools, weapons and jewellery, and the choice of currency. Ethiopian architecture and handicrafts represent the colourful variety of the material life in northeastern Africa.

Houses

The Ethiopian landscape is divided into three climatic zones. The south-eastern lowlands are arid and flat, inhabited by semi-nomadic pastoralists who live in simple dwellings with their animal herds. The farming region, higher in elevation with lush vegetation and rolling hills of coffee, give rise to the last remaining forests in Ethiopia. Here we find neat compounds encompassing thatched wooden huts housing extended families. The highlands are punctuated by high plateaus separated by deep gorges reminiscent of the Grand Canyon in the United States' southwest. In the highlands, people live in isolated house clusters at great elevations separated from their neighbours by steep cliffs and valleys.

While climate, materials, access to resources, issues of defence, inhabitants, and safety all play a role in how a home is constructed, house styles in Ethiopia are as easily influenced by cultural practices and belief systems. In addition, urban dwellers have access to modern building materials and today make their houses of brick with cement floors and gabled roofs. While materials change, the general shape and use of the new structure may mimic that of more traditional models.

The Ethiopian highlands are dominated by the *tukul*, a circular dwelling made of straw, dung and mud adobe walls plastered over a skeletal structure of eucalyptus branches supported by a central poll. A downturned broken ceramic vessel is placed over the central pole to keep rainwater out and to serve as an escape for smoke. During the colder months, all activities take place inside this one room home. The walls are fitted with benches that serve as sitting and sleeping spaces with storage underneath. A smaller structure outside the house may provide further storage space and a kitchen; otherwise, the cooking will be done over a central fire pit in the home. The interior space is dark so during the warmer months, most daily activity and life events including festivals, rituals, and life cycle ceremonies take place outside.

Amhara. The traditional Amhara house (*bet*) is built of stone or wattle and daub. The round houses with their conical grass roofs, topped with an earthenware dome (*gullelat*) are placed in the landscape for maximum protection from wind and rain and integrate well with the landscapes of the Amhara highlands. Since relatively cheap, locally manufactured corrugated iron became available, many Amhara houses also in the rural areas are constructed with iron sheet roofs, and as a consequence, these houses are rectangular.

Amhara households live on their land, or close to it, often in fenced compounds (*gebbi*) with at least one domestic building. In some regions one may find larger clusters of households forming small hamlets. In previous times the nobles would have a number of houses with different functions in their compounds, such as kitchen (*mad bet*), reception house (*addarash*) and guest house (*engeda bet*). Such specialised houses are no longer common.

In the extreme highlands (*daga*), dwellings are typically built with thick stone walls, often with two layers of stone with clay in between. At lower altitudes (*wayna daga*) the climate is milder and timber is more readily available. Here the walls of the houses are built with strong saplings or split trunks (mainly of eucalyptus) which stand upright from the ground, each quite close to the next. They are bound together with horizontally placed wood or bamboo. The walls are then plastered on both sides with a mix of mud and straw. In the lowlands (*qwalla*), the climate is warm and dry, and houses are simpler constructions which provide airy shelters.

Inside the building the floor, walls and the clay benches that run along a part of the wall are smeared with a mixture of mud (*cheqa*), dung, *tef* straw and ashes. The house may be divided into several rooms by semi-permanent walls of bamboo or cloth. The hearth is placed in the main room a good distance from the wall and the centre pole. There are clay benches along the walls, for household members and guests to sit on, and for children to sleep at night. There is little furniture; small wicker tablets (*masob*) are used for serving meals, and most residential houses have at least one master bed (*alga*), consisting of a wooden frame with interlaced strips of hide.

Tegray. In Tegray, the northernmost region of Ethiopia, the soil is rocky and there is little in the way of pastures for animals. Homes are commonly rectangular and built out of stone with a large singular room (*hedmo*) braced by a central post and a fireplace. Other smaller rooms may be connected to the *hedmo* with interior passages. Here the household entertains, sleeps, eats, and stores their belongings. Animals, usually donkeys, mules, calves, and goats are also kept here overnight.

Homes are erected inside a rectilinear courtyard often hidden behind a high stonewall. The *hedmo* consists of a clay or dung plastered floor and benches along the walls. A covered area in the courtyard also has plastered benches and walls to serve as a meeting place for the afternoon coffee ceremony. Both spaces are often painted.

Women are responsible for maintaining and sweeping the interior earth floor, the annual wall plastering, painting, and supplying all the furnishings for the *hedmo*.

Much of materials she brings to the marriage are part of her dowry. However, at least until 1991, men legally owned the house and its possessions.

Men in Tegray are responsible for supplying the wood for the home. As the Ethiopian highlands are today almost completely deforested, wood is a precious commodity and valuable resource. Trees are visible landmarks in Tegray and the only groves left are those that surround churches. Large trees are often the sites where local, regional, and even national policies are still decided by a council of elders who gather there to hear cases.

Traditional Konso architecture in combination with modern construction, Eco Lodge, © Horst Böge

Homes are ideally constructed of hardwood from slow growing trees like juniper and olive. The male owner and his relatives create the flat, earthen roof with wooden beams and perpendicular rafters. The same vernacular architectural style was traditionally utilized for noble and peasant houses alike, but noble houses were notably created using more wood. Often more wood was needed to create a second story loft and decorated roofs. Just as wood embellishments during the Aksumite building program differentiated elite and non-elite residences, the use of wood is still a status symbol in home construction today.

Tegray and Amhara farmers, who live just south of the Tegray region, grow *tef*, barley, oats, and other hardy vegetables on terraced hillsides beyond their small villages on the plateaus. They also have livestock and use animal fur for clothing and wool blankets for bedding. Most identify as Christian and follow the Orthodox Christian faith that includes many religious observations and dietary restrictions. Villages are comprised of ten to thirty homes that each support an extended family and these, in turn, are clustered around a circular Orthodox church. Often the church is the only building with a metal roof in these remote highland communities. The circular configuration of the church building corresponds to the division of sacred architecture in the Orthodox faith, where the most holy space is considered the centre, a space where a replica of the Ark of the Covenant resides and only the highest priests can enter. This space remains unseen by others and mimics the amuletic pouches that practitioners wear around their neck – that which is most sacred and powerful is hidden. The next part of the church is for lower clergy, then the devoted laymen and then, women. Thus, the hierarchical arrangement of power is visually apparent.

Dorze. In the central and southern plateau regions of Ethiopia, houses made with thatched walls and dirt floors are more common. The Dorze in the Guge Mountains are famous for their weaving and domical or beehive-shaped houses consisting of a bamboo structure with thatching made from *ensat* ('false banana'). The houses can reach up to twelve meters high. But over time, the structure is consumed by termites that devour the structure from the ground up. At that time, the structure may change from a home to a kitchen. A domical house can last about fifty years, the lifetime of a human in Ethiopia, before it must be replaced. Animals sleep inside the house in their own section that affords them protection and provides warmth for the family.

While the Dorze home consists of one large room, there may also be one small separate structure intended for a recently married couple. This honeymoon suite is provided for newlyweds to allow them privacy and a brief vacation from the demands of everyday life. Once newlyweds leave to create their own beehive house, this space can be converted to a kitchen.

In the middle of the Dorze hut is an open fire for cooking. There are also low wooden benches for seating around the fire. Along the walls are sleeping places and places for storage. Beyond the house are personal gardens.

Roof construction, South Ethiopia, © Martina Drewes

Gurage. The southern Gurage cultivate *ensat* and live in compounds of thatched round homes. Building specialists who are part of an artisan occupational class are employed to construct their homes, creating rounded roofs with an inverted pot at the top. The occupation of house building along with weaving and potter is a caste-like social position. Gurage women may personalize their dwellings by painting the entranceway and interior walls with diamond shape patterns.

Harar. Some of the most unique houses in Ethiopia are found in the old walled city of Harar. The wall is punctuated by five gates that historically served as points of entry for traders during its heyday as a trading centre during the 16th century. Narrow lanes paved in stone navigate between houses, each tucked away behind a high, whitewashed walled compound. Each compound had a hole in its floor to get rid of waste. Waste would be channelled into an open sewer system in the street. There were larger holes in the walls surrounding the town to let hyenas in at night to scavenge for food and clean the streets.

Referred to as *gegar*(*ach*) ('house[s] of the city') in the Harari language, the traditional homes are made of solid, whitewashed clay bricks. Each home is fitted with piped water, separate kitchens, and pit latrines. The main room (*gidir gar*) is designed for the activities of the central family. It is here where meals are served and visitors entertained, and where men chew *chat*, read the Koran, and sleep at night. This room is moulded to accommodate seated or more often, lounging guests propped up on rows of pillows. These earth platforms have a hierarchical division with the most senior male or important guest on the highest platform. Women may have a space next to this house that is considered their domain. Women are responsible for decorating the *gidir gar* walls with handmade baskets and enamelware. The placement of each piece is calculated and represents a woman's familial connects. When a son marries, for example, his wife must weave a fine Harari basket for her mother-in-law within the first year of marriage. By hanging these baskets on her wall, a woman announces how many married sons she has. A special room off to the side or in an upper loft accessible by stairs is built for honeymooning couples among the young men in the family.

The floor of the traditional and modern Harari house has either a red earth floor or a painted red concrete floor in the main room. This red floor is symbolic of the blood shed by the peoples of Harar during the battle of Challenqo. The battle of Challenqo in 1887 is remembered with sadness by the Harari as the day they lost their independence and were incorporated into the Ethiopian empire by Menilek II.

Afar. Afar nomadic and semi-nomadic in the eastern deserts of the Danakil depression live isolated and nomadic lives as herders of camel, goats, and cattle. Their fibre mats used to cover their homes are made by women from the grasses that grow near the Awash river with a structure of wood and palm fibre. This simple, temporary hut is transported by camel and is the property of women. Afar women assemble and disassemble their homes as their families migrate with their animals from one water source to the next.

Literature: JOE ARANHA, "Hidmo': Stone houses of the Tigray, Ethiopia', *Traditional Dwellings and Settlements Review*, 22/1 (2010), 57; HARALD ASPEN, ULRICH BRAUKÄMPER, ELISABETH-DOROTHEA HECHT, KERSTIN VOLKER-SAAD, 'House(s)', *EAE* III, 76–84.

Peri M. Klemm, California State University, Northridge, Amharic houses: Harald Aspen, NTNU, Norwegian University of Sciences and Technology, Trondheim

Ethiopian handicrafts

Ethiopia has a rich craft tradition. Craft shops in Addis Ababa, which cater to local elite and tourist clientele, attest to the rich assortment of functional art. They are usually stocked full of goatskin lunchboxes, horsehair fly whisks, ceramic figures, hippopotamus-hide shields, hand spun silks, buffalo horn cups, carved crosses, amber and glass beads, filigree silver necklaces, wooden headrests, and paintings on cow hide of the battle of Adwa or the Queen of Sheba meeting King Solomon. This small example reflects the geographical, cultural, and historical diversity of aesthetic traditions in Ethiopia.

Baskets. Baskets of diverse shapes, sizes, and designs are found throughout Ethiopia. Tall round baskets with conical lids, *masob*, serve as tables where northerners gather to eat *enjara* and *wat*, the Ethiopian flat bread with sauce. Tiny-lidded baskets hold rock incense and spices.

Some of the most lavish baskets come from Harar in eastern Ethiopia. Here a Harari girl is taught the coiled stitching technique at an early age. She is expected to produce baskets for use and display in her marital sitting room and during her teenage years, she may be part of a weaving collective with other girls of her age. Tradition dictates that once she marries, she has one year to complete a large, intricate basket for her mother-in-law who will proudly display it on her sitting room wall. This mother-in-law basket, *hamat mot*, is the most narrowly coiled and tightly woven of all thirty or so Harari basket types. The basket will be rimmed with leather or more commonly today, red vinyl and accented with cowry shells near the outer loops used to hang the basket. Today, many Harari girls live abroad and they hire professional weavers to make their dowry baskets with their complex patterns. These baskets are always displayed on her wall with the functional side turned inward and the decorative side outward for guests to admire.

Boorana women in southern Ethiopia weave containers to hold milk, butter, and water and make them watertight by lining the inside with the juices of the euphorbia cactus and smoking them over the fire. Each woven container differs in size and shape and while they function as vessels for liquid, the milk containers made by married women figure prominently in ritual practice, especially during engagement ceremonies and during funerals. While Boorana woven containers vary in shape size and decoration depending on their use, giraffe tail hair and cowry shells can be added to all for decoration.

Amhara peasant on the way to the Saturday market, Gorgora region, © Serge Dewel-Mouton

Baskets throughout Ethiopia are made from dried indigenous grasses that can be dyed. Today, weavers are also experimenting with acrylic yarn and plastic ribbon.

Weaving. While basketry is a women's occupation, weaving is primarily in the men's domain and is very common in central Ethiopia. Men in the highlands weave two basic garments – one that is plain, heavy and coarse used both for everyday wear and as a sheet at night, called *gabi*, and a gauze-like textile bordered with an embroidered band of colourful threads, called *natala*. The *natala* makes up the national costume for women of the Christian highlands consisting of dress and shawl, or *shamma*, that can be worn over the shoulders and head or wrapped around the shoulders and torso. During mourning, this shawl will be reversed and used to cover the head.

The Dorze and Manz areas are known for their weavers who create cotton textiles on pit-style wooden looms. Men are responsible for growing the cotton and women prepare and spin the yarn for the male weavers. Wool is also woven into rugs, hats, and blankets in natural grey and brown tones.

Preparing a loom for weaving, © Charlene Glacy

Gourds. Gourds (calabashes) are used by most cultures in Ethiopia as bowls, ladles, and cups. Undecorated gourds might serve as cups for water, beer, or honey wine (*tajj*) but decorated gourds are created for special occasions and for special people.

Gourds are planted throughout Ethiopia. After a gourd is brought from the field, the exterior is allowed to harden while the inside rots over time. It can then be cut, cleaned, and rubbed with butter. They can then be incised with decoration and adorned with leather straps for carrying, cowrie shells, fibre, or beads. Often gourds are stored over the fireplace so their contents take on a smoky flavour. The function of a gourd is determined by the shape in which it grows and how the artist choses to cut and decorate it. Some gourds are decorated with an awl and fitted with leather netting for carrying. The artist creates gourd containers based on the liquid they will hold so that milk, butter, honey, water and grain alcohol each have their own shape and size. Gourds can be repaired with fibre or metal staples when they crack. The gourds used to hold water for ablutions before the Muslim prayers are now being replaced by plastic manufactured bottles in the shape of the original gourd.

Calabashes, © Charlene Glacy

Headrests. In southern Ethiopia in the Omo River area, nomadic and semi-nomadic pastoralists carry headrests that they use as seats and pillows. As men often have elaborate hairstyles created with mud packs, ochre, and braids, these pillows keep their hairstyles intact and free of dirt and bugs. They also allow men to touch up each other's hairstyle while following their herds and away from their dwellings. Wooden headrests come in a variety of shapes attributed to regional styles. Some are made with rope handles at the base, engraved designs, and metal stitches. Over time and with much use, headrests take on a rich, dark patina.

Pottery. Pottery production in Ethiopia tends to be the domain of women who fashion cooking vessels and household objects from local clay. Coffee pots, tea sets, pitchers, bowls, cooking pots, jars, candle holders in a red or black finish are typically found in most rural households. Large pots are still the primary means of transporting water. They are skilfully made with three handles at the top so female carriers can secure them across their foreheads with a cloth or leather strap.

Female potters use their hands and simple tools to create vessels with a coiling technique. Some pots used for baking are resin coated or glazed to make them waterproof. And many potters also sell their pieces in the local markets.

Potters in most cultures are regarded as belonging to an artisan group and work in symbiotic relationship with farming and smithing. Historically, these groups do not intermarry and potters are considered socially taboo by farmers due to their occupational specialty. For example, the Gamo in southwest Ethiopia who live west of the Lakes Abaya and Chamo, recognize three endogamous castes that are restricted socially from one another but who need one another for trade: farmers and weavers are highest on the social strata, potters are next followed by smiths and leather workers. Potters may also play an important socio-cultural role to these other occupations as ritual experts, performing rites, dancing and singing at life cycle stage, and circumcising boys and girls.

The Ari in southwest Ethiopia make fifty different types of cooking pots that are classified by shape and use and are named after the food cooked in it. A typical household will own about twelve pots. Ari women may receive help from their husbands in digging the clay and firing the pots but they are the sole creators of the vessel. A girl learns the craft from her mother and is expected to excel at all pottery types by the time she's a teenager. Among the Beta Esrael, women create small ceramic figurines and scenes of daily life that may also be painted after they are fired. Today industrial wares and plastic containers have minimized the use of traditional pots, especially in urban areas.

Jewellery. Women and men wear a range of necklaces, rings, bracelets, anklets, and hair ornaments made of colourful beads, shells, bone, leather, clay, grasses, coins, and metal. The first item of jewellery given in the orthodox Christian tradition is a baptismal cord (*matab*) made of silk or cotton thread and tied around the neck. Later in life, women may add a thick silver ring, an earpick, beads, or a cross to their *matab*. Crosses can be made of wood, stone, bone or leather, or if one can afford it, a silver cross either cut directly from large silver coins or melted down and cast using the lost wax process. Over time, different styles developed and became associated with the towns where they originated. For Muslim children it is often an amulet made of leather, metal, or paper that can contain medicines or sacred substances that is first gifted a child. Among the Muslim Wallo Oromo, for example, this amulet called *kudhaama* may contain the dried liver of a hyena. In both the Christian and Islamic contexts, these necklaces bless, protect, and designate the sacrality of the child while asserting the child's religious heritage.

Aksum in the highlands has historically been an important site for metalworking and the production of fine silver jewellery and liturgical crosses. Using an anvil, hammer, and pliers with a fire stoked by bellows, smiths fashion filigree and soldered necklaces and bracelets for local consumption. For affluent clients, the metal of choice is silver, although gold is becoming more popular and for others, nickel, tin or copper alloys.

Silver often comes from the smelting of the Maria Theresa Thaler introduced during the Egyptian Occupation of Harar. The Maria Theresa Thaler, a silver coin with the portrait of the Austro-Hungarian Empress and a minting date of 1780, has remained the main source of silver for jewellery and other decorations throughout the eastern highlands.

On special occasions, affluent Muslim Harari, Somali, Argobba, and Oromo women in Eastern Ethiopia who still possess family treasures in silver or their modern replicas made of nickel, brass, or aluminium, wear cylindrical metal containers called *wakari*, hollow, granulated silver bead necklaces called *muriyya*, and metal chain headpieces with five or seven suspended chain triangles called *siyassa*. These objects, especially those of finer quality like the *siyassa* forehead band, bear direct correspondence to Arabic sources introduced at the time of the Egyptian Occupation.

Square *mergaf* pennants often accentuated with hollow silver beads, made up of thin sheets of pounded silver with a central pocket to contain Koranic verses or medicinal plants are also very popular among Muslim women. In some cases honey-coloured amber beads are added. Today, it is most likely that these beads are copal or phenolic resin rather than true Baltic amber.

Afan Qallo Oromo women have begun creating seed bead necklaces, *ambarka*, over the past three generations. *Ambarka* are constructed either of two thick, single beaded bands joined at the bottom in a series of beaded rows or two double beaded bands connected at the bottom and fringed. In both cases, the sides of the necklaces rest flat on the chest reaching from the breastbone to the collarbone of a young woman. The young women who make these necklaces thread imported seed beads onto twine in diamond shaped patterns framed within broad registers of a single colour. These seed beads from the Czech Republic are purchased in single-colour strands sold in abundance since 1990 in the markets of Harar, Fedis, and Baabbile and most readily available in white, green, yellow, blue, and red. *Ambarka,* along with the beaded headbands, *bishanni* and *challee qarmaa*, make up a complete set of torso adornment. These items are most commonly worn together by unmarried girls who are taught to bead in seclusion and who wear only those beaded items they themselves have assembled.

In the Omo Valley, Hamar women in a polygamous marriage wear metal rings around their neck to symbolize their wife ranking. The first wife's collar ring is much larger and heavier than her co-wives. While neighbouring smiths create these collars for the Hamar, women are responsible for creating their own beaded designs on their leather tunics with beads, cowry shells, and metal fringes.

Mursi women in villages near Jinka wear many bracelets, plastic and seed bead necklaces over their leather wraps, and the beaded hairstyle common to Mursi women. The clay lip plate, however, is usually only inserted when foreigners with cameras make an appearance as a means of generating income. Arsi women in Shashamane use plastic beads almost exclusively now to create their neck, forehead, and wrist adornments.

Today, men and women have begun incorporating new, imported materials into their traditional jewellery including plastic beads, buttons, metal watchbands, soda tops, and even discarded syringe caps.

Literature: John W. Arthur, 'Transforming Clay: Gamo Caste, Gender, and Pottery of Southwestern Ethiopia', *African Study Monographs*, 46 (2013), 5–25; Morie Kaneko, 'Variations in Pottery Making in Southwestern Ethiopia', in Svein Ege et al. (eds.), *Proceedings of the 16th International Conference of Ethiopian Studies*, Trondheim 2009, 383; Raymond Silverman, Neal W. Sobania, 'Silverwork in the Highlands. The Life and Work of Gezahegn Gebre Yohannes and Abib Sa'id in *Ethiopia*', in Raymond Silverman (ed.), *Traditions of Creativity,* Seattle 1999, 183–199; Belle Asante Tarsitani, 'Revered Vessels: Custom and Innovation in Harari Basketry', *African Arts*, 42 (2009), 64–75.

Peri M. Klemm, California State University, Northridge

Coinage and currency in Ethiopia

Through the ages various means of payment were used, particularly several long-lasting forms of so-called natural ('primitive') money. It was only in the 2nd century

CE that the highlands of Tegray became acquainted with coins, at a time when the Aksumite state began to flourish both economically and politically. At first there were Roman and South Arabian coins brought by foreign traders, of which the latter might have even been imitated in Aksum. Shortly before 300 CE an indigenous coinage system was established utilising the three classical metals gold, silver and copper. The coin weights were prompted by the monetary reforms of the Roman emperor Diocletian, but the pictorial programme shows distinctive features.

Aksumite coins. Traders who were busy on the route from the Mediterranean to India via the Red Sea appreciated the gold coins which they could barter when landing en route at Adulis, the port of Aksum. But, of course, they served the Aksumite king equally well for disseminating his image and building his treasury. Furthermore, they had a real economic function: the smaller change circulated at the local market centres. Nowhere in Africa south of Egypt had a comparable, coinage-based economy developed at that time; numismatically speaking Aksum was an island at the southern edge of the then-known world.

Aksumite coins cover a period of about 320 years during which they were struck more or less continuously. They make reference to a number of kings' names, most of which would be unknown otherwise as the different historical sources are less eloquent for ancient Ethiopia. These names may be allocated to 18 individual kings, each carrying more than one name (thus complicating their identification). Numismatic studies have largely been able to reconstruct their sequence, beginning with a certain Endybis and ending with a certain Hethasa, but the length of the particular reign remain unknown – the kings' lists which were compiled in medieval times, are far from helpful. All the coins identify the king with an image and an inscription, but his name is not always mentioned. Initially his title was throughout displayed in Greek as *basileus Aksomitōn* ('king of the Aksumites'); during the 5th century CE *Abassinōn* was also used (apparently the earliest reference to Abyssinia) and during the 6th century the Ge'ez term *negusa Aksum* ('king of Aksum', written in Ethiopic characters and mostly unvocalised) became regular on silver and copper coins, whilst gold coins kept to the Greek as *lingua franca*. In addition, the typological composition conveyed a religious message: in pagan times the symbol of the state god Mahrem (a crescent) legitimised the king, and later on crosses in various elaborated shapes performed this function and were accompanied by appropriate mottoes. A speciality is the partial gilding on several silver and copper types, a labour-intensive procedure by which a bicoloured impression was achieved and certain details of the images highlighted; possibly it was also meant to add to the material value, at least symbolically.

What is usually called the conversion of Ezana, i.e. the official adoption of the Christian cult by the Aksumite king in the wake of the Roman trend, is explicitly expressed on the coins, thus confirming the existence of this king and event, both of which are also attested by monumental inscriptions and tradition. This is a significant date in Ethiopian history, usually given as 333/340 CE (based on a rather legendary source), but a somewhat later assignment to 360 CE can firmly be argued.

There is a second holy king well known not only by his plentiful coinage: Kaleb Ella Atsbeha (Ellēstheaios in Greek, reigning in the 510s to 530s). Hoards of his gold coins were discovered in Yemen where he campaigned as a defender of Christianity in alliance with the Byzantines. After him six more kings are known to have minted coins, but their fates are rather obscure. It seems that they became involved in the Byzantine-Persian wars from the 570s onwards. After the occupation of Palestine (614) and Egypt (618) by the Persians the ties with the Byzantine empire and the far trade to India were disrupted, even before the rise and expansion of the Islamic state in the 630s. These developments hastened the decline of Aksum and its coin production finally ceased.

Later developments. The long centuries following till the establishment of the new Ethiopian empire of Menilek II saw no minting of coins in Christian Ethiopia; the economy got by with trade by barter as elsewhere in Africa, using certain forms of standardised primitive money, preferably salt bars (*amole*), but also iron shovels and needles whilst gold rings were appropriate for paying tribute and hoarding. Very few foreign, e.g. Islamic coins have been found and these were possibly lost by traders. Precious western coins only infiltrated during the Age of Discovery, mainly Venetian ducats and Spanish pesos. Finally the Austrian Levantine Dollar (Maria Theresa Thaler) was favoured throughout East Africa because of its reliable standard of one ounce (*waqet*). Especially after the Suez Canal was opened in 1869, an increasing influx took place and for the British military intervention of 1868 and the later colonial activities of the Italians the Maria Theresa thalers were indispensable.

At the same time in the regions under Muslim sway only the large emporium of Harar needed petty currency for its market place. Therefore the amirs issued a small denomination coin called *mahallaq* which was made of a much-debased alloy and hammer-struck with simple dies. According to the Islamic coin tradition the mint name and, mostly, the *Hijra*-year are quoted on them, the earliest certainly attested being 1197 AH (= 1792 CE); the latest were manufactured in 1885/1886, the year before the city was taken by Menilek's forces. A short time before Harar had had an Egyptian garrison (1875–1885) which was supplied with modern Khedival coins and Indian rupees were also known there. In 1892 Menilek's first small, machine-struck silver coins originated from Harar keeping to the standard of the Egyptian piastre (1/20 Thaler). In the treaty of Wechale Menilek agreed to monetary union with Italy in 1889, which provided for a common circulation of coins. Accordingly the mint of Rome produced special Italian *Talleri* and divisional coins between 1890 and 1896. However, when Menilek cancelled the treaty in February 1893 he decided on the introduction of a national coinage system which was, of course, based on the Maria Theresa standard and underlaid by the Egyptian fractions. These coins were ordered from the Paris mint (1894–1928). The Thaler, called ('male') *berr*, could not replace the huge masses of Maria Theresas (called 'lady *berr*'), but the fractional coins (*alad* = 1/2, *rub* = 1/4, *tamun* = 1/8 and *gersh* = 1/20, later 1/16) were acceptable to the urban market centres whereas the centime (*matonya*) in copper, having no metal value, met with little response.

20th century. Fond of technical toys, Menilek II wanted to have a mint of his own and one was erected and equipped in the Addis Ababa palace grounds in 1903/1904 by a Viennese firm, at that time the only mint operating on African soil. The dies were also made in Vienna and differed from the Paris models in details only. Coin production in Addis Ababa continued with interruptions due to technical problems till 1936. Presentation pieces were also struck there in gold, on demand, by Menilek, Zawditu and Hayla Sellase.

In the course of the Great Depression a coinage reform was launched in 1931 by which the fractional silver coins were replaced by fiduciary nickels and for the higher values banknotes were printed. The Italian regime during the time of the occupation (1936/1941) shut down the mint in Addis Ababa and, with limited success, tried to call in the silver money in exchange for Italian fiduciary coins and special banknotes. Only when Hayla Sellase returned from exile could complete currency re-

Coinage of Ethiopia:
1 King Ezana, Aksum, gold coin (*chrysos*), *c.*350 CE; **2** Anonymous Aksumite silver coin (*argyros*), early 5th century CE; **3** King Hataz (Ethasas), Aksum, copper coin (*lepton*), early 7th century CE; **4** Sultan Muhammad ibn Ali of Harar, brass coin (*malalaq*), AH 1279 (1862/1863 CE); **5** Emperor Menilek II, half *berr* (*alad*), Addis Ababa mint 1904/1912 CE; **6** Emperor Hayla Sellase (*warq*), Addis Ababa mint 1930/1936 CE; **7** Emperor Hayla Sellase , 20 *santim*, Philadelphia mint 1944/1974 CE; **8** Socialist Ethiopia, 50 *berr* 1984 CE, © Wolfgang Hahn

form be carried out with American aid, based on a gold dollar of account represented by banknotes; consequently the Maria Theresa Thaler was finally demonetised in 1945/1947. Thereafter the fiduciary coins were ordered from various mints abroad. The commemorative silver and gold issues still issued (with fictional denominations indicated on them) are to be viewed as merchandise for collectors.

Literature: STUART MUNRO-HAY, BENT JUEL-JENSEN, *Aksumite Coinage*, London 1995; WOLFGANG HAHN, *Numismatische Betrachtungen zur Geschichte von Akßum*, Wien 2015; DENNIS GILL, *The Coinage of Ethiopia, Eritrea and Italian Somaliland*, New York 1991.

Wolfgang Hahn, Wien

Clothing

Cloth versus skins. The clothing preferences of Ethiopians have long been determined by the availability of leather and skins, cotton, wool in some highland areas, and imported silk whose use was once reserved for royalty and the nobility. There is no indication that the widespread cultivation of cotton for woven textiles was established in Ethiopia before the 12th or 13th century, when it would have been reserved largely for use by the upper classes. For the others, early clothing needs were most likely met primarily by the use of leather and skins. During the 1st millennium there is good reason to suspect that fine leather was highly acceptable as apparel for the upper classes. More than eight hundred years later, Father Manoel de Almeida noted that the 'poorest [women] have no pieces of cloth except dressed ox skins', while many highlanders were bare to the waist and wore only a sheepskin. In the late 20th century, among the Gujji, who do not have indigenous weavers, most women still wore a traditional leather dress. This is generally the case in the less prosperous regions of the country. Over the centuries, however, there has been a general process of substitution of textiles for leather and skins.

Cotton: influences from Arabia and the Indian Ocean. Cotton weaving in Ethiopia was until recently carried out only on the pit-treadle loom, whose specific characteristics are unknown elsewhere in Africa. The type is common to Arabia and the Indian subcontinent, however, and was very likely brought from one or other of these places at the same time as the introduction of cotton itself. That date is not known, but in the late 13th century Marco Polo reported the manufacture of good cotton cloth in Ethiopia. Amharic vocabulary describing the basic stuff of textiles supports the theme of previous importation. The term *shamma* is frequently used among the highlanders for cloth and clothing. It serves to denote both a length of material as it comes off the loom, or the traditional shawl-like garment made from it. There are many types of *shamma*, all distinguished by individual modifiers which describe the physical appearance of the material or the garment.

The term *shamma* itself may derive from Persian *jamah*, meaning garment (whence the English pyjama, or leg garment). *Shamma kuta* may be related either to Arabic *qita*, 'piece' of cloth, or *qutn*, 'cotton', and *shamma gabi* to Arabic *jubbah*, a wide garment.

Other words for garments are equally revealing of a link with Arabic. The dress commonly worn by women and called *qamis* has a precise counterpart in Arabic (*qamis*) signifying 'blouse' or 'shirt' (hence Latin *camisia*, Italian *camicia* and French *chemise*). A silk *qamis* is referred to as a *qeftan* (Arabic *quftan*). Another term for *qamis* is *qas* (Arabic *qassa*, a piece of white cotton cloth). The dress made of imported black silk, called *atlas*, worn by Muslims in the region of Harar, may derive from the Arabic loanword, *taylas*, denoting oriental silk satin cloth. Amharic *maqannat*, 'sash', resembles Arabic *miqna* meaning 'headcloth' or 'veil'; *shash* in Amharic, a muslin cloth for covering the head, and *shash* sometimes meaning turban in Arabic; the *shash chera*, used primarily by the priesthood, and in Arabic *al-sayra*, a fine silk cloth. The hooded woollen highland cloak called *barnos,* has a precise equivalent in name and garment in Arabic. Similarly, people from the Dokko region of the Gamu highlands weave the *fota* (Arabic *futa*), a plaid cloth worn as a wrap-around skirt. The evidence suggests that the names for these different materials and garments entered the Ethiopic vocabulary when Arab traders brought piecework to the shores of East Africa from Arabia, Persia and India.

Even at the turn of the last century, large quantities of *shamma* cloth were being imported to Ethiopia not only from India, but also from America, England and France. Shortly thereafter, however, the availability of inexpensive imported warp thread led to a decrease in the import of cloth and a corresponding rise in local production. It may be, therefore, that the diffusion of weaving outside the highland market towns and areas of cotton production is a development of the 20th century.

Types, uses and 'language' of the *shamma*. Woven on the pit-treadle loom, the *shamma* designates woven cotton of widely varying qualities, as well as a broad range of cotton articles. One of these is the traditional wrap-around garment of the country, worn by men, women and children alike of all social classes. The lightest in weight is the most sought after: a single layer of white cotton muslin handsomely decorated with a colourful, patterned border of varying width at each end. This type is worn as a sign of elegance and wealth. Women wear it over a dress of the same material. Today, the finest muslin *shamma* cloth is often woven in Addis Ababa by men of the Dorze tribe. This highly popular material is carried by tradesmen to the major marketplaces of the country, where it is replacing regional costumes with the fashionable style preferred in the capital.

A more practical *shamma*, the *gabi*, already documented in the sixteenth century, is woven of considerably heavier cotton and is undecorated. The length varies from about two to over three metres, and the width from about 120 cm to 180 cm. The *gabi* is generally of double thickness; thus, to achieve the necessary width, four loom-widths of material are sewn together along one selvedge and opened out down the middle.

The *shamma* serves a myriad of protective uses. It is an over-garment by day and a bedroll, blanket, or sheet by night. When a woman mounts a donkey, it is not unusual for her family or attendants to raise the large rectangle of cloth around both her and the animal for the sake of modesty. In the baptism of adults, men and women awaiting the holy water squat naked behind *shamma* curtains held up by godfathers and godmothers. Infants are carried on their mother's back inside the garment. Those who have taken the Eucharist at communion hold a *shamma*-covered hand over their mouths, the whiteness of the material seeming to represent purity or to act as a means of purification. The heavy cotton blanket, or *buluko shamma*, is known once to have been offered by tenants as annual payment for a 23-ha unit of land which came to be known as 'spinner's land'.

A Shawan woman celebrating *Masqal*, © Christian Sefrin

The *shamma* reflects the mood or status of its owner according to the manner in which it is worn. When draped around the torso and thrown over the shoulders, it symbolizes an open, optimistic mood, but if one corner trails on the ground and the other is thrown across the opposite shoulder, sadness is indicated. To protect himself against *buda*, or sickness from the evil eye, the wearer will raise the edge of the garment to cover his mouth. For additional protection, or as an expression of pride, the same section might be raised even higher to cover the nose. On the other hand, self-abasement or servitude is indicated if the *shamma* is not wrapped around the upper body, which is left naked. As a sign of respect, in or near a church or in the presence of a person of stature, one is expected to drape the flaps of the garment across the chest in the form of a cross, and to leave the head uncovered. This garment language, which includes numerous other forms, probably developed because the *shamma* was everybody's everyday garb for every occasion. Only the very wealthy could distinguish mood, manner and social status by wearing different types of apparel, such as silk.

Shirts, knickers, dresses, blouses and sashes. Below the *shamma*, men commonly wear only a shirt and knickers. Ecclesiastics and the upper classes wear ankle-length breeches. Women wear the 'dress' called *qamis*, a straight-cut garment consisting of two pieces of *shamma* cloth rendered double by folding back half the length, and then folded again to form the front and back of the garment, both of double thickness. The pieces are then sewn together along the selvedges giving a central front and back seam. A small section in the central front is left unsewn, at the top of which a half-moon cut is made across the selvedge for the neck. The sides are sewn together, leaving 20 cm openings at the top for the arms. The arm-openings serve as 'sleeves' which can be pulled up over the shoulders to leave the arms free for working. The voluminous width of the *qamis* is gathered at the waist and covered by a long sash, or *maqannat*, which today invariably incorporates a 3.5 cm brightly coloured, decorative band at either end. Another sash, worn by married women, is the *denqo*.

There are a number of variations of the basic *qamis*. One common form, which has attached sleeves, seems to derive from the Arabic version of the Coptic shirt. In this case, one of the two pieces of *shamma* cloth is cut in half. One half is again divided, then folded lengthwise and the edges sewn to make the two sleeves. The remaining half is folded lengthwise and then doubled over to provide four thicknesses, two for the front and two for the back of the garment. The long edges are sewn to the corresponding edges of the other piece of *shamma*, resulting in an off-centre seam both front and back and a width only three-quarters that of the basic *qamis*. A 25cm long

Traditional clothing, southern Ethiopia, © Martina Drewes

vertical centre cut is made in front as a neck opening. A typical *qamis* of this type from the Gondar region would be embroidered on the cuffs and down the centre front from neck to hemline, with a cross at the bottom. A similar cross would extend below the neckline down the centre back to a depth of at least 15 cm.

Historically, silk garments made of imported cloth were much in demand by the upper classes, whose use of them was protected from at least the 16th century by sumptuary laws. They were presented de rigueur as gifts by emissaries to the court. Silks imported from Arabia, China, Egypt, India and the Yemen are frequently mentioned in the reports of foreign travellers from the early 16th century onwards. There was a preference at court for garments of 'Turkish style', but velvet and silk in 'Ethiopian style' were also noted. Now, as then, the silk cord necklace, or *matab*, often intertwined with a chain of precious metal, identifies its wearer as a Christian.

Literature: MICHAEL GERVERS, 'Clothing', *EAE* I, 2003, 757–761; MICHAEL GERVERS, 'Shamma, Gabi, and Kamis', *Rotunda*, 16 (1983), 38–44.

Michael Gervers, Toronto

Food

In Ethiopia, as elsewhere in the world, what has become characterized as 'national' food (i.e. Chinese, Italian, French etc.) is, in fact, a combination of different regional cuisines which have evolved over time and have also been heavily influenced by trade connections and imports. Historically the diets of Ethiopians varied depending on climate, geography, and locale, as well as ethnicity, religion and mode of subsistence (agriculture, pastoralism, hunting etc.). However, during the course of the late 19th and especially 20th centuries as the influence of the Ethiopian empire spread, elements of different ethnic or regional diets were incorporated into the 'Ethiopian' menu. In recent years, these have been supplemented by imported products, particularly in urban areas.

Breads. The most recognizable Ethiopian food is the slightly sour pancake-like bread known in Amharic as *enjara* or *tayta* in Tegrennya. Ideally made from *tef*, other grains, particularly sorghum, are also used. *Enjara* is prepared in a pan over an open fire and served on an eating plate or breadbasket (*masob*). The bread is used to soak up the stew (*wat*) which has been placed on it. Eating with the right hand only, small pieces of *enjara* are torn off and held between the fingers. The sauce is scooped up and put in one's mouth. Usually friends and more often relatives sit around a single large serving dish and eat together. A special mark of affection is known as *gursha*, whereby couples or other intimates scoop up the food and feed each other. Given its iconic status, it is not surprising that *enjara* is used as a metaphor for wages much in the manner of the English term 'breadwinner'. Thus a job seeker is said to be searching for *enjara*. This is only one example of many in which the selection, preparation and consumption of food carries with it deep social and symbolic meanings.

Although *enjara* is seen as the quintessential Ethiopian staple, there are other forms of bread eaten throughout the country. *Dabbo* is a thick, solid, oven-baked bread made from wheat which is usually served in squarish chunks after ceremonial or religious occasions. In contrast to *enjara* it is served along side the stew and other foods, not under them. In Ethiopia's southern and south-western highland regions most meals centre around *qocho*, a dense rubbery bread made from the fermented pulp of the *ensat* root and eaten with grain or meat dishes.

Wat and sauces. If *enjara* is the archetypal Ethiopian bread, its classic accompaniment is a spicy stew called *wat* which may be made from chicken (*doro wat*), lamb, mutton, beef, or particularly during *Lent* or other fasting periods vegetables, lentils, chickpeas, etc. Other dishes placed on the *enjara* include *gomman* (cabbage/kale/collard greens) and *tebs* (lightly roasted meat).

Beans and legumes including chickpeas and lentils figure prominently in the Ethiopian diet. They are eaten fresh in the months of Maskaram and Teqemt (September–November), and as the basis for stews during the rest of the year. They are an essential part of every meal either as a main course or an accompaniment. During long fasts such as *Lent* they are a staple. Legumes and grains may be toasted or boiled and toasted to be eaten as a snack. Onion and garlic are the most important vegetables in the diet, although tomatoes and potatoes (both New World imports) are today ubiquitous.

Ensat leaves being scraped for *qocho* bread, © Martina Drewes

Spices. Given Ethiopia's venerable place on the Red Sea/Indian Ocean trade routes, it is no surprise that from ancient times spices played a vital role in the preparation and preservation of food. By far the most characteristic and popular spice in Ethiopian cooking is *barbare* powder, whose essential ingredient is red pepper. Since chilli peppers are a product of the New World and the Columbian exchange, its use in Ethiopia cannot predate the 16th century. The pepper is mixed with garlic, ginger, *bassobella* (a variety of basil), *korarima* (Ethiopian cardamom), rue (known in Ethiopia as *tena adam* ['Adam's health'], ajwain (Bishop's weed), nigella (black cumin) and fenugreek. It is particularly popular in the northern highlands where it is used in the preparation of various types of red (*qayy*) *wat*. *Barbare* is also used in the preparation of hot paste (*awaze*), *shero* (a hot sauce made from oil, onion and chickpea or lentil flour). Yet another spice powder, *mitmitta*, uses a different type of chilli pepper as well as cardamom, cloves and salt.

Meats. In many Ethiopian traditions it is common to eat meatless meals. Indeed, among Christians much of the year is restricted to 'fast food', a vegan diet. This makes all the more important the many occasions on which meat plays a major role in a meal. These include Christian and Muslim feasts, initiation and other life cycle rites, and the visits of important guests. Lamb stew is commonly consumed in the highlands, while goat meat is more common in lowland areas. The slaughtering of a cow or ox is an act replete with communal significance as the meat is divided into equal portions for sale by lottery to neighbours. Among some Nilotic speaking groups oxen are sacrificed and divided up according to a code which designates specific parts of the animal to different social groups – priests, elders, in-laws – according to a fixed basis.

One oft-commented element in the Ethiopian diet is the consumption of raw meat. In some cases such as *berendo*, this consists of strips of meat. *Ketfo*, ground meat very lightly sautéed in butter and served with greens and farmer's cheese is an example of ethnic (Gurage) food, which has entered the national menu.

Chicken, although relatively cheap and easily accessible, is a status food used for special occasions including hosting a guest. It is not eaten on a daily basis. Poultry is also eaten to mark life-cycle events and is served on holidays. To serve chicken to a guest is an open declaration of deepening relations with the hosts.

Religion. Traditionally, many food avoidance taboos were practiced in Ethiopia on the basis of religion, ethnicity or gender. There is, for example, a widespread avoidance of pork among Orthodox Christians, Muslims and Jews; many Cushitic-speaking people do not eat fish. Both Christians and Jews also abstain from consuming 'fish' which do not have fins and scales, based on biblical prohibition. When members of different religious groups share a celebration, they do not eat from the same animal, because of different religious rules which govern ritual slaughter. Muslims will, for example, only consume *halal* meat. When neighbours of different religions do celebrate together, the hosts will usually provide their guests with an animal which they can slaughter themselves.

Drinks. Beverages are not usually consumed with a meal, other than coffee (whose economic and cultural significance is the subject of the following article). Milk, tea and in recent years soft drinks are prominent among non-alcoholic drinks. *Tajj* (also known as *boke* or *daadhii*) is a common form of honey-mead. *Tullu* beer is made from barley, corn, wheat, or sorghum or some mixture of these. In general non-imported alcoholic beverages were produced and sold by women

Literature: JAMES C. MCCANN, 'Stirring the National Stew: Food and National Identity in Ethiopia', in JAMES C. MCCANN, *Stirring the Pot: A History of African Cuisine*, Athens, OH, 2009, 63–106; ABBEBE KIFLEYESUS, 'Food', *EAE* II, 560–565.

Steven Kaplan, The Hebrew University of Jerusalem

Coffee

Coffee stands out as one of the major symbols for contemporary Ethiopia's national culture and economy. The labels of geographic origin from Harar, Bale, Sidamo and others are famous to coffee addicts worldwide. The ritual process of the Ethiopian coffee ceremony is promoted as the typical Ethiopian lifestyle through postcards and staging in restaurants. If these clichés say something about the importance of coffee for Ethiopians today, the history of this commodity requires to be observed beyond the boundaries of its cradle land.

Evidence and legends on the origin of coffee. The variants of the words 'coffee' in European languages find their etymology in Turkish *kahve*, borrowed from the Arabic *qahwa*.

The frequently mentioned etymology drawn from the Ethiopian region of Kafa is a later construction and confusion, initially proposed by the 18th century Scottish explorer James Bruce. While *qahwa* refers to the drink, the Arabic language has another word, *bunn,* for the green 'bean' or kernel itself. This word is found in different forms in Ethiopian languages (Amharic: *bunna*; Oromiffa: *buna*; Kafa: *buno*).

Besides these linguistic indications, the fact that coffee had been used by Ethiopian populations long before it was commercialized worldwide, is also suggested by the variety of cooking methods in different parts of the country: a paste of butter mixed with crushed berries (ripe or roasted); infusions of leaves, barks or twigs of the coffee tree in milk; whole berries cooked in butter. The latter processing is performed as a ritual by the Oromo people who call it *buna qalaa* ('coffee sacrifice') because the berries are incised with the teeth (as an oxen slaughtered with a knife) before stewed in melted butter and served in a large clay-pot to be eaten collectively during ceremonies.

The Oromo people have invested with a rich set of symbols all aspects of coffee from its cultivation to its consumption. According to a story kept in their tradition, this plant was originally grown from the tears of *Waaqa* (the Sky-God) on the corpse of a man named Buno who was condemned to death and tried to escape his fate by seeking refuge in the highlands, where he found his grave already dug, falling stone-dead into it. This story may reflect historical dynamics of conflict resolution and cultural exchange between the peoples of the wet forests, where coffee was originally grown, and the Oromo pastoralists who migrated from drier lands to settle in these areas. This narrative also indicates that the historical roots of coffee have to be understood in intercultural exchanges on a sub-regional scale rather than in the ownership by an ethnic group in particular.

Beyond Ethiopian traditions, the most celebrated legend on the origins of coffee, originally published in 1671 by a Christian Lebanese author, Faustus Nairon, is that of a herder in Yemen who was worried that his goats (or camels) were unusually restless at night. He reported this to the abbot of a neighbouring monastery (a figure corresponding to the *shaykh* of an Islamic Sufi shrine in other stories), who found that the cause of the goats' excitement was the red berries of an evergreen shrub. Trying the berries on himself by boiling them, he discovered that this decoction had an exhilarating effect and inhibited sleep. Consequently he advised his fellow monks to take this drink to keep awake during the religious services of the night. In Ethiopia other legends, probably linked to these early traditions, credit the discovery of coffee to ascetics (Christian or Muslim) who were recluse in the wilderness and received signs from God to roast and boil coffee berries to help them endure hunger during their mystical exercises.

The development of a global drink. If the good taste of coffee and its stimulating effects were originally experienced by Ethiopian peoples, this commodity was promoted and traded on a global scale through Yemen from the early 15th century. (One can note that *chat* (*khat*) was also introduced into Yemen from Ethiopia in the same period, this other stimulant being consumed through the infusion of dry leaves.)

The first treatises on the history of coffee, published in the 16th and 17th centuries by Arab and Turkish authors, ascribed the 'discovery' of this product, i.e. its spread outside Ethiopia, and the ritual codification of its brewing to the Islamic Sufi

Coffee shrub, © Serge Dewel-Mouton

networks that connected Yemen and Ethiopia. The most celebrated figures for this religious promotion of coffee are Ali ibn Umar al-Shadhili (d. *c.* 1420), known as the patron saint of Mokha, and Abu Bakr al-Aydarus (d. 1508). Even if their actual role in fostering the development of coffee can be discussed, they share common features that have historical significance: both of them belonged to the Shadhiliyya order, and both of them travelled in Ethiopia. In the early 16th century, the trade in coffee imported from Ethiopia spilled over to Sufi religious circles of the southern Red Sea and was disseminated in cosmopolitan urban areas, first in Mecca through pilgrims, then in Cairo, through the students of al-Azhar. Despite some puritan reactions and bans on coffee houses condemning the exciting effects of this new beverage, this vogue quickly became popular and soon won Istanbul where it was officially approved and became an essential component of Ottoman lifestyle. The harvesting of wild coffee in Ethiopia was not enough, however, to supply the booming demand, and coffee plantations were developed on a larger scale in Yemen.

At the end of the 17th century, when coffee won over Europe, only the upper classes could afford this high-value exotic fashion. It became a social and cultural habit through the praise of its virtues by European enlightenment philosophers and the popular success of coffee houses. Coffee has thus become one of the ingredients of the advent of globalized modernity. From one bank to another in the Mediterranean, coffee houses played a stimulating role in social and intellectual history by participating in the genesis of new autonomous public spheres. Until the 18th century, the production of coffee was confined to the terraced gardens of South Arabia (hence the name Arabica given by Linnaeus in 1753), supplemented with limited production in Ethiopia (mainly in the areas of Harar, Kafa and Lake Tana). High inflation in coffee prices, exclusively exported from the Yemeni port of Mokha, encouraged European commercial companies to break this monopoly by transplanting coffee seedlings in tropical countries to develop colonial plantations. In the late 17th century, the Dutch were the first to introduce coffee cultivation in Java. Then, via Suriname, coffee was spread throughout the Caribbean and Brazil. The growing of Arabica coffee requires a tropical climate, high altitude, shade, and constant care.

Later, in the late 19th century, Robusta coffee was discovered in the rainforests of Central Africa. Despite its being less tasty, it has the triple advantage of being resistant to rust fungus, to be cultivable at low altitude, and to have a high caffeine content worthwhile for the industry, for instance in the production of soft drinks with plant extracts.

Today, caffeine has become one of the indispensable substances in modern societies to maintain wakefulness and alertness, especially in a professional setting. On the global scale, coffee represents one of the most important commercial crops. With about half a trillion cups drunk per year, it is said to be the second most traded international commodity, after oil. In 2014, Ethiopia exported $350 million of coffee, representing 34% of the total exports, the country being the fifth producing country, with only 4.4% of the world production.

The modern expansion of coffee in Ethiopia. Today nearly half of Ethiopian coffee production is sold on the national market. This is an exception among coffee producing countries, where the bulk of the harvest is exported. Ethiopians are heavy coffee consumers. Until the early 20th century, however, coffee was prohibited by the Ethiopian Orthodox Church, for it was reserved for Muslims. Drinking coffee could even be considered an act of conversion to Islam. Ethiopian Christians began to consume coffee in the second half of the 19th century. Two historical factors have contributed to this evolution. Firstly, coffee cultivation was developed as a cash crop in the southern territories recently subjugated by the Christian armies. This production rapidly became the country's main source of income. Secondly, the integration of Muslim societies in a state dominated by Christians implied finding ways to resolve the long history of antagonistic relations. Coffee was particularly conducive to processes of reconciliation because its preparation and consumption create a convivial atmosphere that contributes to maintain good neighbourly relations. The most common oral tradition about the adoption of coffee by Ethiopian Christians states that they started to have this drink during the great famine that struck northern Ethiopia from 1888 to 1892, because they found that Muslims resisted better hunger and epidemics. For Jacques Mercier, this narrative 'expresses the state of mind of the Christians: a great misfortune reduced them to eat unclean foods like the donkey or horse, before they came to drink coffee in the company of Muslims'. A slightly different interpretation can be proposed, however. This severe famine was locally understood as a curse to punish the excesses of the religious unification policy that Yohannes IV undertook after the synod of Boru Meda in 1878, forcing Muslims to convert through mass baptism campaigns. When afterwards a more peaceful situation of coexistence had to be restored, sharing coffee was conceived as a means of reconciliation, to repair social ties that had been ruptured between these two communities. This is confirmed by the attitude of Menilek II, the successor of Yohannes, who was a fervent promoter of coffee. He expressed his taste for the drink by having it served at royal banquets, compelling high-ranking officers and the clergy to follow him. The king encouraged his Christian subjects to drink coffee openly. Through this he was committed to overcoming religious differences in order to promote a common political identity oriented towards modernity and international trade.

The Ethiopian coffee ceremony. The 'Ethiopianness' of coffee is the result of long and complex historical processes that have involved religious networks, interreligious issues, international trading communities, political strategies, and cultural adaptations. Nowadays, the ritual of coffee making has been promoted as a typical component of the Ethiopian lifestyle widely shared between cultural and religious communities. The ceremony consists of three main phases:

1. Installation: coffee can be prepared on several occasions during the day. The full ceremonial is implemented at times of holidays or to welcome visitors. Fresh herbs, ideally rushes, are spread on the floor. They may be replaced by the urban green carpet of plastic straw. The utensils are then installed. The porcelain cups without handles are positioned on a tray table. A few pinches of incense are lit in a terracotta burner. During this time, guests are given roasted grain or popcorn to nibble.
2. Preparation: once washed, the green coffee beans are roasted in an iron pan. When they are golden brown, a fragrant smoke is emitted, mingling with the scent of incense. The pan is presented to the guests who sniff the smell, drawing the smoke to their nostrils with a small movement of the hand. When the coffee is considered properly roasted, it is crushed in a mortar. Meanwhile the narrow-necked coffee pot made of terracotta, called *jabana*, is placed on the fire until the water boils. The ground coffee is then poured into the pot. After having boiled for several minutes, the coffee pot is removed from the fire and left to settle. The coffee is then ready to be served. The last stage of preparation is seasoning with various kinds of condiments: salt, sugar, honey, butter, pepper, rue (leaves or seeds), cardamom, ginger, cinnamon or cloves. Sugar, sold in grocery stores in small cones of newspaper, is currently the most used.

Serving at the coffee ceremony, © Maija Priess

3. The triple service: the first cup is passed to the head of household, or the person (usually a man, the most respected among the guests) followed in more or less descending order of respectability. Once the coffee pot is empty after the first service, it is again filled with water, without addition of coffee. The second round of coffee is lighter. Guests can politely refuse this second cup, and the rest of the coffee

is served to those who possibly had not tasted the first round. A third and final service closes the ceremony. These three services are referred to in Amharic and other Ethiopian languages by words borrowed from Arabic: 1. *abol* (from *awwal* ['first']), 2. *tona* (from *thanwa* ['second']); 3. *baraka* ('blessing'). These terms are indications of processes of diffusion and secularization of Islamic Sufi rituals mixed with vernacular beliefs in spirits that have been turned through this ceremony into a national symbol and a trademark of authenticity of Ethiopian coffee culture throughout the ages.

Literature: RALPH S. HATTOX, *Coffee and Cofeehouses: The Origins of a Social Beverage in the Medieval Near East*, Seattle 1988; JACQUES MERCIER, 'Un mythe éthiopien d'origine du café et du khat', *Abbay*, 11 (1988), 143–180; MERID WOLDE AREGAY, 'The Early History of Ethiopia's Coffee Trade and the Rise of Shawa', *Journal of African History*, 29 (1988), 19–25; MICHEL TUCHSCHERER, 'Coffee in the Red Sea Area from the Sixteenth to the Nineteenth Century', in WILLAM GERVASE CLARENCE-SMITH, STEVEN TOPIK (eds.), *The Global Coffee Economy in Africa, Asia, and Latin America, 1500–1989*, Cambridge 2003, 50–66.

Éloi Ficquet, École des hautes études en sciences sociales, Paris

Salt

Salt is an ancient trade product of Christian Ethiopia and of its immediate historical neighbours, mentioned in sources already starting from Aksumite times. It was and is not only important for its evident crucial role in nutrition for humans and livestock, but also because of its role in cultural and economic traditions of the societies of the Horn of Africa. The most notable role of salt historically was its use as a local currency, which was more widely accepted as a universal means of exchange than international silver coinage. In some regions, such as eastern Tegray, salt was the major product and political leaders obtained much of their income through taxes on salt. In addition, it is important in cultural traditions linked with food and traditional medicine. Politically, the salt regions played specific roles in land claims by polities in past times and during the creation of modern boundaries, and sociologically the salt trade helped form specific cultural sub-groups and occupational groups.

The main source of supply of salt for Christian Ethiopia was the Afar Depression, especially Dallol and Arho, where rock salt has been produced since antiquity. Further south and east, there were other sources of salt, such as the remote Afar salt lakes in the eastern deserts, supplying eastern Ethiopian regions and the kingdom of Shawa, and in the southern Oromo regions especially the crater lake of Booqee in Borana. Through the establishment of modern salines in Metsewa in Eritrea from the early 20th century, Eritrea became one of the suppliers and regional exporters of salt, like Djibouti, which facilitated the rise of salt as a cheap, daily consumed product.

Salt as currency. In historical Ethiopia and southern kingdoms, such as Jimma and Kafa, bars of salt, called *amole* (from an Afar term), were widely used as money until the 20th century, and were already reported by Cosmas Indicopleustes in the 6th century. The size and form of these bars were traditionally defined and are still traded today in the same format. Their value was higher the further from their place of origin, due to transport costs and taxation. In the market of Anderacha in Kafa, e.g. four *amole* corresponded to one Maria Theresa dollar in the late 19th century; in 1840 one silver dollar corresponded to 10 to 12 *amole* in Ennarya, but to between 100 and 110 *amole* in Atsbi in eastern Tegray. In traditional scholarship, salt bars were regarded as 'primitive money', in contrast to international coinage. They were perceived as being similar to money, but would not yet fulfil all the functions of money. This was, among other things, due to the fact that salt bars were less stable than metal and could deteriorate during the rainy season and thus the accumulation of capital wealth was possible only in a limited way. However, it has been recently argued that salt bars fulfilled all the requirements of fully developed money, based on observation of local practices. Even in the 20th century, in some regions of Ethiopia salt bars were always accepted for payment, while silver coins were rejected in some market places. In some remote areas it was still in use as currency even in the 1970s, and so well over 100 years after silver coins started dominating internal and international trade of Ethiopia. This shows that within the local economic system salt bars fulfilled all the requirements of money, i.e. were a universally accepted means of exchange. In order to make it practical as small money, to cope with differentiated prices, *amole* were also used in smaller monetary sub-units such as half *amole* (*gemmash*), a quarter (*kurman*, in Oromo: *kurmana*), and down to one-sixteenth.

The socio-political and cultural role of salt. The workers and traders who extracted salt bars from the Afar Depression and transported them formed peculiar social groups within Tegray and the Afar, were called Arhotay (from Arho, in Afar). The governor of Endarta in eastern Tegray, with his seat in Kwiha, controlled the salt routes and high taxes. His title was *baalgada* ('master of the salt'). Nearby Meqele still serves as the interregional salt market, which was one factor why in the 1880s it was chosen as capital by Yohannes IV. The salt workers in Afar (called *fenewti*) are Christians and Muslims, the trade being dominated since the mid-19th century by Christian Arhotay from Tegray. Among the Afar, a special sub-group existed, called Amole, active in the salt area until the 19th century. Also in other regions of Ethiopia, salt played an important socio-political role in local societies. In south-western Ethiopia (e.g., Beni Shangul) the value of salt for interregional trade played a role in slavery and slave raiding, slaves being purchased with precious salt. In the Oromo territory of Borana, the salt-rich Booqee crater lake attracted workers from neighbouring ethnic groups, such as Konso, who specialized in salt extraction and were assimilated by the Borana. When Borana was incorporated into Ethiopia, their first taxation was in salt. Black salt mud is still used today in a small cult site above Booqee to guarantee a safe descent into the crater lake.

Salt is extensively used in traditional and modern food and drinking practices. Traditionally, coffee was consumed with salt, a sign of wealth and care for the guest, rather than with sugar, which is a recent addition to the Ethiopian diet. In the north, this practice is almost forgotten, but it is still a standard in southern regions. In traditional medicine, a reddish rock salt called *ashaale* is popular in northern Ethiopia (it is named after an Afar area near Arho, where it is produced). In case of digestive problems it is diluted in warm water, with red honey, and is consumed, causing diarrhoea, which is considered purifying. In Borana, in southern Oromiyaa, soda with salt (from Magaadoo salt lake) is chewed with tobacco as a stimulant.

Salt in territorial politics. Salt supply also played a historical role in territorial politics: when in the 1870s the Egyptian Empire expanded into the border areas of Ethiopia near the coast and into the Afar kingdoms, it also annexed the salt plains of Dallol, with an Egyptian border post there. However, after the bankruptcy of Egypt, the Christian Ethiopian state took control over it and the area was included into the kingdom of Yohannes IV,

Salt mining, Danakil depression, © Stefan Warwas

with the governor of Endarta ruling over the Arho salt region. The southern expansion of Christian Ethiopia, led by Shawa in the 19th century, was evidently also guided by the traditional interest in salt producing areas, which did not exist in the highlands.

Control was established over the Borana salt lake Booqee, the major supply of salt in the south for humans and cattle, Magaadoo and other saline lakes.

The last lake incorporated under Amhara rule was called by them Chaw Baher ('salt lake') because of its brackish water (in Europe it was known as 'Lake Stephanie', named by European explorers in Kenya). However, it never served as a major source for salt extraction.

To the east of Christian Ethiopia, in the Afar lowlands, a claim was made to the important salt lake Asal, as this was a source of salt for Shawan traders. When the French founded their colony in Djibouti, a border treaty subsequently granted access to this lake, thus confirming the highlanders' claim.

Literature: Richard Pankhurst, 'Amole', *EAE* I, 248–249; Wolbert Smidt, 'Salt', *EAE* IV, 500–503; Wolbert Smidt, 'Salz und Amolé in Tigray, Zur Geschichte und sozialen Funktion einer traditionellen Währung', *money-trend*, 2 (2013), 166–170.

Wolbert G.C. Smidt, Mekelle University

Chat

Chat (Amharic, *jimaa* Oromo, *Catha edulis* Latin) is an evergreen shrub, endemic to Ethiopia, that is used as a mild herbal stimulant. Its use goes at least back to the 14th century and thus predates that of coffee.

Cultivation. Although *chat* can grow higher its height is normally pruned to 3–5m in order to facilitate regular harvesting. For centuries its cultivation was limited to regions in Ethiopia with a predominantly Muslim population such as Yifat or Hararge and later eastern Wallo and Gurage. Today it is cultivated as a cash crop in several regions of Ethiopia. Facilitated by modern infrastructure the trade of *chat* grew immensely during the last decades of the 20th century. This led to an increase and spread of cultivations to other regions. Current important *chat* producing regions are the area around Shashamane in the Rift Valley, the highlands around Harar and Galamso, and the Gurage region, and even Baher Dar.

Chat grows on altitudes between 900 m–2,000 m where it needs considerable care, enough watering and manure in order to produce the desired yield. Under good conditions a farmer can harvest several times a year from one plant. He breaks off young branches and chips off the older, leathery leaves before the *chat* is bound in bundles for the transport to the market. Since it looses steadily its stimulating effect after being cut it has to reach as quickly as possible its consumers.

Trade. There are three different markets of *chat*. First there are local markets in different regions like Wallo where *chat* is sold from local cultivations. Usually the type of *chat* sold at these markets can't be transported over long distance because it quickly looses its freshness and stimulating effect. The market of Addis Ababa is the most important in Ethiopia. More durable sorts like *awadey* and *galamso* come from the east, *balache* and *wando gannat* from the southern Rift Valley, Gurage-*chat* and *columbia* from Baher Dar. These sorts differ in terms of length and form of the branches, colour, taste and effectiveness. Since *chat* is normally consumed in the afternoon it is transported every night by trucks to the capital so that it reaches the markets at noon.

The *chat* export plays a considerable role in the external trade. At the end of the 1990s it was the second largest export product after coffee. Now *chat* occupies with $ 236 million per year the fourth position after coffee, gold, and oilseeds.

In urban areas *chat* is usually sold at specific locations called *chat tara*. In Addis Ababa it is also sold in shops advertising their merchandise with big billboards. While bargaining is common in the *chat tara*, it is sold in shops in pre-portioned bundles for fixed prices. In most regions the sale is dominated by men. But in eastern Ethiopia *chat* is almost exclusively sold by women.

Chat is also exported to neighbouring countries like Djibouti and Somalia. Prior to its ban in Great Britain and the Netherlands it was also exported legally to Europe.

Social and religious role. Chewing *chat* is time consuming. The soft young leaves and smooth shoots are chipped from the branches and chewed so that slowly a paste of *chat* is collected in a cheek. While new leaves and shoots are constantly added the soluble ingredients are ingested with the saliva. Thus, it usually takes time to achieve the desired state. Usually water or soft drinks, sometimes also tea or coffee, are drunk in order to extenuate the bitter taste of the *chat*. Chewing habits may differ depending on personal preferences and the type of *chat*. Some keep the paste in a cheek until the end of the chewing session while others swallow it. Depending on the specific occasion the duration of a chewing session can vary from a short period of one or two hours up to the whole afternoon and even a complete night.

The pharmacologically active ingredient of *chat* is cathinone. The actual amount a consumer ingests is influenced by factors like the sort, the amount and freshness of the particular *chat*.

Chat is consumed because of its pleasurable, stimulating and euphoric effects. It also suppresses hunger and fatigue. While it doesn't create medical addiction regular chewers might develop a certain psychological addiction.

Originally, the consumption of *chat* was limited to a Muslim religious context where it helped scholars and believers to stay alert during the night for the study of texts or religious practices like *zikr* recitations.

In the 20th century its use spread to other social groups who use it for different purposes. *Chat* cultivating farmers, who usually chew only one or two hours a day, consume it for its energizing effects which assists them in their daily work. Truck drivers use it as a means to remain awake and alert during long distance tours. *Chat* is also widespread among university students who use it to study for long hours. But the most common use in the urban context is the consumption for social and recreational purpose. Since *chat* is usually chewed while sitting on the ground, often a room is prepared with mattresses and cushions for the joint *chat* session and some incense or other scented material is burned.

Thus, *chat* chewing is basically a social activity. People discuss all kinds of matters during these gatherings. While the recreational function dominates among urban, non-Muslim consumers, *chat* can also be part of social occasions in Muslim communities, like weddings or *taziya* ('mourning').

Chat sellers in Awaday, Oromia, © Philipp Hedemann

Literature: Ezekiel Gebissa, *Leaf of Allah. Khat & Agricultural Transformation in Harerge, Ethiopia 1875–1991*, Oxford 2004; Dechassa Lemessa, *Khat* (*catha edulis*): *Botany, distribution, cultivation, usage and economics in Ethiopia*, Addis Ababa (UN-Emergencies Unit for Ethiopia) 2001.

Andreas Wetter, Berlin

VI Intellectual culture

Introduction

The Horn of Africa is home to some of the oldest pre-human remains, such as the famous 'Lucy'. After the beginning of the Christian era, the meeting of around a hundred different peoples, along with ancient trade routes and several major religions, formed a vast melting pot in the region. Influences from the Near East, Africa and the Mediterranean world combined in Aksum to form a high culture with a militarily successful kingship, an administrative system, urban structures, a centre of trade, with its distinctive architecture, its own written culture and a religion that spread across the new dominions. The people assimilated elements of culture and language from the Semitic regions of Arabia, the Greco-Judaic Mediterranean world and Africa. These cross-fertilized one another and produced a new culture. At the same time, the rugged geography of the North African Rift Valley preserved archaic societies that have remained unaffected by the so-called civilization of our times.

The introduction of a language and script which the settlers from Arabia brought across to the African shore of the Red Sea, and which is documented in Sabaean inscriptions on stone and later in Ge'ez language in inscriptions and in manuscripts on parchment, proved to be the constitutive impulse for cultural development. This is unique in sub-Saharan Africa and can hardly be estimated highly enough as a pillar of Ethiopian-Eritrean identity. The Church and literature have made extensive use of this medium. Over the course of centuries Amharic developed alongside the language of religious practice and literature that is Ge'ez. In addition, as in all pre-modern societies, oral culture in particular reflects everyday life and has produced an array of specific genres.

The visual arts have also incorporated elements from neighbouring regions, borrowing geometric figures from Arabia; adopting motifs and themes from the Mediterranean region; and plasticity, colour and vitality are African contributions – and up to the present day they have shaped these into distinctive art forms.

Christianity has exercised a great influence, dominating all areas of intellectual life: language, written and manuscript culture, literature, education, music and visual arts. In many areas, especially in the east of the wider region, Islam took on this decisive role and helped Ethiopian Islam forge its own character. The traditional co-existence of Christians and Muslims had a fruitful effect and provided the framework in which both could develop. In the past, the Jewish religion also formed isolated pockets of religion and population within Christian Ethiopia, represented by the Beta Esrael until they emigrated to Israel in two waves some decades ago.

Although Christian dominance determines the cycle of festivals and the religious calendar across a wide area, separate calendar systems still exist alongside one another, such as the Christian and Islamic calendars.

The culture of the Horn of Africa has fascinated Europe and the Western World since the early Middle Ages; it has stimulated fantastic ideas; it has kept alive through all the periods of cultural encounter the desire for an African utopia close to us, and thereby created an extensive literature.

Writing and script

In Ethiopia there can be found Sabaean, Greek, and Ge'ez inscriptions, which tell us a great deal about the early history of the country. These languages reflect, respectively, the origin of the Ethiopian Semites (Sabaean), the influence of Hellenistic culture (Greek), and the new indigenous Ethiopian culture.

Old South Arabian (Sabaean) inscriptions. The earliest Old South Arabian inscriptions were written by Semites who, migrating from North Arabia, penetrated into South Arabia (modern Yemen and adjoining regions of southern Arabia and Oman) before 1000 BCE. One of the various South Arabian groups, the Sabaeans, settled in the highlands of northern Yemen and in the highlands of northern Ethiopia. In Ethiopia they left a little less than 200 inscriptions, dating from the first half of the 1st millennium BCE. In addition to 'pure' Sabaean inscriptions, we also find inscriptions containing phonological characteristics presaging the later Ge'ez language. Of particular historical interest is the mention, in six inscriptions (8th–7th century BCE), of the kingdom of Da'amat in the area of Aksum and eastern Tegray. In Pre-Aksumite inscriptions we can see the ethnonym *ygʿḏ*, which, much later, was to resurface in the form 'Ge'ez' as the name for the language.

Pseudo-Sabaean inscriptions. Even while Sabaean continued to be used in South Arabia, it enjoyed a renaissance of sorts in Ethiopia in several inscriptions of King Ezana (4th century CE), which are known as Pseudo-Sabaean. They are written in finely formed Sabaean script, but the language is Ge'ez. Thus, even after the Sabaean language was forgotten in Ethiopia, there was a continuing desire to express affinity with South Arabian culture, and this was achieved through the use of the old script.

Inscription from Almaqah, Addi Akaweh, Tegray 2008, © Deutsches Archäologisches Institut, Pawel Wolf

Greek inscriptions. Some thirty inscriptions in Greek are attested from the 3rd century BCE to the 6th century CE, and there are Aksumite coins in Greek from the 3rd–7th century CE. The two oldest Greek inscriptions, by Ptolemy III of Egypt and an unnamed Ethiopian ruler, were set up in the mid-3rd century CE in the Red Sea port of Adulis and hence are jointly referred to as the Monumentum Adulitanum. Of greatest significance are the Aksumite inscriptions of King Ezana, which also exist in a Greek version. Here we can see Hellenistic influence at work in the Horn of Africa. There is also another Greek inscription by Ezana from the 4th century which quotes the opening lines of a psalm, thus demonstrating that Christianity had already arrived in Ethiopia.

Ge'ez inscriptions. The indigenous Ethiopian language was committed to writing at the time of the expansion of the Aksumite empire, from the 3rd century CE onwards. The earliest inscriptions were still unvocalized. The inscriptions of King Ezana, excavated by Enno Littmann et al. during the Deutsche Aksum-Expedition of 1906, have pride of place among Ge'ez inscriptions. North Ethiopia at that time belonged to both the Greek and the South Arabian world, but was also becoming conscious of its own special cultural and linguistic identity. Accordingly, a number of the inscriptions appear in parallel versions involving three scripts (Greek, Sabaean, Ge'ez) and two languages (Greek and Ge'ez), with Ge'ez also appearing in its Pseudo-Sabaean guise (i.e. Ge'ez in Sabaean letters).

The inscriptions tell of military campaigns and resettlement of peoples, and a good many of the names of places and peoples are quite recognizable today, e.g. Barya, Beja, and Habashat (Abyssinia). Testimony to Ezana's conversion to Christianity comes from an inscription in which the divinity is invoked, not as 'the undefeated Mahrem [Sabaean]/Ares [Greek]', but as the 'Lord of Heaven'. A Ge'ez inscription from around 600 CE, which was discovered in South Arabia, contains quotations from the Psalter (called by its Ge'ez name *mazmur* in the inscription itself), thus indicating the special importance of the Psalter for the Ethiopian Church already at this early date. This is evidence for an early translation of at least parts of the Bible into Ge'ez.

In the course of time, Greek and Sabaean ceased to play any role in Ethiopia. But the language of the north-central Ethiopian highlands took on greater and greater importance.

Vocalizing the Sabaean script. In Old South Arabian, as in the other old Semitic inscriptional languages, the vowels were not written. This makes some sense, inasmuch as, to a certain degree at least, the vowels can be inferred from the structure of the language. Thus the perfect form of the verb *q-t-l* 'he killed' is read as *qatala,* since most verbs follow the vowel pattern *.a.a.a* in the 3rd person masculine singular. With the advent of Christianity and of missionary activity, however, the desire arose to prevent misreadings of the Holy Scriptures. In the Orient this held true not only for Christianity but also for the Hebrew Old Testament and the Muslim Koran. Thus in Syriac, Hebrew, and Arabic a system of diacritic signs (especially vowel signs) was developed – circles, curves, dots and strokes – which were placed above and below the consonant letters in order to unambiguously convey a particular reading.

For Ge'ez, by contrast, a very different and remarkable path was taken which is unparalleled in the Semitic world. Crucial here is the fact that Ethiopia was in close contact with India; maritime trade went via the island of Soqotra, located east of Somalia and south of Yemen, where in fact Indian inscriptions were recently discovered in a cave. Following the model of the Indian writing system, the principle was taken over whereby each basic consonantal sign was now to be vocalized with *-a*, while the other vowels were expressed by various strokes and curves that were added directly to the consonantal sign itself. Not all of the Ge'ez signs are transparently recognizable as being of South Arabian origin (e.g. the sign ለ *la*, see Table); but the differences are not great. Indeed, there was little difficulty in deciphering Old South Arabian in the 19th century, on the basis of Ge'ez.

By way of illustration, the Sabaean sign *b* is read in Ge'ez as በ *ba*; with the addition of a short stroke halfway up the right side, as ቡ *bu*; with a short stroke at the bottom right, as ቢ *bi*; with a lengthening of the right leg (or shortening of the left leg), as ባ *bā*; etc. Another example: ቀ *qa*, ቁ *qu*, ቂ *qi*, ቃ *qā*. Altogether, for every consonant, there are seven consonant-vowel syllabic signs.

The consonant signs themselves sometimes underwent modification. Thus some South Arabian signs are turned upside down, e.g. ሐ *ḥa*; or tipped to the left, መ *ma*; or to the right, ደ *da*, ሠ *śa*. In conformity with Greek and Indian writing, the direction of the script was inverted, so that – unlike Hebrew, Arabic, and Syriac – Ge'ez writing runs from left to right.

In the following Sabaean-Ge'ez comparative table, the letters are presented in the traditional Ge'ez alphabetical order; the Old South Arabian letters (which in fact had a partly different ordering) are made to conform to this ordering schema. The table omits those South Arabian letters which, because of sound changes, were not necessary for writing Ge'ez and were not taken over. On the other hand, Ge'ez writing created new letters for plain p and glottalized p (*p̣*), primarily in order to write Greek words, e.g. *P̣awlos* 'Paul', *P̣eṭros* 'Peter'.

Sabaean letters	Ge'ez alphabet	Sabaean letters	Ge'ez alphabet
𐩠 *h*	ሀ *ha*	𐩫 *k*	ከ *ka*
𐩡 *l*	ለ *la*	𐩥 *w*	ወ *wa*
𐩢 *ḥ*	ሐ *ḥa* (strongly whispered *h*)	𐩲 *ʿ*	ዐ *ʿa* (strong glottal stop)
𐩣 *m*	መ *ma*	𐩹 *ḏ*	ዘ *za*
𐩦 *ś*	ሠ *śa* (lateral sound)	𐩺 *y*	የ *ya*
𐩧 *r*	ረ *ra*	𐩵 *d*	ደ *da*
𐩯 *s*	ሰ *sa*	𐩴 *g*	ገ *ga*
𐩤 *q*	ቀ *qa* (glottalized *k*)	𐩷 *ṭ*	ጠ *ṭa* (glottalized *t*)
𐩨 *b*	በ *ba*	–	ጰ *p̣a* (glotalized *p*) (modelled on Eth. ጸ)
𐩩 *t*	ተ *ta*	𐩮 *ṣ*	ጸ *ṣa* (glottalized *ts*)
𐩭 *ḫ*	ኀ *ḫa* (ch as in German Bach)	𐩳 *ṣ́*	ፀ *ṣ́a* (glottalized lateral *ts*)
𐩬 *n*	ነ *na*	𐩰 *f*	ፈ *fa*
𐩱 *ʾ*	አ *ʾa* (glottal stop)	–	ፐ *pa* (modelled on Gk. π Π *pi*)

Table 10: Sabaean and Ge'ez script

Literacy and the literary language. It can be assumed that only a small fraction of the population of the greater Aksumite empire had a command of the language of the royal household, the dialect of Aksum. As texts became easier to read (thanks to the vocalized writing system), this language spread. This assumes, of course, an increase in the use of writing in the administration and above all in the Church and in schools. Later, alongside religious subjects, the monastery schools also taught singing, grammar, poetry, and literature. Until the 19th century education lay in the hands of the Ethiopian Orthodox Church, whose schools taught the Ge'ez language, the Bible in its Ge'ez translation, and the rich literature in Ge'ez.

It was only in the mid-19th century, in Protestant (and Catholic) schools, that the various modern Ethiopian languages began to be used and, to a degree, the modern western curriculum was instituted. The Bible and other religious writings – and gradually other works, for example texts on arithmetic and folk traditions – were translated and circulated in Amharic, Tegrennya, Oromo, and other languages of the Horn of Africa. As a result of this activity, many local languages were committed to writing, although until the time of Emperor Hayla Sellase only Amharic was used in the public sphere.

The modern Ethiopian-Semitic languages Tegre, Tegrennya, and Amharic are written in the Ge'ez script. The Cushitic languages Oromo, Somali, and Afar are written in the Latin alphabet. This represents the official language policy of Ethiopia and Eritrea. In Ethiopia, however, this policy is not totally strict. Nothing stands in the way of Cushitic languages being written in Ge'ez script, and Oromo in particular is still sometimes written in its older Ge'ez orthography. For the major Ethiopian languages Sidamo (*c.* 2 million speakers), Hadiyya (over 1 million), and Wolaitta (*c.* 2 million), the Ge'ez script competes to a degree with the Latin alphabet. Among Muslim communities across Ethiopia, numerous local languages are on occasion written in Arabic letters (so-called *ajami*).

Of the smaller languages, only Harari and various Gurage idioms can claim to be written languages. Harari, formerly written in Arabic letters, is written today in the Ge'ez script. In the city of Harar, written Harari can be seen on signs in schools and public buildings. There is also a more recent and relatively rich literature in this language spoken by approximately 20,000 Harari.

Literature: Alessandra Avanzini, Norbert Nebes, Walter W. Müller, Gianfranco Fiaccadori, Serguei A. Frantsouzoff, Alessandro Gori, 'Inscriptions', *EAE* III, 2007, 152–167; Enno Littmann, *Deutsche Aksum Expedition*, IV: *Sabaische, griechische und altabessinische Inschriften*, Berlin 1913; Serguei A. Frantsouzoff, 'Script, Ethiopic', *EAE* IV, 580–585.

Rainer Voigt, Berlin

Manuscript tradition

In Ethiopia and the Horn of Africa the term 'manuscripts' is usually used to mean handwritten documents on parchment or, less frequently, on paper, either in book form, called codices in manuscript studies, or in the form of scrolls. The Christian, Islamic and Beta Esrael cultures of Ethiopia and Eritrea have developed and been transmitted mainly through the production and preservation of numerous texts in manuscript form. These texts cover a range of fields, mostly religious, but also historical and literary, and are expressed in a range of languages, especially Ge'ez, Arabic and Amharic, and to a lesser degree Harari, Tegrennya and others. The exceptional importance of manuscripts in Ethiopian culture is due to the comparatively late introduction of the extensive use of printing to the region in the late 19th century. Ethiopia and Eritrea are among the few countries in the world where the production of manuscripts on parchment is still alive. The tradition of producing manuscripts is firmly rooted in the distinct past of the region, where unlike most sub-Saharan countries, there is an ancient tradition of writing, in the case of Ethiopia and Eritrea, going back to the 1st millennium BCE, which has played a major role in the development of civilization.

Ethiopic manuscripts. The overwhelming majority of Christian manuscripts from Ethiopia and Eritrea are written in Ge'ez (or Ethiopic). Some, mostly non-religious manuscripts in Amharic appear from the mid to late 19th century onwards. The total number of extant Ethiopic manuscripts is not known, but an estimate of over 200,000 in book or codex form seems realistic for those in Ethiopia and Eritrea, bearing in mind the minimum number needed by every church for religious and liturgical use, as well as the sometimes extensive collections still preserved in monastic libraries such as those at Dabra Hayq Estifanos, Dabra Bizan, Gunda Gunde and Aksum Tseyon. There are also rich institutional collections in the Library of the Institute of Ethiopian Studies and the National Archives and Library of Ethiopia, both in Addis Ababa. The number of manuscripts abroad must run into several thousands, most of them in national and other public collections in Europe (e.g. Vatican City, Paris, London and Berlin) and elsewhere (e.g. Princeton, UCLA Los Angeles). There are also a few, quite extensive collections in private hands.

Although writing in Ethiopia and Eritrea predates the adoption of Christianity in the 4th century CE, it was undoubtedly the latter that gave the greatest impulse to the production of manuscripts, ostensibly for use in the daily life of the church. The oldest surviving manuscripts, however, date from long after this. Aside from two illustrated Gospel books that have now been dated to the 7th or perhaps the 5th/6th century and a few more datable to the 12th to 13th centuries, the oldest surviving Ethiopic manuscripts date to the 14th century. The number of manuscripts increases exponentially from the 16th and 17th centuries onwards. Tradition ascribes the destruction of many manuscripts to the upheavals of the mid-16th century, but other vagaries of time (including the 1935–1941 war) are likely to have reduced the number of survivals.

Dating Ethiopic manuscripts can be a difficult or at least an imprecise exercise as only some give a formal indication such as mention of a king or another known individual or event. Otherwise, dating has to be done on the basis of the form and style of the script (known as palaeography) or any paintings incorporated in the text, which is why many manuscripts can only be given an approximate date. Though Ethiopian calligraphy and religious art are conservative by nature, letter forms and features of painting style do change over time and can usually be used to give an approximate date to a manuscript.

The art of producing manuscripts on parchment is still alive in Ethiopia. Manuscripts are even today more highly prized than printed books, especially in church circles. Manuscripts are produced today in much the same, if not the identical way as they have been for centuries. It is undoubtedly this fact that lies behind the continuing interest in Ethiopian manuscripts and manuscript culture today. Though nowadays often made for the tourist market, manuscripts are still produced for their original function as an important part of Ethiopian Orthodox culture and life. In particular, despite the great changes that have occurred in Ethiopia during the 20th century, Ethiopian manuscript culture can still be found in a few places in settings

Gospel of St Luke, Gannata Maryam Church, Lalibala, © Michael Gervers

which continue the original medieval context and manuscripts are revered as sacred objects of the church, especially in conservative rural areas. The commonest texts reflect the place of manuscripts in the devotional lives of many Christian Ethiopians, with Psalters (Book of Psalms together with some other texts), Miracle books (especially the Miracles of Mary) and collections of prayers being the most popular.

The commonest form of manuscript is the book or codex of varying sizes (called *mashaf*), comprising gatherings or quires of parchment sheets folded to form a number of leaves and sewn together and fastened between wooden boards, which may in turn be covered with fine leather which is often tooled with designs incorporating crosses. Smaller and middle-sized manuscripts are often provided with a hide case complete with carrying strap. Quires are sometimes numbered as an aid to binding, but individual leaves or pages are not traditionally numbered. Sometimes extra leaves or pairs of leaves are sewn on to the quires, often to accommodate paintings. Blank pages or sections of pages, especially at the front or at the back of a manuscript, were traditionally used to record contracts, deeds of gift or historical events relevant to the church that owned the manuscript. As such, manuscripts can be valuable historical sources particularly for local history. The blank leaves which are to be used for written text are first scored with a sharp instrument to mark the lines and margins before writing.

Usually, two columns are prepared for the text, though very small manuscripts may only have a single column, which is also the norm for some texts, most notably the Book of Psalms. This latter always has lines of unequal length relating to the stanzas of the psalms. Some texts, especially in large-format manuscripts of church liturgy are often written in three columns.

Gospel of St Matthew, Sawna Maryam Church, Tegray, © Ethio-SPaRe, Hiob Ludolf Centre for Ethiopian Studies, Hamburg

The text or texts themselves are typically written in black ink traditionally made from soot and vegetable substances, often with opening lines of sections and textual divisions, key phrases and especially sacred names (e.g. Mary, Jesus, Michael, Gabriel, etc.) in red ink made of vegetable substances. In recent years, commercially produced inks and colours have started to be used. Very rarely, other coloured inks have been used for writing the text since the mid to late 19th century. During the writing process scribes would leave spaces for the insertion of the red sections (rubrics), which were occasionally never filled in.

The more prestigious manuscripts contain paintings, sometimes on separate leaves bound separately at the beginning and end of the book. At other times, blank pages are left in the text for the incorporation of paintings, and at other times half-page or smaller paintings are placed within the text. These are especially common in manuscripts with extensive cycles of paintings or miniatures, for example such as the Miracles of Mary. The painting of miniatures is mostly entrusted to specialists, some of the most outstanding and sumptuous examples of whose work can be seen in the great museum and library collections. As may be appreciated, the production of such manuscripts is a long process especially when the preparation of the parchment from goat or sheepskin is taken into consideration. Some especially large manuscripts may take up to a year and a half to produce, and medium-sized ones such as a Gospel book or a Psalter may take half a year. The entire process including writing and painting is done outdoors and so in daylight, typically in the grounds of a church or monastery. The class of Ethiopian cleric known as *dabtara* plays an important part in manuscript production. Perhaps oddly to non-Ethiopians, copying skills and writing manuscripts are traditionally considered tasks of lower prestige. Perhaps equally strange to non-Ethiopians, new copies of manuscripts are often regarded as more valuable than old ones, though it sometimes happens that older paintings are incorporated into newer texts. In 1911 Menilek II established a royal scriptorium in Addis Ababa to supply the churches of the new capital with the necessary manuscripts and this was later re-organized by Hayla Sellase, surviving until the revolution.

The codex format is used primarily for religious texts: parts of the Old Testament, the Gospels, the Pauline and apostolic epistles, the Apocalypse of John, the Psalter, Lives of Saints, Miracles of Mary, the Archangels and Saints, liturgical books for use during church services, private prayer and other devotional, theological and canonical books, and so on. Also to be found in this format are books of magical and medicinal remedies, including books of astrology and numerology and other divination techniques, as well as manuals for the preparation of 'magic' scrolls. Royal chronicles and other histories are also recorded in codex format. It should also be noted that many manuscripts contain more than one text and individual 'books' are not always provided with an overt title.

Not all Ethiopic manuscripts have the book or codex format. Another format consists of a strip of parchment, or two or three strips sewn together, folded in concertina fashion. This format is called *sansul* ('chain') and is usually used for a series of paintings, often of saints or sometimes events from a narrative, such as martyrdoms or the Passion of Christ. Occasionally, these contain more than just a few lines of descriptive text. A third, very common manuscript format is that of the so-called magic scrolls, called *ketab*. These consist usually of one, two or three pieces of parchment sewn together and rolled up lengthways, and are used for 'magical' prayers or spells for protection from sickness and other ills, often understood as the work of evil spirits. Magic scrolls also usually contain talismanic drawings at the top, in the middle and at the bottom and sometimes talismanic symbols and designs elsewhere in the text. They are rarely produced with the care and finesse that can be seen in the production of codices. They are after all meant as amulets either rolled up and worn on the person, or suspended on a wall by the owner's sleeping place.

Arabic manuscripts. The situation with Ethiopian and Eritrean manuscripts in Arabic, or in another language such as Harari or Amharic written in Arabic script (called *ajami*), is much more poorly researched than that of Ethiopic manuscripts. We cannot even be certain how many Arabic and *ajami* manuscripts there are in the region. Collections in Ethiopian libraries may only run to a few hundred, though there are doubtless many more in private hands or stored in places unsuitable for proper preservation. This latter aspect is quite different from the situation of Christian manuscripts, where a central role is assigned to Church institutions both for production and storage. Whilst the natural assumption is that Arabic manuscripts must be Islamic, we should not forget that Arabic is not exclusive to Muslims. A considerable amount of Ethiopic (Ge'ez) Christian literature was translated from Arabic, especially from Egyptian sources, and Arabic manuscripts must have been circulating in Ethiopia since earliest times, although no model manuscripts have survived. Additional notes also in Christian manuscripts are at times written in Arabic. However, as Arabic is the language of religion and education in Islam, Arabic texts are naturally widely spread among Muslim communities in Ethiopia and Eritrea, as well as of course in Somalia and Djibouti. Undoubtedly many Arabic manuscripts were imported by itinerant clerics or traders, though because of the habit of copying and commenting on texts locally a good number are of Ethiopian or Eritrean origin.

Three regions that are known as centres for the copying and distribution of Arabic manuscripts are Harar, Wallo and Jimma, as well as most probably Gurage-Land.

Most Arabic manuscripts in Ethiopia are of relatively recent date and do not have the antiquity of Ethiopic manuscripts. No surely dated Arabic manuscript seems to be earlier than the 18th century, though a handful containing 16th century dates of copying have been reported. Some of these may have been imported from Yemen. All Arabic manuscripts are written on paper and exhibit all the features typical of the broader Islamic manuscript culture. The size of Arabic manuscripts varies from just several pages to voluminous works that can include several texts, and sometimes loose pages are inserted into larger manuscripts. Purely Arabic works, whether local or foreign, are occasionally found in one and the same manuscript with texts written in local languages written in Arabic script (*ajami*). For example, the Library of the Institute of Ethiopian Studies in Addis Ababa possesses three mixed Arabic and Harari manuscripts. Whilst no complete study has yet been undertaken of styles of handwriting used in Arabic manuscripts in Ethiopia, there are some features that call to mind some Arabic manuscripts originating from northern Somalia. Older manuscripts from the region of Harar seem to show a more careful calligraphy, whereas more modern ones often show the more clumsy and thicker hand found elsewhere. As yet, however, it is not possible to discuss the relationship between different handwriting styles in the Horn of Africa. Some Ethiopian Arabic hands, like those from Somalia, may nonetheless have been influenced by Yemeni styles.

Literature: Alessandro Bausi et al., *Comparative Oriental Manuscript Studies: an Introduction*, Hamburg 2015 (also at http://www1.uni-hamburg.de/COMST/handbook.html); Sergew Hable Selassie, *Bookmaking in Ethiopia*, Leiden 1981; Siegbert Uhlig, Alessandro Bausi, 'Manuscripts', *EAE* III, 738–744; Ewald Wagner, *Afrikanische Handschriften*, Teil 2: *Islamische Handschriften aus Äthiopien*, Stuttgart 1997.

David Appleyard, SOAS, London

Ge'ez literature

Ge'ez (also called Classical Ethiopic or just Ethiopic) was the language of Aksum. The oldest survivals of Ge'ez are inscriptions dating from the early 3rd century CE, but it was the adoption of Christianity around a hundred years later, in the first half of the 4th century, that provided the impetus for and governed the nature of Ge'ez literature. It is more than likely that there was a Ge'ez oral literature before then, but we do not know if any was ever committed to writing. Ge'ez literature is predominantly religious and Christian, comprising not just the Bible and a whole range of texts used in daily Church practice and ritual such as liturgies and hymns, but also writings of Church Fathers, theology and spirituality, Lives of saints and religious poetry. The major exceptions to this religious character are the royal and other histories (or chronicles), and the exception to its Christian nature is the much smaller religious literature of the Beta Esrael.

Two things stand out about Ge'ez literature when compared, for instance, with Western European literatures. In the first place, it is in large part a literature of translation. There are exceptions (i.e. original Ethiopian compositions) such as the chronicles and some religious treatises and discourses (homilies), as well as Lives of indigenous saints and religious poetry. The second notable feature of Ge'ez literature is that a great deal of it, including the later translations, were written after Ge'ez had ceased to be a spoken, vernacular language. In this it somewhat resembles the use of Latin in medieval Western Europe. We do not precisely know when Ge'ez, or what would be a recognizable form of Ge'ez ceased to be spoken, but it is likely to have been no later than the 10th or maybe the 11th century at the latest. Of course, the language will have evolved continuously and indeed the Ge'ez of the Aksumite inscriptions is slightly different in some details from that of the later Christian literature.

Once established as a written language of literature, the form of the language will have gradually become standardized and fixed, which will have happened during the time of the Bible and other early translations in the 4th to 6th centuries. This is the form of Ge'ez that has continued in all subsequent literature, aside from a few small influences from the spoken languages (Amharic, Tegrennya) of translators, authors and scribes.

Early period. In the following brief survey of Ge'ez literature, it is customary to speak of two periods: an Aksumite or Early Period and a Post-Aksumite or Later Period. The former runs from the adoption of Christianity circa 330 CE to the end of the kingdom of Aksum as a political and institutional entity, not much later than the 7th century CE. During this period Ge'ez literature comprised translations, primarily from Greek, and possibly a local production that has not been transmitted as such, but reworked in later compositions. At this time most of the Christian East, including the Coptic Church of Egypt with which the Ethiopians had a close relationship, used Greek as the main written language.

The first and most important text to be translated was of course the Bible. Evidence strongly suggests that translation was a long and somewhat piecemeal process, beginning with the Gospels perhaps already in the late 4th or early 5th century. By the end of the 6th century the translation of most of the Bible text was completed and there is no reason to doubt that all had been finished by the start of the 7th century at the latest.

Ethiopian tradition speaks of missionary monks coming to Ethiopia from the Eastern Mediterranean world bringing their books with them, presumably written in Greek, and these must have provided a great impetus to the translation process. Other early Christian texts translated into Ge'ez at this time include the collection of homilies by Church Fathers called the *Qerellos*, named after St Cyril of Alexandria, the monastic rules of the Egyptian Abbot Pachomius, and most interestingly a handful of non-canonical works that only survive in their entirety in the Ge'ez translations, such as the Books of Enoch and Jubilees. Tradition also ascribes the composition of the Liturgy, known as the *Deggwa*, to this period and specifically to the Ethiopian

St Yared, who reportedly flourished during the first half of the 6th century, although the earliest evidence about him dates from the 15th century.

Later period. Most Ge'ez literature, both translations and original works, was produced in this period and specifically following the rise of the so-called Solomonic dynasty in 1270. One piece of literature that has aroused some interest outside Ethiopia and which seems to have first reached the country prior to this date during the Zagwe Dynasty is the *Kebra nagast* or Glory of the Kings, which relates how the Ethiopians became the chosen people of God in place of Israel and was used to establish the legitimacy and descent of the Solomonic Dynasty. The original was, therefore, translated from the Arabic original into Ge'ez only after 1270. Throughout this Later Period Arabic, and specifically Christian Arabic, was the language from which Ge'ez translations were made. At the same time, original works in Ge'ez began to be written, both religious and, from the mid-14th century onwards, historiographical in the

Pupils memorizing Psalms in Ge'ez, Koholo Maryam, Tegray, © Ethio-SPaRe, Hiob Ludolf Centre for Ethiopian Studies, Hamburg

form of royal chronicles. Some Christian Arabic literature from Alexandria seems to have reached Ethiopia in the previous century or so, but it was the arrival of *Abba* Salama as the Head of the Ethiopian Church (1348–1388) that marked the flourishing of Ge'ez literature over the next two centuries. He was given the nickname of 'The Translator' because either directly or indirectly he brought about the translation of a host of religious works, and from this period date many important texts such as the Lectionary for Holy Week, numerous Lives of saints, desert fathers and martyrs, the *Filkesyos* (a major work of monastic literature), the funerary ritual, as well as two source works of Ethiopian canon law (the *Senodos* and the *Didesqelya*), while the Synaxarion (*Senkessar*) or compendium of saints with short commemorations and biographies for the whole year was accomplished a few decades later.

During the late 14th and 15th centuries Ethiopian scholars began to expand Ge'ez literature into topics beyond what direct translations could provide, though still building on that translated literature. The first (pseudo)historical work that is more epic in form, namely the so-called Chronicle of Amda Tseyon I, may be mentioned here. Most famous of all are the writings of King Zara Yaeqob (r. 1434–1468). He is credited with expanding the Book of the Miracles of Mary, the translation of which was begun under his father. He is also credited with writing a number of theological and Christological works at a time of great debate, controversy and dispute. From around this same time also dates the creation of a special style of hymn, known as *malke* ('likeness'), praising part by part the body of a saint, and the distinctive type of originally religious poetry known as *qene*, which uses layers of imagery and meaning. Lastly, also dating from this period is the translation of a most important work, the *Fetha nagast* or 'Law of the kings', a collection of ecclesiastical and civil laws which remained in use by the Ethiopian state until the first half of the 20th century and is still used by the Church. Despite the turmoil of the 16th and early 17th centuries caused by the invasion of the Muslim forces of Ahmad Grany and then the migrating Oromo, this period saw a flourishing of literature, both translations and original works, including the chronicles of Kings Galawdewos, Minas, Sartsa Dengel and Susenyos. Another important work from this period is Abba Bahrey's 'History of the Galla', a brief ethnography of the Oromo and account of their migrations into Ethiopia.

With the rise of writing in Amharic and later Tegrennya during the 19th century, the production of new Ge'ez literature faded. Existing texts of course continued to be copied and some religious poetry created, whilst the only new creations (and perhaps even these are copied from older sources) are in the 'fringe' area of magic spells, curses and charms.

Literature: ENRICO CERULLI, *La letteratura etiopica: L'Oriente cristiano nell'unità delle sue tradizioni*, 3rd edn, Milano 1968; GETATCHEW HAILE, 'Ge'ez literature', *EAE* II, 736–741.

David Appleyard, SOAS, London

Amharic literature

Early writing. For many centuries Ethiopian literature was written almost exclusively in Ge'ez. Amharic played the important role of medium of communication at the royal court and functioned as a *lingua franca* of the Ethiopian highlands but it appeared only sporadically in writing. The few Amharic texts composed between the 14th and the mid-19th century include praise poems dedicated to the emperors, religious treatises, biblical commentaries, prayers translated from Ge'ez and historical accounts. The archaic form of Amharic evidenced in these texts, different from the modern language, is known as Old Amharic.

The establishment of Modern Amharic as a literary language, and then as the main vehicle of Ethiopian literature, occurred in the second half of the 19th century when the secretary of Emperor Tewodros II, *alaqa* Zannab, turned to Amharic instead of Ge'ez to write Tewodros's royal chronicle. Amharic also gradually supplanted Ge'ez in religious works and took over almost all the traditional Ge'ez genres. Subsequently, Ethiopian writers adopted the novel and the stage drama from European literature, introducing along with them new, 'secular' themes. *Lebb wallad tarik* ('A Story Born of the Heart') by Afawarq Gabra Iyasus, published in Rome in 1908, is considered as the first Amharic novel and the forerunner of modern Amharic literature.

The real founder of Amharic fictional writing was Heruy Walda Sellase who authored, among others, an allegoric narrative *Wadaje lebbe* ('My Heart is My Friend', 1922/1923) and a novel *Addis alam* ('The New World', 1932/1933). The latter work develops a recurring theme in modern African prose: the young man who finishes college abroad and returns to the backward place of his ancestors. In the literary activity of Heruy and many other Ethiopian writers, especially of the early period, the emphasis was moralistic and didactic. The idea of literature as a form of entertainment did not catch on until the late 20th century. The dramatic art was initiated by Takla Hawaryat's *Fabula Yaawrewoch komediya* ('Fable: the Comedy of Animals', 1921) but popularized in the 1930s by Yoftahe Neguse who wrote allegoric plays, such as *Teqem yallabbat chawata* ('Play Containing Something Useful', 1930/1931).

Post-war literary revival. Literary production in Amharic substantially increased and diversified after the end of the Italian occupation in 1941. Writers improved the level of artistic sophistication of their works and focused on portraying lives of individuals and on depicting the society at large. Although didacticism was still present, most often it took a more subtle form. Thus, Germachaw Takla Hawaryat shows in his novel *Araya* ('Good Example', 1948/1949) the generational conflict and, at the same time, he advocates a wide-ranging modernisation of Ethiopia. In contrast, Makwannen Endalkachaw, an adherent of traditional privileges for the feudal lords, was preoccupied with showing life as a source of suffering and the vanity of the world (*Alam waratannya*, 'The Inconstant World', 1947/1948; *Yadehoch katama*, 'The City of the Poor', 1956/1957).

Kabbada Mika'el with his allegoric (*Yatenbit qataro*, 'Appointment with Prophecy', 1945/1946) and historical plays (*Anibal*, 'Hannibal', 1955/1956) revived and firmly established Ethiopian drama. All of them are modelled on Greek and classical French tragedy. Tsaggaye Gabra Madhen, an outstanding playwright, introduced current social themes to the drama. In *Yakarmo saw* ('The Seasoned', 1965/1966) he portrays the life of a conformist clerk juxtaposed with rebellious acts of his brother. *Ha hu baseddest war* ('ABC in Six Months', 1973) and his other three plays deal with the chaotic years just before and during the Revolution of 1974. A sequel to this drama, *Ha hu waym pa pu* ('ABC or XYZ', 1990), concerns the political situation after the fall of the *Darg* regime. Mangestu Lamma wrote two comedies which he himself translated into English: *Talfo bakise* ('Snatch and Run or Marriage by Abduction', 1968/1969) and *Yalacha gabecha* ('The Marriage of Unequals', 1964/1965). Ayalnah Mulatu wrote and staged a number of musical plays.

In 1949 Taddasa Liban published the first collection of Amharic short stories, entitled *Maskaram* ('September'). The genre has been continued by such writers as Pawlos

Nyonyo (*Debleqleq*, 'Muddle', 1964/1965), Sebhat Gabra Egziabher (*Ammest seddest sabatt enna* ..., 'Five, Six, Seven and ...', 1988; English tr: 'Seeds and other stories' by Wendy Kindred, 2004), Adam Ratta (*Mahlet*, 1988/1989) and Asammenaw Barega (*YaTroya faras enna leloch achacher tarikoch*, 'The Trojan Horse and Other Short Stories', 2001/2002).

Bitter discontent with a society riddled by corruption pervades Abbe Gubannya's political novel *Alewwalladem* ('I Will Not Be Born', 1962/1963). In 1966 Haddis Alamayyahu published one of the best realistic novels in Amharic, *Feqer eska maqaber* ('Love unto the Grave'), a love story set in feudal Gojjam around 1900. A number of successful novels appeared from the 1970s. Baalu Germa's debut book *Kadmas bashaggar* ('Beyond the Horizon', 1969/1970) is a psychological study of a disheartened artist, who represented many young Ethiopians of that period. In his later novels *Yaqayy kokab terri* ('The Call of Red Star', 1979/1980) *Haddis* (1983/1984) and *Darasiw* ('The Writer', 1980) he deals with the Revolution, at first explicitly sympathising with the Communist government but later severely criticizing it in his last work *Oromay* ('It is Over', 1983). The theme of Revolution, shown from the perspective of two families, also emerges in the trilogy *Maebal* ('The Flood', 1979/80) by Berhanu Zaryehun. Dannyachew Warku in *Adafres* (1970) treats the conflict between the traditional and the modern ways of life, being critical of the superficial man of the Revolution period.

The most unconventional Ethiopian writer is Sebhat Gabra Egziabher whose novels incorporate obscene scenes while some of his stories exhibit absurdity. Sebhat uses naturalism to render the characters in his three creative works written in the 1960s but, because of censorship, published only much later. These are: *Letum aynagalleny* ('I will not See the End of the Night', 2004; French tr 2004 by Francis Falceto), set in the red-light district of Addis Ababa; *Tekkusat* ('Fever', 1997) and *Sabattanyaw malak* ('The Seventh Angel', 1999/2000). Mammo Wudnah penned a considerable number of works including novels (*Mahbartannyochu*, 'Members of the Association', 1989/1990) and spy stories. The peoples of south-western Ethiopia are portrayed in Feqramarqos Dasta's trilogy *KaBuska bastajarba* ('Behind the Buska Hills', 1994/1995), *Ivangadi* (1997/1998) and *Yazarsiwoch feqer* ('The Love of People', 1999; English translation of the trilogy 'Land of the Yellow Bull' by the author, 2003). Aside from short

Tsaggaye Gabra Madhen, © Chester Higgins Jr.

stories, Adam Ratta also authored a novel *Gracha qacheloch* ('Grey Bells', 2004/2005) and two others. The writer employed stream of consciousness to give a psychologically detailed picture of an adolescent mistreated by his family.

Lyric poetry. Early Amharic poetry, in form and content, was strongly influenced both by oral folk poetry and by the Ge'ez genre known as *qene*. A new trend was initiated by Mangestu Lamma who in his well-received collection *Yagetem gubae* ('Synod of Poetry', 1957/1958), turned to describing and stirring inner feelings. Poets who sought new poetic forms and means of expressions were Solomon Deressa (*Lejennat*, 'Childhood', 1970) and Sayfu Mataferya (*Yatasfa eger berat*, 'Shackles of Hope', 1976). Gabra Krestos Dasta experimented with visual representation of his poems written from ca 1955–1973 (*Mangad setuny saffi*, ['Give me a Wide Way']: 'Expansive Pathway ... Lifetime Traveler', 2006; English tr and renderings in the same volume by Heran Sereke-Brhan). In a famous volume *Esat way ababa* ('Fire or Flower', 1973/1974) Tsaggaye Gabra Madhen published poems that broach an array of topics such as unconfessed love, death, chasm between urban and rural life, historical events and nature. Other renowned Amharic poets include Yohannes Admasu (*Eski tatayyaqu*, 'May You Be Asked', 1997/1998), Dabbaba Sayfu (*Yaberhan feqre*, 'My Love of Light', 1987/1988) and Faqade Azzaza (*Chuhat*, 'Outcries', 1993). A promising young poet is Bawqatu Seyum, whose collection of poems was translated into English (*Hesasa sega*, 'In Search of Fat', 2012).

In recent years the memoirs of numerous public figures have appeared (e.g. *Dersana heywate*, 'The Story of My Life' by Abarra Jambare, 2009/2010). Additionally, there is a significant increase in the production of books for children, thus far a much-neglected readership. The writings mentioned above represent literature of high artistic value. There is also a large amount of popular literature for the general public.

In contrast to other literatures of sub-Saharan Africa, which are composed in both vernacular languages and European tongues, often considered more prestigious, the Ethiopian literary scene is dominated by Amharic. Writing in English is marginal. The successive governments, including the current one, have censored the production of literary works in Ethiopia, more or less overtly and tightly. Some writings were confiscated (*Oromay*), some plays were banned from the stage (*Ha hu waym pa pu*) and some creative works may well have been nipped in the bud.

Literature: Thomas Leiper Kane, *Ethiopian Literature in Amharic*, Wiesbaden 1975; Thomas Leiper Kane, Denis Nosnitsin, Galina Balashova, 'Amharic literature', *EAE* I, 238–246; Renate Richter, Denis Nosnitsin, Magdalena Krzyżanowska, 'Poetry, Amharic', *EAE* V, 481–485.

Magdalena Krzyżanowska, Hiob Ludolf Centre for Ethiopian Studies, Hamburg

Oromo literature

The literature of the Oromo has mainly been an oral one until recent decades. The earliest published examples are from the mid-19th century: a few short poems on wisdom, love, social satire and other topics, a prayer, and three folk stories. The large area where the Oromo-speaking communities are settled, the different social settings they have been living in during the last two centuries (the traditional rural one governed by the *gadaa* generation-set system, local kingdoms, urban environments, incorporation into the Ethiopian state, etc.) and their different religions (traditional *Waaqeffannaa*, different varieties of Islam, and various denominations of Christianity) have produced a considerable degree of variation in the many genres of their oral literature.

Oral literature. In Tutschek's dictionary and grammar, published in 1844 and 1845, there are a few short wisdom poems that he calls *makmaaka* and *weedduu* 'songs'. The first word is now more commonly used for 'proverbs', while the other one refers to short poems on love, social satire and other topics, like the following complaint of a returning warrior:

Silaa simalan yaaba	'Should I climb on a bamboo cane?
Simalli dameen qabu	Bamboo canes have no branches;
Silaa gandarran gala	Should I come back to the village?
Gandatu wareen qabu.	The village has no respect for fame'

Some of the major formal features of Oromo poetry can be gleaned from the text of this song:

i.) rhyme, that in this particular song follows an A–B–A–B pattern;
ii.) lines have the same number of syllables, here 7 in each line;
iii.) vowel parallelism: *i–aa–*(x–)*a–a–a*(*a*)*–a* in lines 1 and 3, vs (x–)*a*–(x–)*a–ee–a–u* in lines 2 and 4;
iv.) parallelism in the number of syllables in each word of rhyming lines: 2 syllables – 3 syllables – 2 syllables in lines 1 and 3, vs 3 syllables – 2 syllables – 2 syllables in lines 2 and 4;
v.) word repetitions and syntactic parallelism are appreciated stylistic devices, e.g. *silaa* 'perhaps, maybe, should I' at the beginning of lines 1 and 3, and *-n qabu* 'doesn't have' at the end of lines 2 and 4; *simala-* 'bamboo cane (Object)' and *simalli* 'bamboo cane (Subject)' in lines 1 and 2; the order Subject – Object – *-n* 'not' – Verb in lines 2 and 4, etc.

One of the major Oromo poetic genres is the *geerarsa*, traditionally a poem of triumph by a warrior regarding his exploits. Among several Oromo groups this was performed in a loud recitative form and could recount the killing of a large wild animal or an enemy. But it could also describe raids, challenges from war leaders, laments for dead heroes, pleas for mercy addressed to the victors, or could criticize someone's lineage, explain specific events, or contain self-reflection. In recent decades, long *geerarsa* dealt with the political situation of the poets' countries, and thus frequently have political and nationalistic overtones.

Religious texts are particularly sensitive to cultural changes in the communities where they are performed. Traditional rituals and festivals generally involve not only prayers and blessings, both in prose and in verse, but also hymns and songs such as the *gadaa* songs described by many authors, *Ateetee* and rainmaking hymns, etc. Spirit-possession cults have their own songs, while different brands of Christianity have produced their own religious hymns such as the Sabbath and *masqala* songs of Orthodox western Oromos, or the Pente songs of the Gujjii Pentecostals. Muslim *manzuuma* in praise of major local saints and *Mawlid* hymns are widespread among all the Oromo-speaking Muslims, and the special *baahroo* hymns connected to the cult of Shaykh Hussein in Bale have been extensively studied by several authors.

Western Oromo *weedduu jaalalaa* is a genre of love songs that can also be of considerable length, with an elaborate vocabulary and complex literary tropes. Other poetic genres are the *asmaarii* poems (from Amharic *azmari*) sung for entertainment during marriages and other festivals in the Naqamte area. Minor poetic genres are known from most Oromo-speaking groups, and are frequently characterized as male or as female songs. For instance, the short Arsii *weelluu* love songs described by Baxter are sung only by young men and, because of their very personal and humorously vulgar language are never performed in the presence of elderly people. Among the Kenyan Gabra, young men sing *faaruu* love songs while those by young women are called *qarillee*. Other kinds of minor poetry include farewell songs, work songs such as beekeepers' songs, women's work songs, men's songs performed when tilling the soil or threshing collectively, etc., as well as different kinds of children's songs.

An important aspect of Oromo oral literature is that early sources mention famous performers but not major poets, even though a few instances of authorial poems are known. In the second half of the 20th century, however, prominent *asmaarii* poets such as Abbaa Qashuumee have been active among the western Oromos, while in the east and south prominent poets such as Sheek Tahaa Umar and Jaarsoo Waaqoo Qootoo have composed long poems of social critique and commented on current events.

Soothsayers who foretell future events are known from several Oromo areas, such as Areeroo Boosaaro, who died at the beginning of the 20th century. Their prophecies were composed both in verse and in prose. The Italian scholar Cerulli provides examples of prophetic prose texts by Jijjoo Bachoo, also known as Abbaa Rajjii, from the western Oromo. In the 19th and early 20th centuries decisions and laws passed by traditional Oromo councils were frequently in verse. Very little is known about the oral poetry that was performed at the courts of the western Oromo kings, but it probably included major political poetry and praise poetry. Yet prose genres such as historical chronicles and jesters' tales were also performed at their courts. Such oral historical chronicles were performed to exalt the noble origin and deeds of those rulers, and already at the beginning of the 20th century they were known only to the elders. Other Oromo-speaking groups also had oral chronicles about the deeds of their ancestors, and among the Boorana of south-western Ethiopia and northern Kenya they appear to survive still now.

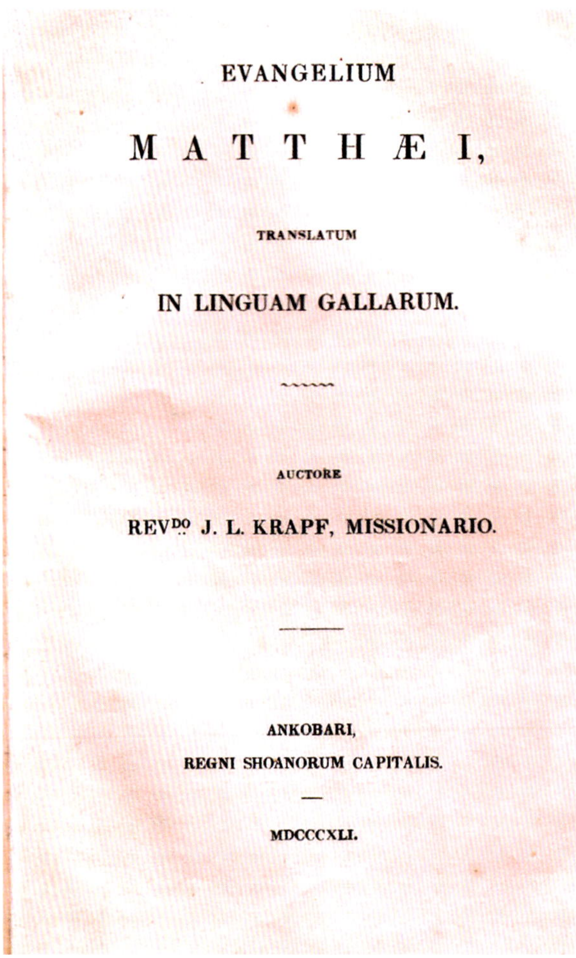
EVANGELIUM

MATTHÆI,

TRANSLATUM

IN LINGUAM GALLARUM.

AUCTORE

REVDO J. L. KRAPF, MISSIONARIO.

ANKOBARI,

REGNI SHOANORUM CAPITALIS.

MDCCCXLI.

Gospel of Matthew in 'Galla' language by Krapf, Ankobar 1841

Cerulli mentions 'professional jesters' such as Abbaa Wadaajoo, and provides some examples of their witty *haasaa* tales. They were maintained at the expense of western Oromo courts, and were quite similar to the *acchawach* or jesters of the Amhara. Oromo oral narratives have been published since the 19th century, and considerable collections of them are now available. They have been classified into different subgenres, e.g. one collection published in 1963 distinguishes (1) the creation of the world and men, (2) cattle, (3) pious and moralising tales and themes from the Old Testament, (4) demons, (5) animal tales, and (6) fairy tales, adventures, and tribal legends.

Minor oral prose genres include proverbs and riddles. The former (*makmaaka* or *mammaaksa*, the term also used for short wisdom poems and tales) are of quite diverse types, e.g. short sentences, sequences of two or three clauses, etc. When they consist of two or more parts, these tend to have several of the formal features that have been seen above in Oromo poetry, e.g. parallel vowels and syllable numbers. On the other hand, riddles (*hiibboo*) also have a strongly formalized structure like proverbs. The game of asking and answering riddles is a highly ritualized one; among the western and central Oromo it has to be introduced by saying '*hiibboo*!', that requires the answer '*hiibbakka*!' from the person who is willing to answer.

Written literature. The earliest written literature in Oromo mainly had a religious character. Muslim hymns written in *ajami*, i.e. adapted Arabic script, are known from Wallo and the area of Harar. Translations of the Bible or of portions of it, such as those by Krapf and Ruufoo or Onesimos Nasib, were produced both in the Latin and Ethiopian scripts from the 19th century, and recent ones have been published both in Ethiopia and Kenya.

A major literary work is Onesimos Nasib and Ganon Aster's *Galla spelling book – Jalqaba barsiisaa*, published in Ethiopian script in 1894, that includes translations of legends about Christian saints from the time of the Roman persecutions, and collections of traditional Oromo folk stories, proverbs, poems and songs. Many of these were reproduced by Cerulli.

A few collections of traditional poetry, proverbs, and narratives were published in later decades, especially after the *Darg* allowed publications in other Ethiopian languages, as long as the Ethiopian script was used. New creative writings appeared, especially in the influential Oromo journal *Bariisaa* that started to be published in Addis Ababa, for instance the revolutionary poems by Mahdi Hamid Muudee. In the 1970s and 1980s also several Oromo expatriates published both poems and fiction in different Latin orthographies. One of the best known among them is Tamene Bitima (Taammanaa Bitimaa) who lived in Germany. But it was after the fall of Mengistu's government in 1991, and the official acceptance of the Oromo Latin so-called *qubee* orthography, that writing and printing in Oromo became firmly established within the new federal structure of Ethiopia. Almost 30 school textbooks were published in 1995 and 1996, and the Regional Administration started to publish extensive collections of oral literature from across the Oromo Region. A succession of magazines also appeared: *Biiftuu*, *Gadaa*, *Madda Walaabuu* and other ones in Ethiopia, while overseas new magazines were published beside those that had appeared earlier such as *Qunnamtii Oromiyaa*, etc.

Modern plays started to appear frequently on TV in Oromo, and were performed even on stage. For instance, *Dukanaan Duuba* by Dhaabaa Wayyeessaa, one of the most prolific and best established authors, was performed at the National Theatre in 1991. Despite harassment and eventual exile, he had other plays performed on the radio and stage and published two novels.

Godaannisa is the story of the tribulations of a student who is trying to realize his talents and of his fraught, but eventually happy, love affair. *Gurraacha Abbayaa*, originally serialized on the national radio, is a tragic story of the sufferings of two Gumuz, i.e., non-Oromo lovers named Teetoo and Yenche. They are prevented from marrying by the traditional rules of sister exchange marriage. The heroine Yenche is forced by her kinsfolk to marry a man who eventually kills her lover Teetoo, while she drowns herself in the Blue Nile. Other well-known novels are Gaaddisaa Birruu's *Kuusaa Gadoo*, about the corruption of officials who take bribes, send people to the front and misuse their power to seduce their victim's wives; *Suuraa Abdii* by Kumsaa Buraayyuu that tells the story of a young high school graduate who comes to Addis Ababa in search of a better life; also *Hawii* by Isaayyaas Hordofaa, Toleeraa Fiqiruu's *Imimmaan hadhaa*, and others.

Finally, after the publication of collections of traditional oral poetry, and the production of poems and songs connected with political militancy and armed struggle, a number of more reflective poets have started to explore personal feelings and themes that are closer to contemporary world poetry, such as Asafaa Tafarraa Dibaabaa, Taha Abdi and Zalaalam Abarra, both in Ethiopia and in the diaspora.

Literature: Giorgio Banti, 'Folktales in Oromiffaa', *EAE* II, 559–560; Giorgio Banti, 'Oromo oral literature', *EAE* IV, 65–69; Paul T.W. Baxter, Gaddisa Birru, 'Contemporary writing in Oromiffaa', *EAE* IV, 70–73.

Giorgio Banti, Università degli studi di Napoli 'l'Orientale'

Oral literature

Oral literature is a term that over the last few decades has been disputed and often redefined. It may be broadly described as any type of orally communicated expressive art. This may include a wide range of forms, such as ritual texts, curative chants, epic poems, folk tales, creation stories, songs, myths, spells, legends, proverbs, riddles, tongue-twisters, historical narratives and so forth. Oral literature is constantly changing by its very nature. In addition, the spread of literacy and the availability of new communication technologies have also triggered significant change. For instance, recent rapid socio-economic changes and the homogenizing effects of globalization raise challenges to preserving cultural diversity, particularly for smaller cultural and linguistic groups.

Our current knowledge of oral literature is informed by the written accounts of adventurers and explorers that were accumulated in the last few centuries, and more recently by scholarly studies on the 'texts' of these traditions. Thus the oldest documentation of oral literatures is available as subjective written descriptions or transcriptions of texts. In the second half of the 20th century, audio recordings have allowed the preservation of the sound element of the performance of these texts. In more recent years, audiovisual documentation technologies have introduced a much richer representation, including the non-verbal elements of communication that play an important part in the performance of many types of oral literature.

The first systematic survey of oral literature in Africa was written by Ruth Finnegan (published 1970), tracing some general features of the historical background and characteristics of oral literatures in the Horn of Africa. However, while we now have detailed studies covering the largest linguistic communities in the Horn, such as the Amhara, Tegrennya speakers, Oromo, Somali and Afar, we only know specific aspects of others and we have very little information about yet others. In Ethiopia we find a long-standing tradition of written literature, associated with Christianity and Islam. Nonetheless, especially among the many pre-literate groups, a rich variety of oral literatures flourish within the numerous cultures of Ethiopia and the wider Horn of Africa. These have been studied from the perspectives of linguistics, anthropology, ethnomusicology, performance studies and cultural studies, rather than as the object of the study of literature.

Types of oral literature. Oral literature in the Horn of Africa can be grouped into major and minor oral poetry and songs, and several other genres. Within the category of major oral poetry we can distinguish between religious and secular genres.

Examples of religious genres include *qene*, hymns praising God and the saints, improvised in Ge'ez and Amharic by *dabtara,* within Ethiopian Orthodox Church liturgy. These are composed according to rigid rules determining form and content, giving an immediate meaning and a deeper, but still discoverable meaning. Within Islamic ritual there is a rich variety of hymns, which often present a written form and an oral performance, composed in Arabic and/or several local languages. Some important examples are *manzuma* poetry in Amharic, Oromo and other languages, *zikri* in Harari, Oromo and other languages, as well as *mablud* in *Afar,* and *nazme* in Saho.

In the realm of secular poetry, praise poems are widespread, such as the Amharic *fukkara* and *qararto*, and the Oromo *geerarsa. Maanso* is a Somali term that can be used to indicate poetry in general, or more specifically a genre of higher status, usually providing serious commentary, with a known author. Somali poetry is characterized by alliteration, by a scansion system based upon vowel length and syllable counting, and by sophisticated poetic diction with frequent use of rare words.

Amongst minor oral poetry and songs, there are widespread repertoires like wedding songs and work songs. Among the many regional traditions, in Harar there developed a repertoire of wedding songs (*gey faqar*) that have been practiced for centuries. Generally performed by one or two women accompanied by a small drum called *karabu*, the songs contain formulaic and improvised elements; the themes, once ranging from religion to patriotism and friendship, today mainly focus on love and marriage. As an example of other minor oral poetry, we can mention the Somali *hees*, a category of rather short poems without named authors associated with work and dance, and of a lower status than the *maanso* genre. Men's work songs include camel-watering and camel-loading songs, and women's work songs cover household chores.

Performance. The performance of oral literature in Ethiopia presents a wide variety of forms that should be described considering the specific cultural and performance context. The most common scenario is that of a performer delivering an oral text to an audience. Performers are often solo, but there are cases of duos (e.g. *jaliyei* and *kotankot* in Harar), and eventually more articulated group performances (e.g. individual-group interactions in the heroic song *geerarsa* and the cattle praise song *faaruu loonii* among Arsi Oromo). The interaction between performer(s) and audience has a very significant role in that it often serves to reinforce social norms and ideologies, as can be witnessed, e.g. in folktale performance among the Gujji-Oromo in southern Ethiopia. Observation of the sonic dimension of performances shows that there is a continuum from ordinary spoken language to proper singing, from the prophetic prose texts of soothsayers (e.g. *raaga* among the Boorana) to the richly ornamented songs performed by singers (e.g. *wali* among the Harari). The performed oral text can be accompanied by other voices, musical instruments, and dance.

Performers. Performers of oral literature can range from specialized figures in a community, to lay members of social groups who partake in day-to-day performance of lullabies, proverbs, riddles, and children's songs.

Azmari are itinerant musicians or minstrels who sing, accompanied by the single-string bowed fiddle *masenqo*, about life, news, Ethiopia, and also about personal situations involving love, conflict, and work. In the past, *azmari* were employed by noblemen to sing praises for their deeds. This earlier role as praise-song performers of notable status was gradually lost until today *azmari* have a reputation as performers who dispense criticism.

Another type of itinerant performer is the *lalibala* (pl. *lalibaloch*) traditional singers of northern Ethiopia who wander from door to door, singing and begging for alms, with the promise of blessing. They usually work in pairs performing a duet or a

Religious chanting, Harar, © Accademia Nazionale di Santa Cecilia, Roma, photo Simone Tarsitani

solo performance according to a set scheme. When invited into houses, they perform a mix of fixed formulas and improvisations about the people they find there. *Azmari* and *lalibaloch* have long practiced their hereditary roles with varying fortunes, however today they are often affected by their low social status: the latter are particularly stigmatized because of the popular belief that, should they stop singing and begging, they would contract leprosy.

Oral literature traditions can also be observed in a range of other contexts, from the solitary performances of Amhara shepherds in the countryside of West Gojjam, to the joyful group singing during the Christian feast of the Transfiguration, or Buhe, when bands of children go round singing 'Hoya-Hoye', a praise song for home owners who may give them sweets, money, or fresh dough (*buhe*) in exchange for their performance. One of the most common occasions to see performances of oral literature are weddings, usually accompanied in many Ethiopian cultures by poetry, providing a mix of entertainment and celebration of the event. Live dance and singing performances of *azmari* can be found in several bars called *azmari bet* in the Kazanchis area of Addis Ababa; this is a common way to get one's first introduction to a very popular form of Ethiopian traditional sung poetry and dance.

Literature: GIORGIO BANTI, 'Maanso', *EAE* III, 610–612; GIORGIO BANTI, 'Oral literature', *EAE* IV, 38–42; GIORGIO BANTI, 'Oromo oral literature', *EAE* IV, 65–69; ELIZABETH LAIRD, *When the World Began: Stories Collected in Ethiopia*, Oxford 2000; *http://www.ethiopianfolktales.com*.

Simone Tarsitani, Durham University

Christian calendar

The Alexandrian calendar. The calendar of the Ethiopian Church follows the Alexandrian year, retaining the ancient Egyptian division of the year into 12 months of 30 days each, plus a 'little month' of five days (six days for the leap year). It begins on Julian 29 August (presently = 11 September of our Gregorian calendar), except in the year of John, which starts one day later because the year of Luke is the Ethiopian leap year and counts 366 days.

The years are grouped in fourfold units. Each of them is named after an evangelist (Matthew, Mark, Luke and John).

The months are shown below; after the Ethiopian names come the Greco-Coptic and Arabic equivalents, then the corresponding dates in the Julian, followed by the Gregorian calendar which differs by 13 days until 2100 CE; in the year of John, add 1 day from Maskaram 1 until Maggabit 4:

Ethiopian	Greco-Coptic/Arabic	Julian	Gregorian
1) Maskaram	Thoout, Tut	29 August	11 September
2) Teqemt	Phaophi, Babah	28 September	11 October
3) Hedar	Athyr, Hatur	28 October	10 November
4) Tahsas	Khoiak, Kihak	27 November	10 December
5) Terr	Tybi, Tubah	27 December	9 January
6) Yakkatit	Mekheir, Amshir	26 January	8 February
7) Maggabit	Phamenoth, Baramhat	25 February	10 March
8) Miyazya	Pharmouthi, Barmudah	27 March	9 April
9) Genbot	Pakhon, Bashans	26 April	9 May
10) Sane	Pauni, Baunah	26 May	8 June
11) Hamle	Epiphi, Abib	25 June	8 July
12) Nahase	Mesore, Misra	25 July	7 August
13) Pagwemen	Epagomenai, Ayyam al-nasy	24 August	6 September

Table 11: Correspondence between Ethiopian, Greco-Coptic/Arabic, Julian and Gregorian calendars

The era is called the 'Year of Mercy' or AM (*Anno Misericordiae*, or *Amata Mehrat*), which is 7⅔ years later than the common era (CE). So, 1 Maskaram 2000 AM is equivalent to 12 September 2007 CE.

The liturgical year: seasons. The whole year is organized into either a fourfold or a threefold structure, in which the liturgical seasons are incorporated:

(a) a four-season division, with: (1) the windy season, *Masaw* (6 October–3 January); (2) the dry season, *Hagay* (4 January–3 April); (3) the sowing season, or that of the small rains, *Balg* (4 April–2 July); (4) the rainy season, *keramt* (3 July–5 October).

(b) a three-season division, exerting a real influence on the chanting of the service, with (1) *Yohannes* (11 September–9 December), covering the beginning of the year; (2) *Astamhero* ('supplication to obtain mercy', 10 December–8 April); (3) *Fasika* from Easter to the end of the year; this season is divided into the cycle of Resurrection and the Season of the Rains (*keramt*).

In addition, the liturgical calendar is arranged according to 20 fixed periods as well as the 10 mobile periods belonging to the cycle of the Resurrection.

The fasts. The fasts exert a great influence on the life of Ethiopian Christians. People fast until noon or, normally, 3pm, not taking any food or drink, and abstaining from eating any food of animal origin. Fasting also requires that married people observe sexual abstinence. Liturgical services follow a different pattern, other liturgical books being used. Liturgy (*Qeddase*) is celebrated every day insofar as the community is able to secure the wherewithal for the service; on week days Liturgy is celebrated after 12 o'clock; on Saturdays and Sundays in the morning, when abstinence only is kept. The chant mode used is normally the 'Ge'ez' one.

There are seven fasts in the Ethiopian Church, some being compulsory only for monks and priests: the fast of (Mount) *Qwesqwam* (40 days, 6 October–15 November); the fast of the *Prophets* (43 days, 25 November–7 January, which includes Christmas, while the eves of Christmas and Epiphany are called *Gahad*, and all the faithful fast; the fast of *Nineveh* (3 days, on Monday, Tuesday and Wednesday of the tenth week before Easter); the Great Fast lasting 55 days, including Saturdays and Sundays when abstinence only is required, is composed of three parts: the Fast of Heraclius (1 week), the Fast of Christ (40 days), and the Passion or Holy Week (8 days, starting on the Saturday [rather than Friday evening] before Palm Sunday until Easter Sunday [rather than morning]); the fast of the *Apostles* (variable length, from 7 to 42 days, starting on the Monday after Pentecost until 12 July, the feast of Saints Peter and Paul); the fast of *Salvation* every Wednesday and Friday of the year, except from Easter to Pentecost and on Christmas or Epiphany, should they occur on such a day; the fast of the *Assumption* (15 days, August 7–21).

The main feasts and the Sanctorale. The Sanctorale, or the Proper of the Saints, includes the commemorations made on fixed days of the months throughout the whole calendar year, as well as a monthly cycle which runs in parallel. There are feasts of the Lord, of our Lady and of the saints. For the sake of comparison, when the Ethiopian name differs from the translation, the usual Western name is also given in brackets, with the corresponding date of the Julian calendar followed by the Gregorian equivalent after the sign '=' (without accounting for the leap year).

The feasts of Our Lord Jesus Christ

1) The Incarnation (*Tesbeet*), 29 Maggabit (Annunciation, 25 March = 7 April)
2) The Nativity (*Ledat*), 29 Tahsas (25 December = 7 January)
3) The Baptism (*Temqat*), 11 Terr (6 January = 19 January) and the miracle at Cana of Galilee (*Qana za-Galila*), 12 Terr (commemorates the return from exile of Emperor Hayla Sellase on 12 Terr 1933 AM = 20 January 1941 CE)
4) The Transfiguration, i.e. Mount Tabor (*Dabra Tabor*), 13 Nahase (6 August = 19 August).
5) The (Exaltation of the) Cross (*Masqal*), 17 Maskaram (14 September = 27 September); this feast is assimilated to the major feasts of the Lord and is therefore celebrated everywhere in a similar manner.
6) The Circumcision of the Lord (*Gezrat*), 6 Terr (1 January = 14 January).
7) The Presentation of the Lord (*Semon*), 8 Yakkatit (2 February = 15 February)
8) The Cross (*Masqal*), 10 Maggabit (6 March = 19 March)

... and several others.

Temqat procession, © Serge Dewel-Mouton

The feasts of Virgin Mary

Emperor Zara Yaeqob (r. 1434–1468) instituted the celebration of a total of 33 annual feasts in honour of Our Lady, 'to be kept like Sundays'. However, the five main commemorations are the following, the Assumption being celebrated in all churches and having precedence over a Sunday:

1) The Dormition (*Erafta*), 21 Terr (16 January = 29 January)
2) The Covenant of Mercy (*Kidana mehrat*), 16 Yakkatit (10 February = 23 February)
3) The Nativity (*Ledata*), 1 Genbot (26 April = 9 May)
4) The Consecration of her church at Philippi (*Qeddase beta*), 21 Sane (15 June = 28 June)
5) The Assumption *Felsata*, 16 Nahase (9 August = 22 August)

The commemorations of saints

The saints commemorated are found in both the *Getsawe* and the *Senkesar*, two books which differ in their nature, contents and history. As well as the saints common to the whole of Christianity (Old Testament prophets, Apostles, Angels, St George, etc.) and the Coptic saints (e.g. Peter of Alexandria), there are a number of specifically Ethiopian saints (e.g. Kings Abreha and Atsbeha, Gabra Manfas Qeddus, Yared the Hymnographer, and so on).

The monthly cycle of the Sanctorale

The Ethiopian monthly cycle groups the commemorations dear to the people. Being a convenient calendar it has a wider practical use, even outside any specifically religious purpose.

Here are some of the more popular commemorations, with the main date of the commemoration.

1. *Ledata*: the Nativity of Our Lady Mary (1 Genbot).
3. *Baata*: the Entry of Mary into the Temple (3 Tahsas).
7. *Sellase*: the Holy Trinity (7 Hamle and 7 Terr).
12. *Mikael*: the archangel Michael (12 Hedar and 12 Sane).
16. *Kidana mehrat*: the Covenant of Mercy (16 Yakkatit).
21. *Egzeetena Maryam*: Our Lady Mary (21 Terr).
23. *Giyorgis*: St George of Lydda (23 Miyazya).
27. *Madhane Alam*: the Saviour of the World (27 Maggabit and 27 Teqemt).

Literature: Emmanuel Fritsch, Ugo Zanetti, 'Calendar, Christian', *EAE* I, 668–672; Emmanuel Fritsch, *The Liturgical Year and the Lectionary of the Ethiopian Church. The Temporal: Seasons and Sundays*, Ethiopian Review of Cultures, Special Issue, 9–10, Addis Ababa 2001.

Emmanuel Fritsch, Lyon, Ugo Zanetti, Chevetogne

Islamic calendar

The general structure of the Islamic lunar calendar is based on two verses of the Koran (= Quran) according to which the year is divided into 12 months of alternately 30 and 29 days (Koran 9:36) and only the actual observation of the lunar phases marks the flowing of time (Koran 9:37 which abrogates the pre-Islamic practice of intercalating a month to reduce the gap between the lunar calendar and the course of the seasons). As a consequence of these Koranic instructions, the Islamic calendar is made up of a total of 354 days, but there are 11 leap years in a space of 30 years to fill the gap between this fixed number of days and the real lunar yearly cycle of 354 days, 8 hours, 48 minutes and 36 seconds. Nor is the calendar connected to the seasons, so that within 32 solar years every Islamic lunar month passes through all the different seasons. The beginning of the Islamic lunar era traditionally starts from the so-called *hijra*, the emigration of the Prophet Muhammad and his followers from Mecca to Yathrib (Medina) on 16 July, 622 CE (= beginning the era *Anno Hegirae*, AH). Mathematical formulas, conversion tables and more recently computer software have been elaborated to convert the Christian solar dates into Islamic lunar dates and vice versa.

The names of the months of the Islamic calendar are originally in Arabic: *Muharram* (30 days); *Safar* (29 days); *Rabi al-awwal* (30 days); *Rabi al-thani* (29 days);

Collective prayer at the end of Ramadan, © Ethiopian Tourism Organization

Jumada al-ula (30 days); *Jumada al-akhira* (29 days); *Rajab* (30 days); *Shaban* (29 days); *Ramadan* (30 days); *Shawwal* (29 days); *Dhu al-qada* (30 days); *Dhu al-hijja* (29 days).

The dates of Muslim celebrations and festivals are fixed according to the observation of the lunar phases and the succession of the months in the Islamic calendar: e.g. the beginning and the breaking of the fast during the month of *Ramadan*, the ninth month of the lunar calendar; the feast of the sacrifice (*Id al-adha* or *al-Id al-kabir* in Arabic; *Arafo* among Ethiopian Muslims, and the commemoration of Abraham's sacrifice) on 10 *Dhu al-hijja*, the 12th month of the calendar; the birthday of the Prophet Muhammad (*Mawlid*) on 12 *Rabi al-awwal*, the third month of the calendar; the festival of *Ashura* on 10 *Muharram*, the first month of the calendar; the end of the fast of *Ramadan* (*Id al-fitr* or *al-Id al-saghir*) on 1 *Shawwal*, the tenth month of the calendar. In areas where the cult of the saints and holy men is particularly felt and practiced yearly pilgrimages to the shrines (*ziyara*) are organized according to the Islamic calendar.

Days always start at sunset. Weeks are made up of seven days whose Arabic names are: *al-Sabt*, *al-Ahad*, *al-Ithnayn*, *al-Thulatha*, *al-Arba'a*, *al-Khamis*, *al-Juma*. Friday is considered to be a festive weekly day, as it is the day of the congregational prayer (*salat al-juma*) which is preceded by a sermon (*khutba*) and performed at noon in the mosque.

In Ethiopia (as in many other non-Arab Islamic countries) local denominations are also used for the months which sometimes derive from the main festival occurring during the month. In Harar, e.g., the following names are common: *Ashura* (= *Muharram*); *Nadi mawlud* (= *Rabi al-awwal*); *Kuottan mawlud* (= *Rabi al-thani*); *Shishtan mawlud* (= *Jumada al ula*); *Ragu soman* (= *Rajab*); *Suti wahri* (= *Shaban*); *Arafa* (= *Dhu al-hijja*). Among the Somali, different names are used the most widespread of which are: *Cashuro* (= *Muharram*); *Sako* (= *Safar*) *Mawlid* (*Rabi al-awwal*); *Rajal* (or *Malmadoone*; = *Rabi al thani*); *Subbuux* (= *Rajab*); *Soondheere* (= *Shaban*); *Soonqaad* (= *Ramadan*); *Soonfur* (= *Shawwal*); *Sidataal* (= *Dhu al-qada*); *Carrafo* (= *Dhu al-hijja*).

The Islamic calendar has been used by the Ethiopian Muslims since the very beginning of the Islamic presence in the region on both public and private occasions. Islamic funerary and memorial inscriptions, historiographical texts and private letters are all dated according to the Islamic calendar.

The earliest Islamic date attested so far in Ethiopia is that on a funerary inscription found in Endarta: 8 *Dhu al-qada* 396 (6 August, 1006 CE). Chronological lists of rulers, historiographical texts, historical notes and official registers in the Islamic regions of Ethiopia (especially in the city of Harar) are all dated according to the Islamic calendar. In this kind of literature the most ancient date recorded is 283 AH (= 896–897 CE). Colophons of Islamic manuscripts also use the Islamic calendar (the oldest so far known Ethiopian Islamic colophon is 1104 AH = 1693 CE).

The usage of the Islamic calendar together with the Christian Ethiopian date is not uncommon in Ethiopia especially in the modern era. This practice was especially widespread in letters addressed by Ethiopian Christian authorities to Muslim Ethiopian and foreign rulers. Nowadays the Islamic periodical press, manuscripts and printed literature in Amharic and other local languages are almost invariably dated according to both calendars. Some Muslim peoples of Ethiopia (especially the Oromo and Somali) still use pre-Islamic traditional timekeeping systems beside the Muslim calendar.

Literature: ALESSANDRO GORI, 'Islamic calendar', *EAE* I, 673–675.

Alessandro Gori, University of Copenhagen

Oromo calendar

Despite their large territory the Oromo share a common system of time reckoning, with only minor variations. The basic elements of the calendar are a cycle of twelve lunar months – *ji'a*, 'moon' – and a cycle of 27 named days, called *ayyaana*. With the exception of the Gabra-Oromo in northern Kenya there is no week. A lunar month starts and ends the day the new moon appears in the sky. The twelve months are *Birra, Chiqa, Sadaasa, Abraasa, Ammajjii, Guraandala, Bitotessa, Caamsa, Buufaa, Wacabajjii, Obora guddaa, Obora diqaa.* The 27 *ayyaana* are *Gardaduma, Sonsa, Rurruma, Lumasa, Gidada, Ruuda, Areeri duraa, Areeri ballo, Adula duraa, Adula ballo, Garba duraa, Garba balla, Garba dullacha, Bita qaraa, Bita balla, Sorsa, Algajima, Arba, Walla, Basa qaraa, Basa balla, Chaaraa, Maganatti jaaraa, Maganatti Britii, Salbaani duraa, Salbaani balla, Salbaana dullacha.*

Ayyaana is a complex concept in Oromo, bearing a number of meanings referring to *Waaqa* (Sky-God) and recalling the ideas of time, fate, and a classificatory principle ordering the universe. Accordingly each day-name implies certain qualities that make it appropriate or inappropriate for ritual. In addition, the Oromo structure time by different types of longer cycles, connected to their *gadaa* system of generational classes, enabling their oral historians to recall past events with extraordinary precision and time depth.

Lunar calendars are the most common ancient system of time reckoning in all continents. However, since the 354 days of twelve lunations do not correspond to the solar year, they soon fail to anticipate seasonal events. One known way to keep correspondence was to add intercalary lunar months by independently checking the progress of the solar year. This was achieved in three main ways. The first is by checking the declination of the sun against either natural or man-made benchmarks on the land. The declination of a celestial body is its angular distance north or south of the celestial equator. The declination of the sun annually ranges from 23.5° north (summer solstice) to 23.5° south (winter solstice). The second way is to monitor the heliacal risings of the constellations, namely the time of the year when the constellation just appears above the eastern horizon at dawn. The last method was to observe the time of regular natural events on earth. Systems using intercalary lunar months are known as lunisolar calendars. Where mathematics and astronomical knowledge developed in connection to bureaucratic centralized states, the lunar calendar often developed into a solar calendar. In some civilizations the lunar calendar has survived, whereas other civilizations, such as those of the Jews and Muslim Arabs, have maintained a lunisolar or a lunar calendar, in connection to ritual.

The lunar calendar of the Oromo keeps correspondence with the seasons. The *ayyaantu*, the Oromo experts in astronomical observation and calendar, were able to maintain the correspondence by checking the right ascension position of the moon in relation to eight stars or star groups. Right ascension is the angular distance measured eastward along the celestial equator. As explained to the writer in 1986, the 27 day cycle is actually the sidereal month of the moon (27.3 days), the time required by the moon to get back to the same right ascension position. The 0.3 cumulative difference is immediately corrected based on empirical observation of the conjunction of the moon with the *Urji Dahaa*, on eight consecutive nights. This means that every recurrence of *ayyaana* exactly corresponds to an exact astronomical position of the moon in relation to the stars. The adjustment of the eleven days deviation between the lunar and the solar year is equally done on an empirical basis. The sidereal month of the moon being about two days shorter than its synodic period, each month starts on a different sequence of two or three days. The *ayyaantu* keep this correlation fixed, having months always starting on the same 2–3 *ayyaana.* When they monitor that there is no longer any correspondence, they repeat the month name, thus adding an intercalary month. Only the months *Guraandala* or *Obora diqaa* can be repeated. To current knowledge, the Oromo are the only people on earth with a pure lunar-sidereal calendar, capable of keeping correspondence with the solar year by only evaluating the right ascension position and the synodic period of the moon against the stars, without reference to the sun, to the heliacal rising of stars, or to regular natural events.

Abba Gadaa celebrating *Ireecha* ('Oromo Thanksgiving'), Jimma, © Ezekiel Gebissa

Literature: Marco Bassi, 'On the Borana calendrical system: a preliminary field report', *Current Anthropology*, 29/4 (1988), 619–624; Gemetchu Megerssa, Aneesa Kassam, 'The 'Rounds' of Time: Time, History and Society in Borana Oromo', in Wendy James, David Mills (eds.), *The qualities of time: anthropological approaches*, Oxford, New York 2005, 251–265.

Marco Bassi, Università degli Studi di Trento

Traditional painting

Aksumite Christianity and the visual culture of the eastern Mediterranean. The visual culture of the ancient Aksumite civilization in northern Ethiopia appears to have been defined by architecture, ceramic items and ornamental objects, as well as kingly portraits on coins that circulated from the late 3rd century CE until Aksumite power declined following Arab control of the Red Sea in the 7th century. King Ezana's adoption of Christianity in around 350, only a few decades after Constantine the Great had declared Christianity a legal religion in the Roman Empire, brought Aksumite culture within the theological sphere of the Egyptian Christian Church, and laid the foundations for a link between Christianity and the Ethiopian state that would remain active until the last emperor was deposed in 1974. Ezana's conversion was accompanied by the emergence of a literate tradition inspired by the Gospels as well as a Christian painted artistic tradition.

Extensive destruction resulting from the incursions of the Muslim general Ahmad ibn Ibrahim al-Ghazi (known as Ahmad Grany, 'the left-handed") in the 16th century limits our understanding of this early painted production. Recent radiocarbon dating of two parchment texts known as the Garima Gospels has delivered date ranges of 390–570 for Garima 2 and 530–630 for Garima 1, the average of the mid-points of the two ranges being 530.

This was a time of documented diplomatic exchange between the courts of Aksum and Constantinople, suggesting that the flux of ideas could have led to the translation of the Greek Gospels into Ge'ez and the introduction into northern Ethiopia of Late Antique techniques of book production and illumination. Stylistically and iconographically, the paintings illustrating the Garima Gospels reflect these cultural and artistic exchanges, and include common late antique themes such as the portraits of the four Evangelists (Garima 2) and the depiction of the Canon Tables harmonizing the four Gospels (Garima 1 and 2), albeit expressed in a distinctly local visual language. In subsequent centuries, the increasing numbers of missionaries arriving from the Eastern Roman Empire contributed to the spread of rigorous ascetic and monastic practices of Egyptian and Syrian origin: hermits began to occupy natural features in the mountainous northern Ethiopian landscape that would previously have been used for indigenous practices, and churches began to be hewn into cliffs and caves, some of which were later decorated with cycles of wall-paintings.

The emergence of an Ethiopian medieval painting tradition. The disintegration of Aksum's centralized economy and its coinage in the 9th century involved the disappearance of an archaeologically recognizable political and cultural centre. Possible successor 'chiefdoms' are being investigated, for instance at Degum, in the Garalta area of Tegray, with its complex of subterranean structures reminiscent of Aksumite funerary church architecture. Evidence of painting production, however, only seems to re-emerge later, in the context of the southward shift of power to the Lasta region, which was the seat of the Agaw-speaking Zagwe dynasty from the 9th century until its replacement by the Amharic-speaking Solomonic dynasty in 1270. This period of transformation of Aksumite and Post-Aksumite culture into the so-called medieval civilization of Christian Ethiopia is marked by important cycles of wall paintings decorating rock-hewn churches in centres of Zagwe power.

David Phillipson has argued that the oldest rock-hewn features in Lalibala could date back to the 7th or 8th centuries, some 500 years earlier than the traditional attribution of all the churches to King Lalibala in the late 12th century; his hypothesis has been largely confirmed by the French team of archaeologists working there. It is equally difficult to firmly attribute and date the cycles of wall paintings that decorate these churches, as they may well be later than the fabric of the churches themselves.

Political and cultural links with Egypt appear to have been frequent during both the Zagwe and the early Solomonic periods, providing valuable comparative stylistic and iconographic material. The eight paintings depicting New Testament episodes and equestrian saints in the church of Yemrehanna Krestos (about 19km north of Lalibala), for instance, show iconographic elements that are close to Byzantine art produced between the 10th and 13th centuries and not normally found in Ethiopian painting, and reveal striking parallels with Coptic paintings of the early 13th century, recalling the depictions of brick buildings and portrayals of equestrian saints found, for instance, in the Monastery of Saint Antony of the Red Sea, some of which can be firmly dated to 1232–1233.

The active monastic community at Dabra Hayq Estifanos, founded on an island in Lake Hayq in Wallo near the southern frontier of christianized territory by Abbot Iyasus Moa in 1248, also appears to have maintained close contacts with Coptic Egypt. Its prolific scriptorium produced new versions of Aksumite texts and numerous translations, revisions and adaptations of Arabic texts from Egypt, as well as illustrated manuscripts, in a process of 'Copto-Arabization' that brought together the Greek heritage of Aksum and the Arabic heritage of Egyptian Christians. This process of active cultural reception, supported by an expanding monastic network that produced centres of learning and workshops for the training of scribes engaged in manuscript copying and illustration, profoundly marked the cultural environment that accompanied the spread of Solomonic rulership in northern Ethiopia until the 15th century. The fact that the first ruler of the new dynasty, Yekunno Amlak, had been educated at Dabra Hayq Estifanos suggests he was acquainted with this literate and painterly environment, and it may have influenced the production of the cycles of late 13th century wall-paintings associated with this king that decorate rock-hewn and cave churches in Lasta at Belbala Charqos, Emakina Madhane Alam and Gannata Maryam, where a well-known donor portrait directly names the king. Active cultural reception is shown by their similar stylistic and iconographic traits to Egyptian wall paintings of the same period, together with their unmistakable originality of conception. The same association is also found in the cycle of paintings decorating the walls of Washa Mikael Church in Wadla – a site that local oral sources suggest was an Amhara power-base in the region at that time.

Theology, politics and the cult of the Virgin Mary. Although Kings Amda Tseyon I and Sayfa Arad brought the northern regions of Ethiopia under royal Amhara control in the 14th century, their successors, Dawit I and his sons Yeshaq and Zara Yaeqob, continued to face a threat from the surrounding Muslim and other non-Christian communities. Zara Yaeqob in particular (whose throne name was Constantine, in a desire to emulate Constantine the Great's unification of Church and state in the 4th century) was a forceful ruler and a theologian, who developed a policy of centralisation and ethnic assimilation of non-Amhara groups designed to stamp out indigenous cultural and religious practices that engaged with natural phenomena such as rain and drought, famine and epidemics. His brutal campaigns laid down the foundations for Amhara royal state dominance over the Church, in which the king's own radical innovations in theology and Church life and policy were upheld. In this process, both Dawit I and Zara Yaeqob used the visual arts as a tool for the unification of the land around their own political aims and theological beliefs, and developed a sustained programme of royal patronage of painting. Under Dawit, the Miracles of Mary

Mary with the Holy Child, wall painting Washa Mikael Church, second half of 13th century © Solomonic-Zagwe Encounters Project

(*Taammera Maryam*) were translated from Arabic into Ge'ez, and a distinctive court style of manuscript illumination to express his personal devotion to the cult of the Virgin Mary was produced by his scriptorium, revealing familiarity with recent Byzantine iconography, including the use of gold detail. Zara Yaeqob ordered the reading of three miracles of Our Lady Mary to church congregations and the mandatory use of her icon in every church, gradually requiring an ever more elaborate church ritual and generating increased demand for portable devotional images on wooden panels. Courtly patronage allowed the development of local talent, in particular the monk Fere Tseyon, whose images in tempera on gesso panels reveal an original style marked by gentle, round faces, almond eyes, and exuberant reds and yellows. New iconographic themes inspired by Syrian, Egyptian and Byzantine workshops were brought into Ethiopia, while artists arriving from the Republic of Venice and the Kingdom of Aragon led to the emergence of new motifs in local icon painting, such as the Virgin holding a flower or the Holy Child holding a bird. Saint George became the most popular military saint in Ethiopia after King Zara Yaeqob had attributed his victory over a Muslim adversary to the dual help of Saint George and Our Lady Mary.

Independent-minded Ethiopian ascetics also flourished at that time, either expanding the influence of the monarchy or challenging it. At the church of Abuna Abreham Dabra Tseyon (hewn out during the reigns of Kings Dawit I and Yeshaq) in Garalta, several untrained hands portrayed local holy figures, include Abuna Abreham himself miraculously parting the waters of the river Geba, together with Egyptian saints. Gunda Gunde monastery, on the border between Tegray and Eritrea, however, followed the principles put forward by the monks Ewostatewos and Estifanos, who were hostile to the orthodoxy of the Amhara rulers, leading Zara Yaeqob to regard them as heretics. Both monks were familiar with the cultural environments of Egypt and other eastern Christian regions and fostered a cultural milieu in which a unique, sophisticated style of manuscript illumination was able to develop, employing bold, flat areas of colour, detailed linear motifs, and highly stylized expressive figures.

A number of works produced during the 15th century seem to have responded to the production of a few European artists working in Ethiopia, particularly the Venetian Niccolò Brancaleone. His icons, illustrated books, and decorated churches suggest a preoccupation with texture and volume reminiscent of Italian Renaissance concerns and remained influential until the 18th century.

Diptych with Mary and Her Son flanked by Archangels, Apostles and St George, Followers of Fere Tseyon, late 15th century © The Walters Art Museum, Baltimore

Christian Orthodoxy under attack. A complex array of different styles emerged throughout the 16th and early 17th centuries, showing varied degrees of adherence to foreign sources and introducing new pictorial themes, such as scenes of the Passion of Christ and the resurrection of Adam and Eve. An extensive use of curved or straight parallel lines and rigidly schematized figures began to be cultivated in Tegray (known as the Parallel Lines Style), indicating the continuing importance of regional workshops.

The wars of conquest waged by Ahmad Grany in the 16th century spread destruction and brought large areas of Ethiopia under the power of the Muslim Sultanate of Adal. In 1541 the Portuguese came to the aid of King Galawdewos with 400 musketeers and a number of non-combatants, including artisans, and Ahmad Grany was killed two years later. The exposure of Ethiopians to Portuguese cultural influence and European art forms increased in 1555, when the Society of Jesus sent a group of missionaries to the Ethiopian kingdom hoping to establish a province under their jurisdiction. In around 1603, the introduction of painted copies of a famous 5th-century icon of the Virgin Mary holding the Child, with a handkerchief and the Gospel book, known as *Protectress of the Roman People* (*Salus Populi Romani*) and kept in the Santa Maria Maggiore Basilica in Rome, came to supplant all other representations of the Virgin and Child in Ethiopia, often with the addition of Ethiopian motifs such as the archangels Michael and Gabriel flanking the Virgin and Child. A radical reorganization of the Ethiopian physical space also began to take place as castles inspired by Indo-Portuguese architecture were erected.

The abdication of the Catholic Emperor Susenyos in 1632 and the re-establishment of Orthodoxy by his son Fasiladas ended Jesuit influence. A period of stability ensued, marked by an expanding economy, growing agricultural production, the use of commodities, and substantial trade with the agricultural communities of the surrounding countryside. The foundation of the capital city at Gondar in the late 1630s fundamentally redefined the traditional Solomonic imperial camp layout, rendering permanently visible a hierarchical but more peaceful world, dominated by bureaucratic offices and elaborate religious and courtly ceremonies. Gondar became a cultural hub that witnessed a large-scale revision of traditionally accepted theological truths, the emergence of an important school of religious commentary and exegesis, major developments in liturgical music and the renewal of Ethiopian artistic life. In his support of Orthodoxy, King Fasiladas commissioned lavishly illustrated manuscripts of the Gospels and the Miracles of Mary in particular, which made use of iconographic motifs inspired both by the legacy of Brancaleone and by the Arabic Gospels illustrated by the Italian Antonio Tempesta and printed in Rome in 1591. Supported by royal patronage, the new forms of visual expression became increasingly sophisticated and came to be known as the First Gondar style. Reflecting a variety of traditions dating back to the 15th century, it employed soft, warm tones and was defined by clearly marked areas of flat colour with each figure depicted as a separate entity, in which the Virgin's drapery folds were portrayed with the parallel lines inherited from the early 1600s.

The Second Gondar style and beyond. Under Emperor Iyasu I (r. 1682–1706), Western missionaries were no longer welcome although Eastern Christians – Egyptians, Syrians, Armenians and Greeks – did come to trade and practise their arts. The so-called Second Gondar style began to emerge during this time, characterized by more crowded compositions, heavy ornamentation and lush colours, which were now more fluid and gradated. Shading and delicate facial modelling were developed, while the flat backgrounds previously used in Ethiopian painting were superseded by a greater concern for representing the spatial reality of the scenes depicted; this also included the rendering of clothing, which became more detailed and sumptuous. New iconographic themes were also adopted, such as the *Kwerata Reesu*, an icon of Christ wearing the crown of thorns on which allegiance to the ruler was sworn. As well as church walls decorated with portraits of saints and biblical scenes, striking apotropaic archangels were painted inside the doors to the holy sanctuaries, revealing the influence of Indo-Persian, Turkish and Western textile design, and the Devil began occasionally to appear along with the Crucifixion. Queen Mentewwab, the wife of Emperor Bakaffa (r. 1721–1730) and a

Diptych with Mary and Her Son flanked by Archangels, themes from the lives of Christ and the Virgin, and Saints, First Gondar Style, 17th century, © The Walters Art Museum, Baltimore

major political figure during the reigns of her son Iyasu II and grandson Iyoas I, succeeded in promoting reconciliation between rival monastic orders and became a great patron of the arts in the mid-18th century, using pictures to legitimate her status and influencing the development of the Second Gondar style. At this time members of the ruling class also possessed their own copies of illuminated manuscripts illustrating the Miracles of Mary and the tales of Our Lady Mary (*Dersana Maryam*). The styles and iconography developed during the Second Gondar period have continued to influence the production of religious and popular paintings in Ethiopia to this day.

Literature: MARILYN E. HELDMAN, *The Marian Icons of the Painter Frē Seyon: A Study in Fifteenth-Century Ethiopian Art, Patronage, and Spirituality*, Wiesbaden 1994; ANNEGRET MARX, EWA BALICKA WITAKOWSKA, MARILYN E. HELDMAN, 'Painting' , *EAE* IV, 90–101; TANIA C. TRIBE, 'Place, Space and Representation in 18th-Century Gondarine Painting', in MANUEL JOÃO RAMOS, ISABEL BOAVIDA (eds.), *The Indigenous and the Foreign in Christian Ethiopian Art: On Portuguese-Ethiopian Contacts in the 16th–17th Centuries*. Papers from the Fifth International Conference on the History of Ethiopian Art, Arrábida, 26–30 November 1999, Farnham 2004, 61–72.

Marilyn E. Heldman, American University, Washington, DC; Tania C. Tribe, SOAS, London

Contemporary art

Contemporary painting in traditional style. In 1886 Emperor Menilek II, then still king of Shawa, founded Addis Ababa as his capital city. Like his predecessors, he and his wife Empress Taytu erected churches and had them decorated with pictures. The new capital, like Gondar before it, became a magnet for painters. And as more and more foreigners and legations took up residence in the city in the wake of Menilek's modernisation programme, the demand for Ethiopian souvenirs grew and church painters began also to paint for the new clientele, alongside their production for churches and the nobility. Thus, for the first time, painting was being done outside of the church context. The traditional themes of church painting continued to be produced, such as religious subjects, equestrian saints, portraits of rulers, or battle and hunting scenes, but were augmented by a wealth of new themes such as daily life, church rituals, banquets, court scenes, or legends – above all the legend of the Queen of Sheba. Later, current events such as the first airplane landing in Addis Ababa or the Ethiopian railway were captured in painting. These new subjects represented either the painter's own inspiration or the wishes of his clientele; if the themes met with approval, they were incorporated into the artist's repertoire.

This new category of painting has been given different names; in the literature it is known variously as 'secular painting', 'traditional painting', 'folk painting', 'popular painting', or 'contemporary painting in traditional style'. New themes indeed arose, but the traditional style of church painting continued to be adhered to. Thus, for example, central perspective is ignored, important personalities are drawn large and unimportant people small. All scenes and important figures are explained in captions. When a painter painted multiple scenes of (e.g.) a legend, he would lay them out in linear succession, comic-strip fashion.

One of the first painters to work for foreign patrons was Balachaw Yemar (1894?–1957); according to his son Solomon Balachaw his father was the first to have painted the legend of the Queen of Sheba in 44 scenes for the American legation. In the 1920s, series of pictures began to be produced in commercial studios, and starting in 1931 at the newly founded Empress Manan Handicraft School. As the demand for paintings grew, above all during the tourist boom of the 1950s and 1960s, pictures were mass-produced in workshops, and self-taught artists also tried their hand – with a resultant decline in quality. Over time these very large-format paintings, which not infrequently could be as large as 90cm x 170cm, gave way to smaller pictures executed on parchment. Parchment calls to mind valuable manuscripts, has an air of ethnicity much valued by foreigners, and the pictures will fit in the traveller's luggage and on the living room wall at home.

The Dragon slayer and the Queen of Sheba, artist unknown, oil on canvas, © Ethnographic Museum Zürich (Inv. No. 16856), photo: Kathrin Leuenberger and Silvia Luckner

During the socialist period (1974–1991) very few tourists came to Ethiopia, and the market for paintings collapsed. Traditional painters also faced competition from institutions such as 'Handicrafts of Ethiopia' and the 'Ethiopian Tourist Trading Corporation'. These organizations were able to adapt quickly to the changing tastes of a heterogeneous public, and had a more extensive network for the marketing of their productions as well as access to international markets. Older artists, who painted large canvases in the relative isolation of their studios, had only qualified success in adapting to the changes in consumer taste. These artists, all of whom had a traditional education, included such figures as Berhanu Yemanu (1908–1991), Qanygeta Jambare Haylu (1913–1994), Wandemmu Wand (1917–2002), and Alamu Hayla Maryam (1918–1991). Much sought-after are the works of Qanna Sambata (1945–1991), who studied painting with Berhanu Yemanu. Paintings by all of these artists are still sold today in souvenir shops. Active until recently was the artist-priest Adamu Tasfaw (born 1930), a church painter who also worked for the tourist market.

Modern art. Academic and modern art began to develop in Addis Ababa in the 1930s. Thanks to the western educational system embraced by Emperor Hayla Sellase, it was now possible for Ethiopians to study abroad; thus painters could now get training at art schools overseas. Later, new stimuli for art education in Ethiopia came from the Fine Arts School (FAS), founded in Addis Ababa in 1958. The teaching staff, at first composed of foreigners, increasingly gave way to indigenous art professionals toward the end of the 1960s. The FAS was integrated into Addis Ababa University in 1998 as the School of Fine Arts and Design (SFAD); in June 2010 it received the name Alle School of Fine Arts and Design, in honour of the founder and first director of the FAS, Alle Felege Selam (Alafallaga Salam, b. 1929).

In the 1950s painters and sculptors produced above all religious and secular works in conventional academic style, which were commissioned by the church and the state. But tendencies to stylization and abstraction can already be seen in the work of Afewerk Tekle (Afawarq Takle) (1932–2012). Among his most important masterpieces are the internationally renowned stained glass windows in the foyer of Africa Hall, built in 1961. In 1968 he created in Harar an equestrian statue of *Ras* Makwannen, the governor of Harar and father of Hayla Sellase.

New forms of artistic expression arose in Addis Ababa in the 1960s with the development of a financially strong middle class and an increase in the number of foreigners in the city, who represented potential customers for the artists. Foreign cultural institutes and galleries mounted exhibitions which proved very popular. The new artistic impetus came first of all from Gebre Kristos Desta (Gabra Krestos Dasta) (1932–1981). He studied in Cologne (1958–1961), where he drew inspiration from German Expressionism, and created abstract compositions in oils and mixed media. Another artist who decisively influenced Ethiopian art was Alexander Boghossian (1937–2003), who called himself Skunder (Eskender) and lived in Washington DC from 1969–2003. In Paris (1957–1966) he came under the influence of the art and philosophy of 'négritude'. His abstract compositions blend motifs from magic scrolls, manuscript illumination, legends, and African art. Both of these artists taught at the FAS, Gebre Kristos Desta from 1962–1974 and Skunder from 1966–1969, where they left a lasting impression on their students. Two artists who were particularly inspired by Skunder are Wosene Worke Kosrof (Wassene Warqe Kosrof, b. 1950), who today lives in the US, and Zerihun Yetmgeta (Zaryehun Yatemgeta, b. 1941). Zerihun's work 'Research from the Art of Magic' draws particularly on magic scrolls in both style and motifs.

A cultural revolution followed in the wake of the political revolution of 1974. The plastic arts, like literature, theatre, and music, were now to convey anti-feudal and anti-imperialist content, that is, to serve as a weapon in the fight against feudalist and imperialist oppression and to educate the masses in the spirit of socialism. The FAS now taught primarily socialist realism, and artists would go to the eastern bloc countries for further training. Among the best-known of those artists who chiefly portrayed the life of workers, peasants, and soldiers in a realistic style were (alongside the above-mentioned Afewerk Tekle) Worku Mammo (Warqu Mammo, b. 1936), Tadesse Mesfin (Taddasa Masfen, b. 1952), and Eshetu Tiruneh (Eshatu Terunah, b. 1953). At the same time, there also existed a broad palette of forms of artistic expression, although on occasion paintings fell victim to censorship. Artists in this category included the already-mentioned Zerihun Yetmgeta; Desta Hagos (Dasta Hagos, b. 1952), a woman painter who often treated the burden of women; Tibebe Terffa (Tebaba Tarfa, b. 1948), with his abstract compositions of forms and colours; and Getachew Yossef (Getachaw Yosef, b. 1957) who, influenced by Rastafarian philosophy and religion, painted anti-war and anti-hunger pictures. Getachew was also the creator of the 'African Union' and 'China-Africa Forum' sculptures (2003) at Addis Ababa's Bole Airport; these were commissioned by the government.

After the overthrow of the military regime in 1991, the art scene in Addis Ababa re-emerged into vigorous life. Numerous galleries opened their doors, such as the Asni Art Gallery, the Lela Art Gallery, and the Laphto Art Gallery, and foreign cultural institutes like the Alliance Ethio-Française and the Goethe-Institut once again hosted exhibitions. Young artists experimented with new forms of expression, e.g. abstractions, and with new media and techniques, such as mixed media, recycled objects, digital compositions, photography, installations, and performance art. Among these artists are Elias Simé (Elyas Seme, b. 1968) and Assefa Gebrekidan (Asaffa Gabra Kidan, b. 1973); they have attracted international attention for their installations and

'Research from the Art of Magic', Zerihun Yetmgeta, mixed media on bamboo, © Ethnographic Museum Zürich (Inv. No. 20999), photo: Kathrin Leuenberger

'Untitled', Tibebe Terffa, oil on canvas, © Ethnographic Museum Zürich (Inv. No. 21387), photo: Kathrin Leuenberger

mixed media works, which employ (among other things) buttons, cardboard, household containers and utensils, and string. In 2004 these two artists were among 28 African exhibitors at Dak'Art, the Biennale for Contemporary African Art in Dakar, Senegal. Mickaël Bethe-Sélassié (Mikael Beta Sellase, b. 1951) has created sculptures of colourful papier maché; he lives and works in Paris and has exhibited (*inter alia*) at the Haus der Kulturen der Welt in Berlin, in 1994. Tesfahun Kibru (Tasfahun Kebru, b. 1978) is likewise known for his sculptures, in which he utilizes materials such as baskets, gourds, metal, rubber, leather, wood, and clay. Since the artists are not government-sponsored, the new graduates of the SFAD organize collective studios, where they have a place to work and exhibit. As most of them lack the financial means to travel abroad, they are frequently cut off from the latest artistic trends and developments in the West.

Eritrea. Early 20th-century Asmara was a place of dynamic development, under the influence of Europe and Ethiopia. Italian artists were active predominantly in the Italian colonial period from 1890–1941. The demand for works of art grew especially in the 1920s, when Eritrea was going through a period of rapid urbanization. Reliefs and murals employing classicist and pseudo-antique motifs enjoyed popularity. Contemporary painting in traditional style, aimed at a small tourist market, developed at the same time as in Ethiopia. At the time of the federation (1952–1962) and later union (1962–1991) with Ethiopia, Eritrean art students studied at the FAS in Addis Ababa, but also at art schools in India. During the military clash with Ethiopia, the Eritrean People's Liberation Front (EPLF) founded in 1978 a group of fighter-artists with the goal of creating 'art for the masses'. Thus a style developed which was closely bound up with socialist realism, and art glorified the war and the life of the people. After 1991 art received a new impetus from various forms of modern art, and artists organized exhibitions chiefly in Asmara. Alongside free art forms, which were promoted by art teachers from India and China, realistic painting predominated. After the war with Ethiopia (1998–2000), former soldiers again painted war scenes in increasing numbers.

Artists earn a living as illustrators of books and magazines, or as theatre designers, or they work for the government. They tend to paint idealized scenes from the war of liberation, such as dancing soldiers, shared meals in the bush, or other group activities. But there are also artists who, alongside politically inspired forms of expression, also create works combining abstract forms and folk motifs with human figures. These include Mikael Adonay (b. 1962), who combines modern decorative elements and motifs from church painting in a colourful oeuvre and connects these with themes from the war.

Literature: ELISABETH BIASIO, 'Contemporary Painting in Traditional Style', *EAE* V, 260–261; LEAH NIEDERSTADT, 'Modern and Contemporary Art', *EAE* V, 257–260; WOLBERT G.C. SMIDT, 'Modern and Contemporary Art in Eritrea', *EAE* V, 262–264.

Elisabeth Biasio, Zürich

Music

As a result of widespread population migration as well as the circulation of music through rapidly proliferating virtual networks, the music of Ethiopia, Eritrea, and other countries in the Horn of Africa is beginning to reach listeners worldwide. Ethiopian musicians are performing in clubs and restaurants across North America, Europe, Australia, Africa and the Middle East. Recordings, in particular the Paris-based Buda Music series *Éthiopiques*, which now numbers nearly thirty compact discs, is available online offering a selection of Ethiopian and Eritrean popular and traditional styles. If Ethiopia and Eritrea have become famous in recent decades for their distinctive cuisine, today served internationally, the music of the African Horn is also gaining a new audience abroad.

Music in Ethiopian religious life. Ethiopia is a source of important historical traditions in the literature, religion, and the arts. None has been more generative in the past than the body of church music associated with the Orthodox Christian Church founded in the early 4th century CE. This body of sacred chants, termed *zema*, is traditionally attributed to the divine inspiration of a 6th-century saint named Yared. The chants are divided into three melodic categories, each with different associations: one category represents God the Father, the second the Son, and a third, the Holy Spirit.

Qabaro (church drums), Lalibala, © Serge Dewel-Mouton

While the Ethiopian musical tradition is the only one in Africa that has a system of musical notation, invented by Ethiopian church musicians in the 16th century, the chant is transmitted by highly trained, non-ordained Church musicians (*dabtara*) primarily as an oral tradition. Accompanying the chant on holidays with drums and small metal rattles, as well as with liturgical dance, the musicians perform Church rituals that last throughout the night. Most church musicians specialize in one area of sacred music, some becoming authorities on chant, others on instrumental practice and dance. Due to their literacy, some musicians acquire skills as healers and magicians, writing amulets and performing oral therapies to cure illnesses. The entry of Protestant missions into the country in the 19th century, and the flowering of 20th-century evangelical churches, has exerted strong influences on Christian innovations in musical practices throughout Ethiopia and in its diaspora.

Ethiopia and Eritrea are also home to many Muslims who celebrate their religion with recitation of the Koran in local mosques. Particularly well known are the performances of Islamic *zikri* (devotional) rituals in the south-eastern Ethiopian city of Harar, which both celebrate the birth of the Prophet and mark different occasions in his life cycle. Other peoples in the region perform their own unique sacred musical styles, such as the Oromo people in the central and western regions of the country for whom musical performance is integral to their indigenous *Qaalluu* religion and worship of their sky god.

Ethnic and regional musical styles. Beyond music traditions associated with their religious life, Ethiopia and Eritrea have many music traditions associated with different regions and the particular ethnic communities that live within them. These secular music traditions, generally referred to as *zafan*, vary greatly in their musical structure and performance styles. The music of Eritrea, highland Ethiopia, and Islamic areas on the eastern borders of both countries is closely related to the music of the Middle East. Most distinctive is the relationship of voices and instruments which sound in a texture called heterophony, where the performers sing or play the same melody together but with slightly different elaborations. The vocal and instrumental styles of the highland plateau region of the Horn often have a nasal sound and in general, melodies are heavily ornamented. With regard to rhythm, music and dance of many regions of the Horn have distinctive rhythmic patterns, although Ethiopian rhythm does not generally have the multi-part complexity heard in West Africa. In addition to their distinctive rhythms, secular dances often have movement styles associated with different regions and certain ethnic communities. Some dance styles, such as the dance *eskesta*, which uses a wide range of shoulder motions, are closely associated with Amhara culture, while a wide range of foot motifs and other motions characterize Oromo circle and line dances.

There are many special types of secular song and instrumental styles from the Ethiopian highland areas known as cultural music (*bahelawi*). These styles are associated with ethnic groups such as the Amhara, Oromo, Gurage, and others while also being associated with the regions these people live in, such as Gojjam, Wallaga, and Shawa.

Secular music along the western and southern borders of Ethiopia differs from that of the highland plateau in that it variously features multi-part musical styles. Among the Dorze people of Gamu Gofa region, polyphony (*edo*) is particularly prominent in songs of homage to individuals, called *halaqa*, and for the celebration of the annual *Masqal* festival. The complex textures of Dorze music share an aesthetic of elaborate patterns similar to that which Dorze weavers produce in cloth.

Musicians. Much of the secular music in the Horn is transmitted and performed by professional musicians, some of whom often inherit their profession from their parents. Perhaps most notable are the minstrels of the highland plateau area, known as *azmari*. In the past the *azmari* were itinerant and played a role as social critics, improvising sophisticated texts of praise or criticism. They continue to perform today in various settings ranging from village drinking houses, to church processionals and wedding ceremonies, as well as in their own clubs in urban areas.

Azmari perform many song genres, including the *shellala*, which incite patriotism and fervour for battle, and the *fukkara*, which commemorate or praise prominent warriors. Another cohort of unusual singers in the highland area of Ethiopia are the *lalibaloch*, who tend to perform as husband and wife couples, descended from individuals who suffered from Hansen's disease (leprosy). Early in the morning, the *lalibaloch* go from house to house singing songs of praise to garner alms. If they are not rewarded with food or money, they improvise songs criticizing the resident. *Lalibaloch* are also associated with strophic songs performed at weddings, as well as songs improvised for memorial services.

Each community has its own singers who transmit local traditions and oral history. Among the Arbore and Hamar peoples in the southwest, songs are sung for recreation

Konso men and women performing music, © Serge Dewel-Mouton

and to accompany work. Hamar musicians sing songs about their ancestors (*aeke gadi*) that recall occasions of historical importance and narrate the past.

Musical ensembles. By the early 20th century, musical ensembles began to proliferate, some organized to represent the state and to unify its multi-ethnic population. These ensembles helped introduce western instruments and music to the Horn of Africa. The Ethiopian Imperial Bodyguard Orchestra, founded in 1929, performed Western music at state events and to welcome visiting dignitaries. From the 1950s onward, the Hayla Sellase Theatre Orchestra brought together a synthesis of cosmopolitan and Ethiopian sounds in a new modern cultural style (*bahel zamanawi*). In 1963, Orchestra Ethiopia was founded, which brought together musicians from all regions and many ethnic groups to perform at official government functions as well as on Ethiopian television and radio. Orchestra Ethiopia inspired other groups in Ethiopia and throughout the Ethiopian diaspora, some of which follow the Orchestra Ethiopia model of having dancers costumed in the dress of particular ethnic communities or locales, and performing music that emphasizes the distinctive melodies, beats, and song texts associated with these people and places. These ensembles today perform in hotels and restaurants in Ethiopian cities for both tourists and urban Ethiopians interested in a range of music from across their country. Some of these musicians were trained at the Yared Music School, established in Addis Ababa in 1967, which offers instruction in both Ethiopian and in western musical styles.

Global musical styles. From the middle of the 20th century onward, many Ethiopian musicians were attracted to popular music styles such as jazz, rock, and a range of African American genres. Mulatu Astatke went abroad to study in the 1950s, acquiring skills on the vibraphone and exposure to the broader world of Afro-Caribbean music and jazz first in England, and then in the United States. His 'Ethio-jazz' has engaged outside listeners to the Ethiopian popular music orbit, as demonstrated by his music's use in the soundtrack of Jim Jarmusch's 2005 film, *Broken Flowers*. While

Mulatu's music is cosmopolitan, his 'Ethio-jazz' also speaks to Ethiopians, especially those who share his social (cosmopolitan, urban), regional (highland), and ethnic (Amhara) affiliation.

Popular music and jazz flowered in Addis Ababa in the decade before the Ethiopian revolution began in 1974. In addition to Mulatu Astatke, other pre-revolutionary Ethiopian musicians, such as Tilahun Gessesse (1940–2009), Alemayehu Eshete (b. 1940), Mahmoud Ahmed (b. 1941), and Aster Aweke (b. 1959), established their careers performing with important ensembles in the Ethiopian capital. All spent considerable time abroad during and after the revolution. Tilahun Gessesse was associated with at least three institutions, including the Patriotic Association Theatre, the Imperial Bodyguard Band, and the National Theatre, building a career based almost entirely among what became devoted Ethiopian audiences both at home and in the diaspora. Mahmoud Ahmed began his career with the Imperial Body Guard Orchestra, but gained international fame following the 1986 release of his recording *Era Mela Mela* on the Crammed Discs label from Belgium. Alemayehu Eshete began singing with the Police Orchestra in 1960, and drew on rock and soul music to the extent that he was dubbed 'the Ethiopian Elvis'. Aster Aweke began performing at the Patriotic Association Theatre early in her teenage years, and sang with a number of bands until she left Ethiopia for the diaspora in 1981. Although she broke through to a broader audience with her 1989 recording *Aster* on Columbia Records, Aster's subsequent career has been divided between Ethiopia and the diaspora. The popularity of these four musicians crosses musical styles as well as transcends ethnic heritages: Tilahun Gessesse was an Oromo, Mahmoud Ahmed, a Gurage, and Alemayehu Eshete and Aster Aweke, Amhara. That these Ethiopian musicians in the popular domain drew both on aspects of Ethiopian music and the musical worlds beyond the borders of the Horn of Africa became a crucial factor that enabled them to initiate musical careers in the Ethiopian diaspora during and after the revolutionary years, with eventual return to their homeland.

Literature: KAY KAUFMAN SHELEMAY, 'Music in the Ethiopian American Diaspora: A Preliminary Overview', in SVEIN EGE, HARALD ASPEN, BIRHANU TEFERRA, SHIFERAW BEKELE (eds.), *Proceedings of the 16th International Conference of Ethiopian Studies*, Wiesbaden 2009, 1153–1164; KAY KAUFMAN SHELEMAY, 'Music', *EAE* III, 1082–1086.

Kay Kaufman Shelemay, Harvard University

Musical instruments

In a country as rich and diverse as Ethiopia, music is unsurprisingly also rich and diverse. Musical instruments in Ethiopia vary according to region, context, ethnic group and sometimes the availability of materials used to make them. However, it is possible to briefly point out some characteristics of musical instruments found in Ethiopia today.

Wind instruments. Wind instruments found in Ethiopia are mainly flutes and horns. Flutes are usually made of bamboo or reed (and nowadays plastic pipes) and are end-blown, without a duct. Flutes played solo (*washent* on the high plateaus; *ululle, gari* or *faga* in Oromo) usually comprise two to four fingerholes. Flutes played in a group (such as the *embilta* in the high plateaus, the *weyssa* in Aari or the *bol* in Berta) have no fingerholes; the melody is generated with the combination of each pitch produced by individual instruments (hocket technique). In some regions, panpipes (*fanfa* in Konso) and globular flutes (Maale *umburko*) are played.

The horns or trumpets are instruments played by the vibration of the musician's lips, placed either at one extremity of the instrument (end-blown trumpet) or at an opening on its side (side-blown or lateral trumpet). They are made from different materials: bottle gourd, wood, metal, bamboo or animal horn. Even though they are without finger holes, musicians can often play more than one tone, either by producing different harmonics, or by covering with the hand all or part of the extremity of the instrument. In several cases, trumpets are symbols of power such as the *malakkat* in the Amhara and Tegray regions, which are used to signal information such as a gathering, or play a part in funeral ceremonies. The Berta, near the Sudan border, play horns in impressive ensembles (*waza*), comprising ten to twelve instruments (from 50cm to 1.80m in length). Finally, it is interesting to note that the small curved trumpet *turumba*, probably of Western origin but manufactured locally out of brass or copper, can be found in some localities of Ethiopia.

Alamu Aga playing *bagana*, © Stéphanie Weisser

Stringed instruments. The lyre is one of Ethiopia's most emblematic instruments. It can be played either by strumming the strings altogether, usually with a plectrum, or by plucking the strings individually with the fingers. Lyres can be played in different contexts: for example, in the highlands, the large buzzing lyre *bagana* is only played in religious contexts, whereas the *krar* is used for both secular and spiritual occasions, although the presence of the *krar* in paraliturgical occasions is relatively recent. Both can be played by strumming the strings with a plectrum or by plucking the strings individually with the fingers.

The fiddle *masenqo*, played in the

Ethiopian highlands, is also emblematic, as it is closely associated with the poet-musician-comedian-entertainers or *azmari*. Even though the *masenqo* has only one string, made of horsehair, players often demonstrate impressive virtuosity. Mostly played by traditional musicians (*azmari*), it is employed in most rituals on the high plateaus, private or public, such as mourning occasions, weddings, *zar* possession rituals, baptisms, etc. The *masenqo* also accompanies, though played outside the church, the celebration of Epiphany (*Temqat*), which is the most important and holiest holiday of the Ethiopian Orthodox Church.

It is worth noting the existence of the *tingle*, a musical bow used in the Southern Region by Kara adolescent boys for personal meditation. Comprising three strings, the *tingle* is played with its end inserted in the musician's mouth.

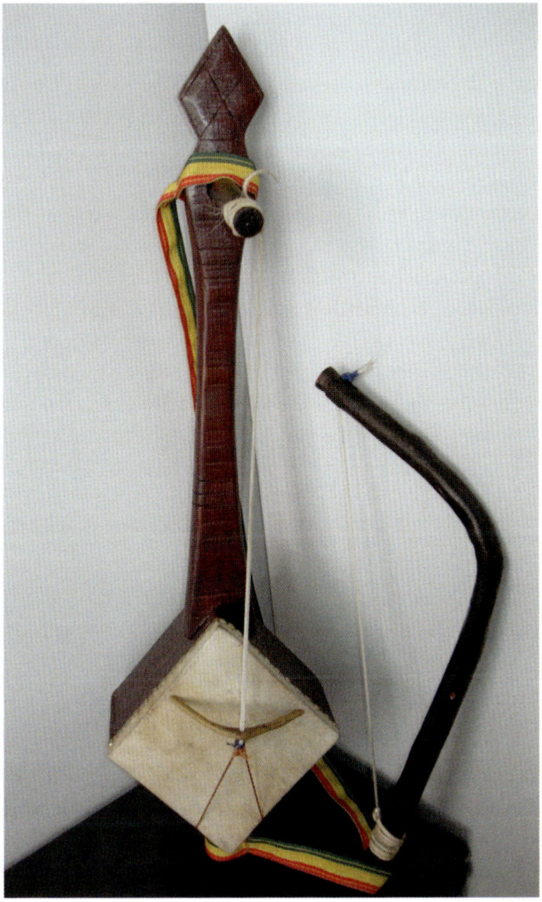

Masenqo, © Stéphanie Weisser

Drums and percussion instruments. In Ethiopia drums are of many different types and sizes. In several societies, the possession of a drum is associated with a specific social status (political power or belonging to a caste). Bells made of metal or stone are often present in church compounds on the high plateaus, and are used for the call to prayer. Wooden blocks are found all over Ethiopia, as well as rattles made of gourds, tortoise shell and other materials. They are used for rhythmic accompaniment. Among the rattles, the hand-held metallic sistrum (*tsanatsel*) is, together with the wooden prayer stick (*maqqwamiya*) and the large two-headed drum (*kabaro*), used in Orthodox Church accompanying group singing and dancing. Finally, one should note that xylophones are found amongst the Aari and lamellophones ('thumb pianos') in the southwest.

Singing and the human body. It is worth mentioning that several musical sounds can be produced with the human body: singing of course, but also clapping, ululating and sonorous breathing.

'Globalized' instruments. Western instruments have been sporadically introduced in Ethiopia since the end of the 15th century by merchants, travellers, diplomats and missionaries. However, they did not find their way into Ethiopian music until the end of 19th century, when brass instruments were adopted, at first by military bands. Other foreign musical styles had an important influence on Ethiopian musical life and instruments. After World War II, American popular musical styles such as jazz, rhythm&blues, soul, rock and pop were brought to Ethiopia, namely through Kagnew army base and radio station (Asmara, 1943–1977). Owned by the American government, the radio station broadcasted the latest songs from the USA. This led to the creation in the 1950s of several theatre orchestras and, from the 1960s onwards, of private bands. Western instruments such as the saxophone, piano, cello, double bass, trumpet, trombone, drum set, etc. were introduced into the then expanding Ethiopian urban musical scene and nightlife during the period commonly called the 'golden age' of Ethiopian music. It is also important to mention the influence of Mulatu Astatke (b. 1943), who led the integration of the vibraphone, conga drums and organ into Ethiopian music and contributed to the development of the genre nowadays known worldwide as 'Ethio-jazz'.

Changes have always occurred in music; in Ethiopia, as in the rest of the world, globalization tends to amplify and accelerate these, especially in urban areas. Urban pop musicians frequently use electric guitars and synthesizers, and amplified or electrified *krar* lyres can also be found. Also, over the last decade, computers are more and more used for musical purposes, including the use of virtual instruments and sound effects. However, musical expressions, whether 'modern' or 'traditional', enrich each other, as do the sounds of the various, numerous and fascinating musical instruments played today in Ethiopia.

Literature: ANNE DAMON et al., 'Instruments, musical', *EAE* III, 169–174; TIMKEHET TEFFERA, 'Western Wind Instruments and the Development of Ethiopian Popular Music', *Studia Instrumentorum Musicae Popularis* III, *New Series*, III 2013, 349–376; TIMKEHET TEFFERA, 'Tradition and Modernism: Emergence and Development of Popular Music in Addis Ababa: The Golden Years', in *Beiträge zur Jahrestagung des Nationalkomitees der Bundesrepublik Deutschland im International Council for Traditional Music* (*ICTM/UNESCO*) *am 15. und 16. Februar 2008*, Münster 2010.

Stéphanie Weisser, Université Libre de Bruxelles

Ethiopia and Eritrea in literature

The Horn of Africa has been extensively described and fantasized by writers, travellers, historians and geographers from different countries, thus constructing long-lasting images and narratives of a mythical ancestral land, rich in religious and cultural heritage. The work of many renowned writers and intellectuals abounds with allusions to Ethiopia and Ethiopians: from Marco Polo to Immanuel Kant, from John Milton, to Ludovico Ariosto, from John Mandeville's account of Prester John to Samuel Johnson's Ethiopian prince Rasselas, from Samuel T. Coleridge's 'Abyssinian maid' to Derek A. Walcott's 'Lion of Judah' in his postcolonial Caribbean drama 'O Babylon!'

Throughout the centuries, representations and constructions of Ethiopia and Eritrea have thus shaped a vivid cultural imagery that has included works as diverse as Johnson's moral tales and the Rastafarian movement that saw in Ethiopia the promised land and the origin of a diasporic culture. Although the Horn of Africa has been mainly portrayed as a sort of Eden by Western writers, in more recent times an additional complementary facet has been added to this picture: that of a region of poverty and famine and a point of departure for many asylum seekers who have also produced their own memoirs and narratives.

The middle ages. The regions beyond Egypt (roughly identified as Ethiopia) exercised a particular fascination for European writers in the modern era, as this unique region was perceived as both Christian and 'exotic' at the same time. Some elements were crucial in the literary representation of Ethiopia, in particular: the utopian fascination of the Queen of Sheba and the literary and religious popularity of the *Kebra nagast*, the Solomonic national saga, as well as the legends of Prester John, which were very popular in Europe between the 12th and the 17th century, while he was often identified with the Ethiopian king, especially from the 14th century on.

However, *Aithiopia* (an unspecified 'land of the black people') was the subject of literary compositions even in Pharaonic Egypt and later. From Ancient Greek through Hellenistic, Imperial Roman and late antique times, not only historians and geographers wrote about Ethiopia and Eritrea, but also poets and literati (such as Heliodorus in *Aithiopika*) often used *Aithiopia* as a fruitful, imaginative background, so much so that the mention of Ethiopians (*Aithiopes*) became a mandatory *topos* in the epic genre, from Homer to the last epic poet Nonnus of Panopolis in the 4th century CE.

From Roman to medieval times, the concepts of 'India' and 'Ethiopia' tended to become interchangeable and could cover territories that spanned a vast area from the East African coast, along the Red Sea to the Indian Ocean, thus including the Horn of Africa. One of the first mentions of 'Ethiopia' in modern Western Europe was made in the anonymous medieval French poem *La Chanson de Roland* (1075–1110). Around 1200 in Germany, Wolfram von Eschenbach in his monumental epos, *Parzival*, referred to a legendary, black 'oriental queen', Belacane, who conceived a 'mixed son', Faireviz, by a Christian French crusader. Geographic works, fictional literature, and even maps came to identify Ethiopia with 'Abassia' or 'Habassia' (from the Arabic *al-Habash*). In particular, towards the end of the 13th century, Marco Polo's influential travelogue, *Milione*, refers more than once to *Abasce* (Abyssinia) and mentions its king *Lo re d'Abasce*. In the 14th century, the moving of the legend of Prester John to Africa and the relationships that Ethiopian communities started developing outside Ethiopia (Jerusalem, Sinai, and later Rome) provided European writers with further imaginative and literary elements.

The first known reference to 'Ethiopia' in English texts is found in 1387, in John of Trevisa's translation from Latin of Ranulf Higden's chronicle *Polychronicon*, while 'The Three Kings of Cologne' (a translation of *Historia Trium Regum*) was another extremely popular text of the late 1300s that provided information about Prester John, Saba, and 'Ethiopes'. Many of the histories and geographies translated from Latin into English in the 15th and 16th centuries mention Ethiopia; while in Spain, Heliodorus' *Aithiopika* was rendered in Castilian by Fernando de Mena as *Historia etiópica de los amores de Teágenes y Cariclea* (1554). But also more reliable studies on Ethiopia appeared in the 16th century: in particular, the first detailed eye-witness report of Ethiopia by the Portuguese missionary and explorer Francisco Álvares (translated into Italian in 1550 by Giovanni Battista Ramusio), the first historiographic attempt by Mariano Vittori, and the first ever printed Ge'ez text, published in 1513 by Johannes Potken. The Reformation had a special influence on the shaping of the image of Christian Ethiopia, as reformers continued the quest of the humanists for lost knowledge and manuscripts that were expected to help understanding the biblical word of God.

16th–18th centuries. In the 16th and 17th centuries, the Jesuits' missionary enterprise on the one hand and then the important linguistic, historical and ethnographical works by the eminent German scholar Hiob Ludolf, on the other, fostered in Europe an increasing interest in Ethiopia and Eritrea, often driven by religious motivations. In Italy in the 16th century, both Ludovico Ariosto's and Torquato Tasso's masterpieces, respectively 'Orlando Furioso' and 'Gerusalemme liberata', referred in different ways to Ethiopia and its Christian king. Around 1640, the Portuguese Jesuit Jerónimo Lobo wrote about Ethiopia in his 'Itinerario e outros escritos inéditos', which circulated amongst European readers, mostly thanks to French translations. Later on, Samuel Johnson translated Lobo's work into English as 'A Voyage to Abyssinia' and this experience had a profound effect on Johnson's fiction. The Portuguese Jesuit Manoel de Almeida, relying on Pedro Páez's unpublished work, wrote a history of Ethiopia, 'Historia de Etiopía', which appeared posthumously in 1660, and which also contained some information about the *Kebra nagast*.

In the 17th century, a recognizable Ethiopia already appears regularly in English literary texts. In particular in Thomas Peyton's poem about paradise, 'The Glasse of Time', that probably served as a model for an extremely famous literary work, John Milton's 'Paradise Lost'; here Milton mentions 'Abassin kings' living on 'Mount Amara', which 'some supposed True Paradise'. In the following century, Ethiopia appeared more frequently in English literature, often as a type of Eden (for instance in the works of Samuel T. Coleridge, Ellis C. Knight, Archibald Campbell and George Colman). Geographic works that in the same period described the Horn of Africa were often rich in details but tended to mix facts with legends and misinterpretations (for instance 'De Nili et aliorum fluminum origine' by the Dutch author Isaac Vossius). In the 18th century, the philosopher Immanuel Kant in his 'Sämmtliche Werke: In Chronologischer Reihenfolge', following a German legend on the existence of a paradise-like land of plenty, referred to Ethiopia (Abessinien) as a 'land of plenty', while the Spanish author Dom Pedro Caldéron de la Barca wrote a play on Makedda, Queen of Sheba, 'La sibila del Oriente y gran reina de Saba'. Samuel Johnson's novel 'The Prince of Abyssinia' (also known as 'Rasselas'), published in 1759 and promptly translated into French, was the first piece of English literature to deal with Ethiopia at length, while the second English novel set in Ethiopia would be, almost a century later, William Dalton's children's adventure story 'Tiger Prince'. Travelogues were proper to English literary representations of Ethiopia at the end of the 18th century, James Bruce's 'Travels to Discover the Source of the Nile' having the strongest impact. Ethiopia was also long believed to be the place of origin of Russia's most famous slave, Abraham Ganibal, the great-grandfather of Alexander Pushkin; the Russian poet often mentioned his African roots in his work and even dedicated to his African ancestor an unfinished seven-chapter novel, 'Arap Petra velikogo', usually translated as 'Peter the Great's Negro'.

19th century. As a result of the enlightenment and its new approach to science, soon fuelled by Positivism and eventually followed by formal colonialism, in the 19th century the Horn of Africa, like most of the continent, became the object of geographic explorations and ethnographic expeditions. Among the numerous 19th century explorers who wrote on the Horn of Africa, we may mention Carlo Piaggia, Henry Salt, Nathaniel Pearce, Antonio Cecchi, Gustavo Bianchi, Giuseppe Sapeto and Mansfield Parkyns.

The British Napier expedition to Maqdala of 1867–1868 and Emperor Tewodros II's resistance to it proved to be fruitful sources for European writers, among others

George MacDonald Fraser in his English novel 'Flashman on the March' and Emil Jonveaux in his French travelogue 'Deux ans dans l'Afrique Orientale'. In the same period, German Protestant missionaries became very active in Ethiopia and produced influential writings about the country; in particular Johann Ludwig Krapf's writings on the Oromo exercised a long-term influence. In the 1880s, Ernest Alfred Wallis Budge began to translate the *Kebra nagast* into English; Rider Haggard was a good friend of Budge and the latter's influence can be detected in Haggard's famous work 'King Solomon's Mines'. In *fin-de-siècle* Germany, following the wide popularity of explorers' travel accounts, Karl May wrote the adventure novel 'Der Scheik von Harrar'.

Meanwhile, missionaries, travellers, explorers, historians, anthropologists and geographers had not only been producing long-lasting narratives, influential travelogues and pieces of literature, but they had also unintentionally opened the path to the European colonization of the region at the end of the 19th century. Colonialism obviously also impacted literature and left a multifaceted mark in European literatures, especially Italian. Italian colonialism in northeastern Africa started in the 1880s. In the 1890s, Ferdinando Martini, writer and governor of Eritrea from 1897 to 1907, wrote semi-literary accounts that combined literary, documentary and administrative scopes. He described 'Affrica' not only as a miserable place, but also as a pure and primordial one, where the human spirit can elevate itself and meet God. Italians also hoped to gain control of Ethiopia, but their strategies proved to be unsuccessful as they were defeated by the Ethiopians more than once: in Dogali in 1887 and, most of all, near Adwa in 1896. Menilek II's unexpected victory in Adwa had a strong, symbolic impact, both nationally and internationally, as for instance in François de Courel's play 'La fille sauvage: Pièce en six actes', and it also inspired Rastafarianism and Panafricanism.

Modern times. Adwa left a strong mark in Italian culture until, at least, the Italian occupation of Ethiopia in 1935–1936, as proven by Gabriele d'Annunzio's work, among others. During Fascism in particular, the fascination with Ethiopian female bodies and sexuality became quite evident in Italian popular culture (literature included), despite Fascism's efforts to ban 'mixed' relations and 'miscegenation'. The Italian invasion of Ethiopia also produced strong, unfavourable reactions among African American authors such as Theodore J. Ward, Joseph Harvey Lowell Baxter and Pauline Hopkins.

Emperor Hayla Sellase's coronation in 1930 was attended by many international observers who wrote about it, including Evelyn Waugh, who travelled again to Ethiopia during the Italian war of occupation and produced the influential travelogue 'Waugh in Abyssinia'. A large number of literary and semi-literary texts on Ethiopia and Eritrea were published in Italy during the Fascist period, for instance the works of Alberto Pollera, while the most prolific French author of this period was Henry de Monfreid.

In the rest of the 20th century, Western literary output that deals with Ethiopia and Eritrea is so vast that it is impossible even to sketch it here. In Italian literature, we cannot fail to mention Ennio Flaiano's 'Tempo di uccidere' and Pier Paolo Pasolini's several works of the 1960s and 1970s, which both retained elements connected to the memory of colonialism, erotic fascination and the image of a mythical ancient land. French writers produced several semi-literary and historical novels on the region, including works that focus on the years spent by French poet Arthur Rimbaud in the city of Harar.

In the 21st century, Western literatures have continued to display a multifaceted interest in the Horn of Africa, as for instance the American novel by Abraham Verghese 'Cutting for Stone', and an increasing number of works written by writers of Ethiopian or Eritrean descent, often with autobiographical goals, has been appearing in various languages, notably German, English, and Italian.

Literature: GIOVANNA TRENTO, WOLBERT G.C. SMIDT, RICHARD PANKHURST, WENDY LAURA BELCHER, 'Literature: Ethiopia and Eritrea in Literature', *EAE* V, 390–405.

Giovanna Trento, University of Cape Town

VII Religion

Introduction

No aspect of Ethiopian cultural life is more interesting and vivid than its great religious diversity. The tremendous variety of the country's traditional indigenous religions is dealt with in some detail in the Chapter on Peoples. From a historical perspective much of Ethiopia's history has been dominated by Orthodox Christianity and Islam. Both religions have been present in the country almost from their inception. However, their history and interactions in Ethiopia differ from much of the neighbouring countries, where Islam quickly rose to a dominant position. In Ethiopia, Christianity was from its beginnings associated with the State and its ruler. From the conversion of King Ezana in the 4th century, through Zagwe kings of Lalibala, to the 'restoration' of the Solomonic rulers in the 13th century to the fall of the Emperor Hayla Sellase in 1974, the Church was linked to the throne. Moreover, its clearly defined hierarchy added to its association with the control of land, literacy and effective power. In many ways the pre-eminent institution of the Church itself was monasticism, and the exploits of many of its greatest monastic leaders are commemorated in hagiographic texts including especially *gadlat* (Vitae) and *taammerat* (miracles). However, Christianity was not limited to rulers and their clergy. It also played a major role in the passage through life of simple believers through both the sacraments and the seasonal rhythms dictated by its numerous feasts and fasts. In a number of cases including circumcision, diet and the Saturday Sabbath these elements also buttressed Ethiopian Christians' visions of themselves as a chosen Israelite people.

According to Muslims, Islam's history in Ethiopia began in the earliest days of Muhammed's activities when his followers were sent to seek refuge in the court of the Ethiopian king, the *najashi*. Whatever the historicity of this event, Ethiopia was not conquered like so much of the surrounding area in the Nile and Red Sea basins. Rather it was largely represented in the country through traders, scholars and nomads, with a single person possibly holding two or even all three of these roles. Many of the greatest figures of Ethiopian Islam are commemorated by pilgrimage to their graves or other shrines, which perhaps more than any other feature 'places' Islam in the country.

Until comparatively recently relations between Muslim and Christians were, if unequal, generally peaceful. While representatives of the two groups struggled throughout the centuries, and at time this led to considerable bloodshed, daily interactions were bolstered by the complementary role played by members of the two faith communities. In recent years this has changed somewhat. In part this can be attributed to the rise of Islamist movements which as in other parts of the world, have heightened Muslim self-awareness and limited the possibilities of compromise. However, it is also connected to the arrival in Ethiopia in modern times of Christian missions, both Catholic and Protestant, which have been less tolerant than traditional Orthodoxy. While the earliest Christian missions can be dated to the middle ages and the Catholic Jesuits, who briefly succeeded in the country, in the 19th and especially the 20th century both Protestants and Catholics have arrived in unprecedented numbers. Their appeal to members of ethnic groups neglected by the dominant Orthodox State has been remarkable. In addition to the religious message they brought, they also were often the vehicles for the introduction of new technologies and institutions particularly in the realms of education and medicine. They have also, despite their universal message, done much to strengthen ethnic awareness. Although not strictly speaking of a missionary group, one of the most interesting recent arrivals are the Rastafari. Representatives of a religious movement with symbolic connections to Ethiopia (Zion) and the Emperor Hayla Sellase ('*Ras* Tafari'), they have spread Ethiopia's fame throughout the world and settled in small numbers in their symbolic homeland.

History and faith of the Ethiopian Orthodox Church

Introduction. Initially as a daughter and, since 1950, a sister of the Coptic Orthodox Church of Alexandria, the Ethiopian Orthodox Tawahedo Church is a member of Oriental Orthodox Churches, identified as non-Chalcedonians for rejecting the decisions taken at the Council of Chalcedon in 451 CE on the issue of Christology. The Church's history and faith are best narrated following the tradition of dividing the time into eras, or dynasties that ruled the country.

The first is one of the several ruling houses of the Aksumite era during which Christianity was introduced into Ethiopia. After the fall of Aksum, the Houses of Zagwe in Lasta, and of Amhara (in Shawa and later in Gondar) had their turns on the royal throne.

Beginnings during the Aksumite kingdom. Ethiopia is geographically well situated to have come in contact with Christianity within a century or two of the faith's establishment. It is close to the Middle East, the birthplace of Christianity, and the region from which it was launched. Moreover, the Red Sea, which was routinely travelled by Middle Easterners, constituted much of the country's eastern border. During the Byzantine era, voyagers must have frequented Adulis, Ethiopia's seaport, whose importance as an emporium has been recorded by many.

According to a remarkable story from the 4th century, Meropius, a philosopher, boarded a boat in Tyre, the one-time famous Syrian seaport in the south of today's Lebanon, and embarked upon a voyage to visit 'India'. Meropius took with him two of his students, Frumentius and Aedesius. The vessel anchored at an Ethiopian port, possibly Adulis. But the voyagers were attacked as the vessel had no permission to anchor in Ethiopian territory. All of the travellers were massacred, save for the two students who 'were found under a tree preparing their lessons'.

The boys Aedesius and Frumentius were taken to the king, who kept them against their will. The king made Aedesius his cupbearer and Frumentius his treasurer and secretary. On his deathbed, the king granted them their freedom. However, by then the two had become such trusted royal advisors that the queen dowager pleaded with them to stay until the crown prince had matured enough to be able to govern the country. They agreed to stay and helped the royal family remain in control of the throne. Frumentius, who after the king's death became a man of higher authority, used his good offices to firmly establish Christianity in Ethiopia. He visited Aksum's traders and business people with the aim of locating Christians among them. He encouraged these Christians to build, as they did, oratories with schools attached to them. This way, Frumentius established the first Christian churches in Ethiopia. In time, Aedesius returned to Tyre where he became a priest of a parish church. Frumentius, however, felt that the seed he had sown needed to be tended. So he went to Alexandria, the nearest centre of Christianity, and pleaded with Athanasius, its Archbishop, to look after the new and growing Christian community by sending them 'some worthy man' to serve as the local bishop. Athanasius found no one worthier than Frumentius himself. In telling him of his election, Athanasius said, 'What other man shall we find in whom the Spirit of God is as in thee, who can accomplish these things?' When Frumentius returned to Aksum, consecrated as its first bishop and apostle, he was filled with grace and the divine power to work miracles. This story is credible. In addition to the numismatic and epigraphic sources discovered by archaeologists, the letter of the Arian Constantius to Princes Ezana and Shaizana of Ethiopia provides clear evidence in support of this incident. Constantius wrote the letter to the Ethiopian princes demanding, in vain, that they send Frumentius back to Alexandria so that he could be instructed in Arianism and consecrated again by George, the Arian Archbishop who had usurped the throne of Athanasius.

It is not recorded who came to Aksum with Bishop Frumentius from Egypt or what religious literature they brought with them. But a Christian community that has a bishop must have clergy who serve with him and service books for performing the different rituals. The biblical Scriptures needed to be translated into the local language, and they gradually were. It did not take long for monasticism to follow, and become firmly rooted. Monks from the Mediterranean world made Ethiopia their home very early in the history of the introduction of Christianity, ultimately becoming founders and fathers of Ethiopian monasticism. Their rules were among the first to be translated into Ethiopic or Ge'ez, and their religious philosophy made monasticism the highest form of Christianity. In the course of time, their centres became the country's institutions for higher education. The translation of the Christian literature of the Mediterranean world, and the composition of others locally, are credited to these monasteries.

Under the Zagwe dynasty. Aksum's significance as an administrative centre of the kingdom ended in about the 10th century. The cause of its fall was most likely a revolt of a non-Christian ethnic group against the power of the Church. The revolt put members of the ruling house into flight and inflicted damage on Church property, including the destruction of the first churches in Aksum. The rebels did not, however, hold power for long. Another Christian dynasty, known by different names, but most commonly referred to as the Zagwe, took power in about 1137, making Adafa or Roha (later known as Lalibala) in Lasta its centre.This new dynasty was more concerned with spiritual matters than political affairs. Its kings constructed the several rock-hewn churches in their home province of Lasta, which became their lasting and monumental legacy. Some of their kings, who were priests as well, are remembered among the saints of the Church. Nevertheless, the dynasty is not famed for having enriched the Church educationally. For example, no literary work of any significance, original or in translation, can be attributed to their time. To the contrary, even some manuscripts copied during the Aksumite era did not survive the Zagwe era.

The Amhara dynasty. The Amhara dynasty, later called Solomonic, was founded in 1270 CE by a strong man who claimed to be a descendant and the legitimate heir of the defunct Aksumite kingdom. The political rulers of this house gave the monks every help they needed to evangelize the Pagan regions, and made the Church a vibrant institution to reward their collaboration in overthrowing the Zagwe. Their leaders were Yohanni in the north (Dabra Dammo, in Tegray), Iyasus Moa and Batsalota Mikael (respectively, Dabra Hayq Estifanos and Dabra Bahrey) in the centre (Amhara), and Takla Haymanot (Dabra Asbo/Libanos), in the south (Shawa and beyond). The major problem at this time and for a long time after was that the Church, with such highly motivated clergy, had only one metropolitan who was authorized to ordain priests and deacons, and even to bless the *tabot* (consecrated altar slab). Those who sought ordination and the blessing of the *tabot* had to come to him from near and far. When he died, an envoy had to take the perilous travel to Alexandria or Cairo to bring a replacement. This arrangement continued from the time of Frumentius to the mid-20th century when the Church became finally self-governing, and appointed a patriarch and metropolitans and bishops as needed within and outside the country.

Faith. The Church, following the Coptic Orthodox Church of Alexandria, recognizes the first three ecumenical councils and their decisions, Nicaea (325), Ephesus (341), and Constantinople (381). It rejects the Council of Chalcedon (451) – which recognizes and identifies two natures in Jesus Christ after the union – and all subsequent councils. Its heroes are Saints Cyril and Dioscorus of Alexandria who taught that there is in Christ one nature out of two natures, as opposed to Chalcedon's one Christ in two natures. The appellation Tawahedo (from the verb *tawahada*, 'to be one by unity') in the Church's name emphasizes its belief in the existence, in Christ, of humanity and divinity but in oneness. All acts of Christ are performed by one Christ with no division of labour to his divinity and humanity. For the Church, Jesus Christ is one person, the Word of God Incarnate. He is perfect man and perfect God. Two events in the history of the Church impelled the clergy to put the faith of the Fathers on the table for discussion: The reformation of the Church's order introduced by Emperor Zara Yaeqob (r. 1434–1468), and the efforts of the Jesuits in the 16th century to bring the Church under Rome. The sources the emperor used for his arguments were challenged by the ZaMikaelites, a group of the most well-informed and finest theologians the country has ever seen. They challenged his belief that God has a form, his Trinitarian theology – three suns (the persons) and one light (divinity) – and his demand for extreme reverence of the Blessed Virgin. Among the other opponents of this emperor were the Estifanosites (Stephanites), who refused to bow to anything but the Father, the Son, and the Holy Spirit – not even to the monarch, the icon of the Madonna and Child, or the Cross, as an expression of respect – and the Ewostatewosites (Ewostateans), who insisted that the Sabbath should be observed as prescribed in the Ten Commandments.

The challenge of the Jesuits and its consequences. From 1527 on the Church faced a series of trials that threatened its survival, at least as an Orthodox Tawahedo institution. First, there came the revolt of the Muslims from the east that inflicted incalculable damage on the Christian heritage through a *jihad* that lasted 15 years. With military help from Portugal, the Muslims were defeated in 1543. But the Portuguese posed another threat: They claimed that they had provided assistance on condition that the Ethiopian Orthodox Church be under the Pope of Rome. Their demand was rejected. Most of the Portuguese left the country, feeling betrayed, but later renewed their efforts following another disastrous event. This time the challenge was a popular migration. Immediately after the defeat of the Jihadists, the country was overwhelmed by Oromo tribes who migrated from the south to the north in epic proportions, bringing with them all the consequences of mass migration. They destroyed many of the churches and threatened much of the heritage that had escaped the Muslim conquest. This incident and renewed Islamic raids from the east and northeast, forced the monarchy to move its centre westward – to found a Gondarine dynasty – and to surrender ultimately to the Catholic pressure in a vain hope of receiving help. Resistance against the Emperor Susenyos' (1606–1632) command that the nation embrace Catholicism was widespread. For the first

Temqat procession at night, Lalibala, © Ethiopian Tourism Organization

time in its history the country saw a peaceful and successful popular uprising against its monarch. The emperor was forced to abdicate and the Catholics were expelled from the country. However, their teaching took a local form and created a lasting division among the clergy. The question became what does unction or anointment mean to Christ (e.g. Acts 10: 38; Ps 44 [45]: 7). As the Son of God, did Christ need, as other men do, to be anointed to receive the spiritual authority of priesthood, kingship, and prophesy? But the concept of anointment regarding the Son of God was undoubtedly a thinly veiled attempt to persuade the Orthodox teachers to accept the formula of two natures in Christ as adopted at the Council of Chalcedon, from which the *tawahedo* Churches had distanced themselves. Further debates in the subsequent decades can be separated into three teachings: (1) the *qebat* 'Unctionists', who believed that Jesus Christ became the natural Son of God by the unction of the Holy Spirit at conception; (2) the *Tsagga* 'Grace', who believed in *Sost Ledat* 'Three births' and maintained that Christ became the Son of God by grace (i.e. by adoption) at baptism, which they called a third birth, and (3) the *Tawahedo* or *Karra* 'Unionists' who taught that Christ became the natural son of God when his divinity was united with his humanity at conception. A royal council held at Boru Meda in 1878 officially declared the formula of the *Sost Ledat* heresy.

Challenges of modernity. Throughout the 19th and 20th century the Church faced challenges connected to international forces and modernisation. Catholic and Protestant missions, although limited in their activities, provided alternative understandings of the Christian faith. Moreover, the overwhelmingly conservative leadership of the Church was ill prepared to confront the challenges of modernisation in areas such as education, development, diplomacy, healthcare and politics.

Whether dealing with the succession issues after the death of Menilek II (1913–1916) or the Fascist conquest (1936–1941) the lack of full self-government was also an impediment. Only in 1951 did a local cleric come to lead the Church, and it was another eight years until full autocephalous status was achieved. Although the Church's disestablishment and loss of its property in the wake of the overthrow of the emperor (1974) was predicted by some to be its death knell, popular support and innovation gave new meaning to Church membership. Despite or perhaps because of the oppressive policies of the *Darg,* grassroots support for the Church rose to unprecedented levels. However, the Church hierarchy became unavoidably involved in the internal politics of Ethiopia and particular regional-political loyalties. Rival camps emerged based not (as in the past) on theological differences, but on regional loyalties and the Church grew perilously close to a schism. Moreover, the flight of hundreds of thousands of Ethiopians to foreign lands created an unprecedented diaspora presence. Thus, as it entered the 21st century the Church was internally divided and faced continued challenges from both new forms of Christianity and increasingly vocal Muslim groups.

Literature: SERGEW HABLE SELASSIE, *Ancient and Medieval Ethiopian History to 1270*, Addis Ababa 1972; TADDESSE TAMRAT, *Church and State in Ethiopia 1270–1527*, Oxford 1972; DONALD CRUMMEY, *Priests and Politicians: Protestant and Catholic Missions in Orthodox Ethiopia 1830–1868*, Oxford 1972.

Getatchew Haile, Hill Museum & Manuscript Library, St. John's University, Collegeville, MN

Organization of the Ethiopian Orthodox Church

Traditional organization. From its beginnings in the 4th century until the mid-20th century the Ethiopian Orthodox Church had a very unusual organization. The Church was officially headed by a Coptic bishop appointed by the patriarch of Alexandria to serve in what was viewed as diocese of the Coptic Church. However, although he consecrated all priests and deacons, the bishop (called *abun* or *pappas*) had only limited authority over the Ethiopian clergy. In practice, the ecclesiastical system of the Ethiopian Church was extremely complex and decentralized with clerical and secular authorities (emperors, bishops, abbots, princes, etc.) having different ecclesiastical powers as determined by agreements or tradition. These authorities competed for control over churches and monasteries. In theory the emperor had authority over churches and monasteries of the kingdom, but this 'national' authority never existed in practice: monasteries belonged informally to different monastic 'schools'; an abbot could control several monasteries; a governor could impose his authority on churches located in his lands; monks and local populations could designate themselves as the head of the local religious institution; and finally local clergy of parish churches were largely autonomous and could manage local religious life free from external interference.

A new organization in 20th century. This complex system gradually disappeared during the 20th century and was replaced by a hierarchical administration. The emperor finally had enough power to deeply reform the ecclesiastical system, in an attempt to control all the elements of the Ethiopian Orthodox Church. Through successive reforms concerning the introduction of Ethiopian bishops in 1929, 1948 and 1951, the creation of a central treasury for the Church in 1942, the creation of the Patriarchate in 1959, and the reform of the parish system in 1972. Hayla Sellase (r. 1930–1974) gradually created a totally new administration in which a central administrative body, the Patriarchate, controlled all churches and monasteries of the Ethiopian Orthodox Church. The revolution of 1974 did not disturb this evolution and the centralisation process was even improved and intensified through a second parish reform in 1978.

The patriarch. Since the separation from the Coptic Church and the creation of the Ethiopian Patriarchate in 1951–1959, the patriarch is the official head of the Ethiopian Orthodox Church. Although he has considerable influence, he represents only one part of the decision making apparatus. He shares this responsibility with the Holy Synod (the assembly of Ethiopian bishops), and the Parish General Assembly, which includes representatives of local clergies and parishioners. During the period of Baselyos (first as Ethiopian archbishop in 1951–1959; and as the first Ethiopian patriarch in 1959–1970), the decision making body was an ecclesiastical council including the patriarch, all the Ethiopian bishops and eight persons directly appointed by the emperor. His successor, patriarch Tewofelos (1971–1976) worked in a similar fashion until the revolution in 1974. He then had to share power, from 1975 until his arrest and removal in 1976, with the Provisional Council of the Ethiopian Orthodox Church, an organ created by the *Darg* for controlling and reforming the institution. Finally, during the

Patriarch *Abuna* Pawlos, © Siegbert Uhlig

time of patriarch Takla Haymanot (1976–1988), several limitations to the power of the patriarch were introduced: the Parish General Assembly, according to the regulation of 1978, participates in the decision making process and a regulation in 1979 decreed that the patriarch is responsible to the Holy Synod. In 1991 the reigning patriarch resigned (or was deposed) by the new regime and replaced by Pawlos (1992–2012). In 2013, Matiyas succeeded Pawlos as the sixth patriarch of the Ethiopian Orthodox Church.

Bishops and dioceses. Until the 19th century, Ethiopia was considered as a single diocese of the Coptic Church. However, during the reign of Yohannes IV (1872–1889), Ethiopia received three Coptic bishops, Petros (1881–1917), Matewos (1881–1926) and Luqas (1881–1900). The kingdom was divided into three dioceses whose limits corresponded to the political realms of the three most powerful princes of the time (Yohannes IV, Menilek and Takla Haymanot). After the deaths of Luqas and Petros, Ethiopia once again became a single diocese under the supervision of Matewos. After the consecration of the first five Ethiopian bishops in 1929–1930, Hayla Sellase assigned each of them to a diocese in Ethiopia. Here again, each diocese corresponded to a local political entity. This system was abolished under the Italian occupation. Finally, after the consecration of Baselyos as the first archbishop of Ethiopia in 1951, Ethiopia was divided into fourteen dioceses, each corresponding to the civilian division of the kingdom. The establishment of the federal system in Ethiopia in 1995 did not change this custom. Even if the number of dioceses dramatically increased, they continue to follow the political and administrative divisions of the country. In 2009, the Ethiopian Orthodox Church had 39 bishops in 44 dioceses in Ethiopia.

Parish council reform. Throughout the imperial period the bishop had only limited control over the local clergy even if he was an Ethiopian: he was only in charge of the ordination of priests and deacons, and of consecration of churches. He could rarely impose his decisions concerning discipline or management of Church properties. patriarch Tewofelos sought to change this and launched a great reform of the Ethiopian parish system in 1972. This reform aimed at establishing in all parishes a council responsible for managing the parish incomes and organizing parish life. Priests and laymen shared posts within this council after being elected by the parishioners. However, the Patriarchate placed these councils under the control of the diocese. The election of the council members and their decisions were to be submitted to the diocese. Bishops could thus supervise the spiritual and secular management of the parishes. However, bishops were also involved in an administrative chain linking the parishes with the central authority. The Patriarchate created three other types of councils gathering clergymen and laymen at the level of the district, of the diocese and of the Patriarchate (the Parish General Assembly). Each level of the administration had to elect representatives for the next level, and had to report to it, thereby creating a hierarchical administration. This reform was slightly amended in 1978 under the *Darg* and at which time the reform was even hailed as a democratization process of the Ethiopian Church.

Local clergy organization. There are three types of churches: *gatar* (rural church), *dabr* (main church) and *gadam* (monastery). A *gatar* church is a small rural church where the liturgy is celebrated only once a week for a small community of parishioners. Most of the churches in Ethiopia are of this type. The number of officiants is usually small, the minimum number of clergy for celebrating liturgy being two priests and three deacons. A *dabr* church is larger. The parish includes more than 500 households and the liturgy can be celebrated every day. Before the land reform of 1975, a *dabr* church, unlike a *gatar* church, owned land. Before the parish reform of 1972, a *dabr* could supervise several *gatar* churches. A *gadam* church represents the church of a monastic community. This church is served only by ordained monks living within the community. It can be considered as *dabr* or as *gatar*, according to the local situation. Both *gatar* and *dabr* church should have a parish council. A *gadam* can be without if it does not serve as parish church to laymen. Some told there were over 30,000 parish churches in 2000. The head of the parish council is always the ecclesiastical chief of the church, usually called *alaqa* for a *dabr*, *marigeta* or simply *qes* for a *gatar* and *mamher* for a *gadam*. The heads of important or famous churches bear honorary titles as in the case of the head of Qeddest Sellase Cathedral called *liqa seltanat*, 'head of the authorities'. Within the parish council, only clergymen can supervise religious life and assign tasks to priests and deacons. However, parishioners of the council manage, in collaboration with the clergy, properties and finances of the church. Each parishioner is supposed to pay an annual contribution to his parish church in order to support the parish administration. These annual dues are usually the only source of income for the Ethiopian Orthodox Church since the land reform of 1975. By paying his/her dues, a parishioner is authorized to elect members of the council or to be elected, and s/he can receive religious services for him and his family (baptism, funeral, etc.) without charge.

Church and state. In the constitutions of 1933 and 1955, the Ethiopian Orthodox Church was considered as part of the Ethiopian State. The monarch was acknowledged as the protector of the Church and the defender of the orthodox faith. Orthodox Christianity as professed by the Ethiopian Orthodox Church was the State religion of the Ethiopian kingdom and discriminatory regulations targeted other religious institutions whether Muslim, Catholic or Protestant. Theoretically the revolution of 1974 put an end to religious discrimination. However, the place and the role of religious institutions within the political and social scene were not clearly defined, and the Marxist military junta clearly interfered in internal affairs of the Church as well as other religious bodies. After the fall of the military junta, the new constitution of 1995 tried to define more clearly the place and the role of religious institutions in Ethiopia: it declared that 'the state and religion are separate, there shall be no State religion and the state shall not interfere in religious matters and religion shall not interfere in state affairs'. So it focused on putting an end to discrimination, a heritage of the revolution, and on the prevention of conflicts between state and religion at least in part to avoid interference of the state in religious institutions, a heritage of both the monarchy and the revolution. However, old habits die hard. The Ethiopian Orthodox Church is today the most powerful religious institution of Ethiopia. It has a predominant place on the social and economic scene of Ethiopia and is still the necessarily ally of the political power. Despite the official religious policy of the new regime and a prudent public distance from Church affairs maintained by Prime Minister Mallas Zenawi (r. 1991–2012), the separation between Church and state has sometimes been belied by the reliance of the state on the Church as a unifying symbol of patriotism, particularly during times of crisis such as the war with Eritrea (1998–2000).

Literature: DENIS NOSNITSIN, EMMANUEL FRITSCH, DIMETROS WELDU, 'Churches and church administration', *EAE* I, 740–742; GETATCHEW HAILE, 'Ethiopian Orthodox Church', *EAE* II, 421–432; STEPHANE ANCEL, 'The Centralization Process of the Ethiopian Orthodox Church', *Revue d'Histoire Ecclésiastique,* 106/3–4 (2011), 497–520.

Stéphane Ancel, Institut des Mondes Africains, Paris

Customs in the Ethiopian Church

As in many religious communities, the faith of Ethiopian Orthodox Christians is expressed not only through theology and scriptures, but also through rituals, and other acts and customs which regulate the lives of believers and determine the rhythm of their lives. These include the administration of the sacraments and the annual, monthly and weekly cycles of festivals and fasts.

Sacraments. In keeping with the oft-remarked 'Hebraic-biblical molding' of Ethiopian Christianity, boys are often circumcised on the eighth day after birth. This is not, however, required or considered a sacrament (*mestir*). The sacrament of baptism (*temqat*) of a boy child takes place 40 days after birth; that of a girl after 80 days (Lev. 12:1–7 and Luke 2:21–24). At that time the child also receives his or her baptismal name which differs from one's normal daily appellation and is known only to a small circle of intimates including family members, close friends and his/her confessor (*nafs abbat*). Infants are usually baptized in a baptismal font outside the church after which the child is immediately anointed with oil in the sacrament known as Chrismation (*meron*). S/he is then brought (literally and figuratively) into the Church and receives Holy Communion (*qwerban*).Various forms of marriage exist in Ethiopia and even within Christian society. Historically most people have preferred to marry within their own ethnic group, religion and class (nobles, priests, peasants etc.). Tradition dictated that one did not marry a person who shared a common ancestor even as far back as the sixth generation. Close family members and relatives played a major role in arranging marriage for young people. In the past only a minority of Christians chose a marriage consecrated as a sacrament. This is known as *qwerban* ('Eucharist') marriage because the couple share communion wrapped in a large garment, which symbolizes their unification. This form of marriage is often also referred to as *taklil* ('coronation'), because if they are virgins the couple wear crowns. Priests (who cannot remarry) and the elderly were the primary participants in this sacramental marriage, which was irrevocable. In contrast, civil marriage by contract was much more common. Known as *samanya* ('80') following the tradition that Eve wed Adam on her 80th day, this form of marriage might be blessed by a priest but was not a sacrament.Throughout their lives, Ethiopian Christians confess their sins and engage in the sacrament of Penance (*nesseha*). Although believers routinely request absolution from their spiritual father/confessor in passing, there is also a far more formal procedure. After discussions with his/her confessor, the two meet and the believer confesses his/her sins. The confessor imposes acts of penance such as fasting, pilgrimage and/or alms. When these have been accomplished, the two meet again and after praying together, absolution (*fethat*) is granted. Confession and penance are necessary if one is to receive Holy Communion and thus is particularly common during *Lent* and particularly Holy Week leading up to Easter. While penance is administered in cases of spiritual 'disease', the Unction for the sick (*qandil*) is intended to heal both spiritual and bodily ills. It should be stressed that the Ethiopian Church is firm on the idea that it is not the anointing with oil which 'magically' heals the sufferer, but rather prayer and belief in the Lord. It is administered by a priest and is not a 'last rite' granted only to those who are dying. Unction with oil is also used for Chrismation (see above), the consecration of the *tabot* ('ark') and other church vessels, at marriages and in the past, coronations.

Funerals and burial ceremonies are among the most elaborate rituals and often of great social significance. According to the canon of the Church a deceased person should be commemorated (*tazkar*) daily in the church until the 40th day after his/her death. Special attention is paid to the third day after the burial, which commemorates Jesus' resurrection and the seventh day when the soul is believed to ascend to the seventh heaven. On the 40th day, the person's soul appears before God and his/her fate until the Second Coming is decided. An elaborate banquet is prepared by the family of the deceased for the clergy who perform the prayers for his/her soul. The local clergy and dignitaries, neighbours and even the poor attend. The costs are often so large that they create a significant financial burden for the family of mourners.

One way in which Ethiopian Christians have coped with this problem is through the institution of the *edder*, or burial society. Each member of an *edder* pays a certain amount monthly to the organization. This serves as 'insurance' which is supplemented at the time of a death by an additional supplemental contribution from members. These serve to defray the heavy costs of the funeral. Over time the *edder* became a far broader organization often assisting in a variety of other circumstances including accidents, fires and other misfortunes.

Ordination is the only sacrament which is not open to all members of the Church. Only men can become deacons and in the course of time, priests. A priest must marry prior to his entry into this status, otherwise he cannot marry and becomes a monk. The process of becoming a monk extends over years and is gradual. A novice is distinguishable by his simple garb and acquires other parts of the monastic habit as he progresses spiritually.

Feasts and fasts. Fasting is one of the central ritual acts demonstrating one's adherence to the Ethiopian Orthodox Church. On fast days believers eat only one meal a day (usually in the mid-afternoon) and consume a vegan diet with no meat, fats, eggs, milk, butter or cheese. All told there are about 250 fast days, of which 180 are obligatory and the remainder are observed only by clergy or particularly devout individuals.

Deacons with processional crosses, © Philipp Hedemann

These include the weekly fasts of Wednesday and Friday as well as various fasting periods, most notably *Lent* (*abiyy tsom*, the great fast) which is most strictly observed and extends for 56 days; the fast of the Apostles (*tsoma hawaryat*) which begins immediately after Pentecost and may last as long as 40 days, and Advent (*tsoma ledat*), which lasts 40 days before Christmas and is mainly observed by the clergy.

While the portion of the population which fasted declined precipitously in the wake of modernisation, it remains an important part of Church custom and even enjoyed something of a revival during the period of the *Darg*, which placed barriers in the way of much religious practice, but could not stop people from not eating.

In addition to fasting practices, Christian Ethiopians observe dietary taboos including the abstinence from pork (which they share with Muslims and Jews) and the avoidance of meat slaughtered by members of another religious group.

Taken as a whole the cycle of feasts construct the rhythms which compose the Christian year. Usually the major feasts come at the end or in the midst of a period of extended fasting, and thus provide relief for the believers. It is also significant to note that the annual observances are reprised on a monthly basis through the commemoration of the same day of every month. Thus the first of every month commemorates the Birth of Mary, the 3rd her presentation at the Temple, the 16th her intercessory role as the Covenant of Mercy etc. These monthly commemorations embed these festivals in the daily lives of the faithful.

From a sociological perspective the feasts can be seen as occasions which define community on a variety of levels. Thus the major festivals such as Easter, Epiphany, and Christmas are celebrated in all churches and define the community of believers versus non-believers. In contrast, there are numerous festivals which are only fully celebrated at churches which have a *tabot* dedicated to a specific figure such as Mary or a particular saint or archangel. In such circumstances the local parish or religious association (*mahbar*) celebrates and asserts its identity in contrast to that of its Christian neighbours.

The *mahbar* fraternal organizations exist to assist in the organization both socially and financially of monthly celebrations in honour of particular patron saints. The *mahbar* is formed by believers who feel a particular devotion to a specific saint and thus usually form a subset of the larger parish community. However, since membership is primarily defined by devotion to a particular saint and not geography, membership often includes members of several parishes thus creating a social bond over a broader geographic area. Members meet on the saint's day of each month rotating from house to house of each member in turn. Although a priest is usually included in the celebration, he does not have a sacramental role. In addition to their ritual ceremonial role, the *mahbar* usually acts as a broader form of social support in which members assist each other in times of need, for orphans etc.

Festivals are also a major occasion for the support of the church and the giving of alms to the poor. Abstinence, voluntary poverty and charity all occupy a central place in the culture of Ethiopian Christianity. Lay people, clergy and rulers were all expected to give generously to the needy. Charity was especially given on the celebration of festivals and when congregants celebrated rites of passage. Offerings on festivals include widely varying sums of money, prepared foods, livestock, church utensils (oil, incense). On saints' days, devotees of a saint give alms in honour of their patron. In return, they acquired merit and expiation for their sins.

It is impossible in the limits of this chapter to describe all the feasts of the Church, however, a few of the major celebrations are described below.

Ledat (The Nativity-Christmas) falls on the 29th day of the month of *Tahsas* (7 January) People attend church services and then share a family meal. (Even if *Ledat* falls on a Wednesday or Friday, no fast is observed.) Gift-giving is not an important part of the holiday, although children may take bread to their parents and receive a blessing or gift in return. A game similar to field-hockey called *ganna* is traditionally played in the afternoon, and the holiday is often referred to by this name.

Temqat (Epiphany 11 *Terr* = 19 January) commemorates the baptism of Christ by John the Baptist in the River Jordan. On the eve of the feast processions set out from each parish church with the priests carrying the *tabot* and deacons carrying crosses, censers and ringing bells. They arrive at a water source which symbolizes the River Jordan and spend the night in prayers. Many churches are located near springs or other sources of water which are believed to have holy/healing properties. In a number of large or historically important cities (Addis Ababa, Gondar, Aksum, Lalibala) pools have been artificially constructed to accommodate a large number of participants. On the day of the holiday believers either immerse themselves in the water source or are sprinkled with water (if the source is not large enough for immersion), although immersion in or sprinkling with water is a central part of the celebration, it is not intended as a repeat sacramental baptism of the individual believer.

Fasika ('Easter'), which is also known as *Tensae* ('Resurrection') is the most important festival in the calendar of the Ethiopian Orthodox Church. (It is preceded by the Lenten fast which lasts 56 days.) Since it is a moveable feast celebrated according to the lunar calendar the date varies. Throughout the weeks preceding Easter other moveable feasts are observed culminating in Holy Week, which commences on Palm Sunday (Hosaena). No drums are used in the church during this preparatory period. The final 48 hours of the holiday weekend are spent in intense fast and prayer, which are only broken around midnight of Easter Sunday when the resurrection is declared.

The Cross is, of course, a symbol of the Ethiopian Church shared with Christians around the world. It is carried by priests and worn by believers. It decorates churches, their furnishings, vessels and vestments. The 15th-century Emperor Zara Yaeqob decreed that it be affixed to all belongs and placed on the forehead of every believer. The Cross became particularly prominent through the celebration of the festival celebrating the 'finding of the True Cross'.

Masqal ('the exaltation of the Cross') 17 Maskaram = 27 September celebrates the discovery of the True Cross by Empress Helena, the mother of the Emperor Constantine. This pan-Christian festival was given a particularly Ethiopian significance when the Emperor Dawit II (1380–1412) received a relic of the True Cross from the Coptic patriarch. Although officially considered a 'minor' feast, *Masqal* is one of the most popular celebrations of the Ethiopian Church. It falls close to the end of the rainy season (*keramt*) and close to the New Year (11 September). It is particularly symbolized by the large yellow 'masqal' flowers, which are ubiquitous in the fields and carried by believers. On the eve of *Masqal* people bring twigs and flowers to a central location to prepare a pyre for a bonfire (*damara*). Large processions from the different parishes set out from the churches and come together. The fire is lit and dignitaries march three times around the fire. The order of procession represents the societal hierarchy.

Marian devotion. No discussion of the practice of Ethiopian Christianity would be complete without special attention to the intensity of believers' devotion to the Blessed Virgin Mary. The Blessed Virgin, Mother of God is the most venerated saint of the

Church. Countless churches are devoted to different aspects of her holiness and no less than thirty-three Marian feasts exist on the calendar of the Church, although many receive only minor commemoration. Of special importance are feasts such as *Erafta* ('her falling asleep') = Dormition and *Felsata* ('the assumption [to Heaven]') which fall on 29 January and 22 August respectively. Although there have been both internal and external critics of what they see as 'excessive devotion' to her, this has done little to reduce the reverence of believers. Her miracles are endlessly recounted, her icons venerated and she is ceaselessly approached in petition and prayer to intercede on behalf of believers.

Literature: CHRISTINE CHAILLOT, *The Ethiopian Tewahedo Church Tradition: A brief introduction to its life and spirituality*, Paris 2002; STEVEN KAPLAN, 'Feasts, Christian', *EAE* II, 510–514.

Steven Kaplan, The Hebrew University of Jerusalem

Hagiography and monasticism in the Ethiopian Church

Hagiography. Hagiography is a pervasive genre in Ethiopian Christian literature attested to in various categories of literary works, which differ in both their structure and their narrative style. The main intent of all of these is to celebrate a saint. Along with the production of literary texts, other elements play a central role in the official acknowledgment and adoration of a saint, sustaining and strengthening his memory, veneration, and ritual devotion by means of a complex system of practices. These are typically represented by the liturgy, the iconography, the veneration of relics, the burial place, the church or monastery dedicated in his (and rarely her) memory.

Because of its prominent role in the liturgy, hagiography contributes – more than other material evidence – to securing the reminiscence of the saint in the collective memory. Through reiterated ritual forms, it provides the faithful with a concrete *modus vivendi* to be followed and contributes to nourishing his/her spirituality. The most popular hagiographic compositions in the Ethiopic literature are the *gadl* ('spiritual combat', but usually translated with 'Acts' or 'Life'); the *dersan* ('homily'); the *taammer* ('miracle'); and a series of hymns and compositions in verses, among which are the *salam* ('peace' but in this case 'salutation') or the *malke* ('effigy, portrait, image').

Hagiographic literature and canonization: The role of the manuscripts. The Ethiopic hagiographic literature is transmitted in manuscripts written in Ge'ez and generally dating from the 13th century onwards. Some of the texts attested in these manuscripts must have circulated much earlier than the 13th century. The first examples of hagiographic texts in Ethiopia (such as Phileas; Arsenofis; Tewoflos, Patroqya and Damalis, etc.) indeed present some peculiar linguistic and material features which indicate that they were translated from Greek into Ge'ez in the Aksumite period. Unfortunately, no hagiographic manuscripts dating from this period have survived. The translation of foreign hagiographic texts continued in later periods, in particular from Arabic in the 13th and 14th century. This was a crucial period in the development of hagiographic literature in Ethiopia, because alongside the copying of more ancient texts and the translation of new texts, an indigenous literature with local saints as its protagonists finally began to emerge. The Lives of these local saints were at the beginning included in manuscripts, which contained foreign Lives. This combination was probably intended to facilitate the circulation and liturgical use of the new texts. One consequence of that is that the foreign Lives had a profound influence on the local ones.

Dabra Dammo monastery, © Wolbert G.C. Smidt

Beside the circulation of texts in collections, a parallel transmission of individual works is also attested. This is the case with both foreign and local saints. The manuscripts that contain individual hagiographies show different features compared to those containing collections: they are usually enriched with miracles, *salam*, *malke*, monastic genealogies, etc. Furthermore, the Lives of the foreign saints present *post mortem* miracles set in Ethiopia, although these saints had never actually lived in the country. This feature of Ethiopian hagiography is representative of the complex process of the acculturation of these foreign elements to the local milieu.

Texts and manuscripts played an essential role in the official recognition of sainthood in Ethiopia and in the establishment of the veneration of the saints. This is due to the fact that in the past the process of canonization did not take place in a formal centralized institutional context and consequently, because of its official nature, the manuscript was often the only testimony to the holiness of the characters described in the texts. Copies of the Synaxarion, the Acts of the Martyrs, the Acts of the Saints, and the Homiliaries were diffused in all significant monasteries and used officially and publicly for the liturgical service. The limited circulation of some manuscripts may be the reason why – for the most part – the saints in Ethiopia are known and venerated at a local or regional level. National saints are few and, apart from rare exceptions, they are mostly foreign saints whose hagiographies were transmitted in larger collections, which circulated throughout the entire country. The process of writing, assembling, structuring and transmitting hagiographic texts within a manuscript reflected therefore the need to create an institutionalized instrument in which a perfect model of life, achievable through sacrifice and perseverance, was made accessible to the members of a community.

Foreign models adopted in the local hagiographic literature. The Byzantine and, later, Egyptian models provided by the texts translated into Ge'ez had a deep influence on the emergence and further development of the local hagiography. This influence mainly concerns the criteria and the rules according to which the authors chose and classified the events they narrate and can be observed at least on three different levels: stylistic, ideological and narrative.

1. The stylistic level deals with peculiar features which are common to hagiography as a literary genre. In describing the Life of a certain saint, the authors can decide to create, out of whole cloth, the story of his life and of his sainthood (i.e. Liqanos; some of the *tsadqan* texts); using oral material at their disposal; copying in part or completely the Life of a saint whose hagiography was already known, changing only some information, i.e. the names of the saint and his parents, the place where he was born, etc. In describing the saint as an intermediator, the authors gleaned their models of virtues from the characters of the Bible. Furthermore, the authors made ample use of *topoi*, or elements having a standardized form which occur in a more or less consistent manner: the origins of the saint, born to noble and pious parents; the barrenness of the parents of the saint before his birth; the *puer senex*, namely the fact that the saint as a child or even as a baby behaved like a grown up, etc.
2. The ideological level deals with the legitimization of certain traditions. A classic example of this is the role attributed to the fathers of the Egyptian desert in the direct consecration of the early Aksumite monks known as the Nine Saints. This tradition is reflected in both Shawan (Takla Haymanot, Iyasus Moa) and Tegrayan monasticism (i.e. Garima; Guba; Alef, etc.). It is an anachronistic attempt to establish a prestigious lineage for Ethiopian monasticism. The Life of Antony and the Rules of Pachomius were among the first hagiographic texts translated into Ethiopic and, as a result, their fame reached Ethiopia very early. The importance of Egyptian monasticism in Ethiopian hagiography is also evident in the Lives of the so-called Egyptian saints of Abyssinian hagiography (Bula/Abib, Gabra Krestos/Alexis, Latsun, Gabra Manfas Qeddus, John the Oriental, etc.).
3. The narrative level is often influenced by episodes which first appeared in the foreign Lives and were interpolated into the local Lives. One of the clearest examples of this is the episode of the Ethiopian military expedition to Nagran, which is found in some Lives translated into Ge'ez and also in some of the first examples of local hagiography (i.e. *Gadla Pantalewon* and *Gadla Kaleb*).

It stands to reason that sometimes these levels, as well as their individual models described, can overlap or be combined in an infinite number of associations. Two features peculiar to the Ethiopian hagiography are represented by the *kidan* ('testament, pact') and the *tazkar* ('commemoration'). The *kidan* is an official promise given by Jesus Christ to the saint in which He pledges to take care of everyone who entrusts himself to the prayers of the saint and celebrates his *tazkar*.

Modern scholars tend to evaluate the hagiographic texts as the expression of several cultural conditions proper to the setting and the period in which they were composed. Ethiopian hagiographies are mines of information for understanding a wide range of aspects of the society and the mentality from the late antique period to the present day.

Monasticism. The Ethiopian monastic milieu played an essential role in the translation, creation and dissemination of the hagiographic literature, and it is not an accident that the overwhelming majority of saints venerated in Ethiopia are monks. Monasticism in Ethiopia must have arrived very early and must have been closely related to the introduction of Christianity in the country. Local traditions number among the first monastic figures the Nine Saints, the *tsadqan* ('the righteous') and Libanos, foreign monks who are believed to have evangelized the Ethiopian and Eritrean highlands between the 5th and the 6th century. Although the existence of monastic communities at that time is difficult to prove, because of the lack of archaeological investigations, some of the monasteries that are nowadays dedicated to these monks are built on ancient sites. Furthermore, the translation of monastic literature from Greek into Ge'ez in the Aksumite period may point to the fact that monastic communities already existed at that time, although today it is difficult to localize them.

Monastic movements and central power. From the 13th century onwards, during the Solomonic dynasty, monasticism became a dominant force in Ethiopia. This also brought about a deep transformation in the production of hagiographic literature. Between the 13th and the 15th centuries several monastic movements emerged and spread. These movements were linked to the main monasteries of the country and were led by charismatic monks, like Takla Haymanot (Shawa), Ewostatewos (Shire, Saraye, Hamasen, Bur, etc.), Estifanos (Agama). Although rooted in a shared monastic background, they emerged independently in different social and cultural contexts. The literature produced in these monastic communities shows that often they did not share a common understanding of theological issues and matters of monastic organization. The disciples of these monks founded other monasteries where they perpetuated the teaching and the rules of their masters in a system of monastic networks. Their relationship with the central powers, Emperor and *abun* was often conflictual. One example is portrayed in five texts of the hagiographic cycle of the monks of the 'house of Takla Haymanot', who clashed with King Amda Tseyon I. Other hagiographic texts linked to the Stephanite and Ewostatean movements show struggles between them and the Emperor Zara Yaeqob. These divisions were exacerbated during the 17th–19th centuries, because of Christological controversies, and were resolved only in the 19th–20th centuries.

Monasticism and hagiography. In general, the circumstances in which the hagiographics were produced are often, but not exclusively, related to the promotion of specific monastic centres, to the legitimation of ancient monastic tradition, to the exercise of the power, to the claim of feudal properties, etc. In some cases the copying or composition of hagiographic texts were sponsored by rulers and kings, as part of a conscious political project, in order to strengthen local or regional identities.

Hagiographic literature and monastic normative texts provide information about the different practices of monastic life (= in secluded religious communities) diffused in the past, some of which survive to this day. The coenobitic and semi-coenobitic forms are the most prevalent, but also eremitism is intensely present. The system of monastic regulations is extremely flexible in Ethiopia and the individual monasteries possess a high degree of autonomy in the organization of their social structure and daily activities. Ethiopian monasticism also has a long-standing tradition of asceticism characterized in some cases by strict and extreme ascetical practices, some of which are attested since ancient times also in other provinces of the Oriental Roman Empire.

Literature: STEVEN KAPLAN, 'Monasticism', *EAE* V, 443–447; ANTONELLA BRITA, *I racconti tradizionali sulla «seconda cristianizzazione» dell'Etiopia. Il ciclo agiografico dei Nove Santi,* Studi Africanistici, Serie Etiopica 7, Napoli 2010.

Antonella Brita, Universität Hamburg

Islam in Ethiopia

Early roots. According to Islamic tradition Muslims first arrived in kingdom of Aksum in 615 when the Prophet Muhammad encouraged some of his followers to emigrate to Ethiopia (al-Habasha) to escape persecution by the pagan inhabitants of Mecca. The event is commonly known as the first *hijra*. The refugees were warmly welcomed by the Ethiopian king (called al-Najashi Ashama b. Abjar in Arabic sources). He protected them from the Meccan polytheists who tried to have them sent back to Arabia and granted them the freedom of practicing Islam. Muslim historiography relates how the *najashi* ('ruler of Aksum') eventually embraced the new religion and exchanged letters and gifts with the Prophet, who prayed for him when he heard of his death. It is difficult to fully assess the historical reliability of this episode.

The idea that Islam began to spread in Ethiopia through the presence of these refugees at the court of the *najashi*, and that the Ethiopian king was one of the first local converts is cherished by Ethiopian Muslims, but is hardly verifiable. It can certainly be considered as a foundation myth for Ethiopian Islam, which shaped the way the Muslim world has perceived Ethiopia to this day.

Scholars agree that Islam was diffused in Ethiopia by three major agents: traders, learned men and Sufi scholars (an individual could belong to one, two or even all three of these groups). In fact, the trade routes linking the Red Sea and the Indian Ocean to the Ethiopian highlands were the paths along which Islam spread into the country. The first Islamic stronghold in the region was on the Dahlak archipelago where epigraphic evidence testifies to the existence of a Muslim community since the 10th century and of an independent sultanate since the 12th century. From there Islam spread into Eritrean coastal regions and then further into the hinterland. Funerary inscriptions discovered in Tegray point to the presence of Muslims as early as 1006. In eastern and central Ethiopia, Islam moved inland from the port city of Zayla following the trade routes towards Shawa. Once again, inscriptions testify to the early existence of Muslim communities in the Harar region and in southern Shawa.

Sultanates. The expansion of Islam in the Ethiopian hinterland triggered the emergence of several minor Muslim states ruled by local family dynasties claiming an Arab origin and competing for supremacy over the region. The oldest Islamic sultanate in Ethiopia controlled Shawa and parts of southern Ethiopia already in 896/897 CE and was founded by a family descending from the Makhzumi Meccan clan. The sultanate of Shawa fell at the end of the 13th century when the Walashma dynasty (also of distant Arab origin) ruling in the Ifat area expanded east and southwards. According to Arab historians and geographers in the first half of the 14th century there were seven major Islamic states in Ethiopia: Ifat, Dawaro, Arababni, Hadiyya, Sharkha, Bale and Dara. Other sources hint at the existence of more or less Islamized polities also in Fatagar, Gidaya and Mora. All these states often encroached on the territories of their neighbours causing countless skirmishes and clashes. It seems that all of the main Islamic states were at first tributaries of the Christian Empire. When in 1299 a Muslim rebellion broke out against the *negus* (king) a long series of battles and wars began between the Christian emperors who were trying to expand their domains southwards and the Muslim sultans and religious leaders who were striving to preserve and extend their area of influence. Periods of coexistence, when the Christian Empire and the Islamic states enjoyed peaceful and cooperative relationships, were overshadowed by sustained tension and recurrent warfare.

Ahmad Grany, *jihad*, and its aftermath. The Christian-Muslim conflict culminated in the first half of the 16th century when *Imam* Ahmad b. Ibrahim al-Ghazi (nicknamed Grany, 'the left-handed', by the Christians) assumed the leadership in Adal, the main Muslim state of that time centred in the city of Harar. The *imam* overthrew the sultan, gathered a heterogeneous army and launched a *jihad* against the Christian state. By 1540 Ahmad b. Ibrahim had completely overrun the Christian kingdom. The intervention of a Portuguese military unit backing the Christians and the Ottoman support granted to the *imam* made the Christian-Islamic war in Ethiopia a truly international conflict with clear geopolitical and strategic importance. The *imam* was killed in battle in 1543 by a Portuguese soldier, and his army was subsequently defeated and dispersed by the joint Ethiopian and Portuguese forces. A subsequent attempt to resume the *jihad* carried out by Nur b. Mujahid (a former military leader of the *imam*'s army) was partially successful, as the Muslim forces defeated and killed the Christian Emperor Galawdewos in 1559. However, the long and bloody war left both sides almost completely impoverished and worn out. The weakness of the local Christian and Muslim states paved the way for the northward and eastward expansion of the Oromo and for the Ottoman occupation of the Red Sea coast. Recovering from the post-war critical situation, the city of Harar managed to establish an Islamic emirate at the middle of the 17th century while the Christian Ethiopian kingdom moved its centre to Gondar, out of the reach of the Oromo migrations. Starting from the second half of the 17th and until the first part of the 19th century Islam spread widely among the Oromo people in the Harar region, in Arsi, in Wallo (there some local Islamic dynasties were created) and in the Gibe region (where some Islamic states emerged, especially in Jimma).

Early modern challenges. The second half of the 19th century was probably the most fateful period in the history of Ethiopian Muslims. Pressured by the expansionist policies of the Christian emperors Tewodros II, Yohannes IV and Menilek II the independent Islamic states were successively defeated and their territories absorbed into the Christian empire. Many Muslim leaders were forced to convert to Christianity or obliged to flee from their native regions. Muslims as a whole came to be treated as marginalized second-class subjects and the public practice of the Islamic cult was strictly limited, if not completely prohibited.

Growing recognition. Starting from the first half of the 20th century, the modernisation of Ethiopian society and culture initiated by Menilek II and more deeply and widely pursued by Hayla Sellase led to a partial liberalization of the state attitude towards Islam and Muslims. Especially after the Italian occupation (1936–1941), during which Ethiopian Muslims had been granted some freedoms and benefits, a few aspirations of the Ethiopian Islamic community were satisfied (e.g. the creation of the *sharia* courts and easier access to land ownership). However, it was only with the revolution in 1974 that Muslims gained full recognition as citizens of the Ethiopian state obtaining the same status as the Christians. However, the *Darg* followed a dogmatic Marxist-Leninist ideology and quickly lost the sympathy of the Muslim population which was hurt economically by the nationalization of the Islamic charitable trusts (*waqf*) and by the restrictions on foreign trade implemented by the communist government.

In 1991 the *Darg* was overthrown and the new federal state promoted a policy of cultural, religious and linguistic liberalization from which the Muslims benefitted. For the first time in the history of Ethiopia, Islamic religious associations, schools, colleges, periodical press, literature became completely legal and almost free from control and restrictions. New and sometimes beautifully imposing mosques were built everywhere in the country and Muslims acquired visibility and increasing prominence in the public sphere both in urban and in rural environments. Moreover, Ethiopian Islam could resume its international connections with the wider Muslim world: Islamic books were imported, pilgrimage to Mecca became easier and foreign learned men could enter the country to preach and teach. The influence of different and often clashing interpretations of Islam elaborated e.g. in Saudi Arabia, Iran, Lebanon, Egypt and Pakistan started to be felt also among Ethiopian Muslims creating harsh tensions within the Islamic communities and between Muslims and Christians. The process of globalization of the Ethiopian Islam is continuing at a speedy pace, and its future can be foreseen only within the framework of the regional and international contexts.

Tomb of *Emir* Nur, Harar, © Serge Dewel-Mouton

Demographics. According to the figures published in the last official census (which has been considered inaccurate by many) in 2007, Muslims make up 33.9% of the Ethiopian population (they were 32.8% in the census carried out in 1994). Muslims are found in every Ethiopian administrative region but they represent the overwhelming majority in the eastern and southern part of the country (Somali region 98.4%; Afar region 95.3%; Dire Dawa 70.9% and Harari region 69.0%). Muslims are almost the half of the population of Oromia (47.5%) and Beni Shangul (45.0%), but they are a minority in the highlands (Amhara 17.2%; Tegray 4.0%) and in Gambela (4.9%) and in the Southern Nations, Nationalities, and Peoples' Region (14.1%). Also in the capital city region, Muslims are estimated to represent only 16.2% of the population.

It is impossible to accurately trace more recent trends in the religious affiliation of the population, as no census has been conducted since 2007. After the fall of the *Darg,* the more visible presence of Islam in the Ethiopian public sphere may have fostered some conversions. However, most of the Islamic social and cultural activities were in fact aimed at strengthening (or redefining) Islamic identity and the self-awareness of Ethiopian Muslims themselves to encourage a wider and stricter observance of the tenets of the faith.

Diversity. Islam is practiced by many different Ethiopian peoples and ethnic groups, e.g. Oromo, Somali, Harari, Berta, Hadiya, Selti. Amharic and Tegrennya-speaking Muslims live in the highlands (especially in Wallo and in the city of Gondar) together with the Argobba.

Ethiopian Islam is multifaceted, as it is practiced by peoples who live in markedly different geographical and human environments and have diverse social structures and cultures. The main common features of everyday lived Ethiopian Islam can be briefly sketched as follows.

Ethiopian Muslim show a very deeply felt devotion to holy men and perform a variety of practices connected with the cult of their saints: pilgrimage to the shrines, supplications at the tombs and communal festivals to honour the memory of the deceased holy person during which the devotees sing and dance together chewing *chat.* The cult of holy men in Ethiopian Islam is the result of the fusion of two different cultural constellations: local pre-Islamic beliefs and rituals (e.g. the belief in spirits, the cult of the *zar*, exorcism, divination and healing rituals) and components of the main-stream Islamic mysticism (e.g. devotion, pietism, emotionalism, belief in the supernatural powers of holy men and organized activism and proselytism).

Islamic shrines. Shrines are a widespread feature of the sacred landscape of Ethiopian Islam. They host the mortal remains (and sometimes other relics) of different kinds of individuals who can all be categorized as Muslim holy men: eponymic founders of lineages and families (especially those who are considered to be descendants of the Prophet Muhammad), ancient and modern rulers, e.g. the *najashi* in Nagash, Tegray; *amir* Nur in Harar, famous representatives of the Islamic community (e.g. the fighters in *Imam* Ahmad's 16th century *jihad*), learned men (e.g. *Shaykh* Husayn in Bale), Sufi masters affiliated (or not) to a mystical brotherhood (e.g. *Shaykh* Jawhar in Shonke, Wallo, Ahmad ibn Umar in Yaa, Beni Shangul). Shrines can also be cenotaphs ('empty tombs') to honour and keep alive the memory of a person who is buried elsewhere (e.g. the famous Muslim saint Abd al-Qadir al-Jilani, who is buried in Baghdad has a shrine in Harar). They can be urban (e.g. in Harar) but more commonly are built in rural areas, sometimes in quite remote locations (e.g. Muhammad Shafi's shrine in Jama Negush, Wallo).

Architectonically Islamic shrines show very different shapes (round or squared) and structures (from a very simple single room to more complex plans with a wide central room and small lateral annexes). They are made of different materials (wood, stone) and are most commonly characterized by the presence of a domed roof (often painted green) which makes them easily identifiable even from a distance. They can be situated within a fenced (or even walled) compound and are often built next to natural elements (a tree, a rock, a spring, or brook), which contributes to or is part of the holiness of the place and is somehow directly related to the individual buried in the shrine.

A systematic survey of the Islamic shrines in Ethiopia has not been carried out. It is thus impossible to retrace the development of the architecture of the shrines, and assess the historical background of the buildings. Most of the shrines (also those related to ancient personages) are in fact recent or even very recent, and cannot be used as an evidence for an early tradition of shrine building in the Islamic communities of Ethiopia. The first definite reference to an Ethiopian Islamic shrine is contained in the historical work 'Futuh al-Habasha' (mid-16th century) where the site of Ahmad al-Najashi is mentioned.

Shrines are almost invariably destinations of pilgrimages, as the personages who are supposed to be buried inside are considered to be gifted with supernatural powers (*baraka*) and with the capacity to intercede for the faithfuls' sins and wrong deeds. Devotees of the enshrined person visit him on the anniversary of his death and on other public and private festivities and occasions but also when they have health problems or face difficulties in their daily life. Prayers and supplications at the shrine are considered to be strengthened by the mysterious forces possessed by the holy personage and thus become more acceptable to God.

Other common features of a shrine can be summarized as follows: 1) a descendant of the person buried in the shrine is the guardian of the sacred place; he is considered to have inherited the invisible powers that his ancestor had and therefore can act as a mediator in conflicts among the faithful and between rulers and their subjects; 2) if the shrine contains the body of a learned man (particularly if he was member of a mystical brotherhood) an educational institution (*madrasa*) is commonly established in the vicinity of the shrine to circulate and transmit the teachings of the deceased master and to offer asylum, spiritual instruction and moral guidance to students and common people.

To accommodate and feed the pilgrims visiting the holy place and the students who come there to study in the *madrasa*, several other buildings can be found next to the shrine including libraries, schoolrooms, dormitories, kitchens, mosques, repositories and granaries. A cemetery often grows around a shrine, as it is believed that the holy man can intercede for the dead and help them enter paradise. Eventually the shrine may become the focal point of a small village.

The intellectual and devotional activities carried out around shrines have decisively contributed to the spread and entrenchment of the Islamic belief and practices among the common faithful and to the enhancement of the Islamic culture among the educated elite.

Theology and Law. Ethiopian Muslims also pay great attention to theology and law. The tendency to discuss the tenets of the faith and the legal aspects of the daily practices of the faithful clearly appears in the curricula of the Ethiopian Islamic educational institutions and in the literature circulating among the Muslim learned men as well as the common faithful (theological and legal treatises, collection of legal opinions and decisions of the *qadi*-courts). Ceremonies marking the main phases of the life of a Muslim individual and family (birth, circumcision, engagement, wedding, and death), dietary rules (*halal* vs *haram* foods; *halal* slaughter), consumption of local alcoholic drinks (*tajj, talla*/*faarso*) and *chat* chewing have been shaped in the past and still are nowadays under the strong influence of pre-Islamic local cultures (*adat*). This influence is considered to be dangerous for the faithful and therefore many of the widespread practices of the Ethiopian Muslims have been repeatedly scrutinized on the basis of the principles of the Islamic law becoming objects of discussion not only among learned men but also among simple believers.

The variegated nature of Ethiopian Islam is reflected also in the manifestations of its higher culture such as the theological and legal schools and the mystical brotherhoods.

Three of the four main schools of Islamic law (Hanafi, Shafii and Maliki) are present in Ethiopia where they coexist peacefully. The history of the diffusion and implementation of Islamic law in Ethiopia has yet to be reconstructed. A steady and strong connection of Ethiopian Muslim learned men with the Islamic educational centres in Yemen (especially Zabid and Hadramaut) has been ascertained, but it is not clear yet to what extent this relationship influenced the way Islamic law and theology were implemented in Ethiopia. According to historical sources in the sultanate of Shawa there was a chief *qadi* administrating justice in a court of law already by the middle of the 13th century. *Sharia* courts were active in Harar during the emirate but they were closed when the city passed under the rule of the Christian kingdom. They were partially restored by Hayla Sellase in 1960, but the scope of their jurisdiction has been so far a much debated issue.

All the major mystical brotherhoods (*tariqa*; pl. *turuq*) spread among the Ethiopian Muslims but mysticism is popularly practised also without a clear affiliation to a specific organized group. Mystical Islam played a decisive role in indigenizing the basic tenets and rituals of Islam and in mediating between them and the pre-Islamic local religious practise and belief. It was thus one of the most effective ways of Islamization of Ethiopia and is still nowadays one of the strongest connective tissues in the body of the Muslim community (*umma*). However, in contemporary Ethiopia, as elsewhere in the Islamic world, a growing sharp criticism has been addressed to the mystical brotherhoods (and to mysticism in general).

Literature: Hussein Ahmed, Alessandro Gori, 'Islam', *EAE* III, 198–202; Hussein Ahmed, 'History of Islam in Ethiopia', *EAE* III, 202–208; Alessandro Gori, 'Zawiya', *EAE* V, 159–60.

Alessandro Gori, University of Copenhagen

Islam and Islamic reformism

Ethiopia is in much popular discourse considered a Christian country – with reference made to the long history of the Orthodox Church and to the central position of Christianity in cultural life. This has often concealed the fact that Ethiopia has a significant Muslim population comprising approximately 34% (*c.* 43% Orthodox and *c.* 18% Protestants) of the total population. Moreover, like Christianity, Islam has a long history in Ethiopia, and is represented by a rich variety of communities and cultures. Most importantly, Islam has undergone significant changes over the past several decades – from being a peripheral 'other' to becoming a more integral part of Ethiopian society.

Sufism and local cultures. Islam in Ethiopia has obviously been shaped by the local cultures with which it interacted. Islamization entailed the adaptation to local customs, which created a fascinating rich variety of local Islamic cultures. Traditional sacred sites were often re-appropriated as Islamic ones, and local religious rituals were integrated into Islam, as were concepts for divine beings.

An example of the latter is how the Muslim Oromo's pre-Islamic notion about spirits – the *ayaana* – continued to have relevance in the form of *jinn* or as *baraka* (benevolent force of blessing). As different ethnic groups kept many of their traditions, Islam in Ethiopia constituted both an overarching framework as well as allowing for local particularities.

It also saw a strong presence of Sufism, making inroads already in the 16th century, and becoming a significant force during the 19th century. Sufism became an important factor in the further expansion of Islam, and played a considerable role in reforming many of the existing religious practices. A distinctive feature of Ethiopian Sufism is that it never saw the formation of popular Sufi brotherhoods. Organized Sufism was instead a rather elitist phenomenon, and initiation into Sufi brotherhoods was limited to the *ulama* (Islamic scholars), who never sought to recruit the broader population into the brotherhoods. Sufism was thus closely connected with learning and Islamic scholarship, and the locales of these Sufi *ulama* were important places for religious teaching. This does not mean, however, that Sufism as such was absent among the broader Muslim communities. Religious symbols and practices were clearly coloured by Sufi traditions, paving the way for a religiosity that was a creative merger between Islamic scholarship, local customs, and elements drawn from Sufi traditions.

Particularly – and increasingly relevant during the 19th century – were the Sufi shrines dotting the landscape. Initially places for Islamic teaching and connected, as noted, to a particular scholar, their prominence was enhanced when the scholar passed and the site turned into his blessed burial place. Most of these shrines were local in character, yet could also draw pilgrims from a wide area.

Islam and political change. The establishment of Ethiopia's current boundaries by the end of the 19th century led to the inclusion of a number of Muslim groups. The country's rulers were forced to adopt policies that could accommodate this increasing religious pluralism. Such policies of guarded tolerance nevertheless meant that Muslims were excluded from higher public offices, and that restrictions on religious activism were maintained. The Revolution in 1974 initially promised an amelioration of the Muslims' situation, particularly as the power and status of the Orthodox Church were curtailed, and formal religious equality was institutionalized. However, the *Darg's* repressive policy towards religion in general and particularly those with international links meant that Muslims soon faced severe restrictions on religious expressions.

The change of government in 1991 brought unprecedented changes for Ethiopia's Muslims. The new regime, the Ethiopian People's Revolutionary Democratic Front (EPRDF) reversed former restrictions on religion, and made a point of recognizing the country's ethnic and religious complexity. This created a political climate in which religious rights were constitutionally enshrined. Muslims responded to this enthusiastically, and this led to an increase of Muslim activities throughout the country, evidenced by the emergence of a wider range of Muslim organizations, the importing of religious literature, and through the mushrooming of mosques all over Ethiopia. This meant that Islam gradually moved from the periphery to becoming a more visible factor within society. Muslims actively carved out their own public space, and sought to assert themselves as an integral part of the Ethiopian nation.

Islamic reformism. The 1990s also saw the arrival and expansion of several Islamic reform movements. These played a pivotal role in transforming the religious landscape, and were catalysts for the formation of religious identity, the enhancement of religious knowledge, and the production of a far more conscious Muslim community. Prominent among these movements was the *Salafi* movement, which arrived already in the 1940s, and had grown stronger in the southeast during the 1960s. The *Salafi* movement expanded rapidly beginning in the early 1990s, and has managed to be a major religious point of orientation for Ethiopian Muslims. Emphasizing religious purity, the *Salafi*s put much effort into reforming religious practices, which includes condemning existing localized versions of Islam, and which, inevitably, exacerbated religious fragmentation. Other reform movements included the *Jamaa al-Tabligh* and the so-called Intellectualist Movement; the latter inspired by ideas from the Muslim brotherhood and other modernist discourses.

The EPRDF government has – particularly since the middle of the 1990s – argued that Islam in Ethiopia has become increasingly radicalized, and has responded with a more assertive policy towards Islam, entailing a narrowing of operational space, as well as control and co-option of religious actors. Developments took a dramatic turn in 2011, when the regime invited the Lebanese *al-Ahbash* movement to Ethiopia. A self-proclaimed moderate organization devoted to combatting any form of 'extremist' Islam, the *al-Ahbash* became instrumental in an enforced campaign of teaching the Muslims about moderate Islam. This campaign spurred repeated Muslim demonstrations (until August 2013) protesting what was seen as the regime's unwarranted interference in religious affairs. The demonstrations were remarkably disciplined and peaceful, but were nevertheless brutally ended by the authorities, who also imprisoned the organizers and accused them of inciting terrorism.

In spite of the regime's charges, there are arguably few indications of any radicalization of Islam in Ethiopia – in the sense of attempts to seize political power for the establishment of an Islamic order. While it is clear that Islamic reformism has revitalized religious adherence and strengthened Muslim identities, one should be careful to equate this with Islamic militant movements with explicit political goals. On the contrary, there seems to be a movement towards increased moderation – something clearly seen in relation to most recent Muslim protests. The slogans embraced, speeches made by the leaders, and messages posted in the social media were all clothed in a language which referenced the constitution, democracy, and human rights. Thus the protests became a pedagogical tool through which democratic and secular values penetrated the minds of the Muslims and gained new meaning – strengthening their understanding and support of the secular state.

In sum, Islam in Ethiopia constitutes an important part of Ethiopian history and cultural life. From being rather peripheral and invisible, Muslims have over the last decades moved more centre-stage, working for religious parity, and for inclusion in the Ethiopian nation – both as Muslims and as Ethiopians. We are also seeing increased intra- and inter-religious tensions – pointing to the critical role religion might play in Ethiopia's future.

Literature: HUSSEIN AHMED, *Islam in Nineteenth-Century Wallo, Ethiopia*, Leiden 2001; TERJE ØSTEBØ, *Localising Salafism: Religious Change among Oromo Muslims in Bale, Ethiopia*, Leiden, Boston, MA, 2012.

Terje Østebø, University of Florida

Interfaith relations between Christianity and Islam in Ethiopia

A longstanding coexistence. Unlike other ancient Christian communities in Africa (in Egypt, the Maghreb or Nubia) that were reduced to the status of political minorities by Arab conquerors and gradually converted to Islam, the ancient Ethiopian Christian kingdom of Aksum established early relations with the emerging Islamic power and contained the expansion of Islam on the fringes of its realm. The establishment of this *modus vivendi* is recalled by the famous story of the first *hijra* (migration), when the first followers of Prophet Muhammad took refuge in Aksum under the protection of the king (*najashi*). Despite competing interpretations, in particular on the question whether the *najashi* eventually converted to Islam, this episode reflects how a certain level of mutual respect and understanding has generally been maintained over centuries between Christians and Muslims in Ethiopia.

As the two religions share a wide set of common references, concepts and values, the interactions between the Christian-populated highlands and their regional environment of the arid lowlands of the Nile and the Red Sea basins were translated into an agreed ideological dualism, facilitating exchanges through a clear-cut division of socio-economic roles. This could not work without competition. Peaceful local inter-

Blessing ceremony of an Orthodox priest and a Muslim *shaykh*, Jimma, © Wolbert G.C. Smidt

actions were historically overshadowed by clashes on a larger scale (most notably the 16th century invasion by Ahmad Grany), which have remained archetypal conflicts in the collective memories of both communities.

Muslims from minority to citizenship. In the second half of the 19th century, the foundations of the contemporary Ethiopian state were established in the wake of the expansion of the Christian kingdom and the imposition of its values over large swaths of territory inhabited by Muslim societies. The authorities viewed these newly incorporated and dominated Muslim subjects with suspicion, for they had been rivals for centuries. However, through their links with the neighbouring countries, Muslim trading communities represented the economic backbone of Ethiopia. Their distinctiveness was thus accepted as long as they practised their faith discreetly and accepted the Christian political domination. After the abolition of imperial rule, the authorities moved toward more secular orientations. Muslims have been gradually recognized as having equal rights in a pluralistic society.

Under the current federal regime, characterized by a constitutionally secular state, the main factor supporting the preservation of generally peaceful interfaith coexistence is a consensus by the majority of the population that the longstanding tradition of tolerance between Christians and Muslims should be retained as a value that fortifies the entire nation. An optimistic picture of peaceful and harmonious relations has been emphasized in official discourse and praised by foreign observers. In practice, everyday forms of coexistence oscillate between permanent stress on denominational differences and their occasional resolution.

Differentiation and tolerance. Clothing and food habits are the most common markers of difference. The most broadly observed is the prohibition of eating the meat of animals not slaughtered in the name of one's own faith. This religious boundary is also expressed in derogatory representations of the other community (that may be mitigated by jokes), or by sustaining memories of conflicts of the past (that may be tempered by stories of individual friendships). Within the religious sphere, differentiation is counterbalanced by occasional transgressions, for instance in pilgrimages where Orthodox Christians and Muslims converge owing to shared beliefs in spiritual and charismatic powers of holy figures. Cases of interreligious marriages, involving the conversion of one of the two spouses, are rare but not excluded. Conversion can be accepted as well, as a marginal phenomenon, for individuals who want to reshape their faith to suit their aspirations.

In the social sphere at large, there are a number of common cultural practices that are not identified as religious norms. This kind of 'interstitial space of secularism' has played an important role in the circulation of individuals beyond denominational identities for purposes of social and professional mobility. The currents of religious radicalization have worked against these 'grey areas' by erasing the remnants of 'secular culture' and struggling against modern irreligious standards through the prescription of alternative models of behaviour determined by conformity to revisited norms and antagonized identities. Indeed, a common trope in reformist speeches is the alleged threat of being overcome by rivals from other denominations who are generally portrayed as 'fanatic' and 'aggressive' (the same terms are often applied to reformers by their coreligionists who see them as internal rivals).

Competitions and controversies. Besides reciprocal invectives, carried out through the publication of controversial pamphlets, the most frequent expressions of tensions between religions concern their competition for dominance in the public sphere. This is made audible by the intensification of the use of loudspeakers broadcasting sermons and spiritual melodies. The greatest arena of conflict is the construction of places of worship, especially mosques. In Addis Ababa, as well as in most of the major towns of the country, the authorization given to Muslim communities after 1991 to build large, visible and architecturally ambitious mosques transformed urban landscapes. In many cases, this was strongly challenged by Orthodox Christian residents of the neighbourhoods where new mosques were built only after dragged out lawsuits over the ownership of the land had been resolved. Another form of expressing enmity has been the throwing of stones at mosques (under the cover of darkness). In the Christian sacred city of Aksum attempts at building the first ever mosque have been foiled by angry protests of members of the Orthodox Church. Some disputes have even culminated in bloodshed. In the last ten years, sporadic interreligious clashes have been reported in the southwest of Ethiopia, particularly in Oromia, where Christian communities (generally Protestant-Evangelical, rarely Orthodox) have been harassed or attacked. Churches have been attacked by factions within the numerically dominant Muslim population, who, for their part, have been infuriated by acts of provocation, such as incendiary speeches or desecration of the Koran.

This current hardening of cleavages and tensions between (and within) religious communities in Ethiopia is linked to the global deterioration of interfaith relations. However, the historical depth of encounters, intermingling, controversies and dialogue between Ethiopian Christians and Muslims still plays a moderating role, by fostering the consciousness that a shared identity should prevail. Preserving the possibility of moving between the blurred segments of religious boundaries is felt more protective to individuals than discriminatory attitudes inspired by hatred and ignorance.

Literature: JON ABBINK, 'Religion in public spaces: Emerging Muslim–Christian polemics in Ethiopia', *African Affairs*, 110/439 (2011), 253–274; JÖRG HAUSTEIN, TEERJE ØSTEBØ, 'EPRDF's revolutionary democracy and religious plurality: Islam and Christianity in post-Derg Ethiopia', *Journal of Eastern African Studies*, 5/4 (2011), 722–755; HUSSEIN AHMED, 'Coexistence and/or confrontation? Towards a reappraisal of Christian Muslim encounter in contemporary Ethiopia', *Journal of Religion in Africa*, 36/1 (2006), 4–22.

Éloi Ficquet, École des hautes études en sciences sociales, Paris

Missions

Early missions. The first proselytizing mission to the Horn of Africa may have been led by Salama Kasate Berhan ('Frumentius') in Aksum and concluded with King Ezana's momentous conversion to Christianity around 340 CE. Hagiographical traditions recount that during successive centuries, waves of Christian missionaries reached the Ethiopian highlands. Among the most famous of these were the Nine Saints, who are said to have reached Ethiopia towards the late fifth or early 6th century. Although not confirmed by solid historical evidence, their activities appear to have coincided chronologically with another important wave of Christianization, the one affecting neighbouring Sudanese Nubia.

Medieval missions. During medieval times a series of missions or rather individual journeys with proselytizing intentions were carried out by Catholic Mendicant orders. Around 1237, the prior of the Dominican convent in Jerusalem, Philip, was contacted by Ignatius II, Jacobite patriarch of Antioch, who as part of his rivalry with Alexandria named a certain Thomas metropolitan of the Ethiopian church. Although they never established permanent missions, the Dominicans could have reached Ethiopia by the second half of the century. In the 14th century, attempts to contact Ethiopia gained momentum, in particular owing to the creation of important Catholic dioceses in the East, such as the Dominican archbishoprics of Sultaniyyah in Persia and of Khanbaliq (today Beijing). Around 1315–1316 the preachers Guillaume Adam, Archbishop of Sultaniyya, and Raymond Etienne reached the Indian Ocean island of Socotra, which centuries earlier had hosted a Nestorian community. Later, the friar Jordanus Catalani was entrusted with a mission to the Ethiopian ruler, but it never came to fruition. At the beginning of the 15th century, another friar, John of Sultaniyyah, attempted a similar trip. During the same century, the renewed unionist projects between the Eastern and Western churches gave a new élan to religious missions. The Observant Alberto da Sarteano played an important role during the Council of Florence (1438–1445), bringing to Italy a Coptic–Ethiopian delegation in which monks from the Ethiopian community in Jerusalem were also active. Around 1455, another friar, Ludovico da Bologna, was entrusted by Popes Nicholas V and Calistus III with a mission to *Negus* Zara Yaeqob (which failed) and in the 1470s, the friar Nicola da Oliveto managed to reach Ethiopia.

The Jesuit breakthrough. In the 16th century religious missions reached a new stage with Portuguese expansion in the East. Under the aegis of the royal Portuguese patronage a Jesuit mission was established in Christian Ethiopia. The mission was initially sponsored by the founder of the order, Ignacio de Loyola, by Pope Paul III and by the Portuguese ruler Dom João III. A Bishop (Andrés de Oviedo) and a 'patriarch of Ethiopia' (João Nunes Barreto) were appointed with the aim of guiding the new

Catholic Ethiopian Church. The first delegation of missionaries reached Ethiopia in 1557 but it was a failure: the Ethiopian King Galawdewos refused to accept Roman authority. Half a century later, the mission was renewed with the arrival of better trained men, who had also spent longer periods in the East. Among them were Pedro Páez, António Fernandes, Francesco Antonio de Angelis and Luis de Azevedo. Slowly but surely they gained the trust of a large part of the Ethiopian ruling elite, including Emperor Susenyos and his half-brother Seela Krestos. By the early 1610s they were organizing religious disputes at the court, and by the end of the decade they built their first Catholic church. In the 1620s the mission reached its climax, with the public announcement of the emperor's conversion, the arrival of the Portuguese Catholic patriarch Afonso Mendes and the foundation of about ten missionary residences north and south of Lake Tana. Yet, their success was short lived. In 1632 Susenyos was forced to abdicate in the face of Orthodox opposition to his policies. He was succeeded by his son, Fasiladas, who brought the Catholic project to a sudden end: the missionaries were banned from the country and the Orthodox Alexandrian faith was restored.

Proselytizing during the Gondarine period and later. The Jesuit experience had a deep impact on the country, influencing fields as varied as religious painting, theological thought and royal architecture. Moreover, it also provoked a major social trauma and, consequently, during the Gondarine period no large missions could be established in Ethiopia. Towards the turn of the 18th century, however, a few Franciscan and Capuchin friars sponsored by the Roman missionary agency *Sacra Congregatio de Propaganda Fide* made inroads into the country and even lived for some years in Gondar. Among them, were the Franciscans Giuseppe Maria di Gerusalemme, Remedius Prutky (who left a valuable report on the city) and the Jesuits Grenier and Paulet.

In the 19th century, with the mounting intervention of European powers in sub-Saharan Africa and the Red Sea, religious missions gained momentum. This time, the Catholics were not alone for Protestant missionary groups joined in in the quest to convert the Africans. One of the pioneers was the Swiss priest Samuel Gobat, who in 1830 arrived in Ethiopia on behalf of the Anglican Church Missionary Society. He travelled extensively throughout Tegray and the Lake Tana region and opened the way for the important Swiss-based St Chrischona-Pilgermission, which from about 1855 onwards worked among the Oromo and the Beta Esrael. During later periods, other Protestant groups set up influential missions, including the British London Society for Promoting Christianity amongst the Jews, the German Hermannsburger Mission, the Swedish Evangelical Lutheran Mission (Evangeliska Fosterlands Stiftelsen) and the American Sudan Interior Mission. With their work they laid the ground for the foundation, in the 20th century, of local Protestant churches that are today active nationwide, such as the Evangelical Church Bethel, the Ethiopian Evangelical Church Mekane Yesus, the Masarata Krestos Church, the Pentecostal Mulu Wangel and the Qala Heywat Church. Catholic pioneers from the same period were the Lazarist priest Giustino De Jacobis and the Capuchin Guglielmo Massaja who worked in Tegray and Oromo areas respectively. A novelty of the colonial era were the Jewish missions to Ethiopian Jewry, the so-called Falasha or Beta Esrael, which were initiated by Jacques Faitlovitch in the early 20th century. The missions became fundamental in making this minority group aware of its 'distinct' identity, thereby setting in motion a process that culminated, a century later, between 1977 and 2015, with the migration of almost all Ethiopian Jews to Israel.

The attitude of Ethiopian rulers towards foreign missionary incursions was ambivalent; at times sponsoring or tolerating them, at times banning them. In general, political rulers were interested in the connection to Europe, its political power and technology (particularly firearms), and they thus saw the missionaries as valuable intermediaries. During most of his rule *Atse* ('Emperor') Tewodros II tolerated missionaries, and he ably employed them as skilled craftsmen and advisors. Yet, his decision to imprison missionaries at Maqdala eventually led to his downfall. His successor, Yohannes IV, systematically attempted to eradicate the missions in the name of religious unity, but his death, in 1889, brought a return to pragmatism under Menilek II. Local rulers also sponsored missionary activities.

Another dimension that needs to be addressed are 'internal' missions, namely those proselytizing efforts organized by Orthodox Ethiopians. Earlier instances of Orthodox missions were those led by monks affiliated with Dabra Libanos community throughout the Shawan plateau and those of Ewostatean monks during the 14th and 15th centuries in the Ethiopian-Eritrean regions of Saraye, Hamasen, Shire and Bur. Other 'schools' of medieval monasticism and strong rulers such as Zara Yaeqob supported proselytizing campaigns that expanded Christianity further south. In the 19th century, perhaps following the example of foreign missionary groups, Ethiopian rulers set up their own proselytizing agenda. Thus, immediately following the church council of Boru Meda (1878), *Atse* Yohannes IV appointed a couple of church scholars to implement the Christianization of Muslim Wallo. The policy was a complete failure and was soon discontinued. It prefigures, however, more consistent policies of church expansion carried out under the rules of Menilek II and Hayla Sellase.

Missions in contemporary times. During the short-lived Italian occupation of Ethiopia, Italian-led missions thrived under such groups as the Istituto della Consolata and the Capuchin friars. In contrast, non-Italian missionaries (Protestant or Catholic) from countries such as the United Kingdom, Sweden, France and the United States were banned from the country. With the liberation of Ethiopia, Hayla Sellase, who had himself been educated by French Capuchins, continued with the pragmatic approach, which he had previously established following in the footsteps of Menilek II. He encouraged European missionaries provided that they direct their proselytizing efforts to the non-Christian peoples of Ethiopia, and that they establish schools and hospitals.

As a consequence of Hayla Sellase's policy, in the 1950s and 1960s an unprecedented number of missionaries were active throughout Ethiopia. Missions played a vital role in the introduction of modern education. The Swedish Evangelical Mission, the Brothers of Saint Gabriel, the Adventists and the United Presbyterian Church operated schools in the first decades of the 20th century. Besides teaching, foreign missions have become fundamental during the 20th century in providing medical and health care. Dr Thomas Lambie of the Sudan Interior Mission was probably the best known of the numerous medical missionaries active in Ethiopia in both primary care and the construction and maintenance of hospitals. Missions became increasingly involved in filling the gap left by a dearth of governmental services in such areas as rural and urban development, famine relief, medical assistance and care for the poor. This was especially true during the last decades of the 20th century, when various Ethiopian and Eritrean governments sought to limit the presence of foreign groups in the country. During periods of famine or war, the collaboration between the Orthodox, ecumenical Christian agencies (who provide a big part of the help) and Muslims intensified.

Today the relations between the different religious and missionary denominations in Ethiopia are characterized in some areas by respect, while in others by overt competition and tensions. The freedom of religion proclaimed by the 1994 Constitution of Ethiopia (art. 27) has paved the way for more open proselytism by foreign groups. Additionally, the expanding urban centres have become arenas for competition between the different religious denominations. Rapid economic development and the intensification of social inequalities have also smoothed the expansion of new sects and religious groups, some with their origin in the African continent itself.

Literature: Verena Böll, Steven Kaplan, Andreu Martínez d'Alòs-Moner, Eugenja Sokolinskaia (eds.), *Ethiopia and the Missions: Historical and Anthropological Insights*, Münster 2004; Getatchew Haile, Aasuv Lande, Sven Rubenson (eds.), *The Missionary Factor in Ethiopia: Papers from a Symposium on the Impact of European Missions on Ethiopian Society. Lund University, August 1996*, Frankfurt–New York 1998.

Andreu Martínez d'Alòs-Moner, University of Gondar

Protestant churches

According to the 2007 Population census 18.6% of Ethiopians are Protestants. While in the north and east of the country they make up less than 1% of the population, they represent 70.1% in the Gambela Region and over 55% in the south and west. Protestantism is the third largest religion in Ethiopia, and it continues to grow rapidly.

Beginnings. European Protestants first came to Ethiopia in the 17th century with the aim of strengthening and reforming the Orthodox Church. In the 19th century new envoys followed, translating the Bible into Amharic, Oromo and other vernaculars, teaching and distributing scriptures. In some places Bible readers gathered, but were oppressed. In the 20th century Protestant churches were presented with new opportunities. Vast areas with a population practising traditional African religions had been incorporated into the empire and the ruling emperors sought modernisation. Lacking personnel and funds to establish schools and medical institutions, they invited foreign organisations to enter the country. In the 1920s mission societies from Sweden, the United States, Germany and England started work in Ethiopia. They were of Lutheran, Presbyterian, Baptist, Adventist or Pentecostal background. At their stations, which usually included a school and clinic, they were allowed to teach the Christian faith of their own denomination.

Ethiopianisation. The Italian invasion in 1935 ended the initial period. At that time the number of Evangelical Christians hardly exceeded 1,000. But while the foreign missionaries were expelled from the country, Ethiopian believers came to the forefront. In Wallaga, Walaytta, Kambaata and Addis Ababa these pioneers gathered people in private homes for Bible studies and prayer in spite of oppression. After the liberation in 1941 Emperor Hayla Sellase granted permission for Protestant churches to be built in areas declared 'open'. The movement grew and national churches were constituted, the Evangelical Church Bethel in 1947, the Ethiopian Evangelical Church Mekane Yesus in 1959, the Lutheran Church Bible True Friends in 1960, the Masarata Krestos Church in 1964, the Pentecostal Mulu Wangel in 1966 and the Qala Heywat Church in 1974. All these Ethiopian Protestant Churches engaged in educational, medical or social programmes.

Persecution. Under the Marxist *Darg* (1974–1991) Protestants were suppressed and harassed. Church leaders were imprisoned, tortured or killed. Places of worship were closed, buildings expropriated and meetings forbidden. Where possible the Christians, however, did not stop their social activities and bore witness to the faith. The number of believers actually grew considerably during this period. Also changes took place. Church hymns, formerly translations from Swedish or German hymns, were replaced by Ethiopian language songs and choruses. Choirs of young people were formed and worship services were conducted not only following a set liturgy, but also included charismatic features.

Growth and activities. The Ethiopian Evangelical Church Mekane Yesus (MY, Makana Iyasus) is the oldest and largest Protestant Church in Ethiopia. It dates back to 1898 when the first believers gathered in Wallaga. (The first Evangelical Church in Eritrea was established several decades earlier.) The MY is notable for her holistic approach, combining the Proclamation of the Gospel and human development. Its membership grew from 25,000 in 1959 to 8,308,857 in 2016, having 8,565 congregations and 3,968 preaching places, served by 3,940 pastors, 7,549 evangelists and 580,171 volunteers. Ethiopian missionaries were sent to Mali and Asia. The MY Development and Social Services Commission implemented 241 projects in 2014, reaching 6 million direct beneficiaries and 5.5 million indirect beneficiaries.

The Qala Heywat Church (KHC, Kale Heywet Church), with some Baptist roots, is another large Protestant Church in Ethiopia. During and after the Italian occupation local congregations arose and an independent indigenous church leadership developed. By 1955, 538 congregations, mainly in Walaytta, Kambaata and Hadiyya had been established. Thereafter, growth was dramatic and by 2015 the KHC had about 6.7 million members and 7,774 congregations. Alongside spiritual and social programmes the KHC stresses theological training and operates over 300 Bible schools on different levels.

Another widespread Protestant group are the Pentecostal churches. More than 20 registered churches can be found, the Full Gospel Believers' Church, Mulu Wangel, being the largest. There are differences in teaching, emphasis or practice, but most of them are organized in the Ethiopian Pentecostal Churches Fellowship. When the movement started in Ethiopia among university and high school students, there was a lot of opposition and persecution. They persisted and many young people were attracted by the appearance of the spiritual gifts like healing and speaking in tongues.

There are several other Protestant churches or Assemblies. Most of them are members of the Evangelical Churches Fellowship, which embraces around 28 denominations and more than 35,000 local congregations. It is evident, that Protestant programmes, teaching and practice attract many Ethiopians and give them inner strength, self-respect and hope.

1959	*c.* 25,000	1967	72,976
1976	283,000	1980	508,201
1991	1,002,863	2000	3,359,683
2005	4,312,407	2008	5,012,486
2015	7,886,595	2016	8,308,857

Table 12: Membership development of the Ethiopian Evangelical Church Mekane Yesus

Literature: GUSTAV ARÈN, *Envoys of the Gospel in Ethiopia: in the Steps of the Evangelical Pioneers 1888–1936*, Stockholm 1999; JOHANNES LAUNHARDT, *Evangelicals in Addis Ababa (1919–1991)*, Münster 2004; DEBELA BIRRI, *Divine Plan Unfolding. Story of Bethel Church*, Minneapolis, MN 2014.

Johannes Launhardt, Hermannsburg

Rastafari

The Rastafari movement emerged in Kingston, Jamaica, in the early 1930s when a number of people (Archibald Dunkley, Joseph Nathaniel Hibbert, Robert Hinds, Leonard P. Howell), most of whom had been travelling in Central and Northern America, returned home preaching the divine character of Emperor Hayla Sellase. The coronation of *Ras* Tafari Makwannen as Emperor Hayla Sellase on 2 November 1930 was interpreted as a sign announcing the opening of the seven seals unleashing God's judgement (Rev. 5:5). Coronation day remains a major celebration of the Rastafari, as is the birthday of the emperor (23 July). During the mid-1930s, the Rastafari movement was strengthened in the wake of Italy's Fascist conquest of Ethiopia.

The social and ideological roots of Rastafari. The social and ideological roots of the Rastafari movement can be traced to popular religions which had been a means of resistance during slavery; the tradition of Ethiopianism, through which blacks identified with Ethiopia through biblical symbolism; and the works of Marcus Garvey (1887–1940) who strived for Black pride and sovereignty, and for going Back to Africa. Rastafari first took root among the poor and destitute black population of Kingston and met strong resistance from the broader Jamaican society and the British colonial government. It is characterized by a wide diversity of practices, and has often been understood as an allegory for individual freedom. However, beyond their shared faith in God's presence in man as represented by Emperor Hayla Sellase, commonalities can be pointed out among Rastafari: the inversion of symbolical values attributed to black and white identities; identification with the ancient Hebrews taken into and out of slavery; a world vision expressed by the term Zion, representing Africa as the land of origins and the promised land; and Babylon, representing the western world and its regimes.

The cultural system of the Rastafari took form in the 1940s. Their *livity*, or way of life, is characterized by the growing of the hair in dreadlocks; an *Ital*, i.e. vegan and

Binghimam Shashamane, © Giulia Bonacci

natural diet; and the ritualized use of the herb (*cannabis sativa*). The *Italk* (from the pronoun '*I*'), a subversion of the Jamaican patois, expresses their confidence in the power of the word and in the sovereignty of the individual subject. *Nyahbinghi*, their sacred music, is played with three types of drums (bass, fundeh, repeater). A *nyahbinghi* may last as long as seven days and nights. A ritual of purification by fire and of praises for the Ethiopian emperor, it stages a mythical confrontation between godly and evil forces.

The Rastafari movement has been a major source of inspiration for artists, poets, filmmakers, writers and intellectuals. Rastafari, by restoring pride in black identity came to embody cultural change in Jamaica after its independence in 1962. Despite its severe repression by the Jamaican government, Rastafari have become a central part of Jamaica's national identity. Rastafari faithful have always claimed the right to leave the island and to go back to Africa, where they expect their redemption to take place.

The Shashamane land grant. In 1950, Hayla Sellase granted 200 hectares of land on the outskirts of Shashamane, a southern market town, to the 'black people of the world' to thank them for their support during the Italian war. Beginning in the late 1960s, Rastafari took up the invitation and started settling in Shashamane. Despite the loss of their land grant through the 1975 land reforms, and harsh living conditions under the *Darg*, arrivals resumed in the 1990s. About 800 'returnees' are living in Shashamane, and a couple hundred more live in Addis Ababa, Baher Dar, and other secondary towns. The majority are Jamaicans, but about twenty other citizenships are represented. Shashamane has become the 'capital city' of the international Rastafari movement despite the absence of a policy regarding these unusual settlers on behalf of either the Ethiopian government or the African Union (AU). Because of their lack of documentation, difficulties are acute, in particular for those who are born in Ethiopia but remain foreigners. Legal challenges in Ethiopia have prompted numerous 'returns' to other countries including Ghana, Benin, South Africa, and Tanzania. A puzzling phenomenon for many Ethiopians, Rastafari have nonetheless contributed to grass-roots development and to the growth of the cultural and musical scene in Ethiopia, where many Ethiopian artists now play reggae music.

Thanks to Rastafari's involvement in reggae music, the Rastafari movement has undergone international diffusion since the 1970s. Rastafari's organizations, like the Ethiopian World Federation, the Twelve Tribes of Israel, the Ethiopia Africa Black International Congress and the Theocratic Order of *Nyahbinghi* are kept alive by growing communities in the wider Caribbean, England, and the United States. In addition, numerous communities emerged in various places: continental Europe, Asia and Pacific, Central and Latin America and, of course, Africa, where locally grown Rastafari have a vibrant voice.

Literature: GIULIA BONACCI, *Exodus! Heirs and Pioneers, Rastafari Return to Ethiopia*, Kingston 2015; ERIN C. MACLEOD, *Visions of Zion: Ethiopians and Rastafari in the Search for the Promised Land*, New York 2014.

Giulia Bonacci, Institut de recherche pour le développement, Nice

VIII Society and politics

Introduction

The eight short articles contained in this chapter offer vivid insights into the complexity and ever changing nature of the Politics and Society of the region.

Although the average reader probably thinks first of Ethiopia's long history of Imperial rule as the *sine qua non* of Ethiopian political tradition, the country has in fact been the 'laboratory' for a wide variety of political systems. Not only has the historical core witnessed the rise and fall of a centralized Christian monarchy, but in more recent years Marxism and Federalism have had their impact. Moreover, if what looks at what might be considered the country's periphery we see Muslim sultanates, complex and ever revolving age-grade systems, as well as 'tribes without rulers' with extremely low levels of political centralism.

Returning for a moment to the Imperial legacy, it was Ethiopia's sustained independence from colonial rule as well as its solidarity with many of the African continent's anti-colonial and independence movements which made it not only an obvious choice for the institutions of Pan Africanism. The Organization of African Unity (OAU) followed by the African Union (AU) continue to enable it to play a meaningful role in regional and continental politics.

The aforementioned diversity of political systems is echoed and perhaps even exceeded in Ethiopia's traditions of legal pluralism. Even at the height of central state power, many issues of family and personal status remained *de facto* under the jurisdiction of local law and custom. Today with the enhanced respect for Ethiopia's multiple nations and traditions, this has been enshrined in law with different courts taking responsibility for different realms of jurisprudence.

Medical pluralism might be an apt description for Ethiopia's health care systems. Alongside countless ethnic and religious practices and practioners, who have provided care for centuries, a modern bio-medical system began to emerge in the late 19th and early 20th century. Aided by considerable foreign involvement, it provided improved but very unevenly distributed care. Even today many isolated areas suffer from a distinct lack of access to bio-medical care and pharmaceuticals.

Ethiopia's economy has struggled through upheaval and turmoil as successive regimes have sought to guide it to greater success and most importantly an improved ability to meet the needs of the poorest. The deeply conservative policies of the last years of Hayla Sellase were followed by the radical centralisation and socialism of the *Darg*, which left much of the economy in tatters. Since 1991 there has been impressive growth and increased investment in infrastructure and industry. However, much of this has come at the price of displacement of populations, and great controversy over land policy and sustainability.

While obviously each of Ethiopia's peoples offered education and training to its members, prior to the late 19th century this took place almost exclusively within the context of religious education. Throughout the 20th century secular education slowly expanded, but was limited by a dearth of trained staff and resources, as well as war and upheaval.

Media: Prior to the 20th century even print technology had limited impact on Ethiopia. Thus the 'Gutenberg revolution' was rapidly followed by modern telecommunications. Successive governments have with greater or lesser success tried to retain control over the press, radio, television and most recently internet. But in an era of information explosion and in the wake of the emergence of a vibrant and vocal diaspora this is an almost impossible task.

Of the countless games and sports found among the nations of Ethiopia, only a few have achieved an institutionalized modern form. Ethiopia today participates in a full range of regional, continental and international sport frameworks. Ethiopian distance runners have achieved the greatest international success, while soccer (football), also has tremendous popularity.

Pan-Africanism

Pan-Africanism postulates the unity of cause and destiny of Africans and descendants of Africans, and it remains the most ambitious and inclusive ideology Africa has produced for itself. Formulated at first in the African diaspora by black intellectuals, it has fed popular cultures throughout the Americas. By the 1950s, Pan-Africanism was re-appropriated by the rising African leadership and shaped the political destiny of the continent. Ethiopia holds a special place in the Pan-African movement. Embedded in the ideological foundation of Pan-Africanism thanks to Ethiopianism, deeply involved in African liberation movements and in the development of regional and continental institutions, Ethiopia represents a cornerstone of Pan-Africanism.

Ethiopia and early Pan-Africanism. From the time the name 'Ethiopia' appeared in the King James Version of the Bible (1611), it became a reservoir of symbolic, religious and racial values, and featured prominently in the collective thought and social practices of black people in the Americas and southern Africa.

A biblically derived myth of black nationality and destiny, Ethiopianism ordains global black redemption from the sovereignty of other races. In the wake of Ethiopia's victory against the Italians at Adwa (1896), Ethiopianism was reconfigured to integrate the modern territory of the East African country. Thus the convergence between mythical and racial representations, and a political reality was sealed, and the state of Ethiopia entered the 20th century imbued with attributes of royalty, sovereignty, and independence.

As early as the reign of Emperor Menilek II (r. 1889–1913), black people were welcome in Ethiopia. Haitian born lawyer and activist Benito Sylvain came to Ethiopia four times after the battle of Adwa and represented both his native land and Ethiopia at the first Pan-African Conference held in London in 1900. Guadeloupean (French Antilles) Joseph Vitalien was Menilek's personal physician. In 1919, when Tafari Makwannen was heir to the throne, black professionals were targeted for recruitment by Ethiopian delegations visiting the United States. In 1922, official letters were sent to Marcus Garvey's Universal Negro Improvement Association to invite black people to come to Ethiopia. In 1930, about a hundred African Americans and Caribbeans were living in Addis Ababa. Most of them left with the Fascist invasion of the country.

Africa Hall, Addis Ababa, © Derejeb

The second war between Ethiopia and Italy (1935–1941) led to a major Pan-African mobilization. Black American pilots like Colonel John Robinson fought on the frontline and later trained the first generation of Ethiopian cadets. In the 1940s and 1950s, the Ethiopian government employed many black teachers, educators, technicians, artisans, journalists, editors, etc., for the reconstruction and development of the country. In addition, to thank black people for their moral and financial support during the war, 200ha of land was set-aside for them in 1950 in Shashamane, southern Ethiopia (the present Oromia Region). In the late 1960s, Rastafari from Jamaica and elsewhere took up the invitation. Today they form a community of about 800 'returnees'. Since the late 1950s, hundreds of students from various African countries have received scholarships to study in Ethiopia, and many of them subsequently held senior positions in their home countries. One of the best-known recipients of an award from the Hayla Sellase Foundation was Leopold Sedar Senghor, who was president of Senegal from 1960 to 1980.

Institutionalizing Pan-Africanism. The task of bringing African states to a summit conference was not easy, as they had to be convinced to set aside their respective ideologies to establish the OAU in 1963 in Addis Ababa. However, building on the spirit of the continental Pan-African movement, particularly support for the decolonization process and the quest for political freedom and integration, Ethiopia prepared a draft charter, which was endorsed as the Charter of the OAU. The organizational structure that Ethiopia proposed (an inter-state association of heads of state and government with a diluted authority of the council of ministers and a secretariat) was also accepted. Addis Ababa became the host of the OAU and, in 2002, of its successor, the AU.

Ethiopia's involvement in African liberation movements demonstrated its dedication to the African cause and remains one of its major achievements in the arena of the continental political arena. Irrespective of the frequent ideology-driven frictions within the OAU Liberation Committee, both the imperial regime and the military junta (*Darg*) exerted considerable efforts towards the realization of one of the major agendas of the Pan-African Movement: African emancipation from colonialism. In the process, it irrevocably associated itself with the anti-colonialist struggles of the peoples of South Africa, Namibia and Zimbabwe.

Prominent liberation fighters like Nelson Mandela and Robert Mugabe benefitted from their training in and association with Ethiopia on different occasions. The material, logistical and moral support rendered to liberation movements in southern Africa endeared Ethiopia to the people and politicians of this region.

Ethiopia also played a significant role in the creation and stabilization of regional institutions. Its timely intervention salvaged and revitalized the Pan-African Freedom Movement of eastern, central and southern Africa in 1962; its active involvement in the Intergovernmental Authority on Drought and Development (founded in 1986, revitalized as Intergovernmental Authority on Development (IGAD, in 1996); and in the Common Market for eastern and southern Africa (COMESA, founded in 1994). The pro-active role of Ethiopia demonstrates the strategic importance of the country in concerted regional efforts to establish political and economic associations. In spite of its weak economic stature, Ethiopia proved instrumental in the struggle to establish these regional units. However, both the idea of membership to the East African Federation and a viable IGAD later haunted Ethiopian governments. They have envisioned such regional bodies as vehicles for advancing immediate goals, without anticipating major long-term challenges. Like other African organizations, these regional associations remained weak and bound to specific goals. Similarly, Ethiopian authorities and the business community have not yet internalized the actual objectives of COMESA, including the formation of a fully integrated, and internationally competitive regional economic community.

Ethiopia and African politics. Ethiopia's efforts at mediating inter- and intra-state conflicts in post-independence Africa represent another dimension of the country's involvement in the affairs of the continent. Generally speaking, these interventions demonstrated Ethiopia's sense of belonging and commitment to collective peace and security in Africa. The country's prominence in African politics, its adherence to the principle of the peaceful resolution of conflicts and its carefully nurtured principle of non-affiliation with ideologically-driven associations in the continent contributed to its successes in most of its mediations. Nonetheless, the policies adopted by successive Ethiopian regimes were primarily based upon the possible implications each case might have on Ethiopia. Ethiopia also steadfastly advocated for resolution of African problems without intervention from external forces. In particular, the meddling of ex-colonial powers elicited the strongest of reactions. For the imperial regime, disputes had to be resolved within the framework of national unity and without interference in the internal affairs of other nation-states.

The *Darg*, similarly, adhered to these principles, although at times its assessment of ongoing African conflicts was overly influenced by ideological affinity. The post-1991 government has also demonstrated its commitment to the Pan-African agenda through mediation, peace keeping missions and championing regional as well as continent-wide discussions for integration and development. Deployment of Ethiopian peacekeepers in Rwanda, Burundi, Liberia, Sudan (Abyei and Darfur), and Somalia are cases in point. Leadership roles in IGAD and OAU/AU proved instrumental in resolving conflicts in Somalia, Sudan and recently South Sudan. At a larger scale, Ethiopia emerged crucial in coordinating African agendas through the New Partnership for African Development and climate change talks. These activities were not without their shortcomings and possible repercussions that might limit the country's future position in African politics.

Ethiopia's traditional approach of restraint and detachment in its external relations determined the degree of its involvement in regional and continental affairs. The commitment to shield the 'sacrosanct' Ethiopian nationhood from any external interference has somehow contributed to the resistance towards the creation of viable supranational organizations at regional or continental levels and the realization of African political unification. In addition, successive governments often designed their foreign policy with the aim at securing and consolidating their power. Ethiopia's overall involvement in African affairs can be assessed in light of what it managed to accomplish in the process. Ethiopia simultaneously tried to safeguard its strategic interests and to establish a position of reverence amidst the euphoria of post-independence Africa. Ethiopia has been part of both the successes and failures of the Pan-African movement. It has been harshly criticized and even condemned for some of its positions while fervently applauded for others. The country has equally benefited from the services of African states and their organizations in times of difficulties.

Literature: BELETE BELACHEW YIHUN, *Black Ethiopia: a Glimpse into African Politics, 1956–1991*, Los Angeles, CA 2014; GIULIA BONACCI, *Exodus! Heirs and Pioneers, Rastafari Return to Ethiopia*, Kingston 2015.

Giulia Bonacci, Institut de recherche pour le développement, Nice, Belete Belachew, Jimma University

Political systems of Ethiopia

Aksum and its legacy. The process of state formation in northern Ethiopia goes back to ancient times. The best-known and most highly developed state was the city state of Aksum on the Red Sea littoral, which came into existence around the 2nd century BCE. Aksumite civilization thrived in the 3rd century CE as is evident from its spectacular monuments and currency that it left behind as part of its material culture. The Aksumite polity is characterised as an archaic society which exhibited craft literacy and deified royalty. Literacy was confined to priests and those who kept royal records and administrative accounts. Besides craft literacy, Aksumite society also harboured the other key-defining trait of an archaic society, an all-powerful ruler who embodied the intimate tie between the religious and political domains. The kings of Aksum were tied to the religious order through the belief that they were descendants of gods, in particular, of the god of war Mahrem (Greek *Ares*). The king's politico-military prowess was symbolized by the imperial title of *negusa nagast* ('king of kings').

Aksum is also considered to have been the 'seedbed' for the medieval Christian empire. The introduction of Christianity and the conversion of the Aksumite Emperor in the 4th century have largely defined the subsequent history of state formation in Ethiopia. Ethiopian emperors sought to create a nation state not only through political centralisation, but also through cultural homogenisation such as the imposition of the Orthodox Church and the Amharic language on the country's diverse cultural and religious communities. The ruling class comprised the emperor, the nobility, the clergy and the military. The Church laid the ideological foundation for the Ethiopian empire and supported the claim of kinship ties with the biblical King Solomon of Israel. Ethiopian monarchs justified their power as descendants of King Solomon. For this ideological service the Orthodox clergy was entitled to one-third of the land of the empire. In contrast to what might have been possible under the kings of Aksum, the differentiation of an autonomous stratum of literati made it possible for the clergy of the medieval Christian empire to diffuse the Ethiopian national religious system far and wide. They could also develop an indigenous literary tradition that formed a point of reference for a more inclusive collective identity. Unique to the political system of the Ethiopian empire was also the fact that power was derived not from controlling the land, but rather from controlling the people (the peasantry). The *rest* system, a kind of corporate ownership system based on descent, allowed the peasantry to have access to land. In the *rest* system, all male and female descendants of an individual founder or occupier were entitled to a share of land. Superimposed on the *rest* system was the *gult* right, a type of fief right that required the *rest* holding peasants to pay tribute and taxes in cash, kind, or labour to landlords.

Muslim polities. There were also other centres of state formation in Ethiopia. If Orthodox Christianity had served as the main ideology for state formation in the northern highlands, Islam served the same ideological purpose in the central and southeast and southwest highlands. Sultanates, of which Ifat and Adal were the most prominent, emerged in central Ethiopia as early as the 10th century CE. These competed with the Christian kingdom to control trade and trade routes and political hegemony from the 13th to the 16th centuries. In this political struggle the Christian kingdom had the upper hand except when it briefly succumbed in the first quarter of the 16th century when Ahmad Ibn Ibrahim al-Ghazi (Ahmad Grany), managed to defeat the Christian empire. Subsequent to Grany's defeat the medieval Islamic sultanates declined as major power contenders, but survived in the much reduced, albeit economically important, city state of Harar in eastern Ethiopia, which was also a centre of Islamic learning.

There was a third centre of state formation in southern Ethiopia partly tributary to and partly autonomous from the Christian kingdom. These kingdoms were connected to indigenous religions. The most politically developed kingdoms of these were the kingdom of Kafa and the kingdom of Walayyta. Ritual kingship represents yet a different form of political system in Ethiopia. The Anywaa of Gambella in western Ethiopia are the most representative polity of this type. Called headmen and noblemen these political leaders were attached to specific villages, and they rarely embarked on missions of territorial expansion.

While inter-village warfare was rife among the Anywaa, none of these inter-village fights resulted in territorial encroachments. The object of the struggle between the headmen and the noblemen were primarily royal emblems or other emblems of authority. The insignia of the offices of headmanship and kingship consisted especially of precious beads, a royal stool and special spears.

The Oromo and age-groups. Very different from the indigenous kingdoms of the south we find age-group-based societies built along a more inclusive and non-hierarchical principle of a political community. The generation-based *gadaa* system of the Oromo is the most representative of this type of political system. (As are the Konso, Dirasa and Sidaama.) All males are gathered into sets defined neither by their age nor by their patrilineal lineage, but according to their membership of a generation. All sons of men belonging to one generation form a single generation set. As a generation gathers individuals of very different ages, it is divided into five more sub-classes according to age. Every eight years each class progresses into a different grade. Each grade is characterized by its own set of rights and responsibilities, from infant shepherds to young warriors, mature decision-makers and wise elders. In this way social roles are distributed in a life-long sequence, the exercise of leadership transferring from one generational class to another. What is more, the members of the generational class in charge of leadership and decisions of justice vote some of their fellows to become their representatives or chiefs. The gathering of generational class assemblies under the shade of venerable trees like the sycamore fig (*odaa*) is one of the most powerful symbols of the democratic ideal of the Oromo, oriented towards preservation of peace (*nagaa*) through the maintenance of a flow of arguments and blessings.

Segmentary systems. A very different political system existing among the pastoralist communities in western and eastern Ethiopia is the segmentary lineage system. The Nuer who live in western Ethiopia and also in South Sudan have become a paradigmatic case of a political organization in 'tribes without rulers' (see also the Somali and Gurage). Among them patrilineal descent serves, in the absence of central institutions of political power, as a basis of solidarity. In the segmentary lineage system, descent through the male line is the fundamental value upon which the political system is built. The lineage system and the political systems operate in two different domains, corresponding to patrilineal descent groups (clans and lineages), in the first case, and to territorially based tribes, in the second. Apart from serving as an ideological frame of reference for the Nuer, lineages are also relevant points of reference in articulating the rules of exogamy, and further serve as basic units in the performance of rituals. In segmentary lineage political systems tribes are much more flexible and inclusive than the conventional understanding of the term 'tribe' would allow. Both members of other clans and even more so outsiders often attach themselves to an original tribe associated with a certain clan through marriage and other forms of social exchanges ultimately creating an expanding political community. As such, societies whose political system is built along the principle of segmentary lineage system are very assimilationist.

Christian expansion. These diverse political systems were incorporated into the expanding Christian empire by the end of the 19th century. After the two major challenges of the Islamic states and the Oromo migration of the 16th and 17th centuries the Christian kingdom was revived, thanks to its offshoot in the central highlands that emerged as the Shawan kingdom. Due to its politically and militarily astute leaders, the Shawan kings kept aloof from the destructive wars of the 17th and 18th centuries, known as the 'Era of the princes' (*Zamana masafent*) when the monarchy declined and the regional warlords competed to be the king-makers. Instead, they consolidated their hold by continuously expanding into the south well beyond what the medieval Christian kingdom managed to achieve. The Shawan kings also managed to forge closer diplomatic ties with European countries for commerce and access to firearms. With greatly increased firepower Emperor Menilek II embarked on a major territorial expansion into the south, east and west. The economic riches of the newly conquered territories in turn enabled him to claim the imperial throne from the northern kings, ultimately becoming 'king of kings' of imperial Ethiopia. The task of consolidation and modernisation of Menilek's empire was left to Emperor Hayla Sellase (r. 1930–1974).

Recent upheaval. The modernisation of the Ethiopian empire generated various social contradictions and rising demands from the various sections of the society. First challenged by regional and ethnic autonomous movements, particularly the separatist liberation movements in Eritrea, the ideological foundation of the Ethiopian empire was further questioned by the student movement of the 1960s and 1970s, which called for political and land reform. After a decade of protests by students, the military finally stepped in and toppled the emperor, thereby bringing an end to one of the oldest monarchies in history. Subsequently the military government, known as the *Darg*, sought to institute a new political order built on socialist principles. Claiming to be 'more genuine' socialist organizations, the various political parties and liberation movements that sprung up from the student movement challenged the *Darg* politically as well as militarily. The *Darg* managed to violently suppress the urban-based Marxist parties such as the Ethiopian People's Revolutionary Party (EPRP), whereas the rural- based Marxist liberation movements such as the Tigray People's Liberation Front (TPLF) not only survived but eventually also military defeated the *Darg*. By the end of the 1980s the TPLF was the strongest of the liberation movements and forged a coalition with splinter groups from the EPRP and other ethnic-based political organizations. These formed a new national organization known as the Ethiopian People's Revolutionary Democratic Front (EPRDF). Following a UN-supervised referendum, Eritrea declared its independence in 1993.

The EPRDF overthrew the *Darg* in 1991 and took control of the Ethiopian state, which it has radically restructured. Reversing the centuries-old nation-building project through political centralisation and cultural homogenization, the EPRDF has instituted a new political order based on multiculturalism. The country has been reorganized as a federation based on the ethnic principle. Ethnic groups, 'Nations, Nationalities and Peoples' in the Ethiopian parlance, are accorded constitutional rights to self-determination up to and including secession when they feel their rights are violated by the federal government. The new Ethiopian federation comprises nine Ethno-regional states, and two city-states (the nation's capital Addis Ababa and the cosmopolitan town of Derre Dawa).

Literature: DONALD CRUMMEY, *Land and Society in the Christian Kingdom of Ethiopia: From the 13th to the 20th Century*, Chicago, IL 2000; EDWARD EVANS-PRITCHARD, *The Nuer: A Description of the Modes of Livelihood and Political Institutions of a Nilotic People*, Oxford 1940.

Dereje Feyissa, Addis Ababa University

Legal systems of Ethiopia

The legal realities of the Federal Democratic Republic of Ethiopia (FDRE) reveal the coexistence of multiple interacting local (or 'customary'), religious and state legal orders.

Historically, the overall Ethiopian legal system has been shaped by numerous overlapping legal orders: Local and religious laws have always regulated the daily life of the different communities. In addition, there were imperial rules to regulate various relations within the 'Highland empires' and the Ethiopian Orthodox Church from the 14th century onwards. These included legislation in the form of codices, statutes and decrees, e.g. the *Fetha nagast* ('The law of the kings'), the *Kebra nagast* ('The glory of the kings') and the *Serata mangest* ('procedural laws of the state'). Beginning in the 1950s a comprehensive process of codification, mainly drawn from European sources and guided by modernising ambitions of Emperor Hayla Sellase (1892–1975), took place. Beside the promulgation of the first written constitutions of Ethiopia (1931 and 1955), between 1955 and 1965 five major legal codes were enacted: a Penal Code (1957), a Civil Code (1960), Commercial Code (1960), Maritime Code (1960), a Criminal Procedure Code (1961) and a Civil Procedure Code (1965).

However, given the vast rural population and the minimal application of state rules, to this day the state legal order has very limited influence on the lives of the overwhelming majority of Ethiopians. Earlier attempts to create one formal system could not succeed due to the state's inability to penetrate the deeply-ingrained local legal cultures. This legal pluralism is particularly visible in the arena of personal and family law.

Traditional law: Thief asking for forgiveness by placing a stone on his back, thus ending legal action against him, Mikael Amba, Tegray, © Wolbert G.C. Smidt

Legal pluralism. The present Constitution of the Federal Democratic Republic of Ethiopia, 1995 (FDRE-Constitution) and subsequent public policy mark a change in official dealings with the needs of the 'multicultural' citizens. Ethno-linguistic and religious diversity have officially become co-organising principles. State actors have realised that the state policy of a 'nation state' and uniform laws is not suitable in light of the cultural diversity of the country.

The FDRE-Constitution reflects this diversity in numerous ways: Firstly, Ethiopia's political arrangements reveal the coexistence of federal and regional state laws with partly overlapping scopes (see art. 50, 52, 55). Moreover, for the first time in Ethiopian legal history the application of local and religious laws to specific personal matters has been accorded constitutional recognition (see art. 27, 34, 78). Hence, in the federal state there is the possibility that more than one law applies to a single legal domain.

Secondly, the constitution recognises an unconditional right to self-determination of every 'Nation, Nationality and People in Ethiopia' including the right to develop and promote their own cultures, customs and history (art. 39), including methods of dispute resolutions. At the same time the state regulates the application of local and religious laws and their respective conflict resolution mechanisms. Criminal law also remains officially in state hands. Thus, the state has established a legal framework in which the various legal orders are 'permitted' to operate.

In order to not entirely relinquish their authority for co-regulating the 'private' sphere, Ethiopia's state actors follow similar dualistic strategies as their predecessors within the broader policy of 'unity and diversity'. Beside the constitutional recognition of legal pluralism, a comprehensive state family law reform promoting gender-equality has been initiated. However, state family law is primarily implemented through religious and local dispute resolution mechanisms. As in the earlier Civil Code, the Revised Family Code (RFC) of 2000 under certain procedural conditions acknowledges various forms of marriage: civil, 'customary' and religious. The enactment of the RFC did not significantly change the huge discrepancy between the 'law in the books' and the 'living law', in particular regarding access to state family courts.

Constitutional recognition of Islamic law and *sharia* courts as an example. Ever since Muslims first settled in Ethiopia, Islamic law has been used to regulate their secular as well as their religious affairs. Islamic law and the religious courts of the Muslim communities (who constitute more than one-third of Ethiopia's population) had already existed within the borders of contemporary Ethiopia for centuries prior to their official recognition in 1942 by Emperor Hayla Sellase. Since that time the jurisdiction of *sharia* courts (*Sharia Ferd Bet*) has been officially restricted to personal matters. Only since 1995 have Islamic dispute resolution mechanisms been constitutionally recognized. Parallel to the state judicial branch, a three-layered *sharia* court structure has been established at federal and regional levels: First Instance Court of Sharia, High Court of Sharia, and Supreme Court of Sharia. Unlike state courts, a precondition for the jurisdiction of *sharia* courts is the mutual consent of both parties to a dispute to be adjudicated in this forum. In the course of state actors' demands of ensuring legal certainty and procedural justice, the *sharia* courts are supposed to apply solely the Civil Procedure Code of Ethiopia (CPC) as procedural law. Despite the various state mechanisms of regulation such as: financing of *sharia* courts, consensual jurisdiction and the requirement of applying the state CPC, the state has only limited possibilities to regulate material decisions of *sharia* jurisdictions. However, Ethiopian legal system has introduced mechanisms of judicial review: The power to review final judicial decisions rests with the cassation divisions of the federal and regional Supreme Courts. Another control mechanism for guaranteeing the appropriate application of constitutional principles has been established: The political organ the House of Federation has the power to interpret the FDRE-Constitution in conjunction with the Council of Constitutional Inquiry.

Ethiopia's unique state legal pluralistic arrangement leads to tensions as well as to mutual adaptations as reactions to divergent legal concepts. A precondition for the smooth application of the existing procedure rules is a mutual knowledge transfer. Without ensuring for example adequate training in the state procedural law as well as in constitutional principles for the appointed *qadi,* and without teaching Islamic legal principles to state actors, it appears to be difficult to reach a successful implementation of this legal plural arrangement.

Literature: Aberra Jembere, Woldetensay Woldemelak, *An Introduction to the Legal History of Ethiopia 1974–2009*, Addis Ababa 2011; Katrin Seidel, 'State-recognised Legal Pluralism in Ethiopia: The Relationship between Islamic Family Law and State Law', *Law in Africa*, 2 (2012), 223–237.

Katrin Seidel, Max-Planck-Institut für ethnologische Forschung, Halle/Saale

Modern economy of Ethiopia

Background and trends. With a population of about 100 million (2016), a large geographic area with fertile soils and good rainfall in many areas, Ethiopia is potentially one of the richest countries in Africa. Historically, the economy has depended largely on subsistence agriculture that has remained a major source of employment and a contributor to the national economy. Until recently (around 2010), agriculture accounted for over 50% of the Gross Domestic Product (GDP), – the value of all goods and services in an economy – employed over 85% of the labour force and accounted for 80% of export earnings.

Despite its many riches, Ethiopia is one of the poorest countries in Africa with 36.8% of the population being below the poverty line of $1.25 a day in 2011. It also ranks 173 out of 186 countries based on the 2015 United Nations Development Programme's Human Development Index. During the previous decades, the Ethiopian economy has experienced repeated setbacks because of droughts that contributed to the loss of millions of lives, an unstable political climate, and a high rate of poverty. In the last few years, despite some positive trends in the growth of the economy, the country is still struggling to extract itself from this dismal economic condition. To have a better insight into this seemingly paradoxical economic condition (rich in resources, yet poor in economic development), it is imperative that we examine economic trends under the different regimes in the last several decades.

	Average							
Indicator	1980–1990	1990–2000	2001–2010	2011	2012	2013	2014	2015
GDP in constant prices (in billion *berr*)	124.06	152.20	279.23	466.22	507.43	556.46	602.07	653.00
GDP growth (%)	2.54	3.15	8.65	11.39	8.84	9.66	8.20	8.46
GDP at current prices (in billion US-$)	9.53	9.45	16.83	31.37	42.63	46.00	49.86	55.52
Per capita GDP at current prices (in US-$)	228.67	167.42	217.69	370.25	491.33	517.71	547.98	597.11
Inflation index, average concumer prices (2000–100)	40.91	84.98	164.00	380.32	472.11	510.21	549.58	599.51
Government net debt (as % of GDP)	nd	109.32	61.19	20.74	17.86	19.11	20.47	21.46
General government gross debt (in billion *berr*)	nd	56.99	78.22	132.56	156.47	186.37	227.73	278.59
Current account balance (in billion US-$)	-0.19	-0.06	-0.99	-0.78	-2.99	-2.78	-3.53	-4.04
Current account balance (as % of GDP)	-2.03	-0.81	-5.89	-2.50	-7.00	-6.05	-7.09	-7.27
Source: IMF, based on Ethiopian government sources and IMF estimates								
Date for 2014 and 2015 are estimates. Computation by author								

Table 13: Macroeconomic indicators, © Mulatu Wubneh

In 1941 following the end of the Italian occupation, Hayla Sellase's government sought to modernize the country's economy by improving and expanding the infrastructure left behind by the Italians; rebuilding small-scale industries; expanding commercial farms; and restructuring the bureaucratic system. The main focus was to create a modern economy based on agro-industrial development. This push for the transformation of the economy was accomplished through centrally administered national plans supporting a market-based economic policy. Between 1957 and 1973, there were three national plans. Although these plans helped to modernize the economy, they fell short of achieving meaningful results because of a number of problems including the lack of accurate data to refine the plans, weak institutional mechanisms to implement them, and a bureaucratic administrative system that lacked technical capabilities and was reluctant to accept major reforms including the transformation of the archaic land tenure system that constrained the expansion of the economy. Overall, during the latter years of the Hayla Sellase's rule (1960–1974), the economy grew at an average annual rate of 4.1%, which was higher than the population growth rate of 2.3%, but per capita income growth remained at 1.5%.

The *Darg*, the military junta that took power in 1974, was bent on developing a politico-economic system based on the socialist ideology. It started out by nationalizing land, housing and many of the major economic sectors including commercial farms, manufacturing, mining and service establishments. This led, on one hand, to the emergence of many opposition groups that challenged the *Darg*'s policies and its heavy-handed measures to eliminate the opposition, and on the other, to the deterioration of the national economy. This economic dislocation along with the unstable political climate led to the pauperization of millions of people. According to the World Bank, under the *Darg* (1974–1990), GDP grew at an average annual rate of less than 2.0% and per capita income inched from $203 in 1981 to $250 in 1990. Thus, by the end of this period, Ethiopia remained among the most economically distressed countries in Africa.

Cereal mill in the outskirts of Lalibala, © Wilfried Hofmann

In 1991, the Ethiopian People's Revolutionary Democratic Front (EPRDF) took control of the country. It inherited an economy that had been shattered by failed socialist policies and political turmoil, and whose government's coffers were virtually empty with no foreign exchange reserves to speak of. It adopted many of the liberal economic policies initiated toward the end of the *Darg*'s rule – a market-based economy that encouraged competition, with state protection for some strategic industries (notably telecommunications and banking), and an economic policy that focused on enticing private investment. The EPRDF also adopted a policy of decentralisation and reorganization of regions along ethno-linguistic lines. The major thrust of the EPRDF's economic policy was guided by a growth strategy known as the Agricultural

Development Led Industrialization (ADLI), aimed at strengthening the ties between agriculture and industry by increasing the productivity of small farmers through increased use of fertilizers and improved seeds; expanding large-scale commercial farming; restructuring manufacturing to use more local inputs; and promoting export-led and labour-intensive industrial development. In short, ADLI's primary objective was to transform Ethiopia's subsistence economy into a modern economic system.

In terms of investment, the EPRDF channeled a significant percentage of resources to the development of infrastructure and expansion of export-oriented sectors. The government identified four major sectors – horticulture, floriculture, textiles and leather and shoes – as the primary export sectors that would receive significant state investments. For instance, public investment between 2008 and 2013 was around 17.9% of GDP; the corresponding figure for sub-Saharan African countries was 7.1%. Total government investment between 2004 and 2014 averaged about 25.6% of GDP; the corresponding figure for oil-importing sub-Saharan African countries was 23.1%. There were plans to increase total government investment to 30.0% of GDP by 2015. The EPRDF government also attracted a number of foreign investors to invest in commercial farming by making thousands of acres of land available at rock bottom price of $1.0–$10.00 dollars per acre. This remarkably generous price attracted large stakeholders from Saudi Arabia, India, Turkey and Malaysia, as well as other countries. Other investment incentives included exemption from custom duties and taxes on capital goods and raw materials imported for exports, easy access to credit and other facilitating services such as a 'one-stop' investment processing system. According to the Oakland Institute, the Ethiopian government has leased over 3.6 million hectares of land to foreign investors to produce agricultural products for exports. Its policy of leasing agricultural land at low prices and the decision to remove/displace local farmers that were settled on these lands has been characterized as 'land grab', and is being implemented at the expense of thousands of local farmers.

City rail, Addis Ababa, © Stefan Warwas

Growth performance of the economy. Ethiopia's economic growth in the first decade of the EPRDF's government was comparable to the growth rate during Hayla Sellase's regime despite the transition problems that the government faced. Some of the factors that contributed to a better performance of the economy in the first decade were the new government's decision to liberalize the economy, the decentralisation of the local government, and more importantly, the relatively good weather conditions that helped the agricultural sector reap bumper crops. Other sectors such as manufacturing and services also did fairly well during this period – increased at an average annual rate of 3.0% and 21.0%, respectively. According to government data during the period from 2002–2010, the economy increased at an average annual rate of 11.0%. Although the World Bank maintains that the rate was probably around 7.0–8.0%, this growth rate is still robust by sub-Saharan Africa standards for the period.

Based on the successes of the poverty reduction and sustained development strategies, the EPRDF launched the Growth and Transformation Plan (GTP) in 2010. The objective of the program was to achieve the Millennium Development Goals by 2015 and to catapult Ethiopia to middle-income country status by 2025. The GTP, while emphasizing macroeconomic stability, set an economic growth target of 11.2% for the period. Critics have maintained that this growth target was ambitious given the limited role that the private sector is playing in the economy; the high level of debt the country is carrying; the high inflation rate; the increasing current account deficit; and the volatility of export prices on Ethiopia's commodities. A preliminary assessment of the GTP by the IMF shows that the economy has fallen short of meeting the targets set by GTP.

Recent developments and prospects

1. Recent Developments. Ethiopia's recent economic performance continues to show a growth trend for the tenth consecutive year, with real GDP growth in 2012/2013 reaching 9.6%. Most of Ethiopia's robust GDP growth was accounted for by the service sector (45.0%), followed by agriculture (42.7%), and the industrial sector (12.4%). The service sector growth is associated with the increase in wholesale and retail trade, transport and communications, and hotels and tourism. The growth of the manufacturing sector is fuelled by the continued construction boom and the expansion of mining and manufacturing initiatives. Also, the poverty rate has declined from 54.6% in 2000 to 36.8% in 2011.

   Although the share of agriculture in GDP continues to decline, it still remains the backbone of the national economy, contributing to 43.0% of GDP in 2013. Despite the continued expansion in cultivated areas and the relative improvement in yields, the agriculture sector is still beset by a number of problems. These include the uncertainty in land ownership due to the complete ownership of land by the government and the practice of redistribution of land and relocation of small farmers to make way for foreign investors, increase in the price of inputs including fertilizers, and the decline in size of farms (average size of farms is about 0.93 ha), particularly in the highland areas where the population density is increasing and a farming practice that is highly influenced by hydrological and climatic variability. According to the World Food Program of 2014, about 2.7 million people were dependent on emergency food aid and another 7.0 million were chronically food insecure in 2012/2013.

2. Economic growth in Ethiopia has been accelerating steadily for the past decade – GDP has increased at a higher rate than the average for sub-Saharan Africa; the poverty rate has declined and infrastructure, particularly roads, has improved in many areas. According to IMF, GDP is expected to grow at 8.0–8.5% in 2014 and 2015, respectively. In 2010, the GTP set a goal of achieving the Millennium Development Goals by 2015. The important question is: will Ethiopia be able to sustain the projected level of economic growth in the coming decade.

   The macroeconomic picture seems to suggest that Ethiopia is facing some challenges – the growth rate for GDP is slowing down; inflation is on the rise; total national debt is increasing and the current account and balance of payment deficits continue to rise (Table 1). More importantly, the country faces both structural and policy issues that must be addressed if Ethiopia is to reach the goal of joining the middle-income countries by 2025.

Some of these problems include the following:

The land insecurity problem caused because of government control (no private ownership right of land) and periodic redistribution of farms in some areas (irrigation lands) has contributed to an atmosphere of uncertainty among farmers; although land users can buy and sell lease rights. Also, state-owned and party-owned businesses receive preferential access to land lease and credit thereby contributing to the marginalization of non-government and non-party businesses.

Ethiopia's development strategy has focused on promoting growth through public investment with limited participation from the private sector. The reality is that the domestic resources are limited because of the low savings rate and external resources are becoming increasingly difficult to leverage because of global economic conditions. Ethiopia has to entice and allow the private sector to play a major role in development.

Financing the GTP requires having the capacity to raise resources from local and external sources. The continued large share of borrowing from domestic resources is crowding out investment in the private sector putting a squeeze on the availability of credit and foreign exchange for the rest of the economy. Also, external borrowing is constrained by a number of structural adjustment conditions set up by lender countries.

Ethiopia's economic strategy uses import substitution and export expansion to promote industrial development and to generate foreign exchange earnings. Ethiopia's export sector is stagnating because of overvalued exchange rate decline in primary commodity prices and lagging productivity. Export earnings in 2015/2016 declined by 7,0% from the previous year. The lack of foreign exchange will have a major impact on the economy.

The economic transformation pattern shows that Ethiopia's economy is transitioning from an agriculture-based to service-based economy, which often tends to be a lower productive sector. This pattern of growth is different from the economic experience of the Asian countries where the economy transitioned from agriculture-based to manufacturing-based economies. Manufacturing in Ethiopia, instead of increasing, has stagnated over the years accounting for 13.0% of the GDP in 2012/2013. Also, wages in the service sector (which is mostly made up of sales and domestic workers) are relatively low compared to the manufacturing sector thus accounting for the high level of poverty in the country.

Going forward, Ethiopia needs to address the above problems as well as those related to the harnessing of the entrepreneurial initiatives of the private sector, the growing social and political problems caused by the increasingly narrowing democratic system, and the rise in ethnic politics if the country is to join the status of middle-income countries by 2025.

References: Most of the data for the above analysis were taken from the World Bank, 2013. *World Development Indicators, 2012/2013* (*www.worldbank.org*); the International Monetary Fund, *World Economic Outlook Database* (*www.imf.org/external/data.htm*), *The Federal Democratic Republic of*

Ethiopia – Selected Issues.(*http://se.imf.org*), 2014, and the National Bank of Ethiopia, *Annual Report, 2012/2013* (*www.nbe.gov.et*), 2013; Alemayehu Geda, Befekadu Degefe, 'The Political Economy of Growth in Ethiopia', in Benno Ndulu et al., *The Political Economy of Growth in Africa* (*Country Case Studies*), Oxford 2007.

Mulatu Wubneh, East Carolina University, Greenville

Modern education of Ethiopia

Education before the coronation of Hayla Sellase. For centuries, formal education in Ethiopia was mainly carried on through religious instruction by the Ethiopian Orthodox Church. Modern education started only in the late 19th century when Emperor Menilek II permitted foreign Catholic and Protestant missionaries to establish a number of schools. The missions, viewing education as an effective means of proselytizing, frequently taught in local languages and sent promising students abroad. Over the years, additional denominational schools were founded throughout the country.

Following the battle of Adwa in 1896, the failure of the traditional education system to meet the needs of a modern nation in preparing people for work in statecraft, diplomacy, commerce, and industry was apparent. To address this concern, Menilek set up the first modern state-sponsored school in 1908, the Menilek II Secondary School in Addis Ababa. In 1925, the regent Tafari Makwannen opened Tafari Makwannen Lyceum in Addis Ababa.

Public education during the reign of Hayla Sellase. After the coronation of Hayla Sellase in 1930, the progress of public education quickened. A central Ministry of Education and Fine Arts was established, and in addition to the education tax, the ministry received 2% of the national treasury revenue. In Addis Ababa, Empress Manan started public education for girls by founding the Etage Manan School in 1930. The same year that Hayla Sellase School was established. At the time of the Italian invasion there were 21 government schools with an enrolment of 4,200 students and about 2,000 students enrolled in denominational schools.

During the Italian occupation from 1936 to 1941, schools in Ethiopia were closed and all meaningful education suspended. In addition, many educated Ethiopian men and women were executed by the Fascists.

After the restoration in 1941, the British were the dominant force in the empire's education. In 1944 the government made English the medium of instruction of all subjects taught in schools. In the 1940s, significant secondary schools were established in Addis Ababa. Technical, vocational, and special schools were also operated by governmental departments or private societies. Education received about 20% of the national budget during the 1940s, the second largest allocation of funds. By 1952 there were 60,000 students enrolled in 400 primary schools and eleven secondary schools throughout the empire.

During the 1950s the government made a concerted effort to expand its education system. From 1953–1955 American advisers under the Point Four Program worked with the Ministry of Education and encouraged Ethiopians to adapt the education system to the conditions and needs of the empire. Amharic was made the language of instruction for the first six school years; with English used in the later grades. By 1960–1961 there were 26 secondary schools, 14 of them in the provinces and 310 mission and privately operated schools with an enrolment of 52,000.

Despite these gains, the 1961 UNESCO Conference of African States on the Development of Education ranked Ethiopia's primary and secondary education at the bottom among African nations. Challenged by these findings, the Ministry of Education developed a new education policy that was in effect until 1974. The grade structure was reconfigured into six years of elementary school (taught in Amharic), two years of junior secondary, and four years of senior secondary schooling (taught in English). The curriculum was revised to provide a mix of academic and non-academic subjects, and precedence was given to establishing technical training schools.

Pupils at school, © Deminoff

Between 1961 and 1971, the government, using a series of World Bank loans, expanded the public school system more than fourfold and declared universal primary education a long-range objective. In 1971 there were 1,300 primary and secondary schools with an enrolment of 600,000. The US Peace Corps provided teachers with college degrees for secondary, special, and middle schools and increased the number of instructors in those schools by 50 %. Expenditures on education increased from 10% of total government expenditures in 1968 20% in the early 1970s, but funding remained inadequate. By 1974, despite efforts by the government to improve the situation, more than 90% of the population remained illiterate. Primary education was available to 12% of primary school age children, and only 1 million students were enrolled in all the nation's schools.

Post revolution education. After the 1974 revolution, emphasis was placed on increasing literacy in rural areas. Practical subjects were stressed, as was the teaching of socialism. Eastern European governments provided policy advisors to develop a curriculum based on their socialist systems. School construction at all levels was impressive: primary school enrolments grew to 2.5 million students, and the number of junior and senior secondary schools almost doubled. Despite these gains, large segments of the student-age population remained without schools, while civil war, severe drought, and famine had a negative effect on educational improvements that had been achieved.

Following the ousting of the *Darg* in 1991 by the Ethiopian People's Revolutionary Democratic Front, there was a massive expansion throughout the educational system. By 2013, enrolments exceeded 22.3 million pupils in 35,414 government schools. Basic education now consists of four year cycles of Lower Primary schools (grades 1 to 4) taught in the regional 'mother' language and Senior Primary schools (grades 5 to 8) taught in English. Secondary schools also have two cycles from grades 9 to 10 and grades 11 to 12 with instruction in English. About 26.5% of the school-age population is in school. Attrition is high at all levels, and the Ministry of Education places a high priority on reducing the drop-out and repetition rates, as well as improving learning outcomes and increasing educational management skills. Obstacles to the Ministry's announced aims include large class sizes, poor resources, low pay for teachers, and evidence of corruption including the forgery of certificates in some areas. Girls' education is adversely affected by gender stereotypes, violence, and the lack of sanitary facilities (only 43% of schools have separate girls' latrines).

Ethiopia's recent gains in education are generally impressive. Adult literacy has increased to 83% of the population, and the government spends 25.2% of its annual budget on education. The nation has made very significant increases in student enrolment, the number of teachers, the level of the training of its teachers, and the number of textbooks.

Literature: THEODORE M. VESTAL, 'Modern Education', *EAE* II, 234–237; THEODORE M. VESTAL, 'The United States Peace Corps', *EAE* IV, 127–128.

Theodore M. Vestal, Oklahoma State University

Ethiopian health care systems

A medical system consists of the entire range of therapeutic resources available in a given place, irrespective if they are part of the biomedical process. Thus, in describing the Ethiopian medical system we need to take into account all the resources which are presently available. In Ethiopia one can find very diverse therapeutic tradition: biomedicine, religious medicine, an Ethiopian traditional medicine as well as many local medical practices.

Local medicine. There are countless traditions of local medicine belonging to the different peoples which are part of ethnic 'puzzle' of the Ethiopian state. Many of these are used within a single group, but often the search for healing provides a motive for cross-cultural encounters. Hundreds of plants are used in whole or in part to heal diseases such as tapeworm (*kosso* is administered) or rheumatism (henna). Animal products such as milk, butter, honey and blood are also an important part of the traditional pharmacology, especially among the southern groups incorporated into the Ethiopian empire during the 19th and 20th centuries. As for the northern regions there is also the psychotherapeutic zar cult, which is spread through the Horn of Africa and beyond, and has been studied extensively by anthropologists.

Religious healing. Muslims, Jews and Christians also made use of these easily available remedies often supported in their activities by written manuals. Sacred texts might not only reveal the path to a cure, but bring the remedy itself. Thus, the physical object of the book, both the Bible and the Koran might be no less important than the words or instructions it held. Visits, journeys and even pilgrimages to a sacred stream or the grave of a saint might also be part of one's road to healing. The main ones are the holy water sources (*tsabal*) where people go to bath and drink water in order to be healed from any kind of sickness. People use holy water to heal any sort of ailments as well as very serious diseases, or for preventing sicknesses or misfortunes.

Apart from these, there is an Ethiopian written traditional medicine, developed through the centuries in the highlands. It has been influenced by the Greek, Arabic and Jewish traditions through the migrations and the trade exchange between Ethiopia and Arabic peninsula. It is practiced by *dabtara* who are part of the ecclesiastical hierarchy of the Tawahedo Orthodox Church. They work as therapists using in their activities prayers and herbal drugs. They act as therapists in their houses, but not in churches: their therapeutic activities are seen as different from their religious work. Sometimes, at least some of them, are regarded with suspicion by the people that think they have relations with demons. There are also Muslim therapists (*hakim*) who follow the religious and therapeutic precepts of Islam in their activities.

Western bio-medicine. Western medicine first arrived in Ethiopia around the 16th century. However, the French physician, Charles Poncet, who arrived at the end of the 17th century and worked at the Gondarine court, was the first trained doctor to practice in the country. He mainly dealt with the imperial family. While other western doctors visited the country on medical missions in subsequent years, it was only in the reign of Menilek II that biomedicine was firmly established in Ethiopia. At the beginning of 20th century the first hospital was established in Addis Ababa in 1897 by Russian doctors. At the same time, doctors from both western and eastern Europe reached Ethiopia to work there. One of whom, the Frenchman Pierre Mérab established the first pharmacy in the country.

In the next decades some missionaries from Protestant churches reached the country, especially the southern regions. In many cases they founded small dispensaries and clinics to meet the health needs of the local populations.

Seeking holy water from the Entoto mountain to heal a paralysed child, © Philipp Hedemann

Subsequently biomedicine started to spread throughout the country, becoming the leading medical resource, in terms of diffusion of facilities. Throughout the first half of the 20th century, biomedical facilities, such as clinics and hospitals, were found primarily in major cities. Rural areas largely lacked those kind of resources, relying only on religious and traditional healing.

After the fall of Emperor Hayla Sellase (1974), Ethiopia experienced with the *Darg* regime the worst period of its recent history. During that time, due to the harsh economic conditions, and to the progressive deterioration of infrastructure, the biomedical facilities also deteriorated.

After the civil war and the fall of the *Darg* (1991), the situation gradually improved. In recent years, new hospitals and clinics have been established throughout the country. Moreover, the gradual opening of the country to a market economy has also permitted the growth of a private sector, both in the medical sector and in the pharmaceutical ones. New clinics and hospitals run by private concerns have been established, especially in larger towns and cities. Nevertheless, the countryside remains underserved by the biomedical resources.

The private hospital and clinic cover quite all the spectrum of diseases. They are of different size; some of them are based on outpatient services, while others have some beds. Along with them there are clinics and hospitals belonging to the religious and charity organizations. These are spread throughout the country.

Currently, public medical resources are present in all the country. Following the federal organization of the state, they are managed by the central Ministry of Health and by the various regional health bureaus. There are hospitals and health centres in all the regions, even though the number of healthcare professionals such as physicians, nurses, and doctors' assistants are limited.

The biomedical care delivery system is organized in a four-tier system which comprises: Primary health care unit, District hospital, Zonal and regional hospital, and Specialized referral hospital.

The Primary health care unit consists of a network of health centres and health posts. They normally do not have beds and function as outpatient services. The District hospital is normally a small hospital which has to meet the needs of the local population. The Zonal and regional hospitals are intended to serve a larger portion of population, and normally they offer services for a wider range of diseases.

For pharmaceuticals, there are two distribution systems: public and private. The public is organized with a state wholesaler that supplies the public pharmacies. These are located in both urban and rural areas. Some pharmacies are found within hospitals and health centres.

The number of private wholesalers is growing very rapidly. Normally they buy pharmaceuticals from abroad and distribute them to private pharmacies which are located throughout the country. There are three different types of shops where it is possible to buy pharmaceuticals: the pharmacies, the drugstores and the rural drugstores. Each is run by a different level of professional staff. To own a pharmacy one needs to have a degree in pharmaceutical sciences, but for a rural drugstore it is enough to be a pharmaceutical technician. Moreover, these less trained professionals can only sell a limited spectrum of medicines. Trained pharmacists, are of course, far more comprehensive.

Even if biomedicine has spread throughout the country, especially in the cities, one can easily find biomedical facilities both public and private, people in their search for health normally use different medical resources belonging to diverse traditions.

Literature: Ronald A. Reminick, Rachel Chambers, Joachim Persoon, 'Healers', *EAE* III, 3–5; Richard Pankhurst, *An Introduction to the Medical History of Ethiopia*, Trenton, NJ 1990.

Pino Schirripa, Sapienza Università di Roma

Media and communication in Ethiopia

The development of modern media and means of communications was closely connected to the emergence of the Ethiopian nation-state at the end of the 19th century. In this context it must be noted that from the outset the government sought 1) to communicate information about Ethiopia to the outside world, 2) to provide an inward sense of national identity, and 3) to use media for the education and development of the country's population. These elements clearly demonstrate the close link between modern means of communication and the state which continues to the present. This strong link has always resulted in tight control of the media by successive governments.

Print. The formation of the modern print sector in Ethiopia at the beginning of the 20th century combined state and private initiatives. For example, the editor of what is considered to be the first formal Amharic newspaper, *Aemero*, was a Greek businessman, Andreas E. Kavvadias. This was also one of the first newspapers that appeared in a local language on the African continent. Another important newspaper *Berhanenna salam*, founded in 1917, offered early Ethiopian intellectuals a forum to express their thoughts on the country's future. This newspaper, as well as other print media, were shut down during the Italian occupation (1936–1941).

After the end of the Italian occupation, the second phase of the development of modern print media in Ethiopia began. The quantity of circulating newspapers and magazines increased and their quality improved. The press was under the direct control of the Ministry of Information, and was ostensibly a mouthpiece of the government. Notably, publications were expected to convey the image of a modern, progressive Ethiopia. Student publications of the 1960s offered some critical opinions vis-à-vis the government press. However, they circulated in very small numbers. At the time of the Ethiopian revolution (1974) there was a flourishing of freedom of expression and political issues were hotly debated in the press. After the final seizure of power by the military government (1976) control of the media was reasserted, and served the 'education' and 'enlightenment' of the population in keeping with the prevailing state ideology – socialism. After the fall of the military government (1991), freedom of the press was declared in an official government proclamation. As a result, numerous private newspapers were founded. Initially around 250 newspapers and 120 magazines were licensed, but only a few could be sustained long term. In addition, circulation of newspapers is low, usually in the range of a few thousand copies and limited mostly to the capital, Addis Ababa. Over the course of the past decade, the press has been exposed to tighter control again. Some publications were banned by the government and according to critical opinions the press law adopted in 2008 gives the government too much leeway to restrict the freedom of the press. According to the Ethiopian Broadcast Authority in 2014, 16 newspapers and 19 magazines were published regularly.

Television. Television in Ethiopia is firmly in the hands of the government, and there are no privately operated television stations. In 1964, the Ethiopian Television (ETV) was established to document the meeting of the founding members of the Organisation of African Unity in Addis Ababa. In 1982 on the occasion of the founding of the Workers' Party of Ethiopia, colour television was introduced by the military government. After the fall of the military government, ETV survived and was renamed the Ethiopian Broadcasting Corporation (EBC) in 2014. In keeping with current pluralistic cultural policies EBC transmits its programmes in Amharic, Oromo, Tegrinya, Somali, Afar, Harari, as well as in English. Only a very small part of the population owns a television. The growing middle class in the cities increasingly has access to foreign channels via satellite, including the programme of the Ethiopian Satellite Television produced by members of the Ethiopian diaspora, programs from the Arabic-speaking world, and English channels such as BBC and CNN.

Radio. Radio is still one of the most important media through which Ethiopians obtain information. This is especially true for the rural population. According to a study from 2011, 80% of Ethiopians use radio as a source of information. The first radio station was established in 1935. Today, there are about a dozen radio stations the majority of which are in government hands. In the capital Addis Ababa private FM-radio stations, which mainly transmit entertainment formats, also operate. From abroad via shortwave also Deutsche Welle and Voice of America transmit programs in Amharic and other languages spoken widely in Ethiopia. Both lament that in the recent past the Ethiopian government has repeatedly used 'jammers' to prevent the reception of their programs in Ethiopia.

Telecommunications and internet. The publicly run Ethiopia Telecommunications Corporation was originally founded in 1952 and since that time it has been the only provider of telecommunications services in Ethiopia. In 2010, Telecommunications Corporation was renamed as Ethio Telecom. Today it controls access to the telephone network and Internet. The Ethiopian government has resisted pressure to liberalize its telecommunications sector. The reasons given for this are: the large investments in this sector by the government and its importance as a source of revenue for the state, as well as the desire to control means of communication. However, subcontracts in this sector have been transferred to foreign companies.

For example, the expansion and modernisation of the telecommunications infrastructure was assigned to a Chinese company in 2006, and the management of Ethio Telecom was temporarily transferred to a French company in 2010. The latter was contracted to modernize the management capacities of Ethio Telecom.

Cell phone usage has grown rapidly in recent years, but the total number of users is still low in comparison to other countries in the region.

According to the data of the International Telecommunication Union, Ethiopia has 23.7 mobile subscribers per 100 inhabitants. In comparison, in neighbouring Kenya there are 72 mobile subscribers per 100 inhabitants. The owners of mobile phones are largely to be found in cities, whereas the rural population mainly uses the phones at local kiosks or telecom shops. Internet use in Ethiopia is still in its infancy, less than 1.5% of Ethiopians have access to the Internet. A growing number of Internet cafés offer people the opportunity to access the Internet. In addition, web-enabled mobile phones are used increasingly. Connection speeds are often slow and the costs are high by international standards. The current expansion of fast Internet via mobile phones is supposed to fix at least the former problem.

It should also be noted that numerous diaspora Internet sites host lively political discussions and foster links between the diaspora and the homeland.

Literature: RONNNG RANDI BALSVIK, RICHARD PANKHURST, 'Press in Ethiopia', *EAE* IV, 205–207; TERJE S. SKIERDAL, HALLELUJAH LULE, 'Uneven Performances by the Private Press in Ethiopia: An Analysis of 18 Years of Press Freedom', *Journal of Communication and Language Arts, Spe-*

cial Issue on Media and Democracy, 3/1 (2009), 44–59; THE INTERNATIONAL TELECOMMUCATION UNION (ITU), 'ITU Regional Office for Africa, Ethiopia', 2014, *http://www.itu.int/ITUD/afr/memberstates/country_details.asp?countryIndex=ETH* (accessed 17 February 2015).

Julian Tadesse, Leibniz-Zentrum Moderner Orient, Berlin

Sports in Ethiopia

'Ethiopians have always done sport.' With these words Emperor Hayla Sellase laid the foundation for Ethiopia's first stadium in Addis Ababa in 1947. Today, eight traditional games and sports are promoted by the Ethiopian Cultural Sports Federation because they are practiced throughout the country. These are *Ganna* (hockey), *Korbo* (spear-throwing through a moving ring), *Kegel* (wrestling), *Faras gugs* (horseback riding with spear and shield), *Faras shart* (horse racing) and the board games *Bub* (Nine Men's Morris), *Shah/Santaraj* (chess) and *Gabata* (a game with stones and holes).

Sport institutions. Modern physical education (PE) was introduced into the secondary schools in the capital in the 1920s. Its content heavily depended on the preferences of the non-Ethiopian teaching personnel. Historical photographs hint at the widespread popularity of gymnastics. In 1948, the introduction of PE on all levels of the educational system was approved by the Department of Physical Education and Scouting of the Ministry of Education. The Ethiopian Inter-School Athletic Association, founded in 1950, organized annual contests in athletics, football and volleyball in district and regional capitals. The finals always took place in the presence of the emperor in Addis Ababa. PE teacher education started with summer courses in 1957. In 1965, Hayla Sellase I University offered Physical Education as a diploma course. Since 1970 Addis Ababa College of Teacher Education (renamed Kotabe College of Teacher Education in 1976) has become the most important centre for sports teacher training.

As in many places, sports have been closely linked to the armed forces. Top athletes such as Abbaba Bikila, captain of the Imperial Body Guard and Olympic marathon winner in Rome (1960) and Tokyo (1964), and Darartu Tulu, police major and winner of Olympic Gold in the 10,000 meter in Barcelona (1992) and Sydney (2000) are the best known examples. Already the Imperial Body Guard Cadet Training School in Qabena (1946–1953), as well as Hayla Sellase I Military Academy in Harar (founded in 1958) had the most modern facilities, best-qualified foreign coaches and sufficient food supply to train excellent sportsmen. In addition to athletics, the military especially supported boxing. Olympic team members such as Abbaba Makwannen (Tokyo 1964) or Ayyale Muhamed (Munich 1972, Moscow 1980) trained within the armed forces sport clubs.

From 1953 until 1976, the Young Men's Christian Association (YMCA) supported modern sport through its ideas on the unity between religion, character building and physical fitness. The YMCA hosted the national volleyball and basketball federations and trained the national teams. From the 1960s onwards, heavy athletics, particularly boxing and weight-lifting became important elements of the YMCA sports scene. Subsequently weight lifting developed into a popular element of the urban leisure culture with public performances in cinemas, theatres and hotel lobbies.

Internationalization. Ethiopian sports' first connection to the international system of sports competitions came through the Ethiopian Football Federation. Founded in 1943, the federation was recognized as an (official) FIFA member in 1948. Its founding member, Yednaqachaw Tasamma (1921–1987), is undoubtedly the most important

Ethiopian sports official of the 20th century. 1948 also saw the establishment of the Ethiopian Sports Confederation which received official International Olympic Committee recognition in 1954. Two years later, Ethiopia participated for the first time in the Olympic Games (Melbourne 1956) with eight athletes and four cyclists. From 1968 onwards, boxers also qualified for participation. In 1962, Ethiopia hosted and won the Africa Cup of Nations (football). It organized the tournament again in 1976.

Already in 1973, Yednaqachaw Tasamma planned the reorganization of sport in Ethiopia with the aim of systematically developing talented athletes while at the same time supporting mass sports. In the implementation of this program, Ethiopia cooperated with other socialist states such as Cuba, where Ethiopian boxers were trained. Ethiopian coaches and sports officials attended courses at the German College of Physical Culture (Leipzig, GDR) which taught the most modern training methods and socialist sports management. From 1976 onwards, sport was coordinated by the Commission for Sports and Physical Culture. Ethiopia's firm anti-Apartheid foreign policy as well as Cold War politics precluded participation in the Olympics in Montreal (1976), Los Angeles (1984) and Seoul (1988).

Great Ethiopian Run 2009, © Julian Tadesse

Although Ethiopian sports organizations and especially its cadres were critically reviewed after 1991, there has been a clear continuity in personnel. Since the 1990s, the competitive sports sector focuses primarily on long-distance running and football which leads to the neglect of other kinds of sports. In 2001, the Ministry of Youth and Sport formulated an official sports policy which is implemented by the Federal Sport Commission. Successful runners such as Hayla Gabra Sellase invest in private training centres.

Literature: KATRIN BROMBER, 'Muscularity, Heavy Athletics and Urban Leisure in Ethiopia, 1950s–1970s', *The International Journal of the History of Sport* 30/16, 2013, 1915–1928; RICHARD PANKHURST, 'Sports', *EAE* IV, 728–729; PAUL RAMBALL, *Barefoot Runner. The Life of Marathon Champion Abebe Bikila*, London 2007.

Katrin Bromber, Leibniz-Zentrum Moderner Orient, Berlin

IX Recent developments

Introduction

For such a closely interconnected area the latest developments and current political and economic situations of the individual countries could hardly be more different. There is relative stability in one country, namely Ethiopia, which, as an influential regional power, seeks despite its bloody history to establish itself as an honest broker in the area. In contrast, parts of the region lack workable state structures and are dominated by factions or dictatorships that are tearing themselves and each other apart. In the long term, parts of the region seem to have only a meagre chance of viable independent development in the international political arena. Yet, at the same time this 'blind spot' of Africa is witnessing the emergence of a new African state in Somaliland.

Above all Ethiopia, as the core of the region, merits a closer look. Prospering economically, with a democratic constitution and a federal system of government, Ethiopia – despite major shortcomings in the areas of participatory democracy and human rights – is a rising, productive, multinational society with good prospects for the future.

But in spite of unquestioned progress, the most important questions remain unresolved. The decades-long tide of emigration, which shows no sign of abating, needs to be reversed and emigrants motivated to return. Ethiopia needs leaders in the fields of economy, politics and science. The country needs to make huge strides in education and employment in order to keep the youth, who make up the majority of the population, in the country. Ambitious long-range economic plans must be implemented and the economy liberalized all down the line, to attract further investment to the country. The people need to see rapid improvement in the areas of democratization, external and internal security, the war on poverty, and the strengthening of a middle class which is still in the process of formation. In particular, support is needed from academics in pointing the way to future development. And here a promising beginning has been made.

Ethiopia and its neighbouring states

Djibouti

History. Djibouti is a small territory in the Bab-al-Mandab strait, the juncture between the Red Sea and the Indian Ocean. It was under the influence of the Aksumite kingdom before coming under the rule of the Ottoman empire from the 16th to the 19th century, when the Turks ceded it to Egyptian *Khedive* Ismael. At the same time, local rule persisted in the form of Sultanates, and before proclaiming the land a colony in 1896, the French had established protective contracts with the local Afar and Issa leaders, the two ethnic groups that inhabit the area. Both communities followed a pastoral lifestyle owing to the hot and hostile climate, both speak a Cushitic language and follow Sunni Islam, which had been brought to the Red Sea coast by traders from the Arabian Peninsula. However, tensions between the two communities have occurred in the past and continue to the present day. The French fostered conflicts by favouring one group against the other, especially when independence was at stake after WW II. While most Issa opted for independence with the option of later uniting with Somalia, the Afar voted for staying with France in a referendum held in 1967. Djibouti became independent ten years later following a second referendum. However, France has maintained its strong military presence ever since. Conflicts between Issa and Afar culminated in a civil war during the early 1990s, and tensions persist till today. The country has been ruled by only two presidents: Hassan Gouled Aptidon (1977–1999), and his successor Ismaïl Omar Guelleh, who was elected for a fourth term in office in April 2016.

Regional relations. Djibouti has maintained peaceful relations with most of its neighbours in the volatile Horn region with the exception of Eritrea. Violent clashes on the contested border around Ras Doumeira occurred in 1996 and in 2008, when Eritrean troops entered Djiboutian territory. Both governments signed an agreement in 2010 that designated Qatar as mediator, but so far no conflict solution has been reached.

Djibouti has played an active role in mediating Somalia's internal conflicts. In 2008/2009 the government hosted the Alliance for the Re-liberation of Somalia and brokered an agreement between the alliance and the Provisional Federal Government of Somalia, which led to a coalition between both groups. Djibouti has been participating in the African Union Mission in Somalia since 2011. Moreover, it is the host of the Horn's regional organisation Intergovernmental Authority on Development and plays an active role in the AU and the Arab League, while maintaining close relations with most states of the Arab Peninsula. However, between 2014 and 2016 diplomatic relations between Djibouti and the United Arab Emirates were severed due to a conflict concerning the Dubai-based port operating company DP World, which is in charge of Djibouti's port management and was sued for corruption by President Guelleh.

International relations. Djibouti's government aptly utilizes its important geostrategic position on the Bab-al-Mandab strait that connects the Red Sea and the Indian Ocean and is on a crucial international shipping route. The country accommodates several international military bases with the aim of controlling piracy and containing Islamist insurgency. Former colonial power France has stationed close to 2,000 troops, and in the aftermath of the 9/11 attacks in 2001, the USA started to use Djibouti as a base in the 'war against terror' and established a modern military base at Camp Lemonnier that accommodates 4,000 military and civilian personnel. In 2014 the US government secured the rights to use the base for another 20 years. In addition, Djibouti is host to a small Japanese station and has recently signed a contract with China in 2016, which plans to erect its first military base on African soil and is making substantial investments in infrastructural and development projects.

Relations with Ethiopia. Relations between Ethiopia and Djibouti are close, especially since Ethiopia started to use the port of Djibouti as its sea outlet as a consequence of its war with Eritrea (1998–2000). The major part of Ethiopia's exports and imports are handled through the port of Djibouti, and both countries are connected by a jointly operated railway. A new railway line financed by China connecting the port with Addis Ababa was completed in 2016, and the countries signed an agreement to construct a fuel pipeline from Djibouti port to Ethiopia's capital. President Guelleh and Ethiopian Prime Minister Hailemariam Desalegn repeatedly underscored their willingness to enhance cooperation in the political, economic and social sectors, and Hailemariam Desalegn has been promoting ideas concerning the increased political integration of both countries.

Economic and geopolitical perspectives. The government of Djibouti has successfully utilized the geostrategic position of the territory to create stability and solid perspectives for economic growth (6.5 % in 2015) through international military presence and by attracting substantial international direct investment. However, the resulting income has not been used to alleviate widespread poverty among the population and to fight the endemic unemployment of more than half of the population. Today 42 % of Djiboutians are living in absolute poverty, while a small and corrupt ruling elite is reaping the benefits of international currency flows. More than one quarter of the population has not received primary education, and pastoralists in the peripheral regions have suffered from loss of livestock due to worsening drought conditions.

Literature: JENNIFER N. BRASS, 'Djibouti's Unusual Resource Curse', *Journal of Modern African Studies* 46/4 (2008), 523–545; STEPH MATTI, CLAIRE METELITS, *Deserting Democracy: Authoritarianism and Geo-Strategic Politics in Djibouti*, 2013, *http://www.academia.edu/5363276/Deserting_Democracy_Authoritarianism_and_Geo-strategic_Politics_in_Djibouti.*

Nicole Hirt, Hamburg

Eritrea

History. The territory known today as Eritrea is inhabited by nine ethnic groups and received its name and present shape at the time of colonisation by Italy in 1890. The Italians established a central government to stabilise their rule, but left traditional structures of local governance intact. An early attempt to expand their rule to Ethiopia failed when they lost the battle of Adwa in 1896. Mussolini used Eritrea as a base to conquer Ethiopia (in 1936) and invested in industrial production and infrastructure. However, Italy lost her colonies during WW II, and a British military administration was established in 1941, at which time the future status of the territory was still under consideration. While the majority of the Orthodox Christian highlanders favoured unity with Ethiopia thanks to their close cross-border cultural affiliations and organised themselves into the Unionist Party, most Muslims opted for independence and joined the Muslim League. In 1952 the UN took the controversial decision to federate Eritrea with Ethiopia, which annexed the country in 1962. This led to a 30-year long struggle (1961–1991) that was initiated by the Muslim-dominated Eritrean Liberation Front (ELF). However, in the early 1970s the Eritrean People's Liberation Front (EPLF) emerged and ousted the ELF from the field in 1982. The EPLF achieved a military victory over the Ethiopian *Darg* regime in 1991 and Eritrea declared formal independence after holding a referendum in 1993. One year later the EPLF renamed itself the People's Front for Democracy and Justice. It is headed by President Isayas Afewerki, who has never been confirmed in office by popular vote. Today Eritrea is an autocracy without an implemented constitution, where the rule of law and civil liberties are absent. In 2002 the government extended the previously 18-month long national service to an unlimited period of time, and consequently Eritrea has become one of the largest per capita refugee producing countries worldwide.

Relations with Ethiopia. Throughout the centuries, relations between Eritrea and Ethiopia have been characterised by close, yet often conflict-ridden interaction between rulers and local communities. The Eritrean highland provinces were part of the Aksumite kingdom (first to 10th century CE), and remained under the suzerainty of the Ethiopian *negus* during the 14th and 15th centuries, when the *bahr nagash* ('lord of the sea') ruled as governor on behalf of the Abyssinian sovereign. During the 'Era of the princes' (1784–1855) Ethiopian control over the territory vanished. The Red Sea coast and its hinterland had come under the rule of the Ottoman Empire in the 16th century, and the Turks controlled the port city Metsewa until 1865, when they ceded power to Egyptian Khedive Ismail. During the 18th century the rulers of Ethiopia's northern province of Tegray extended their influence to the Eritrean highland, especially following the coronation of Tegrayan ruler *Ras* Kassa as Ethiopian Emperor Yohannes IV in 1872. In the following years the Mahdi uprisings in Sudan and the presence of both British and Italian troops in the region led to complex diplomatic relations, which facilitated Italy's colonisation of Eritrea. However, close societal interaction between Eritrean and Ethiopian cross-border communities remained intact during Italian rule and the economic development of Eritrea's urban areas attracted numerous labour migrants from Tegray.

After the demise of Italian rule, Ethiopia's Emperor Hayla Sellase aimed at incorporating Eritrea into Ethiopia in order to secure the country's access to the sea. He successfully used the geostrategic interests of the USA and the pro-Ethiopian sentiments of the Orthodox Christian population to achieve Eritrea's federation with Ethiopia in 1952, followed by annexation one decade later, which triggered the struggle for independence. In 1974 Hayla Sellase was overthrown by the *Darg*, and due to failed interior policies and loss of Soviet support, the military regime lost the war against the EPLF, which cooperated with the Tigray People's Liberation Front (TPLF).

Initially, there were high hopes that the EPLF and TPLF, which dominated the new Ethiopian government, would maintain cordial relations. Yet, tensions over economic and fiscal policies, a border conflict and lack of diplomatic skills led to a devastating war that raged between 1998 and 2000 and cost up to 100,000 lives and resulted in the deportation of tens of thousands of Eritreans from Ethiopia and vice versa. In December 2000 the Algiers peace agreement was signed by both parties and the independent Eritrea Ethiopia Boundary Commission was assigned to delineate the border. It awarded the contested village of Badme to Eritrea in 2002. Ever since Ethiopia has refused to implement the decision, and a situation of neither war nor peace between the countries prevails. This has resulted in the militarisation of Eritrean society through open-ended military and national service, and in the flight of more than 100,000 Eritreans to Ethiopia, which has been granting them refuge. Both countries have been hosting opposition groups from the other side, and there is little hope for a break in the stalemate as long as the current incumbents remain in power.

Regional relations. Eritrea's relations with its other neighbours have been volatile. The People's Front for Democracy and Justice government clashed with Yemen over the Hanish Islands in 1995, with Djibouti over the contested border around Ras Doumeira in 1996 and in 2008. Qatar has tried to mediate the conflict since 2010 without tangible results. Diplomatic relations with the Sudan were severed from 1994 to 2005 because the Eritrean government accused Sudan of hosting Eritrean Islamist insurgents. However, relations resumed in 2005 and have been increasingly cordial after Eritrea mediated successfully in conflicts between North and South Sudan, as well as between the Sudanese government and eastern front rebels. Eritrea joined the regional organisation, the Intergovernmental Authority on Development (IGAD), after independence, but suspended its seat in 2006 in protest against Ethiopia's US-backed invasion of Somalia in order to bring down the Islamic Court Union. In the following years, the Eritrean government was accused of supporting the *Al-Shabaab* militias in Somalia. Attempts by the government to rejoin IGAD in 2012 were turned down by Ethiopia and Kenya.

International relations. Eritrea's international relations have suffered from the government's mistrust in international organisations and from the persistence of conspiracy theories nurtured by the ruling elite in order to mobilise the population to resist alleged threats against the country's independence. Eritrea joined the UN and the AU in 1993 and received observer status at the Arab League. However, President Isayas repeatedly stressed how the international community had betrayed the Eritrean people when the country was federated with Ethiopia in 1952, ignoring that roughly half of the population had supported union with Ethiopia.

In the immediate post-independence period, relations with Europe and the USA were positive, although the government stressed its policy of self-reliance. During the border war, the government accused the international community and specifically the USA of taking sides with Ethiopia. However, in the early years of this millennium, President Isayas tried to win the favour of the US-government, which planned to establish a military base in the Horn region after the 9/11 attacks of 2001 by joining the 'coalition of the willing' in the invasion of Iraq. However, when the US government decided to establish its base in Djibouti, Eritrean-US relations deteriorated rapidly, and the latter supported Ethiopia's and IGAD's initiative to impose sanctions on Eritrea as a consequence of the government's support for armed insurgent movements in the region. Sanctions were approved by the UN Security Council in 2009 and tightened in 2011. The EU's relations with the country have been strained due to Eritrea's appalling human rights record, but development cooperation resumed in 2015, mainly due to European concerns over the increasing influx of Eritrean refugees.

Economic and geopolitical perspectives. After independence Eritrean ambitions to perform miracles in development and nation-building were high, and prospects were positive: although the countryside was damaged by 30 years of war, the capital Asmara with numerous industrial facilities was unharmed, rudimentary infrastructure existed, and the country had a good potential to benefit from the fisheries, tourism and potentially growing manufacturing and natural resource extraction sectors. In addition, the government profited from Ethiopia's use of the ports of Assab and Metsewa. However, since the Eritrean-Ethiopian war, the country has entered into a steady political and economic downward spiral. In 2001 Isayas cracked down on an internal reform movement, and the introduction of indefinite national service for Eritreans aged between 18 and 50 years in 2002, along with the installation of a militarised command economy based on the forced labour of recruits had catastrophic consequences for the country's development. Today malnutrition is widespread, two thirds of all children of primary school age are not in school, and approximately 5,000 Eritreans per month flee their country to find better opportunities abroad.

Literature: DAN CONNEL, TOM KILLION, *Historical Dictionary of Eritrea*, 2nd edn, Lanham 2011; NICOLE HIRT, ABDULKADER SALEH MOHAMMAD, 'Dreams don't Come True in Eritrea: Anomie and Family Disintegration due to the Structural Militarisation of Society', *Journal of Modern African Studies*, 51/1 (2013), 139–168; KJETIL TRONVOLL, DANIEL R. MEKONNEN, *The African Garrison State. Human Rights and Political Development in Eritrea*, Woodbridge, Suffolk 2014.

Nicole Hirt, Hamburg

Somalia

State formation without end? Since the 16th century, Somalia has seen a long period of tension between Christian Ethiopia and Muslim sultanates; a division of ethnic Somali territory by the colonial powers at the end of the 19th century; religiously and nationalistically motivated guerrilla wars against the British, Italians, and Ethiopians (1899–1920), with heavy casualties; and the founding of the country's first political party (1943), the Somali Youth League. This was followed by the amalgamation of the former colonies of British Somaliland and Italian Somaliland into the Somali Republic (1960); violent, clan-based civil wars; the Somali-Ethiopian Ogaden war (1977–1978), with heavy losses; and the ongoing efforts of Somaliland in the north, thus far unsuccessful, to attain full political independence. Since the turn of the century developments have been marked by the drone-fought, US-supported 'war against terror'; the Ethiopian military intervention against the Islamic courts (2006–2009); and an unrelenting stream of terrorist attacks both in Somalia and abroad, mostly carried out by *Al-Shabaab*, with hundreds of casualties. No jointly negotiated resolution of the conflict is in sight in the near future. The military action of the African Union Mission In Somalia (AMISOM), now almost ten years old, has had only limited success; over 21,500 soldiers are involved from interested neighbouring countries (Ethiopia, Burundi, Djibouti, Kenya, Uganda).

Critics view Somalia as a failed state. Indeed, it seems impossible in the foreseeable future to resolve the notoriously tenacious and violent clash of inner-Somali interests through any politically negotiated settlement that might lead to a lasting peace. How are we to see the Somali Republic? As a victim of geopolitically motivated regional influences? As a male-dominated state controlled by clan leaders and lacking any democratic basis?

Greater Somalia and the Ogaden war. When the Somali Republic gained its independence in 1960, the constitution of the new state envisaged the formation of a 'Greater Somalia', which was to include north-eastern Kenya, French Somaliland (Djibouti), and the Ogaden territory of Ethiopia. To realize these territorial aspirations, the Western Somali Liberation Front (WSLF) was created. After a ten-year 'democratic' transition period, a coup d'état brought Major General Siyaad Barre to power in 1969; an Islamic form of Marxism was instituted, at first with the support of the Soviet Union.

By 1976, Somali-led guerrilla activity had begun in the Ogaden. Mengistu Haile Mariam (Ethiopia) accused the Mogadishu regime of secretly infiltrating soldiers into Ethiopian territory. Siyaad Barre and his military associates responded that only 'volunteers' were allowed to fight for the WSLF. At the end of July 1977, 50,000 Somali soldiers began moving into the Ogaden, and this covert invasion was followed by open war, in which tens of thousands of people lost their lives. Attempts by Somali troops to take the eastern Ethiopian city of Harar failed. The Soviet Union, which shortly before had switched sides, was now allied with the socialist Ethiopian military government. With the help of 1,500 Soviet advisors, 11,000 Cuban soldiers, and 100,000 militiamen who were hastily recruited and incorporated into the armed forces, the 40,000 soldiers of the regular Ethiopian army succeeded in defeating the better-equipped Somali forces.

On 9 March 1978 Siyaad Barre ordered the Somali army to retreat. They had lost one-third of their regular soldiers, three-quarters of their tanks, and half of their military aircraft, supplied by their former ally, the Soviet Union. In 1988 he signed a peace agreement which stipulated a bilateral cessation of support for rebel groups.

A precarious future. At the end of 1991 Siyaad Barre was removed from power and fled into exile first in Kenya and then in Nigeria. His political demise coincided with the collapse of the Ethiopian military regime. In Addis Ababa the Ethiopian People's Revolutionary Democratic Front (EPRDF) replaced the *Darg*. While Somalia sank into civil war, the new Ethiopian regime adopted a policy of 'ethnic federalism', which granted to major ethnic groups their own federal states. In 1992 the first regional elections were held in the newly created Somali region of Ethiopia. At the same time, the UN Security Council approved sending to Somalia a Unified Task Force (UNITAF), also known as Operation Restore Hope. UNITAF was empowered to use all necessary means, including military force. The officially stated goal was to provide humanitarian aid to victims of famine and civil war; at the same time it was charged with restoring law and order and installing a viable central government. The mission was a failure. In early December 1992 the first UNITAF troops landed on the Somali coast. At times they numbered 37,000, mostly Americans. Germany also took part. The Bundeswehr sent a contingent called the Deutsche Unterstützungsverband Somalia. In early October 1993, 18 American soldiers were killed, whereupon the USA and its allies withdrew their troops from Somalia.

Ethiopia then developed a new Somalia policy, still based on Ethiopian interests but with a stronger regional orientation. Partly with an eye to the possibility of making use of the port of Berbera, it has maintained friendly relations with the government of Somaliland (Hargeisa) in the north, which has long cherished hopes of full political independence. In return, Somaliland supports the Ethiopian government in combating armed opposition groups such as the Ogaden National Liberation Front and the Ogaden National Liberation Army.

At the end of 2006 Addis Ababa officially declared war on the ruling Union of Islamic courts, based in Mogadishu and controlling large parts of south and central Somalia, which was suspected of calling for a *jihad* and a reconquest of the Ogaden. Ethiopian forces entered Mogadishu on the side of the transitional government. Their Muslim opponents went into exile in Eritrea, where they founded the Alliance for the Re-Liberation of Somalia. The Ethiopian troops were withdrawn at the beginning of 2009.

A further pillar of Ethiopia's Somalia policy is its military participation in the AMISOM mission. Kenya and Ethiopia, which had already begun intervening bilaterally and unilaterally with 3,500 and 4,500 soldiers respectively, put their troops under the command of AMISOM in 2011 and 2012. But with only limited success. In retrospect one can say that classical military intervention in Somalia has been subject to very narrow limits. Neither the large-scale US-led intervention by the UN nor the invasions by Ethiopia and Kenya and the African Union have had any lasting results. Nor have the numerous peace conferences organized abroad lived up to expectations or borne much fruit.

The case is similar for the creation in autumn 2012 of new Somali institutions (government, parliament) as provided for by the transitional constitution. Similarly, the AMISOM-supported campaign for greater international involvement had only limited success in promoting political stabilization, the building of civilian institutions, and the hoped-for effective training of Somali national security forces.

Much speaks for the view that international attempts to grasp the reasons and dynamics behind the inner-Somali conflict have mostly been poorly informed, with little real strategy, and dominated by self-interest. Short-sighted thinking predominates, instead of trying to keep peace with the ongoing transformation in the actions and motives of Somali groups against a background of accelerating social change, the growing conflicts between largely nomadic, traditional-religious rural pastoralists and urban population groups.

International stakeholders tend to have only fragmentary experience of Somalia, or none at all, which further exacerbates the problem, reinforces the stereotypes put forward by the mass media ('the good guys vs the terrorist bad guys'), and thereby impedes, albeit indirectly and unintentionally, the highly desirable and long overdue re-orientation of local actors in the conflict. A political approach that sees radical Islamic terrorism lurking behind any criticism of the government runs the risk of disregarding and disparaging the valid local social and economic motives of marginalized population groups. Ethiopia is currently host to some 250,000 Somali refugees, and in Kenya 650,000 people live in Dabaab, the world's largest refugee camp.

Despite major initiatives to improve the standard of living, 10.5 million inhabitants of Somalia continue to suffer from weak state institutions, financial dependence on support from abroad, social inequality, corruption, and poverty. An estimated 70% of the population receive no wages and live from agriculture and nomadic pastoralism. One-fifth of the annual monetary income comes from the over one million Somali living in the diaspora. According to the United Nations Development Programme, the average annual per capita income in 2012 was $843. Of the roughly 11 million inhabitants, 85% are under 35 years of age. An estimated 49% of the male population and 25% of the female population can read and write.

It remains to be seen whether the repeatedly postponed election of the new president will improve the situation. He is considered as a man of integrity. His election took place under strict security precautions under military guard within the airport grounds. Clan elders had nominated over 14,000 delegates who elected the 275 members of the national parliament. General elections are expected in 2020 at the earliest.

Literature: ABDIRIZAK SHEIKH, MATHIAS WEBER, *Kein Frieden für Somalia?*, Frankfurt 2010; IOAN M. LEWIS, *Understanding Somalia and Somaliland: Culture, History and Society*, London 2008; STEFAN BRÜNE, *Ratlos in Mogadischu? Europa, die USA und die Internationale Gemeinschaft in Somalia*, Berlin 2015.

Stefan Brüne, Hamburg (February 2017)

South Sudan

Clash of elites and failed politics. Tens of thousands of deaths, unimaginable atrocities, one-fifth of the 12 million inhabitants in flight as refugees, and a dangerous and widespread shortage of food. Five years after winning independence with great sacrifice, the Republic of South Sudan, the world's newest state, threatens to implode on itself. In the index of fragile states maintained by the Fund for Peace, the country occupies first place, topping even Somalia.

Yet everything began with high hopes. There was enormous enthusiasm when, in January 2011, over 98% of the participants in a referendum on independence voted for the secession of South Sudan from Sudan – 3,800,000 vs 45,000. On 9 July 2011 the Republic of South Sudan became an independent state.

The initial euphoria was followed by bitter disappointment. Armed conflict broke out in December 2013. Long-smouldering animosities between factions of the Sudan

People's Liberation Movement (SPLM) – supporters of President Salva Kiir Mayardit, a Dinka, on the one hand, and of Vice-President Riek Machar, a Nuer, on the other – cost the lives of several hundred people, mostly Nuer. The detailed course of events that culminated in civil war, involving the presidential guard and other security forces, remains today unexplained. Riek Machar was able to escape and pressed ahead with the formation of the Sudan People's Liberation Movement-in-Opposition (SPLM-IO).

The consequences have been appalling: armed regional conflict, burnt-down schools and hospitals, 1,600,000 domestic and 600,000 foreign refugees, 17,000 children separated from their families, unpunished war crimes and other offenses, and exceptionally high military spending. The hopes for development attendant upon the attainment of political independence have given way to widespread disillusionment. South Sudan, beset by civil war, counts as one of the poorest undeveloped and underdeveloped countries of sub-Saharan Africa.

Disputed peace accord. At the beginning of 2015 President Salva Kiir Mayardit suspended the free elections that had been scheduled for mid-year – the first in the history of the country – and, with the support of parliament, decreed a three-year extension of his term of office. The international community reacted with concern. It is only since the publication in late 2014 of a UN report – originally held back by the AU – on war crimes and human rights violations on both sides (illegal executions, arbitrary arrests, mass rape, forced recruitment of child soldiers, burning of victims alive) that there has been any real debate over such issues as targeted sanctions, an independent hybrid judiciary, and a weapons embargo under UN auspices.

Among the main weapons suppliers to both sides in the South Sudanese conflict are Ukraine, Israel, and China. The Sudanese regime in Khartoum is suspected of financing parts of the SPLM-IO. Also unclear is the role of Uganda. The 5,000 Ugandan troops sent in December 2013 in support of President Kiir have now left the country, but there is continuing speculation regarding the Ugandan army's role in the acquisition and maintenance of South Sudanese MI-24 combat helicopters and amphibious armoured vehicles.

When Riek Machar and President Salva Kiir, under heavy international pressure, signed a peace agreement in Addis Ababa and Juba on 17 and 26 August 2015, brokered by the regional organization Intergovernmental Authority on Development (IGAD), the move was hailed on all sides. The Agreement on the Resolution of Conflict in South Sudan provided for an immediate cease-fire, the formation of a transitional government, and the temporary establishment of a demilitarized zone around the capital, Juba.

And yet, despite continuing threats of international sanctions by the UN, IGAD, USA, UK, Norway, AU, EU, and China, the parties to the conflict have shown little willingness to compromise for the sake of lasting peace. President Kiir's surprising unilateral decision, immediately after the peace settlement, to create 28 new federal states (later increased to 32) instead of the former ten altered the power-sharing arrangement and remains controversial. It is unclear when and under what conditions the Hybrid Court for South Sudan (demanded by the AU), and the Truth, Reconciliation and Healing Commission can become a viable reality. At the end of 2015 a number of important institutions involved in implementing the peace settlement were able to begin work. Much of the success of the peace process then depended largely on whether and how the 'Joint Monitoring and Evaluation Commission', under the chairmanship of former Botswanan President Festus Gontebanye Mogae, managed to combine past-oriented and future-oriented desiderata: no exemption from punishment for past crimes, but at the same time a striving for future reconciliation. In the words of UN Secretary-General Ban Ki-moon, 'Put peace above politics. Pursue compromise. Overcome obstacles. Establish the Transitional Government of National Unity. And do not delay it.'

In July 2016 the agreement began to unravel when government forces attacked SPLM-IO units inside Juba, forcing Riek Machar, once again, to escape into exile. The political opposition split, with Taban Deng Gai leading the faction that remained in the Transitional Government of National Unity. As violence intensified in other parts of the country the armed opposition in the rural areas continued to fragment into smaller local groups.

In general terms, the peace accord is caught between normative and realpolitik conceptions. On the one hand, there is a general consensus that one is dealing, on both sides, with war criminals who merit punishment. At the same time, the US special envoy for South Sudan, Donald Booth, refrained from directly passing judgment, preferring to see the peace accord, despite multiple violations, as the best hope for a jointly negotiated end to the war. Observers from the US Senate have described the country as a 'violent cleptocracy' and a 'hijacked state' in which 'war crimes pay'.

Financial meltdown. As a former liberation movement, the SPLM is a party without a detailed political programme. Patronage networks, composed mostly of close associates of the president and well-versed in the art of pulling political strings, look out for their own interests by securing for themselves significant advantages and favourable conditions. A neutral, politically experienced middle class, familiar with the complexities of state building and capable of pushing through its programmes, exists only to a limited degree. The majority of the population are poverty-stricken and live primarily from subsistence agriculture. The country has the highest rate of illiteracy in the world: 60% of the men and 84% of the women can neither read nor write. For a while, 47 members of parliament were illiterate.

The long-overdue Security Sector Reform, and concomitantly the politically and socially imperative reduction of the oversized security forces, have thus far been stymied by the constitutionally enshrined power of the president, the crumbling state monopoly on violence, and the presence of armed militias all over the country. Military spending, at 70% of the annual budget, remains extremely high, which, combined with declining oil revenues and the recent currency devaluation, impedes any future-oriented diversification of the 'war economy'. The Republic of South Sudan has the second-highest number of generals in the world, surpassed only by the Russian Federation.

The attempt by the US at the end of 2016 to implement a comprehensive weapons embargo in the UN Security Council did not achieve a majority vote. Only seven of the 15 council members voted in favour of a corresponding outline resolution. Eight countries abstained, including Russia and China as well as thethree African states of the council.

In mid-December 2015 the South Sudanese central bank lifted the constraint tying the exchange rate of the South Sudanese pound to the US dollar and other foreign currencies and allowed the pound to float freely – a move which led to an inflationary devaluation of the national currency. The background to this radical reform was a massive economic and financial collapse. The recent admission of South Sudan into the East African Community is unlikely to bring much change, especially since the statutory requirements for membership in the organization include democracy, good government, tax liability, observance of human rights, and striving for social justice.

In light of the circumstances sketched above, a generationally oriented redirection of the entire political agenda appears as a critical und urgent need. Two-thirds of the 12 million inhabitants of South Sudan are less than 30 years old; 80% of the youth who are eligible for work are underemployed or unemployed. This underdevelopment is connected with high youth unemployment, interethnic violence, and the high prestige attached to cattle theft. The government has announced the goal of creating, by the year 2040, a nation which is literate, informed, and free from dependence on foreign aid.

Literature: 'Gewalt ohne Ende: Elitenkämpfe und Politikversagen im Südsudan', *Zeitschrift für Außen- und Sicherheitspolitik*, 10/1, 2017, 29–38; INTERGOVERNMENTAL AUTHORITY ON DEVELOPMENT, *Agreement on the Resolution of the Conflict in the Republic of South Sudan*, Addis Ababa 17.08.2015; UNITED NATIONS DEVELOPMENT PROGRAMME, SOUTH SUDAN – NATIONAL HUMAN DEVELOPMENT REPORT, *People, Peace and Prosperity*, December 2015; EDWARD THOMAS, *South Sudan: A Slow Liberation*, London 2015.

Stefan Brüne, Hamburg (January 2017)

Ethiopia's developmental state

The notion of Ethiopia as a 'developmental state' emerged as a cornerstone of the ideology of national and organisation renewal in the ruling Ethiopian People's Revolutionary Democratic Front (EPRDF) after the organisation split in 2001, in the wake of a damaging war with Eritrea (1998–2000). Ten years earlier, as it took power in 1991 at the head of a transitional government, the EPRDF had set out a three-pronged reform agenda for the state it inherited from its military Marxist predecessor: decentralisation of its unitary structure; liberalisation of its command economy; and democratisation of its system of single party rule. A decade later, however, the practical impact of these reforms had disappointed most liberal observers. A radically new constitutional architecture of federal 'self-determination' was still offset by strong political and fiscal control from the centre; economic liberalisation was slow and incremental and excluded key sectors the government saw as essential to economic transformation or national security; and electoral politics continued to be dominated by the 'revolutionary democratic' strategy of an activist ruling coalition and its allies, leaving little or no space for competitors.

The 'developmental state'. The emergence of the new strategy in the early 2000s began to crystallise the idea that the EPRDF was establishing a political, economic and administrative order very different from the plural liberal polity envisaged by many of its international partners, critics, and competitors. With pan-Ethiopian nationalist sentiment stirred by the Ethiopian-Eritrean war, and internal dissent within the ruling party marginalised, Ethiopia's Prime Minister Mallas Zenawi now spearheaded the introduction of a new national project: the developmental state – or what the government refers to as 'democratic developmentalism'. This shift ushered in a period of exceptionally high and sustained economic growth. The exact rates of growth are debated, but have been either above or close to 10% each year since 2003. They remained enviably unaffected by the global crash of late 2008, or the transfer of leadership within the EPRDF after the death of the influential Prime Minister in August 2012. By 2014 and 2015 Ethiopia's fast-growing economy was attracting more and more interest from international investors and investment capital.

Enthused by the extremely rapid economic change forged by activist states in Taiwan under the Kuomintang, in Korea under General Park, and (more recently) in China, the late Prime Minister had identified the importance of political leadership and state-led intervention to engineer similar socio-economic transformation in Ethiopia. His view was that if 'improving agricultural productivity and directing the surplus generated as a result of industrialisation' were keys to development, nevertheless 'behind the economic process lies a fundamentally political one: the coming to power of a political class that has both the will and the ability to bring [it] about' (Mallas Zenawi). In a context of chronic food insecurity and poverty, his government saw structural economic transformation as an existential issue, too important to be left to commercial interests or market forces. This is an approach that has (at the time of writing) changed little since Mallas Zenawi's death.

Characteristics of the developmentalism. So how should a developmental state proceed? Four characteristics were identified. First, it should win legitimacy on the basis of a 'single-minded pursuit' of socially inclusive and long-horizon development. Second, this legitimacy should be anchored in broad citizen support and a strong consensus across the population. Third, the state should be 'autonomous': independent of all sorts of influences, but particularly those of the private sector, which it should be able to discipline and guide into developmentally beneficial investment to support national growth. Finally, whilst a developmental state could be either democratic or undemocratic, the late Prime Minister concluded that in Ethiopia it was democratic.

The Ethiopian ruling party's approach is based on a series of important non-liberal assumptions. The first is that the state should be led, over a sustained period of one or several generations, by a political leadership consistent in its commitment to developmentalism. This raises a range of questions: about how to ensure that national leadership *remains* clean and committed to an inclusive balance of pro-poor development and national growth over the long-term; about the potential for electoral changes of power under a constitutional multi-party system; and about the extent of real popular support for the government. After a strong challenge in the 2005 national poll – particularly but not only in urban areas – political opposition parties have been marginalised, as the ruling party rebuilt its structures and reoccupied available

Market day in Bati, Oromia, © Wilfried Hofmann

political space. In May 2015, opposition parties were unable to secure a single seat in the federal parliament. In the EPRDF's view, the extensive system of multi-ethnic representation it has established under federalism, with parliamentary structures at various levels from the local to the centre, gives it 'democratic' credentials. This is not a perspective shared much beyond the ruling party, where critics point to the repressive use of force against opponents.

The second assumption is that the state can and should retain control of key economic levers, both as economic regulator, and economic actor: that a government can be both developmentally activist, and also avoid the 'socially wasteful rent-seeking activities' associated with a dominant public sector (Mallas Zenawi). This sets the approach apart from the neo-liberal view attributing efficiency exclusively to competition. Ethiopia's leaders reject the notion that markets are the ideal tool for boosting production and allocating surplus in a transformatory developmental context, sharing a number of the ideas of economist Joseph Stiglitz. Believing this to be in the interests of accelerated socio-economic transformation for the majority of smallholder farmers rather than the wealthy elite, EPRDF seeks a developmental state with the will and the capacity to discipline market and private sector forces, both domestic and international, which it sees as likely to threaten the integrity and pro-poor orientation of policy making and the bureaucracy.

Criticism. Critics have questioned the extent to which this 'capacity and will' exist in practice at federal level, let alone in the federated National Regional States, and at local level. The Ethiopian state has long been regarded as remarkably free of corruption. The extent of emerging corruption amongst both the civil service and a large class of political appointees has now become a widespread concern, along with the unwillingness of both groups to 'speak truth unto power'. This last has been consistently underdeveloped in Ethiopia's traditionally hierarchical political culture. Burgeoning corruption and ongoing weaknesses in many aspects of civil service performance arguably represent the single most important vulnerability of the Ethiopian developmental state model.

Implementation of Ethiopia's national development strategy, then, remains in 2016 overwhelmingly state-led. A second five-year Growth and Transformation Plan (GTP II) was launched in the second half of 2015, continuing the programme of exceptionally ambitious public investment in infrastructure launched in 2010. State leverage is backed by extensive control of strategic sectors and resources, and by a very large public sector. Privatisation has not been extended to many areas of infrastructure or services where national security implications are in play, and in contemporary Ethiopia national security is broadly conceived. Thus, although there is some scope for commercial investment in power generation, transmission and distribution are reserved to the state, and most investment is public: for instance, in the construction of hydropower dams on the rivers that flow down Ethiopia's escarpments, including (controversially) the Nile and Omo. Also closed to the private sector is the telecommunications sector, where large profits subsidise other areas of public investment.

Along with ongoing state-led expansion of the power, transport and telecoms networks, GTPII continues to build in the areas of education, health, and housing, and focuses on the massive expansion of the formal financial sector, in an attempt to encompass the majority rural population. Although 16 Ethiopian private banks operate in a tight regulatory environment requiring them to purchase government bonds to the value of 27% of their loan portfolio, international banks have been precluded from retail activities, and an aggressive state-owned Commercial Bank predominates. There are indications that the Ethiopian financial sector may be further opened up as soon as 2020, not least in the context of World Trade Organisation accession: introducing international competition and a more diverse range of financial products, as well as a secondary market in treasury bills; and beyond 2020 introducing a share capital market. These changes are likely to present stiff challenges to a domestic banking sector still in its infancy by global standards; but will potentially provide much needed new sources of credit to the equally small domestic private sector.

Meanwhile international investors and companies have already moved strongly into the construction, textiles, beverages, cut flower and cement industries. At the same time the public sector dominates engineering and industrial park development; sugar and fertilizer production; and road, sea, rail, and air transport, amongst others. Critics complain that the Ethiopian currency has continued to be overvalued and interest rates kept low: a strategy that favours the import of materials for the public investment programme, but undercuts export competitiveness and national savings accumulation. Job creation to meet the needs of an increasingly aspirational young generation remains an exceptionally tough challenge, with growing migration for work, locally and internationally.

The retention of land in public ownership has also been a highly controversial area of policy. For the developmental state, it facilitates the rapid expansion of infrastructure (roads, rail, dams, power and telecoms networks), expropriation of land for which would be vastly more time consuming and costly under a private property regime; it prevents expenditure of nationally scarce capital resources on the purchase of land for investment or development; and dampens rates of rural-urban migration. Critics have long cautioned that the approach is unsustainable in the longer term, with increasing fragmentation of agricultural landholdings in the highlands barely offset by a gradual increase in land rental arrangements, and tensions emerging between an older generation with land, and a younger one without such access. Land expropriation has been extremely controversial in lowland areas, particularly over the last five years, with large-scale (and often unproductive) leasing to commercial investors coinciding with population resettlement. Since 2014, however, it has also become controversial in the context of urban expansion, with integrated development planning in and around Addis Ababa triggering protests across Oromia.

Government as stakeholder. If the state is the leading stakeholder, the government's view of the range of actors who should desirably be aligned behind its development vision extends far beyond the state. State initiatives have been complemented by the activities of a range of politically allied or aligned institutions established for the purpose. These include government-oriented regional NGOs and development associations; mass membership bodies, micro-credit institutions, and co-operatives; and private endowment fund conglomerates. The existence of this spectrum of state and non-state socio-economic actors all strongly aligned with the government's vision, gives the leadership very extensive leverage over the development agenda. Meanwhile actors in the private and voluntary sectors have been viewed with less favour, and the government has been remarkably assertive in territory normally thought of as that of the private sector. Certain kinds of trade, which distort markets – for instance through sharp practices including hoarding and price gouging – are condemned as 'unproductive rent-seeking'. Government insists that the Ethiopian private sector needs to mature and evolve in order to play a leading role to complement the economic agency of the state, which will be primary in the interim. A somewhat parallel approach has been taken to the voluntary sector, with civil society thought of as usefully 'filling gaps' in service delivery, rather than as a good thing per se.

In sum, the developmental potential of a state-led approach that takes a long-horizon pro-poor perspective, and succeeds in centralising rents and rendering the policy environment predictable seems clear. Its implementation by a civil service and political hierarchy largely unconstrained by external checks and scrutiny, and subject only to internal – often political – systems of evaluation and control raises concerns about probity, integrity and sustainability. Under the EPRDF, the developmental state has become an all-encompassing project, welcomed by supporters, but leaving little space or tolerance for those with alternative ideas. Observers have complained that this comprehensive approach will enhance the scope for crony capitalism, corruption, and complacency to emerge. Meanwhile, the practical progress of processes of decentralisation, liberalisation and democratisation remain issues hotly contested between the government and its critics.

Literature: Emanuele Fantini, *Developmental State, Economic Transformation and Social Diversification in Ethiopia*, Istituto per gli studi di politica internazionale, Analysis no. 63, Milan 2013 (*http://193.205.23.8/sites/default/files/publicazioni /analysis_163_2013.pdf*); Meles Zenawi, 'States and Markets: Neoliberal Limitations and the Case for the Developmental State', in Akbar Noman, Kwesi Botchwey, Howard Stein, Joseph Stiglitz (eds.), *Good Growth and Governance in Africa: Rethinking Development Strategies*, Oxford 2012, 140–174.

Sarah Vaughan, Edinburgh

Emigration and diaspora

Since Ethiopia is located near the ancient commercial networks of the Red Sea and the Arabian Sea, it is not surprising that Ethiopians have been dispersed beyond the frontiers of northeastern Africa for centuries, through voluntary movements or through the larger forced migration that we associate with the slave trade.

Ancient traders and pilgrims. The earliest evidence we have for the existence of overseas Ethiopians dates to the ancient port of Barygaza (modern Bharuch, in Gujarat, India), which in the early centuries of the 1st millennium may have sustained an Ethiopian merchant community. However, most early references relate to the history of Christianity in Ethiopia. Abyssinian pilgrims probably travelled to Jerusalem in the first centuries following the conversion of the kingdom of Aksum in the 4th century CE. Soon after the rise of Islam in the 7th century, an Abyssinian community was considered to be one of three resident nations there. When Salah ad-Din regained Jerusalem from the Crusaders for Islam in 1187, he apparently recognized their distinct claims as long time representatives of their branch of the Coptic Church. Certainly, the fact that Ethiopians are again named as one of the 'nations' of the Holy Land in the second half of the 13th century leaves no doubt as to their being well established in Jerusalem. The Ethiopian presence in Jerusalem persists to this day at both the Church of the Holy Sepulchre and the Ethiopian Church that was financed by Emperor Menilek II at the end of the 19th century.

Enslavement and forced migration. The community at Jerusalem was atypical because its members were individuals who had been sent to serve their Church in the very heartland of their faith. By contrast, most Ethiopians in the diaspora found themselves enslaved in foreign lands and converted to Islam, although there were also many free Christian Ethiopian traders and craftsmen in Arabia. Honoured among Muslims is the Ethiopian slave Bilal ibn Rabah, an early convert to Islam and the first muezzin of Islam. As a consequence of the slave trade from Ethiopia, Ethiopians were scattered across the Islamic world from Arabia to India, Egypt to Zanzibar, where they were commonly known as 'Habash' or 'Habashi' from the Arabic name for all the different peoples of Ethiopia or the Horn of Africa.

Islam offered a social system that enabled the bonded to acquire significant power and authority, thus enslaved Ethiopians played a prominent role as soldiers, concubines, and eunuchs in Muslim India. As early as the second quarter of the 13th century, Habashi slaves had become one of several factors in the military and political arena of the new Turkish Sultanate of Delhi.

Habashi also reached the kingdom of Bengal directly by sea and became important as military slaves under Rukn al-Din Barbak Shah (r. *c.*1459–1474). In 1486, the Habashi usurped power, ruling Bengal for seven years before themselves being overthrown in 1494. Consequently, the Habashi were expelled from Bengal and migrated south to the Deccan, where the rulers of the Bahmani Kingdom had been employing Habashi military forces since earlier in the century and where eventually several Habashi also emerged as major military and political leaders.

In the late 15th century, Habashis ruled as governors of two of the kingdom's four provinces; another served as minister of revenue under Sultan Mahmud (r. *c.*1482–1518). Following the collapse of the Deccani kingdom and its replacement by several new, independent kingdoms, Habashi rose to positions of authority in the 16th-century kingdoms of Ahmadnagar, Bijapur and Golconda. Related to the renown enjoyed by Habashi military and court officials in the Deccan at this time was the emergence of a Habashi force called Siddis as the dominant naval power along the coast of western India. Based on the island-fort of Janjira, Siddis were unchallenged masters of the coasts until 1870, when they submitted to British overrule.

Habashi were also prominent during the centuries of Muslim domination of northern India in Gujarat, where they were found as soldiers in the armies of its rulers and as sailors in its ports as early as the 13th century.

Prominent Habashi rose to occupy positions of leadership under successive rulers of Gujarat during the middle decades of the century until Akbar's conquest of Ahmadabad in July 1572. We should note, however, that not all Habashi were enslaved. A network of Islamic Sufi saints' shrines that are associated with Habashi pioneers in the agate bead trade to Africa was established during this era, perhaps in the 14th century.

Ethiopian slaves are recorded as a significant group among other enslaved peoples in Arabia during the 19th century. Throughout Arabia and in Cairo, Abyssinian female slaves were greatly admired and desired as concubines. Many of these women were manumitted and some inherited their own property, although many lived at the edges of society.

Liberated by the British Royal Navy, in 1890 a handful of Oromo captives ended up at Lovedale Mission in South Africa. The grandson of one of the Oromo women was South African anti-apartheid activist and language policy expert, Neville Alexander (1936–2012). Local slavery as well as the export slave trade gradually ended in the early 20th century.

Political opposition and the birth of a diaspora. As early as the 1920s, some elite Ethiopians began to study abroad and, as opposition to the imperial regime increased after WWII, some remained in exile. Until the period of Italian hegemony in Ethiopia, when some Ethiopians settled in Italy, the diaspora phenomenon was dormant.

The phenomenon of a new diaspora dates to the 1960s as part of the struggle between imperial Ethiopia and the Eritrean liberation movement. From 1967 thousands of Eritreans fled into the Republic of the Sudan; by 1991 there were over 500,000 Eritreans refugees in Sudan. With the Revolution of 1974 and the *Darg*'s brutal campaigns against civil opponents in Ethiopia, various groups of Ethiopians soon joined the ranks of Eritreans in Sudan. In the mid-1980s, drought and forced resettlement schemes caused another 50,000 to leave Ethiopia, so that the total population in the Sudan reached at least 656,000. Much of this population movement was temporary, but uncertainty about political conditions at home caused many thousands of these refugees to remain in Sudan. Some moved on to Egypt, while still others made their way as secondary refugees to Italy and elsewhere in Europe, in particular in the United Kingdom and northern European countries.

During the same period, over 15,000 Beta Esrael (Ethiopian Jews) were taken to Israel, mainly from Sudan, during the late 1970s and early 1980s. In the 1990s another 35,000 reached Israel directly from Ethiopia. By 2014 there were almost 140,000 Israeli citizens of Ethiopian descent. Lacking western education and work experience, the Beta Esrael have a higher level of unemployment and earn less than most other Israeli citizens.

The Refugee Act of 1980 and the Immigration Act of 1990 establishing the Diversity Visa program opened the doors of the United States of America to refugees from Ethiopia and Eritrea, who may have numbered over 150,000 by 2011. When one adds the number of second and third generation Ethiopian and Eritrean descendants in the United States, their number swells to perhaps as many as 450,000. While some have returned or visited home, continued political instability in both countries and establishing roots where they settled have combined to create true diaspora communities of Ethiopians and Eritreans in the United States. Many of them belong to the Ethiopian Orthodox Tawahedo Church, however, as in Ethiopia, the growth of Pentecostal churches has been very significant. There are many Ethiopian and Eritrean businesses and community organizations, in particular in Washington, DC, Los Angeles, and in the larger New York City region. In addition to sending remittances to family members still living in Ethiopia, Ethiopian-Americans increasingly are investing in Ethiopia. In 2002, the Diaspora Engagement Affairs General Directorate was established within the Ethiopian Ministry of Foreign Affairs with the objective to liaise with the Ethiopian diaspora and to encourage its investment in the country. The same year, a new legal status was proclaimed for foreign nationals of Ethiopian origin, entitling them to all rights and duties of the Ethiopians except the right to vote. At the same time, charges that the Ethiopian government has employed digital surveillance tools to spy on Ethiopians suggest that political opposition is no more tolerated outside of Ethiopia than within.

It is clear that the vast majority of Eritrean refugees chose not to return to independent Eritrea after 1991. The Eritrean diaspora maintains a strong collective national consciousness, encouraged through community organizations and the celebration of Eritrean national holidays. Both as individuals and as families, but often as communities too, the diaspora maintains strong links with Eritrea. At an individual or family level, money and other goods are regularly remitted to family members in Eritrea. During the struggle for independence, the diaspora played a crucial role by financing the Eritrean People's Liberation Front. Since independence, many within the diaspora have continued to contribute by making regular financial donations to the State, or more recently by buying state-issued bonds. Nevertheless, in 2011 the UN banned the Eritrean government from collecting a 2% diaspora tax that has raised particular opposition among the 40,000 Eritreans living in the United Kingdom.

Archpriest Merawi Tebege during the feast of *Kidana Mehrat* 2010, Hamburg, © Maija Priess

A dramatic increase of economic migrants. Seeking employment abroad where none was available at home, in recent decades many Ethiopians, young women for a large part, flocked to Saudi Arabia and to the Gulf States. However, at the end of 2013 the Saudi government decided to expel about one million undocumented non-Saudi workers including approximately 150,000 Ethiopians. Although the Ethiopian government has established funding to reintegrate these labour migrants, the unprecedented numbers have overwhelmed official efforts. With the same economic objectives, Ethiopians with various statuses are present in all the countries of the region including Djibouti, Kenya and Uganda. Regular and irregular migrations by air and by land towards South Africa have dramatically increased in the past decade. Southern Ethiopians, in particular from Hadiyya and Kambaata are over-represented in South Africa, from where they keep tight bonds with their relatives in Ethiopia. The roads of migration through the continent and through the Mediterranean remain very perilous, and numerous people die on the way or fall victims to smugglers' networks. Since 2009, 50,000 Eritreans passed through Sinai and about a fifth of them never came out. The systematic kidnapping, torture and ransom of Eritreans in Sinai is a well organized crime, which only a few human rights activists are determined to voice. With an increasing presence through information technologies, the Ethiopian and Eritrean diaspora communities are on the move, they are well connected to their homelands, and contribute to a quickly changing social landscape as increasing number of youths seeking to move out of their countries toward greener pastures.

Literature: Edward A. Alpers, Khalid Koser, 'Diaspora', *EAE* II, 150–153; Giulia Bonacci, 'In and Out of Ethiopia: Migrations, Diaspora and Contemporary Ethiopia', *African Diaspora*, 8

(2015), 1–13; MINISTRY OF FOREIGN AFFAIRS, DIASPORA ENGAGEMENT AFFAIRS GENERAL DIRECTORATE, *Basic Information for Ethiopians in the Diaspora*, Addis Ababa 2011 (*http://www.ethiopianembassy.org/pdf/doc-information-book-diaspora-2012.pdf*).

Edward A. Alpers, University of California, Los Angeles,
Giulia Bonacci, Institut de recherche pour le développement, Nice

Poverty eradication in Ethiopia

Introduction. Ethiopia is one of the few African countries whose economic development trajectory seems to suggest that it is on the right track towards making significant progress with regard to meeting the United Nation Millennium Development Goal 1 – eradicating extreme poverty and hunger – in the next ten to fifteen years. According to the World Bank (WB), between 2000 and 2012 the Ethiopian economy grew at an average annual rate of 8.3%; double the average rate of sub-Saharan African countries. The poverty rate (headcount ratio at $1.25/day) also dropped by 33% between 2000 and 2011. Ethiopia has also seen a significant improvement in expanding access to primary and secondary education, widening basic health service coverage, reducing the infant mortality rate, and increasing life expectancy. These improvements are the consequences of the significant investment the country has made in infrastructure (particularly roads), schools, health clinics and establishing safety net programs in food deficit areas.

United Nations Development Program (UNDP). Yet, the 2014 Human Development Report ranked Ethiopia as 173rd out of 186 countries in its Human Development Index (HDI). More importantly, over 25 million people still live in poverty, and millions more are just above the poverty line, often vulnerable to climatic and economic shocks and food insecurity. In 2012/2013, over 7.1 million people were under the government's Productive Safety Net Program (PSNP) – a food transfer program to areas where there is a food consumption deficit. The central questions are: Why does Ethiopia rank so low on the UNDP development index after two decades of a significantly high rate of economic growth? Why do we still have over 25 million Ethiopians in poverty and millions more just above the poverty line? How broad and inclusive has economic growth been? How likely is Ethiopia to meet Millennium Development Goal 1 in the next ten to fifteen years? What are the major challenges that seem to undermine Ethiopia's effort to extricate itself from the poverty trap? This brief chapter will try to answer some of these questions as we examine trends in the economic development of Ethiopia and government policies toward eradicating poverty in the country.

Poverty eradication – definition, measures and government strategy. Poverty is a multidimensional concept and any effort to eradicate poverty must be viewed in the total context of human development which, according to the UNDP, incorporates changes made in the social, economic and political life of people. These changes are related to economic growth; a decent standard of living; access to resources necessary to attain a healthy life; opportunities for education; and freedom to engage in productive economic activities. They also should provide choices that guarantee political freedom and protection of rights and allow individuals to voice their concerns freely. More importantly, as numerous studies on development have demonstrated, any effort to eradicate poverty must be inclusive, sustainable and receptive to embracing a broad definition of human development.

In this article we use this broader definition of human development as a framework for gauging Ethiopia's efforts to eradicate poverty for two reasons. First, the concept will enable us to evaluate the effect of the Ethiopian government's economic policies in addressing many human development issues. Second, it will help us assess the extent to which the economic progress achieved in the last two decades has been effective in improving the lives of people and in eradicating poverty.

In 1999, the World Bank (WB) and the International Monetary Fund (IMF) introduced the Poverty Reduction Strategy Papers (PRSP) to form the basis for Bank and Fund lending. These strategy papers were to be 'country-owned' and 'country-driven', so that borrowing countries would be able to identify their own priorities and also take ownership of the process. They were also to be action-oriented and specifically targeting the extreme poor with the objective of developing strategies on how to eliminate poverty within a short period of time.

Following the WB and IMF's initiatives, the Ethiopian Peoples' Revolutionary Democratic Front, the current ruling government, launched the Sustainable Development and Poverty Reduction Program (2000–2005) and the Plan for Accelerated and Sustainable Development to End Poverty (2005–2010). The main objectives of both programmes were to pursue a sustainable broad-based economic development and to pave the way toward achieving the Millennium Development Goals (MDG). Based on the experience of these earlier programmes, in 2010 the government introduced the Growth and Transformation Plan (GTP) that covered the period 2010–2015. The national vision, according to the GTP, was to create conditions whereby Ethiopia could make significant economic progress, eliminate poverty and attain the level of a middle income economy by 2025 (later changed to 2030). The GTP also set several specific targets related to building the capacity of institutions, improving access to primary health, education and other social safety net programs, job creation, poverty reduction, gender equality and the provision of basic economic and social infrastructure such as roads, water, electricity and telecommunications.

As part of the effort to accelerate economic growth and eradicate poverty, the government channelled significant resources to the development of infrastructure. For instance, according to the IMF, public investment in infrastructure and key economic sectors between 2000 and 2013 averaged 17.9% of the Gross Domestic Product (GDP), two and half times the average for sub-Saharan Africa. Also, the share of pro-poor spending (spending on agriculture, education, health, water, and food security) as a percent of total public expenditure continued to increase – from 57.0% in 2005 to 70.0% in 2013. However, a large part of this pro-poor spending is financed through foreign aid – for instance, the salaries of primary school teachers, agriculture development agencies, health extension workers depend to a large extent on foreign aid. In 2008, the government established a disaster risk management system that focuses on institutionalizing disaster risk management programs and developing social safety networks.

Trends in development and poverty eradication. Ethiopia's rapid economic growth, as demonstrated by the relatively high GDP and per capita income growth, has helped to reduce poverty in the country. According to the Central Statistical Agency's (CSA) Household Income and Consumption Expenditures surveys, millions of Ethiopians have been lifted out of poverty: by a national headcount poverty declined from 45.5% in 1996 to 29.6% in 2011. Similarly, based on the extreme poverty measure of $1.25/day (after equalizing the purchasing power parity [PPP] of *berr* and dollar), the poverty rate declined from 63.2% in 1995 to 30.7% in 2010. At the same time, the Gini coefficient (a measure of income disparity) remained consistently below 30% between 2000 and 2010, indicating a relatively low income disparity between the high and low income household groups (Table 1).

Konso children, © Clemens Schlüter

The national poverty line in Ethiopia is set at 3,781 *berr* (approximately: US$ 185; USD 1.00 = 20.5 *berr*), and those who fall below this line are considered poor. In 1996, one in every two Ethiopians lived below this line; this figure has improved to one in three Ethiopians in 2011. However, despite these remarkable achievements, about 25 million people still live below the poverty line. Many million more are impacted by various kinds of shocks associated with risks, vulnerability, and economic and environmental setbacks thereby challenging Ethiopia's continued effort to eradicate poverty. Historically, almost half of Ethiopia's rural population has suffered from recurring droughts leading to family dislocation and famine in many communities. Moreover, according to the WB, 14% of non-poor rural households are vulnerable to falling into poverty if the current level of progress in ending extreme poverty is not maintained.

Unemployment and underemployment are also problems that threaten Ethiopia's effort to eradicate poverty. According to a 2011 CSA's survey, youth (15–29 years) unemployment is around 23.3%. This high rate is compounded by the addition of an estimated 1.4million new job seekers (expected to rise to 3.2million by 2050) entering the labour force every year. The percentage of unemployed and underemployed women is 42% while that of men is 17.5%. The government's public investment in infrastructure and other development programs is helping to reduce the unemployment rate. However, this strategy is not sustainable as the government will be unable to continue this level of public investment in the foreseeable future. Thus, it is crucial to attract private sector investment in job creating enterprises.

In the area of governance, the Ethiopian government has given considerable attention to decentralisation and devolution of power to regional governments. It also recognizes the importance of good governance in building a sustainable economy and in promoting human development. However, the data on transparency, accountability and corruption, as well as on political rights and civil liberties, show that political and social conditions have deteriorated over recent years. An analysis which gauges the general political condition including the electoral process, political pluralism and the functioning of government, as well as other human and political conditions such as individual rights, the rule of law, freedom of expression and belief shows that citizens are not free to enjoy many of the basic human and political rights guaranteed in the Constitution.

Challenges. In relatively short period Ethiopia has made major strides towards meeting the UN MDG 1 – eradicating extreme poverty and hunger. But there are a number of challenges, some structural and some policy-based, that the country still faces as it makes an effort to eliminate poverty. These include

- The population dynamics. Ethiopia's population is growing at 2.5%, and according to the UN estimate, the population will reach 130 million by 2025, placing Ethiopia among the ten largest countries in the world by population. This level of population growth will be followed by a correspondingly rapid increase in demand for social and economic services including education, health, housing and employment opportunities. It will also pose a major challenge to the country's effort to eliminate poverty. The decline in the fertility rate and the drop in overall population growth experienced in the last decade are encouraging. However, they have to be further slowed so that Ethiopia could benefit from the demographic transition dividend (as fertility and mortality rates decline, the dependency ratio – non-working age over working age ratio declines) in order to create a situation whereby the demand for services will be matched by the country's capacity to provide services.

  A related problem of population dynamics is the age profile of the population. About 60% of Ethiopia's population (some 54 million people) is under 25 years of age creating a high dependency ratio. As was noted above, the unemployment rate among the young is close to 25% and well over one million new job seekers enter the economy each year. Currently, the high level of public investment is helping reduce unemployment, but only increased private investment in job creation can resolve this problem in the long term.
- Structure of the economy. Agriculture is the backbone of the Ethiopian economy and the source of livelihood for over 85% of the population. The growth of agriculture has also been effective in reducing poverty. A recent WB study found that, on the average 1.0% growth in agricultural output is associated with a 0.9% decrease in poverty. But the performance of the agriculture sector is highly dependent on climatic conditions. In the last few decades, drought and inconsistency of rainfall have affected the productivity of the agriculture sector often putting a large proportion of the rural population at risk and vulnerable to famine. The government has established safety net and risk management programs, but the geographic coverage of these programs is not as wide as it should be. Some areas, particularly those in the pastoralist areas, are excluded from benefiting from government safety net programs, as well as receiving direct services including extension services, improved seeds and fertilizers. Also, the increase in food prices (Consumer Price Index [CPI] increased by 400% between 2000 and 2013), hurts the poor and contributes to an increase in the number of households that need a safety net. A survey by CSA found that the number of households with a food gap of less than 3 months increased from 25% in 2005 to 42% in 2011.

  The GDP share of agriculture has started to decline (from 47% in 2000 to 38% in 2011) suggesting a structural change in the economy. However, this change has not been accompanied by a corresponding growth in the non-agriculture sector, particularly in the manufacturing sector, which has the capacity to employ more people. Rather, there has been an increase in the share of the service sector (made up of trade, domestic and other social service workers) from 35% in 2000 to 43% in 2011. Employment in the service sector consists of workers who may be characterized as 'working poor', often struggling to make ends meet. The government has to make every effort to increase the share of the manufacturing sector.

Amhara peasants on the way back from the market, © Serge Dewel-Mouton

- Role of the private sector. As was noted above the private sector has a crucial role to play in generating sustainable economic growth and reducing poverty by creating employment opportunities. Unfortunately, the role of the private sector in Ethiopia has been limited. The government has tried to introduce legislation and incentives to entice private investment and increase the role of the private sector, but these efforts have thus far yielded limited results. Among the critical factors that determine the participation of the private sector is the ease of doing business and the impact that government rules and regulations and the bureaucracy have on business operations. In 2014 Ethiopia ranked 132 (3 rank points down from the previous year) among 189 countries surveyed by the WB's Doing Business Survey. The transaction costs incurred by the private sector in Ethiopia are significantly higher than the rate among some African or Asian countries. Factors such as starting a business, getting credit, trading across borders were scored poorly in the 2014 Survey, and the government has to improve the business climate to reduce the transaction cost of the private sector.
- Safety net for urban areas. The current safety net program does not cover urban areas, many of which are experiencing high rate of unemployment and underemployment and increases in the price of rental homes and food prices. The urban

unemployment rate in 2012 was 17.5%, but this figure does not include the self-employed, who are working out of necessity (example, as daily labourers) while searching for waged employment. There is also a general misperception that poverty in urban areas is not as high as in rural areas, although poverty in urban areas, particularly in major urban areas, has continued to increase.

A 2011 CSA's Welfare Monitoring Survey found that more than half of those surveyed believed that their standard of living was worse than it was twelve months ago. This perception that living standards have deteriorated was particularly prevalent in urban areas. Safety nets to support the urban poor are more needed than ever in urban areas. Also, safety nets for urban areas can encourage the self-employed out of necessity to become more enterprising and to establish self-sustaining businesses.

- Governance and Institutional structure for inclusive growth. The Ethiopian government has put in place legislation and processes to improve the governance structure and widen the political space. But as the data in Table 1 show, there are major challenges in improving political rights and civil liberties and in guaranteeing individual freedom, the rule of law and an effective legal system. Political rights and civil liberties have deteriorated over the years, and the Ethiopian public is not free to enjoy the liberties of democracy.
- Improving quality of services. In the last decade, Ethiopia has made an impressive move in enhancing the level of services in education, health, road and water services. But the country still faces many daunting human development issues, particularly in improving the quality of services in infrastructure and social services.

Whether Ethiopia will be able to eliminate poverty and reach the level of middle income countries by 2030 depends on how much the government is able to address many of the challenges outlined above.

In 2016, the Ethiopian government launched the GTP II (2015–2020) whose primary objective is to catapult Ethiopia to a middle income country by 2020. The plan identified major strategies including sustaining the rapid economic growth achieved in GTP I, enhancing the capacity of the agriculture and manufacturing sectors, improving the infrastructure base, expanding the role of the private sector in the economy and strengthening urban expansion management including job creation. The government has set very ambitious targets and strategies on how to implement these plans some of which include achieving a 10% GDP growth rate, reducing the share of agriculture in GDP to 35.6% while increasing the share of the manufacturing sector to 22.8%, reducing the poverty rate to 16.7%, expanding electric power service coverage to 90% and improving the social, health and education service coverage of the country.

Ethiopia's experience in meeting the targets set in GTP I shows that the economy continues to face major challenges including lack of capital to finance projects, high inflation rate, food shortage caused by drought, significantly high unemployment rate, and a shrinking of private sectors as party-sponsored corporations continued to dominate the economy. As we look forward it is imperative that the government recognizes that the structural and policy-based issues that the economy faces must be addressed if the targets set in GTP II are to be achieved.

References: Most of the economic and poverty data for this analysis was taken from the following reports, which in turn, cite national sources, including Central Statistical Authority and Ministry of Finance and Economic Development as the original sources; National Human Development Report 2014, *Ethiopia: Accelerating Inclusive growth for sustainable human development in Ethiopia*, Addis Ababa 2015; World Bank, *Ethiopia: Poverty assessment*, Addis Ababa 2015.

Mulatu Wubneh, East Carolina University

	Years				
Item	1995	2000	2005	2010	2013
Economic growth measures					
GDP – annual growth rate (%)	6.13	6.07	11.80	11.20	10.49
per capita GDP (annual growth rate %)	2.73	3.08	8.70	8.30	7.70
Major economic sectors – growth					
Agriculture value added (annual growth rate %)	3.80	3.10	13.50	5.10	5.40
Manufacturing value added (annual growth rate %)	8.89	6.66	13.03	9.21	16.93
Service value added (annual growth rate %)	10.59	10.89	12.32	16.24	8.78
Consumer Price Index (CPI) – 2010 = 100	34.10	35.00	44.80	100.00	176,80
Poverty – Income measures					
National absolute poverty headcount (%)	45.50	44.20	38.70	29.6 (11)	
Poverty head count ratio at $1.25 a day (ppp) (% of population)	63.20	55.60	39.00	30.70	
Gini coefficient index	0.39	0.28	0.30	0.30	
Poverty – Non-Income measures					
Health					
Life expectancy	49.3	52.2	56.6	61.5	63.6
Infant mortality rate (death per 1,000 live births)	106	97	74	59	44
Under 5 yr. age mortality rate (death per 1,000 live births)	175	146	110	76	64
Maternal mortality ratio (death per 100,000 live births)	1.200	990	740		420
Education					
Literacy rate – 15+ age who can read and write (as % of population)	27.0 (94)	35.9 (04)	37.9	39.0 (07)	46.7 (11)
Primary ed. gross enrollment (as % of population)	29.3	54.9	79.2	87.0 (06)	85.7
Water – National water supply coverage (%)	19.1	27.9	35.9	52.6	68.5
Road – Average distance from main road (in kms.)			14.9	11.3	6.4
Governance – Political rights and civil liberties (scale of 1 to 7)*					
Political right	4	5	5	6	6
Civil liberties	5	5	5	6	6
Status	PF	PF	PF	NF	NF
Transparency, accountability and corruption in the public sector**		2.5	2.5	2.5	3.0

* Rating on political rights and civil liberties, 1 = most free, 7 = least free; Status = freedom status (PF = partly free; NF = not free).

** Rating on transparency: 1 = low, 6 = high

Figures in parenthesis indicate year of data.

Source: World Bank, *WDI 2015*; *PovcalNet* – Poverty Index calculator.
Freedom House, *Freedom in the World 2015*. http://freedomhouse.org/report-types/freedom-world.
CSA, *Household income and consumption expenditure survey* (*HICES*), CSA, Addis Ababa (various years).
CSA, *Ethiopian welfare monitoring survey 2011* (Summary Report), Addis Ababa 2012.
WHO, *Trends in maternal mortality, 1990–2030*, WHO 2014; *Ethiopia: Fact sheet of Health Statistics*, 2014

Table 14: Trends in poverty reduction, © Mulatu Wubneh

Internal and external security – Ethiopian aspects

Ethiopia is a multi-ethnic country with more than 80 nations and nationalities (ethnic groups). Nevertheless, because many of these nations and nationalities were marginalized from the economic and social benefits of the state, the modern history of Ethiopia became a history of armed conflicts. Moreover, until very recently, these groups were also prohibited or at least discouraged from developing their cultures and languages. As a result, Ethiopian history, in the last century, has been associated with authoritarian government tyranny and absolute poverty, which resulted in protracted armed conflicts within its borders and hostile relationships with its neighbours. Moreover, colonial borders that divided members of the same ethnic/national groups between territories of different countries triggered wars with neighbouring countries such as Somalia. These protracted armed conflicts ended when the *Darg* military junta that took power in 1974 was ousted in 1991. Since then conflicts in the peripheries of the country have taken place at a much reduced level.

An Afar man with machine gun, © Wolbert G.C. Smidt

Internal security. Ethiopian internal security primarily depends on the management of diversity, the reduction of poverty and the exercise of democracy. Following the downfall of the military regime, the country introduced a federal system which devolved power to regional states established primarily on the basis of identity markers. This federal arrangement empowered identity groups to be fairly represented in federal political institutions and has encouraged most of the armed oppositions groups, which fought against the central government, to disarm. Moreover, the separation of state and religion has created favourable conditions for tolerance between the religious groups in the country. Taken together these changes have created a relative internal stability in the past quarter century. Nevertheless, the government has to work further to address issues such as lack of accountability and transparency in state institutions, perceptions of marginalization, centre-periphery relations, interregional and interethnic conflicts, all of which could affect the stability of the nation in general and some regional states in particular.

According to the government internal security is closely linked to development efforts which seek to reduce absolute poverty in the country (see the article 'Poverty eradication in Ethiopia'). Around 80% of Ethiopians depend on rain-fed subsistence agriculture. This has made the country vulnerable to droughts and famine, which contributed not only to the 1974 revolution that overthrew the imperial regime, but also to protracted armed conflicts fought against the military regime. Still today drought related to climate change challenges the food security of the country. While Ethiopia has tremendous potential for carbon free natural energy sources such as hydroelectric power, significant investment is required to achieve energy security. Therefore, poverty reduction and achievement of food security have become the heart of internal security of the country. The country has registered more than 10% economic growth in the past twelve years and consequently more than 22 million people have been lifted from absolute poverty. Moreover, it is hoped that the country as a whole will reach a middle-income by 2025. Nevertheless, food security and lifting the rest of the population from absolute poverty will remain as main issues of internal security of the country.

The issue of democratisation of the state and good governance is also a question of internal security for the country. The Ethiopian state is one of the oldest states in the world, but was traditionally highly centralized and hierarchical. The devolution of power through the federal structure has created regional and local state structures relatively closer to their citizens. This has created opportunities for the wider mobilization of citizens to implement government development plans such as reforestation, increase of agricultural production and so forth. Nevertheless, a single party domination of the political system and a top down approach of the state hinders wider participation of citizens in state affairs. Hence, issues of justice, lack of accountability and transparency in service delivery and corruption remain critical problems, and these may provoke civil strife unless the government takes some corrective measures by reforming the state institutions at all levels. The public protests that have happened in Oromia and Amhara regional states in 2015/2016 are manifestations of the above problems.

External security. Ethiopian external security depends on the stability of the Horn of Africa. The Horn of Africa is a very unstable region (see the article 'Ethiopia and its neighbouring states'). There are ongoing armed conflicts in and between Sudan and South Sudan. Somalia has not fully recovered from clan-based conflicts and insurgencies of terrorist groups, and is generally classified as a 'failed state'. Ethiopia also has unsettled border issues with Eritrea and a water-use related dispute with Egypt concerning the Nile River. These regional security problems challenge the security of Ethiopia.

For example, the border issue with Eritrea erupted into a bloody war from 1998–2000. Moreover, since the end of that war there has been a state of 'cold war' between the two countries. In 2006 Ethiopia confronted the al-Qaeda affiliated *Al-Shabaab* in Somalia due to the security threats posed by this terrorist group. Today it is also fighting against *Al-Shabaab* within Somalia in collaboration with African Union Mission in Somalia troops. Ethiopia hosts more than 700,000 refugees as a result of the conflicts in the neighbouring countries.

However, regardless of these security challenges, Ethiopia continues to be relatively stable and has become the main security player in the region. Ethiopia is the fourth largest contributor of peace keeping force in the world and the largest in Africa. It is also the main peacekeeping actor in the region including in South Sudan, Sudan and Somalia.

The country has also created a consensus concerning the use of the Nile River water with the Nile basin countries in general and with the newly established Egypt government in particular. Moreover, Ethiopia, with the second largest population in Africa, has the potential to be a hub of economic integration and stability of the region. The recent electric power connection with Djibouti,

Kenya and Sudan is an indicator of the Ethiopian potential to bring regional economic integration and stability to the Horn of Africa.

The fact that the country hosts the AU's headquarters, more than one hundred diplomatic missions and international organizations' headquarters, is also an asset for extending its influence towards regional stability and security.

Ethiopian foreign security policy also supports the external security interests of the country. The foreign security policy focuses on fighting against regional security threats such as terrorism and boosting its economic interest and regional economic integration. This has helped the country to become a major regional player in the UN, AU and regional platforms such as the Intergovernmental Authority on Development, and including hosting international conferences on climate change.

Security institutions. Ethiopia has established relatively disciplined and functional security institutions since 1991. Historically the military was the main actor in civil conflicts in Ethiopia. This made the military a major player in the civil administration and it was the most feared institution in the country until the downfall of the military regime. On the basis of the Federal Constitution enacted in 1995, the army was re-established again with a mandate confined to maintaining the territory integrity and sovereignty of the country. In establishing the new national army, the former army of Ethiopian People's Revolutionary Democratic Front (EPRDF), which overthrew the military regime, became the basis for the new institution. Former leaders of the EPRDF forces still play a major role in the leadership of the army today. This has created a basis for bringing the military infrastructure of the military regime and the practices of indoctrination of EPRDF forces together and developing them through reforms which have created a professional and disciplined army in the country. The Ethiopian military, which is the fourth largest military in Africa, is the major fighting force against *Al-Shabaab* in Somalia and one of the main peacekeeping force contributors in the world and the region as indicated above.

The Ethiopian police are administered at two levels: the federal and the regional. The federal police are responsible to maintain peace and security at the federal level, whereas the regional police are responsible for maintaining peace and security of the regions. The regional police are the main institutions that closely work with communities in resolving local conflicts. However, the Ethiopian police still require considerable professional capacity development to enable them to handle civil strife without bloodshed and violations of human rights.

In conclusion the internal and external security of Ethiopia depends on striving to become a middle income country and lifting most Ethiopians from absolute poverty. In addition, the democratisation of the state and providing good governance is as critical as the level of absolute poverty, which in turn determines the stability and speed of economic development in the country. Ethiopia has registered significant progress in reversing its recent history of instability and conflict. This development has also created a favourable condition for the country to be a major player of stability and economic integration of the Horn of Africa.

Literature: David Turton, *Ethnic Federalism: The Ethiopian Experience in Comparative Perspective*, Oxford 2006; United Nations High Commissioner for Refugees, The UN Refugee Agency, *2015 UNHCR country operations profile-Ethiopia* (*http://www.unhcr.org/pages/49e483986.html*).

Mesfin Gebremichael, Addis Ababa University

Chances and challenges for Ethiopia's development in the regional context

Compared with various crisis plagued countries and regions on the African continent, Ethiopia today seems to be a cornerstone of political stability and economic improvement in the Horn of Africa. And indeed there are a range of developments that give reason for optimism.

Economic development. This shows a strong, almost two-digit annual growth over recent years, as well as a declining rate of inflation since mid-2012. The Ethiopian government is deeply engaged in making the country more attractive for investors and – in the East African context – more competitive. Compared with Africa as a whole and based on the Mo Ibrahim Foundation Index (2015 Ibrahim Index of African Governance), Ethiopia is currently above the continental average with reference to conditions for sustainable economic development – better than Kenya and Djibouti – and by far better than Eritrea and Somalia.

Despite the basically reform-oriented Ethiopian economic policy, the business environment for private investment is not without risks and problems, not least of which include the chronically low foreign exchange reserves and the preferential treatment of public projects for the allocation of credit.

In what is still one of the poorest countries of the world, in 2010 the Ethiopian government launched the first five year Growth and Transformation Plan (GTP I), followed by GTP II in 2015. The overarching objective of Ethiopia's national development strategy is the realisation of its vision of becoming a lower middle-income country by 2025. Thus GTP II aims to achieve an annual average real GDP growth rate of 11%. With substantial support from the international donor community Ethiopia has made commendable progress towards reaching the Millennium Development Goals by the

The future looks hopeful, © Wilfried Hofmann

end of 2015, particularly regarding the overall decline of poverty. But there is still a long way to go in other areas, such as maternal health, sanitation and gender equality.

Development of the agricultural sector. This is of outstanding importance for Ethiopia (around 80% of the population lives and works in rural areas) and, because of this, it is one of the priorities of European Development Cooperation. Selling large and fertile agricultural areas or leasing them to foreign investors remains controversial in view of the ongoing lack of food security in some regions of the country. While critics warn against a 'sell off' of fertile land in the interest of short-sighted foreign exchange gains, the government defends this policy, pointing out that Ethiopia has abundant land reserves and that modern agricultural technology and management methods are supported by that policy.

One of the biggest challenges for Ethiopia with a view to socio-economic development is the rapid growth of its population. Already today every second Ethiopian is under age 21. Providing adequate education and work facilities for the next generation will therefore be one of the most difficult tasks for the future. Sustainable support of Ethiopia's endeavours for a country-wide promotion of education is therefore one of the priorities in the development cooperation with the European Union and her member countries.

For quite some years Germany, e.g. has been engaged in building schools and universities, supporting vocational training as well as establishing and developing academic cooperation. In the same spirit the planned Stiftungsprofessur (endowed junior professorship) at Hamburg University is meant to support the young academic generation in Ethiopia.

One important and encouraging element for a broad civil society debate about the future of the country are the relatively relaxed relations between the country's two largest religious denominations – Orthodox Christians and Muslims, which other countries in the region and beyond may take as an example (see the article 'Interfaith relations between Christianity and Islam in Ethiopia').

Foreign and security policy. In these issues Ethiopia traditionally plays a prominent role as a regional power in the Horn of Africa. As a founding member of the OAU and, while holding the presidency of the AU in 2013, Ethiopia underlined its claim to be one of the opinion leaders in Africa. One measure of the continental and regional engagement of Ethiopia is the fact that the country is the largest African troop contributor to the United Nations and the African Union with about 12,000 soldiers for peacekeeping missions. As a member of the East African regional organization Intergovernmental Authority on Development (IGAD) and, since the outbreak of the South Sudan conflict in December 2013 (see also 'South Sudan' in the article 'Ethiopia and its neighbouring states'), Ethiopia has taken a leading and lasting role in mediation efforts for a settlement of hostilities.

Stability and security in neighbouring Somalia are of vital importance for Ethiopia (see also the articles 'Somalia' and 'Ethiopia and its neighbouring states'). Since early 2014 Ethiopian troops have been engaged in Somalia as part of the AU-Mission AMISOM: The African Union Mission In Somalia. Together with other AMISOM troops, they have been successful in fighting *Al-Shabaab* militias. From an Ethiopian point of view, which is shared by partners and allies, a solely military solution will not be feasible. Therefore, Addis Ababa is actively engaged in driving the inner Somali peace process in which Ethiopia regards itself as an 'honest broker' – a role which is viewed with some mistrust at least in parts of the Somali leadership in Mogadishu, bearing in mind the tense relationship in the past history of the two countries.

Following the death of the former leader, Prime Minister Mallas Zenawi (2012) the relationship with its northern neighbour, Eritrea, remains tense under his successor, Hailemariam Desalegn. Particularly sensitive is the issue of the mutual recognition of the border between the two countries. Ethiopia supports a tightening of UN sanctions against Eritrea and ultimately pins its hopes on early regime change in Asmara.

The future distribution and use of the Nile waters is of vital importance for neighbouring countries Ethiopia, Sudan and Egypt (more than 80% of all Nile waters come from the Ethiopian highlands). Therefore negotiations between these countries on this issue are of high political and economic relevance. In March 2015 the Khartoum Declaration, where the principles of cooperation regarding the Blue Nile were laid out, was signed by Ethiopia, Sudan and Egypt.

As in 2010, the ruling Ethiopian Peoples' Revolutionary Democratic Front (in power since the fall of the *Darg* in 1991) won the parliamentary elections held on 24 May 2015. The opposition did not win even a single seat in parliament, which is elected under a 'first past the post' voting system. In April 2013 EPRDF had also already cemented its overwhelming majority at the local level. For the time being, the transitional process following the death of Prime Minister Mallas Zenawi has been completed without notable political friction (as was anticipated in some quarters). However, expectations directed towards the new government under Prime Minister Hailemariam Desalegn for a noticeable opening of political space, for greater pluralism in the political landscape, freedom of the press and room for opposition parties and civil society have been utterly disappointed. Ongoing tensions with considerable losses of lives in the Oromo and Amhara regions of Ethiopia about plans of the central government for a partial redistribution of land around the capital Addis Ababa are alarming signals for an erosion of political and social stability in a multi-ethnic country like Ethiopia. This development is a matter of growing concern for friends and partners of Ethiopia.

In Africa there are many well documented examples of the view that there is an undeniable correlation between sustainable economic and social development on the one hand and good governance in the widest sense on the other hand. In short: in

Two Sidaama girls, © Clemens Schlüter

a country or in a region where globally accepted principles of good governance are permanently ignored or where transparent and legitimate implementation is lacking, a secure future for its citizens cannot be expected. As much as economic and developmental progress in Ethiopia in recent years and its positive role in the efforts to stabilize the situation in the Horn of Africa deserves appreciation, well-meaning friends and partners of the country plead for greater pluralism in society, rather than the increased restriction we are witnessing. A start could be made, e.g. by a step-by-step change of the present voting system. In a country with more than 80 ethnic groups (and almost as many different languages) proportional elements could be introduced which could then lead to a stronger participation of the peoples of Ethiopia in shaping their future. As a complementary measure a Round Table might be established, elsewhere a proven, valuable method for providing a platform for political dialogue about a peaceful future of a country. Admittedly this is a tall order for a country of such complexity, and at the same time, so rich in potential and history. But finally, it would be in the interest of all Ethiopians and even for the whole region. Friends and partners of Ethiopia stand ready to assist the country and its people and the whole region with advice and action on this difficult path.

Literature: GÉRARD PRUNIER, ÉLOI FICQUET (eds.), *Understanding Contemporary Ethiopia: Monarchy, Revolution and the Legacy of Meles Zenawi*, London 2015.

Claas Knoop, Bremen

X Travelling and sightseeing

Introduction

The present book is not a travel guide, and this final chapter does not change that. What we wish to do here is simply to provide appropriate travel information for visitors to the region. Here three points stand out:

- Northeastern Africa is not generally considered a 'classic' tourist destination; it is not flooded with mass tourism, and typical amenities such as nationwide hotel chains, smoothly functioning infrastructure, European-quality medical care, or a large spectrum of organized leisure activities are not to be found.
- On the other hand, Europeans have been travelling to the region regularly ever since the Middle Ages and have brought back reports on their impressions of the land and its people.
- Furthermore, for over 80 years now visitors have been able to explore this fascinating and unfamiliar world along established itineraries, following the Historic Route or visiting the national parks, travelling in small Land Rover groups or as individuals.

It is not possible to describe here every tourist attraction. Some, like Aksum or the southern 'peoples and cultures route', have been mentioned in previous chapters. Many other sites, in themselves highly worth a visit, are currently inaccessible to most travellers for political or security reasons, e.g. in Eritrea or Somalia.

Since the time of Hayla Sellase, Ethiopia has promoted itself as a tourist destination. The country is making a major effort to attract tourists and is working to expand its tourist industry and give it international visibility. This includes the construction of museums to preserve and study the history and culture of the many smaller peoples that are threatened by 'civilization'.

In travelling to northeastern Africa, we encounter the people with a respect for their own identity. We do not gape at them like animals in the zoo, as they put their exotic customs on display for our cameras. Rather, our encounter represents a chance for both parties to come to know better the unknown 'other'. And from our perspective this offers an opportunity to make an urgently needed contribution to the preservation of irreplaceable cultures.

Travel and exploration in Ethiopia and the Horn of Africa

Ancient travellers. Since ancient times, traders, diplomats, pilgrims, missionaries and soldiers have visited and crossed the lands of the Horn of Africa and the Red Sea. The earliest written records of travel to these regions go back to the beginning of Christian times. They were chiefly the work of Greek, Roman and Byzantine authors.

Hamar region at dusk, © Matthias Ansel

One such document is the anonymous Greek text 'Periplus of the Erythrean Sea' or 'Periplus of the Red Sea'. Written around the middle of the 1st century CE, it is a description of the Red Sea harbours, coasts and hinterland for Roman traders. Although the text does not provide identifiable ethnic names, it includes valuable geographical information, such as the first reference to Aksum. The activities of the 4th century Arian missionary and envoy of Constantius II known as Theophilus the Indian, who travelled extensively to Himyar and Aksum were recounted by a contemporary, the Arian Philostorgius, in his 'Historia ecclesiastica'. Two centuries later, the 'History' by Nonnosus, a Byzantine ambassador under Justinian I (518–527) reported on the Red Sea area, Aksum, Himyar and Arabia. His work, now lost, is transmitted in excerpts by Photius, Ecumenical patriarch of Constantinople from 858 to 867.

From the mid-6th century dates a major text with valuable information on the political vicissitudes in the region: the so-called 'Christian Topography'. It was also written in Greek by a Christian monk who is known under the pseudonym of Cosmas Indicopleustes. The book records the author's visit to Adulis, when this port was under the control of a governor appointed by the Aksumite King Ella Atsbeha, also known as Kaleb. Cosmas provides the entire text of two inscriptions he copied at Adulis on behalf of the king (the so-called 'Monumentum Adulitanum'). Furthermore, he provides insightful descriptions of trading activities and political conditions in the kingdom of Aksum and mentioned the Agaw ethnic group.

The next important corpus of travel literature on Ethiopia and the Horn of Africa belongs to Muslim authors. From the times of the *hijra* to about 1500 several Arabic and Muslim authors report on the Red Sea and the Horn of Africa, attesting to the intensifying contacts between this region and the Muslim world. Some important authors from this period are al-Yaqubi (9th century), Ibn an-Nadim, Ibn Sulaym al-Aswani (10th century), Ibn Said al-Maghribi (13th century), Ibn Battuta, Ibn Khaldun (14th century) and al-Maqrizi (14th and 15th centuries.).

Medieval travellers and the myth of the Prester John. During medieval times western authors increasingly travelled to the Horn of Africa and wrote reports about their experiences. A valuable early account is the 'Masaot Binyamin' ('The Travels of Benjamin'), written in Hebrew by the Spanish Jew Benjamin of Tudela. In this book Benjamin recounts his travels to Europe, Africa and Asia between about 1159 and 1172/1173. According to his narrative he (or his informants) travelled across the Red Sea, from Aden to Suez and gathered information on Cush and the Sultan of Al-Habash. Later on, the emergence of the myth of the Prester John in Europe and its progressive association with Christian Ethiopia spurred excursions to the Horn as well as diplomatic exchanges between European states and the Ethiopian monarchy. One of the earliest European agents and diplomats to travel to Ethiopia was Filippo, envoy of Pope Alexander III in the second half of the 12th century. A century later, Marco Polo's 'Il Milione' offered the first reliable account of 'Abasce', i.e. Abyssinia, although he was relying only on informants, as he never reached Africa or the Red Sea.

In the 13th and 14th centuries, the emergence of the mendicant orders, chiefly the Franciscans and Dominicans, was also responsible for an increase of travel to the Orient and East Africa. Thus, mendicant missionaries and prelates such as Guillaume Adam, Jordanus Catalani, John of Sultaniya and John of Montecorvino led religious missions to the East that at some point also encompassed the Horn of Africa and the Red Sea. Similarly, mendicant friars in Europe played an important role in disseminating knowledge related to the Horn of Africa. These included an anonymous Franciscan who authored the 'Libro del Conoscimiento', the Dominican Pietro Ranzano (informing on Pietro Rómbulo), and the Franciscans John of Wintertur and Francesco Suriano (informing on Giovanni Battista da Imola).

In the 15th century, several European states and royal houses exchanged envoys with such Ethiopian rulers as Yeshaq (1414–1430), Zara Yaeqob (1434–1468), Baeda Maryam I (1468–1478) and Eskender (1478–1494). In consequence Christian Ethiopia became the target of numerous embassies as well as the goal of a handful of individuals attracted by this distant Christian monarchy. It can be assumed, that by the end of the century a relatively safe route connected Egypt, via Sudanese Nubia, with highland Ethiopia.

The Portuguese and Jesuit periods. In the 16th century, the dominant European partner of Christian Ethiopia was the Portuguese monarchy. For over a century and under the aegis of the Portuguese empire in Asia, numerous European and Indian diplomats, agents, soldiers, missionaries and technicians travelled to the Horn of Africa. The reasons bringing them to Africa were manifold but diplomatic, military and proselytizing intentions prevailed throughout this period. This intensification of travel resulted in the production of numerous written accounts describing in detail the lands and peoples encountered. With the help of the printing press, the travelogue authored by the Portuguese Francisco Alvares in 1540, 'The Prester John of the Indies: A True Narration about the Lands of the Prester John', became widely popular in Europe. In the next century, another popular account on Ethiopia was the so-called 'Itinerário' by the Jesuit Jerónimo Lobo. In Europe this literature spurred the interest for the Horn of Africa, and Christian Ethiopia in particular, and, in its turn, stimulated further travelling activities. Yet, perhaps more importantly, it is thanks to the travelogues, treatises and missionary letters written from 1500 onwards that we know much more about the conditions of travel in the early modern times.

Among the different routes undertaken to reach the Horn of Africa a privileged one was that connecting the important Indian ports of Gujarat, via the coasts of Oman and Hadramaut, with the ports of the Red Sea. This was the route that for centuries Asian merchants and pilgrims had been using to reach the holy sites of Arabia as well as the spice-thirsty markets of the Levant and Europe. The route was overseen by folks from different religions (mostly Muslim, Hindu Jain) and different ethnic groups (predominantly Indian, Persian, and Arab), but the Banyan group, with its worldwide network of outposts (stretching from Malakka to Sawakin), stands out as the chief brokers. The Banyans provided travellers with credit and intelligence and, to some extent, granted them also an atmosphere of protection and trust. Additionally, the Ottoman colonisation of the Red Sea, in spite of the traditional rivalry between the Porte and European powers, created a politically homogeneous area where, provided one carried the appropriate *firmam* (a primitive form of the modern passport system and similar to the Portuguese *cartaz* system) and enough cash to pay for the *sagoate* (present, bribe), travelling was relatively safe. Another important piece of information gleaned from the historical literature is the fact that more often than not European travellers used a disguise (typically Armenian dress) to avoid being identified as westerners. This method must have been in use until early colonial times. Additionally, the use of interpreters (*lingoas* in Portuguese and *dragomen* in the international language) was widespread; interpreters seem to have had different origins but those from such groups as Jews, Levantines (Greeks), Armenians and European renegades must have been numerous.

Travellers during the Gondarine period. Contrary to what is often assumed in the historical literature, Gondarine Ethiopia was not isolated from the outer world, not even from Western Europe. The expulsion of the Jesuits in 1632 severed the ties between Ethiopia and the Spanish and Portuguese-speaking world, but by no means did it stop foreign travel into the country. Thus, it can be assumed that the diplomatic exchanges between Fasiladas (1632–1667) and such Muslim powers as Yemen and Mughal India resulted in a continued presence of Arab and Indian agents, traders and technicians in the Gondar state. Moreover, late into the 17th century and under the reign of Iyasu I (1682–1706) the living conditions for Europeans (*faranji*) must have improved for at his court a continuous presence of Europeans (such as the physician Charles Poncet, the Franciscans Giuseppe Maria di Gerusalemme and Benedetto and the Jesuits Grenier and Paulet) is recorded.

By then, however, unlike what occurred during the Portuguese period, the favourite route used by Europeans to reach the Ethiopian highlands was the one that began in Cairo and that, by water or land, reached the southern Sudanese outposts. The journey typically started sailing the Nile southwards towards upper Egypt until reaching Qina. There the route would split in two directions: eastwards to Al-Qusayr to take the maritime route towards the ports of Sawakin and Metsewa; and southwards in an overland journey through Aswan and further south to Sudanese Nubia until reaching Sennar and the escarpments of Chilga. Towards the end of the 18th century, the famous traveller James Bruce reached Gondar using the first variant of that route.

Explorers and colonizers. In the 19th century, the introduction of steamboat service as an efficient and economic means of transportation and the opening up of geographical and exploration societies throughout Europe gave a boost to travel to Africa, in general, and to the Horn of Africa, in particular. Little by little, travel lost its connotation as a risky and unique experience and began to assume its modern features, as a standardized, touristic-like activity. As a testimony to this, it is during this period that the practice of immortalizing one's visit to a famous, exotic place becomes widespread. This was initially carried out by carving graffiti bearing the name of the traveller on a site (such as it was done by the British officer Charles Beke around 1810 in the monastery of Martula Maryam, Gojjam) and, later, from about 1850, with the conspicuous use of engraving and photography.

European travellers to the Horn of Africa during this period were thus plentiful and a handful of them produced travelogues. Writing an account once the journey was over became a 'requirement' that fulfilled many purposes. On the one hand, it functioned as authorized evidence of the 'discoveries' claimed by the explorer. On the other hand, the narrative made it possible to reach a wide readership – with potential gains in economic terms and in prestige – and, eventually, obtain sponsorship for further 'explorations'. Among the earliest examples of this literary genre were Henry Salt's 'A voyage to Abyssinia' (1816), Nathaniel Pearce's 'Life and Adventures' (1831), Arnauld d'Abbadie's 'Douze ans de séjour dans la Haute-Éthiopie' (1868), Eduard Rüppell's 'Reise in Abyssinien' (1838, 1840), Wilhelm Schimper's 'Reise von Adoa in Abyssinien an den Tacazé und in das Semengebirge …' (1843) and Edmon Combes and Maurice Tamisier's 'Voyage en Abyssinie' (1838).

Tourism and 'adventure' travel in contemporary times. Today Ethiopia is an important tourist destination in tropical Africa. In an addition to the classic Historic Route it is also one of the most popular destinations for a kind of 'adventure travel' that seeks to visit 'exotic' and still 'isolated' populations. This is exemplified by the Omo valley human tours in south Ethiopia, which has gained recently significant touristic pedigree. Additionally, the genre of exploration literature has not died out yet as it is still practiced by a few journalists and tourists.

Literature: O(SBERT) G(UY) S(TANHOPE) CRAWFORD, *Ethiopian Itineraries circa 1400–1524*, Cambridge 1958; SVEN RUBENSON, *The Survival of Ethiopian Independence*, London 1976 (chapter 1, 'A survey of sources').

Andreu Martínez d'Alòs-Moner, Gondar University

Tourism in Ethiopia

Ethiopia has much to offer tourists in terms of archaeological and cultural heritage, and natural resources. Often described as the 'cradle of civilization' and 'the home of Lucy' (Amharic *Denqenash* = 'wonderful'), one of the earliest known human ancestors (*australopithecus afarensis*), the country's rich biodiversity and unique cultural and historic assets include nine World Heritage Sites listed with UNESCO. Among these are the famous complex of 13th-century rock-hewn churches in Lalibala, the city of Aksum with its world-famous stelae and ancient centres of Orthodox Christianity, the historic walled Muslim holy city of Harar, the valleys of the Awash and Omo Rivers, Semen National Park, and the recently inscribed (2011) 'Konso Cultural Landscape'. Tourism in Ethiopia is based mainly on these sites and promoted through two main tourism routes: the northern, historical route and the southern, cultural route. The roughly half million tourists who travel to Ethiopia each year engage in predominantly cultural heritage tourism, cultural tourism and/or nature tourism. Business and conference tourists also contribute to making tourism a significant foreign exchange earner for Ethiopia. While tourism is an important sector for economic growth and social development in the country, its full potential has yet to be realized, especially in terms of service standards, livelihood enhancement and conservation. Other underdeveloped areas of tourism include eco-tourism and community-based tourism, both of which have the potential to increase mutual respect and understanding of the diverse ethnic groups of Ethiopia.

Tourism standards and development potential. Accommodations for visitors and travellers in the capital Addis Ababa range from single rooms and apartments via online portals to guest houses and hotel resorts in all star categories. Along the northern and southern routes accommodation is available in hotels, resorts, motels, lodges, or campsites. Much of the lodgings along these popular tourist destinations do not yet meet international standards, especially in terms of security and sanitary conditions. However, a commitment to improve standards for health, safety and security, and to meet environmental requirements for waste management was made in 2015 by the Ministry of Culture and Tourism, supported by the UNs' World Tourism Organization, which has started a system of grading and accreditation of hotels in Ethiopia.

The potentially transformative role of tourism, especially in relation to conservation, poverty reduction and economic development is acknowledged by the Ethiopian Government and is supported by international agencies such as the World Bank and the German Federal Enterprise for International Cooperation. However, as anthropologist Tamás Régi reminds us, 'while the travel industry increasingly contributes to most developing countries' GDP, it does not necessarily follow that international tourism fosters microeconomic stability'. This is certainly the case in many peripheral areas of Ethiopia where local communities affected by tourism do not share equitably in the benefits of tourism revenue.

The northern route: historical heritage and nature-based tourism. Tourism across Africa focuses primarily on cultural and nature-based tourism. Ethiopia is rather unique, since a major attraction is historical heritage tourism. Among the many historical sites included in tour packages to the north are: Aksum and its famous stelae parks, 17th-century castles in Gondar, and the monolithic rock-hewn churches of Lalibala and Lake Tana with its more than 20 island monasteries, the oldest of which have their origins in the 14th century. Most of these churches still function as centres of worship and prayer for Ethiopian Orthodox Christians. The northern route also has great potential to cultivate nature-based tourism attractions (see also the article 'Historic Route'), which are still in the early stages of being fully developed into eco-tourism destinations, like the Semen Mountains described below.

Conservation, national parks and cultural landscapes. Increasing biodiversity conservation is one important way in which nature-based tourism is advancing in Ethiopia. One of the showcase examples of this is the first tourist lodge in Semen National Park, a protected area that is home to numerous rare animal species, including the near-endemic gelada baboon (*Theropithecus gelada*) and animals like the Walia ibex and the Simien fox (*Canis simensis*).

An extreme and awe-inspiring landscape is the Danakil depression of Afar, well-known for its active volcanoes and lava lakes, such as the Erta Ale, which the Afar people call 'smoking mountain'. Another remarkable initiative that promotes both nature-based and cultural tourism is the newly recognized 'Konso Cultural Landscape', which brings together sustainable rural development, local ecological knowledge, ritual practices, sacred sites, as well as, an increasing number of tourists.

However, creating linkages between local communities, protected areas, conservation and tourist-related initiatives still remains a challenge in many parts of Ethiopia. This became evident in 2005 when the African Parks Foundation (now African Parks Network) arrived in the Southern Nationalities, Nations and People's Region (SNNPR) to try to improve infrastructure deficiencies that continue to hamper tourism growth. While SNNPR and the communities living in and around the parks could have benefited from improved wildlife management and community-based tourism in Nech Sar and Omo National Park, ultimately the conservation projects did little to improve the lives of local communities. Due to public pressure from the communities in the Lower Omo valley, who were excluded from full participation in conservation management, the African Parks Foundation left Ethiopia in 2008.

One lesson that can be learned from this case is that unless local communities are given the opportunity to meaningfully participate in the expansion of tourism and equitably share in the benefits of tourism, economic growth and poverty reduction will be limited. In the case of the Lower Omo, one of the reasons for the exclusion of local communities in the planning, implementation and benefits of community-based conservation and tourism development is that many agro-pastoralist communities are still ill-perceived of, not as partners, but as 'underdeveloped' cultures.

The southern route: intercultural encounter. The southern route includes visits to wildlife destinations such as the Mago National Park and the Lake Stephanie area. Most tours concentrate on visits to the diverse ethnic groups living in the Omo Valley of southern Ethiopia. From Addis Ababa tourists travel mainly by car through Arba Mench and Konso, a UNESCO world heritage site, and continue towards Jinka with its South Omo Museum and Research Centre. Ethnic groups visited are the agro-pastoral Mursi, Kara, Dassanech who live along the Omo River as well as the Tsamakko, Hamar, Banna, Borana and Arbore. Unfortunately, the people of the Lower Omo Valley, who are promoted by tour agencies, brochures, and newspaper articles, which stress their exoticism, have yet to benefit from tourism in their areas. While people's daily working patterns and private spheres are often disturbed by tourist visits, they do not receive fair compensation for their time dedicated to hosting tourists (i.e. posing for pictures, dancing, guiding, etc.).

As a result of these continuous inequitable and disrespectful tourist encounters, the world-famous ethics of Ethiopian hospitality have become distorted. While exposure to other cultures can teach tourists to respect and understand others, and at the same time enable people like the Mursi, Bodi, Hamar, Arbore, Kara, Nyangatom to create meaningful relationships with tourists, this is often not the case. These unpleasant encounters have led to different reactions of local groups towards tourists, ranging from animosity to indifference, or to changes in behaviour, some of which are negative, others more innovative.

One of the more 'innovative' responses to tourism is the often exaggerated way in which people of the Lower Omo 'dress up' for tourists (e.g. the wearing of cattle headdresses among the Mursi or exaggerated body painting among the Kara). These are cultural distortions that have been introduced in order to compete for tourist revenue (see mursionline.org). Tourism has also changed how people treat outsiders. For instance, the aggressive behaviour tourists might experience from the Mursi is something rarely found elsewhere in Mursiland. One explanation has to do with the 'pay per picture' logic, which is still perceived by locals as the most profitable form of tourist income. These brief financial exchanges (typically a few Ethiopian *berr* for a photo), are often unsatisfactory and unpleasant interactions that create a negative

Adventure tourism in southern Ethiopia, © Horst Böge

experience for tourists and for those being photographed. What has also emerged from these encounters is a culture of begging, especially among children (see photo), who one can often be seen chasing tourist cars with the hope that a few candies, coins, or plastic water bottles will be passed through the window.

This 'begging culture' is a negative experience for tourists and a negative change in many communities in southern Ethiopia. Another problematic change has to do with increased alcohol consumption in some areas where people are objectified and exploited by tourists.

Towards respectful and equitable tourism. Anthropologists at the South Omo Research Centre (Jinka) found in comparative and participatory research on community-based tourism that encounters with tourists could be improved through culturally sensitive methods of conflict management and innovative and collaborative planning led by local communities. These approaches are closely related to notions of respect and cultural self-esteem of the respective groups. Whereas, for example, in Kara and Hamar tourists are increasingly met with playful and staged cultural performances, e.g. the 'leap across the cattle'; in Arbore, a tourist village was established so local people could choose whether they wanted to meet tourists or continue their daily routines undisturbed. In recent years, the Mursi have also started to find inventive ways to avoid hostile encounters (e.g. clearing areas for camp sites) in order to host tourists for longer periods and foster more meaningful exchanges.

The rejection of tourism, or certain types of tourism, is grounded in people's experience that the majority of tours to visit 'exotic cultures' or the last 'untouched tribes of the world' lack serious engagement with and respect for the particular culture, realities, shareholder rights, opinions and potential of the people visited. As a consequence, the often tense meetings result in disappointment for both sides. The tourist practice of 'dropping by' or watching people in their homes lies outside the concept of proper behaviour in the face-to-face societies of South Omo. Moreover, it would also be unthinkable in many other places in the world. One solution to these challenges was to establish local tourist associations. Although these were meant to integrate local perspectives and secure funds for local institutions, tour guides and operators interested in personal profit, instead of fostering mutual understanding in informed ways, endanger the initial idea that members from the local communities who have an understanding of the culture and language, manage tourism and benefit from it.

While some tour operators and guides have cultivated personal bonds with the local hosts, which provide a basis for communicative processes and build long-term trust and commitment, still too few individuals from the respective local communities are employed or empowered in ways that they can influence tour programs in their areas.

The future of tourism in Ethiopia. The historical heritages and bio-cultural diversity found in Ethiopia makes the country an attractive tourist destination. With this promising potential to develop more sustainable tourism, there still remains the critical need to bridge the nature-culture gap in conservation strategies, which are often not consistent with indigenous views, and to build tourism infrastructures that integrate the expectations of local communities, tourist enterprises and tourists alike. Better distribution of direct and indirect tourism revenue and mutual awareness of cultural particularities are important to enable good relationships and to enhance the tourism infrastructure in socially-sustainable ways. This could be well supported by tourism policies which envisage a good balance of national coordination and local particularities. Although sharing in the financial benefits for local populations is essential to make tourism equitable, it should be taken into account that foreign tourists are equally benefiting from cultural and natural wealth. This understanding sees tourism as means for mutual international exchange between hosts and guests as equal global citizens and neighbours. Combined with a culture of respectful communication this carries the potential to enhance global tourists' encounters in Ethiopia in the future.

Literature: JONATHAN MITCHELL, CHRISTOPHER COLES et al., *Enhancing Private Sector and Community Engagement in Tourism Service in Ethiopia*, London 2009; JON ABBINK, 'Tourism and its Discontents – Suri-Tourist Encounters in Southern Ethiopia', *Social Anthropology*, 8/1 (2000), 1–17; TAMÁS RÉGI, 'The art of the weak: tourist encounters in East Africa', *Tourist Studies*, 13/1 (2014), 99–118; SHAUNA LATOSKY, *Predicaments of Mursi (Mun) Women in Ethiopia's Changing World*, Köln 2013.

Shauna LaTosky, Echi Christina Gabbert, Max-Planck-Institut für ethnologische Forschung, Halle/Saale

Museums in Ethiopia

Museums are a recent addition to the Ethiopian cultural landscape. However, in some regions the tradition of collecting historical items has been established for long time. In reaction to the rise of tourism and to the creation of a new urban middle class, the first museums were founded starting from the 1950s, mainly in Addis Ababa, and quite recently in great numbers all over Ethiopia. Some museums are usually included in any tourism route and urban sightseeing, while others are on their way to being 'discovered'. For the purpose of this article, the concept of 'museum' has been extended to also include important outdoor sites and cultural landscapes, presented as 'open-air museums'.

A peculiar role is played by church collections, which preserve different kinds of memories in their storehouses (*eqa bet*), including epigraphic and archaeological remains. While they act as centres of memory, objects are not in public display. Yet, all over Ethiopia, in response to increased tourism, some church communities now convert them to museums, often with access for the public.

Generally, local initiatives for the foundation of museums are increasing, including plans for several regional universities to create their own museums (Gondar, Meqele, Dabra Marqos), parallel to new museum foundations in collaboration with foreign partners.

Addis Ababa. The oldest and most important museum is the National Museum of Ethiopia, founded as the Archaeological Museum (1958). Recently it was conceptually rearranged in collaboration with the French Centre of Ethiopian Studies, Addis Ababa. Most important are its archaeological collections, built up in the era of Emperor Hayla Sellase during decades of excavations directed by French archaeologists. These comprise various items from Pre-Aksumite and Aksumite times. In addition, there are ethnographic collections representing major ethnic groups, modern art collections, which were created during the first peak of modern art in Ethiopia in the 1960s, regalia and golden crowns of recent emperors, an imperial throne and other imperial objects. Another section of the National Museum contains palaeontological collections, with remnants of ancient animals and early humans, among which the *australopithecus* skeleton known in Ethiopia as *Denqenash* (or 'Lucy'), which is by now inseparably linked with the modern self-definition of Ethiopia as the cradle of mankind.

Recent history is the focus of the Addis Ababa Museum, in the former residence of *Dajjazmach* Berru at Masqal Square. The experience of war and suppression in the time of the military dictatorship (*Darg*) is the theme of the nearby Red Terror Museum (2010). Another older museum of tremendous interest is the Ethnographic Museum of the Institute of Ethiopian Studies of Addis Ababa University (1963), where objects from all over Ethiopia are presented. Its greatest importance lies in its very fine collections of Christian icons and in its Christian and Islamic manuscripts.

Aside from the so-called Historic Route (Aksum, Gondar, Lalibala, and the monasteries of Lake Tana), Addis Ababa offers the best sightseeing opportunities. In its

Museum of the Institute of Ethiopian Studies, Addis Ababa, © Ethiopian Tourism Organization

environs travellers usually visit the Entoto mountain with the original palace of Emperor Menilek II and his wife Taytu, the church collection of Entoto Maryam, which has been turned into a museum (1986). The 'Piyassa' quarter (Arada) with the St George Church (with collections linked to Emperor Hayla Sellase), is visited due to the numerous older, sometimes Indian-style, houses. Former palaces of the old Shawan nobility are usually not open for visits, as they have been turned into offices, army quarters etc., similar to the palaces which house the Prime Minister and President today. The commercial quarter Markato is one of the largest market areas in Africa, and thus regarded as worth a visit by tourists.

Tegray. The Tegray Region possesses the largest number of museums in Ethiopia. The ancient historical centre, Aksum, has two museums. The State Museum (1974), with archaeological objects, including coins and inscriptions from Pre-Aksumite times onwards, was relocated in 2007 to the restored former residence of governor *Dajjazmach* Gabra Sellase Barya Gaber besides the stelae park. Within the compound of the church of Aksum Tseyon, a new museum will house the rich collections of precious objects donated to the church over centuries, including silver drums (*nagarit*) of rulers, votive and royal crowns, such as the first crown of Menilek II (before 1896) and the crown of Yohannes IV, precious vestments of nobles etc. In the nearby monastery of Abba Garima, the church collections have been turned into a museum, housing two of the most ancient illuminated Christian manuscripts in the world, the Ethiopian Abba Garima Gospels, which have been dated to Late Antiquity. Likewise, the church collections in nearby Yaha have currently been transferred to a new museum, constructed by the German Archaeological Institute in collaboration with the local community. It also holds Sabaean inscriptions and rare artefacts dated to the early 1st millennium BCE. The recent discovery of remnants of a temple and inscriptions of the same period in Maqaber Gaewa nearby Weqro has led to the foundation of the 'Society for the Promotion of Museums in Ethiopia' (Berlin), which in collaboration with the Tourism and Culture Agency of Tegray created a museum in Weqro to house these discoveries (2015). In Meqele, the Martyr's Museum houses artefacts and huge photographic collections from the time of the struggle of the Tigray People's Liberation Front against the central government until 1991. The palace constructed in the 1880s by the German-trained engineer *Lej* Engedashat alias Schimper and the Italian craftsman Naretti, commissioned by Emperor Yohannes IV, houses the important Mekelle Museum with collections from Yohannes IV (including his throne in non-Ethiopian style), Tegrayan governors from his dynasty, important Tegrayan artworks, especially church icons, as well as Arabic inscriptions from the historical Muslim quarters of nearby Kwiha. Large cultural areas are labelled 'open air museums', especially Garalta with its numerous rock-hewn churches.

Other regions. Regional museums have come into existence mainly during the past two decades. An important example is the Harar City Museum which displays Harar manuscripts, Harar coinage etc.

Formerly composed of the private collection of Abdullahi Sherif, it was taken over by the state in order to assure its preservation.

The historical Islamic town of Harar in eastern Ethiopia is remarkable for the Indian-style residence of its one-time governor *Dajjazmach* Tafari Makwannen (later Emperor Hayla Sellase), the house ascribed to the poet and trader Arthur Rimbaud, and several other places.

Some other ancient Muslim centres of learning, such as in Arsi, preserve important manuscript collections, not yet turned into museums. In Dase, a palace building of *Negus* Mikael of Wallo has been converted into the Regional Museum.

Many regional museums preserve memories of local history, sometimes of formerly independent kingdoms, with objects and documents. An older example is the Jimma Museum (*Muuziyemii Jimmaa*) with memorabilia of its former kings, local crafts, and a section devoted to coffee; also the palace of king Abbaa Jiffaar in Jiren can be visited. The Naqamtee Museum (1989) documents Oromo cultural traditions of Wallaga, and in Soddo a cultural museum preserves artefacts of the Walaytta (1966). A new museum (2011) in Semera in Afar was opened, and the private Black Lion Museum in Shashamane presents objects related to the Rasatafarian movement. Another recent foundation is the Coffee Museum of Bonga in Kafa (2007).

A totally different concept is followed by the South Omo Research Centre, Jinka (2002). Founded by German researchers with Japanese colleagues, in partnership with Ethiopian authorities, and both a museum and a cultural centre, it is used by researchers and local communities of the Omo for encounters, workshops and documentation of local cultural knowledge and traditions. Other museums in Ethiopia usually follow a concept of static documentation, but the idea of integration of local communities is increasingly discussed.

Literature: ALKE DOHRMANN, DIRK BUSTORF, 'Museums', *EAE* V, 452–455; D. JAMES NARENDRA BONDLA et al. (eds.), *Cultural Landscapes of Ethiopia: Conference Proceedings*, Meqele 2015.

Wolbert G.C. Smidt, Mekelle University

Addis Ababa

Addis Ababa, the capital and major city of Ethiopia, is at the virtual geographic centre of Ethiopia and was built near the watershed of two great river systems: the Blue Nile and the Awash. The Entoto range of hills dominate the capital to the north, while the city lies on a well-watered plateau surrounded by mountains: Yarar to the east and the Mannagasha and Wachacha to the west and south-west. Its altitude of 2,300 m is a challenge for many visitors to this cosmopolitan and dynamic city.

Establishment and early development. Addis Ababa was the last in a series of moving provincial capitals of Shawa, including Ankobar, Dabra Berhan and Entoto, which built on a previous tradition of dispersed national capitals in Aksum, Lalibala and Gondar. In 1886 Empress Taytu persuaded Emperor Menilek II to move his capital from the cold and windy Entoto hills to the warmer plains below and the hot springs of Finfinnee (still near the centre of the old city). It was she who named the new city Addis Ababa ('new flower'). By the next year large plots of land had been allocated to the major nobility, other important personages and some churches. The local Oromo tribes had their lands confiscated and many were removed. It is important to note that the city was originally founded as a military encampment mirroring an army on the march. The lands of the general of the advance guard, Habta Giyorgis, were furthest to the west, while the palace (*gebbi*) of Menilek was in the centre, bracketed on each side by the leaders of the left and right wings of the army. The rear area to the east of the palace was allocated to another prominent noble. Many of these original lands can still be traced back to military grants. Each encampment continued to be settled by each noble's retainers and slaves, usually brought from the lands and ethnic groups he controlled.

Shopping and commercial street, Addis Ababa, © Matthias Ansel

Among those ethnic groups, the Amhara, the Oromo, the Gurage, the Dorze and the Tegrayans would come in the largest numbers and make Addis Ababa the major melting pot of Ethiopia. From its very earliest days Addis Ababa has grown spontaneously without significant control from the centre.

When Emperor Yohannes IV died in battle, and Menilek of Shawa succeeded as emperor, his coronation in 1889 was not held in Addis Ababa, but in a church on the hill of Entoto. However, during the 1880s and 1890s the new capital steadily grew in importance.

The fledgling administration of the new city was severely strained by major national crises, including, the famine, cattle plague and cholera epidemic of 1889–1892. While the population of Ethiopia decreased substantially, there is reason to believe that many from the countryside took refuge in Addis Ababa to take advantage of the alms distributed by the emperor, empress and nobility.

The palace was the centre of the administration of the capital. The Emperor retained ultimate control over Addis Ababa. However, he partially delegated authority to key imperial officials, the most important of whom was the *naggadras*, or head of the merchants. Ethiopia's victory in the battle of Adwa in 1896 confirmed Menilek's personal domination and also solidified Addis Ababa's role as the nation's political centre. It led to international recognition of Ethiopia's independence. Representatives of provincial and international powers came in increasingly large numbers to Addis Ababa to take up residence, helping to make it a national and regional diplomatic centre.

Menilek was keen on modernizing and experimenting – if only selectively – with western technology. Of the many foreign minorities, Greeks, Armenians and Italians had the largest impact on the city's history and development. During this early period Addis Ababa saw its first telegraph and telephone service, electrification of the *gebbi*, flour mills, soap factories, cars and traction engines. New churches were erected, like St George Church in the centre of town. The beginning of the 20th century saw a new building program in the capital: a new mint was begun, new bridges financed, a concession for a cartridge factory let, as well as the concession for the Bank of Abyssinia and a new school, the Menilek II Secondary School was established. The central market area (*arada*) was reorganized, and many more permanent buildings planned and built.

The next major period of Addis Ababa's history, from 1907 to 1916, was a period of transition and instability. Hayla Giyorgis, its first mayor, consolidated his power, becoming the most powerful man in Ethiopia in the wake of Menilek's illness, death and troubled succession. During this period major international import and export traders, mainly Indians, French and Armenians, moved their headquarters to Addis Ababa. The city's market grew larger than Harar's for the first time, making the capital the economic as well as the political centre of Ethiopia. Its population steadily grew from about 45,000 in the late 19th century to 100,000 by 1918. However, before the first real census in 1984 all population figures are only rough estimates.

1916–1935. The 1916 coup d'état marks another major turning point in the history of the capital as well as of Ethiopia as a whole. *Lej* Iyasu, Menilek's grandson, was overthrown and replaced by the Empress Zawditu with *Ras* Tafari Makwannen (the future Emperor Hayla Sellase) as second in command and regent. As the leader of the reformist faction in Ethiopia, Tafari used the restructured Addis Ababa municipality as a training ground for future national and provincial administrators. It became the showcase for reform and modernisation in Ethiopia. As Tafari slowly increased his power, centralisation of power and resources in Addis Ababa grew apace. The capital's role as the primary city dominating the empire grew significantly.

By 1917 the railway, which had begun in Djibouti in 1897, reached the outskirts of the city and became the city's major transport link with the outside world. New schools, most notably the Tafari Makwannen School, were founded. A new and prolific printing press, *Berhanenna salam*, was established. These and other factors led to Addis Ababa becoming the intellectual and cultural centre of Ethiopia. Modernisation and westernization reached a climax with a flurry of activity in honour of Emperor Hayla Sellase's coronation in 1930. The first girls' school, the Empress Manan School, was founded by the emperor's consort, and the Empress Zawditu Memorial Hospital was set up in the capital by the Adventists. Significant road building also took place.

1935–1941. In 1935 the Italians invaded Ethiopia and soon made Addis Ababa the capital not only of Ethiopia but of the whole of Africa Orientale Italian (Italian East Africa), which included Eritrea and Somalia. During their rule from 1936 to 1941 they planned to make Addis Ababa the showcase of their empire, and the centre of a vast road system. Grandiose city plans were also drawn up to transform it through a major building campaign. The city was to be segregated into white and indigenous areas, and the indigenous areas segregated by religion and ethnicity. A separate market for Ethiopians was created, today's Markato, and the old market, *arada*, was reserved for the whites.

Italians clearly reinforced Addis Ababa's role as Ethiopia's primary city, despite many of the plans never reaching fruition. The road system funnelled increasing numbers of ethnic groups from throughout the empire to settle the capital. The housing designed for Italians was mostly in the art deco style, and some of it still survives. They also greatly expanded the city's water supply system with new sources from Gefarsa and expanded the electric grid. The Italians also greatly exacerbated an already existing problem when they systematized and organized prostitutes and prostitution, to ensure that white and non-white troops were serviced. Probably the greatest impact that the Italians had on the city was economic, for they established an

Taxi traffic, Addis Ababa, © Horst Böge

urban labour market with monetary remuneration for services and abolished slavery. This was a marked change from the previous system where most labour was linked to landowners who were mostly aristocrats and few workers had been paid. Addis Ababa's population during the Italian occupation probably grew to about 300,000.

1941–1974. In May, 1941 Addis Ababa became the first capital to be liberated from the Axis powers during WWII. The late 1940s to 1974 marked the most rapid period of expansion in the capital's history. By 1960 its population was about half a million. Over half of the manufacturing industries in Ethiopia were found in the capital and 60% of their fixed assets. Foreigners owned and/or managed most of the industrial enterprises. Wealth and land were also concentrated in the hands of the Ethiopian elite and aristocracy. In 1966 5% of the population owned 95% of the private land in Addis Ababa. Land speculation was rampant and as a result one-third to one-half of the capital's land was under-utilized. Furthermore, the few industrial plants tended to be concentrated in the growing southern regions of the city, like Nafas Selk. These were prime contributors to the revolution which was to come in 1974.

During this period Addis Ababa became more and more cosmopolitan and increasingly not just a national and regional centre, but also an international one. In 1960 it became in effect the capital of Africa when the OAU was established in the city. It also hosted other regional and international organizations like the Economic Commission for Africa and a wide variety of NGOs.

Addis Ababa also continued to be the major national melting pot. The major ethnic groups in the capital still were the Amhara, the Oromo, the Tegrayans, the Gurage and the Dorze. Measured by the indices of amount of travel to homelands and land ownership in Addis Ababa, the Oromo assimilated most into the dominant Amhara culture, and the Gurage and Dorze the least. By 1967 56% of the population of Addis Ababa were migrants. There were more economic, educational, and employment opportunities in the capital than anywhere else in Ethiopia. Transport facilities, especially the road network for buses and taxis, were centred there and encouraged migration not only from rural areas but also from smaller towns. Finally, natural disasters, especially the periodic famine and droughts, influenced many to migrate to Addis Ababa.

1974–the present. With the revolution of 1974 the *Darg* became the focus of political power. After it consolidated its control, it tried to carry out a radical break with the past, implementing a 'socialist plan' for the development of Addis Ababa.

In 1978 a new planner, the Hungarian C.K. Polony was hired, and a steady shift to the south of the centre of the city was implemented. Symbolically Masqal Square (traditionally used for the celebrations for the Feast of the Finding of the True Cross) was renamed 'Revolutionary Square' and became the centre of most revolutionary activities. However, eight years later a new Italian planning committee was appointed to draft a new master plan.

The city has continued to grow in the spontaneous and unplanned way. The famine of 1983–1985 was a major spur to the growth of the capital helping to increase its population to one and a half million. However, overall it grew more slowly than it had before 1974 and would after 1991. A great deal of low cost housing was built, much of it with mud wattle walls and corrugated iron roofs. According to the 1994 census, the main religious groups found in Addis Ababa were: The Ethiopian Orthodox Tawahedo Church (85%), Muslims (12.7%), Protestants, including Seventh Day Adventists, Pentecostals, Lutherans, Baptists, Anglicans, Presbyterians, Masarata Krestos, Mulu Wangel, Qala Heywat etc. (3.9%), Catholics (0.8%) and followers of traditional and other religions (0.6%). The rapid spread of urbanization, the increase in the population of the city, the expansion of the city and the concentration of economic and social activities created a strong demand for transportation. The two common carrier systems that coexist in the city, buses and privately owned taxis, both grew in size and extent. Finally, Addis Ababa was connected with Djibouti through the railway and a true international airport was built in the Bole area southeast of the city centre.

After the flight into exile in 1991 of Mengistu Haile Mariam, the leader of the *Darg*, the new government of Mallas Zenawi implemented a federal, and in theory decentralized system of government. This slowly resulted in a decline in the rate of growth of the capital, while regional capitals like Dire Dawa, Gondar and Meqele began to grow much more swiftly. Addis Ababa has remained the primary city throughout this time, but is no longer as dominant as it had once been. In 2003 the 1986 master plan was revised, highlighting two new initiatives. First, there was a focus on the revitalization of neighbourhoods in Addis Ababa, which in effect attempted to decentralize the city. Second, there was a new emphasis on improving the city's gravely underdeveloped infrastructure. A new traffic grid was set up with ring roads and widened highways which transformed the city's transportation.

Sightseeing. Addis Ababa remains the political and economic centre of Ethiopia. Furthermore, it is still the intellectual centre of the country. Hotels, restaurants, coffee shops and bars cover the full range from *deluxe* and *gourmet* to inexpensive and simple. Although there are today many other universities, schools and hospitals throughout the country, Addis Ababa continues to boast a higher concentration in numbers and quality of educated and trained professionals than anywhere else in Ethiopia. It also has a higher concentration of museums, theatres and art galleries. Its population is now said to have reached four million.

The most important museum is the National Museum of Ethiopia, founded 1958 (see some details in the article 'Museums in Ethiopia').

Addis Ababa is home to countless Orthodox Churches. Several of these are of major historical significance. St George's Cathedral, which also houses a small museum, was dedicated to the saint whose *tabot* ('ark', i.e. 'altar slab') was carried into the Ethiopian victory over the Italians at Adwa in 1896. Both Empress Zawditu and the Emperor Hayla Sellase were crowned at this site. Holy Trinity Cathedral (Qeddest Selassie) is (after the church of Mary of Zion in Aksum), the holiest site of the Church. It was built to commemorate the expulsion of the Italian Fascists. Emperor Hayla Sellase, Empress Manan, Prime Minister Mallas Zenawi, Patriarchs *Abuna* Takla Haymanot and *Abuna* Pawlos, and the suffragette Sylvia Pankhurst are among the notables buried in its cemetery. Madhane Alam cathedral in the trendy Bole neighbourhood, near the international airport, is Addis Ababa's newest major church and its largest. It has a clear modern feel.

The large open market, known as the aforementioned Markato, is said to be the largest open market in Africa. Nearby is the Anwar Mosque, the most important religious centre for Muslims in and around the capital, and the Roman Catholic Church of the Nativity, both testaments to the city's religious diversity.

There has also been a cultural revival in the city. One symbol of this has been the return of 'Ethio-jazz' to the city once the curfew imposed during most the 1970s and 1980s was revoked.

In conclusion it needs to be said that Addis Ababa was formed from a wide range of peoples, from all parts of the nation. This diversity has given the capital a unique character and energy, helping to create unity out of diversity. Addis Ababa has been in many ways a melting pot, helping Ethiopia to forge a new national identity in the 21st century.

Literature: PETER GARRETSON, *A History of Addis Abäba*, Wiesbaden 2000; PETER GARRETSON, MEKETE BELACHEW, 'Addis Abäba', *EAE* I, 79–88.

Peter Garretson, Florida State University, Steven Kaplan, The Hebrew University Jerusalem

Historic Route

The Historic Route is a good way to gain insight into Ethiopian history and can be completed in around seven to ten days. The combination of the words 'historic' and 'route' points to the possibility of personally exploring the past by travelling along a predefined itinerary. This circuit was first described by the Portuguese Francisco Alvares, who lived in Ethiopia from 1521–1525 and whose 'historical' account of his travels is the prototype for the travel diaries of today.

The Historic Route is well-established with most stops on it located in what is now the Amhara region in the northeast of the country. The five standard destinations of Baher Dar and Lake Tana, Gondar, Aksum, Lalibala and Harar can be supplemented with additional stops such as Dabra Dammo and Yaha. The sites visited bear witness to Ethiopia's cultural and religious heritage, with each a window on a particular period in history. The past always leaves its mark: a building's architecture and materials reveal its time of construction, artefacts reference stories of religion, trade, hierarchy and war. Even though this journey through time exploring the cultural history of Ethiopia begins over 2,500 years ago, some of the sites visited are still very much alive – for example the rock-hewn churches of Lalibala. They can be marvelled at not only as bygone monuments, but also as part of Ethiopia's contemporary Christian culture.

The route can either be booked as a small-group package (flights/transfers, hotels, entrance fees, local guides) or organised independently. Numerous hotels have sprung up along the route over the last few years. The best time to travel is between November and February, with the processions at Christmas (6/7 January) and *Temqat* (Epiphany, 13 January) as particular highlights. Shoes are to be removed upon entering churches, and it is recommended that women drape a scarf over their shoulders. This journey through Ethiopia's eventful and fascinating history begins in its modern capital, Addis Ababa, built in 1886. From there, the circuit continues to Baher Dar and Lake Tana, which can be reached by air (from Bole Airport), car or bus.

Baher Dar and Lake Tana. The provincial capital of the Amhara region, Baher Dar, stands on the shores of Ethiopia's largest lake, Lake Tana (3,600 km^2). It is the source of the Blue Nile and home to 30 island monasteries scattered around the lake.

These monasteries were built (according to scholars) from the late 13th century, although local tradition claims they began to be established already in the 4th century. Each monastery consists of a church and monks' huts spread over the island. Despite the monasteries' isolation they have amassed sizeable collections of texts, including glorious illuminated manuscripts. These testify to Ethiopia's rich literary history. The monasteries are spiritual centres where life is dedicated to God and the community alone. They are largely self-sufficient, with literature and clothes delivered by boat. The island monasteries are representative of the importance of monasteries to the Ethiopian Church. Their uniqueness and ascetic simplicity have been admired for centuries by travellers.

Only two of these monasteries are open to women (Werra Kidana Mehrat [Zage]) and Narga Sellase. Trips to the monasteries can be arranged in Baher Dar. By crossing the water in *tankwa*, narrow but highly stable papyrus boats, the passengers get a feeling of what lies in store on the islands: timelessness.

The first monastery is Kebran (a 90-minute boat trip). The church of Kebran Gabreel (14th century) was rebuilt under Emperor Iyasu I (r. 1682–1706) from red stones. Its wall-paintings have some vivid scenes including the beheading of John the Baptist. In the monastery's library is a particularly beautiful illuminated manuscript of the Four Gospels, on which some miniatures are enhanced with gold. The 14th-century church Werra (*Ura*) Kidana Mehrat stands on the Zage peninsula on the south-west shore of the lake. The church boasts a conical ceiling as well as gloriously colourful murals. Over 300 manuscripts, the oldest from the 15th century, are in its library.

The other seven churches on Zage are less frequently visited. The oldest monastery Daga Estifanos (13th century) lies on the island Daga in the middle of the lake. Its church of St Stephen was rebuilt in 1880 after having been destroyed by fire. Its treasury houses the opulently decorated liturgical robes and crowns of several rulers. Daga Estifanos was the burial site of emperors Zara Yaeqob (15th century) and Fasiladas (17th century). New glass coffins allow visitors to view their mummified bodies. Legend has it that in the 16th century the Ark of the Covenant was hidden at this site from the conquering Ahmad Grany.

East of Daga lies the islet of Narga. Empress Mentewwab erected the church of Narga Sellase in 1737/1738. The church has many engravings on wood and stone and wall-paintings and is well worth seeing. Tana Qirqos is situated to the eastern shore of the lake. According to local tradition, the Holy Family took refuge here during Herod's persecution. Invaluable manuscripts, a stone with Jesus's footprints, a necklace of St Mary and Sabaean inscription on a bowl are shown to visitors.

It is worth visiting the Church of St George upon returning to Baher Dar. Possibly the oldest two-storey building in Ethiopia stands close to the church (16th century).

Ura Kidana Mehrat Church on Zage Peninsula, Baher Dar, © Ethiopian Tourism Organization

An excursion (35 km) to the Blue Nile falls is an established feature of most visits. These spectacular waterfalls illustrate the Egyptians' historical concern that the Ethiopians could cut off the flow to the Nile, thus robbing Egypt of its fertile silt. Known as Tis Esat (Amharic 'smoking water'), the 45-metre waterfalls vary between a trickle and a raging tumult from season to season. The oldest preserved stone bridge (1626) in Ethiopia is located nearby. The construction of the Ethiopian Renaissance dam on the Nile began in 2010 and is slowly changing the region's entire topography.

While en route to Gondar it is worth taking a detour to the peninsula of Gorgora where there is a castle built for Emperor Susenyos (r. 1604–1632). Not far away is the circular church Dabra Sina (17th century). The Annunciation with Gabriel represented as an old man is seldom seen.

The visit is an excellent way to get in the mood for the old imperial city of Gondar (35 km). The city is built at an elevation of 2,200 m at the foot of the Semen Mountains in north-west Ethiopia.

Gondar. Built as the royal seat of the emperors, Gondar remained the imperial capital from 1636 to 1855. The palace of Fasil(adas) (*Fasil gemb*) is an impressive, monumental complex (70,000 m²). Emperor Fasiladas (r. 1632–1662) is said to have chosen the site based on a dream. A lion's cage draws attention to the fate of the last lion kept here, which died in 1965. The grave of the British consul Walter Plowden (1820–1860) is also located within the Royal Enclosure. Plowden was murdered by insurgents and laid to rest by order of Emperor Tewodros II (r. 1855–1868).

Gondar was long a centre for religious training, its ecclesiastical schools famed for their tradition of biblical exegesis. Visitors are welcome to the Madhane Alam Church school (see also the article 'Gondar and surroundings').

The circuit continues northwards.

Aksum. Modern Aksum may just be a small town in northern Tegray that mainly lives off tourism, but it remains steeped in history. Aksum is the cradle of Ethiopian history, and was once the capital and commercial centre of a powerful kingdom (1st–7th centuries CE). Not too far way Adulis in Eritrea flourished during this period serving as the port of Aksum.

Aksum's most famous landmarks are its stelae (obelisks), palace ruins and the Church of Our Lady Mary of Zion. Northern Aksum is home to a large stelae park, which is a cemetery containing the graves of the Aksumite monarchs. The coins found in the town tell the story of the conversion to Christianity of King Ezana about 340, the crescent above the monarch's portrait being eventually replaced with a cross. The religions of Aksum and its wars are documented by inscriptions on stelae and palaces, some of which are in three scripts (Sabaean, Greek and Ge'ez) and two languages, Greek and Ge'ez (the latter also in Sabaean script). Other sites worth seeing include stone thrones and the large palaces and temples in the west of the town. The Church Maryam Tseyon (Church of Our Lady Mary of Zion, 16th century) was built on the foundations of an older 6th-century church. Its treasury houses the Ark of the Covenant. Although women are not allowed inside the church itself, church treasures such as imperial crowns are on display to all visitors. The Aksum Museum features artefacts such as carafes, coins, manuscripts and crowns (see also three articles on Aksum in the chapter History).

The tour now turns back towards the south.

Dabra Dammo. The oldest church in Ethiopia dates back to the 6th century and is located at Dabra Dammo monastery. It lies at an altitude of 2,216m on an *amba* (table mountain) in the region of Bizat, East Tegray. According to the hagiography of Abba Aragawi, God sent down a serpent with which he was able to pull himself up onto the mountain. To this day, in order to ascend one has to use a rope let down by monks some 25m above. Women are not admitted. The church reveals Aksumite architecture; beams and the ceiling are decorated with carved animals. A fire caused by lightning in 1996 destroyed some of Ethiopia's oldest manuscripts. Today around 100 self-sufficient monks, who have enough space to grow essential foodstuffs, live here.

Yaha. Located in the Tegray region, Yaha was once a centre of Pre-Aksumite civilisation. It is home to the 2,500-year-old Moon temple of the Daamat kingdom. The rectangular temple building reflects the light during the full moon nights. In Tiya one can find a collection of 36 stelae resembling small anthropoid figures, dated to the Neolithic period.

A detour to the rock-hewn churches of Weqro Cherqos and Abreha Atsbeha near Addigrat is particularly worthwhile due to their wall-paintings and the recently discovered Ethiopian-Sabaic temple in Weqro (6th to 8th centuries BCE).

Lalibala. Lalibala has been a UNESCO World Heritage Site since 1978. The $50 entrance fee paid for a visitor's pass covering all churches ensures the preservation of a site often referred to as the 8th wonder of the world. Located in Lasta at an altitude of 2,600m, the site is famous for its eleven churches carved out of the red volcanic tuff. The rock-hewn churches are built down into the ground and only come into sight a short distance from their edge. These architectural masterpieces are characterized by a variety of styles. Four churches have been carved from a single block of stone, the others were excavated from a vertical rock face. The churches are in daily liturgical use and welcome large numbers of pilgrims at Christmas and Temqat (Epiphany).

Emperor Lalibala (*c.* 1180–1225), was the most powerful ruler of the Zagwe dynasty (*c.* 1137–1270). According to Ethiopian tradition, he was instructed by God to build a copy of Jerusalem in Ethiopia. The 'River Jordan' (Yordanos) divides the rock-hewn churches into two groups.

The northern group comprises six churches: Beta Golgota, Beta Qeddus Mikael (Dabra Sina), Beta Maryam, Beta Masqal, Beta Danagel and Beta Madhane Alam. Madhane Alam ('Saviour of the World') is the largest of the churches and unique in terms of its construction. Despite being built in the form of a temple and surrounded by rectangular pillars, it nevertheless adopts the outline of a basilica with five naves. Its open windows feature a variety of patterns based on elements such as swastikas and the Greek cross. The oldest church, Beta Maryam, boasts striking details such as frescos, a frieze depicting saints and ornamental carvings. Beta Golgota, together with Qeddus Mikael refer in their architecture to the Holy Sepulchre in Jerusalem. The figural reliefs in Beta Golgota are unique for Ethiopia. The tomb of Emperor Lalibala and of Adam and the Chapel of the Holy Trinity inside this church are making it the holiest place in Lalibala.

South of the Jordan are the churches Beta Amanuel, Beta Marqorewos (Mercurius), Beta Abba Libanos and Beta Qeddus Gabreel-Rufael. The elegant rock-hewn church Beta Qeddus Giyorgis (St George), has the form of a Greek cross with four arms of equal length (12.5 m). Some connecting tunnels feature small recesses housing the remains of deceased monks.

The route now turns to the east.

Harar. The old city of Harar (13th century) is famous for its more than 100 mosques, 200 shrines, Koranic schools and the unique architecture of its houses. Precious manuscripts in Harari and Arabic are on display. Harar boasts a rich heritage of craftsmen, and visitors are welcome in their workshops. Menilek II conquered the city in 1887 and appointed *Ras* Makwannen as its ruler. His son, who became the Emperor Hayla Sellase made frequent visits to his native town.

The journey back provides an opportunity to visit the monastery of Dabra Libanos, which was founded by the monk Takla Haymanot (13th century). The new church features glass windows designed by the artist Afewerk Tekle. The 'Spring of the Madonna' is visited by sick people seeking healing.

Back in Addis Ababa the travellers expand their knowledge of history in the city's several museums. Further excavations continue to provide new insights into the more than two millennia of Ethiopian history. Some sights may one day be added to the Historic Route.

Literature: Charles Fraser Beckingham, George Wynn Brereton Huntingsford (eds.), *The Prester John of the Indies. A True Relation of the Lands of the Prester John, being the narrative of the Portuguese Embassy to Ethiopia in 1520, written by Father Francisco Alvares*, I–II, Cambridge 1961; Klaus Dornisch, *Sagenhaftes Äthiopien: Archäologie, Geschichte, Religion*, Darmstadt 2015.

Verena Böll, Dresden

Lalibala

Lalibala is situated at 2,600 m a.s.l., *c.* 340 km north of Addis Ababa, in the Amhara region, offering a good year-round climate and exhilarating mountain views. It is a town of 15,000 inhabitants and is famous for its unique monolithic rock-hewn churches hewn from the reddish volcanic rock mostly more than 700 years ago. Lalibala is an ecclesiastical centre of the Ethiopian Orthodox Church and a place of pilgrimage and devotion for worshippers, attracting yearly *c.* 100,000 visitors. Religious celebrations are central to the life of the town, with regular processions, extensive fasts and crowds of singing and dancing clerics. This, combined with its extraordinary religious architecture and simplicity of life, gives Lalibala a timeless, almost biblical atmosphere. The town is testimony to the ancient civilization of Ethiopia, with its traditional, circular two-storey stone houses with exterior staircases and conical, thatched roofs. The relative isolation of the small town helps to explain more closely the piety and hard lives of the rural poor. The weekly market on Saturdays, where such as spices, agricultural products, handicrafts and livestock are sold, offers an insight into local life.

Rock hewn church Madhana Alem, Lalibala, © Serge Dewel-Mouton

According to legend, Lalibala and his older brother travelled to the city of Roha and constructed rock-hewn churches over a period of 25 years assisted during the day by many workmen and by angels overnight. Constructions dated to that period bear names which mirror places visited by pilgrims to Jerusalem and its environs. Early in King Lalibala's reign, the Muslim Salah ad-Din (Saladin) had captured Jerusalem in 1187, and for this reason Ethiopians may have felt excluded from making their pilgrimages to the Holy Land. The Ethiopian Orthodox Church later canonized the king and changed the name Roha to Lalibala.

The eleven churches are within walking distance of each other and are divided into two main groups plus one church which stands alone. Although the church exteriors and interiors are carved from rock, their architecture is extremely diverse: there are different styles of doors, windows, floors, and pillars. The roofs of the churches are level with the ground and are reached by stairs descending into narrow trenches. A complex system of drainage ditches, tunnels and subterranean passageways, some with cavities and chambers filled with mummies of pious monks and pilgrims, connects the underground structures. Establishing a sequence or chronology for rock-hewn buildings is much more difficult than for conventional ones, especially when the churches are in daily use. Consequently, there have been long running scholarly disputes as to both the period and duration of construction. Some researchers argue that the first monuments were not originally churches. In any case, the churches retain clear evidence of their Aksumite inspiration.

The churches. The northern group: Beta Madhane Alam ('Church of the Saviour of the world') is the largest monolithic church in the world, probably a copy of St Mary of Zion in Aksum. It is a basilica measuring 33.7m x 23.7m x 11.5m, surrounded by square columns and two lines of windows of different styles. It is home to the Lalibala Cross. It is linked by walkways and tunnels to Beta Maryam (St Mary's church) which is possibly the oldest of these churches standing in a spacious courtyard. It has three doors with a large porch and Aksumite-style windows. The interior is richly decorated with mural paintings of biblical subjects and decorations of stars and crosses. Among other pillars, there is a 7.6m high one kept shrouded in cloth (hiding paintings and texts), known as *amda berhan* ('pillar of light'). In the northern wall of Beta Maryam, there is the excavated small chapel of Beta Masqal ('Church of the Cross') currently used as the church treasury. The west and south doorways of Beta Danagel ('Church of the virgins') have Aksumite features inside, the north door does not. According to legend, it was built in honour of maidens martyred in Rome in the mid-4th century. A tunnel at the southern end of the courtyard outside Beta Maryam leads to the interconnected churches of Beta Mikael (Dabra Sina) and Beta Golgota, which is known for its artwork and which includes early Christian carvings of saints on the walls. It contains a separate room called the Sellase Chapel ('Trinity', accessible to priests only) containing the tomb of King Lalibala and an empty room called the Tomb of Adam.

The Eastern group: Beta Amanuel ('Emmanuel') is architecturally sophisticated having Aksumite-style external walls and doorways. A spiral staircase leads to an upper storey. Sacred bees living inside are a reminder of the prophecy of Lalibala's kingship. There is a subterranean tunnel leading to the partially collapsed Beta Marqorewos; its early wall paintings on cotton have been removed and can now be seen in the National Museum in Addis Ababa. Between Beta Marqorewos and Beta Gabreel-Rufael (the Archangels Gabriel and Raphael) there is a small room called *beta lehem* ('House of bread'). All these may not have been originally in ecclesiastical use. Beta Abba Libanos dedicated to an Ethiopian saint is a cave church having a façade with detailed carvings and a wall separating it from the surrounding area on three sides but not on top. Beta Giyorgis dedicated to St George, the patron saint of Ethiopia, is the most finely executed and best

A bronze processional cross, © University Collection, Addis Ababa 4651

preserved; its roof in the shape of a Greek cross is used today as a symbol of the Lalibala monuments. It is a nearly perfect cube, hewn in the shape of a cross, and is oriented so that the main entrance is in the west and the holy of holies in the east. The church is set in a deep pit with perpendicular walls and it can only be entered via a hidden tunnel carved into the rock.

Inside Beta Maryam Church, Lalibala, © Serge Dewel-Mouton

Outside of Lalibala proper lie the monasteries of Naakweto Laab and Ashetan Maryam as well as the famous church of Yemrehanna Krestos from the 12th century built in the Aksumite fashion but in a cave.

Conservation of national heritage. For centuries, the church and the state have been jointly responsible for the holy site of Lalibala. There has been seismic activity in the area resulting in severe degradation of the monuments from water damage, and most of churches are now considered to be in a critical condition having structural problems with risk of collapse and degradation of paintings, sculptures and bas-reliefs. The Authority for Research and Conservation of Cultural Heritage wants to have tighter planning controls over the setting of the churches to address housing and land-use tourism, and to have a management plan. It wants to develop the Conservation Action Plan for the overall sustainable development of the area, with the involvement of the local population. Temporary light-weight shelters were installed over some churches and these, while offering protection have impacted on visual integrity.

In 2011, UNESCO with help from the EU launched a new project to erect protective metal shelters to shield four of the churches at risk. The shelters may be unsightly, but they are preserving the integrity of the churches. This project has effectively preserved traditional craft skills, while also generating income in an area affected by poverty. In recent years, a conscious effort to develop Lalibala's infrastructure has also brought further attention to this remote place, leading to the arrival of even more pilgrims and tourists.

Literature: Marilyn Heldman, 'Churches of Lalibäla', *EAE* III, 484-489; Kellen McClure, *No Shelter: UNESCO's efforts to save Lalibela's Culture*, University of Vermont, Addis Ababa 2007; David W. Phillipson, *Ancient Churches of Ethiopia*, New Haven–London 2009.

Maija Priess, Universität Hamburg

Meqele

Meqele ('Mekele') is the second largest city in Ethiopia and the capital of the National Regional State of Tegray. Economically, it is a centre of industrial investment and thus a major contributor to the growth of the Ethiopian economy. Since the 19th century it has established itself as a political and economic centre, even at times serving as the capital of imperial Ethiopia in the 1880s, as is witnessed to this day by historical monuments. The international Ras Alula Abba Nega Airport links Meqele with five to six daily flights to Addis Ababa, and to other destinations in the region.

Sightseeing includes the town itself, mainly its pleasant palm tree alleys with fruit and coffee bars in the quarters below the former imperial palace, and several museums. The former palace of Emperor Yohannes IV is now a museum. In addition, the museum in the Hawalti area, marked by a huge monument commemorating the deaths of fighters form the Tigray People's Liberation Front's (TPLF) war against the central government is worth a visit. It has collections of photos and documents from this struggle which ended in 1991. A smaller palace of governor Abraha Araya (ruling 1899–1909), near Hawalti imitates the style of the imperial palace, and today serves as a hotel. There are also several impressive natural sites in the area, such as the dramatic waterfall of Chala'anqwa in Dabri, with ruins of medieval hermit settlements, the fertile valley of the Mikael Tsellamo church behind Dabri, or the waterfall of Romanat nearby the village of Gambala near Masabo. In recent years Meqele has incorporated the town of Kwiha and surrounding villages such as Aynalam, Gambala, and Dabri, where new streets are about to be constructed. In 1994 the population of Meqele was around 100,000 inhabitants, in 2007 215,914, and by 2015 410,217. Its climate is moderate and dry, with an altitude of around 2,100 m a.s.l.

Origins. Some local accounts claim that the history of Meqele goes back to the 13th century, which is at best a misinterpretation of existing historical accounts, and in any case a gross exaggeration. As a royal town it was newly founded only in the early 1880s in an open grazing plain shared by several surrounding villages. Some of these, however, were definitely ancient: their history dates far earlier than the 13th century, as Aksumite ruins within today's city limits demonstrate. Starting from its foundation, Meqele grew and subsequently took over the lands of these much older, but mostly small villages. This dynamic process has reached a further climax in the years around 2005 to 2015. One of the first small settlements to be incorporated was the few peasant's houses around the 13th-century church of Madhane Alam, and one of the last the nearby town of Kwiha, an Italian colonial foundation around one of the most ancient sites of the region, the Aksumite Enda Charqos church of Wegra Hariba.

Originally, Meqele was a large plain below Wegra Hariba, which was a seat of a toll station for salt trade and at times of the governor of Endarta (as mentioned in the tax registers of Emperor Tewodros II). The name means 'shared' in Tegrennya, which refers to the fact that its grazing lands were commonly used by the surrounding villages, such as Dabri, and Aynalam, who also had a common market place in the plain, mainly for salt. The name usually used for the area was, as old maps and the local oral tradition show, Gambala, after a small river originating in Kwiha above the plain.

When Emperor Yohannes IV was looking for a site for his palace in Tegray, he first chose Aksum. However, he had to give up this choice after failed negotiations with the local clergy who were not ready to give up their status as a free, autonomous city.

Meqele, © Wolbert G.C. Smidt

His decision to settle down in Agula, the ancient seat of the governors of Tsara north of Meqele, to which he had hereditary claims, had to be abandoned, as it could not feed his army.

The lands of Meqele and its water-rich villages, however, were fertile enough so that he could establish his permanent seat there. In contrast to his previous capitals, he did not take over an already existing seat of governors, but established a totally new settlement.

Palace and museum. The historical accounts tell us that he built his palace in Meqele, on a small hill, from 1882 to 1884. Interestingly, this palace was an early example of modern civil engineering realized by a foreign-educated Ethiopian, together with a foreign craftsman. The emperor gave this task to his Italian architect Giacomo Naretti, who had already completed other buildings for him. He planned and erected this palace together with the first Ethiopian engineer, *Lej* Engedashat from Adwa, who had just returned from his university studies in Germany in 1877. This palace served as a seat of the princely governors of Tegray until the military coup of 1974, when the last governor, a descendent of Emperor Yohannes IV, fled into exile. It was then used as an administrative seat and by the military. After 1991 it was converted into a museum hosting icons, manuscripts, two Arabic inscriptions from Kwiha, and memorabilia of Emperor Yohannes IV and his family. It has been renovated and reopened in 2016.

History. The rather rich history of Meqele and its surroundings has not yet been fully explored and rediscovered. In the early 19th century the plain of Meqele and the surrounding villages belonged to the ruler of the princedom of Tegray, *Ras* Walda Sellase, who used the fertile village of Dabri, where his descendants still live today, as a resort. In 1867 when the huge British-Indian army led by Robert Napier against Emperor Tewodros II arrived in Tegray, they established a camp in Dolo above today's Meqele.

During its time as capital of the Ethiopia in the 1880s, it was the scene of a successful ruse and political drama: Emperor Yohannes IV had for years been challenged by his cousin Dabbab Araya, who controlled the trade routes to Metsewa as a bandit, causing significant insecurity on the northern borders of Ethiopia. The emperor's ministers offered his cousin the Ethiopian crown in the palace of Meqele, which he naively accepted – only to be arrested after entering the gates.

In 1895 Meqele was officially incorporated into the Italian colony of Eritrea, and the Italians built their administrative centre and military fort on the hill above it, in Endayasus (today's main campus of Mekelle University). However, the Tegrayan forces had just retreated in order to create the illusion of an easy victory. They soon laid siege to Endayasus, and cut the fortress off from its water supply. After a short battle, the Italian garrison capitulated in January 1896 and moved to Adwa, where they were decisively defeated.

During successive governments, Meqele remained the seat of the governors of Tegray. When Tegray was split into several provinces, such as around 1900, it was the seat of the governors of Endarta. Among the most active was *Leul Ras* Seyyum Mangasha, who in the 1960s developed a modern city plan and greatly shaped Meqele (similarly to Hawasa). Meqele, like all of Ethiopia, was occupied by the Italians from 1936 to 1941. After the return of the emperor the city was marginalized due to his earlier experiences of opposition from the side of Tegrayans, who largely perceived Emperor Hayla Sellase as illegitimate. That opposition had culminated in the direct support of the Italians by the Tegrayan governor of Meqele and parts of the local population. The marginalisation, finally, culminated in a rebellion, which was crushed in 1943 by British RAF bombers, attacking Meqele in a move to support their WW II ally Hayla Sellase. When marginalisation continued, a younger generation of students entered into an armed struggle in the 1970s, forming the TPLF (coined the 'second *wayyana*'). Meqele fell into the hands of the TPLF in 1989. The seat of the rebel administration remained in the caves of Addi Gazaeti in the Tamben mountains until it moved to Meqele in 1991. In the same time, the TPLF business college, and the agriculture faculty of Asmara University, which had been evacuated to southern Ethiopia, moved to Meqele and were established as independent academic colleges. Both colleges merged in 2000 and formed Mekelle University, with its seat in the deserted military camp of Endayasus. Today it has seven colleges, eight institutes, six campuses, more than 160 undergraduate and post graduate programs and over 30,000 students.

Economy, urban development and population. The economic importance of Meqele lay originally in its ancient salt market due to its closeness to the Afar salt routes and its location at the north-south trade route linking the Red Sea with inner Ethiopia through eastern Tegray. Since the 1990s it has witnessed a sharp increase in investments, many of them private from abroad (e.g. by Tegrayan diaspora). The Masabo cement factory, owned by Endowment Fund for the Rehabilitation of Tegray, is one of the most important industries of the north, as is Mesfin Engineering, which assembles Ethiopian trucks and most recently also cars. The Maa Garment and Textiles Factory (1991) is one of the most important textile producers in Ethiopia. A new centre of the city is under construction, below the second (business) campus of the University of Addi Haqi and the Hawalti monument, with government buildings, a church and a mosque, a stadium and 5-Star hotels all planned. New residential neighbourhoods have been added during the last two decades, such as Addi Ha, Addi Hawsi, Addi Haqi, Diyaspora, Qalqal Dabri, Lachi, soon expanding to the surrounding villages. A planned railway will connect Meqele to the Afar plains, to the economically important pottash production, and further to Djibouti. The population still predominantly consists of Tegrayans, with a considerable number of workers who migrated from Eritrea during the 1998–2000 war, and rural migrants especially from Agama, Wajjarat, Rayya and surrounding Endarta. The large majority (over 90%) are Christian Orthodox, but an important Muslim community has dominated trade since the period of the city's foundation. There is a Catholic community (mainly based on the community of migrants from Agama and Irob) and new Protestant, mainly Pentecostal, churches. Due to a rising small and large trade, enterprises, colleges and the university the number of Amharic-speakers from different regions is increasing.

Literature: YOHANNES ABERRA, TSEGAY BERHE GEBRELIBANOS, 'Mäqälä', *EAE* III, 761–763; NOBUHIRO SHIMIZU, 'An Analysis of the Construction Method of Emperor IV's Buildings in Tigray Region, Ethiopia', in D. JAMES NARENDRA BONDLA et al. (eds.), *Cultural Landscapes of Ethiopia: Conference Proceedings*, Meqele 2015, 27–38; RUMI OKAZAKI, 'A Study of the Formation of an Imperial City in Tigray, Ethiopia, at the turn of the 20th Century', *Journal of Architectural Planning* 79/702 (August 2015), 1753–1759.

Wolbert G.C. Smidt, Mekelle University

Gondar and surroundings

Gondar and the Historic Route. Gondar (12°36' N, 37°28' E) sits at an elevation of about 2,200 m, and is surrounded on three sides by a ring of 3,000 m-high mountains. To the south, the landscape opens to a valley formed by the Angarab river and further down to Lake Tana. The city stretches along a ridge centred on a complex of castles and palaces built during the 17th and 18th centuries, when Gondar was the capital of the Christian Ethiopian state.

Gondar is today one of Ethiopia's major tourist destinations. Together with Harar, Lalibala, Aksum and Yaha, the city represents one of the main stops in the Historic Route. It is also from Gondar that several historical and religious sites from the former Gondarine state and the Lake Tana area can be visited. Additionally, the city is the traditional jumping off point for visiting the Semen Mountains National Park, established in 1959 and situated about 100 km to the northeast.

Gondar's tourism potential, however, is far from being exploited to its maximum. While the choice of accommodations has increased in recent years with the construction of several new hotels, only a few meet international standards. Additionally, while the city is well connected by a paved road to Baher Dar, the capital of the Amhara regional state, to reach Dase (to the east) and Enda Sellase (to the north), one still travels on a difficult and partly gravel road. Although regular flights connect Gondar with the capital Addis Ababa as well as with Aksum, Lalibala and Baher Dar, a direct connection with the rest of the regional capitals is still lacking. Moreover, the city would benefit greatly from hosting international air connections. However, this does not seem to be on the agenda of the present government.

Gondar's heritage. Gondar's main attractions for tourists are its art and architecture, that encompass nearly four centuries of history. The most elevated area of the city is occupied by the royal enclosure (*Fasil gebbi*), an area of historical elite buildings surrounded by a 900 m-long wall. This is where Ethiopian Christian rulers fixed their capital for over 150 years. The enclosure features about 15 buildings erected between the mid-17th to the mid-18th century. Among these are the massive castle of King Fasil (Fasiladas) (the *Fasil gemb*), the elegant castle of Iyasu I, Bakaffa's U-shaped monumental hall and Queen Mentewwab's stylish palace. The compound also hosts three historical churches, Atatame Mikael, Elfen Giyorgis and Gemja Bet Maryam and other minor buildings, including Turkish baths, towers and cisterns. Outside of the royal compound, about 200m to the north there is the Ras Gemb, a Gondarine palace that faced several vicissitudes throughout its lifetime: initially it hosted high dignitaries of the Gondarine state, including Mikael Sehul, and during the Italian occupation it was the residence of the governor of Amhara. Later, during the period of the *Darg* it served as a prison, and presently it hosts the Museum of the city of Gondar, which was recently set up with the help of French experts. Further on a ridge stretching northeast towards the Angarab river there is the church of Dabra Berhan Sellase. Built by Iyasu I at the end of the 17th century, the church is an impressive sanctuary built of mortar and stone masonry and with a thatched roof made of papyrus; its interior contains one of the most famous painting collections of Gondarine art.

Bath of Emperor Fasiladas, © Andreu Martínez d'Alòs-Moner

Down the hill to the west, near the Kaha river, two important sites are found. The first is Fasil's bath, a water pool with a central pavilion that was built by the king in the 1640s. The bath is part of a larger complex that includes a garden with century-old banyan trees and a second historic building, the Tomb of Zobel, Fasiladas's horse! The bath is an elegant construction that resembles in its design and function those built in Mughal India by such rulers as Akbar, Jahangir and Shah Jahan. Once a year, in early January, the gardened complex becomes the stage for the *Temqat* festivity, attracting thousands of foreign tourists. Further to the east, there is the complex of Dabra Tsahay Qwesqwam, built between 1733 and 1746 by Queen Mentewwab. The site, which includes a church, a private chapel and a palace, served as the headquarters for the Qwara faction that dominated state politics for decades.

On the outskirts of Gondar several other historical buildings can be mentioned, some of which have suffered from decay and destruction. Along the 'College Road', near Lammergayer Hotel, stands the church of St John the Baptist (Yohannes Matmeq), which includes a ring of fortified walls with domed towers similar to those in Dabra Berhan. To its southwest there is the church of Ledata Maryam, which only preserves a few pillars of its original structure. The city's outskirts also include notable examples of civil engineering, such as two historical bridges, both on the Angarab river: the first to the east of the city, on the path to Dafacha, and the second towards the south, on the ancient path to Tsadda.

The short period of the Italian occupation from 1936 to 1941, also left remarkable modernist architecture throughout the city. This is most conspicuous in the downtown area, in the area of 'Piasa': among the remarkable examples of this period are the Poste e Telegrafi building (today Ethiopian Telecom), Comando truppe (today South Gondar Administrative Zone), Circolo militare e coloniale (today Zonal Court), Albergo CIAAO (today Tarara Hotel) and Opera nazionale dopolavoro cinema (today Cinema Ethiopia and Camelot Restaurant). Moreover, villas and apartment blocks in the north quarter of the town that once housed occupation officials and colonists are also of interest.

Gondar's intangible heritage also works as an important magnet for visitors and tourists. The city thrives during the *Temqat* festival. Additionally, the traditions of *eskesta* dancing and improvised singing (*azmari*) find there their most elaborate expressions. They can be easily appreciated in the *azmari bet* around Piasa.

Outside Gondar. In the environs of Gondar several sites of historical, cultural and natural relevance are found. However, it is to be noted that only a handful of them are well connected with the capital by a paved road. This may account for the fact that most of Gondar's historical heritage outside of the city remains largely unknown to the international tourist.

12km to the south of Gondar there is the village of Azazo, where Gondar's history started. Around 1621, Emperor Susenyos, aided by his trusted adviser, Spanish Jesuit Pedro Páez, founded a capital there, Gannata Iyasus. Over the years the complex grew to include a palace garden, built with the help of Indian engineers, and a fortified church complex. Susenyos's son, Fasiladas, came of age in this setting and once he came to power, in 1632, he set to reproduce the same spaces further north, in Gondar. Recent excavations carried out by a Spanish archaeological team have studied most of the structures of this once imposing city. Immediately to the southeast of Gannata Iyasus is found the church and monastery of Takla Haymanot. Established after the expulsion of the Catholic missionaries, in the late 1630s or early 1640s, for over 250 years it was the headquarters of Dabra Libanos monastic community. Today it features some of the earliest instances of Gondarine-style architecture.

About 50km to the southwest, Gorgora peninsula hosts a handful of remarkable sites. At Gorgora port one can visit the church of Dabra Sina Maryam that preserves a series of outstanding examples of early Gondarine painting. Up the hill, on a promontory overlooking the whole peninsula, stands the imposing 'Vetta Mussolini', erected by the Italian military to celebrate their victory. More to the southwest is found monastery of Mandabba Madhane Alam, founded around the 14th century and once one of the most powerful monastic communities of the region. Further west and about 12km southwest of the village of Aburja, there are the ruins of the former Jesuit residence of Gorgora Nova. The site was also the subject of recent excavations by Spanish archaeologists. It once comprised a fortified building of stone masonry that hosted the missionaries' houses and their seminary and a Catholic church dedicated to Iyasus (Gorgora Iyasus), an admirable transposition of Indo-Portuguese architecture in Ethiopia.

In another direction, along the asphalt road from Azazo to Addis Zaman, several Gondarine and pre-Gondarine sites can be visited. At the outskirts of Tsadda to its north, there is the church of Egziabeher Ab, built by Emperor Yohannes I, which features the fortified-like structure of many Gondarine churches. A few km further in the direction to Addis Zaman, to the left of the road stands the church-monastery of Bahrey Gemb, an almost unique example of Gondarine sanctuary with an external domed *maqdas*. Shortly after Bahrey Gemb a gravel track turns eastwards. After a difficult drive climbing the mountain, in the area known as Gomenge, the imposing ruins of Danqaz can be seen: they comprise the old palace of Emperor Susenyos and the Catholic church dedicated to Iyasus and erected by the Jesuit priests. Back on the asphalt road to Addis Zaman, past the village of Enfraz, on an elevated promontory to the left there is the imposing castle of Guzara. Often attributed to Emperor Sartsa Dengel, it was probably contemporary to the main Gondarine structures in the capital. Further inland in the same area, at the foot of Amba Maryam and on an elevated promontory, the ruins of the house of the Catholic patriarch Afonso Mendes can be visited. For a short period, between 1626 and 1632, it was here that the highest Catholic authority resided.

The northern part of Gondar has fewer important historical sites, but several of them are remarkable. Around the village of Amba Giyorgis, some 40km to the north-east, two important Gondarine churches are found, both attributed to Emperor Iyasu I: Daqwa Kidana Mehrat and Gorenko Maryam. Closer to Gondar, 5km to the north, there is the so-called Falasha (Beta Esrael) village of Wallaqa, where 'Falasha' pottery is produced and sold to tourists. However, nowadays there are few, if any, Beta Esrael in the country, almost all having emigrated to Israel during the 1980s and 1990s.

Literature: Eduardo Martín Agúndez, Christina Charro Lobato, Agustín Carria Ramos, *Gondar City Tourist Map*, Madrid 2013; Gian Paolo Chiari, *Guide to Gondar and Lake Tana*, Addis Ababa 2012; David Rifkind, 'Gondar: Architecture and Urbanism for Italy's Fascist Empire', *Journal of the Society of Architectural Historians*, 70 (2011), 492–511.

Andreu Martínez d'Alòs-Moner, Gondar University

Baher Dar

Baher Dar (at 11°36'N and 37°25'E) is a town on the central highland plateau of north-western Ethiopia at the mouth of the Abbay (Blue Nile) river on Lake Tana. It is situated at an altitude of 1,802m and 578km from Addis Ababa, at a location commanding the fertile region of the Lake Tana–Abbay basin. It is the capital of the Amhara National State.

Formerly called Baher Giyorgis, its foundation is attributed to Emperor Iyasu I (r. 1682–1706). In 1856 and 1866 Tewodros II visited Baher Dar on his return from his Shawan and Gojjam campaigns. Still in the 19th century, several foreign travellers who visited the site via Metsewa, Addis Ababa or Sudan described it either as a village or a town and estimated its population at around 1,200–1,600 inhabitants.

Amhara men on a *tankwa*, Lake Tana, Baher Dar, © Serge Dewel-Mouton

The 20th century. During the first half of the 20th century both the Ethiopian and British governments agreed that a barrage be constructed on the Abbay. The former hoped this would become a good source of revenue in support of its efforts at modernisation. However, the project did not materialize because the Ethiopian government insisted that Baher Dar should be connected by road with Addis Ababa and not with the Sudan. In 1930 the Ethiopian team of experts sent by the government described Baher Dar as a village with a considerable trading activity, characterized by various traditional settlement areas, each of which was distinguished by the social position its members occupied. The *kahenat* (clergy) and *balabbat* ('noble') communities were the most important, while other groups of tenant-craftsman communities lived on the *balabbat* lands. All communities were economically interdependent, but there was no intermarriage.

The Italian army captured Baher Dar in April 1936 and soon used it as a gateway to occupy the rest of Gojjam. They gave Baher Dar modern urban features introducing a new secular administration and private land ownership. Moreover, they allocated land for administration, the army, an airstrip and port facilities. Residential and commercial zones were demarcated, the latter soon hosting different types of shops, tearooms, tailor shops, bars and restaurants run by Italians, Arabs, Somali and Sudanese. However, Ethiopian participation in this realm was insignificant. Furthermore, Baher Dar was connected by motorboats with other Lake Tana ports and by motor roads with Gondar, Dabra Marqos and Addis Ababa. A wooden bridge connecting Gojjam and Bagemder along the mouth of the Abbay from Lake Tana was built. A considerable number of the *balabbat* opposed the new masters and joined the patriotic resistance in the surrounding forest.

The Italians gave Baher Dar political and economic importance making it an administrative centre of the semi-autonomous Lake Tana southern territories of Yilmana Densa, Macha and Achafar. Yet they cut off the existing relationship among the communities of Baher Dar.

The Italians showed interest in the possibility of developing the Lake Tana and Abbay basin agriculturally and of exploiting their waters for hydro-electric power, but when they left Ethiopia, they destroyed the wooden bridge they had built at Kanfaro ('mouth') Abbay and the Alata Bridge near the Blue Nile falls.

After an alliance of the Ethiopian patriots and the international anti-Fascist forces liberated Ethiopia from Italian occupation in 1941, the Ethiopian government realized the huge potential of the area and made the town a centre of a *warada* ('district') administration with all facilities. In 1945 the status of Baher Dar was raised to a municipality. Soon, other considerations accorded the town the rank of an *awrajja* ('subprovince') capital in addition of being a *warada* capital.

Modern developments. Baher Dar's strategic location for economic development and tourism, with availability of historical relics and natural beauty and resources, drew more government attention. In the early 1950s there also arose the idea in higher government circles that an alternative administrative capital of the country be constructed. Baher Dar was considered the best site for this purpose. In 1950–1951 the Emperor Hayla Sellase visited Baher Dar several times, and British town planners recommended that more scientific studies be carried out in Baher Dar and its surrounding.

The Cooperative Program (1950–1956) between Ethiopia and the USA, and the 'Regional Tana Basin Project of 1958–59' showed that Baher Dar could grow as an important centre in the basin, but the idea of making the town an alternative national capital was dropped, although Baher Dar continued to grow.

In 1960–1962 a comprehensive master plan of the town prepared by a group of German experts led by Max Guther focused on the physical layout of Baher Dar and a comprehensive economic plan in connection with regional and national economic interests. New administrative, residential, commercial, industrial, recreational and educational zones were demarcated. Baher Dar was provided with a modern hospital, educational institutions like the Polytechnic Institute and Academy of Pedagogy (later called Baher Dar Teachers College). Separate areas for bus, railway and airport were assigned. Private houses, shops, bars and restaurants were expanded. Air and water transport were revived and expanded. A modern bridge that connected Gojjam and Bagemder was constructed at Kanfaro Abbay in Baher Dar.

The economic development component of the master plan recommended that over 20 industries be established in Baher Dar, making it a centre of 'industrial chains' integrated with trade, handicraft and cottage and home industries, in order to accommodate about 300,000 inhabitants within a period of 50 years.

However, until very recently, with the exception of the textile industry, only small private enterprises were expanded. Baher Dar grew as a significant centre for tourism, speeded up by the ease in air, land and water transport and hotel accommodations in the town.

Since the early 1990s, Baher Dar has experienced remarkable growth and expansion, encouraged by the government's free market economic policy. Today, Baher Dar is not only an administrative centre, but also a nucleus of commerce, industry, transport, health, education and tourism. Baher Dar University was formed in 2000 through the unification of Baher Dar Polytechnic Institute and Baher Dar Teachers College. It has more than 50,000 students in over 200 programs. The city is serviced by a local airport, which has daily flights to both Addis Ababa and Gondar. According to the 2007 census, the population of the city and its rural environs was over 220,000 made up overwhelmingly of Orthodox Christians (90%), who are Amhara (96%).

Sightseeing. Baher Dar with its wide, palm lined avenues and gardens overflowing with tropical vegetation and birds, has a growing number of modern shops, hotels, and restaurants. Baher Dar's two markets are worth of visit: the general market, displaying colourful woven cloth and a wide range of supplies (including coffee); and the roadside market, specialized in baskets. There are also a variety of handicraft and weaving centres. In the compound of St George's Church, there is still a building erected by the Jesuit Pedro Páez (1564–1622).

Baher Dar provides access to both the lake and its many islands, and to the Blue Nile falls. The visitor will see among modern motorboats also *tankwa* ('papyrus canoe'), bigger or smaller according to their transporting purposes, made by the lake side Wayto people.

Until the 1950s, Wayto were hunters-fishers whose culture and economy mainly rested upon hippopotamus. Besides fishing, they are now mainly involved in *tankwa* building or in stone hewing, while women's occupation is basketry.

Visiting the Blue Nile falls Tis Esat 22 km outside of the city or, boating on Lake Tana and exploring its churches and monasteries, are among the attractions. The monks will often display their communities' icons, manuscripts and other religious objects. Note, however, that some do not allow entrance to women.

Literature: SELTENE SEYOUM, *A History of Bahir Dar Town, 1936–1974*, M.A. Thesis, Addis Ababa University, Addis Ababa 1988; SELTENE SEYOUM, 'Baher Dar', *EAE* I, 442–444.

Seltene Seyoum, Addis Ababa University, Maija Priess, Hamburg

Dabra Berhan

History. The capital of the North Shawa Administrative Zone of the Amhara Regional Administration, Dabra Berhan ('mountain of light') is located 120 km northeast of Addis Ababa (9°41' N 39°32' E) at an elevation of 2,840 m. It is at the heart of the Christian highland and formerly known as Dabra Eba. Dabra Berhan is closely connected with the Emperor Zara Yaeqob, who founded it as his new capital in 1455.

According to various sources, an apparition of light brought about the naming of the new capital, although the traditions diverge as to why and how the light from heaven descended. The earliest of these say the light descended from heaven, 38 days after a group of heretics (followers of the Stephanite monks) were killed. Emperor Zara Yaeqob then proclaimed that the place should henceforth be called Dabra Berhan. A later and probably more reliable tradition associates the light with Halley's Comet, which could have been observed in Shawa around this time.

According to his chronicler, Zara Yaeqob stayed in Dabra Berhan for twelve years 'without leaving'. After the king's death, Dabra Berhan seems to have been relatively neglected. During the conquest of Imam Ahmad Grany, the area around Dabra Berhan offered fierce resistance to the invasion. But the *imam* was eventually successful, and it was at Dabra Berhan that he proclaimed, 'Abyssinia is conquered'. He made the town a central military garrison from which his troops were deployed and where his generals carried out a military parade.

In the centuries following the defeat of Ahmad Grany, Dabra Berhan and its territories witnessed another phase of continual ethnic clashes, this time between the Oromo and the Amhara. The Oromo pushed the Amhara inhabitants to the lowland while they themselves settled on the plateau. Around the mid-18th century, the Amhara under the leadership of Amha Iyasus (1745–1775) once again gained control of part of the highlands including Dabra Berhan by pushing the Oromo out. Later in the first half of the 19th century, in the wake of the rising power of the Shawan dynasty, *Ras* Wasan Saggad (1808–1813) attempted to rebuild the town. However, shortly after his death it was reportedly destroyed again by the Abbicho Oromo. The area was reconquered by King Sahla Sellase (1813–1847), who made Dabra Berhan his residence. This period was one of flourishing and growth, thanks to the strong interactions with distant regions. The town 'was frequented by heterogeneous races' and had become 'one of the principal depots for the numerous royal slaves of the Shoan King', who were employed in various types of manual labour including the construction of a bridge at Barressa. It was during this time that Dabra Berhan became the only centre in Shawa where mules and horses could be obtained.

The progress of Dabra Berhan was halted yet again with the conquest of Shawa by Emperor Tewodros II (1855–1868). The urban growth of Dabra Berhan was resumed following the accession of Menilek II to the Shawan throne.

Cherubs and christological scenes painted on cloth, Dabra Berhan Sellase Church, Gondar, © Michael Gervers

The contemporary city. As a medieval town with a high historical importance, Dabra Berhan has different archaeological sites which deserve attention from field specialists. Among these is the palace of Emperor Zara Yaeqob which according to his chronicle, had 'never been built by any of his predecessors' and was situated about 50m west of the Sellase Church, a medieval church in town with magnificent wall paintings. The British diplomat William Harris observed the remnants of the palace in the first half of the 19th century, '… the vestiges that remain of his [Zara Yaeqob's] abode, certainly exhibit an order of architecture far superior to that of the present degenerate day'. He also stated that the surrounding area was covered by impenetrable forest of particularly juniperus trees with only a single path. In front of the presumed site, there is Zara Yaeqob *addababay* ('Zara Yaeqob square') which still serves the community for different public events.

According to the 2007 national census, the total population of Dabra Berhan was 65,231 and marked a growth of about 60 % since 1994. The population of 110,408 inhabitants (2012), mainly Amhara (90 %), shows that it is one of the fastest growing towns in Ethiopia. The majority of its inhabitants (95 %) practice Ethiopian Orthodox Christianity, while 2 % of the population are Protestants and 3 % are Muslim.

Dabra Berhan has different surrounding 'suburbs' (*safar*) which make it a 'middle sized' town.

Arada Safar is located at the heart of the town facing the Addis Ababa-Dase road, noted for its taverns and pensions. To its north is Ankobar Safar which is known for its *talla* and *araqi* houses. Tabase Safar borders the Beressa river. According to tradition, the area got this name during the reign of Emperor Yekunno Amlak (r. 1270–1285) because of its cold weather. Wealthy people of the town reside in the Asmara Ber area which is on the eastern extreme of the town. Qes Amba, which once was the centre of the town, is an area which except for some peasant dwellings has been abandoned since the Italian period. Eslam Amba, located opposite the Sellase Church, is the area where the Muslim community of the town, who are largely merchants reside surrounding their mosque.

Dabra Berhan has long been preferred by governments to be part of the manufacturing corridor of the nation. During Zara Yaeqob's period, the town was known for its crafts, a term that applies to a wide range of creative and design activities like tanning, pottery, weaving, sewing traditional clothes and woodworking producing wooden stools, chairs and other artefacts. The Dabra Berhan Blanket Factory PLC was established in 1965 by Emperor Hayla Sellase as Dabra Berhan Wool Factory, which is still known as the first and largest blanket manufacturer in the country. In recent years, the town has attracted massive investment. Among the mega manufacturing industries, the Dabra Berhan Construction Machinery Industry, Dabra Berhan Tractor and Agricultural Equipment Assembly, Dabra Berhan My Shoes and Leather Manufacturing Industry, Dabra Berhan PBC Products Manufacturing Factory, Dabra Berhan Glass Manufacturing Company, Dabra Berhan Dashen Beer Brewery are particularly important.

The town hosts few modern academic institutes among which the Dabra Berhan Teacher Training Institute (1957) is the oldest. Dabra Berhan University is a young university which was established in 2007 with a current intake capacity of more than 13,000 regular academic trainees.

Literature: WILLIAM C. HARRIS, *The Highlands of Ethiopia*, London 1844; RICHARD PANKHURST, *History of Ethiopian Towns from the Middle Ages to the Early Nineteenth Century*, Wiesbaden 1982; RICHARD PANKHURST, *History of Ethiopian Towns from the Mid-Nineteenth Century to 1935*, Wiesbaden 1985.

Mersha Alehegne, Addis Ababa, Maija Priess, Hamburg

Harar

To the Europeans, Harar was known as the 'Timbuktu of the east'; to its own people, as the 'City of saints'. The comparison with the mysterious Muslim city of Timbuktu reflected the Harar's one-time inaccessibility to Europeans. Only in 1854 did the Englishman Richard Burton manage to visit the city for a few days. Harar is utterly different from other Ethiopian cities. With its wall and narrow alleys, it is a typical oriental city and it indeed resembles Timbuktu more than, for instance, imperial Gondar. The epithet 'City of saints' reflects the fact that Harar is the spiritual and cultural centre of Islam in south-eastern Ethiopia, with influence reaching as far as Somalia. Islam in Harar is characterized by the veneration of large numbers of saints.

The city centre, enclosed within the walls, is only 1.6km x 0.8km in size. Until a few decades ago it was inhabited almost exclusively by a single homogeneous ethnic group, the Harari. The Harari, who call themselves *ge usu* ('people of the city'), speak their own Semitic language, Harari, in contrast to the Cushitic language Oromiffaa spoken in the surrounding countryside. From the 16th century the Harari language produced its own literature, mostly religious in nature and written in Arabic script. Arabic, too, played a significant role in cultural life; it was the administrative language of the *qadi*-court, or *Diwan*.

Harar market in front of the gate, © Ethiopian Tourism Organization

History. According to an indigenous chronicle, the history of Harar began with the arrival from Mecca of the national St Abadir in 1216. Although the chronicle is strongly legendary in character and full of obvious anachronisms, the date may well be correct, for in 1332 Harar is mentioned in an Ethiopian chronicle. The city must already have had some importance at that time, as it was able to send three 'governors' in support of a Muslim insurrection in Ethiopia.

The next we hear of Harar is in 1520, when the Walashma sultans moved their capital from Adal to Harar so that it would be less exposed to Christian attacks. But the sultans had to contend not only with the Christians, but also with radical imams who challenged their rule from within. The best known of these was Ahmad Grany, who in 1525 killed the Walashma sultan and replaced him with a puppet ruler. He then set out from Harar on his march of conquest through Ethiopia.

When Ahmad Grany was defeated and killed by the Portuguese in 1543, the vanquished Muslims returned to Harar. A kinsman of Grany's, Nur ibn Mujahid, once again organized a *jihad* against the Christians and in 1559 defeated and killed the Ethiopian Emperor Galawdewos. However, in the meantime Nur ibn Mujahid was beset by a new enemy, the pagan Oromo who were advancing from the south. Against them he erected the famous walls, which protected the city itself, but did nothing to prevent the ravaging of the surrounding countryside. The destruction of the fields led to two famines, the second followed by a plague to which Nur ibn Mujahid himself fell victim in 1568.

Only one other ruler of Harar attempted an unsuccessful *jihad* against the Christians. The main threat to the city was now the Oromo. In 1576, Imam Muhammad Gasa I moved his seat of government north to Awsa in Afar territory. Harar was ruled by a governor until 1647. In that year Harar regained its independence under Ali ibn Daud. Until the Egyptian takeover in 1875, Ali's dynasty ruled over a city-state which controlled an area of some 50km radius around Harar, but whose political and especially economic influence extended all the way to Zayla on the Red Sea and westward to Aliyu Amba. However, the clashes with the Oromo so weakened the city that, when the Egyptian Khedive Ismail incorporated Harar into his imperialist designs, the emir was unable to offer any resistance.

The Egyptians reformed the administration and system of taxation, erected mosques and administrative buildings, and converted the Oromo of the hinterland to Islam. Under Egyptian rule the city was opened up to foreigners. Indian and European merchants settled in Harar. The French poet Arthur Rimbaud served there for a time as representative of the Bardey Company, and the French Capuchins founded a mission in the city.

In 1885 the Egyptians, hard-hit financially by the Mahdist insurrection in Sudan, had to abandon Harar under pressure from the British. As ruler of Harar the evacuating Egyptian forces installed Emir Abdullahi, thus reinstating a member of Ali ibn Daud's family on the throne. In 1887, using as a pretext the massacre by the emir of the Italian expedition of Pietro Porro, King Menilek of Shawa incorporated the city into his realm. The decisive battle of Challanqo, which remains a traumatic event for Harari even today, spelled the end of Harar's independence. At this time, the Amhara first began to settle outside the city walls as soldiers, administrators, and teachers.

The new governor of the city was *Ras* Makwannen, the father of the future Emperor Hayla Sellase. *Ras* Makwannen tore down the Friday mosque of Harar (built 1771) and replaced it with the Orthodox Madhane Alam Church. In other respects, however, he showed respect for the Islamic faith and in particular left the *sharia* court in place. Only in the 1920s did Amhara officials gradually start to make their way into the city administration. The Amhara were also able to take possession of Harari lands by making loans to the Harari who were in financial difficulties due to the expenses of their elaborate family feasts – loans which the latter were unable to repay. By way of reaction to this foreign domination, leading Harari formed the cultural organization *Firmach* ('signatures'), which (among other things) founded the first Islamic school in which 'modern' subjects were also taught. When the Italians invaded Ethiopia in 1935–1936, they were welcomed by the Harari, for the fascist regime pursued a pro-Islamic policy in order to counter the influence of the Orthodox Church.

Following the defeat of the Italians in 1941 the Amhara attempted to restore the pre-war status quo. This met with resistance in Harar, in the form of the *Jamiyya Wataniyya* ('homeland league'). In 1947, together with the Somali Youth League, they sent a delegation to the UN commission in Mogadishu, which was charged with determining the fate of the former Italian colonies. The Ethiopian government reacted by dissolving the *Jamiyya* and carrying out mass arrests. The first wave of emigration from Harar followed.

The coming of the *Darg* in 1974 brought far-reaching social and ethnic changes to Harar. The wealth of the Harari had been based on the possession of estates outside of the city, which were leased out to Oromo tenant farmers, and on long-distance trade. The laws imposed by the *Darg* destroyed these sources of livelihood. Many Harari were forced to emigrate, either to local urban centres like Dire Dawa and Addis Ababa, or to destinations abroad, Saudi Arabia, Canada, and the USA. Today roughly two-thirds of all Harari live in the diaspora. In their place, other ethnic groups like the Amhara and Oromo streamed into the city walls.

After the overthrow of the *Darg* regime in 1991, Harar acquired a degree of self-administration as the administrative seat of the Harari National Regional State. In conjunction with the Ethiopian campaign to create writing systems for previously unwritten languages, the Harari replaced the Arabic script with the Ethiopic script (whereas the Oromo and many other groups opted for the Latin script). This was a further sign of the gradual integration of Harar into the larger Ethiopian polity.

Life in the city. Today, of the roughly 30,000 inhabitants of the inner city, only half are Harari; yet they are the ones who set the tone for life in the city. Today the combined population of the old and new cities is about 65,000.

Arriving from Dire Dawa, one enters the inner city of Harar today through the western Harar Bari ('Harar gate'), which the Egyptian government built to augment the five traditional gates in the city wall (*jugal*). From there the broad shopping street Amir Uga ('street of the emir') leads to the Faras Magala ('horse market'), directly in front of the Madhane Alam Church. Today the Faras Magala is an inter-urban bus and taxi station. Formerly the road was not accessible to vehicular traffic beyond this point, but today one can drive on the Amir Uga all the way through the city to the Argob Bari ('Argobba gate') in the east. Cars can also reach the Gedir magala ('big market') in the city centre. This is still a functioning marketplace, with Oromo and Argobba women selling their wares. In the Gedir Magala is also found the Italian-built mosque named after the saint Ali Hamdun. It has a single minaret, while the present-day Friday mosque, north of the Amir Uga, has two. The construction of the Friday mosque is traditionally associated with Ahmad Grany, although it was most likely built only in 1560. Most of the more than 100 mosques in the city have no minaret. From the outside they are distinguishable from private homes, if at all, only by the presence of an exterior staircase leading to the roof, which the muezzin uses for the call to prayer.

Ras Makwannen's palace is located east of the Madhane Alam Church; it fell into disrepair in the 20th century, but has recently been partly restored. The Rimbaud house was also built in *Ras* Makwannen's time. The poet changed his residence several times during his stay in Harar, but never lived in the 'Rimbaud house', which was built only after his death. Restored a few years ago by the French, it contains a small museum and a library.

In spite of the presence of numerous newer buildings, the inner city continues to be characterized by narrow unpaved alleys winding between whitewashed (nowadays sometimes also green) windowless houses, whose only access to the street is by a gate, sometimes elaborately carved. Such carved gates, which came into fashion in the Egyptian period, were made by immigrant craftsmen from Gujarat in India. The main room of the house is against the inner back wall, i.e. opposite the entrance, elevated by two steps, so that it has three levels. The highest level is reserved for the master of the house and guests of honour. The walls are decorated with prescribed arrangements of local basketry, for which Harar is famous. The former home of the *qadi* near the Rimbaud House, today a kind of museum, can be visited as a good example of a wealthy Harari residence.

Highly elaborate basketry is still produced today for domestic use. Simpler baskets suffice for the tourist market. Jewellers work with silver, gold, coral, amber, malachite and glass, again producing for local use, but also for the Oromo, Argobba, and tourists. The Somali, however, have their own jewellers. As in other parts of Ethiopia, a number of crafts are practiced only by members of discriminated castes. One of these is blacksmithing, practiced by the Tumtu, who live apart from the rest of the population and are reputed to have the evil eye. The case is similar with potters. Leatherwork is produced by the Bona, a low-caste Somali group. In Burton's time Harar was famous for its bookbinding, which however has nowadays practically died out.

Harar is divided into five quarters, which are named after the five historical city gates. In earlier times the quarters were not only administrative units but also played a role in the city's cultural life: for example, sports competitions were held between the Koranic schools of the different quarters. The quarters are in turn divided into neighbourhoods, over 100 altogether. They are commonly named after locally venerated saints (*awach*) of the neighbourhood, but also after markets, mosques or shops.

Religion and culture. The veneration of saints has always played a large role in the social life of the Harari. Paramount among them is the national saint Abadir, whose grave and mosque, in the southern part of the city near the Saqutat gate, can sometimes be visited. Over 200 other cultic sites, mostly graves but also trees and rocks, are scattered across the city and its surroundings. Several women are included among the saints. Pre-Islamic concepts have also clearly been incorporated into the cult. In honour of the saints so-called *zikri* are performed, prayers and litanies sung to a drum in Arabic, Harari, and today also Oromo.

The veneration of saints is a long-standing hallmark of Harari Islam. Wahhabi influences from Saudi Arabia have opposed the cult of saints, but this has met with resistance; so, Wahhabi adherents have placed themselves outside Harari society. Most recently there have also been modernist currents flowing back to Harar from the Harari diaspora in the West, where Harari come into contact with Muslim emigrants from other countries. The cult of saints has come to be viewed by middle-class people in particular more as a cultural than a religious symbol of the town.

Among the other social relationships and institutions found among the Harari, the *Afocha* stand out. These are mutual self-help associations which come into play above all at weddings and funerals, the former in particular involving lavish and expensive celebrations. Members hold regular meetings featuring communal prayers, where the cult of saints again plays a role. For men, membership of an *Afocha* is compulsory. Although financial obligations and a certain standard of education are expected, members must be able to read and write and to demonstrate knowledge of the Koran. In the women's *Afocha*, which are separate from the men's *Afocha*, only knowledge of the Koran is required. Women normally join an *Afocha* only when their children are of school age; prior to this they may join a voluntary *Baha* club. After the most recent wave of emigration, Harari have also created *Afocha* in the diaspora.

The consumption of *chat* plays an important role in the gatherings of the men's *Afocha*. But groups of friends will also meet privately in the afternoon to chew *chat*. The ceremony begins with the recitation of the *Fatiha*, the opening *sura* of the Koran, and is interrupted at intervals with prayers and drinking of coffee. The *chat* leaves must be fresh. *Chat* has a euphoric effect at first, stimulating the participants to enthusiastic discussion and disputation. After about two hours a soporific effect sets in. *Chat* also plays an important role in the economic life of Harar; it has supplanted coffee as the main cash crop, because it is more profitable.

A major tourist attraction today is the feeding of hyenas in the evening before the city gates. The hyena-man holds a piece of meat in his mouth, calls one of the hyenas by name, and lets it grab the meat out of his mouth. The feeding is said to go back to a pact between the Harari and the hyenas that was made during a famine in the 19th century. In exchange for being fed, the hyenas agreed not to attack the Harari and their cattle.

Literature: Patrick Desplat, *Heilige Stadt – Stadt der Heiligen*, Köln 2010; Ewald Wagner, *Harar: Annotierte Bibliographie zum Schrifttum über die Stadt und den Islam in Südostäthiopien*, Wiesbaden 2003; Belle Asante, Ewald Wagner, Jonathan Miran, Tim Carmichael, 'Harär', *EAE* II, 2005, 1012-1021.

Ewald Wagner, Gießen

National parks

National parks, conceived of as extended natural heritage areas of a country open for tourism and with special protection rules were established in the Horn of Africa in the 1960–1990s, with the exception of Djibouti where a nature protection area was enacted already in 1939 by the French colonial administration.

The origins of the idea of nature reserved in the Horn may be seen in the policy of Menilek II to safeguard forests for fuel production and even for environmental reasons, when he established churches in Mannagasha and on Entoto at the end of the 20th century. Traditionally, trees and bushes growing around churches and sacred grounds are not cut. Only in 1963 was a UNESCO mission, headed by Julian Huxley, sent to survey the country's wildlife and propose the establishment of a Wildlife Conservation Board and Department that prepared a 3-year Wildlife Conservation Plan to create national parks in Ethiopia. The Awash park, a royal game reserve, was established in 1966 as well as the Omo and Semen Parks. The Forêt du Day Park was initially a recreation resort for Europeans during the torrid months in Djibouti city.

The national parks in the Horn of Africa are supposed to conform to the official definition of a park established in 1969 by the International Union for the Conservation of Nature; the defining elements being the protection of the ecosystem(s) of a park from human exploitation and excessive human settlement, and restricted entry, for recreational, educational and scientific purposes. State-funded park staffs were supposed to guard the parks, to enforce these conditions and to further the development of each park as a natural reserve. Yet, due to insecurity and civil war in the 1970–1990s, the parks were neglected and are still under threat in Somalia.

Parks in the Horn of Africa are mainly located on sparsely settled regions: lowlands in the border areas of the Ethiopian and Eritrean peripheries, high mountains towering over the plateaus as well as coastal environments on the Red Sea and the Indian Ocean littorals in Djibouti, Eritrea and Somalia. However, none of the designated areas, even in the highest mountains as well as in the most remote coral reefs and archipelagos, were unused and uninhabited by native peoples. Even the typical natural features and

Termite hill in Yabelo Wildlife Sanctuary, © Matthias Ansel

landscapes of the park areas, such as high-mountain pastures, grass plains, riverine inundated forests, dunes, sand bars and mangroves, have been effected by age-old human activity (periodic burning, shifting cultivation, pastoral nomadism, gathering, fishing, hunting). The parks contain important numbers of common and endemic African species, including birds, plants, reptiles and mammals, that it is deemed important to protect. The native animal and vegetal species are protected only in the Forêt du Day, Bale and Semen Parks. UNESCO listed the Semen Mountains as a World Heritage Site in 1978 and later the valleys of the Omo and the Awash rivers.

National parks		Surface area in km^2	Region
Forêt du Day (Goda Mountains)	1939	30	Tadjourah
Protected areas/Nature reserves			
The 7 Frères Islands	–	–	Obock
The Maskalli and Moucha Islands	–	–	Arta/Djibouti

Table 16: National parks, protected areas/ nature reserves of Djibouti

In Djibouti nature protected areas are under the administration of the Ministry of Agriculture. The Forêt du Day and the Mabla Mountains served as a sanctuary for the 1991 Afar-based rebellion led by the *Front pour la restauration de l'unité et de la démocratie.* Fierce fights occurred between the Army and the rebels, and the whole region was closed for several years. Visitors are now rare in the Forêt du Day where it is difficult to prevent herders from its outskirts from entering with their cattle and cutting down some trees. Tourists prefer to go to the beaches of the Seven Frères, Moucha and Maskalli Islands where they engage in snorkelling and scuba-diving to watch colourful fishes and coral reefs. It seems that no one is in charge of enforcing underwater fishing restrictions.

National parks		Surface area in km²	Region (Zoba)
Dahlak Marine National Park	1960s	–	Semenawi Qayyeh Bahri
Semenawi Qayyeh Bahri Nature Park	1990s	–	Semenawi Qayyeh Bahri
Wildlife Reserves			
Nakfa Wildlife Reserve	1990s	–	Semenawi Qayyeh Bahri
Yobi Wildlife Reserve	1990s	–	Anseba

Table 17: National parks and wildlife reserves of Eritrea

The Ethiopian Wildlife Conservation Organisation ran Eritrean parks before the country became independent in 1993. According to official Internet sites an asphalted road, starting to the North from Metsewa, was opened for 'national and foreign' visitors of the Semenawi Qayyeh Bahri Nature Park. It is not known if the islands in the famous Dahlak Marine National Park, its coral reefs, its fish and its historical heritage, are accessible to tourists. Because of the state of emergency there is no doubt that the Nakfa and Yobi Wildlife Reserves are still closed.

National parks		Surface area in km²	Region
Daallo Forest (*Buuraha Daallo*)	–	–	*Sanaag*
Hargeysa National Park	–	–	*Wokooyi Galbeeb*
Las Caanod-Taleex-Ceel Chebet			*Sool*
Jilib (?) National Park	–	–	Shabeellaha Hoose?
Kismaayo National Park	–	–	Jubbada Hoose
Lag Badana National Park (Bushbush National Park)	1985s	3,340	Jubbada Hoose
Jowhar-Warshek	–	–	Shabeellaha Dhexe
Game/Nature Reserves			
Seylac	–	–	*Wokooyi Galbeeb*
Ras Xaafun	–	–	Bari (Puntland)
Jowhar	–	–	Shabeellaha Dhexe
Balcad Nature Reserve	–	–	Shabeellaha Dhexe
Bush Lake Badana Game Reserve	–	–	Shabeellaha Hoose
Alifuuto National Nature Reserve	–	–	Shabeellaha Dhexe
Beledweyn	–	–	Hiiraan
Hobyo	–	–	Mudug
Mogadiscio	–	–	Mogadiscio
Xuddur	–	–	Bakool
Mandera	–	–	Gedo

Table 18: National parks, wildlife reserves, game/nature reserves of Somalia/Somaliland

Due to more than a quarter century of continuous political violence in Somalia, it is not known how much habitat remains in the nature reserves. Only half of the 40 sites at 'parks.it' are clearly located on maps and only ten are really documented. As a 'clandestine' state, Somaliland has been ignored since 1991 by the UN agencies dealing with the protection of the environment, despite its political and economic stability. The Hargeysa National Park seems to be more a recreation resort for the dwellers of the Somaliland capital than a nature reserve. The Daallo Forest – remains of a juniper forest – is under threat because of its location in a disputed border zone between Somaliland and Puntland. During the second half of the 1980s, the Ministry of Tourism under the Siyaad Barre's regime established Lag Badana, the first national park in united – at that time – Somalia, but this is undoubtedly no longer functional. By 1989 new legislation was initiated governing national parks and nature reserves under the Ministry of Livestock, Forestry and National Range Agency. Following the outbreak of the civil war in 1988–1991, development of the national parks came to a halt. As all Somali public servants, permanent staff (administrators, guards) have given up protection of the sites. In 2014 President Xasan Sheekh Maxamuud announced new development projects of the national parks to strengthen environmental preservation and potential tourism and job opportunities. For the time being it is only a dream because the 25-year civil war still rages all over the country.

National parks		Surface area in km^2	Region
Awash	1966	756	Afar & Oromiyaa
Semen Tararawoch (Semen Mountains)	1969	179/136	Amhara
Abyaataa Shaalaa Haykoch (Abyaataa-Shaalaa Lakes, also Rift Valley Lakes)	1971	887	Oromiyaa
Omo	1966	4,068	South
Yabale Tararawoch (Bale Mountains)	1970	2,471	Oromiyaa
Yangudi Rasa	1977	4,731	Afar
Mago	1979	2,162	South
Nach Sar	1974	514	South
Gambela	1974	5061	Gambela
Game reserves/wildlife reserves			
Merab Awash	1981	1,781	Oromiyaa & Afar
Aldage	1981	1,832	Afar
Bale/Balee	1981	1,766	Oromiyaa
Chaw Baher	1981	4,212	South
Gawane	–	2,439	Afar
Millee Sardo	–	8,766	Afar
Tama Wildlife Reserve	–	3,269	South
Shire	–	5,000	Tegray
Sanctuaries			
Babilee Yazehonoch Matalaya	–	6,982	Somali & Oromiyaa
Yabelo Yadur Ensasat Matalaya	–	2,537	Oromiyaa
Senk Yakorkewoch Matalaya	–	54	Oromiyaa

Table 19: National parks, game/wildlife reserves of Ethiopia

The Ethiopian Wildlife Conservation Organisation has played an important role in the conservation and management of wildlife in the parks. But occasional, restricted hunting by foreign, big game hunters ('sport hunters', paying a substantial sum of money) seems to be still allowed. Traditional hunting by local people has, over the past few hundred years, kept the numbers of game animals fairly constant. In the past two decades this trend was somewhat reversed.

In some areas of Ethiopia, parks are now problematic because of both the eviction of local populations and the growing pastoral and hunting pressure on the parks; e.g. there are at least 13 ethnic groups that partly live in or use the southern parks (Meen, Aari, Mursi, Hamar, Bashada, Gujji, Koorete, Suri, Kara, Nyangatom, Dizi, Anuak and Nuer). Several others (Afar, Karrayyuu) live in the north-eastern parks. Since it was prohibited for them to enter, some pastoralists and cultivators (among them Karrayyuu and Afar) who traditionally used the park areas (also for some hunting), started violent resistance against the guards, raiding in the park and killing game. In addition, since the 1970's, many Afar have been evicted due to the establishment of mechanized farms in their traditional territories in the vicinity of the Awash Park. During the 1975-1991 civil war the Semen Mountains Park served as a high altitude sanctuary for the anti-government guerrillas. In spring 2000 the Bale National Park suffered seriously from widespread fires: it was a protest against the enforcement of protection rules on grazing. Some foreign advisers invited the Federal Government to bring into force again the expulsion of native population from parks. Then authorities were also accused of planning the establishment of buffer zones in the aim to isolate remnants of guerrilla movements. In the 1990s, the parks in southern Ethiopia were given a boost by the EU-funded National Parks Rehabilitation in Southern Ethiopia Project (1993–1998), whereby park development was to go hand in hand with the development of infrastructure, services and school-building for local people, whose cooperation was sought. The project ran fairly successfully during an initial period, but declined when project funding came to an end in 1998 and institutional structures did not function properly. Despite all efforts, there is at present no well-supported or sustainable parks management in Ethiopia. This in the long run will endanger the wildlife, the landscape and the chances of the local populations, which continue to increase in number.

In 2004 the Dutch-based 'African Parks Foundation' (AFP) signed an agreement with the Ethiopian government to manage the parks of Omo, Nach Sar and Mago and develop them for conservation and wildlife tourism. For this purpose the boundaries of these parks were legally established for the first time, and the aim of keeping the local population out was clearly set. Controversies surrounding the government's handling of the local people led the AFP to prematurely withdraw in 2008. Currently, the issue of developing a more community-based protection area strategy instead of an exclusionary protected-area approach to the park is being discussed, but the matter was left dormant.

Due to the civil war in Sudan thousands of South Sudanese Anywaa and Nuer crossed the Ethiopian border to take refuge in the Baro Salient. They were sheltered from violence in camps established in the vicinity of the Gambela National Park. Some of them entered the park to hunt animals, gather fruits, cut trees and graze their cattle. The pressure on arable land started before the land rush in the last five years due to a persistent influx of Ethiopian migrants and refugees. This influx of refugees has modified the ethnic balance of power in the Gambela region: violent clashes broke out between Anywaa and Nuer. Several times the Ethiopian Federal Army had to disperse protesters who took refuge in the park. Since 2009 the Federal and the Gambela regional governments have dispossessed indigenous peoples of their ancestral land on a large scale. They have dramatically changed the agrarian structure and consequently destabilized the political situation in the region and threatened the park. In the Southern region, downstream from the impressive Gelgel Gibe III Dam, 445,000ha irrigated schemes are officially planned 'to improve the livelihood of the population' (*sic*) at the vicinity of the park. But, more than 200,000 agro-pastoralists have been living for centuries in the Lower Omo Valley north of Lake Turkana. Most of them will either be expelled from their grazing land or deprived of an access to the Omo River.

The Ethiopian national parks are the only parks visited in the Horn of Africa for a long time by foreign tourists (from Europe). Most of the visitors are watching wild animals and the falls in the Awash Park because it can be reached in a couple of hours from Addis Ababa on a paved road. Due mainly to the persistence of state of emergency in Eritrea, insecurity, civil wars in the 1970–1990s, as well as lack of tourist infrastructure, the parks in the Horn of Africa, while long established, have never attained the fame of the well-known large natural reserves in Kenya, Tanzania or South Africa.

In the Horn, and in Ethiopia in particular, tourists have been more attracted to ancient monuments: i.e. monasteries, churches, and mosques in Eritrea, Tegray and Wallo, and castles and churches in Gondar. But, in recent years, safaris and treks have been organized to show the flora and fauna and populations of the more remote regions of the Omo, Bale and Semen Parks. Tourism to the Omo Park has become more popular because of the presence of the 'colourful' Suri and Mursi peoples in its vicinity – popular object of tourist photography.

Literature: JON ABBINK, ALAIN GASCON, 'Parks, National', *EAE* IV, 114–117; ASEBEBE REGASSA DEBELO, *Wilderness or Home? Conflicts, Competing Perspectives and Claims of Entitlement over Nech Sar National Park,* Wien 2016; GUILLAUME BLANC, *Une histoire environnementale de la nation. Regards croisés sur les parcs nationaux du Canada, d'Éthiopie et de France*, Paris 2015.

Alain Gascon, Paris

The volcano Erta Ale, © Stefan Warwas

Glossary of selected names and terms

As there is no single way of rendering Ethiopian names and words in the Latin or Roman alphabet, a wide range of spellings appears in the literature. In an attempt to bring some order, the authors have used a slightly simplified version of the academic systems of transcription of the Ge'ez and Arabic scripts, avoiding all the accents and diacritics which may complicate matters for the general reader. Such accents and diacritics are, however, used to mark significant distinctions in actual pronunciation. In the following glossary, therefore to the spelling used in this book the more academic transcription is added in Ge'ez or Arabic script where appropriate for those readers familiar with these.

***Names und Terms* (*Terms marked with* *)**

abun *: *abun*: **አቡን**: alternative form of Abuna (*Abunä*) 'Our Father', honorific for the metropolitan bishop of the Ethiopian Orthodox Church.

Addis Ababa: *Addis Abäba*: **አዲስ አበባ**, often also written as Addis Abeba.

Adwa: *ʿAdwa*: **ዐድዋ**, **ዓድዋ**

Afawarqi: *Afäwärqi*; **አፈወርቂ**

Ahmad ibn Ibrahim, "Grany": *Aḥmad Ibn Ibrāhīm al-Ġāzī* (*Grañ*): احمد ابن ابراهيم الغازي

Alaqa *: *Aläqa*: **አለቃ**: ecclesiastical title given to the head of an important church.

Al-Shabaab: *al-Šabāb*: الشباب

Amole *: *amole*: **አሞሌ**: bar of rock salt traditionally used as a form of currency.

Asmara: *Asmära*: **አሥመራ**, **አስመራ**

Atse *: *Aṣe*: **አፄ**: term of address and reference for an Ethiopian emperor.

Awrajja *: *awrağğa*: **አውራጃ**: administrative division corresponding to 'region' or 'sub-region, province'.

Azmari *: *azmari*: **አዝማሪ**: traditional Ethiopian minstrel, more properly the *masinqo* (one-stringed fiddle)-player, likened to mediaeval European minstrels and troubadours.

Bab al-Mandab: *Bāb al-Mandab*: باب المندب

Balabbat *: *balabbat*; **ባላባት**: originally 'owner (of a) father', a member of the ruling class.

Bale: *Bale, Balee*: **ባሌ**

Barbare *: *bärbäre*: **በርበሬ**: Ethiopian red pepper, which when dried and ground is used as the base of a strong, pungent condiment of the same name.

Baselyos: *Basəlyos*: **ባስልዮስ**

Beni Shangul: *Beni* (*Bela*) *Šangul*: **ቤኒ** (**ቤላ**) **ሻንጉል**

Berta: *Bärta, Berta*: **በርታ**

Beta Esrael: *Betä Əsraʾel*: **ቤተ እስራኤል**; often also written as Beta Israel.

Berr *: *bərr*: **ብር**: the unit of Ethiopian currency, originally meaning 'silver' and first applied to silver dollars or thalers in use from the 18th cent.

Chat *: *čaṭ*: ጫጥ: an evergreen shrub the leaves of which are chewed as a stimulant.

Dabr *: *däbr*: ደብር: a monastic church and/or the relevant cloister, a more important church institution.

Dabra Berhan: *Däbrä Bərhan*: ደብረ ብርሃን

Dabtara *: *däbtära*: ደብተራ: unordained clergy occupying an intermediate position between the ordained clergy and laity, the most educated clerics, ecclesiastic scribe.

Daga *: *däga*: ደጋ: one of the ecological zones of Ethiopia which lies at altitudes ranging from 2,300 to 3,000 m a.s.l.

Dajjazmach *: *däǧǧazmač*: ደጃዝማች: high military title.

Darg *: *Därg*: ደርግ, often also written as Derg. Ruling council or committee of the Marxist regime under Mengistu Haile Mariam.

Dase: *Däse*: ደሴ

Derre Dawa: *Dərre Dawa*: ድሬ ዳዋ

Echage *: *əččäge*: እጨጌ: title of the head of Dabra Libanos (*Däbra Libanos*) monastery in Shawa, also in his capacity as head of Ethiopian monasticism.

Enjara *: *ənǧära*: እንጀራ: flat, round, spongy bread made of *tef* and sometimes other grains.

Ensat *: *ənsät*: እንሰት: so-called 'false banana' plant cultivated in the southern and south-western highlands, the starchy stem of which is used as a food staple.

Ewostatewos: *Ewosṭatewos*: ኤዎስጣቴዎስ

Falasha *: *Fälaša*: ፈላሻ: traditional designation for Beta Esrael.

Faranj: *färänǧ*: ፈረንጅ: designation for a foreigner.

Fasika *: *Fasika*: ፋሲካ: Easter, Passover, also called Tensae (*Tənsaʾe*) 'Resurrection', the most important feast of Our Lord Jesus Christ in the calendar of the Ethiopian Orthodox Church.

Fasiladas: *Fasilädäs*: ፋሲለደስ

Fetha nagast *: *Fətḥa nägäst*: ፍትሐ ነገሥት: 'Law of the kings' often considered the ecclesiastical and civil code of Abyssinia, actually the 16th century Ge'ez translation of a 13th century Copto-Arabic 'Collection of Canons'.

Gabbar *: *gäbbar*: ገባር: tax-paying peasant farmer in the late 19th and much of the 20th century.

Gadaa *: cyclical generation-set or age-grade system in traditional Oromo societies.

Gadl *: *gädl*: ገድል: '(spiritual) contending, struggle, (heroic) life', is the most typical form of Ge'ez literature devoted to saintly figures (hagiography), and one of the most important constituents of Ge'ez literature.

Galawdewos: *Gälawdewos*: ገላውዴዎስ

Ge'ez *: *Gəʿəz*: ግዕዝ: the classical literary language of Christian Ethiopia, also known as 'Classical Ethiopic', 'Old Ethiopic', 'Ancient Ethiopic' or simply 'Ethiopic', first attested as the official language of the Kingdom of Aksum and still used as the liturgical language of the Ethiopian Church.

Gebbi *: *gəbbi*: ግቢ: a compound, including a palace compound, especially used for the Emperor's compound in Addis Ababa.

Gondar: *Gondär*: ጎንደር

Habash(i) *: *Ḥabaš(ī)*: حبشي ,حبش: Arabic name for Ethiopia, Ethiopians, respectively.

Harar: *Ḥarär*: ሐረር

Hayla Sellase: *Ḫaylä Śəllase*: ኀይለ ሥላሴ; often also written as Hayla Sellasie, Haile Sellasie, Haile Selassie.

Hijra *: *hiğra*: هجرة: emigration of the Prophet Muhammad from Mecca to Medina in 622 AD; in the Ethiopian context the 'First Hijra' refers to the emigration of a group of Muhammad's early followers to Ethiopia in 615 AD.

Imam *: *imām*: امام: leader of Muslim prayers in a mosque. The title may also be used for a political leader.

Isayyas: *Isayəyas*: ኢሳይያስ

Jihad *: *ğihād*: جهاد: 'holy war' against non-Muslims.

Jijiga: *Ğiğiga*: ጂጂጋ

Kahen *: *kahən*: ካህን: 'priest'.

Kantiba *: *käntiba*: ከንቲባ: title of a city governor, town major.

Lalibala: *Lalibäla*: ላሊበላ, often also written as Lalibela.

Lej *: *Ləğ*: ልጅ: from the late 19th century title applied to the male children of the nobility and the imperial family.

Leul *: *ləᶜul*: ልዑል: noble title applied to a prince of the imperial house.

Mallas Zenawi: *Mälläs Zenawi*: መለስ ዜናዊ.

Mamher *: *mämhər*: መምህር: lit. 'teacher', by extension particularly the 'abbot' or 'head of a monastery'.

Mengistu Haile Mariam: *Mängəstu Haylä Maryam*: መንግሥቱ ኀይለ ማርያም.

Masqal *: *mäsqäl*: መስቀል: 'Cross' of Christ, and particularly the feast to celebrate the '(Exaltation of the) Cross', on 17 Maskaram, one of the major Christian feasts.

Menelik II: *Mənəlik*: ምንሊክ

Meqele: *Mäqälä*: መቐለ, often also written as Mekelle.

Metsewa: *Məṣəwwaᶜ*, often also written as Massawa: ምጽዋዕ

Mogadishu: *Mogadishu*, *Muqdisho*: مقديشو

Naftannya: *näfṭäñña*: ነፍጠኛ, soldier settler associated with invading imperial army in southern parts of Ethiopia, in the late 19th and much of the 20th century.

Negus *: *nəguś*: ንጉሥ: 'king, ruler, chief, head, commander', is the traditional title of the Ethiopian (pagan and later Christian) monarch from the Aksumite epoch onwards.

Negusa nagast *: *nəguśä nägäśt*: ንጉሠ ነገሥት: 'king of kings', the latter term (*nagaśt*) actually being a plural of *nagaśi* (*nägaśi*) which is an alternative form for *negus*, probably originally with a different meaning.

Qabale *: *qäbäle*: ቀበሌ: small adminstrative division, 'precinct, district', also 'resident's association'.

Qadi *: *qāḍī*: قاضي: magistrate or judge of the *sharia* court.

Qene *: *qəne*: ቅኔ: a poetic genre of Ge'ez literature as well as a branch of traditional higher education; in the liturgical practice of the Ethiopian Orthodox Church, a hymn improvised by the *dabtara* during the celebration of the Divine Office.

Ras (*): *ras*: ራስ: literally 'head' (Amharic), was the second highest rank and title (after *negus*) in the feudal-military hierarchy of the Ethiopian empire.

Salam *: *sälam*: ሰላም: literally 'Peace', also as a formula of salutation, is a poetic genre of Ge'ez literature consisting of a short hymn commemorating a saint's deeds.

Selte: *Səlṭe*: ስልጤ

Semen: *Səmen*: ስሜን, also Samen: *Sämen*: ሰሜን

Shamma *: *šamma*: ሻማ: large shawl-like garment of which there are various types.

Sharia *: *šariʿa*: شريعة: Islamic law forming a comprehensive system of juridical guidance.

Shawa: *Šäwa*: ሸዋ

Shaykh *: *šayḫ*: شيخ: respectful male title for outstanding and revered individuals used throughout the Muslim world.

Tabot *: *tabot*: ታቦት: the altar tablet or slab that rests upon the altar chest, or the altar chest itself; in the Ethiopic Bible, it refers both to the Old Testament Ark of Noah and the Ark of the Covenant in which the Tablets of the Law were placed.

Tajj *: *ṭäǧǧ*: ጠጅ: alcoholic drink produced from honey.

Talla *: *ṭälla*: ጠላ: beer made from a variety of cereals, chiefly barley.

Tankwa *: *tankʷa*: ታንኳ: a boat of papyrus reeds, particularly used for navigating Lake Tana by the Wayto people.

Tef *: *ṭef*: ጤፍ: a cereal crop indigenous to the Ethiopian highlands.

Tegray: *Təgray*: ትግራይ

Tegre: *Təgre*: ትግሬ

Tegrennya: *Təgrəñña*: ትግርኛ

Temqat *: *Ṭəmqät*: ጥምቀት: often erroneously assimilated with 'Epiphany', is one of the most important annual feasts of the Christian calendar, celebrating Christ's 'baptism' by John the Baptist in the River Jordan.

Tewodros: *Tewodros*: ቴዎድሮስ

Wabi Shaballe: *Wabi Šäbälle* (Wabi Shabeelle): ዋቢ ሸበሌ

Walaytta: *Wälaytta*: ወላይታ

Warada *: *Wäräda*: ወረዳ: 'district', a smaller administrative division.

Wat *: *wäṭ*: ወጥ: a general term for various kinds of stews.

Wayna daga *: *wäyna däga*: ወይና ደጋ: one of the ecological zones of Ethiopia which lies at altitudes ranging from 1,500 to 2,300 m a.s.l.

Yeshaq: *Yəsḥaq*: ይስሐቅ

Yohannes IV: *Yoḥannəs*: ዮሐንስ

Zamana masafent *: *zämänä mäsafənt*: ዘመነ መሳፍንት: 'era of the judges', with reference to the biblical history, is the traditional designation of a political period, usually dated from 1769 to 1855, marked by decentralisation and conflicts among regional rulers and warlords.

Zar *: *zar*: ዛር: one of the best known and most widely spread forms of spirit possession, originated in Ethiopia and spread throughout the Horn of Africa, and also in Egypt, Iran, Saudi Arabia, Oman, Yemen, and Israel.

Zara Yaeqob: *Zärʾa Yaʿəqob*: ዘርአ ያዕቆብ

Zawditu: *Zäwditu*: ዘውዲቱ

Ge'ez transcription

The Ge'ez script (***fidal***) and its simplified transcription used, aside from few exceptions, in this book; in parenthesis, when different, the transcription according to the ***Encyclopaedia Aethiopica*** system

<table>
<tr><td>ሀ
ha</td><td>ሁ
hu</td><td>ሂ
hi</td><td>ሃ
ha</td><td>ሄ
he</td><td>ህ
he (hə)</td><td>ሆ
ho</td></tr>
<tr><td>ለ
la (lä)</td><td>ሉ
lu</td><td>ሊ
li</td><td>ላ
la</td><td>ሌ
le</td><td>ል
le (lə)</td><td>ሎ
lo</td></tr>
<tr><td>ሐ
ha (ḥa)</td><td>ሑ
hu (ḥu)</td><td>ሒ
hi (ḥi)</td><td>ሓ
ha (ḥa)</td><td>ሔ
he (ḥe)</td><td>ሕ
he (ḥə)</td><td>ሖ
ho (ḥo)</td></tr>
<tr><td>መ
ma (mä)</td><td>ሙ
mu</td><td>ሚ
mi</td><td>ማ
ma</td><td>ሜ
me</td><td>ም
me (mə)</td><td>ሞ
mo</td></tr>
<tr><td>ሠ
sa (śä)</td><td>ሡ
su (śu)</td><td>ሢ
si (śi)</td><td>ሣ
sa (śa)</td><td>ሤ
se (śe)</td><td>ሥ
se (śə)</td><td>ሦ
so (śo)</td></tr>
<tr><td>ረ
ra (rä)</td><td>ሩ
ru</td><td>ሪ
ri</td><td>ራ
ra</td><td>ሬ
re</td><td>ር
re (rə)</td><td>ሮ
ro</td></tr>
<tr><td>ሰ
sa (sä)</td><td>ሱ
su</td><td>ሲ
si</td><td>ሳ
sa</td><td>ሴ
se</td><td>ስ
se (sə)</td><td>ሶ
so</td></tr>
<tr><td>ሸ
sha (šä)</td><td>ሹ
shu (šu)</td><td>ሺ
shi (ši)</td><td>ሻ
sha (ša)</td><td>ሼ
she (še)</td><td>ሽ
she (šə)</td><td>ሾ
sho (šo)</td></tr>
<tr><td>ቀ
qa (qä)</td><td>ቁ
qu</td><td>ቂ
qi</td><td>ቃ
qa</td><td>ቄ
qe</td><td>ቅ
qe (qə)</td><td>ቆ
qo</td></tr>
<tr><td>በ
ba (bä)</td><td>ቡ
bu</td><td>ቢ
bi</td><td>ባ
ba</td><td>ቤ
be</td><td>ብ
be (bə)</td><td>ቦ
bo</td></tr>
<tr><td>ቨ
va (ḇä)</td><td>ቩ
vu (ḇu)</td><td>ቪ
vi (ḇi)</td><td>ቫ
va (ḇa)</td><td>ቬ
ve (ḇe)</td><td>ቭ
ve (ḇə)</td><td>ቮ
vo (ḇo)</td></tr>
<tr><td>ተ
ta (tä)</td><td>ቱ
tu</td><td>ቲ
ti</td><td>ታ
ta</td><td>ቴ
te</td><td>ት
te (tə)</td><td>ቶ
to</td></tr>
<tr><td>ቸ
cha (čä)</td><td>ቹ
chu (ču)</td><td>ቺ
chi (či)</td><td>ቻ
cha (ča)</td><td>ቼ
che (če)</td><td>ች
che (čə)</td><td>ቾ
cho (čo)</td></tr>
<tr><td>ኀ
ha (ḫa)</td><td>ኁ
hu (ḫu)</td><td>ኂ
hi (ḫi)</td><td>ኃ
ha (ḫa)</td><td>ኄ
he (ḫe)</td><td>ኅ
he (ḫə)</td><td>ኆ
ho (ḫo)</td></tr>
<tr><td>ነ
na (nä)</td><td>ኑ
nu</td><td>ኒ
ni</td><td>ና
na</td><td>ኔ
ne</td><td>ን
ne (nə)</td><td>ኖ
no</td></tr>
</table>

ኘ *nya (ñä)*	ኙ *nyu (ñu)*	ኚ *nyi (ñi)*	ኛ *nya (ña)*	ኜ *nye (ñe)*	ኝ *nye (ñə)*	ኞ *nyo (ño)*
አ *a (’a)*	ኡ *u (’u)*	ኢ *i (’i)*	ኣ *a (’a)*	ኤ *e (’e)*	እ *e (’ə)*	ኦ *o (’o)*
ከ *ka (kä)*	ኩ *ku*	ኪ *ki*	ካ *ka*	ኬ *ke*	ክ *ke (kə)*	ኮ *ko*
ወ *wa (wä)*	ዉ *wu*	ዊ *wi*	ዋ *wa*	ዌ *we*	ው *we (wə)*	ዎ *wo*
ዐ *a (‘a)*	ዑ *u (‘u)*	ዒ *i (‘i)*	ዓ *a (‘a)*	ዔ *e (‘e)*	ዕ *e (‘ə)*	ዖ *o (‘o)*
ዘ *za (zä)*	ዙ *zu*	ዚ *zi*	ዛ *za*	ዜ *ze*	ዝ *ze (zə)*	ዞ *zo*
ዠ *ja (žä)*	ዡ *ju (žu)*	ዢ *ji (ži)*	ዣ *ja (ža)*	ዤ *je (že)*	ዥ *je (žə)*	ዦ *jo (žo)*
የ *ya (yä)*	ዩ *yu*	ዪ *yi*	ያ *ya*	ዬ *ye*	ይ *ye (yə)*	ዮ *yo*
ደ *da (dä)*	ዱ *du*	ዲ *di*	ዳ *da*	ዴ *de*	ድ *de (də)*	ዶ *do*
ጀ *ja (ğä)*	ጁ *ju (ğu)*	ጂ *ji (ği)*	ጃ *ja (ğa)*	ጄ *je (ğe)*	ጅ *je (ğə)*	ጆ *jo (ğo)*
ገ *ga (gä)*	ጉ *gu*	ጊ *gi*	ጋ *ga*	ጌ *ge*	ግ *ge (gə)*	ጎ *go*
ጠ *ta (ṭä)*	ጡ *tu (ṭu)*	ጢ *ti (ṭi)*	ጣ *ta (ṭa)*	ጤ *te (ṭe)*	ጥ *te (ṭə)*	ጦ *to (ṭo)*
ጨ *cha (č̣ä)*	ጩ *chu (č̣u)*	ጪ *chi (č̣i)*	ጫ *cha (č̣a)*	ጬ *che (č̣e)*	ጭ *cha (č̣ə)*	ጮ *cho (č̣o)*
ጰ *pa (p̣ä)*	ጱ *pu (p̣u)*	ጲ *pi (p̣i)*	ጳ *pa (p̣a)*	ጴ *pe (p̣e)*	ጵ *pe (p̣ə)*	ጶ *po (p̣o)*
ጸ *tsa (ṣä)*	ጹ *tsu (ṣu)*	ጺ *tsi (ṣi)*	ጻ *tsa (ṣa)*	ጼ *tse (ṣe)*	ጽ *tse (ṣə)*	ጾ *tso (ṣo)*
ፀ *tsa (ṣ́ä)*	ፁ *tsu (ṣ́u)*	ፂ *tsi (ṣ́i)*	ፃ *tsa (ṣ́a)*	ፄ *tse (ṣ́e)*	ፅ *tse (ṣ́ə)*	ፆ *tso (ṣ́o)*
ፈ *fa (fä)*	ፉ *fu*	ፊ *fi*	ፋ *fa*	ፌ *fe*	ፍ *fe (fə)*	ፎ *fo*
ፐ *pa (pä)*	ፑ *pu*	ፒ *pi*	ፓ *pa*	ፔ *pe*	ፕ *pe (pə)*	ፖ *po*
ቈ *qwa* (q^{w}ä)		ቊ *qwi* (q^{w}i)	ቋ *qwa* (q^{w}a)	ቌ *qwe* (q^{w}e)	ቍ *qwe* (q^{w}ə)	
ኈ *hwa* (ḫ^{w}ä)		ኊ *hwi* (ḫ^{w}i)	ኋ *hwa* (ḫ^{w}a)	ኌ *hwe* (ḫ^{w}e)	ኍ *hwe* (ḫ^{w}ə)	
ኰ *kwa* (k^{w}ä)		ኲ *kwi* (k^{w}i)	ኳ *kwa* (k^{w}a)	ኴ *kwe* (k^{w}e)	ኵ *kwe* (k^{w}ə)	
ጐ *gwa* (g^{w}ä)		ጒ *gwi* (g^{w}i)	ጓ *gwa* (g^{w}a)	ጔ *gwe* (g^{w}e)	ጕ *gwe* (g^{w}ə)	

Index of principal names and terms

The index provides a selection of the most important names and terms. 'Ethiopia' and 'Eritrea' have however not been indexed.
The spelling of northeastern African names and terms follows the rules applied in the Glossary. Living persons, however, are listed according to their own chosen spelling.
Expressions from non-European or ancient languages are placed in italics.

N

O

P

Q

Y

Z

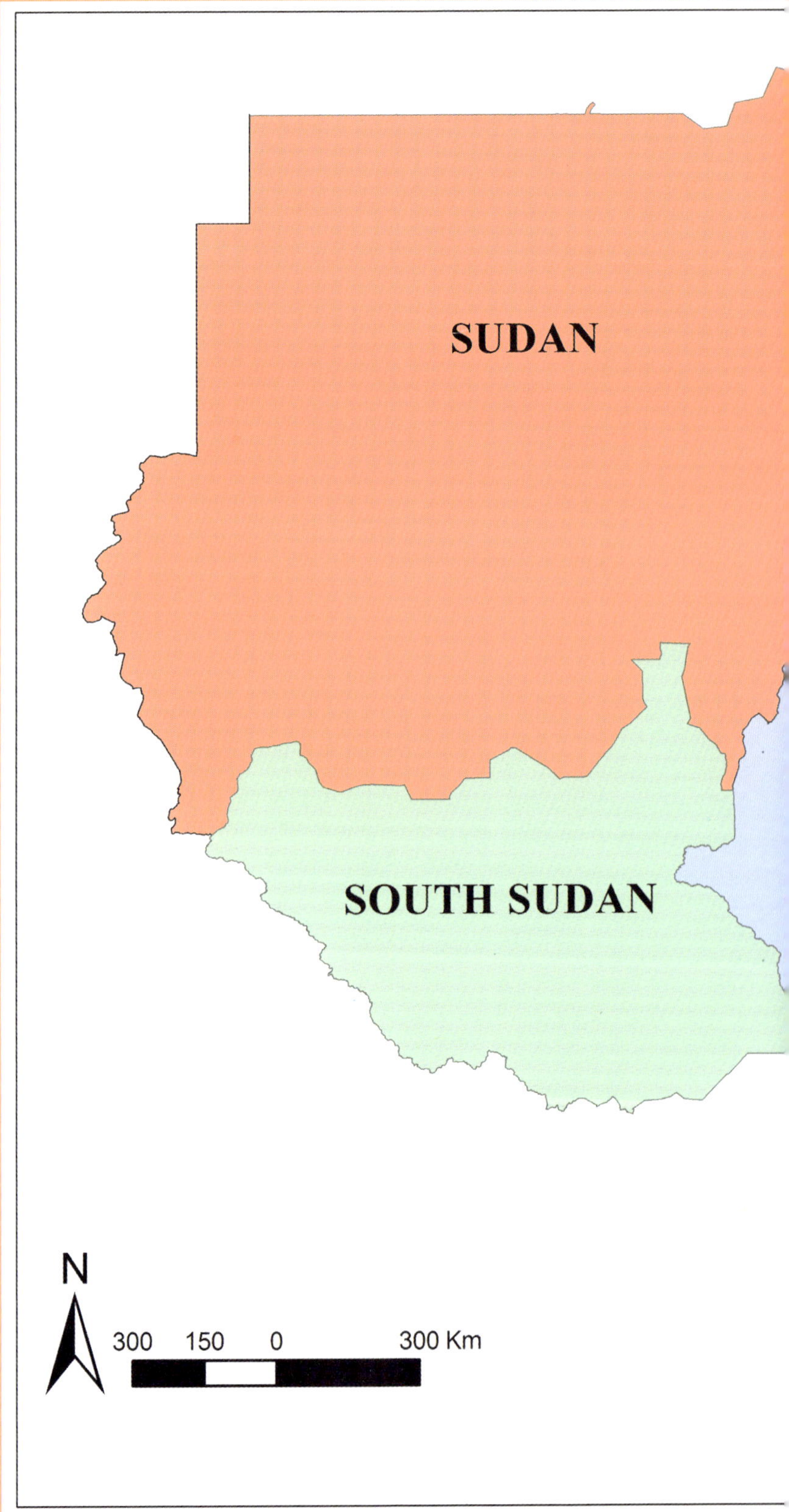
SUDAN
SOUTH SUDAN
N
300 150 0 300 Km